St Annes
Little Crook
Forres IV36 0LN

St Annes
Little Crook
Forres IV36 0LN

St Annes
Little Crook
Forres IV36 0LN

The
Collins
World
Atlas

Wm. Collins Sons
& Co. Ltd.
P.O. Box
Glasgow. G4 0NB

The
Collins
World
Atlas

First Published 1970
Revised 1972, 1973
Reprinted 1974
Revised 1975, 1977
Reprinted 1979
Revised 1980
Printed & Bound in Scotland by Wm. Collins Sons & Co. Ltd.

0 00 447049 4

Contents

REGIONS OF EUROPE

ASIA

AFRICA

AUSTRALASIA

GENERAL MAPS
The symbols used on general maps in this atlas are explained below. Thematic map symbols are explained in keys alongside each map.

Relief

	Land contour
▲ 29028	Spot height (feet)
≍	Pass
▭	Permanent ice cap

Hydrography

	Submarine contour
• 36200	Ocean depth (feet)
	Reef
	River
	Intermittent river
	Falls/Dam
	Gorge
	Canal
	Lake/Reservoir
	Intermittent lake
	Marsh/Swamp

Relief

Feet		Metres
16 404		5000
9843		3000
6562		2000
3281		1000
1640		500
656		200
0		Sea Level
656		200
13123		4000
22966		7000

Communications

——Tunnel——	Railway
——Tunnel——	Road
– – – – – –	Desert track

Administration

————	International boundary
– – – –	Undefined boundary
–·–·–·	Internal boundary
▨ ◉ ◎ ⊙	National capitals

Settlement

▨	**Calcutta**	Over 1,000,000 inhabitants
◉	**Dortmund**	500,000–1,000,000 inhabitants
◎	Veracruz	100,000–500,000 inhabitants
⊙	Timbuktu	Under 100,000 inhabitants

Lettering
Various styles of lettering are used in this atlas, each style for a different type of feature.

Physical features	*ALPS*	*Congo Basin*	*Nicobar Islands*	*Mt Cook*
Hydrographic features	*PACIFIC OCEAN*	*Red Sea*	*Lake Erie*	*Amazon*
Country name	CHILE	Internal division	IOWA	Territorial admin. (Fr.)

BRITISH ISLES GENERAL MAPS
Additional or variant symbols used on these maps.

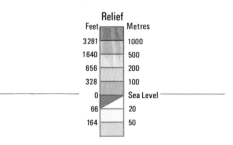

Relief

Feet		Metres
3281		1000
1640		500
656		200
328		100
0		Sea Level
66		20
164		50

Access Point ═══○═══	Motorway
════	Main road
⊕	International airport
✈	Other airport

–·–·–·	National boundary
–··–··–	County or Region boundary

	Built-up area
▨	Over 1 000 000 inhabitants
◉	500 000–1 000 000 inhabitants
◎	100 000–500 000 inhabitants
⊙	25 000–100 000 inhabitants
○	10 000–25 000 inhabitants
•	Under 10 000 inhabitants

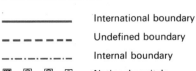

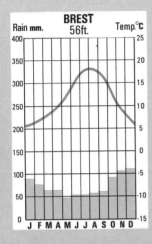

BREST
56ft.
Rain mm. / Temp.°C

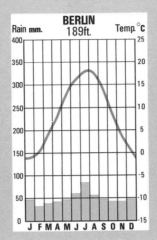

BERLIN
189ft.
Rain mm. / Temp.°C

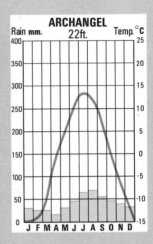

ARCHANGEL
22ft.
Rain mm. / Temp.°C

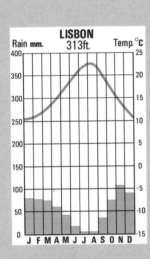

LISBON
313ft.
Rain mm. / Temp.°C

© Collins ◇ Longman Atlases

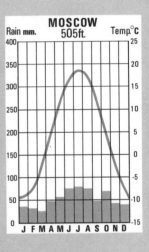

MOSCOW
505ft.
Rain mm. / Temp.°C

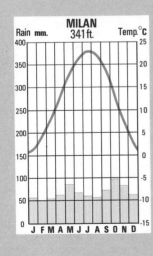

MILAN
341ft.
Rain mm. / Temp.°C

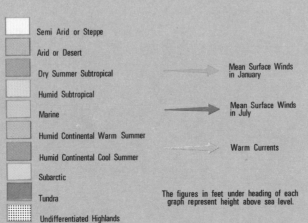

Semi Arid or Steppe

Arid or Desert

Dry Summer Subtropical

Humid Subtropical

Marine

Humid Continental Warm Summer

Humid Continental Cool Summer

Subarctic

Tundra

Undifferentiated Highlands

Mean Surface Winds in January

Mean Surface Winds in July

Warm Currents

The figures in feet under heading of each graph represent height above sea level.

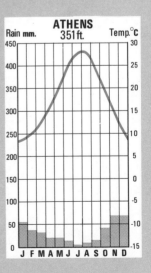

ATHENS
351ft.
Rain mm. / Temp.°C

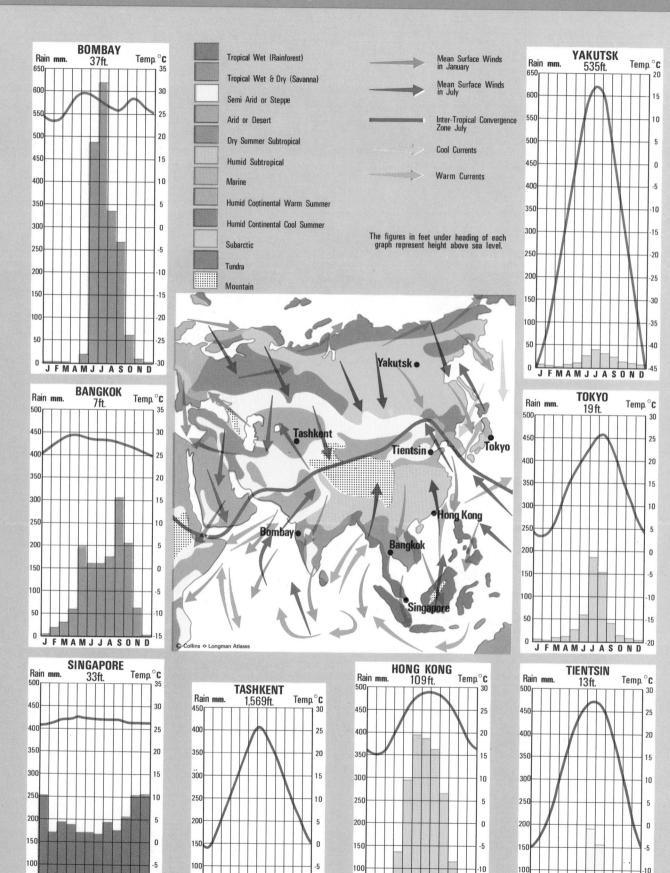

BOMBAY
37ft.
Rain mm. / Temp. °C

YAKUTSK
535ft.
Rain mm. / Temp. °C

BANGKOK
7ft.
Rain mm. / Temp. °C

TOKYO
19ft.
Rain mm. / Temp. °C

SINGAPORE
33ft.
Rain mm. / Temp. °C

TASHKENT
1,569ft.
Rain mm. / Temp. °C

HONG KONG
109ft.
Rain mm. / Temp. °C

TIENTSIN
13ft.
Rain mm. / Temp. °C

Legend:
- Tropical Wet (Rainforest)
- Tropical Wet & Dry (Savanna)
- Semi Arid or Steppe
- Arid or Desert
- Dry Summer Subtropical
- Humid Subtropical
- Marine
- Humid Continental Warm Summer
- Humid Continental Cool Summer
- Subarctic
- Tundra
- Mountain

- Mean Surface Winds in January
- Mean Surface Winds in July
- Inter-Tropical Convergence Zone July
- Cool Currents
- Warm Currents

The figures in feet under heading of each graph represent height above sea level.

Map labels: Yakutsk, Tashkent, Tientsin, Tokyo, Hong Kong, Bangkok, Bombay, Singapore

© Collins ◊ Longman Atlases

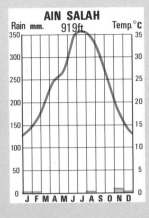

AIN SALAH
919ft.
Rain mm.   Temp. °C
350 — 35
300 — 30
250 — 25
200 — 20
150 — 15
100 — 10
50 — 5
0 — 0
J F M A M J J A S O N D

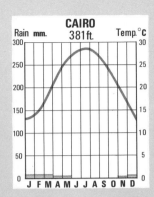

CAIRO
381ft.
Rain mm.   Temp. °C
300 — 30
250 — 25
200 — 20
150 — 15
100 — 10
50 — 5
0 — 0
J F M A M J J A S O N D

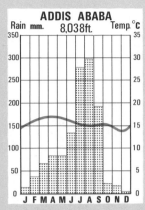

ADDIS ABABA
8,038ft.
Rain mm.   Temp. °C
350 — 35
300 — 30
250 — 25
200 — 20
150 — 15
100 — 10
50 — 5
0 — 0
J F M A M J J A S O N D

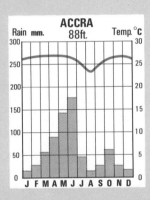

ACCRA
88ft.
Rain mm.   Temp. °C
300 — 30
250 — 25
200 — 20
150 — 15
100 — 10
50 — 5
0 — 0
J F M A M J J A S O N D

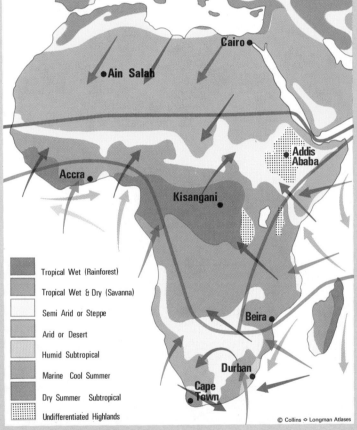

Cairo ●

● Ain Salah

Accra ●

Kisangani

● Addis Ababa

Beira ●

Durban ●

Cape Town ●

Tropical Wet (Rainforest)
Tropical Wet & Dry (Savanna)
Semi Arid or Steppe
Arid or Desert
Humid Subtropical
Marine Cool Summer
Dry Summer Subtropical
Undifferentiated Highlands

© Collins ◇ Longman Atlases

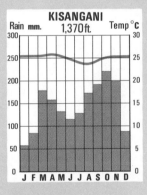

KISANGANI
1,370ft.
Rain mm.   Temp. °C
300 — 30
250 — 25
200 — 20
150 — 15
100 — 10
50 — 5
0 — 0
J F M A M J J A S O N D

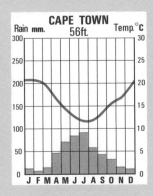

CAPE TOWN
56ft.
Rain mm.   Temp. °C
300 — 30
250 — 25
200 — 20
150 — 15
100 — 10
50 — 5
0 — 0
J F M A M J J A S O N D

Mean Surface Winds in January

Mean Surface Winds in July

Inter-Tropical Convergence Zone January

Inter-Tropical Convergence Zone July

Cool Currents

Warm Currents

The figures in feet under heading of each graph represent height above sea level.

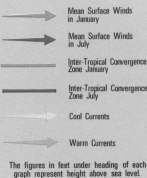

DURBAN
16ft.
Rain mm.   Temp. °C
300 — 30
250 — 25
200 — 20
150 — 15
100 — 10
50 — 5
0 — 0
J F M A M J J A S O N D

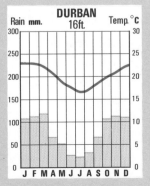

BEIRA
28ft.
Rain mm.   Temp. °C
300 — 30
250 — 25
200 — 20
150 — 15
100 — 10
50 — 5
0 — 0
J F M A M J J A S O N D

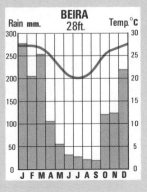

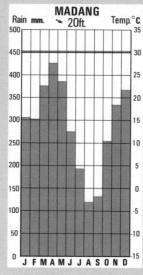

DARWIN 97ft.
Rain mm. / Temp. °C
J F M A M J J A S O N D

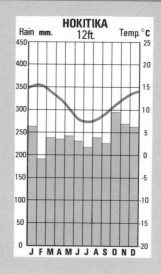

MADANG 20ft.
Rain mm. / Temp. °C
J F M A M J J A S O N D

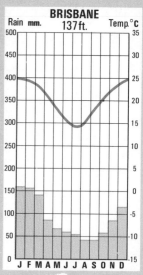

HOKITIKA 12ft.
Rain mm. / Temp. °C
J F M A M J J A S O N D

BRISBANE 137ft.
Rain mm. / Temp. °C
J F M A M J J A S O N D

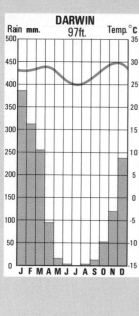

ALICE SPRINGS 1,901ft.
Rain mm. / Temp. °C
J F M A M J J A S O N D

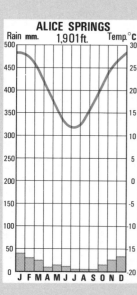

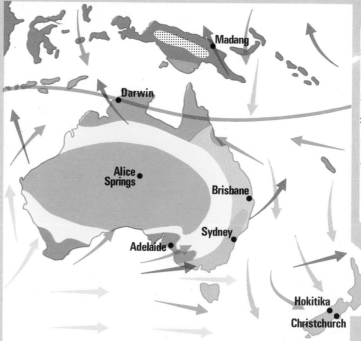

© Collins ◇ Longman Atlases

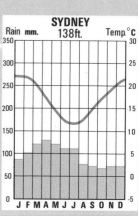

SYDNEY 138ft.
Rain mm. / Temp. °C
J F M A M J J A S O N D

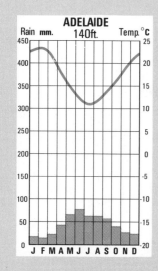

ADELAIDE 140ft.
Rain mm. / Temp. °C
J F M A M J J A S O N D

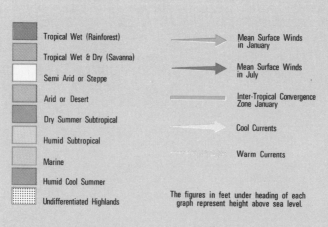

Tropical Wet (Rainforest)

Tropical Wet & Dry (Savanna)

Semi Arid or Steppe

Arid or Desert

Dry Summer Subtropical

Humid Subtropical

Marine

Humid Cool Summer

Undifferentiated Highlands

→ Mean Surface Winds in January

→ Mean Surface Winds in July

→ Inter-Tropical Convergence Zone January

→ Cool Currents

→ Warm Currents

The figures in feet under heading of each graph represent height above sea level.

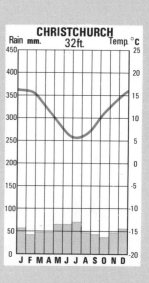

CHRISTCHURCH 32ft.
Rain mm. / Temp. °C
J F M A M J J A S O N D

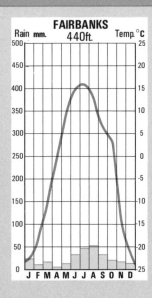

FAIRBANKS 440ft.
Rain mm. | Temp.°C

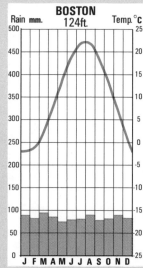

BOSTON 124ft.
Rain mm. | Temp.°C

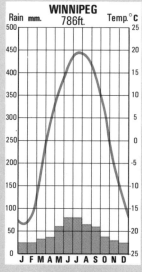

WINNIPEG 786ft.
Rain mm. | Temp.°C

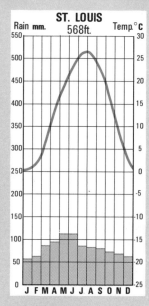

ST. LOUIS 568ft.
Rain mm. | Temp.°C

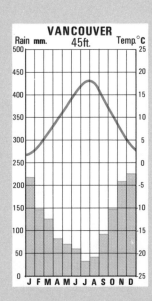

VANCOUVER 45ft.
Rain mm. | Temp.°C

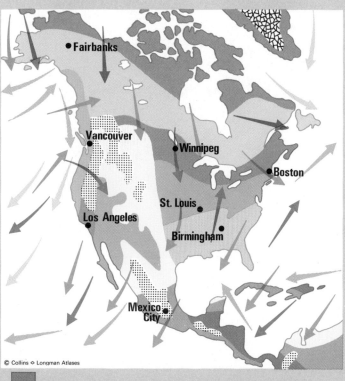

Fairbanks

Vancouver

Winnipeg

Boston

St. Louis

Los Angeles

Birmingham

Mexico City

© Collins ◇ Longman Atlases

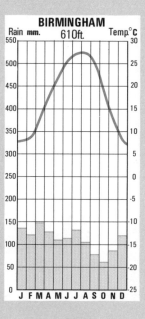

BIRMINGHAM 610ft.
Rain mm. | Temp.°C

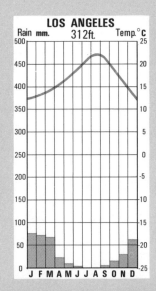

LOS ANGELES 312ft.
Rain mm. | Temp.°C

Tropical Wet (Rainforest)

Tropical Wet & Dry (Savanna)

Semi Arid or Steppe

Arid or Desert

Dry Summer Subtropical

Humid Subtropical

Marine

Humid Continental Warm Summer

Humid Continental Cool Summer

Subarctic

Tundra

Ice Cap

Mountain

→ Mean Surface Winds in January

→ Mean Surface Winds in July

→ Cool Currents

→ Warm Currents

The figures in feet under heading of each graph represent height above sea level.

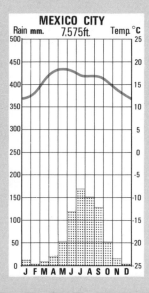

MEXICO CITY 7.575ft.
Rain mm. | Temp.°C

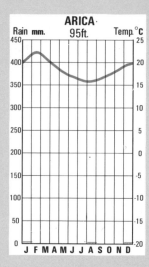

ARICA
95ft.
Rain mm.   Temp. °C
J F M A M J J A S O N D

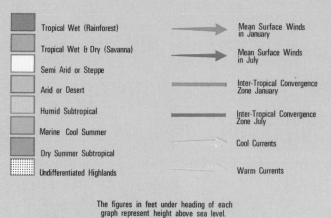

Tropical Wet (Rainforest)
Tropical Wet & Dry (Savanna)
Semi Arid or Steppe
Arid or Desert
Humid Subtropical
Marine Cool Summer
Dry Summer Subtropical
Undifferentiated Highlands

Mean Surface Winds in January
Mean Surface Winds in July
Inter-Tropical Convergence Zone January
Inter-Tropical Convergence Zone July
Cool Currents
Warm Currents

The figures in feet under heading of each graph represent height above sea level.

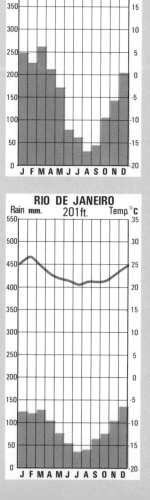

CAYENNE
20ft.
Rain mm.   Temp. °C
J F M A M J J A S O N D

VALPARAISO
135ft.
Rain mm.   Temp. °C
J F M A M J J A S O N D

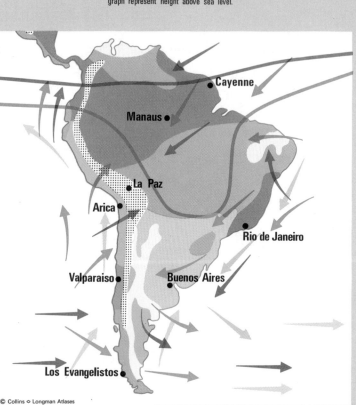
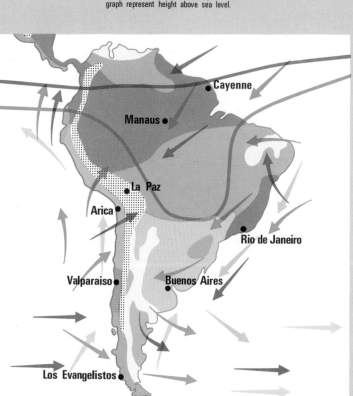

Cayenne
Manaus
La Paz
Arica
Rio de Janeiro
Valparaiso
Buenos Aires
Los Evangelistos

© Collins ◇ Longman Atlases

MANAUS
144ft.
Rain mm.   Temp. °C
J F M A M J J A S O N D

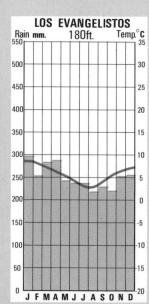

LOS EVANGELISTOS
180ft.
Rain mm.   Temp. °C
J F M A M J J A S O N D

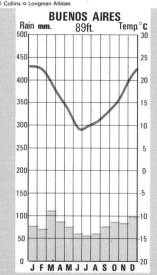

BUENOS AIRES
89ft.
Rain mm.   Temp. °C
J F M A M J J A S O N D

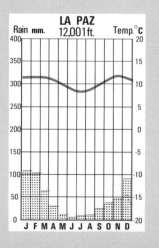

LA PAZ
12,001ft.
Rain mm.   Temp. °C
J F M A M J J A S O N D

RIO DE JANEIRO
201ft.
Rain mm.   Temp. °C
J F M A M J J A S O N D

Urals

Caucasus

Black Sea

Baltic Shield

Baltic Sea

North European Plain

Carpathians

MEDITERRANEAN SEA

North Sea

Alps

Pyrenees

ATLANTIC OCEAN

Scale 1:20 000 000
Bonne Projection

Arctic Circle

500 Miles
800 Kms.
400
600
300
400
200
100
200
0
0

Main trend lines
Rift valleys
Main centres of volcanic activity

Quaternary
Tertiary
Mesozoic
Palaeozoic
Precambrian

Lowland Plains & Basins
High Plains & Plateaus
Scarps & Upland Edges
Fold & Volcanic Mountains

Permanent ice and snow

Tundra and alpine

Desert

Semi-desert

Grassland, heath, marsh and steppe

Forest and woodland

Cultivated land

Scale 1:16 000 000

| 0 | 100 | 200 | 300 | 400 | 500 Miles |

| 0 | 200 | 400 | 600 | 800 Kms. |

Conic Projection

ARCTIC

North Cape

ICELAND

Hekla 4892

NORWEGIAN SEA

Lofoten Is.

Arctic Circle

S C A N D I N A V I A

8103

Tornio

Gulf of Bothnia

Faroe Is.

Mälaren

Åland Is.

Gulf of Finland

L. Peipus

Shetland Is.

Vänern

ATLANTIC

Skagerrak

Vättern

Gotland

Baltic Sea

OCEAN

Hebrides

Orkney Is.

NORTH SEA

Jutland

Bornholm

European

Ben Nevis 4406

Ireland

Great Britain

Weser

Elbe

North

Vistula

Bug

Pripet

Thames

Rhine

Oder

Land's End

English Channel

Meuse

Ardennes

Ore Mts.

Sudeten Mts.

Bay of Biscay

Seine

Vosges

Black Forest

Bohemian Forest

Moravian Heights

Carpathian

Loire

Jura Mts.

Danube

Inn

C. Finisterre

Massif Central

Mt.Blanc 15781

The Alps

Po

Hungarian Plain

Drava

Mures

Cantabrian Mts.

Cevennes

Rhone

Sava

Transylvanian Alps

Douro

Garonne

Pyrenees

Pico de Aneto 11168

Dinaric Alps

M e s e t a

Ebro

Gulf of Lions

Ligurian Sea

Apennines

Adriatic Sea

Balkan

Tagus

Ligurian Sea

Corsica

Tiber

Guadiana

Sierra Morena

Guadalquivir

Balearic Is.

Sardinia

Tyrrhenian Sea

Pindus Mts.

Olympus 9550

C. St. Vincent

Sierra Nevada

Aeg

Str. of Gibraltar

M E D I T E R R A N E A N

Ionian Sea

High Atlas

Tell Atlas

Sicily

Mt Etna 10958

Saharan Atlas

Malta

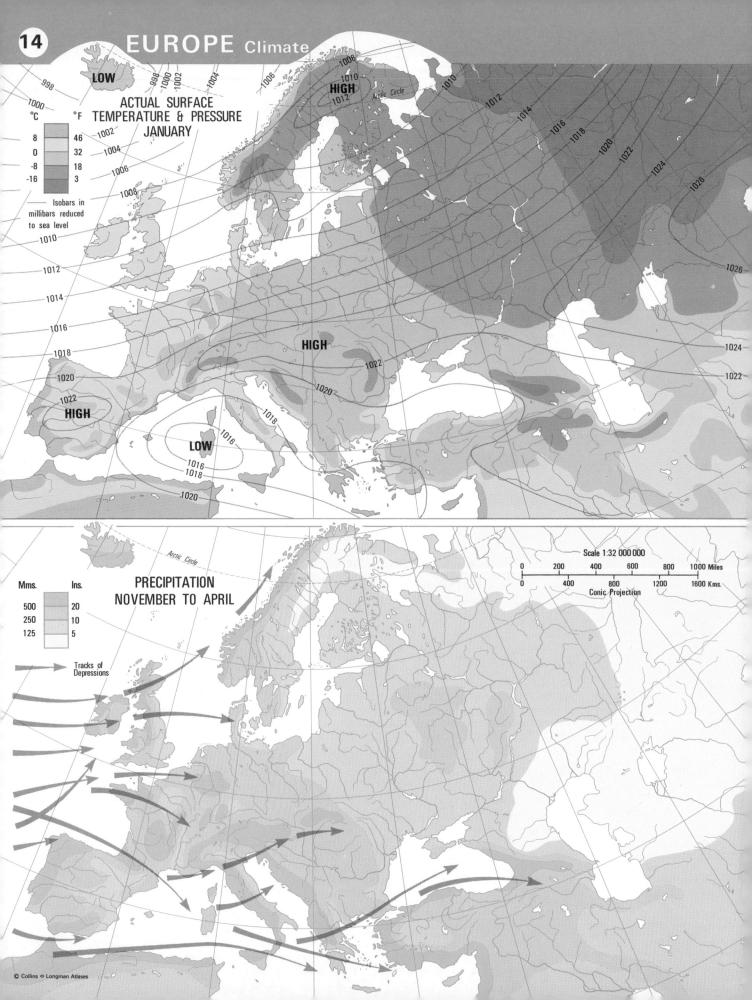

ACTUAL SURFACE
TEMPERATURE & PRESSURE
JANUARY

°C	°F
8	46
0	32
-8	18
-16	3

Isobars in
millibars reduced
to sea level

LOW

HIGH
1012

HIGH
1022

HIGH

LOW

PRECIPITATION
NOVEMBER TO APRIL

Mms.	Ins.
500	20
250	10
125	5

Tracks of
Depressions

Arctic Circle

Scale 1:32 000 000

0   200   400   600   800   1000 Miles
0   400   800   1200   1600 Kms.
Conic Projection

© Collins ◇ Longman Atlases

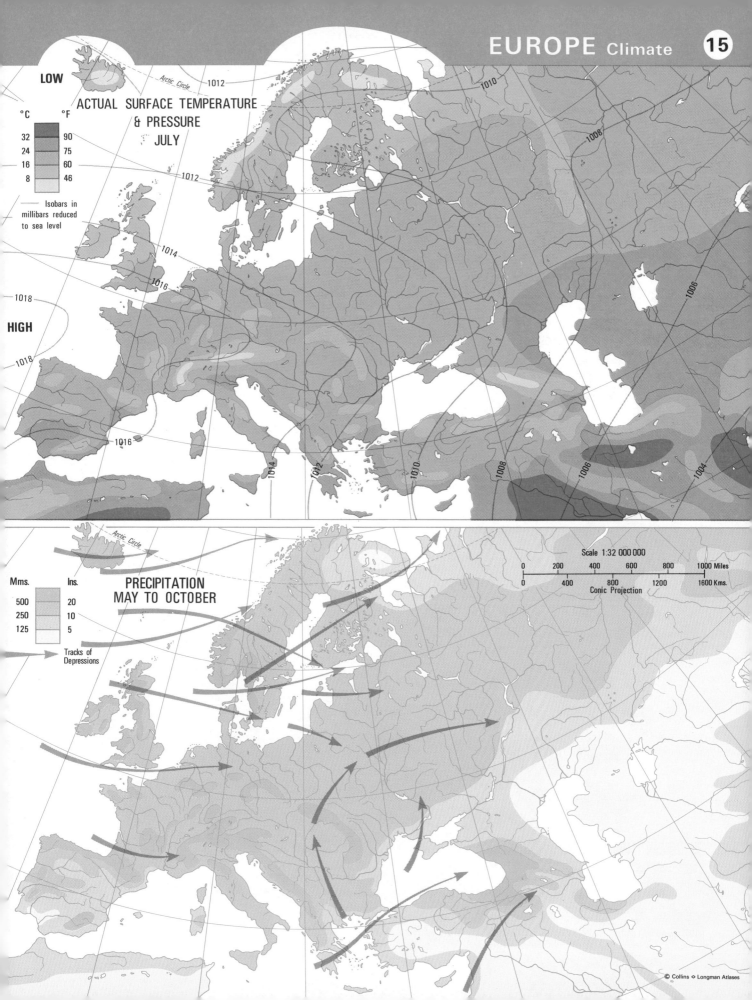

LOW

°C °F
ACTUAL SURFACE TEMPERATURE
& PRESSURE
JULY

32	90
24	75
16	60
8	46

Isobars in
millibars reduced
to sea level

HIGH

Mms. Ins.
PRECIPITATION
MAY TO OCTOBER

500	20
250	10
125	5

Tracks of
Depressions

Scale 1:32 000 000

0   200   400   600   800   1000 Miles
0   400   800   1200   1600 Kms.
Conic Projection

Arctic Circle

© Collins ◇ Longman Atlases

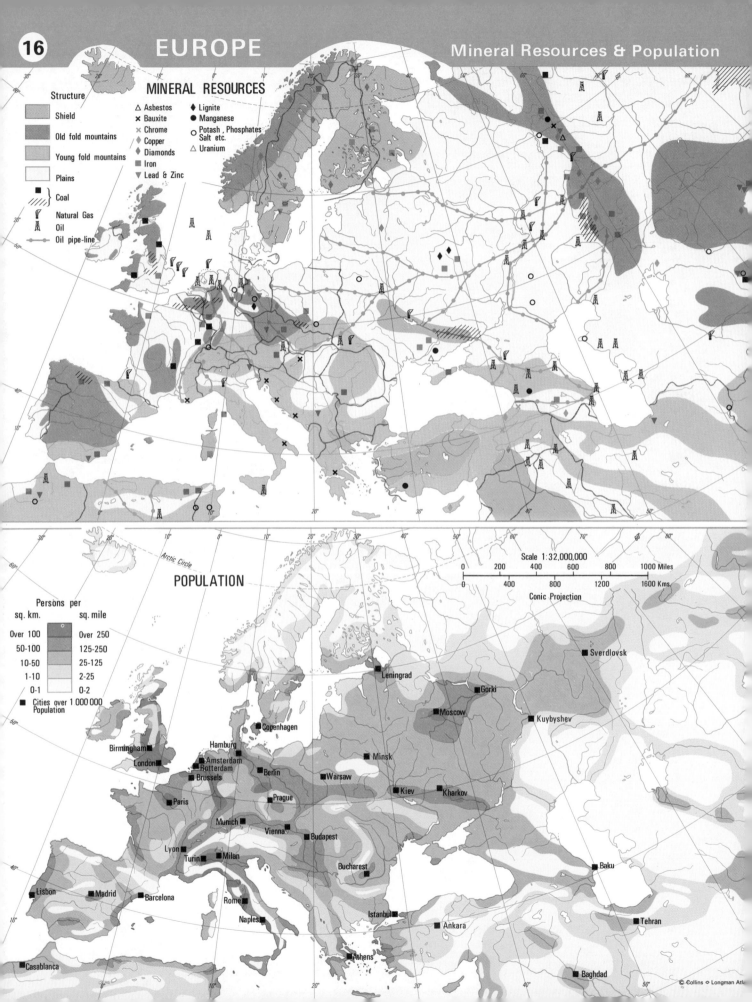

MINERAL RESOURCES

Structure

- Shield
- Old fold mountains
- Young fold mountains
- Plains

- Coal
- Natural Gas
- Oil
- Oil pipe-line

- △ Asbestos
- ✕ Bauxite
- ✕ Chrome
- ◆ Copper
- ◆ Diamonds
- ■ Iron
- ▼ Lead & Zinc
- ◆ Lignite
- ● Manganese
- ○ Potash, Phosphates Salt etc.
- △ Uranium

POPULATION

Persons per

sq. km.	sq. mile
Over 100	Over 250
50-100	125-250
10-50	25-125
1-10	2-25
0-1	0-2

■ Cities over 1 000 000 Population

Scale 1:32,000,000

| 0 | 200 | 400 | 600 | 800 | 1000 Miles |
| 0 | 400 | 800 | 1200 | 1600 Kms. |

Conic Projection

Arctic Circle

Sverdlovsk
Leningrad
Gorki
Moscow
Kuybyshev
Copenhagen
Hamburg
Birmingham
Minsk
London
Amsterdam
Rotterdam
Berlin
Warsaw
Brussels
Kiev
Kharkov
Paris
Prague
Munich
Vienna
Budapest
Lyon
Turin
Milan
Bucharest
Baku
Lisbon
Madrid
Barcelona
Rome
Istanbul
Naples
Ankara
Tehran
Athens
Casablanca
Baghdad

© Collins ◇ Longman Atl

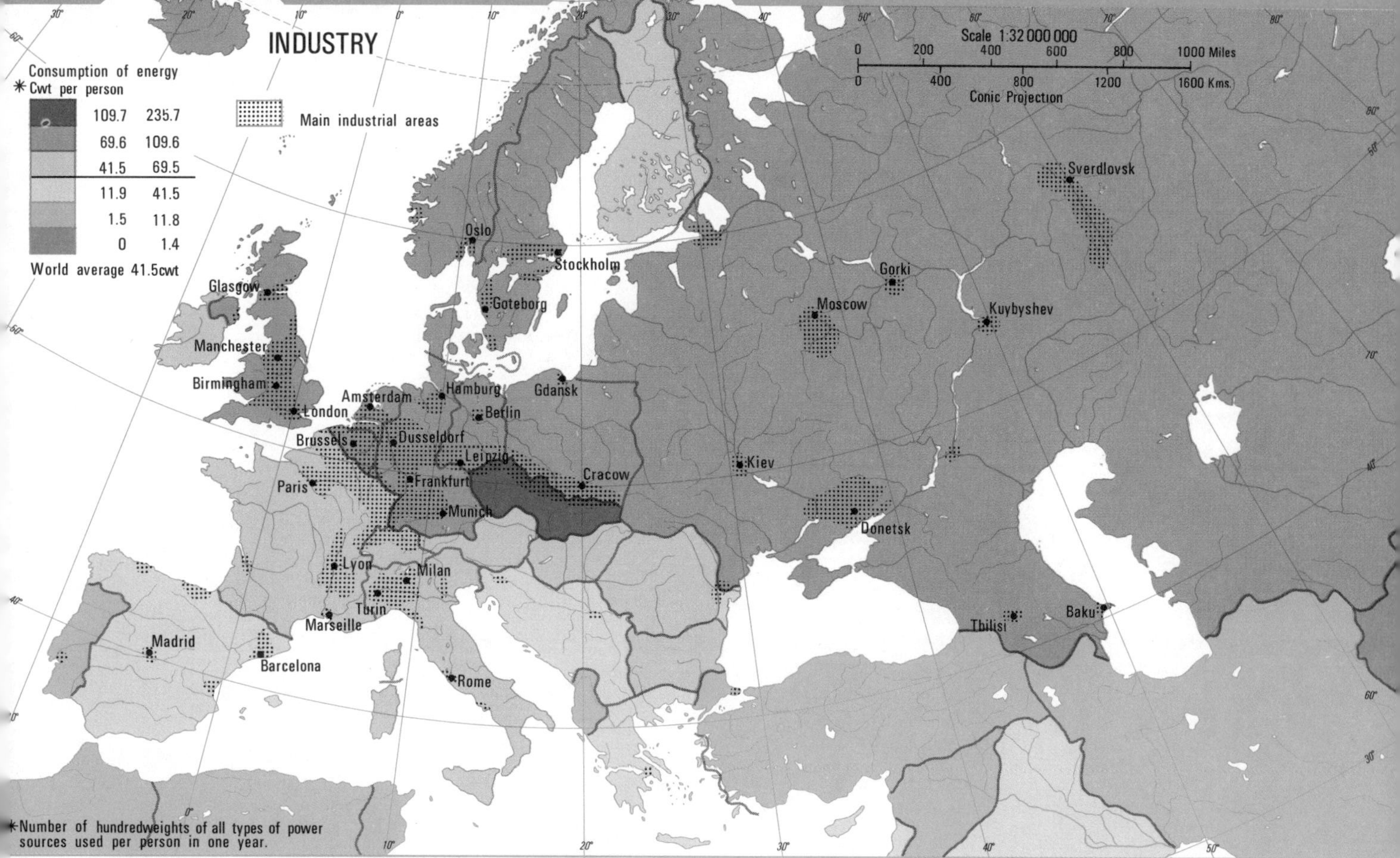
INDUSTRY
Consumption of energy
* Cwt per person
109.7 235.7
69.6 109.6
41.5 69.5
11.9 41.5
1.5 11.8
0 1.4
World average 41.5cwt
Main industrial areas
Scale 1:32 000 000
0 200 400 600 800 1000 Miles
0 400 800 1200 1600 Kms.
Conic Projection
Sverdlovsk
Oslo
Stockholm
Gorki
Glasgow
Goteborg
Moscow
Kuybyshev
Manchester
Birmingham
Hamburg
Gdansk
Amsterdam
London
Berlin
Brussels
Dusseldorf
Leipzig
Kiev
Paris
Frankfurt
Cracow
Munich
Donetsk
Lyon
Milan
Turin
Marseille
Tbilisi
Baku
Madrid
Barcelona
Rome
*Number of hundredweights of all types of power sources used per person in one year.

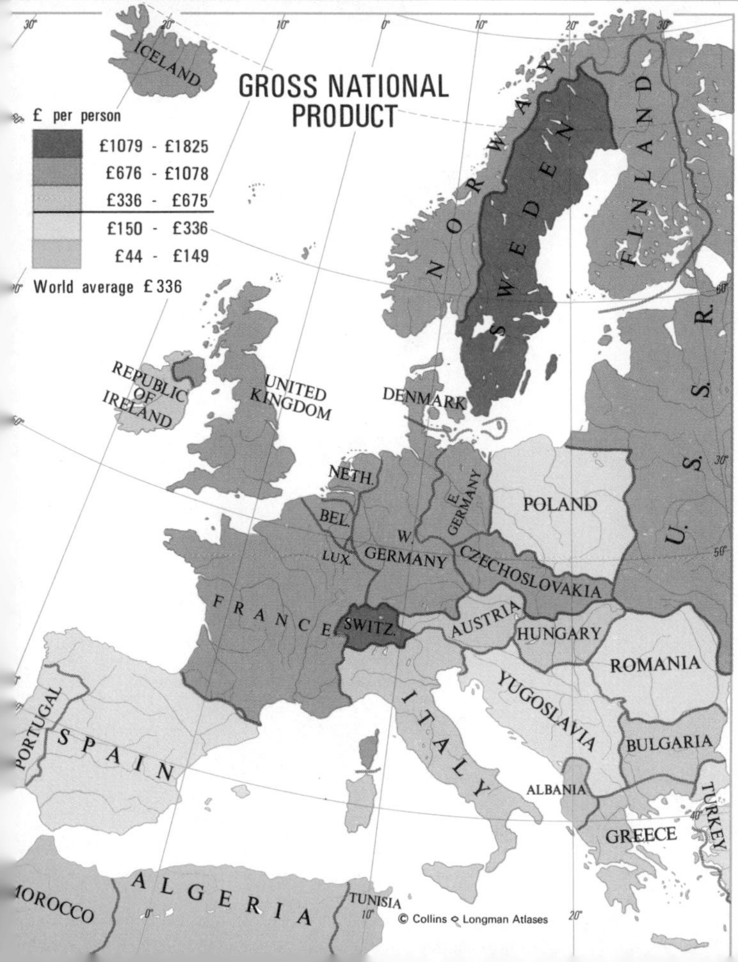
GROSS NATIONAL PRODUCT
£ per person
£1079 - £1825
£676 - £1078
£336 - £675
£150 - £336
£44 - £149
World average £336
ICELAND
NORWAY
SWEDEN
FINLAND
U.S.S.R.
REPUBLIC OF IRELAND
UNITED KINGDOM
DENMARK
NETH.
E. GERMANY
POLAND
BEL.
LUX.
W. GERMANY
CZECHOSLOVAKIA
FRANCE
SWITZ.
AUSTRIA
HUNGARY
ROMANIA
YUGOSLAVIA
PORTUGAL
SPAIN
ITALY
BULGARIA
ALBANIA
TURKEY
GREECE
MOROCCO
ALGERIA
TUNISIA

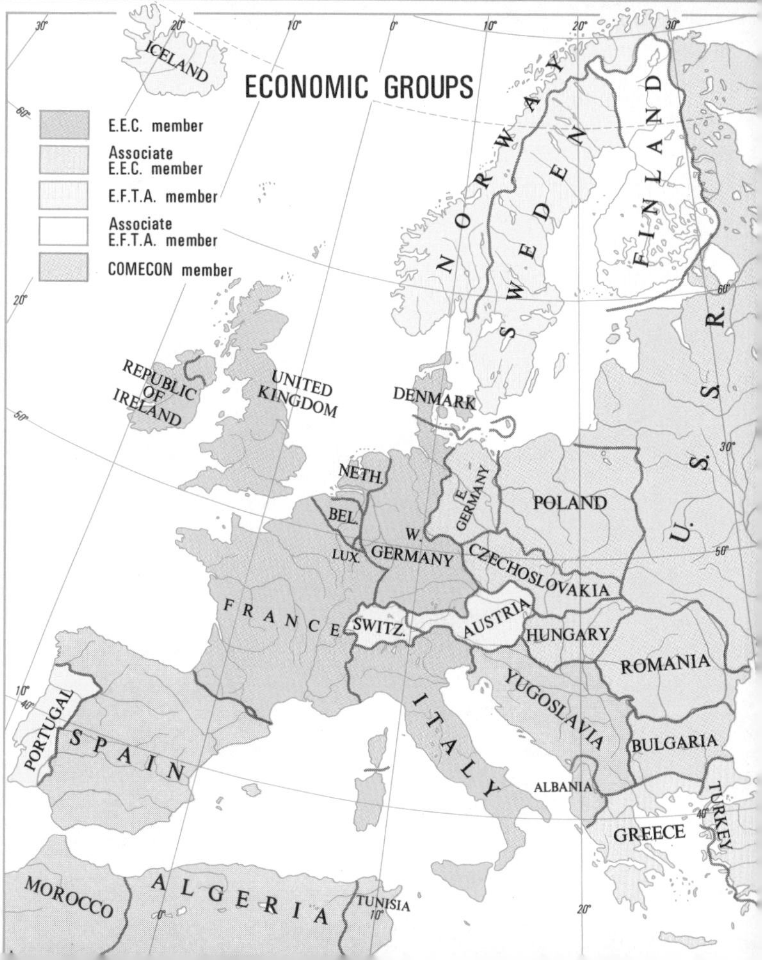
ECONOMIC GROUPS
E.E.C. member
Associate E.E.C. member
E.F.T.A. member
Associate E.F.T.A. member
COMECON member
ICELAND
NORWAY
SWEDEN
FINLAND
U.S.S.R.
REPUBLIC OF IRELAND
UNITED KINGDOM
DENMARK
NETH.
E. GERMANY
POLAND
BEL.
LUX.
W. GERMANY
CZECHOSLOVAKIA
FRANCE
SWITZ.
AUSTRIA
HUNGARY
ROMANIA
YUGOSLAVIA
PORTUGAL
SPAIN
ITALY
BULGARIA
ALBANIA
TURKEY
GREECE
MOROCCO
ALGERIA
TUNISIA

© Collins o Longman Atlases

ARCTIC OCEAN

ATLANTIC OCEAN

SOVIET

UNION

OF

SOCIALIST

REPUBLICS

IRAN

IRAQ

SYRIA

LEBANON

CYPRUS

TURKEY

BLACK SEA

Caspian Sea

Tabriz

Mosul

Aleppo

Homs

Adana

Konya

Antalya

Izmir

Nicosia

Rhodes

Crete

Ankara

Istanbul

Bursa

Edirne

Sinop

Trabzon

Batumi

Ordzhonikidze

Groznyy

Yerevan

Tbilisi

BULGARIA

ROMANIA

GREECE

Athens

Thessaloniki

Sofia

Bucharest

Burgas

Constanța

Ploeşti

Cluj

Belgrade

YUGOSLAVIA

ALBANIA

Tiranë

Patras

Aegean Sea

Ionian Sea

MEDITERRANEAN SEA

Murmansk

Arkhangel'sk

Pechora

Kotlas

Sukhona

N.Dvina

Vologda

Yaroslavl

Gorki

Kazan

Kirov

Kuybyshev

Ufa

Perm

Sverdlovsk

Ob

Kama

Volga

Moscow

Kalinin

Ivanovo

Tula

Orel

Kursk

Voronezh

Penza

Saratov

Volgograd

Astrakhan

Rostov

Don

Donets

Donetsk

Dnepropetrovsk

Zaporozhye

Kharkov

Kiev

Odessa

Kishinev

Krasnodar

Sevastopol

Kerch

Sea of Azov

L. Onega

L. Ladoga

White Sea

Petrozavodsk

Leningrad

Novgorod

Pskov

L. Peipus

Smolensk

Gomel

Minsk

Vilnius

Vitebsk

Riga

Kaunas

Klaipeda

Kaliningrad

Tallinn

FINLAND

Helsinki

Turku

Tampere

Vaasa

Luleå

Oulu

SWEDEN

NORWAY

Tromsø

Narvik

Bodø

Trondheim

Bergen

Stavanger

Oslo

Stockholm

Göteborg

Malmö

Gotland

Öland

Bornholm

Baltic Sea

Gulf of Bothnia

Vänern

Vättern

North Cape

Lofoten

Hebrides

ICELAND

Reykjavik

Arctic Circle

Faroe Is

Shetland Is

Orkney Is

UNITED KINGDOM

Edinburgh

Glasgow

Belfast

REPUBLIC OF IRELAND

Dublin

Manchester

Leeds

Liverpool

Birmingham

Bristol

London

NORTH SEA

DENMARK

Copenhagen

Esbjerg

Kiel

Hamburg

Bremen

Hannover

EAST GERMANY

Berlin

Dresden

WEST GERMANY

Essen

Bonn

Frankfurt

Stuttgart

Munich

NETH

Amsterdam

The Hague

Rotterdam

BEL

Brussels

Lille

LUX

Luxembourg

Strasbourg

Berne

SWITZ

Zürich

Geneva

POLAND

Warsaw

Gdańsk

Poznań

Łódź

Wrocław

Cracow

Białystok

Vistula

Oder

Bug

CZECHOSLOVAKIA

Prague

Plzeň

Bratislava

Košice

AUSTRIA

Vienna

Innsbruck

Graz

HUNGARY

Budapest

Szeged

Miskolc

Zagreb

Sava

Split

Venice

Trieste

Bologna

ITALY

Rome

Naples

Bari

Taranto

Brindisi

Reggio

Palermo

Sicily

Cagliari

Sardinia (It.)

Corsica (Fr.)

Ajaccio

Tyrrhenian Sea

Adriatic Sea

Ancona

Florence

Genoa

Turin

Milan

MONACO

Nice

Marseille

Lyon

FRANCE

Paris

Nantes

Bordeaux

Toulouse

Brest

Cherbourg

Le Havre

English Channel

Channel Is

Bay of Biscay

Seine

Loire

Garonne

Rhône

Rhine

Elbe

ANDORRA

Barcelona

Valencia

Zaragoza

Bilbao

Oviedo

La Coruña

SPAIN

Madrid

Murcia

Granada

Sevilla

Córdoba

Ebro

Duero

Tagus

PORTUGAL

Lisbon

Oporto

Gibraltar (Br.)

MOROCCO

Rabat

Casablanca

Fez

Tangier

ALGERIA

Algiers

Oran

TUNISIA

Tunis

Annaba

Bizerta

MALTA

Balearic Is (Sp.)

Palma

C. Finisterre

Str. of Gibraltar

BEL : BELGIUM
L : LIECHTENSTEIN
LUX : LUXEMBOURG
NETH : NETHERLANDS
SM : SAN MARINO
SWITZ : SWITZERLAND

Scale 1:20 000 000

Bonne Projection

500 Miles
800 Kms.

Mediterranean Sea

Tertiary
Mesozoic
Palaeozoic
Precambrian

Igneous rocks of various ages

Lowland Plains & Basins
High Plains & Plateaus
Scarps & Upland Edges
Fold & Volcanic Mountains

Main fault line

MOINE THRUST

Northwest Highlands

GREAT GLEN FAULT

Grampian Mountains

HIGHLAND BOUNDARY FAULT

Ochil Hills

SOUTHERN UPLANDS FAULT

Southern Uplands

Cheviot Hills

CRAVEN FAULT

Lake District

Pennines

Antrim Mts.

Wicklow Mts.

Macgillycuddy's Reeks

Cambrian Mountains

Cotswolds

Chiltern Hills

North Downs

Exmoor

South Downs

Dartmoor

Scale 1:5 000 000

0   50   100   150 Miles

0   50   100   150   200 Kms.

Conic Projection

2°

0°

2°

N O R T H   S E A

Buchan Ness

Unst

Yell

Mainland

Fair Isle

Foula

Shetland Islands

Orkney

Islands

Pentland Firth
Duncansby Hd.
Dunnet Hd.

Pentland Firth

Dornoch Firth

Moray Firth

Spey

Dee

Ben Macdhui
4300

Cairngorms

Firth of Tay

Firth of Forth

Firth of Forth

Strathmore

Tay

Forth

Ochil Hills

Pentland
Hills

L. Lomond

Clyde

G r a m p i a n s

The Great Glen

Ben Nevis
4406

Northwest
Highlands

C. Wrath

Ben More
Assynt
3273

N. Rona

Butt of Lewis

Lewis

The Minch

Skye

Rhum

Mull
3169

Firth of Lorne

Jura

Islay

Coll

Tiree

I n n e r   H e b r i d e s

Flannan Is.

North Uist

South Uist

Barra

St. Kilda

O u t e r   H e b r i d e s

A T L A N T I C

O C E A N

58°

58°

60°

60°

2°

4°

6°

8°

10°

12°

0°

2°

56°

56°

Sub-alpine

Heath and peat

Grass moorland

Forest and woodland

Agricultural land

Urban areas

Scale 1:3 500 000

Conic Projection

Miles
100   75   50   25   0

Kms.
150   125   100   75   50   25   0

© Collins © Longman Atlases

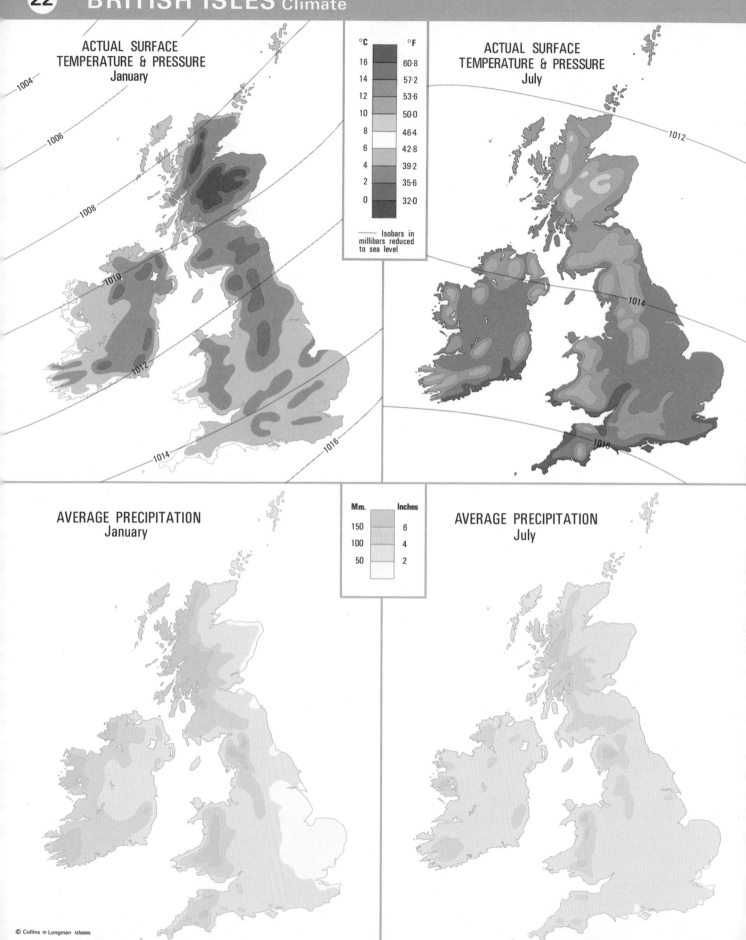

ACTUAL SURFACE
TEMPERATURE & PRESSURE
January

ACTUAL SURFACE
TEMPERATURE & PRESSURE
July

°C	°F
16	60·8
14	57·2
12	53·6
10	50·0
8	46·4
6	42·8
4	39·2
2	35·6
0	32·0

Isobars in
millibars reduced
to sea level

AVERAGE PRECIPITATION
January

AVERAGE PRECIPITATION
July

Mm.	Inches
150	6
100	4
50	2

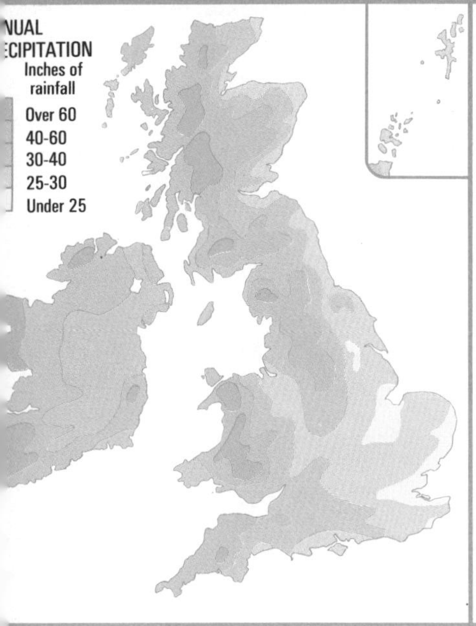

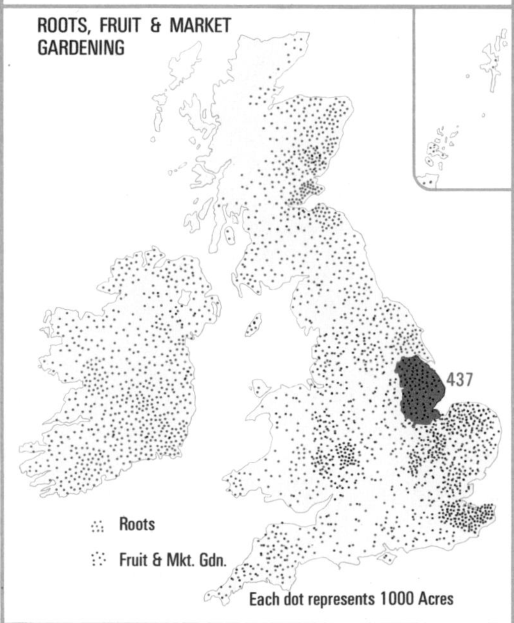

ANNUAL
PRECIPITATION

Inches of
rainfall

Over 60
40-60
30-40
25-30
Under 25

OATS

Each dot represents 2000 Acres

HAY & SILAGE

Each dot represents 2000 Acres

WHEAT

Each dot represents 2000 Acres

ROOTS, FRUIT & MARKET
GARDENING

437

Roots
Fruit & Mkt. Gdn.

Each dot represents 1000 Acres

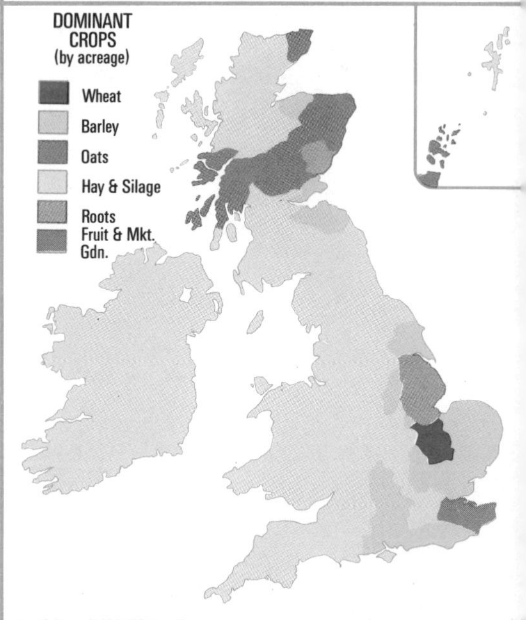

DOMINANT
CROPS
(by acreage)

Wheat
Barley
Oats
Hay & Silage
Roots
Fruit & Mkt.
Gdn.

BEEF CATTLE

Each dot represents 2000 Head

DAIRY CATTLE

Each dot represents 2000 Head

SHEEP

Each dot represents 20 000 Head

ns ◇ Longman Atlases

POPULATION

Persons per sq. km.   Persons per sq. ml.

over 150   over 400
20-150   50-400
0.4-20   1-50
under 0.4   under 1

Cities over 250,000 population ■
Main Road
Main Railway

Scale 1:5 000 000

0   25   50   75   100 Miles
0   50   100   150 Kms.
Conic Projection

Glasgow
Edinburgh
Newcastle upon Tyne
Belfast
Kingston upon Hull
Leeds
Bradford
Liverpool
Manchester
Sheffield
Dublin
Stoke-on-Trent
Nottingham
Wolverhampton
Leicester
Birmingham
Coventry
London
Cardiff
Bristol
Plymouth

ORKNEY
• Kirkwall

SHETLAND
• Lerwick

Legend

— International boundary
— National boundary
— County or region boundary
--- Historic counties in Northern Ireland
▨ Metropolitan county
▦ Greater London
• Administrative headquarters (those underlined contain the offices of more than one county)

The local government boundaries for England & Wales shown on this map were officially approved by an Act of Parliament in October 1972, and those for Scotland and Northern Ireland in October 1973. The sub-division of Counties and Regions is not shown.

SCOTLAND
9 Regions
3 Island Authorities
53 Districts

NORTHERN IRELAND
1 Region
26 Districts

ENGLAND
39 Counties
6 Metropolitan Counties
Greater London
36 Metropolitan Districts
296 Non-Metropolitan Districts

REPUBLIC OF IRELAND
26 Counties

WALES
8 Counties
37 Districts

WESTERN ISLES
• Stornoway

HIGHLAND
• Inverness

GRAMPIAN
• Aberdeen

STRATHCLYDE

TAYSIDE
• Dundee
• Cupar

CENTRAL
• Stirling

FIFE

LOTHIAN
• Glasgow
• Edinburgh

BORDERS
Newtown
St Boswells

DUMFRIES & GALLOWAY
• Dumfries

NORTHUMBERLAND
Newcastle upon Tyne
TYNE & WEAR

CUMBRIA
• Carlisle

DURHAM
• Durham

CLEVELAND
• Middlesbrough

NORTH YORKSHIRE
• Northallerton

HUMBERSIDE
• Kingston upon Hull

LANCASHIRE
• Preston

WEST YORKSHIRE
• Wakefield

SOUTH YORKSHIRE
• Barnsley

MERSEYSIDE
• Liverpool

G.M.
• Manchester

CHESHIRE
• Chester
• Mold

DERBYSHIRE
• Matlock

NOTTINGHAMSHIRE
• Nottingham

LINCOLNSHIRE
• Lincoln

CLWYD
• Caernarfon

GWYNEDD

SALOP
• Shrewsbury

STAFFORDSHIRE
• Stafford

W.M.
• Birmingham

LEICESTERSHIRE
• Leicester

NORFOLK
• Norwich

POWYS
• Llandrindod Wells

HEREFORD & WORCESTER
• Worcester

WARWICKSHIRE
• Warwick

NORTHAMPTONSHIRE
• Northampton

CAMBRIDGESHIRE
• Cambridge

SUFFOLK
• Ipswich

DYFED
• Carmarthen

GWENT
• Cwmbran

GLOUCESTERSHIRE
• Gloucester

OXFORDSHIRE
• Oxford

BUCKINGHAMSHIRE
• Aylesbury

BEDFORDSHIRE
• Bedford

HERTFORDSHIRE
• Hertford

ESSEX
• Chelmsford

WEST GLAMORGAN
• Swansea

MID GLAMORGAN

S.G.
• Cardiff

AVON
• Bristol

WILTSHIRE
• Trowbridge

BERKSHIRE
• Reading

GREATER LONDON
Kingston upon Thames

SURREY

KENT
• Maidstone

SOMERSET
• Taunton

HAMPSHIRE
• Winchester

WEST SUSSEX
• Chichester

EAST SUSSEX
• Lewes

DEVON
• Exeter

DORSET
• Dorchester

ISLE OF WIGHT
• Newport

CORNWALL
• Truro

ISLE OF MAN
• Douglas

Republic of Ireland / Northern Ireland

DONEGAL
• Lifford

Londonderry

Antrim

Tyrone
• Belfast

Fermanagh
Armagh
Down

SLIGO
• Sligo

LEITRIM
• Carrick-on-Shannon

CAVAN
• Cavan

MONAGHAN
• Monaghan

LOUTH
• Dundalk

MAYO
• Castlebar

ROSCOMMON
• Roscommon

LONGFORD
• Longford

WEST MEATH
• Mullingar

MEATH
• Navan

GALWAY
• Galway

OFFALY
• Tullamore

LAOIS
• Port Laoise

KILDARE
• Naas

DUBLIN
• Dublin

WICKLOW
• Wicklow

CLARE
• Ennis

TIPPERARY

CARLOW
• Carlow

KILKENNY
• Kilkenny

WEXFORD
• Wexford

LIMERICK
• Limerick

KERRY
• Tralee

• Clonmel

WATERFORD
• Waterford

CORK
• Cork

G.M.   GREATER MANCHESTER
S.G.   SOUTH GLAMORGAN
W.M.   WEST MIDLANDS

Scale 1:4 000 000

0   20   40   60   80   100 Miles
0   40   80   120   160 km

Conic Projection

© Collins ◇ Longman Atlases

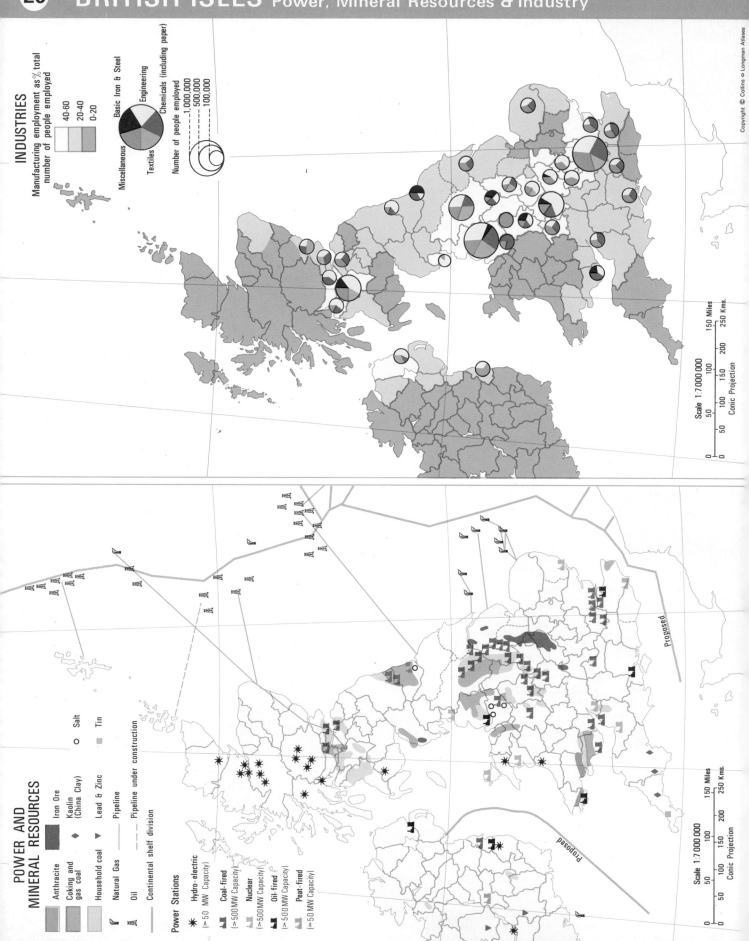

INDUSTRIES

Manufacturing employment as % total number of people employed

- 40-60
- 20-40
- 0-20

Basic Iron & Steel
Engineering
Chemicals (including paper)
Miscellaneous
Textiles

Number of people employed
- 1,000,000
- 500,000
- 100,000

Scale 1:7 000 000
Conic Projection

| 0 | 50 | 100 | 150 Miles |
| 0 | 50 | 100 | 150 | 200 | 250 Kms. |

POWER AND MINERAL RESOURCES

- Anthracite
- Coking and gas coal
- Household coal
- Natural Gas
- Oil
- Continental shelf division

- Iron Ore
- Kaolin (China Clay)
- Lead & Zinc
- Pipeline
- Pipeline under construction

- Salt
- Tin

Power Stations

- Hydro-electric (>50 MW Capacity)
- Coal-fired (>500MW Capacity)
- Nuclear (>500MW Capacity)
- Oil-fired (>500MW Capacity)
- Peat-fired (>50 MW Capacity)

Proposed

Proposed

Scale 1:7 000 000
Conic Projection

| 0 | 50 | 100 | 150 Miles |
| 0 | 50 | 100 | 150 | 200 | 250 Kms. |

SOUTHERN ENGLAND

© Collins ◇ Longman Atlases

LINCOLNSHIRE

NORFOLK

Saxthorpe · Bacton
North Walsham · Waxham
Aylsham · Stalham
Coltishall · Winterton-on-Sea
Hoveton · **Norfolk Broads**
King's Lynn
Market Deeping · Glen · Deeping Fen · Crowland
Wisbech · Nene · Nar
Thorney · Marshland Fen · Outwell
Peterborough · Guyhirn · Downham Market · Swaffham · East Dereham · **Norwich** · Great Yarmouth · Yarmouth Roads
March · Whittlesey · Old Fletton · Stilton · Wissey · ▲267 Watton · Wymondham · Reedham · Caister-on-Sea
Farcet Fen · Methwold · **Breckland** · 244 · Yare
Chatteris · Littleport · Attleborough · Lowestoft
CAMBRIDGESHIRE · Wangford Fen · Brandon · Thetford · Bungay · Beccles · Kessingland
Huntingdon · Isle of Ely · Diss · Harleston · Blyth · Southwold
St Ives · Mildenhall · Lark · Ixworth · Waveney · Halesworth · Southwold
Cottenham · Soham · Kentford · Eye · Yoxford
Burwell · Little Fen · SUFFOLK · Debenham · Framlingham · Saxmundham
Cambridge · Newmarket · Bury St. Edmunds · Stowmarket · Leiston
Great Shelford · ▲420 · Needham Market · Deben · Aldeburgh
Sawston · Linton · Haverhill · Wickham Market · Orford · Orford Ness
Melbourn · Great Chesterford · Sudbury · Hadleigh · Woodbridge · Hollesley Bay
Royston · Saffron Walden · Stour · Nayland · Ipswich · Bawdsey
410 · Newport · Thaxted · Bures · Manningtree · Felixstowe
Letchworth · Stansted Mountfitchet · Great Bardfield · Halstead · Colne · Harwich
Hitchin · Stevenage · Braintree · Coggeshall · Colchester · The Naze · Walton on the Naze
HERTFORDSHIRE · Bishop's Stortford · Great Dunmow · Kelvedon · Wivenhoe · Frinton
Harpenden · Welwyn Garden City · Ware · Chelmer · Witham · Tiptree · Brightlingsea
Hatfield · Hertford · Harlow · ESSEX · Maldon · Mersea I. · West Mersea · Clacton on Sea
St Albans · Hoddesdon · Chelmsford · Blackwater · Bradwell-on-Sea
Cheshunt · Waltham Abbey · Epping · Chipping Ongar · South Woodham Ferrers · Southminster
Potters Bar · Enfield · Epping Forest · Roding · Billericay · Wickford · Burnham-on-Crouch
Barnet · Chigwell · Brentwood · Rayleigh · Crouch · Foulness I. · Foulness Pt
Harrow · GREATER · Redbridge · Havering · Basildon · S. Benfleet · Foulness
London · Hounslow · LONDON · Grays · Stanford le Hope · Canvey · Shoeburyness · Southend-on-Sea
Richmond-upon-Thames · Tilbury · Thames Haven · Grain · Sheerness
Kingston-upon-Thames · Swanscombe · Gravesend · Rochester · Minster · Queenborough
Sutton · Bexley · Dartford · Gillingham · Isle of Sheppey · Leysdown-on-Sea · Margate · North Foreland
Croydon · Bromley · Chatham · Sittingbourne · Whitstable · Herne Bay · Broadstairs
Kingsdown · Borough Green · Faversham · The Swale · Isle of Thanet · Ramsgate · Pegwell Bay
Banstead · Caterham · Westerham · Sevenoaks · Maidstone · ▲645 · Canterbury · Sandwich · Goodwin Sands
Dorking · Reigate · Redhill · Oxted · KENT · North Downs · Charing · Stour · Aylesham · Deal · Walmer
Leith Hill ▲965 · Horley · Lingfield · Tonbridge · Paddock Wood · Headcorn · Great Stour · Wye · ▲583 · Temple Ewell · St Margaret's at Cliffe · South Foreland
Capel · Crawley · East Grinstead · Royal Tunbridge Wells · Marden · Vale of Kent · Kennington · Ashford · Lyminge · Dover
Cranleigh · Forest Row · The Weald · Cranbrook · Tenterden · Bethersden · Hythe · Folkestone · Sandgate
Horsham · Crowborough · Wadhurst · Hawkhurst · Hamstreet · Romney Marsh · Dymchurch · Strait of Dover
Ashdown Forest · ▲646 · Mayfield · Northiam · New Romney · Cap Gris-Nez
Cuckfield · EAST · Ticehurst · Isle of Oxney · Rother · Lydd · Dungeness
Haywards Heath · Burgess Hill · Uckfield · Heathfield · Battle · Brede · Rye · Rye Bay
Ditchling Beacon ▲813 · Lewes · SUSSEX · Hailsham · Polegate · Hastings · Bexhill
Henfield · Steyning · Hove · ▲713 · Eastbourne · Beachy Hd
Shoreham-by-Sea · Southwick · Brighton · Newhaven · Seaford
Worthing

STRAIT OF DOVER
Dunkirk · Grand Fort Philippe · Gravelines · Aa · Calais · Audruicq · NORD · Guînes · Ardres · Marquise · ▲522 · ▲554 · St Omer · Boulogne · Liane · Desvres · Samer · ▲656 · FRANCE · PAS DE CALAIS · Fauquembergues · Hucqueliers

Relief

Feet		Metres
3281		1000
1640		500
656		200
328		100
0	Sea Level	
66		20
164		50

Spot Heights in Feet ▲4406

Scale 1:1 000 000

0 · 10 · 20 · 30 · 40 Miles
0 · 10 · 20 · 30 · 40 · 50 · 60 Kms.

Lambert Conformal Conic Projection

West from Greenwich · 0° · East from Greenwich

Scale 1:1 000 000

Lambert Conformal Conic Projection

Relief

Feet	Metres	
3281	1000	
1640	500	
656	200	
328	100	
0	Sea Level	
		20
		50
		100

Feet | 66 | 164 | 328

Spot Heights in Feet ▲4406

Collins © Longman Atlases

GLOUCESTERSHIRE

GWENT

Chipping Sodbury
Kingswood
Bath
Bristol
A
V
O
N

Chepstow
Avonmouth
Portishead
Clevedon
Weston-super-Mare

Newport
Cardiff
Penarth
Lavernock Pt
Barry
Flat Holm
Steep Holm
Nash Pt
Breaksea Pt
Porthcawl

SOUTH GLAMORGAN
MID GLAMORGAN
WEST GLAMORGAN

Ebbw Vale
Bedwellty
Pontypool
Aberdare
Mountain Ash
Rhondda
Pontypridd
Caerphilly
Merthyr Tydfil
Tredegar

Swansea
Port Talbot
Neath
The Mumbles
Mumbles Hd
Swansea Bay

Llanelli
Burry Port
Kidwelly
Port-Eynon
Worms Hd

Laugharne
Pendine
Saundersfoot
Tenby
Caldy
Amroth

Milford Haven
Angle
Pembroke
Limney Hd
St Gowan's Hd

Skomer
Stackholm
St Ann's Hd

DORSET

Weymouth
Portland
Bill of Portland
Chesil Beach
Abbotsbury
Dorchester
Bridport
Beaminster
Lyme Regis
Lyme Bay
Seaton
Sidmouth
Budleigh Salterton
Exmouth
Dawlish
Teignmouth

SOMERSET

Mendip Hills
Cheddar
Wells
Shepton Mallet
Glastonbury
Street
Wedmore
Bridgwater
Burnham-on-Sea
Bridgwater Bay
Watchet
Minehead
Dunster
Quantock Hills
Nether Stowey
Williton
Taunton
Wellington
Langport
Ilminster
Chard
Crewkerne
Yeovil
Sherborne

DEVON

Exmoor Forest
Lynton
Lynmouth
Foreland Pt
Combe Martin
Ilfracombe
Marte Pt
Baggy Pt
Croyde
Braunton
Barnstaple
Bideford
Northam
Bideford Bay
Clovelly
Hartland Pt
Hartland

Simonsbath
South Molton
Bampton
Tiverton
Cullompton
Crediton
Okehampton
Hatherleigh
North Tawton
Chumleigh
Winkleigh

Dartmoor Forest
High Willhays
Ryder's Hill
Princetown
Moretonhampstead
Chagford
Ashburton
Buckfastleigh
Newton Abbot
Torbay
Torquay
Berry Hd
Brixham
Start Bay
Start Pt
Prawle Pt
Salcombe
Kingsbridge
Bolt Hd
Bigbury Bay

Exeter
Exmouth
Topsham

Tavistock
Plymouth
Saltash
Plympton
Yealmpton
Modbury
Rame Hd
Whitesand Bay

CORNWALL

Launceston
Liskeard
Callington
Looe
Polperro
Fowey
Lostwithiel
Bodmin
Bodmin Moor
Brown Willy
Camelford
Boscastle
Tintagel Hd
Port Isaac Bay
Padstow
Wadebridge
Camel
St Austell
St Austell Bay
Mevagissey Bay
Dodman Pt
Gorran
Grampound
Nare Hd
Veryan Bay
St Mawes

Pentire Pt
Trevose Hd
Newquay
Watergate Bay
Perranporth
St Agnes
Portreath
Redruth
Camborne
Hayle
St Ives
St Ives Bay
Godrevy Pt
Gurnard's Hd

Truro
Falmouth
Falmouth Bay
Manacle Pt
Helston
Mullion
Lizard Pt
Lizard

Penzance
Marazion
Mount's Bay
Land's End
Sennen
Wolf Rock
Seven Stones

Isles of Scilly
St Martin's
St Mary's
Bryher
Hugh Town
St Agnes

FRANCE
Alderney
CHANNEL ISLANDS
Guernsey
St Peter Port
St Sampson
St Martin
St Helier
Jersey
Sark
Grosnez Pt
la Rocque Pt
les Ecréhou
Rozel

BRISTOL CHANNEL

ENGLISH CHANNEL

Lundy

Eddystone

Same Scale

NORTH SEA

Scale 1:1 000 000

0	10	20	30	40 Miles
0	10	20	30	40	50	60 Kms.

Lambert Conformal Conic Projection

West from Greenwich East from Greenwich

Relief

Feet		Metres
3281		1000
1640		500
656		200
328		100
0		Sea Level
66		20
164		50
328		100

Spot Heights in Feet ▲ 4406

Vallsend
South Shields
Jarrow
TYNE AND
WEAR
Sunderland
A194(M)
Washington
Houghton-le-Spring
Seaham
Hetton-le-Hole
Easington
Durham
Peterlee
Wingate
Sedgefield
Aycliffe
Billingham
Hartlepool
Tees Bay
Stockton-on-Tees
Darlington
Redcar
Middlesbrough
Marske-by-the-Sea
CLEVELAND
Thornaby-on-Tees
Eston
Saltburn-by-the-Sea
Brotton
Loftus
Stokesley
Guisborough
Broughton
Cleveland Hills
Whitby
Sleights
Esk
Robin Hood's Bay
▲ 1489
▲ 958
North York Moors
Cloughton
Northallerton
Hambleton Hills
Scalby
Thirsk
Helmsley
Kirkbymoorside
Scarborough
Hovingham
Pickering
Vale of Pickering
Filey
Malton
Staxton
Norton
Flamborough
Boroughbridge
Easingwold
Yorkshire Wolds
Flamborough Head
Knaresborough
Shipton
Burton Agnes
Bridlington
Harrogate
Sledmere
Bridlington Bay
Wetherby
York
Stamford Bridge
Great Driffield
Wilberfoss
Pocklington
Hutton Cranswick
Tadcaster
Middleton on the Wolds
Hornsea
Leeds
Garforth
Market Weighton
Leven
Rothwell
Cawood
Selby
Holme upon Spalding Moor
Beverley
Aldbrough
Castleford
Hambleton
HUMBERSIDE
Kingston upon Hull
Normanton
Knottingley
Howden
South Cave
Cottingham
Wakefield
Pontefract
Goole
Snaith
Whitton
Hessle
Hedon
Withernsea
Ackworth Moor Top
Garthorpe
New Holland
Keyingham
Holderness
Hemsworth
Askern
Thorne
Winterton
Barton-upon-Humber
Patrington
Royston
S. Kirby
Crowle
Humber
Easington
Barnsley
Adwick le Street
Staincross
Scunthorpe
Immingham
Wombwell
Thurnscoe
Isle of Axholme
Brigg
Great Coates
Grimsby
Spurn Hd
Mexborough
Epworth
Cleethorpes
Conisbrough
Doncaster
Caistor
Rawmarsh
Tickhill
Bawtry
▲ 550
Tetney
Rotherham
Maltby
Gainsborough
Market Rasen
North Somercotes
Saltfleet
Sheffield
Anston
Louth
Killamarsh
Worksop
East Retford
Dunholme
Wragby
Burwell
Mablethorpe
Staveley
Clowne
Torksey
Lincoln Wolds
Sutton on Sea
East Markham
Bain
Chapel St Leonards
Creswell
Sherwood Forest
Horncastle
Bolsover
Warsop
Boughton
Bardney
Spilsby
Burgh le Marsh
Chesterfield
Lincoln
Woodhall Spa
Skegness
Clay Cross
Sutton in Ashfield
Mansfield
Lincoln Edge
LINCOLNSHIRE
Witham
Metheringham
Sleeping
Wainfleet All Saints
Matlock
Kirkby in Ashfield
Coningsby
Gibraltar Pt
Alfreton
Southwell
Newark-on-Trent
Navenby
Wrangle
Ripley
Hucknall
North Kyme
Heanor
Eastwood
Arnold
Long Bennington
Sleaford
Holland Fen
Holkham Bay
Blakeney Pt
Sheringham
Ilkeston
Carlton
Heckington
Boston
Cromer
Nottingham
West Bridgford
Beeston
Bingham
Grantham
Donington
Kirton
THE WASH
Hunstanton
Burnham Market
Wells-next-the-Sea
Holt
Long Eaton
Stapleford
Keyworth
Bottesford
Folkingham
Heacham
Docking
▲ 293
Mundesley
Waltham on the Wolds
Bourne
Deeping Fen
Dersingham
Saxthorpe
North Walsham
Melton Mowbray
Colsterworth
Spalding
Holbeach
Sandringham
Fakenham
Aylsham
Shepshed
Sutton Bridge
Long Sutton
The Marsh
King's Lynn
NORFOLK
Coltishall
Loughborough
Coalville
LEICESTERSHIRE
East Dereham
Hoveton

Tees
Ure
Swale
Nidd
Wharfe
Ouse
Derwent
Aire
Don
Trent
Ouse
Witham
Glen
Great Ouse

ATLANTIC

OCEAN

NORTH

CHANNEL

NORTHERN IRELAND

TYRONE

LOUGH
NEAGH

DOWN

LONDONDERRY

ANTRIM

HIGHLAND

West From Greenwich

© Collins ◇ Longman Atlases

Scale 1:1 000 000

Lambert Conformal Conic Projection

Relief

Feet		Metres
3281		1000
1640		500
656		200
328		100
0		Sea Level
66		20
164		50
328		100
656		200

Spot Heights in Feet ▲4406

NORTH SEA

FIRTH OF FORTH

NORTHUMBERLAND

TYNE AND WEAR

DURHAM

CUMBRIA

SOLWAY FIRTH

CLEVELAND

SHETLAND ISLANDS
Same Scale

Scale 1:1 000 000

Lambert Conformal Conic Projection

Relief

Feet	Metres
3281	1000
1640	500
656	200
328	100
0	Sea Level
66	20
164	50
328	100
656	200

Spot Heights in Feet ▲ 4406

PENTLAND FIRTH
Brough Ness
Dunnet Hd
Stroma
Muckle
Skerry
John O' Groats
Duncansby Hd

Durness
L. Eriboll
Whiten
Hd
Ben 1338
Hutig
Kyle of Tongue
Strathy Pt
Portskerra
Dounreay
Dunnet Bay
Dunnet
Thurso
Bettyhill
Tongue
L. Hope
Ben Hope
3042
Ben Loyal
2504
L. Loyal
Strathnaver
Halladale
Halkirk
L. Watten
Reiss
Sinclair's
Bay
Noss Hd
Strath More
L. Naver
Ben Griam
More
1936
Strath of Kildonan
Kinbrace
Morven
2313
Dunbeath
Berriedale
942
Lybster
Wick
Thurso

L. More
Ben Hee
2864
Altnaharra
Ben Klibreck
3154
N O R T H
Beinn nam
Bad Mor
952

Ben More
Assynt
L. Shin
Casiley
Lairg
Strath of Brora
Beinn
Dhorain 2060
Kildonan
Helmsdale

Oykel
Bridge
Oykel
Carron
Fleet
Bonar Bridge
Ben Horn
1706
Brora
Golspie
Dornoch
2302
Dornoch Firth
Tarbat Ness
Portmahomack

Beinn
Tharsuinn
2270
Tain
Hill of Fearn
Easter Ross
L. Morie
MORAY FIRTH
Burghead
Lossiemouth
Spey Bay
Portknockie
Cullen
Portsoy
Banff
Macduff
Troup Hd
Rosehearty
Kinnairds Hd
Fraserburgh

N. Glass
3429 Ben Wyvis
M A N D
Alness
Invergordon
Cromarty Firth
Cromarty
Findhorn
Elgin
Garmouth
Buckie
Spey
Keith
Strichen
New Pitsligo
Tumff
Cuminestown
Buchan
Rattray Hd

Garve
Loch
Luichart
Strathpeffer
Dingwall
Evanton
Black
Isle
Fortrose
Nairn
Forres
Rothes
Fochabers
Knock
Hill
1409
Deveron
New Deer
Mintlaw
Ugie
Peterhead

Glen Orrin
Conon
Muir of Ord
Beauly F.
Beauly
Moray Firth
Nairn
Ferness
Lossie
Dufftown
Charlestown of
Aberlour
Huntly
Strathbogie
Fyvie
Ythan
Boddam
Buchan Ness
571

Cannich
Enrick
Strathglass
The Aird
Inverness
Strathnairn
Dores
Findhorn
Càrn na
Loine
1799
Strathspey
Ben Rinnes
2755
2663
Insch
Garioch
Inverurie
Oldmeldrum
Ellon
Formartine
Newburgh
Cruden Bay

Invermoriston
Loch Ness
Drumnadrochit
Tomatin
2162
Grantown-
on-Spey
Strath Avon
Corryhabbie
Hill
Tomintoul
The Buck
2368
Càrn Mòr
2636
Lumsden
Don
Alford
Kintore
Dyce
Aberdeen

Fort
Augustus
Glen More
2658
Carrbridge
Aviemore
Monadhliath
Mountains
Spey
Geal Charn
2692
Cairn Gorm
4084
3843
Ben Avon
Avon
H I G H L A N D S
Tarland
Hill of
Fare 1545
Don
GRAMPIAN
L. Oich
3087
Kingussie
Newtonmore
4300
Ben
Macdhui
Cairngorms
Braemar
Dee
Ballater
Aboyne
Banchery
Dee

Glen Roy
3700
Creag
Meagaidh
L.
Laggan
Dalwhinnie
3786
3071
Mt Keen
2555
Mt Battock
Glen Dye
1747
Kerloch
Stonehaven

Glen
Spean
Badenoch
Forest of Atholl
Lochnagar
Glen Esk
Fettercairn
Laurencekirk
Inverbervie

Treig
Ben Alder
3765
3502
Glas Maol
Glen Tilt
Beinn a'Ghlo
3671
Glen Clova
West Water
Edzell
Brechin
N O R T H

Spean
3700
Kinloch Rannoch
Blair
Atholl
Glen Garry
Tummel
Glenshee
Glen Prosen
Isla
Montrose
S E A

kwater Rest
L. Laidon
Rannoch Moor
L. Rannoch
3547
Schiehallion
T. Tummel
Pitlochry
Kirkmichael
Strathardle
Kirriemuir
Forfar
Glamis
Lunan Bay

GRAMPIAN
Glen Lyon
3984
Lawers
Ben Lawers
Kennore
Strath Tay
Aberfeldy
Bridge of
Cally
Blairgowrie
Alyth
Sidlaw Hills
Carmylie
Arbroath

Breadalbane
Killin
Loch
Braan
Dunkeld
Coupar Angus
Isla
Tay
Dundee
Monifieth
Carnoustie
Buddan Ness
Bankfoot
West from Greenwich
Collins Longman Atlases

Mull Hd
Noup
Hd
Papa
Westray
North Ronaldsay
N. Ronaldsay Firth
Pierowall
The
North Sound
Start
Point
Westray
Westray
Firth
Eday
Sanday
Sacquoy Hd
Rousay
Eynhallow Sd
Egilsay
Sanday
Sound
Stronsay
Brough Hd
Wyre
Gairsay
Stronsay
Firth
Shapinsay
Auskerry
ORKNEY
Shapinsay Sd
Mull Hd
Stromness
Ward
881
Hill
Kirkwall
Skaill
Hoy Sd
Ward Hill
1565
Quoyness
St Mary's
Copinsay
Rora
Hd
Scapa Flow
Burray
Hoy
Flotta
St Margaret's Hope
Hurliness
S. Walls
South
Ronaldsay
PENTLAND FIRTH
Brough Ness
Dunnet Hd
Stroma
Muckle Skerry
Dunnet
John O' Groats
Duncansby Hd
3° W

Relief
Feet	Metres
3281	1000
1640	500
656	200
328	100
0	Sea Level
66	20
164	50
328	100
656	200

Spot Heights in Feet ▲4406

ST. GEORGE'S CHANNEL

Scale 1:1 400 000

Lambert Conformal Conic Projection

© Collins © Longman Atlases

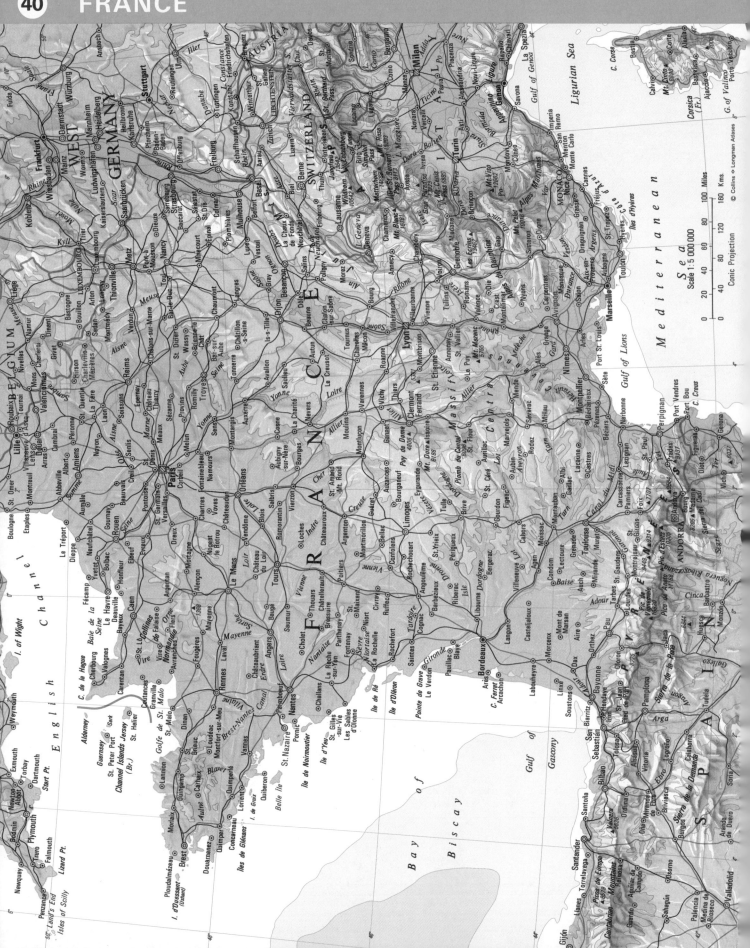

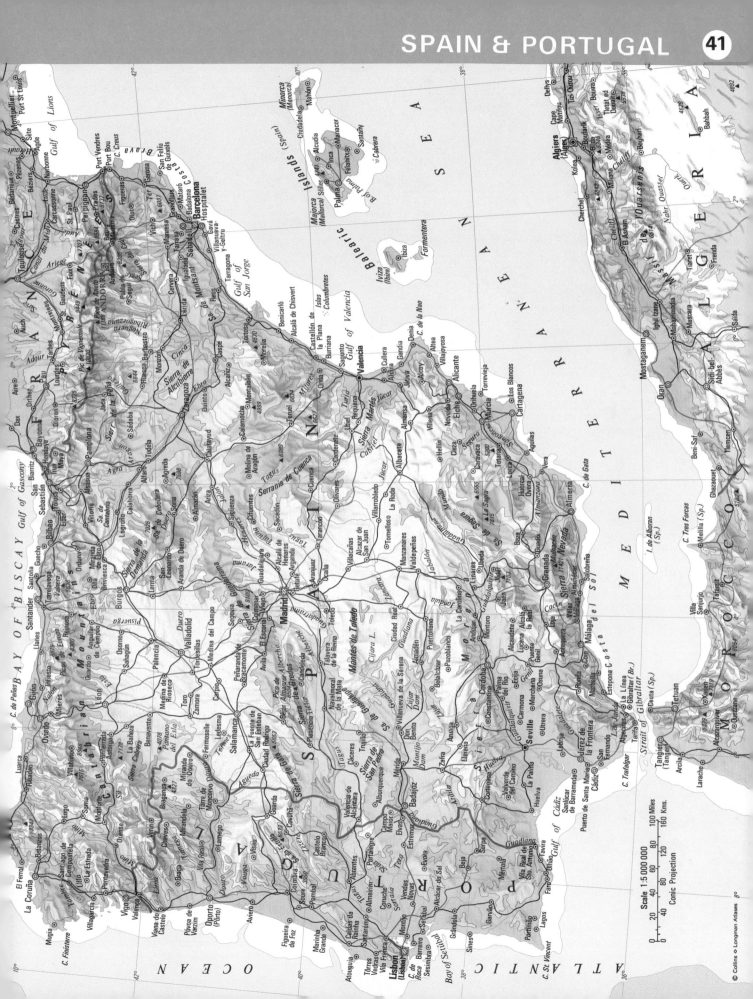

AUSTRIA

FRANCE

SWIZ.

Lyon
Clermont Ferrand
Thiers
Roanne
Villeurbanne
Geneva
Chamonix
Annecy
Mont Blanc 15770
Matterhorn 14690
Mt. Rosa
Simplon Tunnel
Locarno
Como
Maggiore
Milan
Bergamo
Brescia
Monza
Vicenza
Padua
Verona
Venice
Gulf of Venice
Treviso
Udine
Gorizia
Trieste
Ljubljana
Rijeka
Maribor
Celje
Klagenfurt
Villach
Bolzano
Merano
Trento
Trent
Brenner Pass
Bernina 13284
Triglav 9396
Istra
Krk
Cres
Rovinj
Pula
Losinj
Pag
Gospić

St. Etienne
Le Puy
Grenoble
Romans
Valence
Gap
Briançon
Mt. Pelat 10016
Alpes Maritimes
Turin
Asti
Alessandria
Acqui
Mondovi
Cuneo
Mt. Viso 12602
Pavia
Vogherra
Piacenza
Parma
Reggio
Modena
Bologna
Ferrara
Ravenna
Faenza
Forli
Rimini
Cremona
Mantua
Adige
Po

Nîmes
Avignon
Arles
Montpellier
Sète
Béziers
Marseille
Toulon
Hyères
Îles d'Hyères
Gulf of Lions
Salon
Aix-en-Provence
Aubagne
Draguignan
Grasse
Cannes
Fréjus
St. Tropez
Nice
Monaco
Monte Carlo
Menton
San Remo
Imperia
Savona
Genoa
Gulf of Genoa
La Spezia
Massa
Carrara
Pisa
Leghorn
Arno
Florence
Prato
Pistoia
San Marino
Pésaro
Urbino
Senigallia
Ancona
Iesi
Macerata
Ascoli Piceno
Teramo
Pescara
Chieti

LIGURIAN SEA
C. Corse
Capraia
Elba
Pianosa
Montecristo
Giglio
Grosseto
Cecina
Volterra
Siena
Arezzo
Perugia
L. Trasimeno
Assisi
Foligno
Monte Vettore 8130
Terni
Rieti
L'Aquila
Avezzano
Mt. Amaro 9170
Sulmona
Termoli

Corsica (Fr.)
Calvi
Bastia
Mt. Cinto 8890
Corte
Aléria
Ajaccio
G. of Valinco
Sartène
Pto. Vecchio
Bonifacio
Str. of Bonifacio

Asinara
C. Falcone
G. of Asinara
Caprera
Tempio
Olbia
Porto Torres
Sassari
Alghero
Bosa
Macomer
Coghinas
Orosei
Gulf of Orosei
C. Mte. Santu
Sardinia (Italy)
G. of Oristano
Oristano
Arbatax
Iglesias
Villaputzu
Cagliari
San Pietro
C. Carbonara
G. of Palmas
C. Spartivento
G. of Cagliari

TYRRHENIAN SEA

Civitavecchia
Viterbo
L. Bolsena
Rome
Velletri
Frosinone
Pontine Is.
G. of Gaeta
Gaeta
Caserta
Benevento
Naples
Vesuvius
Salerno
Ischia
G. of Naples
Capri
G. of Salerno
Potenza
Campobasso
Foggia
Ariano
Avellino
Melfi
San Severo

MEDITERRANEAN

Minorca
Mahón

Ustica (Italy)
Lipari Is.
Stromboli 3038
Palmi
Messina
Reggio
Str. of Messina
Sicily
Palermo
Cefalù
Barcellona
Termini
Alcamo
Trapani
Marettimo
Favignana
Marsala
Nebrodi Mts.
Mt. Etna 10758
Adrano
Enna
Sciacca
Caltanissetta
Catania
Agrigento
Licata
Caltagirone
Siracusa
Vittoria
Modica
Ragusa
C. Passero

ALGERIA
TUNISIA
Constantine Mts.
Medjerda Mts.
Bejaïa
Annaba
Skikda
Tabarka
La Calle
Bizerta
Mateur
Tunis
Gulf of Tunis
Nabeul
C. Bon
Pantelleria (Italy)
Sétif
Constantine
Souk Ahras
Béja
Medjerda
Malta Channel
Gozo
MALTA
Valletta
Linosa
Lampione
Lampedusa (Italy)
Kairouan
Sousse
Monastir
Mahdia
Enfida
Batna
Biskra
Tebessa
Kasserine
Sbeitla

Feet	Relief	Metres
16 404		5000
9843		3000
6562		2000
3281		1000
1640		500
656		200
0		Sea Level
Land Dep.		200
656		
13 123		4000
22 966		7000

HUNGARY
Nagykanizsa
Kaposvár
Pécs
Baja
Szekszárd
Szeged
Makó
Hódmezővásárhely
White
Arad
Brad
Odorhei
Sighişoara
Stântu
Gheorghe
U.S.S.R.
Bolgrad
Sasyk
Virovitica
Osijek
Sombor
Subotica
Kikinda
Timişoara
Deva
Sibiu
Red Tower
Pass
Braşov
Negoiu
9346
Foscani
Râmnicu
Sarat
Galati
Reni
Izmail
Mouths of
Sulina
the Danube
St. Gheorghe's
Mouth
Dubica
Brod
Novi
Sad
Vršac
Lugoj
Mt. Mindra
8268
Tirgu-Jiu
ROMANIA
Piteşti
Dimbovita
Ploeşti
Buzău
Faurei
Brăila
Tulcea
Portiţei
Mouth
Banja
Luka
Doboj
Ruma
Danube
Belgrade
Orşova
Iron
Gate
Turnu
Severin
Olt
Slatina
Argeş
Bucharest
Călăraşi
Cernavodă
Constanţa
Travnik
Tuzla
Šabac
Pożarevac
Negotin
Craiova
Jiu
Caracal
Olteniţa
Silistra
Mangalia
YUGOSLAVIA
Sarajevo
Višegrad
Titovo
Uzice
Valjevo
Kragujevac
Kraljevo
Kruševac
Morava
Zaječar
Vidin
Calafat
Lom
Ogosta
Oryakhovo
Corabia
Turnu
Măgurele
Giurgiu
Zimnicea
Ruse
Svishtov
Razgrad
Tolbukhin
Balchik
C. Kaliakra
BLACK
SEA
Cvrsnica
7310
Pljevlja
Novi
Pazar
Niš
Kuršumlija
Leskovac
Pirot
Dragoman
Pass
Vratsa
Iskŭr
Lovech
Osŭm
Pleven
Tŭrnovo
Shipka
Pass
Sliven
Karnobat
Varna
Burgas
Mostar
Metković
Nikšić
Žabljak
Dermitor
8274
Hercejna
Tara
Lim
Kosovska
Mitrovica
Priština
Dimitrovo
(Pernik)
Sofia
Botevgrad
Kazanlŭk
1785
Stara
Zagora
Tundzha
Yambol
Elkhovo
Mljet
Dubrovnik
Kotor
Titograd
Cetinje
Bar
Peć
8714
Pržren
Vranje
Kumanovo
Kyustendil
Radomir
Trajan's Gate
Musala
9597
Plovdiv
Dimitrovgrad
Khaskovo
Maritsa
Kŭrdzhali
C. Igneada
Midye
SEA
Shkodër
Drin
8661
Skopje
Titov
Veles
Prilep
Blagoevgrad
Rhodope
Smolyan
Arda
Edirne
Kirklareli
Luleburgaz
Bosporus
Catalca
Istanbul
Üsküdar
ALBANIA
Shëngjin
C. Rodonit
C. Palit
Tiranë
Durrës
Elbasan
Ohridsko
Ohrid
Bitola
Crno
Kočani
Strumica
Petrich
Mesta
Xanthi
Struma
Serres
Drama
Kavála
Kampúni
Kesan
Tekirdağ
Gallipoli
Dardanelles
Çanakkale
SEA OF MARMARA
Marmara
Bandırma
Bursa
Seman
Berat
7930
Vjosë
Prespa
Florina
Kastoria
Kozáni
Mt. Olympus
9570
Edhessa
Kilkis
Thessaloniki
C. Plati
Thásos
Samothráki
Ímroz
Límnos
5797
Edremit
TURKEY
Balikesir
Soma
Bergama
Vlorë
Smólikas
8639
Kardhitsa
Grevená
Ossa
6489
Lárisa
G. of
Thessaloniki
G. of Toronaîos
Singitikós G.
Mt. Áthos
6670
Áyios
Evstrátios
Lésvos
Mitilíni
Dikíli
Akhisar
Manisa
İzmir
Corfu
Igoumenitsa
Arta
Trikkala
Pinios
Vólos
N. Sporades
Skíros
AEGEAN
Psará
Khíos
G. of İzmit
Turgutlu
Ödemiş
Preveza
Levkás
GREECE
Mesolóngion
Kefallinía
Lamía
Pass of
Thermopylae
8235
Parnassós
8061
Khalkís
Euboea
C. Kafirévs
Áyios
Matáthon
Sámos
Ikaria
Aydin
IONIAN
SEA
Zákinthos
Pátras
G. of Patras
Gulf of Corinth
Mégara
Piraeus
Athens
Kéa
Kíthnos
Ándros
Tínos
Kéa
Cyclades
Páros
Náxos
SEA
Sámos
Dodecanese
G. of Kerme
Kálimnos
Killíni
7795
Pirgos
Corinth
Argos
Návplion
Aíyina
Kos
Amorgós
Íos
Rhodes
Kíparissía
Spárti
Milos
Thíra
Rhodes
Píos
Kalámai
Skhíza
G. of Messinia
G. of Lakonia
C. Maléa
Kíthira
SEA OF CRETE
Karpáthos
Andikíthira
C. Spátha
Canea
Réthimnon
Iráklion
Idhi
8058
Crete

© Collins ◇ Longman Atlases

Scale 1:5 250 000
Conic Projection
0   100   200 Miles
0   100   200   300 Kms.

IONIAN
SEA

Str. of
Otranto

Gulf of
Taranto

Táranto
Gallípoli
Lecce
Otranto
C. Sta Maria
di Leuca
Brindisi
Monopoli
Bari
Crotone
C. Rizzuto

Scale 1:2 000 000

Conic Projection

Relief

Feet	Metres
16 404	5000
9843	3000
6562	2000
3281	1000
1640	500
656	200
0	Sea Level

Land Dep.

656	200
13 123	4000
22 966	7000

NORTH

SEA

West Frisian Islands

East Frisian Is.

Wadden Sea

GRONINGEN

FRIESLAND

DRENTHE

IJsselmeer

N.E. Polder

NORTH HOLLAND

Markerwaard (U.C.)

E. Flevoland

S. Flevoland

OVERIJSSEL

Amsterdam

Veluwe

NETHERLANDS

GELDERLAND

The Hague ('sGravenhage)

SOUTH

UTRECHT

HOLLAND

Rotterdam

Waal

Maas

NOORD BRABANT

Schouwen

Overflakkee

Duiveland

East Schelde

Walcheren

South Beveland

ZEELAND

West Schelde

LIMBURG

ANTWERP

FLANDERS

WEST FLANDERS

EAST FLANDERS

LIMBOURG

WEST

GERMANY

BELGIUM

BRABANT

HAINAUT

Brussels

Münster

Essen

Dortmund

Düsseldorf

Cologne (Köln)

Bonn

Koblenz

FRANCE

PICARDY

ARTOIS

NAMUR

LIÈGE

Ardenne

Eifel

Hunsrück

LUXEMBOURG

LUXEMBOURG

© Collins · Longman Atlases

ICELAND
on the same scale

Östero
Strömo
Vaagö
Bordö
Thorshavn
Sandö
Syderö

FAROE IS
on same scale

Scale 1:7 500 000

0   50   100   150 Miles
0   100   200 Kms.
Conic Projection

ATLANTIC
OCEAN

SKAGERRAK

KATTEGAT

DENMARK

BALTIC SEA

N O R W A Y

S W E D E N

FINLAND

LAPLAND

GULF OF BOTHNIA

GULF OF FINLAND

ESTONIA
S.S.R.

LATVIA
S.S.R.

LITHUANIA
S.S.R.

WHITE
RUSSIA
S.S.R.

R.S.F.S.R.

U.S.S.R.

Gulf of
Riga

© Collins ○ Longman Atlases

Relief

Feet	Metres
16404	5000
9843	3000
6562	2000
3281	1000
1640	500
656	200
0	Sea Level
Land Dep.	
656	200
13123	4000
22966	7000

C I N Severnaya Zemlya
Komsomolets
October Revolution
Bolshevik
C. Chelyuskin

I N

New Siberian Is
Bolshoi Lyakhovskiy
Novaya Siberia
Kotelnyy
G. of Tona

L A P T E V   S E A

E A S T   S I B E R I A N   S E A

Wrangel I.
De Long Str.
Bering Str.
Chukotskiy Pen.
Gulf of Anadyr

Taymyr Peninsula
Byrranga Mts
L. Taymyr
Upper Taymyr
Pyasina
Khatangskiy G.
Olenekskiy Gulf
Nordvik
Ust Olenek
Khatanga
Anabar

Norilsk
Kamen 6672
Putoran Mts
Konuy

Central Siberian Plateau

Olenek
Olenek
Tura
Markha

SOCIALIST REPUBLIC

RAL   SOCIALIST   REPUBLIC

dinka
Tunguska
Stony Tunguska
Lower Tunguska
Lena
Vilyuy
Vilyuysk
Markha
Olekminsk
Yakutsk
Aldan
Aldan
Lena

Bulun
Tiksi
Yana
Verkhoyansk
Kazachye
Indigirka
Yana

Cherskogo Range

Mt Chen 8799
Mt Pobeda 10325
Srednekolymskaya
Kolyma
Omolon
Oymyakon
Amga
Amga
Ust Maya
Aldan

Anadyr
Anadyr

Kolyma Range

Koryak Range

Gizhiga
Gizhiga Gulf
G. of Penzhina
Palana
Uka

B E R I N G   S E A

Kamchatka Peninsula
Ust Kamchatsk
Klyuchevskaya
Petropavlovsk Kamchatskiy

Okhotsk

S E A   O F   O K H O T S K

Ayan
Shantar Is
Topko 2253

Dzhugdzhur Range

Okha
Aleksandrovsk Sakhalinskiy
Poronaysk

Sakhalin

Yenisey
Angara
Chuna

Eastern Sayan
Sevo
Kansk
oyarsk
Nizhneudinsk
Tayshet
Bratsk
Bratsk Resr.
Tulun
Cheremkhovo
Angarsk
Irkutsk
Kyzyl
Ola Ra.
Munku Sardyk 11454
Khöbsögöl Dalai

Ust Kut
Kirensk
Vitim Range
Yablonovoy Range
L. Baikal
Ulan-Ude
Petrovsk Zabaykal'skiy
Chita
Shilka

Stanovoy Range
Olekma
Skalimyy 8143

Skovorodino
Zeya
Svobodny
Zeya

Great Khingan Shan
Amur
Blagoveshchensk
Sungari

Nikolayevsk-na-Amur
Amgun
Komsomolsk-na-Amur
Amur
Birobidzhan
Sovetskaya Gavan
Khabarovsk
Uglegorsk

Sikhote Alin Range

Gulf of Tartary
Yuzhno-Sakhalinsk
La Perouse Str.
Wakkanai
Asahi dake 7513

Hokkaido
Sapporo
Hakodate

Ulan Bator
Undur Khan

M O N G O L I A

INNER MONGOLIA

C H I N A

L. Khanka
Ussuriysk
Vladivostok
Olga

Mutankiang
Harbin
Kirin
Sungari

Changchun
Sungari

Nigata

J A P A N

Honshu
Hachinohe

Shenyang
Fushun
Anshan

NORTH KOREA
Pyongyang

Liaotung Bay
Korea Bay
Lüta

Kyoto
Tokyo
Yokohama
Fujiyama 12388
Nagoya
Kobe
Osaka

SEA OF JAPAN

SOUTH KOREA
Seoul

U R G
Paotow
Huhehot
Chiangkiakow
Peking

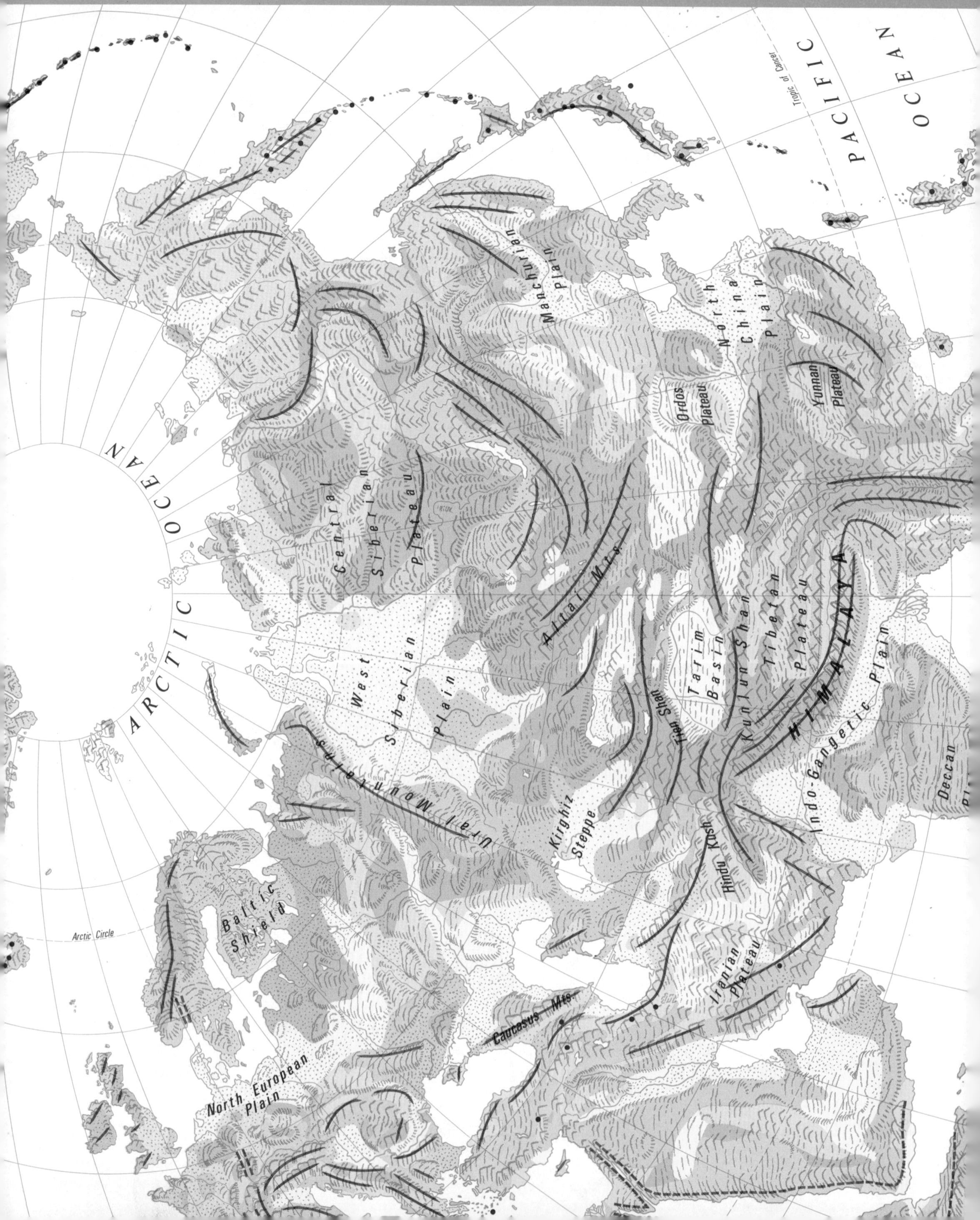

PACIFIC

OCEAN

Tropic of Cancer

ARCTIC OCEAN

Manchurian Plain

North China Plain

Ordos Plateau

Yunnan Plateau

Central Siberian Plateau

West Siberian Plain

Altai Mts.

Tarim Basin

Kunlun Shan

Tibetan Plateau

HIMALAYA

Indo-Gangetic Plain

Deccan

Tian Shan

Ural Mountains

Kirghiz Steppe

Hindu Kush

Iranian Plateau

Baltic Shield

Arctic Circle

Caucasus Mts.

North European Plain

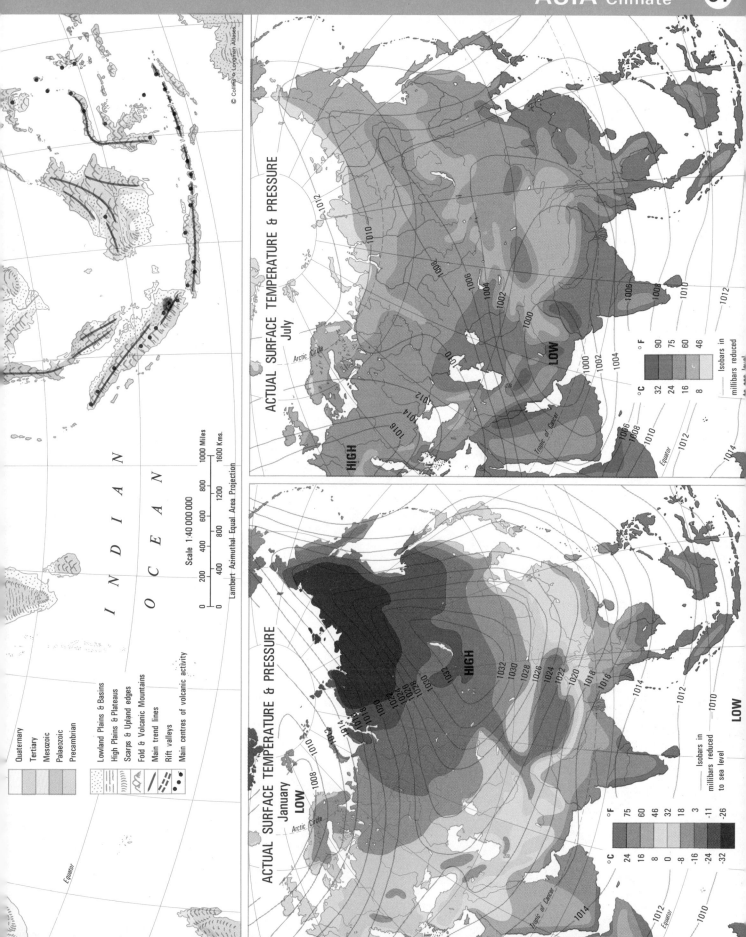

ACTUAL SURFACE TEMPERATURE & PRESSURE
July

°F 90 75 60 46
°C 32 24 16 8

Isobars in millibars reduced

Arctic Circle
Tropic of Cancer
Equator

LOW
HIGH

ACTUAL SURFACE TEMPERATURE & PRESSURE
January

LOW
HIGH
LOW

°F 75 60 46 32 18 3 -11 -26
°C 24 16 8 0 -8 -16 -24 -32

Isobars in millibars reduced to sea level

Arctic Circle
Tropic of Cancer
Equator

Quaternary
Tertiary
Mesozoic
Palaeozoic
Precambrian

Lowland Plains & Basins
High Plains & Plateaus
Scarps & Upland edges
Fold & Volcanic Mountains
Main trend lines
Rift valleys
Main centres of volcanic activity

I N D I A N

O C E A N

Equator

Scale 1:40 000 000

0   200 400 600 800 1000 Miles
0 400 800 1200 1600 Kms.

Lambert Azimuthal Equal Area Projection

© Collins ○ Longman Atlases

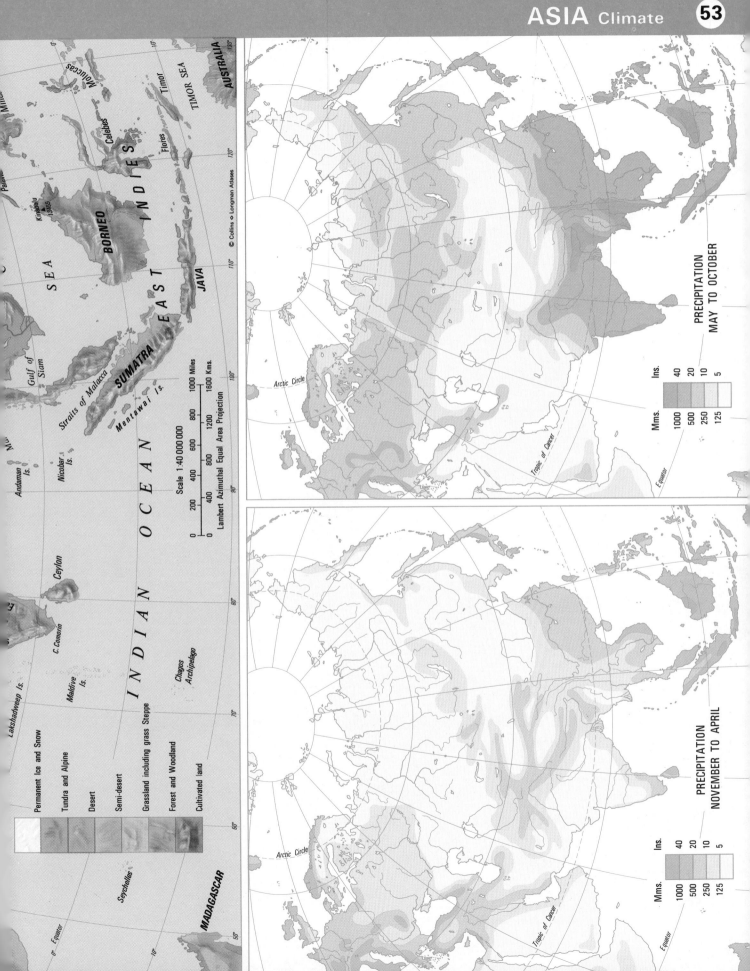

MOLUCCAS
Timor
TIMOR SEA
AUSTRALIA

Milne

Celebes
Flores
Palawan
Kinabalu
1455
BORNEO
JAVA
SUMATRA
Mentawai Is.
Straits of Malacca
SEA
EAST INDIES

Gulf of Siam

Nicobar Is.
Andaman Is.

Ceylon

C. Comorin

Lakshadweep Is.
Maldive Is.
Chagos Archipelago

INDIAN OCEAN

Seychelles

MADAGASCAR

Equator

© Collins ○ Longman Atlases

Scale 1:40 000 000

0   200   400   600   800   1000 Miles

0   400   800   1200   1600 Kms.

Lambert Azimuthal Equal Area Projection

Permanent Ice and Snow
Tundra and Alpine
Desert
Semi-desert
Grassland including grass Steppe
Forest and Woodland
Cultivated land

PRECIPITATION
MAY TO OCTOBER

Arctic Circle
Tropic of Cancer
Equator

Ins.
40
20
10
5

Mms.
1000
500
250
125

PRECIPITATION
NOVEMBER TO APRIL

Arctic Circle
Tropic of Cancer
Equator

Ins.
40
20
10
5

Mms.
1000
500
250
125

PACIFIC OCEAN

ARCTIC OCEAN

Aleutian Is.
BERING SEA
St. Lawrence I.
Bering Str.
Kamchatskiy
Petropavlovsk
Anadyr
Wrangel I.
New Siberian Is.
Severnaya Zemlya
Verkhoyansk
Norilsk
Dudinka
Yenisei
Franz Josef Land
Spitsbergen
BARENTS SEA
Novaya Zemlya
NORWEGIAN SEA
ICELAND
ATLANTIC OCEAN
Arctic Circle
REP. OF IRELAND
Dublin
Glasgow
UNITED KINGDOM
London
Brussels
Paris
FRANCE
Berne
ITALY
NORTH SEA
DENMARK
Copenhagen
Amsterdam
NETH
GER
Bonn
Berlin
Prague
CZECHOSLOVAKIA
Vienna
AUSTRIA
Budapest
HUNGARY
YUGOSLAVIA
Belgrade
ROMANIA
Bucharest
Sofia
BULGARIA
GREECE
Istanbul
Ankara
TURKEY
Izmir
CYPRUS
LEBANON
Beirut
Damascus
SYRIA
Jerusalem
ISRAEL
JORDAN
Amman
Mecca
SAUDI ARABIA
Riyadh
YEMEN
Sana
SOUTHERN YEMEN
Aden
Gulf of Aden
Socotra
OMAN
Muscat
UNION OF ARAB EMIRATES
Dubai
Abu Dhabi
QATAR
Doha
BAHRAIN
Kuwait
Persian Gulf
Basra
Abadan
Baghdad
IRAQ
Tigris
Euphrates
Tropic of Cancer
IRAN
Tehran
Isfahan
Tabriz
Mashhad
Baku
Tbilisi
CASPIAN SEA
Krasnovodsk
AFGHANISTAN
Kabul
Helmand
PAKISTAN
Karachi
KASHMIR
Srinagar
Islamabad
Lahore
Delhi
New Delhi
Agra
Kanpur
Varanasi
Nagpur
Hyderabad
Bombay
Ahmadabad
INDIA
Indus
Ganges
Jumna
Yamuna
Narmada
Godavari
NEPAL
Katmandu
BHUTAN
Brahmaputra
BANGLADESH
Dacca
Calcutta
Patna
BURMA
Mandalay
Irrawaddy
Sadiya
Lhasa
TIBET
SINKIANG-UIGHUR
Urumchi
Lop Nor
Ching Hai
Sinkiang
Ch I N A
Lanchow
Sian
Chungking
Kunming
Yangtze Kiang
Hwang Ho
Si Kiang
Sr. Kiang
Hanoi
Kweichow
Kwangchow
Victoria
HONG KONG (Br.)
Macao (Port.)
Hainan
Kunming
Wuhan
Changsha
Peking
Tientsin
Tsinan
Nanking
Shanghai
EAST CHINA SEA
YELLOW SEA
Tsingtao
Lüta
Pusan
Seoul
KOREA
NORTH KOREA
SOUTH KOREA
Pyongyang
Shenyang
Harbin
Sungari
Amur
Argun
INNER MONGOLIA
MONGOLIA
Ulan Bator
L. Baikal
Ulan-Ude
Irkutsk
Chita
Khabarovsk
Vladivostok
Komsomolsk-na-Amur
Sakhalin
SEA OF OKHOTSK
Magadan
Okhotsk
Kuril Islands
Hokkaido
Honshu
SEA OF JAPAN
JAPAN
Tokyo
Yokohama
Osaka
Kobe
Kyoto
Nagoya
Hakodate
Nagasaki
Kyushu
Shikoku
Korea Str.
Ryukyu Is.
TAIWAN (FORMOSA)
Taipei
PHILIPPINES
Quezon City
Luzon
SOUTH CHINA SEA
UNION OF SOVIET SOCIALIST REPUBLICS
Lena
Aldan
Vilyuy
Yakutsk
Krasnoyarsk
Yenisei
Novosibirsk
Tomsk
Ob
Semipalatinsk
Omsk
Irtysh
Sverdlovsk
Perm
Kama
Karaganda
Ayaguz
Balkhash
L. Balkhash
Alma-Ata
Samarkand
Tashkent
Syr Darya
Amu Darya
ARAL SEA
Aralsk
Petropavlovsk
Kuybyshev
Gorki
Ural
Uralsk
Guryev
Astrakhan
Volgograd
Volga
Saratov
Tula
Moscow
Kharkov
Donetsk
Rostov
Sevastopol
Odessa
BLACK SEA
Kiev
Warsaw
POLAND
Dnieper
Minsk
Riga
BALTIC SEA
Leningrad
Rybinsk
Vologda
Arkhangelsk
Murmansk
White Sea
Petrozavodsk
Helsinki
FINLAND
Stockholm
SWEDEN
NORWAY
Oslo

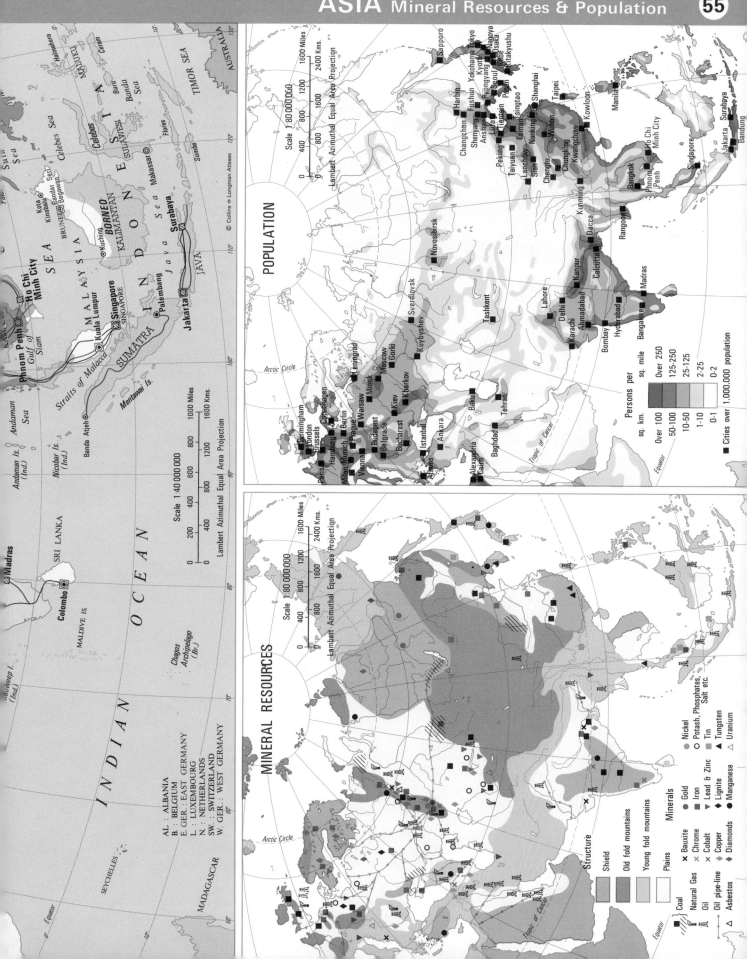

POPULATION

Scale 1:80 000 000

1600 Miles
2400 Kms.
1200
1600
800
400
0
400
0
Lambert Azimuthal Equal Area Projection
© Collins ◇ Longman Atlases

Sapporo
Tokyo
Yokohama
Kyoto
Nagoya
Osaka
Kitakyushu
Seoul
Pusan
Harbin
Fushun
Pyongyang
Kobe
Changchun
Shenyang
Anshan
Dairen
Tsinan
Shanghai
Taipei
Peking
Tientsin
Tsingtao
Nanking
Wuhan
Taiyuan
Lanchow
Sian
Chengtu
Chungking
Kwangchow
Kowloon
Manila
Ho Chi
Minh City
Kunming
Bangkok
Singapore
Phnom
Penh
Novosibirsk
Dacca
Rangoon
Sverdlovsk
Kanpur
Calcutta
Madras
Tashkent
Lahore
Delhi
Ahmadabad
Hyderabad
Bangalore
Kuybyshev
Leningrad
Gorki
Karachi
Bombay
Moscow
Kharkov
Minsk
Kiev
Baku
Tehran
Copenhagen
Warsaw
Budapest
Istanbul
Birmingham
London
Berlin
Prague
Belgrade
Bucharest
Ankara
Brussels
Munich
Vienna
Baghdad
Paris
Hamburg
Milan
Athens
Alexandria
Cairo

Arctic Circle

Tropic of Cancer

Equator

Persons per
sq. km.	sq. mile
Over 100	Over 250
50-100	125-250
10-50	25-125
1-10	2-25
0-1	0-2

■ Cities over 1,000,000 population

MINERAL RESOURCES

Scale 1:80 000 000

1600 Miles
2400 Kms.
1200
1600
800
400
0
400
0
Lambert Azimuthal Equal Area Projection

Arctic Circle

Tropic of Cancer

Equator

Structure
Shield
Old fold mountains
Young fold mountains
Plains

Minerals
✕ Bauxite	● Gold
✕ Chrome	■ Iron
✕ Cobalt	▼ Lead & Zinc
◆ Copper	◆ Lignite
△ Diamonds	▲ Manganese

● Nickel	
○ Potash, Phosphates, Salt etc.	
■ Tin	
▲ Tungsten	
△ Uranium	

■ Coal
Natural Gas
Oil
Oil pipe-line
▲ Asbestos

MALUKU
Halmahera
Ceram
Buru
Celebes
Sea
Banda
Sea
TIMOR SEA
AUSTRALIA
Celebes
Makassar
SULAWESI
Flores
Sumba
BORNEO
Kota
Kinabalu
BRUNEI
Bandar Seri
Begawan
KALIMANTAN
Kuching
Java
Sea
Surabaya
JAVA
Ho Chi
Minh City
MALAYSIA
Singapore
Palembang
SINGAPORE
SUMATRA
Kuala Lumpur
Jakarta
Phnom Penh
Gulf of
Siam
Straits of Malacca
Mentawai Is.
Banda Atjeh
Nicobar Is.
(Ind.)
Andaman Is.
(Ind.)
Andaman
Sea

Scale 1:40 000 000

1000 Miles
1600 Kms.
800
1200
600
800
400
200
0
400
0
Lambert Azimuthal Equal Area Projection

Madras
SRI LANKA
Colombo
MALDIVE IS.
Chagos
Archipelago
(Br.)
I N D I A N   O C E A N
SEYCHELLES
MADAGASCAR

AL. : ALBANIA
B. : BELGIUM
E. GER. : EAST GERMANY
L. : LUXEMBOURG
N. : NETHERLANDS
SW. : SWITZERLAND
W. GER. : WEST GERMANY

CASPIAN

Kara Bogaz
Gol Bay

CAUCASUS
MTS.

S.S.R.

Turkestan   U.   S.   S.   R.

Khiva   Turtkul

Derbent

Telavi

Tbilisi

Dvolti
13553

Alazan
Shirak
Steppe

Zakataly
14698

Nukha

Kura

Kuba

Sumgait

Apsheron
Pen

Krasnovodsk G.   Balkhan Ba.

TURKMENISTAN   S.S.R.

KARA   KUM

(Black Sand Desert)

Bukhara

Chardzhou

Kirovakan
9820

Kirovabad

AZER-BAIJAN

Baku

Krasnovodsk

Nebit Dag

Yerbent

Ashkhabad

Kara-Kum Canal

ARMENIA
S.S.R.

Stepanakert

Salyany

Alyaty (92 feet below sea level)

Cheleken

Vyshka

Kum Dag

Koper

Range

Lutfabad

Kalat

Kara-Kum

Nakhichevan
12808

Moghan
Steppe

SEA

Kizil
Arvat

Sumbar

Attek

Ashkhabad

Barreh Gaz

Qutur   Khoi

Marand

Ahar

Kuh-i-Savalan
15784

Lenkoran

Atrek

Bojnurd

Kuh-i-Afeh

Kuh-i-Shah
10323

Quchan

Mashhad

Kushk

Kala Nao

Maruchak

Ardabil

Bandar-e-Pahlavi

Gorgan

Kara-Su

Kuh-i-Binalud
11207

Nishapur

Torbat-i-
Shaikh Jam

Herat

Parophamisus   Mts
11712

Safed
Koh

DASHT-E-KAVIR
(Salt   Desert)

I   R   A   N

AFGHANISTAN

ZAGROS   MOUNTAINS

PERSIAN   GULF

Shiraz

PERSEPOLIS

STR. of Hormuz

GULF OF OMAN

KUWAIT

BAHRAIN

QATAR

UNION OF ARAB EMIRATES

OMAN

ARABIAN

SEA

Riyadh

Muscat

Tropic of Cancer

80 © Collins ◇ Longman Atlases

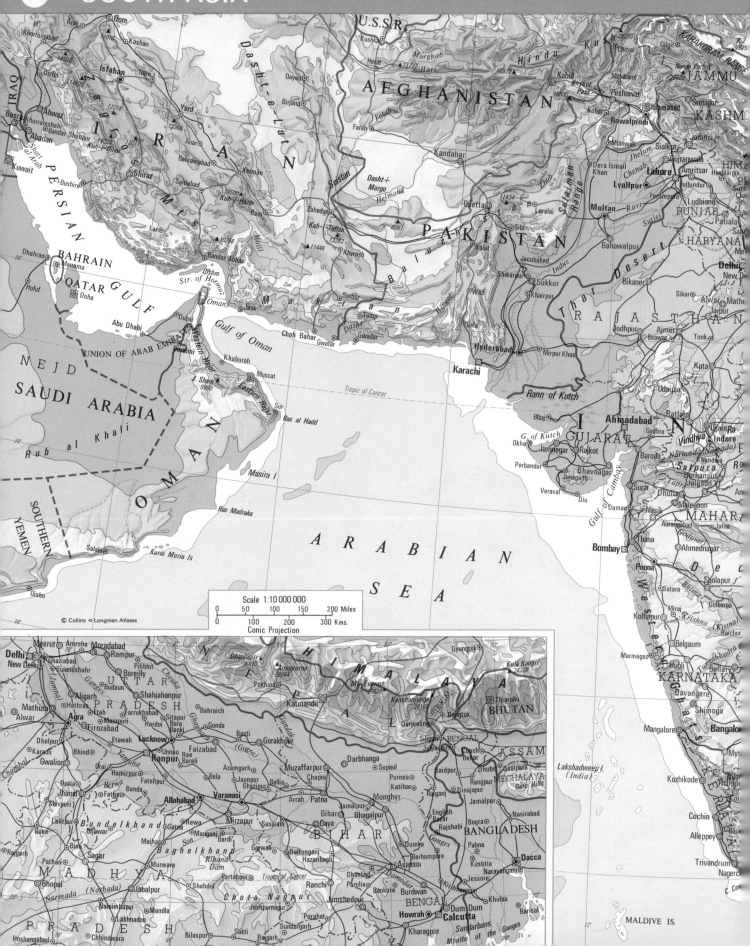

U.S.S.R.

IRAQ

Khorramabad · Arak · Qom · Kashan · Kushka
Dizful · Isfahan · Nain · Murghab
Basra · Ahwaz · Kuh-i-Dinar · Yazd · Qayen · Birjand · Hari · Herat · AFGHANISTAN · Hindu Kush · KARAKORAM RANGE · K2 25230 · JAMMU
Khorramshahr · Shahpur · Dasht-e-lut · Farah · Kabul · Khyber Pass · Peshawar · Srinagar · KASHMIR
Kuwait · Abadan · Shiraz · Anar · Kerman · Seistan · Dasht-i-Margo · Helmand · Kandahar · Kohat · Rawalpindi · Jammu

BAHRAIN · Dhahran · Manama · QATAR · Doha · Str. of Hormuz · Oman · Jask · Makran · Dasht · Gwadar · Karachi · Rann of Kutch · Ahmadabad · GUJARAT

PERSIAN GULF

NEJD
SAUDI ARABIA
Rub al Khali

OMAN

Masira I.

SOUTHERN
YEMEN

Ras Madraka

Salala · Kuria Muria Is.

Qishn

A R A B I A N
S E A

Scale 1:10 000 000
0   50   100   150   200 Miles
0   100   200   300 Kms.
Conic Projection
© Collins ◇ Longman Atlases

BOMBAY · Poona · MAHAR

Meerut · Amroha · Moradabad · Rampur
Delhi · New Delhi · Ghaziabad · Bulandshahr · Pilibhit · NEPAL · Gyangse · HIMALAYA · Kula Kangri 24768 · BHUTAN
Aligarh · Bareilly · Shahjahanpur · UTTAR PRADESH · Pokhara · Mt. Everest 29028 · Kanchenjunga 28168 · Thimphu
Mathura · Etah · Bahraich · Katmandu · SIKKIM · Gangtok
Agra · Firozabad · Farrukhabad · Gonda · Darjeeling · BENGAL · ASSAM
Alwar · Etawah · Lucknow · Gorakhpur · Siliguri · Cooch Behar · MEGHALAYA · Garo Hills
Dholpur · Kanpur · Faizabad · Basti · Darbhanga · Supaul · Purnea · Dinajpur · Lakshadweep I. (India)
Gwalior · Bhind · Rae Bareli · Azamgarh · Muzaffarpur · Katihar · Rangpur · Jamalpur
Jhansi · Hamirpur · Jaunpur · Ghazipur · Chapra · Monghyr · Rajganj · Saidpur · Dhubri · BANGLADESH · Mangalore
Allahabad · Varanasi · Arrah · Patna · Bhagalpur · English Bazar · Bogra · Rajshahi · Nasirabad
Rewa · Mirzapur · Sasaram · Gaya · BIHAR · Dumka · Ganges · Pabna · Dacca
MADHYA · Satna · Maihar · Son · Hazaribagh · Dhanbad · Asansol · Kushtia · Narayanganj · Cochin · Alleppey
Bhopal · Jabalpur · Ranchi · Purulia · Burdwan · Bankura · Krishnanagar · Jessore · Khulna · Trivandrum
PRADESH · Narmada · Mandla · Chota Nagpur · Jamshedpur · BENGAL · Barisal · MALDIVE IS.
Howrah · Calcutta · Dum Dum · Sundarbans · Mouths of the Ganges

Tropic of Cancer

Taiwan
Kaohsiung

TAIWAN
(FORMOSA)

Batan Is
Luzon Strait
Babuyan Is
Cieador
C. Engaño
Laoag
Aparri
Tuguegarao
Pulog
San Fernando
9606
Baguio
Dagupan
San Carlos
Cabanatuan

LUZON

Quezon City
Manila
San Pablo
Daet
Naga
Catanduanes
gas
Legaspi
Mindoro
Burias
Bulan
Catarman
Masbate
Samar
Calbayog
Tacloban
Panay
Iloilo
Leyte
Dinagat
Bacolod
Cebu
Siargao
Negros
Bohol
Surigao
Dipolog
Butuan
Dumaguete
Ozamiz
Cagayan de Oro
Iligan
Zamboanga
Davao
Basilan
Dulawan
Moro
Gulf
Jolo
Sulu
Arch

PHILIPPINES

MINDANAO

Philippine Trench

Davao G.

Cape Johnson
Depth 34439

Parece Vela

Farallon de Pajaros
Asuncion
Agrihan
Pagan
Alamagan
Guguan

M a r i a n a
Sarigan
Anatahan
Farallon de Medinilla

I s l a n d s
Saipan
Tinian
Rota

Agana
Guam
Nero Deep
31618

Challenger Depth
36200

P A C I F I C

Yap
Gaferut

Faraulep

Pigailoe

Lamotrek

Sorol
Ifalik

O C E A N
Palau
Is
Koror
C a r o l i n e
Eauripik
I s l a n d s
(U.S. Trust Territory)

Sonsorol

Merir

Tobi

Helen Reef

L E B E S

Karakelong
Talaud
Is
Sangi
Sangihe
Is

S E A

Menado
Kuandang
Buol
7740
Belang
Gorontalo
6453
omini
ala
Togian Is
Poso
Tulsa
Poh
Peleng
Kolaka
Mekongga
3454
Kendari
Wowoni
Muna
Butung
ubaena
abia

Morotai
Tobelo
M o l u c c a S e a
Djailolo
Ternate
Weda
Halmahera

Waigeo
Dampier Str
Kwoka
9843
Manokwari
Batjan
Sorong
Arfak
9646
Vogelkop
Misoöl
Teluk
Berau
Faktak
Wasior
M O L U C C A S
Obi
Banggai Is
Sula Is
C E R A M S E A
Binaija
10023
Namlea
Ambon
Buru
Buia
Ceram
Adi
Banda
Katmana
Kokenau

B A N D A S E A
Kai Is
Wokam
Kobroör
**Aru
Is**
Trangan

S I A
Nila
Damar
Jamdena
Tanimbar
Is
Selaru
E S S E A
Roma
Babar Is
Leti Is
Sermate

Wetar
Alor
Dili
Timor
Kupang
Roti
Savu Sea
Sawu
Ende
Maumere
1758
Dilikiki

A R A F U R A S E A

Schouten Is
Biak
Japen
Sarmi
Djajapura

Mamberamo
4395
I R I A N
Maoke Rand
Sudirman Mts
Putjak Djaja
16503
Djajawidjaja
J A Y A
Mts
Mandala Pk
15420

Wasior
Teluk
Irian

Manus
Admiralty Is

**Bismarck
Sea**
Aitape
Wewak
Sepik
Madang

Djajapura

PAPUA NEW
Mt Hagen
GUINEA
Mt. Wilhelm
15400

N E W G U I N E A
Dikoel
Fly
Kikori
13100

Kolepom
C. Vals
Merauke
**Gulf of
Papua**
Port Moresby

Mulgrave Is
Banks I
Torres Str.
Thursday I
Prince of Wales I
C. York

**C o r a l
S e a**

Relief

Feet		Metres
16 404		5000
9843		3000
6562		2000
3281		1000
1640		500
656		200
0		Sea Level
Land Dep.		
656		200
13123		4000
22 966		7000

U. S. S. R.

KAZAKHSTAN S.S.R.

MONGO[LIA]

Tashkent

UZBEKISTAN SSR

KIRGIZSTAN S.S.R.

Alma Ata

Frunze

Balkhash

Lake Balkhash

Aktogay

Ayaguz

Zaysan

Altai

Ulan Gom

Hirgis Nur

Uliastai

Bulagan

Möron

Selenga

Khöbsögöl
Dalai

Lake
Baikal

Irkutsk

Slyudyanka

Tula Ula Bat

Yenisei

Kyzyl

Saian Mts.

TADZHIKISTAN S.S.R.

Dushanbe

Dzungaria

Tien Shan

Urumchi

Turfan
Turfan
Depression
–505

Hami

Gobi

NINGSIA
HUI

SINKIANG UIGHUR

Tien Shan

Kashgar

Yarkand

Aksu

Kucha

Kara-Shahr

Baghrash Köl

Ansi

Yumen

Tunchwang

Edsin Gol

Hsinpacher

AFGHANISTAN

PAMIRS

Hindu Kush

KARAKORAM RANGE

K U N

Takla Makan

Guma

Khotan

Charchan

Charchan

Charkhlik

Lop
Nok

Nan

Shan

Karo
Nor

Mangyai

Tatsaitan

TSINGHAI

Ching
Hai

Sining

Lanchow

Linsia

Lintao

PAKISTAN

JAMMU AND KASHMIR

Srinagar

Lahore

Rawalpindi

Peshawar

Gilgit

Karakoram
Pass

L U N

Altyn Tagh

Tibetan
Plateau

T I B E T

C H I N [A]

SZECHWAN

Chengtu

Chungking

Kanting

Tzekung

Ipin

Luchow

HIMACHAL PRADESH

Delhi

New Delhi

HARYANA

PUNJAB

Ludhiana

Ambala

Meerut

RAJASTHAN

Jaipur

Agra

UTTAR PRADESH

Lucknow

Kanpur

Allahabad

Varanasi

Ganges

NEPAL

Katmandu

BHUTAN

Thimphu

Shigatse

Lhasa

Changtu

Paan

Mekong

Salween

Yangtze Kiang

Minya Konka
24900

Kweiyang

KWEICHOW

MADHYA PRADESH

Jabalpur

Nagpur

BIHAR

Patna

Monghyr

Bhagalpur

Darbhanga

Gauhati

Brahmaputra

MEGHALAYA

Shillong

Silchar

NAGALAND

Kohima

MANIPUR

Imphal

Kachin
State

Myitkyina

Bhamo

Katha

YUNNAN

Kunming

Mengtsz

ORISSA

Ranchi

Jamshedpur

BENGAL

Asansol

Dacca

BANGLADESH

Khulna

Calcutta

Howrah

Kharagpur

Sundarbans

Chittagong

Cox's
Bazar

Chin Hills

Akyab

Shwebo

Lashio

Shan

BURMA

Mandalay

Meiktila

MAHARASHTRA

Nagpur

Wardha

Chanda

ANDHRA PRADESH

Vishakhapatnam

Rajahmundry

Vijayawada

Bandar

Puri

B A Y
O F
B E N G A L

Sandoway

Prome

Bassein

Myingyan

KAWTHOOLEI

THAILAND

Chiang Mai

M. Lampang

Uttaradit

LAOS

Luang Prabang

VIETNAM

Hanoi

Vinh

Wentiane

Chita
Ude
Shilka
Shilka
Borzya
Sayn Shand
Erhlien
Huhehot
Paotow
ng Ho
Ningwu
Great
Taiyuan
Fenyang
SHANSI
Shihkiachwang
SI
Loyang
Tungkwan
Sian
HONAN
Shan
CHUAN
HUPEH
Ichang
Kiangling
Shasi
Changteh
Tung Ting Hu
Changsha
Siangtan
HUNAN
Shaoyang
sien
CHUAN
Kweilin
Yinotako
Wuchow
Si Kiang
Kweiping
ning
Chanchiang
Luichow
Peninsula
Haikow
HAINAN
Yulin

Svobodnyy
Blagoveshchensk
Amur
USSR
Khabarovsk
HEILUNGKIANG
Hailar
Tsitsihar
Harbin
KIRIN
Changchun
Kirin
Shenyang
Fushun
LIAONING
Anshan
Penki
Antung
HOPEH
Peking
Tangshan
Tientsin
Gulf of
Chihli
Tzepo
NORTH
Tsinan
SHANTUNG
Tsingtao
CHINA
Kaifeng
Suchow
KIANGSU
PLAIN
Nanking
Shanghai
Wuhan
Hangchow
CHEKIANG
Ningpo
KIANGSI
Nanchang
Wenchow
FUKIEN
Foochow
Amoy
KWANGTUNG
Kwangchow
Kowloon
Macao
Victoria
HONG KONG
SOUTH
CHINA SEA

Sakhalin
Yuzhno
Sakhalinsk
Wakkanai
Asahigawa
Sapporo
HOKKAIDO
Otaru
Muroran
Hakodate
Aomori
Hachinohe
Morioka
Akita
Sendai
NORTH
KOREA
Pyongyang
Nampo
SEA OF JAPAN
HONSHU
Kanazawa
Toyama
Tokyo
Yokohama
Nagoya
SOUTH
KOREA
Seoul
Inchon
Kyoto
Kobe
Osaka
Taegu
Pusan
Hiroshima
SHIKOKU
Kitakyushu
Fukuoka
KYUSHU
Nagasaki
Kagoshima
Osumi
Gunto
PACIFIC
OCEAN
YELLOW
SEA
EAST
CHINA
SEA
Quelpart
Ryukyu Islands
Amami
Okinawa
Naha
Tropic of Cancer
TAIWAN
(FORMOSA)
Taipei
Taichung
Kaohsiung
Tainan
Formosa Strait
Bashi Channel
Batan
Islands
Babuyan
Islands
Luzon Strait
PHILIPPINES
LUZON

© Collins ○ Longman Atlas

Relief

Feet	Metres
16 404	5000
9843	3000
6562	2000
3281	1000
1640	500
656	200
0	Sea Level
Land Dep.	
656	200
13 123	4000
22 966	7000

Scale 1:16 000 000

0 100 200 300 400 500 Miles
0 200 400 600 800 Kms.

Conic Projection

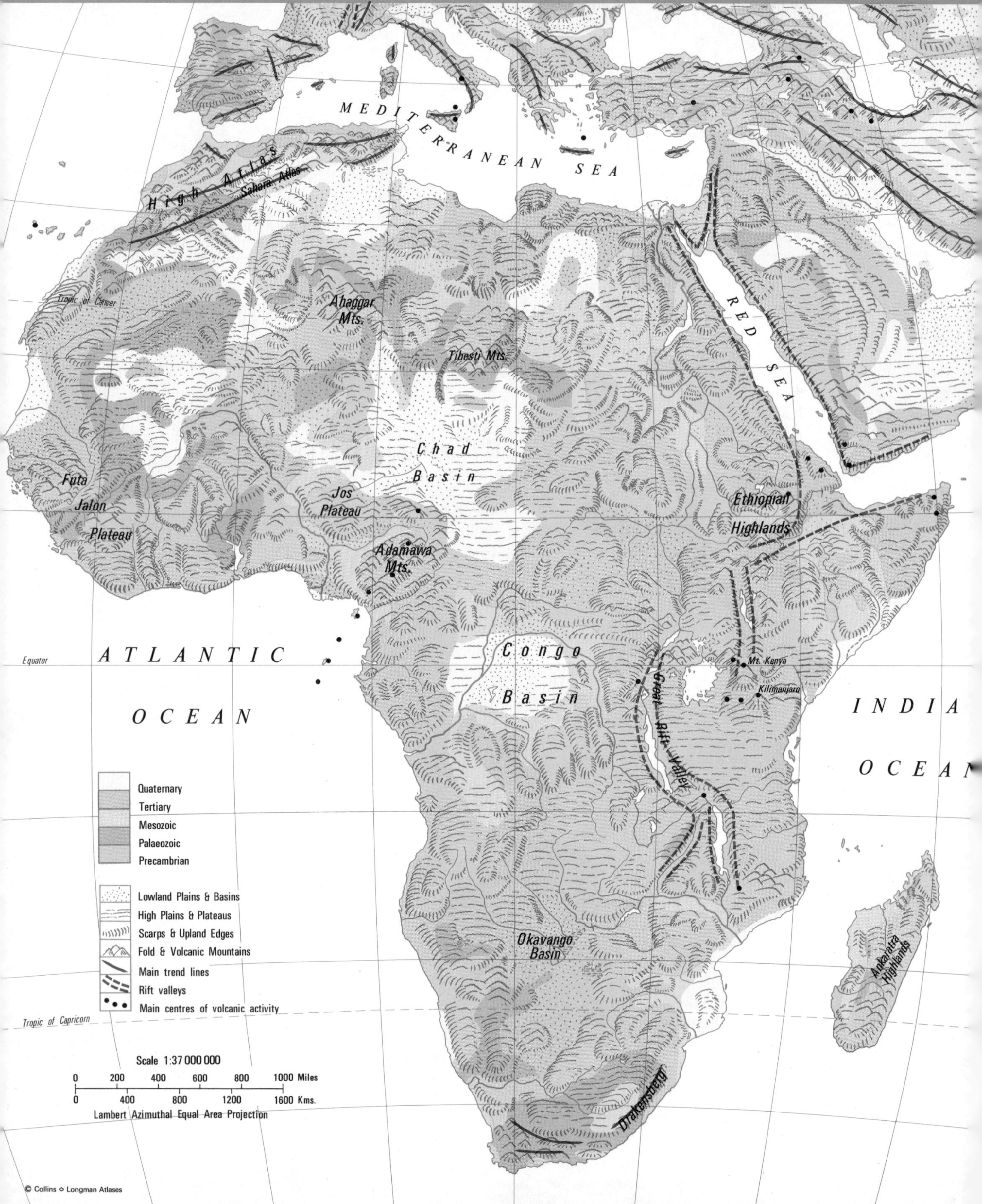

MEDITERRANEAN SEA

High Atlas

Sahara Atlas

Tropic of Cancer

Ahaggar Mts.

Tibesti Mts.

RED SEA

Chad Basin

Futa Jalon Plateau

Jos Plateau

Ethiopian Highlands

Adamawa Mts.

ATLANTIC

Equator

OCEAN

Congo Basin

Mt. Kenya

Kilimanjaro

INDIA

OCEAN

Great Rift Valley

	Quaternary
	Tertiary
	Mesozoic
	Palaeozoic
	Precambrian

Okavango Basin

Ankaratra Highlands

	Lowland Plains & Basins
	High Plains & Plateaus
	Scarps & Upland Edges
	Fold & Volcanic Mountains
	Main trend lines
	Rift valleys
	Main centres of volcanic activity

Tropic of Capricorn

Scale 1:37 000 000

| 0 | 200 | 400 | 600 | 800 | 1000 Miles |
| 0 | 400 | 800 | 1200 | 1600 Kms. |

Lambert Azimuthal Equal Area Projection

Drakensberg

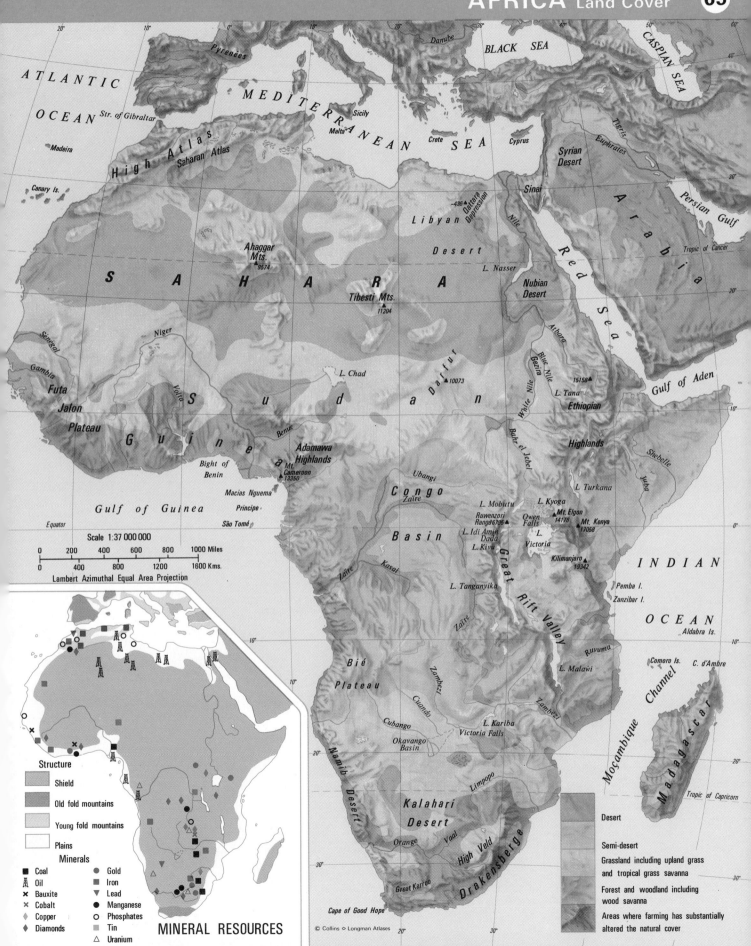

ATLANTIC OCEAN

MEDITERRANEAN

BLACK SEA

CASPIAN SEA

Str. of Gibraltar

Danube

Pyrenées

Sicily

Crete SEA

Malta

Cyprus

Madeira

High Atlas

Saharan Atlas

Canary Is.

Syrian Desert

Euphrates

Tigris

Sinai

Persian Gulf

Libyan

-436 Qattara Depression

Tropic of Cancer

Ahaggar Mts. 9574

Nile

L. Nasser

Nubian Desert

S A H A R A

Desert

Tibesti Mts. 11204

Red Sea

Gulf of Aden

Niger

Darfur

10073

Atbara

15158▲

Senegal

L. Chad

Gezira

L. Tana

S u d a n

White Nile

Blue Nile

Ethiopian

Gambia

Volta

Benue

Futa

Jalon

Plateau

G u i n e a

Adamawa Highlands

Highlands

Shebelle

Bight of Benin

Mt Cameroon 13350

Juba

Macias Nguema

Ubangi

Congo

Zaire

L. Mobutu

L Turkana

Principe

São Tomé

Ruwenzori Range 16795

L. Kyoga

Mt. Elgon 14178

Mt. Kenya 17058

Equator

Gulf of Guinea

B a s i n

L. Idi Amin Dada

L. Kivu

Owen Falls

L. Victoria

Kilimanjaro 19342

I N D I A N

Scale 1:37 000 000

Zaire

Kasai

Great Rift Valley

L. Tanganyika

Pemba I.

Zanzibar I.

O C E A N

0   200   400   600   800   1000 Miles

0   400   800   1200   1600 Kms.

Lambert Azimuthal Equal Area Projection

Aldabra Is.

Ruvuma

Bié

Plateau

Zambezi

L. Malawi

Comoro Is.

C. d'Ambre

Mozambique Channel

Cuando

Zambezi

Madagascar

Cubango

Okavango Basin

L. Kariba

Victoria Falls

Namib Desert

Limpopo

Tropic of Capricorn

Kalahari Desert

Orange   Vaal

High Veld

Drakensberge

Great Karroo

Cape of Good Hope

© Collins ◇ Longman Atlases

MINERAL RESOURCES

Structure

Shield

Old fold mountains

Young fold mountains

Plains

Minerals

- ■ Coal
- ⚒ Oil
- ✕ Bauxite
- ✕ Cobalt
- ◆ Copper
- ◆ Diamonds
- ● Gold
- ■ Iron
- ▼ Lead
- ● Manganese
- ○ Phosphates
- ■ Tin
- △ Uranium

Desert

Semi-desert

Grassland including upland grass and tropical grass savanna

Forest and woodland including wood savanna

Areas where farming has substantially altered the natural cover

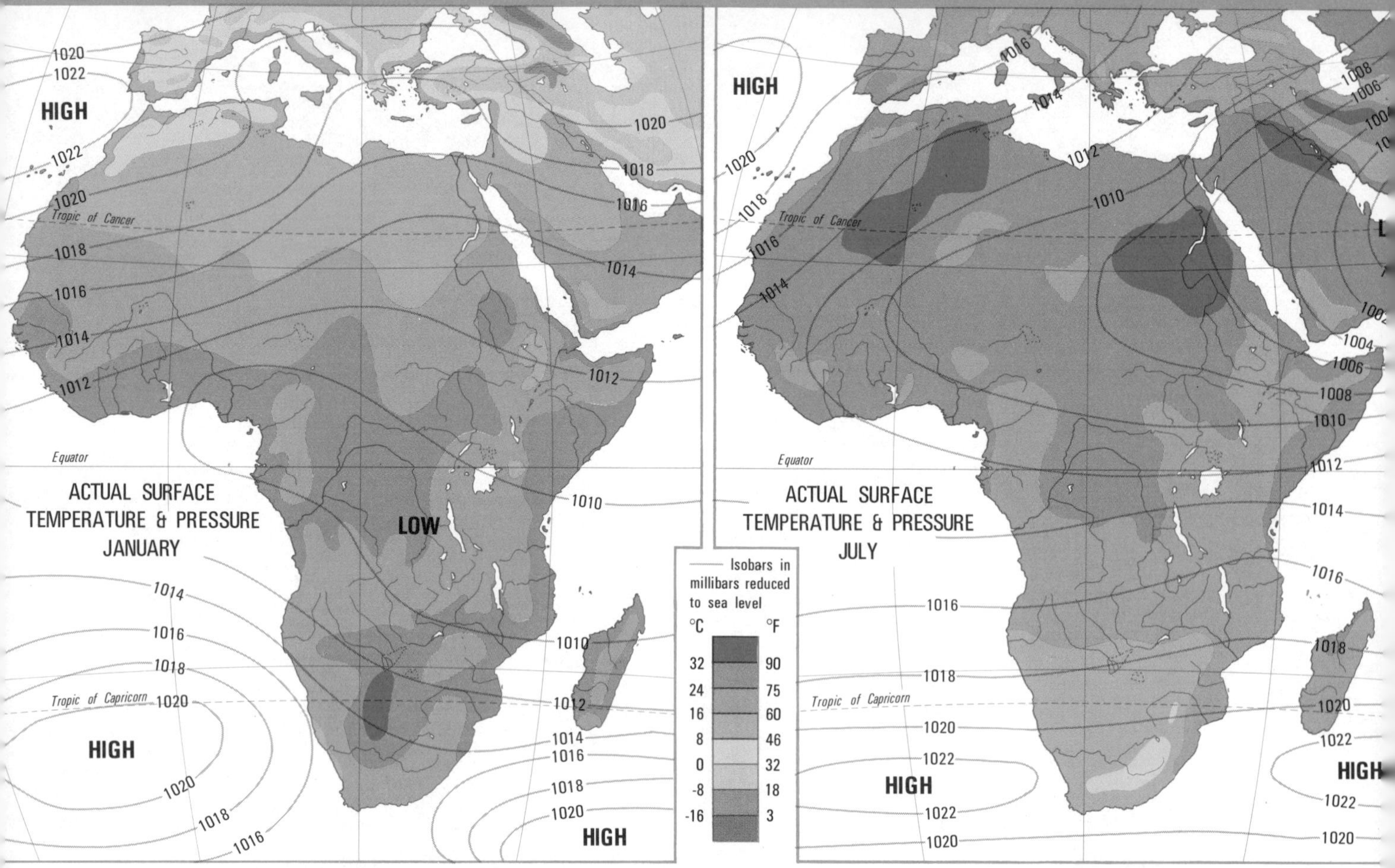

HIGH

1020
1022

HIGH

1022

1020

Tropic of Cancer

1018

1016

1014

1012

1020

1018

1016

1014

Equator

ACTUAL SURFACE
TEMPERATURE & PRESSURE
JANUARY

LOW

1010

1014

1016

1018

Tropic of Capricorn 1020

HIGH

1020

1018

1016

1010

1012

1014
1016
1018
1020

HIGH

HIGH

1016

L

Tropic of Cancer

1010

1014

1008
1006
1004

1002

1004
1006
1008
1010

1012

Equator

ACTUAL SURFACE
TEMPERATURE & PRESSURE
JULY

1016

1018

1020

1022

HIGH

1022

1016

1018

1020

1022

1020

HIGH

Isobars in millibars reduced to sea level		
°C		°F
32		90
24		75
16		60
8		46
0		32
-8		18
-16		3

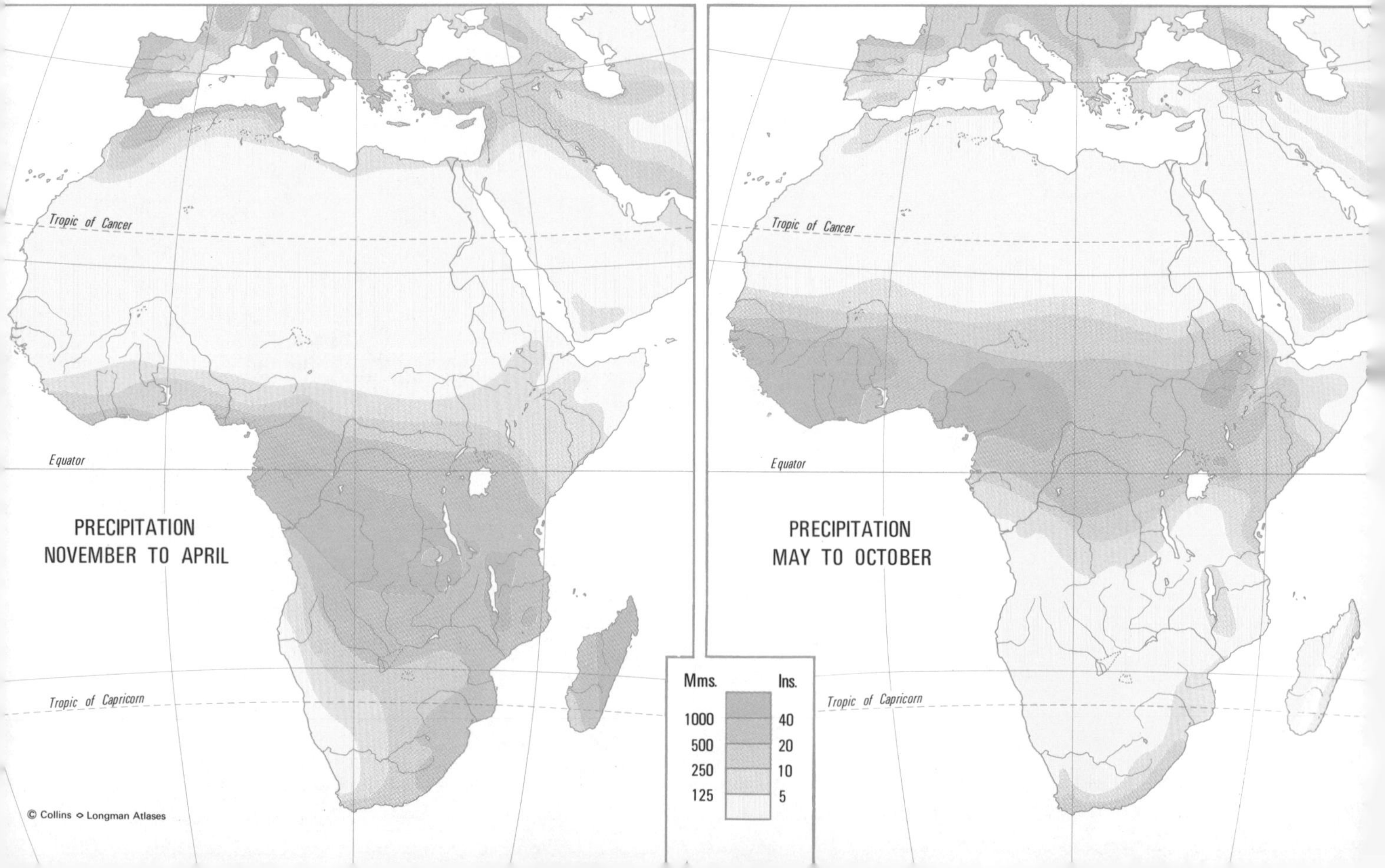

Tropic of Cancer

Equator

PRECIPITATION
NOVEMBER TO APRIL

Tropic of Capricorn

Tropic of Cancer

Equator

PRECIPITATION
MAY TO OCTOBER

Tropic of Capricorn

Mms.		Ins.
1000		40
500		20
250		10
125		5

FRANCE
MONACO
ANDORRA
Madrid
Lisbon
PORTUGAL
SPAIN
Corsica (Fr.)
Sardinia (It.)
Balearic Is.
ITALY
Rome
Tirané
ALBANIA
Belgrade
YUGOSLAVIA
ROMANIA
BULGARIA
Sofia
GREECE
Athens
Black Sea
Caspian Sea
U.S.S.R.
Ankara
TURKEY
Tangier
Oran
Algiers
Annaba
Constantine
Tunis
Sicily
MALTA
Crete
CYPRUS
LEBANON
Beirut
SYRIA
Damascus
ISRAEL
Jerusalem
Amman
JORDAN
IRAN
Tehran
Baghdad
IRAQ
Rabat
Fez
Casablanca
Marrakesh
MOROCCO
Madeira (Port.)
Canary Is. (Sp.)
Tenerife
El Aaiún
WESTERN SAHARA
Mediterranean Sea
Tripoli
Beida
Benghazi
Tobruk
Alexandria
Cairo
Suez
Aswân
L. Nasser
N.T.
KUWAIT
BAHRAIN
QATAR
UNION OF ARAB EMIRATES
Persian Gulf
Tropic of Cancer
SAUDI
ARABIA
RED SEA
Nouadhibou
MAURITANIA
chott
ALGERIA
Reggan
Ain Salah
LIBYA
EGYPT
Wadi Halfa
Dongola
Port Sudan
Massawa
Asmara
Sana
YEMEN
Aden
SOUTHERN YEMEN
DJIBOUTI
Djibouti
Berbera
Dakar
Kayes
SENEGAL
GAMBIA
Bissau
GUINEA
Bamako
Kankan
MALI
Timbuktu
Niger
Gao
NIGER
Agadès
Niamey
L. Chad
CHAD
SUDAN
Khartoum
Nyala
El Muglad
ETHIOPIA
Addis Ababa
Jimma
Diredawa
SOMALI REPUBLIC
onakry
SIERRA
Freetown
LEONE
LIBERIA
Monrovia
Sokoto
Kano
Maiduguri
N'Djamena
Sarh
Garoua
Wau
Malakal
Jos
UPPER VOLTA
Ouagadougou
Volta
Tamale
IVORY COAST
Bouaké
GHANA
Kumasi
BENIN
TOGO
Savé
NIGERIA
Ibadan
Enugu
Port Harcourt
Calabar
CAMEROON
Douala
Yaoundé
CENTRAL AFRICAN REPUBLIC
Bangui
Mobaye
Lisala
Zemio
Niangara
Juba
L. Turkana
Bardera
Mogadishu
Abidjan
Sekondi
Takoradi
Accra
Lomé
Porto-Novo
Lagos
EQUATORIAL GUINEA
Bata
São Tomé
Libreville
GABON
Ndjolé
Franceville
CONGO
Ouesso
Zaïre
Mbandaka
ZAÏRE
Kisangani
UGANDA
Kampala
Lake Victoria
Kisumu
KENYA
Nairobi
Equator
Mombasa
INDIAN OCEAN
ATLANTIC OCEAN
Brazzaville
Kinshasa
Ilebo
Kindu
RWANDA
Kigali
BURUNDI
Bujumbura
Kigoma
Mwanza
Moshi
Tanga
Zanzibar
Dar es Salaam
ANGOLA
Cabinda
Luanda
Malanje
Kananga
Kalemie
Lake Tanganyika
TANZANIA
Lindi
Aldabra Is. (Br.)
Comoro Is. (Fr.)
Lobito
Huambo
Lubumbashi
Mbala
Pemba
Moçambique
Majunga
Moçâmedes
Menongue
Mongu
ZAMBIA
Ndola
Chipata
Lilongwe
MALAWI
L. Malawi
Blantyre
Lusaka
Vila de Sena
Beira
MADAGASCAR
Tamatave
Tananarive
Salisbury
Wankie
ZIMBABWE
Gwelo
Fort Victoria
MOÇAMBIQUE
Moçambique Channel
Tuléar
Tropic of Capricorn
Fort-Dauphin
SOUTH WEST
Grootfontein
Bulawayo
Inhambane
WALVIS BAY
Walvis Bay
Windhoek
BOTSWANA
Francistown
AFRICA
(NAMIBIA)
Gaborone
Pretoria
Maputo
Mbabane
SWAZILAND
Lüderitz
Johannesburg
Karasburg
Gaborone
Kimberley
Kroonstad
Maseru
Ladysmith
LESOTHO
Durban
Port Nolloth
REPUBLIC OF
Calvinia
SOUTH AFRICA
Cape Town
Mossel Bay
Port Elizabeth
East London

POPULATION

Casablanca
Alexandria
Cairo
Ibadan
Lagos
Kinshasa
Johannesburg

Persons per
km.   sq. mile
100	Over 250
100	125-250
-50	25-125
-10	2-25
0-1	0-2

s over 1,000,000 population

Scale 1:37 000 000
0   200   400   600   800   1000 Miles
0   400   800   1200   1600 Kms.
Lambert Azimuthal Equal Area Projection

FRANCE

Oporto
Valladolid
ANDORRA
Nice
Marseille
Florence
Sarajevo
Adriatic Sea

SPAIN
Zaragoza
Corsica (Fr.)
Rome
ITALY
Bari

Madrid
Barcelona
Cagliari
Naples
Taranto

Lisbon
Valencia
Majorca
Sardinia (It.)

Seville
Cartagena
Palma
Balearic Islands (Sp.)
Iviza
Minorca
MEDITERRANEA
Palermo
Messina
Sicily
Catania

Gibraltar (Br.)
Algiers
Bejaïa
Annaba
Bizerta
Tunis
MALTA

Tangier
Ceuta (Sp.)
Oran
El Asnam
Blida
Constantine
Kairouan
Sousse

Melilla (Sp.)
Tetuan
Sidi-bel-Abbès
Atlas
Sfax
G. of Gabes

Rabat
Fez
Oujda
Tlemcen
Atlas
Biskra
Chott Melrhir
Gabès
Tripoli

Casablanca
Meknès
Saharan Atlas
Djelfa
Chott Djerid
Touggourt
Medenine
Misurata

Safi
Khenifra
Chott ech Chergui
Ghardaïa
Ouargla
Nalut
Gulf of Sirte

MOROCCO
Tendrara
Béchar
Hassi Messaoud
Ghadames
Sirte
Age

High Atlas
Ain Sefra
Abadla
El Goléa
Ghadames
Tripolitania
Hun
El Aghe

Marrakesh
Toubkal
Reggan
Ain Salah
Fort Polignac
Sebha
LIBY

Canary Islands (Sp.)
Tademait Plateau
ALGERIA
Ghat
Murzuq
El Qatrun

La Palma
Lanzarote
WESTERN SAHARA
Ahaggar Mts
Mt. Tahat 9574
Tummo
Djado Plateau
Bardai 10335

Tenerife
Fuerteventura
El Aaiún
Tamanrasset
Tibesti M
Emi Koussi 11204

Gran Canaria
Las Palmas
Tropic of Cancer

Villa Cisneros
SAHARA

C. Blanc
Nouadhibou
Fdérik
Kidal
NIGER
TCH

Atar
Agadès
Bodélé Depression

MAURITANIA
Timbuktu
Gao

Nouakchott
Tidjikja
MALI

St. Louis
Nioro
Mopti
Niamey
Birni N'Konni
Nguigmi
Lake Chad

SENEGAL
Dakar
Diourbel
Kayes
San
Sokoto
Maradi
Zinder
Nguru
Yao

Banjul
GAMBIA
Tambacounda
Bamako
Ouagadougou
Sokoto
Katsina
N'Djamena

Bissau
GUINEA BISSAU
Futa Jalon
Sikasso
UPPER VOLTA
Kaura Namoda
Kano
Maiduguri

Bijagos Archipelago
Boké
Labé
Bobo-Dioulasso
Navrongo
Zaria
Bauchi
Maroua

GUINEA
Kankan
Sansanné-Mango
Kaduna
Chari

Conakry
Beyla
IVORY COAST
GHANA
BENIN
Parakou
NIGERIA
Minna
Jos
Logone

SIERRA LEONE
Bouaké
Sunyani
Lake Volta
Savé
Ilorin
Ogbomosho
Makurdi
Garoua

Freetown
Bô
Daloa
Kumasi
Ibadan
Oshogbo
Enugu
Adamawa Highlands
Ngaoundéré

LIBERIA
Abidjan
Lomé
Cotonou
Porto Novo
Benin City
Onitsha
CAMEROON
Tibati
CENTRAL

Monrovia
Sassandra
Accra
Bight of Benin
Lagos
Watri
Calabar
Nkongsamba
Bangui

C. Palmas
Sekondi-Takoradi
Niger Delta
Port Harcourt
Mt. Cameroon 13350
Douala
Yaoundé

Gulf of Guinea
Principe
EQUATORIAL GUINEA
Malabo
Bata
GABON
Libreville
CONGO

São Tomé
Equator
C. Lopez
Lambaréné

Scale 1:20 000 000
0 100 200 300 400 500 Miles
0 200 400 600 800 Kms.
Lambert Azimuthal Equal Area Projection

BULGARIA
Sofia
Varna
Black Sea
Samsun
Istanbul
Thessaloniki
Mt Olympus
9650
Bursa
Ankara
TURKEY
GREECE
Athens
Aegean
Sea
Izmir
Konya
Kayseri
Mt Ercyas
12848
Adana
Antalya
Taurus Mts
Rhodes
Nicosia
Iráklion
Crete
CYPRUS
SEA
Derna
Akhdar
Tobruk
Salûm
Cyrenaica
Jaghbub
El Alamein
Alexandria
Tanta
Cairo
El Giza
El Faiyûm
Qattara Depression
Sialo
Libyan
Caucasus Mts
Batumi
Thilisi
Mt Ararat
16946
Yerevan
L. Sevan
Van
L. Van
Tabriz
15784
Kurdistan
Aleppo
SYRIA
Homs
Euphrates
Mesopotamia
Mosul
Baghdad
IRAQ
Tigris
LEBANON
Beirut
Damascus
Syrian
Desert
Tel Aviv
Amman
Jaffa
JORDAN
Jerusalem
ISRAEL
Dead
Sea
Maan
Suez Canal
Suez
Aqaba
Sinai
G. Katharina
8651
Al Jauf
An
Nafud
Hail
EGYPT
Asyût
7173
Qena
Luxor
Ouseir
El Khârga
Aswân
6488
Aswân High Dam
L. Nasser
HEJAZ
Red
Medina
Nubian
Desert
7271
Wâdi Halfa
Dongola
Karima
Abu Hamed
Port Sudan
Suakin
Merowe
Atbara
Ed Damer
Nile
A
SUDAN
Darfur
Geneina
J Gimbala
10073
El Fasher
Nyala
En Nahud
El Obeid
Kosti
El Muglad
Omdurman
Khartoum
Kassala
Wad Medani
Sennar
Er Rahad
Blue Nile
White Nile
Bahr el Ghazal
Malakal
Sobat
Wau
Sudd
Bahr el Jebel
AFRICAN
C
ngassou
Monga
Zemio
Niangara
Buta
Isiro
Uele
Bomu
Juba
Akobo
ZAÏRE
Kisangani
Boyoma Falls
fa
L. Idi Amin Dada
Ruwenzori Ra
16795
Kasese
Entebbe
UGANDA
Kampala
Owen Falls Dam
Mt Elgon
14178
Soroti
Gulu
Pakwach
Albert Nile
L. Mobutu
Lake Victoria
Kisumu
Eldoret
KENYA
Mt Kenya
17058
Garissa
Kismayu
Equator
U.S.S.R.
Kara Bogaz Gol Bay
Krasnovodsk
Caspian Sea
Baku
Turkestan
Amu Darya
Bukhara
Chardzhou
Ashkhabad
Mary
Kushka
Turkmen
18376
Demavend
Tehran
Elburz Mts
Bander-e-Shah
Aral
Mashhad
Herat
Hari
AFGHANI-STAN
Hamadân
Kermânshâhân
Dasht-e-Kavir
(Salt Desert)
Rasht
Urmia
Zagros
IRAN
Isfahan
Yazd
Mountains
Dasht-e-Lut
Ahwaz
Basra
Abadan
Shiraz
Kuh-i-Dinar
14029
Kerman
Zahedan
KUWAIT
NEUT
Kuwait
Persian Gulf
Bushire
Makran
Bander Abbas
SAUDI
Anaiza
Dhahran
BAHRAIN
Hofuf
QATAR
Dubai
UNION OF ARAB EMIRATES
(Oman)
Gulf of Oman
Mt Hajar
Muscat
E. Hajar
Riyadh
J
Tropic of Cancer
ARABIA
Juddah
Mecca
Rub al Khali
OMAN
Salala
Kuria Muria Is
SOUTHERN
YEMEN
Hadramaut
Mukalla
Sana
YEMEN
Hodeida
Taizz
Perim
Al Shaab
Aden
Gulf of Aden
Socotra
(S. Yemen)
C Guardafui
Berbera
Erigavo
SOMALI REPUBLIC
Agordat
Massawa
Asmara
Kassala
Aduwa
Ras Dashan
15168
Gondar
Birhan
13629
Dessye
Ankober
Addis Ababa
ETHIOPIA
Ethiopian
Highlands
Jimma
Gore
Dembi Dolo
L. Abaya
Shebelle
Lake Turkana
Danakil
Assab
DJIBOUTI
(FR TERR OF AFARS AND ISSAS)
Djibouti
Zeila
Diredawa
Harar
Hargeisa
Obbia
Bardera
Iscia Baidoa
Wajir
Mogadishu
Juba

Relief
Feet   Metres
16404   5000
9843   3000
6562   2000
3281   1000
1640   500
656   200
0   Sea Level
Land Dep.
656   200
13123   4000
22966   7000

© Collins ○ Longman Atlases

WESTERN SAHARA

MAURITANIA

MALI

SENEGAL

GAMBIA

GUINEA BISSAU

GUINEA

SIERRA LEONE

LIBERIA

IVORY COAST

UPPER VOLTA

GHANA

ATLANTIC OCEAN

SAOUR

S A H

Bijagos Archipelago

BRONG-AHAFO
ASHANTI
NORTHERN
WESTERN
CENTRAL
EASTERN
UPPER

Nouadhibou
C Blanc
Fdérik
Zouerate
Akjoujt
Atar
Taoudenni
Araouane
Tidjikja
Nouakchott
Méderdra
Bogué
Kaédi
Kiffa
Néma
Bamba
Bourem
Gourma-Rarous
Timbuktu
Niger
Gao
Goundam
Douentza
Podor
Dagana
Kaédi
Matam
Nioro
Nara
Sokolo
Mopti
Ouahigouya
Dori
St. Louis
Louga
Linguère
Baké
Kayes
Djenné
San
Ségou
Bani
C Verde
Thiès
Diourbel
Rufisque
Dakar
Kaolack
Tambacounda
Bafoulabé
Kita
Kati
Koulikoro
Bamako
Bougouni
Ouagadougou
Banjul
Bignona
Sédhiou
Farim
Ziguinchor
Kédougou
Saradougou
Koutiala
Sikasso
Houndé
Bobo-Dioulasso
Pô
Bissau
Bolama
Boké
Télimélé
Pita
Labé
Yambering
Tinkisso
Siguiri
Bagoé
Lawra
Navrongo
Wa
Tamale
Sansanne-Mango
Fada-N'Gour
Conakry
Forécariah
Boffa
Kindia
Mamou
Dabola
Kouroussa
Faranah
Kankan
Odienné
Boundiali
Korhogo
Ferkéssédougou
Bouna
Bole
Kabala
Makeni
Magburaka
Sefadu
Kissidougou
Macenta
Beyla
Touba
Dabakala
Bondoukou
Kete Krachi
Port Loko
Rokel
Freetown
Bo
Kenema
Pendembu
Pujehun
N'zérékoré
Mt. Nimba
Man
Séguéla
Bouaké
Sunyani
Kumasi
Obuasi
Enchi
Monrovia
Buchanan
Daloa
Bouaflé
Dimbokro
Abengourou
Agboville
Gagnoa
Greenville
Sassandra
Abidjan
Bingerville
Port Bouet
Grand Bassam
Tarkwa
Axim
Sekondi-Takoradi
Accra
Tema
Winneba
Cape Coast
Oda
Koforidua
C Palmas
Tabou

Sherbro I.
Sassandra
Cavally
Bandama
Comoé
Tano
Lake Volta
Black Volta
White Volta
Red Volta
Senegal
Gambia
Falémé
Baoulé
Bafing
Niger
Milo
Bani
Sankarani

Relief

Feet	Metres
16 404	5000
9843	3000
6562	2000
3281	1000
1640	500
656	200
0	Sea Level

Land Dep.	
656	200
13123	4000
22966	7000

Scale 1:10 000 000

0 100 200 300 Miles

0 100 200 300 400 Kms.

Lambert Azimuthal Equal Area Projection

© Collins ◇ Longman Atlases

NIGERIA
Aba
Calabar
Port Harcourt
Bonny
Mt. Cameroon 13350
Victoria
Malabo
Bight of
Bonny
Gulf of Guinea
Principe
São Tomé
Equator
C. Lopez
Port Gentil
Chinchoua
Libreville
Lambaréné
Fougamou
Moulla
N'Dendé
Setté Cama
Tchibanga
Mayoumba
Banda

ATLANTIC

OCEAN

Foumban
Dschang
Banganté
Yoko
Bétaré-Oya
Bafia
N'Kongsamba
M'Bangé
Tiko
Douala
Edea
Kribi
Ebolowa
Campo
Bata

EQUATORIAL GUINEA

GABON
Mitzic
Makokou
Booué
Ndjolé
Lastoursville
5185
Moanda
Franceville
Mbinda
Djambala
Sibiti
Loudima
Dolisie
Pointe Noire
Buco Zau
Necuto
Tshela
Guilherne Capelo Ihe
Cabinda
Banana
S. Antonio
do Zaire
Matadi
Ambrizete
Ambriz
Caxito
Luanda
Catete
Quicama
Muxima
Nat. Park

CAMEROON
Yaoundé
Yokadouma
Lomié
Doumé
Bertoua
Batouri
Berbérati
Doumé
Nola

CONGO
Ouesso
Liouesso
Ikelemba
Impfondo
Bomongo
Mbandaka
Bolobo
M'Pouya
Mushie
Kwamouth
Bandundu

Brazzaville
Malebo Pool
Kinshasa
Kenge
Masi-Manimba
Kikwit
Idiofa
Popokabaka
Feshi
Kasongo-
Lunda
Sanza
Pombo
Uige
Tembo
Aluma
Camabatela
Quibaxi
CUANZA NORTE
Vila Salazar
Falls
Duque de
Bragança
Dondo
Malanje
Cuanza

ANGOLA

CENTRAL AFRICAN REPUBLIC
Bossembélé
Ft. de Possel
Carnot
Bangui
Zongo
Libenge
M'Baiki
Lopi
Dongou
Nouvelle
Anvers
Bolomba
Ingende
Bikoro
L. Tumba
Kiri
Inongo
Mai
Ndombe
Kutu
Fimi
Lukenie
Bandundu
Kasai
Oshwe
BANDUNDU
Ilebo
Basongo
KASAI
Mweka
Gungu
Kahemba
Portugalia
Vila Verissimo
Sarmento
Caungula
Henrique
de Carvalho

LUNDA

Kouango
Mobaye
Bosobolo
Gemena
Karawa
Budjala
Lisala
Bumba
Bomongo
Basankusu
Bongandanga
Befale
Djolu
Boende
Monkoto
Lomela
Dekese
Kolé
Lodja
Lusambo
Luebo
Dimbelenge
Kananga
Mbuji
Mayi
Tshikapa
Kazumba
Luisa
Mwene
Ditu
Kapanga

OCCIDENTAL

Rafai
Bangassou
Monga
Bili
Bondo
Aketi
Komba
Buta
Yahuma
Basoko
Isangi
Yapehe
Opala
Ikela
Katako
Kombe
Lubefu
Tshofa
Gandajika
Kabongo
Kaniama
Kamina
Sandoa

KASAI ORIENTAL

ZAIRE

EQUATEUR

Bomu
Zemio
Bambes
An
Kisang
Boyoma
Falls
Ubundu
Kibon
Sent
Libudi
Lut
Buka
Mwinilunga

Bié
8597
Huambo
V. Silva Porto
5098

MOXICO

HUAMBO

BENGUELA
Lobito
Benguela
Dombe Grande
V. Mariano
Machado
Caconda
Quilengues
Moçâmedes
João de
Almeida
Chibemba
Porto Alexandre
5905
Roçadas
Vila Pereira
de Eça

HUILA

CUANDO-

CUBANGO

Menongue

SOUTH WEST AFRICA (NAMIBIA)
Ovambo
Okavango
Andara
Capriv
Kasane

Relief
Feet   Metres
16404   5000
9843   3000
6562   2000
3281   1000
1640   500
656   200
0   Sea Level
Land Dep.
656   200
13123   4000
22966   7000

Scale 1:10 750 000
0   100   200   300 Miles
0 100 200 300 400 500 Kms.
Lambert Azimuthal Equal Area Projection
© Collins • Longman Atlases

ATLANTIC

OCEAN

INDIAN OCEAN

ATLANTIC OCEAN

ZAMBIA

ZIMBABWE (RHODESIA)

Mashonaland

Matabeleland

MOZAMBIQUE

MANICA

SOFALA

GAZA

INHAMBANE

SWAZILAND

TRANSVAAL

ORANGE FREE STATE

NATAL

LESOTHO

REPUBLIC OF SOUTH AFRICA

CAPE PROVINCE

Transkei

BOTSWANA

KALAHARI DESERT

Ngamiland

Okavango Basin

SOUTH WEST AFRICA (NAMIBIA)

NAMIB DESERT

Great Namaland

ANGOLA

HUILA

CUANDO-CUBANGO

Caprivi Strip

Lake Kariba

Etosha Pan

Table Mt.

Cape of Good Hope

Tropic of Capricorn

Salisbury

Bulawayo

Johannesburg

Pretoria

Bloemfontein

Kimberley

Durban

Cape Town

Port Elizabeth

East London

Windhoek

Walvis Bay

Maputo

Beira

Lusaka

Scale 1:10 750 000

Lambert Azimuthal Equal Area Projection

Miles
0 50 100 150 200 250

Kms.
0 100 200 300 400

Relief

Feet	Metres
16 404	5000
9843	3000
6562	2000
3281	1000
1640	500
656	200
Sea Level	Sea Level
656	200
Land Dep.	
13123	4000
22966	7000

Equator

PACIFIC

OCEAN

Tropic of Capricorn

INDIAN

OCEAN

Southern Alps

Scale 1:27 000 000

0	200	400	600	800 Miles
0	400	800	1200 Kms.	

Lambert Azimuthal Equal Area Projection

GREAT DIVIDING RANGE

GREAT DIVIDING RANGE

Bismarck Ra.

Maoke Range

Barkly Tableland

Lake Eyre Basin

Macdonnell Ranges

Musgrave Range

Nullarbor Plain

Hamersley Ra.

	Lowland Plains & Basins
Quaternary	High Plains & Plateaus
Tertiary	Scarps & Upland edges
Mesozoic	Fold & Volcanic Mountains
Palaeozoic	Main trend lines
Precambrian	Main centres of volcanic activity

Makassar Strait
Celebes
1286 ▲ Rantekombola
Butung
Kabia
BANDA SEA
Misoöl
Vogelkop
Japen
Admiralty Is
New Hanover
New Irela
Bismarck Sea
Sula Is
Buru
10023 ▲
Ceram
Wokam
Aru Is
Maoke Range
Putjak Djaja ▲
16503
Sepik
NEW GUINEA
Mt. Wilhelm
15400 ▲
New Britai
FLORES SEA
Bali
Lombok
Sumbawa
Flores
Alor
Wetar
Jamdena
Tanimbar Is
Trangan
Kolepom
C. Vals
Fly
Gulf of Papua
Mt. Victoria
13280 ▲ D'Entrecastea
Owen Stanley Range
Sumba
Sawu
Roti
Timor
ARAFURA SEA
Torres Strait
TIMOR SEA
Melville I.
Bathurst I.
C. Wessel
C. York
CORAL SEA
Van Diemen Gulf
Cobourg Pen.
C. Arnhem
C. Londonderry
Joseph Bonaparte Gulf
Arnhem Land
Groote Eylandt
Cape York Peninsula
C. Melville
C. Lévêque
Daly
Roper
Limmen Bight
Gulf of Carpentaria
Sir Edward Pellew Group
Wellesley Is
Mitchell
King Leopold Ranges
Ord
Victoria
Barkly Tableland
Leichhardt
Flinders
Gregory Ra.
Atherton Plateau
Mt Bartle Frere
5287 ▲
Great Barrier Reef
Eighty Mile Beach
Great Sandy Desert
Monte Bello Is.
Barrow I.
North West C.
De Grey
L. Mackay
Mt Ziel
4955 ▲
Macdonnell Ranges
James Ra.
Great Dividing Range
Fortescue
Hamersley Range
Mt Bruce 4024 ▲
Ashburton
L. Disappointment
Simpson Desert
Greating Range
Tropic of Capricorn
Gascoyne
Gibson Desert
L. Amadeus
Finke
Artesian Basin
Dirk Hartogs I.
Murchison
L. Carnegie
Mt Woodroffe 4970 ▲
Musgrave Ranges
Everard Range
Warburton
Cooper Creek
B Range
Grey Range
Warrego
Culgoa
Darling Downs
4955 ▲ New England Range
Round Mt. 5300 ▲
L. Barlee
Great Victoria Desert
L. Eyre
Darling
Barwon
L. Moore
L. Cowan
Nullarbor Plain
L. Torrens
L. Gairdner
Flinders Range
Darling Range
Geographe Bay
Swanland
C. Leeuwin
W. Cape Howe
Great Australian Bight
Eyre Peninsula
Spencer Gulf
Murray
Murrumbidgee
Riverina
Murray
Great Dividing Rang
Mt Kosciusko 7316 ▲ Snowy Mts
INDIAN OCEAN
Kangaroo I.
Wilson's Promontory
King I.
Bass Strait
Hunter Is.
Flinders I.
Cape Barren I.
TASMA SEA
C. Howe
Mt Ossa 5305 ▲
South East Cape

Desert
Semi-Desert
Grassland
Forest and Woodland
Cultivated land

Scale 1 : 20 000 000
0 100 200 300 400 500 Miles
0 200 400 600 800 Kms
Lambert Azimuthal Equal Area Projection

© Collins ◦ Longman Atlases

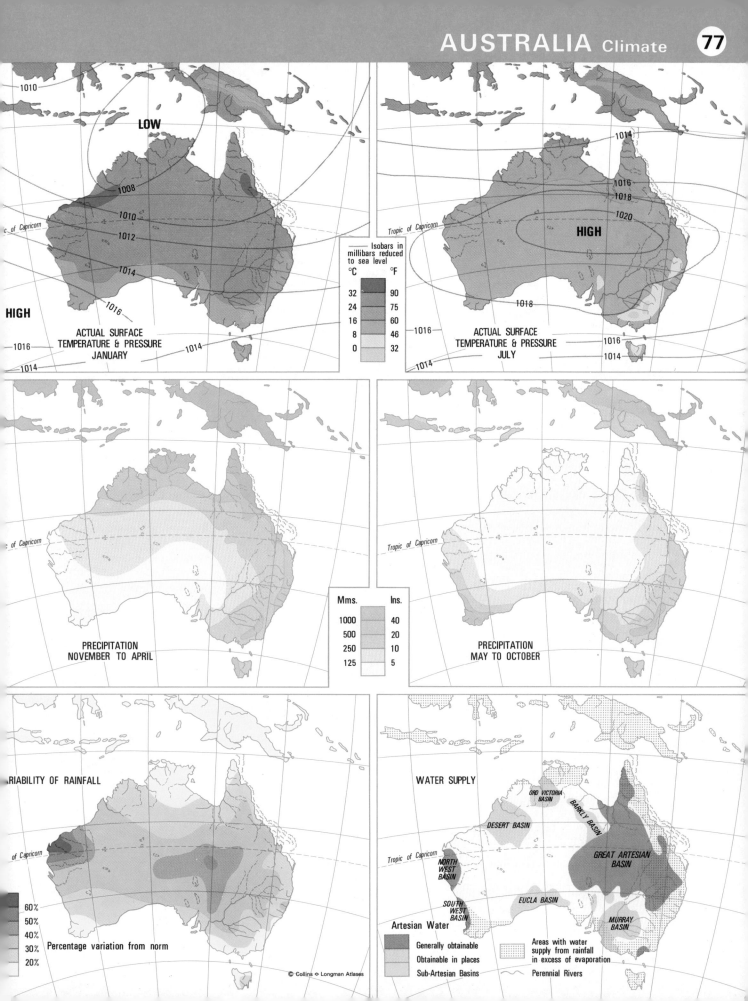

1010

LOW

1008

1010

1012

c. of Capricorn

1014

1016

HIGH

1016

**ACTUAL SURFACE
TEMPERATURE & PRESSURE
JANUARY**

1014

1014

Isobars in
millibars reduced
to sea level

°C	°F
32	90
24	75
16	60
8	46
0	32

1014

1016

1018

1020

Tropic of Capricorn

HIGH

1018

1016

**ACTUAL SURFACE
TEMPERATURE & PRESSURE
JULY**

1016

1014

Tropic of Capricorn

**PRECIPITATION
NOVEMBER TO APRIL**

Mms.	Ins.
1000	40
500	20
250	10
125	5

Tropic of Capricorn

**PRECIPITATION
MAY TO OCTOBER**

VARIABILITY OF RAINFALL

of Capricorn

60%
50%
40%
30%
20%

Percentage variation from norm

© Collins ● Longman Atlases

WATER SUPPLY

ORD VICTORIA
BASIN

BARKLY BASIN

DESERT BASIN

NORTH
WEST
BASIN

GREAT ARTESIAN
BASIN

Tropic of Capricorn

SOUTH
WEST
BASIN

EUCLA BASIN

MURRAY
BASIN

Artesian Water

Generally obtainable

Obtainable in places

Sub-Artesian Basins

Areas with water
supply from rainfall
in excess of evaporation

Perennial Rivers

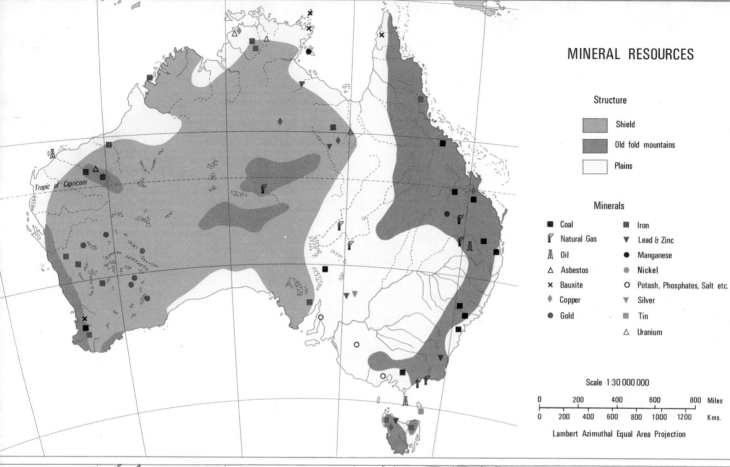

MINERAL RESOURCES

Structure

- Shield
- Old fold mountains
- Plains

Minerals

- ■ Coal
- Natural Gas
- Oil
- △ Asbestos
- ✕ Bauxite
- ◆ Copper
- ● Gold
- ■ Iron
- ▼ Lead & Zinc
- ● Manganese
- ● Nickel
- ○ Potash, Phosphates, Salt etc.
- ▼ Silver
- ■ Tin
- △ Uranium

Tropic of Capricorn

Scale 1:30 000 000

| 0 | 200 | 400 | 600 | 800 | Miles |

| 0 | 200 | 400 | 600 | 800 | 1000 | 1200 | Kms. |

Lambert Azimuthal Equal Area Projection

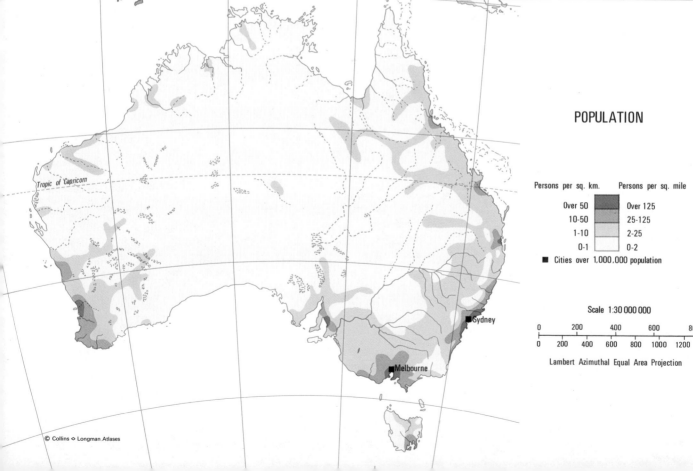

POPULATION

Tropic of Capricorn

Persons per sq. km.	Persons per sq. mile
Over 50	Over 125
10-50	25-125
1-10	2-25
0-1	0-2

■ Cities over 1,000,000 population

Sydney

Melbourne

Scale 1:30 000 000

| 0 | 200 | 400 | 600 | 800 | Miles |

| 0 | 200 | 400 | 600 | 800 | 1000 | 1200 | Kms. |

Lambert Azimuthal Equal Area Projection

INDONESIA

SULAWESI
Rantekombola 1335
Ujung Pandang
Butung
Kabia
Buru
Sula Is.
Misool
Ceram 10023
Wetar
BANDA SEA
Aru Is.
Tanimbar Is.
C. Wessel
C. Arnhem

FLORES SEA
Flores
Sumbawa
Sumba
Roti
Timor

IRIAN JAYA
Maoke Range
Putjak Djaja 16503
Djajapura
Wewak
Sepik
NEW GUINEA
PAPUA NEW GUINEA
Mt Wilhelm 15400
Lae
C. Vals
Gulf of Papua
Torres Strait
Port Moresby

Admiralty Is.
New Hanover
New Ireland
Bismarck Sea
New Britain
Mt Victoria 13280
Owen Stanley Range
Solomon Sea

ARAFURA SEA

TIMOR SEA

C. Londonderry
Melville I.
Bathurst I.
Darwin
C. York
C. Melville
CORAL SEA

Joseph Bonaparte Gulf
Katherine
Roper
Groote Eylandt
Gulf of Carpentaria

C. Lévêque
Wyndham
Birdum
Mitchell
Cooktown

C. Leeuwin
Derby
Broome
King Leopold Ranges
Hall's Creek
NORTHERN
Tennant Creek
Normanton
Cairns 5287
Ingham
Great Barrier Reef

Eighty Mile Beach
Port Hedland
Marble Bar
TERRITORY
Mount Isa
Hughenden
Townsville
Bowen

Barrow I.
Hamersley Range 4024
Ashburton
L. Mackay
Macdonnell Ranges 4955
Alice Springs
Winton
Mackay
Rockhampton

Tropic of Capricorn
L. Disappointment
WESTERN
L. Amadeus
QUEENSLAND
Barcaldine

Gascoyne
AUSTRALIA
L. Carnegie
Musgrave Ranges
Great
Artesian
Bundaberg

Murchison
Meekatharra
SOUTH
L. Eyre
Grey Range
Basin
Charleville
Cunnamulla
Brisbane
Toowoomba
Warwick

Geraldton
L. Moore
AUSTRALIA
L. Torrens
Woomera
Flinders Range
Darling
Bourke
Cobar
Nyngan
Goondiwindi
Narrabri 5300
Taree

Kalgoorlie
Rawlinna
Nullarbor Plain
L. Gairdner
Ceduna
Port Augusta
Broken Hill
NEW SOUTH WALES
Maitland
Newcastle

Perth
Fremantle
L. Cowan
Esperance
Whyalla
Spencer Gulf
Murray
Lachlan
Murrumbidgee
Sydney
Wollongong

Bunbury
Albany
Great Australian Bight
Kangaroo I.
Adelaide
Murray
Bendigo
Ballarat
Mt Kosciusko 7316
Snowy Mts
Canberra
AUST.CAP.TER.
C. Howe

INDIAN OCEAN
VICTORIA
Melbourne
Geelong
King I.
Bass Strait
Flinders I.
TASMAN SEA

TASMANIA
Mt Ossa 5305
Launceston
Hobart
South East C.

Scale 1:20 000 000
0   100   200   300   400   500 Miles
0   200   400   600   800 Kms.
Lambert Azimuthal Equal Area Projection

© Collins ◊ Longman Atlases

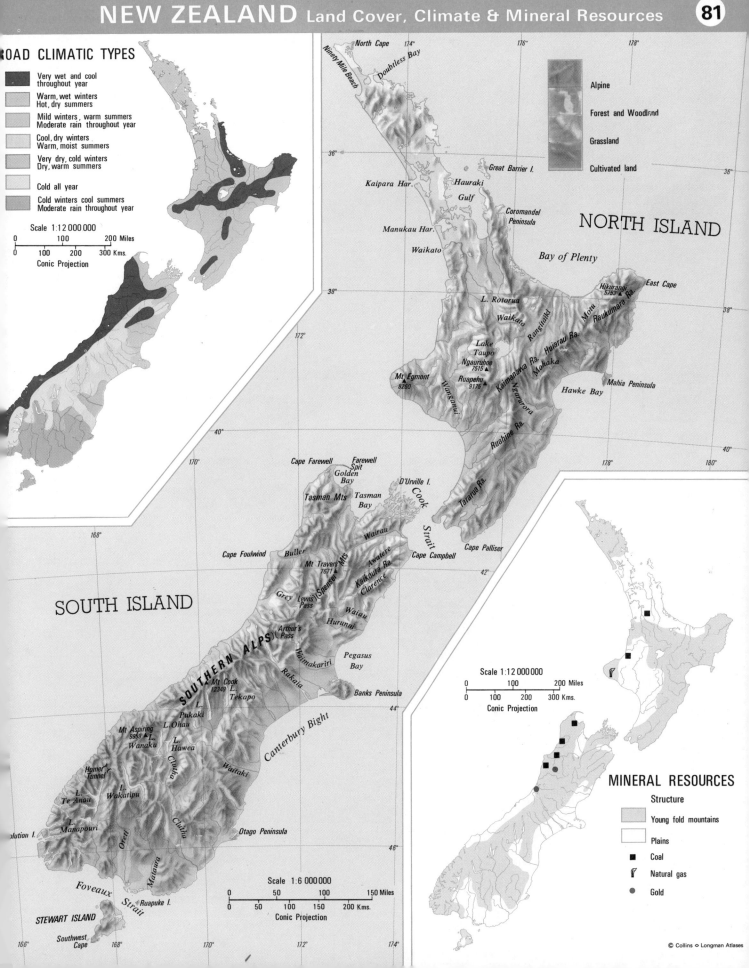

BROAD CLIMATIC TYPES

- Very wet and cool throughout year
- Warm, wet winters Hot, dry summers
- Mild winters, warm summers Moderate rain throughout year
- Cool, dry winters Warm, moist summers
- Very dry, cold winters Dry, warm summers
- Cold all year
- Cold winters cool summers Moderate rain throughout year

Scale 1:12 000 000

| 0 | 100 | 200 Miles |
| 0 | 100 | 200 | 300 Kms. |

Conic Projection

Alpine

Forest and Woodland

Grassland

Cultivated land

NORTH ISLAND

North Cape
Doubtless Bay
Ninety Mile Beach
Kaipara Har.
Great Barrier I.
Hauraki Gulf
Coromandel Peninsula
Manukau Har.
Waikato
Bay of Plenty
L. Rotorua
Hikurangi 5753
East Cape
Waikato
Rangitaiki
Moto
Raukumara Ra.
Lake Taupo
Ngauruhoe 7515
Kaimanawa Ra.
Huiarau Ra.
Mohaka
Mt Egmont 8260
Ruapehu 9175
Ngaruroro
Mahia Peninsula
Wanganui
Hawke Bay
Ruahine Ra.
Tararua Ra.
Cape Farewell
Farewell Spit
Golden Bay
D'Urville I.
Tasman Mts
Tasman Bay
Cook Strait
Wairau
Cape Campbell
Cape Palliser
Cape Foulwind
Buller
Mt Travers 7671
Spenser Mts
Awatere
Kaikoura Ra.
Clarence
Grey
Lewis Pass
Waiau
Hurunui
Arthur's Pass
Waimakariri
Pegasus Bay
Rakaia
Banks Peninsula
Mt Cook 12349
L. Tekapo
L. Pukaki
L. Ohau
Mt Aspiring 9959
L. Wanaka
L. Hawea
Clutha
Waitaki
Canterbury Bight
Homer Tunnel
L. Te Anau
L. Wakatipu
Oreti
Clutha
Otago Peninsula
Mataura
L. Manapouri
Resolution I.
Foveaux Strait
Ruapuke I.
STEWART ISLAND
Southwest Cape

SOUTH ISLAND

SOUTHERN ALPS

Scale 1:6 000 000

| 0 | 50 | 100 | 150 Miles |
| 0 | 50 | 100 | 150 | 200 Kms. |

Conic Projection

Scale 1:12 000 000

| 0 | 100 | 200 Miles |
| 0 | 100 | 200 | 300 Kms. |

Conic Projection

MINERAL RESOURCES

Structure

- Young fold mountains
- Plains
- ■ Coal
- Natural gas
- ● Gold

© Collins ◇ Longman Atlases

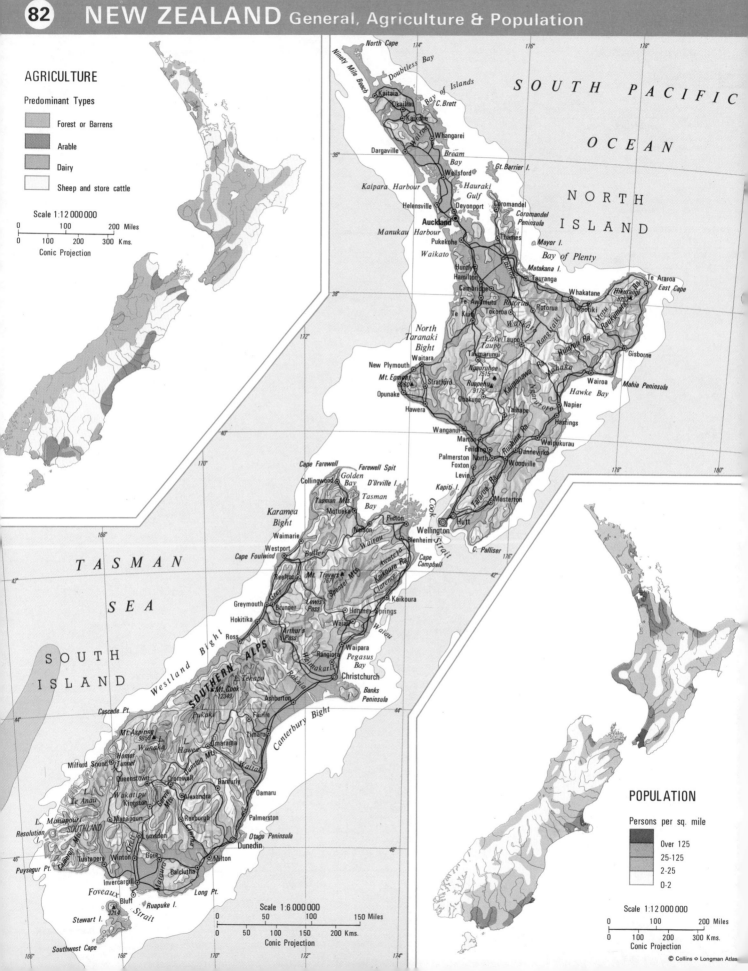

ARCTIC OCEAN

Brooks Range

Alaska Range

Coast Mountains

Rocky Mountains

Canadian Shield

Hudson Bay

PACIFIC OCEAN

Coast Range

Cascade Range

Sierra Nevada

Great Basin

The Great Plains

Ozark Plateau

Appalachian Mts

Blue Ridge

ATLANTIC OCEAN

Sierra Madre Occidental

Altiplano Mexicano

Sa. Madre del Sur

Sa. Madre Oriental

Gulf of Mexico

Tropic of Cancer

Arctic Circle

CARIBBEAN SEA

Sierra Madre

Tertiary
Mesozoic
Palaeozoic
Precambrian

Lowland Plains & Basins
High Plains & Plateaus
Scarps & Upland Edges
Fold & Volcanic Mountains
Main trend lines
Main centres of volcanic activity

Scale 1:35 000 000
0   200   400   600   800   1000 Miles
0   400   800   1200   1600 Kms.
Bonne Projection

© Collins ◇ Longman Atlases

Iceland

Denmark Str.

C. Farewell

Arctic Circle

G R E E N L A N D

G

Davis Strait

Newfoundland

Cape Breton I.
St. Lawrence
Gulf of
Anticosti I.
Nova Scotia
C. Cod
Long I.
Green Mts.
St. Lawrence
L. Ontario
Niagara Falls
L. Erie

L a b r a d o r

C. Chidley

Hudson Strait

Ungava
Peninsula

Baffin
Bay

Baffin Island

Foxe
Basin

Southampton
Island

Hudson Bay

James
Bay

Albany

L. Michigan
L. Huron
L. Superior

Mississi

Ellesmere
Devon I.
Prince of
Wales I.

Baffin

Queen

Elizabeth

Islands

Melville I.

Banks I.

Victoria Island

Black

Gt. Bear
Lake

Gt. Slave
Lake

Mackenzie

Seven

Nelson

Lake
Winnipeg

C a n a d i a n   S h i e l d

Saskatchewan

L. Athabasca

Peace

Missouri

The   Great   P

A R C T I C

O C E A N

Beaufort
Sea

Brooks Range

Alaska Range
Mt. McKinley
20320

Mt. Logan
19850
Mt. St. Elias
18008

R O C K Y   M O U N T A

Mt. Robson
12972

Selkirk Mts

Snake

Great Salt Lake

Si

Peace River Res.

Fraser

Coast Mountains

Mt. Rainier
14408

Cascade Range

Columbia

Vancouver I.

Coast Range

Queen
Charlotte
Islands

Siberia

Bering Str.

Yukon

Kodiak I.

Alaska Pen.

P

ATLANTIC

OCEAN

C. Hatteras

Tennessee

Mt. Mitchell
6684

Appalachian Mts.

Ohio

Mississippi

Ozark
Plateau

Arkansas

Red

Colorado

Rio Grande

Sierra Madre Oriental

Sierra Madre Occidental

Altiplano Mexicano

Sierra Madre del Sur

Sierra Madre

Colorado
Plateau

Gila

Colorado

nevada

Gulf of California

Lower California

C. San Lucas

Guadalupe I.

Tropic of Cancer

PACIFIC

OCEAN

Revilla Gigedo Is.

Clipperton I.

Bahama Islands

C. Sable

Cuba

Greater Antilles

Jamaica

Yucatan Channel

Campeche Bay

Yucatan
Peninsula

Gulf of
Honduras

Citlaltepetl
18700

Gulf of Mexico

Hispaniola

Caribbean Sea

L. Nicaragua

Gulf of
Panama

C. San Francisco

Equator

Galapagos Is.

Scale 1:25 000 000
Bonne Projection

| 0 | 100 | 200 | 300 | 400 | 500 | 600 | 700 | Miles |
| 0 | 200 | 400 | 600 | 800 | 1000 | | | Kms. |

Permanent ice and snow

Tundra and alpine

Forest and woodland

Semi-desert

Desert

Grassland including prairie and savanna

Cultivated land

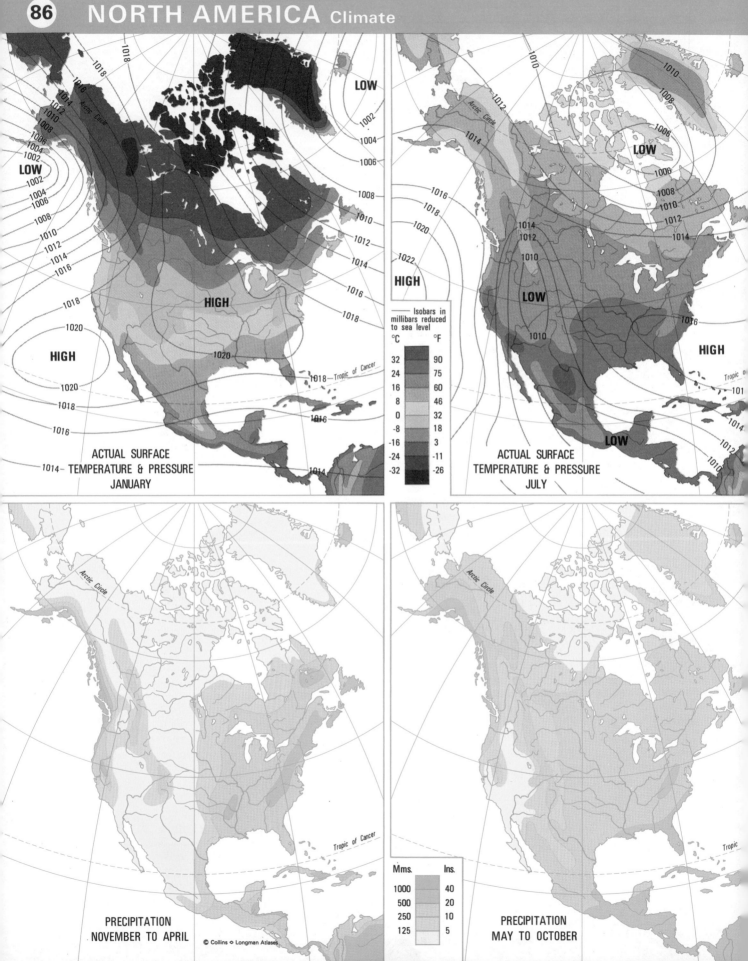

LOW

1018
1018
1016
1014
1012
1010
1008
1006
1004
1002
Arctic Circle

LOW
1002
1004
1006
1008
1010
1012
1014
1016
1018
1020

HIGH

HIGH

1020
1018
1016

1014

1002
1004
1006
1008
1010
1012
1014
1016
1018

1020
1022

1018 Tropic of Cancer
1016
1014

HIGH

**ACTUAL SURFACE
TEMPERATURE & PRESSURE
JANUARY**

Isobars in
millibars reduced
to sea level

°C	°F
32	90
24	75
16	60
8	46
0	32
-8	18
-16	3
-24	-11
-32	-26

LOW

1010
1008
1006
1004
Arctic Circle
1012
1014

LOW
1006
1008
1010
1012
1014

1014
1012
1010

LOW

1010

HIGH

1016

Tropic o
101

LOW

1014
1012
1010

**ACTUAL SURFACE
TEMPERATURE & PRESSURE
JULY**

Arctic Circle

Tropic of Cancer

**PRECIPITATION
NOVEMBER TO APRIL**

© Collins ◇ Longman Atlases

Mms.	Ins.
1000	40
500	20
250	10
125	5

Arctic Circle

Tropic

**PRECIPITATION
MAY TO OCTOBER**

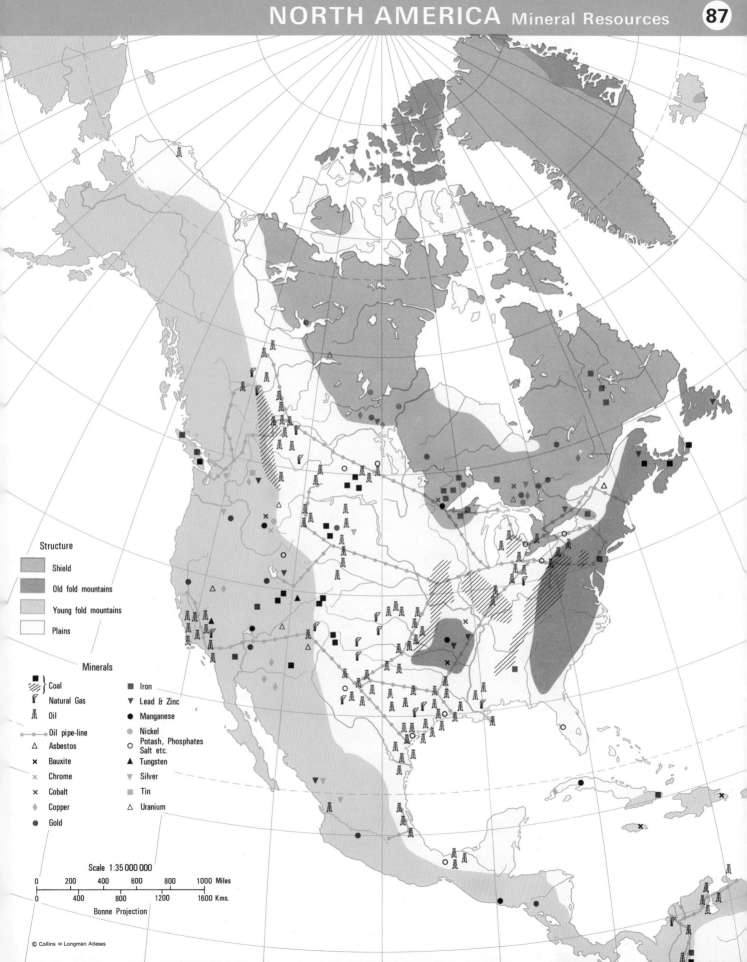

Structure

- Shield
- Old fold mountains
- Young fold mountains
- Plains

Minerals

- Coal
- Natural Gas
- Oil
- Oil pipe-line
- Asbestos
- Bauxite
- Chrome
- Cobalt
- Copper
- Gold
- Iron
- Lead & Zinc
- Manganese
- Nickel
- Potash, Phosphates Salt etc.
- Tungsten
- Silver
- Tin
- Uranium

Scale 1:35 000 000

| 0 | 200 | 400 | 600 | 800 | 1000 Miles |

| 0 | 400 | 800 | 1200 | 1600 Kms. |

Bonne Projection

© Collins ◇ Longman Atlases

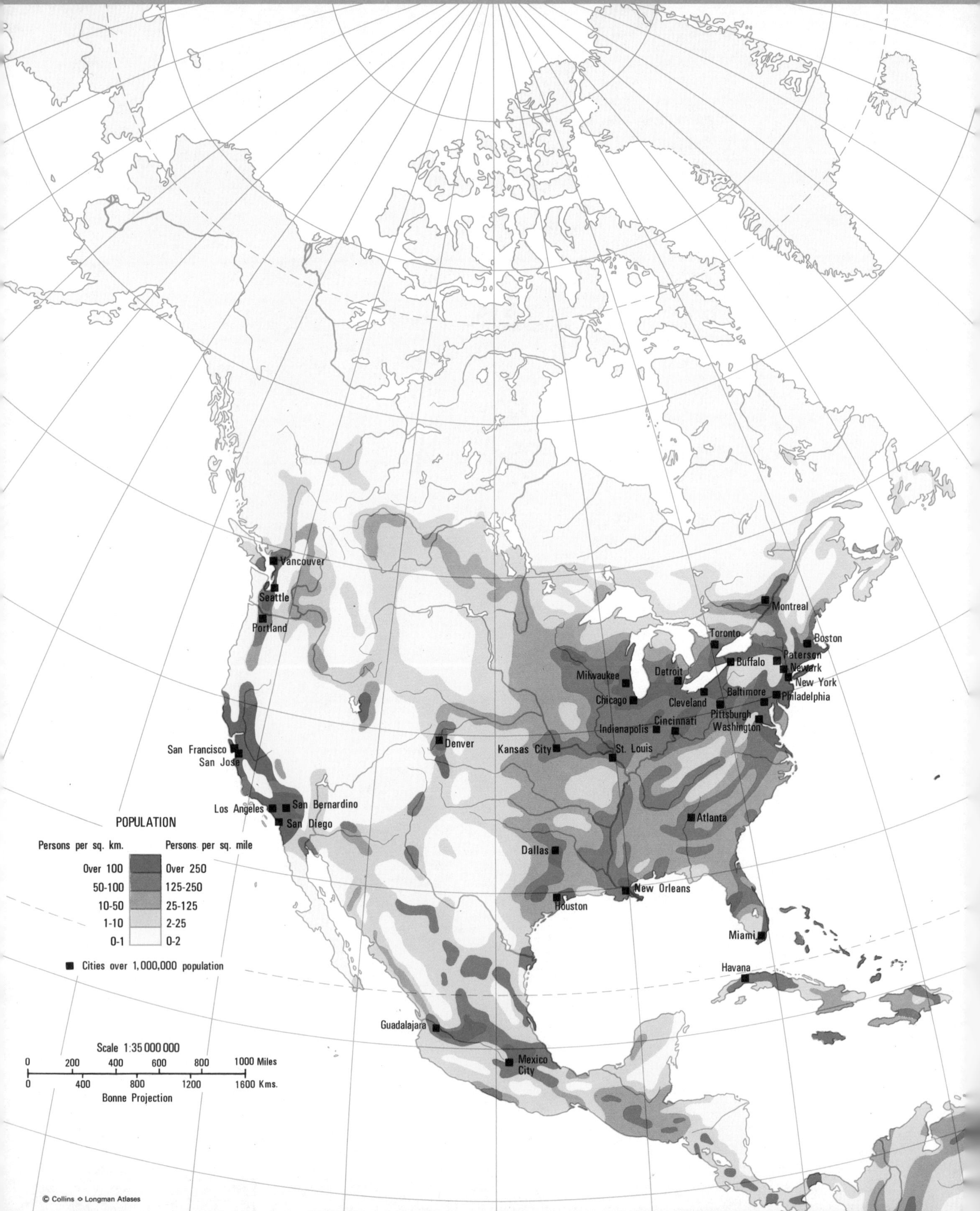

Vancouver

Seattle

Portland

Montreal

Toronto
Boston
Paterson
Buffalo
Newark
Milwaukee
Detroit
New York
Chicago
Cleveland
Baltimore
Philadelphia
Indianapolis
Cincinnati
Pittsburgh
Denver
Washington
San Francisco
Kansas City
St. Louis
San Jose

Los Angeles
San Bernardino
San Diego
Atlanta

Dallas

New Orleans

Houston

Miami

Havana

POPULATION

Persons per sq. km.	Persons per sq. mile
Over 100	Over 250
50-100	125-250
10-50	25-125
1-10	2-25
0-1	0-2

■ Cities over 1,000,000 population

Guadalajara

Mexico
City

Scale 1:35 000 000

| 0 | 200 | 400 | 600 | 800 | 1000 Miles |
| 0 | 400 | 800 | 1200 | 1600 Kms. |

Bonne Projection

U.S.S.R.

St. Lawrence I.
Bering Strait

ARCTIC   OCEAN

GREENLAND
(Denmark)

Arctic Circle

ICELAND
Reykjavik

Ellesmere Island

Parry Islands

Banks I.
Pr. of Wales I.

Baffin Bay

Godthaab

U.S.A.
ALASKA
Yukon
Fairbanks
Anchorage

Kodiak I.

Victoria Island

Baffin Island

Davis Strait

Gt. Bear Lake

Mackenzie

Southampton I.
Hudson Strait

Newfoundland

PACIFIC

OCEAN

Gt. Slave Lake
L. Athabasca
Peace

Hudson Bay

Churchill
Churchill
Nelson

C A N A D A

James Bay

St. John's
St.

Prince Rupert

Fraser

Vancouver I.

Edmonton

Calgary

Saskatchewan
Regina

Lake Winnipeg

Albany

Ottawa
Quebec

Gulf of St. Lawrence

Cape Breton I.

Halifax

Vancouver
Seattle
Portland

Columbia

Spokane

Missouri

Winnipeg

Duluth

L. Superior

Ottawa
Montreal
St. Lawrence
Toronto
L. Ontario

Boston
Paterson

Snake

Gt. Salt Lake

Minneapolis
St. Paul
Milwaukee
L. Michigan
Detroit
L. Huron
L. Erie
Cleveland
Buffalo
Pittsburgh
New York
Philadelphia

San Francisco

Salt Lake City

Platte

Omaha

Chicago

Cincinnati
Indianapolis
Ohio
Baltimore
Washington

ATLANTIC

Bermuda

OCEAN

Colorado

Denver
Kansas City
Arkansas
St. Louis

U N I T E D   S T A T E S   O F   A M E R I C A

Tennessee

Los Angeles

San Diego

Phoenix
Tucson

Albuquerque

El Paso

Oklahoma City

Red

Memphis

Dallas

Mississippi

Birmingham

Jacksonville

Tropic of Cancer

Guadalupe (Mex.)

Gulf of California

San Antonio

New Orleans
Houston

Mobile

Miami

Nassau
BAHAMAS

Monterrey

La Paz

M E X I C O

Rio Grande

Gulf of Mexico

Havana
C U B A

DOMINICAN REP.

Revilla Gigedo Is (Mex.)

Tampico

San Luis Potosi

Mérida

G r e a t e r   A n t i l l e s

HAITI
Port-au-Prince
Santo Domingo

Guadalajara

Veracruz

Kingston
JAMAICA

Mexico City

Belmopan
BELIZE

CARIBBEAN SEA

GUATEMALA
Guatemala City
EL SALVADOR
San Salvador

HONDURAS
Tegucigalpa
NICARAGUA
Managua

San José

PANAMA
Panama City

VENEZUELA

COSTA RICA

COLOMBIA

Hawaiian Islands
(U.S.A.)

Tropic of Cancer

PACIFIC
OCEAN

Kauai
Lihue
Oahu
Honolulu
Molokai
Maui
Hawaii
Hilo
Pahala

Scale 1:20 000 000

PACIFIC

OCEAN

Guadalupe I.
(Mex.)

© Collins ○ Longman Atlases

Scale 1:12 000 000

0   200   400 Miles

0   200   400   600 Kms.

Bonne Projection

Relief

Feet		Metres
16 404		5000
9 843		3000
6 562		2000
3 281		1000
1 640		500
656		200
0		Sea Level
Land Dep.		
656		200
13 123		4000
22 966		7000

Scale 1 : 17 000 000

0	100	200	300	400	500 Miles

0	100	200	300	400	500	600	700	800 Kms.

Bonne Projection

© Collins ◇ Longman Atlases

C A N A D A

MINNESOTA

WISCONSIN

MICHIGAN

IOWA

ILLINOIS

INDIANA

OHIO

UNITED STATES OF AMERICA

MISSOURI

KENTUCKY

WEST VIRGINIA

Lake Superior

Lake Michigan

Lake Huron

Lake Erie

Georgian Bay

North Channel

Green Bay

Saginaw Bay

Keweenaw Bay

L. Nipigon
Long L.
Pic
Hearst
Kapuskasing
Cochrane
Iroquois Falls
Kirk
Timmins
Kenogamissi L.
Elk Lake
Chapleau
Franz
Michipicoten Harbour
Michipicoten I.
Tip Top Mtn. 2142
▲ 1280
Missinaibi
Nakusimi
Groundhog
Mattagami
Oba
Heron Bay
Nipigon
Thunder Bay
Dog L.
Lac des Mille Lacs
Atikokan
Rainy L.
Fort Frances
International Falls
Ely
Eagle Mtn. ▲ 2329
Grand Marais
Isle Royale
Batchawana Mtn. ▲ 2129
Montreal
Whitefish Pt.
Sault Sainte Marie
Sault Sainte Marie
Blind River
Little Current
Manitoulin I.
Sturgeon Fall
L. Nipiss
Ludgate
Sudbury
Capreol
Timagami L.
Biskotasi L.
Missississagi
Virginia
Grand Rapids
Duluth
Two Harbors
Superior
Cloquet
Apostle Is.
Ashland
Hancock
Ontonagon
Keweenaw Pt.
Keweenaw Bay
1959 ▲
Ironwood
Mt. Curwood 1982
Marquette
Negaunee
Newberry
Munising
Mackinaw City
Cheboygan
Beaver I.
Rogers City
Alpena
North Pt.
C. Hurd
Owen Sound
Collingwood
Midla
St. Croix
Mille Lacs L.
Spooner
Park Falls
1873 ▲
Iron River
Iron Mountain
Rhinelander
Escanaba
Manistique
Manitou Is.
Traverse City
Grayling
Au Sable
Au Sable Pt.
Port Austin
Goderich
Waterloo
Kitchener
Missis
Gal
Ladysmith
Antigo
Marinette
Menominee
Manistee
Cadillac
Sterling Heights
Saginaw Bay
Bay City
Saginaw
Stratford
London
St. Thomas
Brant
Minneapolis
St. Paul
Roseville
Richfield
Bloomington
Hastings
Chippewa Falls
Eau Claire
Wausau
1939 ▲
Shawano
Green Bay
Appleton
Ludington
Clare
Midland
Alma
Owosso
Flint
Port Huron
Sarnia
Grand
Wisconsin
Wisconsin Rapids
Marshfield
Winona
Rochester
Sparta
La Crosse
L. Winnebago
Oshkosh
Fond du Lac
Manitowoc
Sheboygan
Muskegon
Grand Rapids
Wyoming
Lansing
East Lansing
Pontiac
Birmingham
Warren
St. Clair
Chatham
Port Burwell
Austin
Turkey
Black
1240 ▲
Madison
Portage
Watertown
2280 ▲
Wauwatosa
Waukesha
West Allis
Milwaukee
Holland
South Haven
Kalamazoo
Battle Creek
Jackson
Ann Arbor
Livonia
Dearborn
Detroit
Windsor
Wyandotte
Leamington
Pt. Pelee
Cedar Falls
Waterloo
Dubuque
Janesville
Beloit
Racine
Kenosha
Benton Harbor
Adrian
Monroe
Toledo
Sandusky
Lorain
Lakewood
Erie
Cedar Rapids
Clinton
Rockford
Freeport
Waukegan
North Chicago
Arlington Heights
Elgin
Skokie
Evanston
Oak Park
Cicero
Chicago
E. Chicago
Gary
Michigan City
South Bend
Mishawaka
Elkhart
Fort Wayne
Defiance
Findlay
Fostoria
Elyria
Parma
Cleveland
Cleveland Heights
Euclid
Mentor
Painesville
Ashtabula
Meadville
Warren
Niles
Sharon
Young
Iowa City
Davenport
Rock Island
Moline
Aurora
Oak Lawn
Joliet
Hammond
Harvey
Chicago Heights
Park Forest
La Salle
Kankakee
Plymouth
Peru
Logansport
Kokomo
Marion
Portland
Lima
Mansfield
Marion
Wooster
Massillon
Canton
Alliance
Boardman
Aliquippa
Glens
Pittsbur
Weirton
Mou
Lebu
Ottumwa
Burlington
Fort Madison
Galesburg
Peoria
Pekin
Bloomington
Lafayette
Danville
Urbana
Champaign
Anderson
Muncie
Piqua
Springfield
Newark
Coshocton
Zanesville
Cambridge
Steubenville
Wheelin
Quincy
Illinois
Decatur
Tuscola
Jacksonville
Springfield
Terre Haute
Indianapolis
Richmond
Fairborn
Dayton
Kettering
Columbus
Scioto
Muskingum
Hannibal
Mexico
Missouri
Florissant
St. Louis
East St. Louis
Belleville
Alton
Effingham
Bloomington
Franklin
M. Miami
Middletown
Hamilton
Chillicothe
Athens
Fairmon
Clarksburg
Parkersburg
Jefferson City
Salem
Centralia
Princeton
Lawrenceville
Vincennes
Bedford
Seymour
Covington
Newport
Cincinnati
Portsmouth
Maysville
Chippewa
Wolf
Fox
Rock
Mississippi
Wabash
White
Kaskaskia
Cedar
Ohio
Scioto
Thames
Maumee
Grand
Wisconsin
1066 ▲

Waswanipi L.

D A
Gouin Res.

Q U E B E C
L. St. John
Dolbeau
Roberval
Chicoutimi-Jonquière

Gaspé Peninsula
Mont Blanc 3474
Ment Joli
Matane

St. Lawrence
Rimouski

Amos
Senneterre
St. Maurice
Saguenay
Tadoussac

NEW BRUNSWICK
Edmundston
Big Bald Mtn. 2205
St. Leonard
Grand Falls

Rouyn
Val-d'Or
Ottawa
L. Kempt
La Tuque
564
La Malbaie
Baie St. Paul

Laurentides Mts.
Rivière-du-Loup

Caribou
Peaked Mtn. 2260
Presque Isle

L. Simard
Cabonga Res.
Baskatong L.
Mont Laurier
Mpunt Tremblant 1176
Matawin
Shawinigan
Quebec
Montmagny
Levis

St. John
Allagash
Mt. Katahdin 5267

Houlton
St. John

Kipawa L.
Coulonge
Maniwaki
Trois-Rivières
Joliette
Sorel
Drummondville
Thetford Mines
Megantic

Moosehead L.
Greenville
White Cap Mtn. 3645

M A I N E
Danforth

Fredericton
Oromocto

Mattawa
Ottawa
R. du Lièvre
Gatineau
St. Jérôme
Montreal
Lachine
Laval
Verdun
Jacques-Cartier
St. Hyacipthe
Granby
Sherbrooke
Megantic Mtn. 3656
Caribou Mtn. 3599
Rump Mtn. 3648

Lincoln
St. Stephen
Calais
St. Andrews

Pembroke
Whitney
Renfrew
Arnprior
Hull
Ottawa
Smith's Falls
Valleyfield
Farnham

Sugarloaf Mtn. 4235
Bangor
Brewer

Grand Manan I.

I
Huntsville
Madawaska
Cornwall
Malone
Plattsburgh
Burlington
Berlin
Mt. Washington 6288

Waterville
Ellsworth

Haliburton Highlands
O
Brockville
Ogdensburg
Lyon Mtn. 3881
L. Champlain
Montpelier
Mt. Lafayette 5249
White Mts.
Kennebec
Augusta

Simcoe
Peterborough
Belleville
Kingston
Watertown
Mt. Marcy 5344
Aditondack
Lebanon
Sebago L.
Portland

Rockland

Oshawa
Cobourg
Picton
Snowy Mtn 3898
Mts.
L. George
Rutland
Killington Mtn. 4242
L. Winnipesaukee
Concord
Biddeford

Toronto
Scarborough
Lake Ontario
Pulaski
Oswego
Oneida L.
Rome
Utica
L.
Claremont
Keene
Manchester
Portsmouth

Niagara Falls
Lockport
Greece
Irondequoit
Rochester
Syracuse
Auburn
Cayuga L.
Cortland
Oneonta
Amsterdam
Schenectady
Brattleboro
Nashua
Lawrence
Gloucester

Buffalo
Lackawanna
Denew
Amherst
N E W Y O R K
Seneca L.
Ithaca
Mohawk
Waterviet
Troy
Albany
Pittsfield
Fitchburg
Lowell
Lynn
Beverly

Dunkirk
Olean
Catskill
Hunter Mtn. 4026
Taconic Mts.
Leominster
Cambridge
Medford
MASSACHUSETTS
Boston
Quincy

Jamestown
Alma Hill 2549
Corning
Elmira
Binghamton
Slide Mtn. 4203
Kingston
Hudson
Northampton
Chicopee
Springfield
Worcester
Weymouth
Brockton
Plymouth
C. Cod

Kane
Du Bois
Williamsport
Bloomsburg
Scranton
Carbondale
Poughkeepsie
Newburgh
Torrington
West Hartford
Hartford
East Hartford
Manchester
Woonsocket
Pawtucket
Providence
Cranston
Fall River
New Bedford
Nantucket Sound
Nantucket I.

P E N N S Y L V A N I A
State College
Altoona
Lewistown
Sunbury
Hazleton
Wilkes-Barre
Delaware
Kingston
CONNECTICUT
Meriden
Waterbury
New Britain
Norwich
New London
RHODE ISLAND
Newport
Warwick
Montauk Pt.
Martha's Vineyard

Ittanning
Johnstown
Mt. Davis 3212
Reading
Allentown
Bethlehem
Easton
New Brunswick
Perth Amboy
Danbury
New Haven
Fairfield
Bridgeport
Norwalk
Stamford
Greenwich
Yonkers
Mt Vernon
Paterson
Clifton
East Orange
Irvington
Newark
Jersey City
New York
Hempstead
Long Island
Long Branch

A T L A N T I C
O C E A N

Harrisburg
Lancaster
Lebanon
Pottstown
Levittown
Norristown
Chester
Camden
Philadelphia
Trenton
NEW JERSEY

York
Susquehanna
Wilmington
DELAWARE
Dover
Atlantic City
Wildwood
C. May
Delaware Bay

Cumberland
Hagerstown
Frederick
Martinsburg
M A R Y L A N D
Baltimore
Parkville
Catonsville
Annapolis
Vineland

Rockville
Silver Spring
Arlington
Alexandria
Washington D.C.
Laurel
V I R G I N I A

Feet	Relief	Metres
16 404		5000
9843		3000
6562		2000
3281		1000
1640		500
656		200
0		Sea Level
Land Dep.		
656		200
13 123		4000
22 966		7000

Scale 1:5,000,000

0   50   100   150   200 Miles

0   50   100   150   200   250   300 Kms.

Bonne Projection

© Collins ◇ Longman Atlases

GULF OF MEXICO

CAMPECHE BAY

PACIFIC OCEAN

Mexican States numbered on map.
1 FEDERAL DISTRICT
2 TLAXCALA
3 AGUASCALIENTES
4 MORELOS

Relief

Feet		Metres
16 404		5000
9843		3000
6562		2000
3281		1000
1640		500
656		200
0		Sea Level
Land Dep.		
656		200
13 123		4000
22 966		7000

Scale 1:12 500 000

0	100	200	300	400	500 Miles
0	100	200	300	400	500	600	700	800 Kms.

Lambert Azimuthal Equal Area Projection

© Collins ○ Longman Atlases

Hamilton ⊚ BERMUDA

A T L A N T I C

O C E A N

30°

Kennedy

West Palm Beach Freeport
Port Lauderdale Grand Bahama I. Great Abaco I.
Miami

25°

New Providence Eleuthera I. BAHAMAS
Nassau
Andros I. Cat I.

W E S T

Gt. Exuma San Salvador
Rum Cay Tropic of Cancer
Long I.
Crooked Samana Cay
Fortune I. French Cays
Acklin's Mayaguana I.
I N D I E S

Archo. de Sabana Archo. de Camagüey
Caibarién Little
LAS Morón Inagua
Spiritus Ciego Nuevitas Great Caicos Is. Turks Is.
de Avila CAMAGÜEY Inagua I. (Br.) (Br.)
Camagüey Holguín
Victoria de las Tunas Banes 20°
Jardines de la Reina Manzanillo Bayamo Baracoa DOMINICAN
Turquino ORIENTE Tortue Puerto Plata REPUBLIC Puerto Rico Trench
Cayman Brac C. Cruz 5467 Santiago Cap Haitien Valverde Santiago Samana
Is. de Cuba G. of Gonâve Gonaives 27980 PUERTO RICO Anegada
St. Marc La Vega San Francisco (U.S.) Tortola (Br.)
Montego Bay St. Ann's Bay Jérémie Gonâve I. de Macorís Arecibo San Juan (Br.) Virgin Gorda
Port Antonio 1820 S. Pedro Mayaguez 4390 (U.S.) Virgin Anguilla (Br.)
Black River Port-au- 8793 S. Cristóbal La Romana Ponce Vieques Is. St. Martin St. Barthélemy
JAMAICA Kingston Prince Santo Saona Mona St. Croix Sint Maarten (Fr.) Barbuda
Les Cayes Domingo (U.S.) (Fr.-Neth.) Saba (Br.)
Barahona St. Kitts (Neth.)
Hispaniola Sint Eustatius ANTIGUA
(Neth.) Nevis ⊚ St. John's
(Br.)

Greater Antilles

Lesser Montserrat
(Br.) Pointe-à-Pitre
Guadeloupe
(Fr.) 4869 Marie Galante
(Fr.)

Antilles Roseau DOMINICA

C A R I B B E A N   S E A 15°
Fort Martinique
de-France (Fr.)

Castries
ST. LUCIA

Lesser Antilles ST. VINCENT Kingstown BARBADOS
The Bridgetown
Aruba (Netherlands) Grenadines
Curaçao Carriacou (Br.)
Bonaire (Br.)
Guajira Willemstad Orchila St. George's GRENADA
Paraguaná Los Roques La Blanquilla
Penin. Pen. El Cardon
Riohacha Gulf of Coro Margarita I. TOBAGO
Sta. Marta Venezuela Tortuga Porlamar Dragon's Mouth
Barranquilla Sa. Nevada Altagracia Araya Carúpano Paria Pen. Port of Spain
Soledad Cristóbal San Felipe Pto. Cabello Tucacas La Guaira Pen. S. Fernando
Cartagena Calamar de Sta. Marta Maracaibo Cabimas Barquisimeto Valencia CARACAS Cumaná Gulf of TRINIDAD
Arjona Lake Carora L. Valencia Barcelona Pto. La Cruz Paria Serpent's Mouth 10°
Colón Maracaibo Trujillo San Juan de Maturín
Panama City Magangue los Morros El Tigre Orinoco
Gulf of El Banco Acarigua Valle Delta
Darien G. of Uraba Montería Bolívar S. Félix Curiapo
Gulf of El Real Magdalena Mérida Barinas Guanare Ciudad Bolívar Barrage
Archo. de VENEZUELA
las Perlas Panama
Bello San Cristóbal Apure S. Fernando GUYANA
El Real Riosucio Cúcuta Arauca
Bucaramanga Pamplona
Barrancabermeja
COLOMBIA Meta
Medellin Málaga Puerto Angel
Sa. Nevada de Cocuy Carreño Falls

Tropic of Cancer

A T L A N T I C   O C E A N

Highlands

São Francisco

Paranaíba

C. São Roque

Equator

Marajó I.

Amazon

Tocantins

Araguaia

Xingu

Tapajós

Mato

Gr

Selvas

Guaporé

Madeira

Purus

Juruá

Mamoré

Bol

L. Titicaca

C. Orange

Guiana   Highlands

Essequibo

Mt. Roraima
9219

Negro

Japura

Amazon

Ucayali

Marañón

Orinoco

Meta

Llanos

S o u t h

Cordillera Oriental

Cordillera Central

Cordillera Occidental

Cataopaxi
19347

Mt. Chimborazo
20577

A N D E S

Trinidad

Windward   Islands

Leeward   Islands

Lesser   Antilles

C a r i b b e a n   S e a

Curaçao

Puerto Rico

Hispaniola

Greater   Antilles

Jamaica

Cuba

Bahama Islands

C. Gallinas

Gulf of
Darien

Gulf of
Panama

Isthmus of Panama

C. San Francisco

G. de Guayaquil

C. Negra

L. Maracaibo

C. Sable

Yucatan
Channel

Yucatan
Pen.

Gulf of
Honduras

Sierra Madre

L. Nicaragua

RELIEF AND STRUCTURE

Quaternary
Tertiary
Mesozoic
Palaeozoic
Precambrian

Lowland Plains & Basins
High Plains & Plateaus
Scarps & Upland Edges
Fold & Volcanic Mountains
Main trend lines
Main centres of volcanic activity

Guiana Highlands

East Brazilian Highlands

Amazon Basin

Mato Grosso Upland

Andes

© Collins ○ Longman Atlases

Tropic of Capricorn

C. Frio

Itatiaya 2823

Serra da Mantiqueira

Brazil

East Serra do Mar

Lagoa dos Patos

Paraná

Uruguay

Rio de la Plata

Chaco

Gran Chaco

Pilcomayo

Paraguay

Salado

Paraná

Entre Ríos

Colorado

Bahia Blanca

Pampas

G. de San Matias

Chubut

G. de San Jorge

Patagonia

Plateau

Desert

Mt. Aconcagua 7021

Andes

Chiloé I.

Magellan's Str.

Magellan's Str.

Tierra del Fuego

C. Horn

Cockburn Channel

Falkland Is.

Antarctic Peninsula

S. Felix S. Ambrosio

Juan Fernandez Is.

PACIFIC OCEAN

Permanent Ice and Snow
Alpine
Desert
Semi-desert
Grassland including mountain grassland and Savanna
Forest and Woodland
Cultivated land

Scale 1:25 000 000

1000 Miles
1600 Kms.

0   200   400   600   800   1000

400   800   1200   1600

Lambert Azimuthal Equal Area Projection

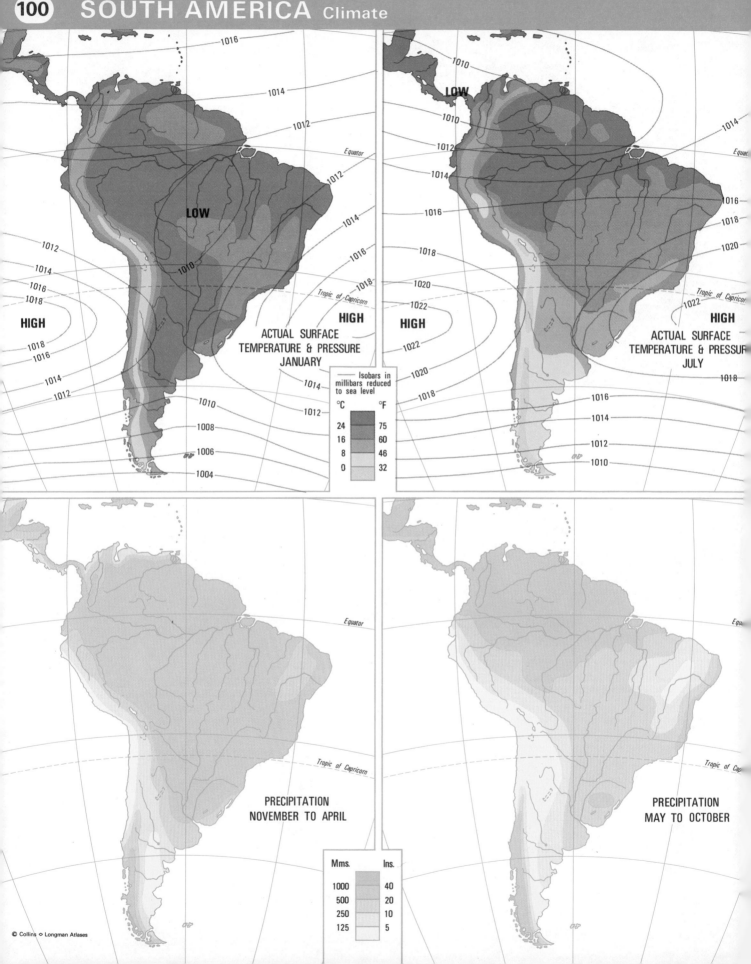

1016
1014
1012
Equator
1012
LOW
1014
1016
1018
Tropic of Capricorn
HIGH
ACTUAL SURFACE
TEMPERATURE & PRESSURE
JANUARY
1012
1014
1016
1018
1016
1014
1012
HIGH
1018
1016
1014
1012
1010
1008
1006
1004

Isobars in
millibars reduced
to sea level

°C		°F
24		75
16		60
8		46
0		32

1010
LOW
1010
1012
1014
1016
Equator
1014
1016
1018
1020
Tropic of Capricorn
1022
HIGH
ACTUAL SURFACE
TEMPERATURE & PRESSURE
JULY
1018
1016
1014
1012
1010
HIGH
1018
1020
1022
1020
1018

Equator

Tropic of Capricorn

PRECIPITATION
NOVEMBER TO APRIL

Mms.		Ins.
1000		40
500		20
250		10
125		5

Equator

Tropic of Cap

PRECIPITATION
MAY TO OCTOBER

MINERAL RESOURCES

Structure

Shield

Old fold mountains

Young fold mountains

Plains

Coal

Natural Gas

Oil

Oil pipe-line

Minerals

△ Asbestos
✕ Bauxite
✕ Cobalt
◆ Copper
● Gold
■ Iron
▼ Lead & Zinc
● Manganese
● Nickel
○ Phosphates, Potash, Nitrates
▽ Silver
■ Tin

Scale 1:50 000 000

| 0 | 400 | 800 | 1200 Miles |

| 0 | 400 | 800 | 1200 | 1600 Kms. |

Lambert Azimuthal Equal Area Projection

Tropic of Capricorn

Equator

tor

POPULATION

Persons per sq. km.   Persons per sq. mile

Over 100	Over 250
50-100	125-250
10-50	25-125
1-10	2-25
0-1	0-2

Scale 1:50 000 000

| 0 | 400 | 800 | 1200 Miles |

| 0 | 400 | 800 | 1200 | 1600 Kms. |

Lambert Azimuthal Equal Area Projection

■ Cities over 1 000 000 population

Caracas

Medellin

Bogotá

Cali

Equator

Lima

Recife

Salvador

Belo Horizonte

Rio de Janeiro

São Paulo

Tropic of Capricorn

Santiago

Montevideo

Buenos Aires

© Collins ♦ Longman Atlases

Tropic of Cancer

Havana CUBA BAHAMAS

MEXICO HAITI DOMINICAN
BELIZE Port-au-Prince REP. PUERTO
Belmopan Kingston Santo RICO
HONDURAS JAMAICA Domingo San Juan Leeward Is.
GUATEMALA Tegucigalpa Lesser
Guatemala NICARAGUA Antilles Windward Is.
City Managua ATLANTIC
San Salvador L. Nicaragua
EL SALVADOR Caribbean Sea
San José C. Gallinas Curaçao
COSTA Barranquilla Maracaibo TRINIDAD OCEAN
RICA Cartagena Port of Spain
PANAMA Panamá City Caracas
Medellín Cúcuta Ciudad Bolívar Georgetown
Manizales VENEZUELA Paramaribo
Bogotá Essequibo GUYANA Cayenne
COLOMBIA Orinoco SURINAM
Cali GUIANA
(Fr.)
Quito
ECUADOR Equator
Guayaquil Negro Manaus Amazon Belém São Luís
Iquitos Amazon Fortaleza
Pucallpa Madeira Tapajós Teresina Natal
Trujillo P E R U Trans Xingu Highway João Pessoa
Amazonian B R A Z I L Recife
Callao Lima Tocantins Maceió
Cuzco Araguaia Aracaju
L. Titicaca São Francisco Salvador
Arequipa Cochabamba Cuiabá
La Paz Santa Cruz Goiânia Brasília
Arica B O L I V I A
Sucre Belo
Iquique Horizonte
C Vitória
H Ribeirão Prêto
Antofagasta I PARAGUAY Paraná Rio de
L Janeiro Niterói
E Salta Asunción São Paulo Tropic of Capricorn
San Miguel
de Tucumán Paraná Curitiba
Salado
Florianópolis S O U T H
Córdoba Santa Uruguay
Valparaíso Mendoza Fé Pôrto Alegre
Santiago Rosario Pelotas
A URUGUAY
Talca R Buenos Montevideo
Concepción G Aires Rio de la Plata ATLANTIC
E Mar del Plata
N Bahía Blanca
T San Antonio Oeste
I
N G. of San Matias OCEAN
A
Puerto Montt
Chiloé I. Trelew

PACIFIC

OCEAN Galapagos Is.
(Ec.)

Juan Fernandez Is.
(Chile) Comodoro
Rivadavia

Scale 1:35 000 000

0 200 400 600 800 1000 Miles

0 400 800 1200 1600 Kms.

Lambert Azimuthal Equal Area Projection Falkland Is.
(Br.)
© Collins ◇ Longman Atlases Punta Arenas Tierra del
Fuego

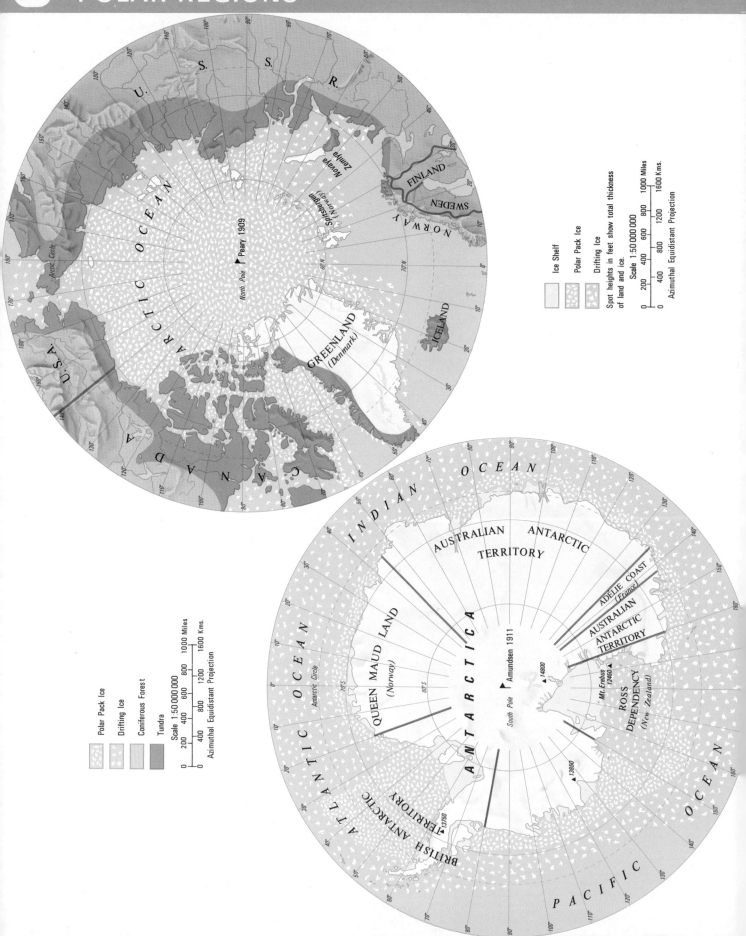

Ice Shelf

Polar Pack Ice

Drifting Ice

Spot heights in feet show total thickness
of land and ice.

Scale 1:50 000 000

0   200   400   600   800   1000 Miles
0   400   800   1200   1600 Kms.

Azimuthal Equidistant Projection

U. S. S. R.

U. S. A.

ARCTIC OCEAN

Arctic Circle

North Pole ▶ Peary 1909

Novaya Zemlya

Spitsbergen (Norway)

FINLAND

SWEDEN

NORWAY

ICELAND

GREENLAND
(Denmark)

C A N A D A

Polar Pack Ice

Drifting Ice

Coniferous Forest

Tundra

Scale 1:50 000 000

0   200   400   600   800   1000 Miles
0   400   800   1200   1600 Kms.

Azimuthal Equidistant Projection

INDIAN OCEAN

INDIAN OCEAN

Antarctic Circle

AUSTRALIAN ANTARCTIC
TERRITORY

ADELIE COAST
(France)

AUSTRALIAN
ANTARCTIC
TERRITORY

QUEEN MAUD LAND
(Norway)

A N T A R C T I C A

South Pole ▶ Amundsen 1911

▲14800

Mt. Erebus ▲12450

▲13850

ROSS
DEPENDENCY
(New Zealand)

▲13750

BRITISH ANTARCTIC TERRITORY

ATLANTIC OCEAN

PACIFIC OCEAN

PACIFIC OCEAN

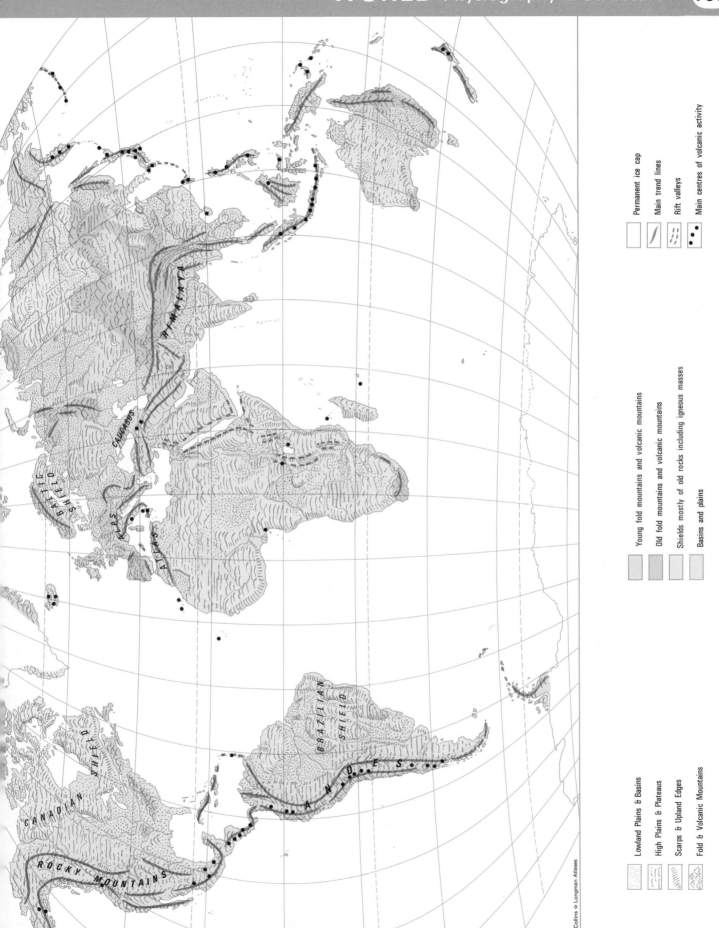

Permanent ice cap

Main trend lines

Rift valleys

Main centres of volcanic activity

Young fold mountains and volcanic mountains

Old fold mountains and volcanic mountains

Shields mostly of old rocks including igneous masses

Basins and plains

Lowland Plains & Basins

High Plains & Plateaus

Scarps & Upland Edges

Fold & Volcanic Mountains

HIMALAYA

CAUCASUS

BALTIC SHIELD

ALPS

ATLAS

BRAZILIAN SHIELD

ANDES

CANADIAN SHIELD

ROCKY MOUNTAINS

© Collins ◇ Longman Atlases

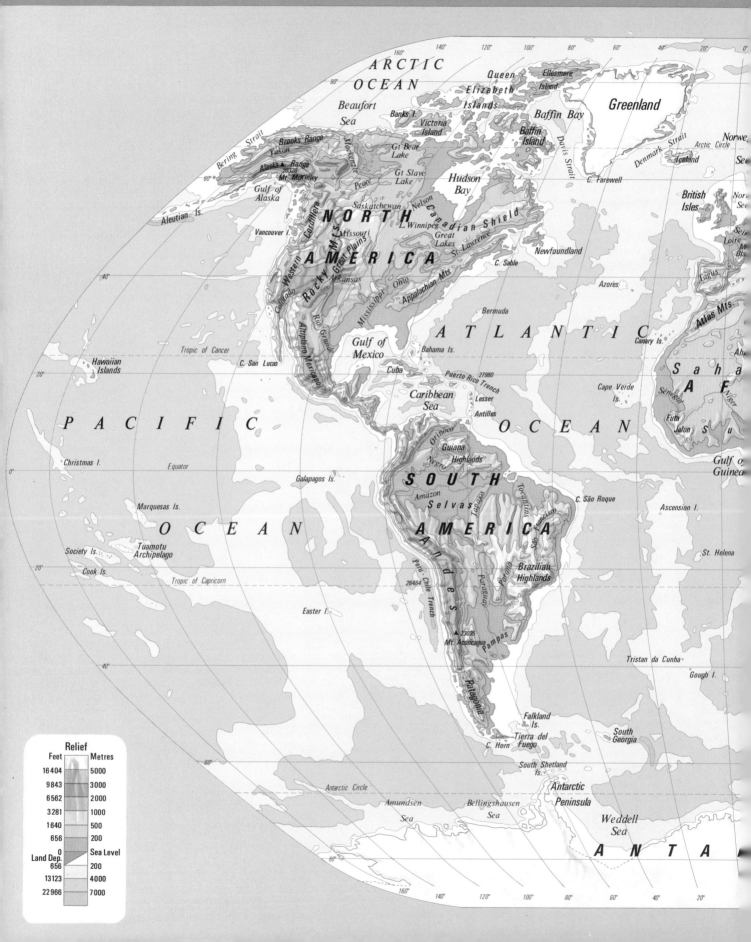

ARCTIC OCEAN

Queen
Elizabeth
Islands

Ellesmere
Island

Greenland

Beaufort
Sea

Banks I.

Victoria
Island

Baffin
Island

Baffin Bay

Davis Strait

Norwe

Brooks Range

Yukon

Alaska ▲ Range
20320
Mt. McKinley

Gulf of
Alaska

Aleutian Is.

Vancouver I.

Bering Strait

Mackenzie

Gt Bear
Lake

Gt Slave
Lake

Peace

Hudson
Bay

C. Farewell

Arctic Circle

Denmark Strait

Iceland

Se

British
Isles

Nor

Sei
Loire
Bla

NORTH

AMERICA

Cordillera

Rocky Mts.

Western

Colorado

Saskatchewan

L. Winnipeg

Missouri

Great Plains

Nelson

Canadian Shield

Great
Lakes

St. Lawrence

Newfoundland

C. Sable

Arkansas

Mississippi

Ohio

Appalachian Mts.

Azores

Tagus

Atlas Mts.

Tropic of Cancer

C. San Lucas

Rio Grande

Altiplano Mexicano

Gulf of
Mexico

Bahama Is.

Bermuda

ATLANTIC

Canary Is.

Sah a

S A F

Hawaiian
Islands

Cuba

Caribbean
Sea

Puerto Rico Trench 27980

Lesser
Antilles

Cape Verde
Is.

Senegal

Niger

Futa
Jalon S u

Gulf o
Guinea

PACIFIC

Christmas I.

Equator

Galapagos Is.

OCEAN

Orinoco

Negro

Guiana
Highlands

SOUTH

Amazon

Selvas

Tapajos

Tocantins

São Francisco

C. São Roque

Ascension I.

St. Helena

Marquesas Is.

OCEAN

AMERICA

Society Is.

Tuamotu
Archipelago

Cook Is.

Tropic of Capricorn

Easter I.

26464

Peru Chile Trench

Andes

Paraguay

Parana

Brazilian
Highlands

Tristan da Cunha

Gough I.

▲ 23035
Mt. Aconcagua

Pampas

Patagonia

Falkland
Is.

Tierra del
Fuego

C. Horn

South
Georgia

South Shetland
Is.

Antarctic
Peninsula

Antarctic Circle

Amundsen
Sea

Bellingshausen
Sea

Weddell
Sea

A N T A

Relief

Feet	Metres
16 404	5000
9843	3000
6562	2000
3281	1000
1640	500
656	200
0	Sea Level
Land Dep.	
656	200
13 123	4000
22 966	7000

20° 40° 60° 80° 100° 120° 140° 160° 180°

A R C T I C   O C E A N

itsbergen

Franz
Josef Land

Novaya
Zemlya

Severnaya
Zemlya

New Siberian
Is.

80°

Barents   Sea

Kara Sea

Laptev Sea

East Siberian
Sea

North Cape

Indinavia

Baltic
Shield

N. Dvina

Ob

West

Siberia

Lena

Siberian

Ob

60°

North

Baltic Sea

European

Drina

Dnieper

Ural Mountains

Siberian

Plain

Irtysh

A S I A

Amur

Sea
of
Okhotsk

Kamachatka
Pen.

Bering Sea

Aleutian Trench
25663

U R O P E

Don

Volga

Caspian Sea

Altai

L. Baikal

Gobi

Manchurian
Plain

Sakhalin

Hokkaido

Kuril Trench
34587

Danube

Balkan Mts.

Black Sea

Caucasus Mts.

Aral
Sea

L. Balkhash

Syr Darya

Tien Shan

Amu Darya

Tarim
Basin

Kunlun Shan

Hwang Ho

North
China
Plain

Yellow
Sea

Sea of
Japan

Henshu

40°

Japan Trench

rranean Sea

Anatolia

Tigris

Euphrates

Iranian
Plateau

Hindu Kush

Tibetan
Plateau

Brahmaputra

Yangtze Kiang

Yunnan
Plateau

East
China
Sea

Kyushu

34449

Marianas Trench

Tropic of Cancer

I C A

Tibesti
Mts.

Arabia

Persian Gulf

Himalaya

29028
Mt. Everest

Ganges

Salween

Mekong

Formosa

P A C I F I C

20°

Nile

Red Sea

Deccan

Bay of
Bengal

South
China
Sea

Philippine Trench

L. Chad

Blue Nile

Gulf of Aden

Arabian
Sea

Andaman Is.

Philippines

34439

36200

Caroline Is.

Marshall
Is.

White Nile

Ethiopian
Highlands

Ceylon

Nicobar Is.

O C E A N

Ubangi

Congo
Basin

Lake
Victoria

19342
Kilimanjaro

Amirantes

Seychelles

I N D I A N

Sumatra

Borneo

Putjak Djaja
16503

New Guinea

Solomon Is.

Equator

Gilbert Is.

Kasai

Zaire

Great Rift Valley

Tanganyika

Celebes

Java

Christmas I.

Timor
Sea

Arafura Sea

Samoa
Is.

Bié
Plateau

L. Malawi

Zambezi

O C E A N

Cocos Is.

Timor

A U S T R A L A S I A

Coral Sea

Vanuatu

New
Caledonia

Fiji Is.

Tonga Trench

Madagascar

Mauritius
Réunion

Great
Sandy Desert

Great
Artesian
Basin

Tonga Is.
35702

Tropic of Capricorn

20°

Kalahari
Desert

Drakensberg

Mozambique Channel

Limpopo

Vaal

Orange

C. of Good Hope

C. Leeuwin

Great
Australian
Bight

Amsterdam I.

A u s t r a l i a

L. Eyre

Murray

Darling

Great Dividing Range

Tasman

Sea

Chatham
Is.

Kermadec Trench
32953

40°

Tasmania

New
Zealand

Prince Edward Is.

Crozet Is.

Kerguelen

Heard I.

60°

Antarctic Circle

Ross
Sea

80°

T I C A

40° 60° 80° 100° 120° 140° 160° 180°

Scale 1:85 000 000

0   500   1000   1500   2000   2500 Miles

0   1000   2000   3000   4000 Kms.

Flat Polar Equal Area Projection

© Collins ◇ Longman Atlases

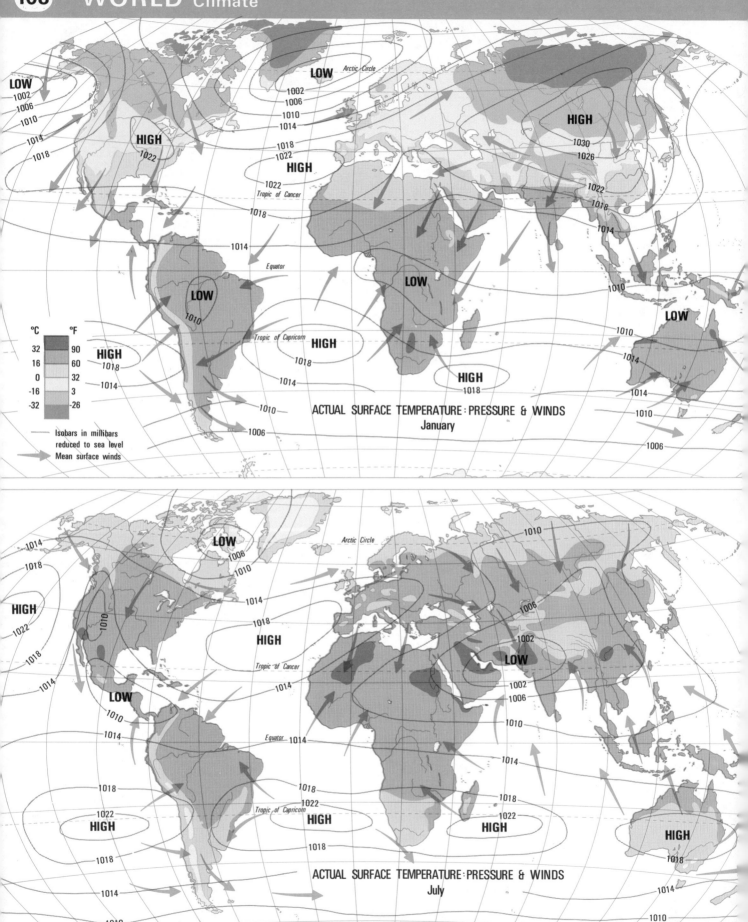

°C °F
32 90
16 60
0 32
-16 3
-32 -26

— Isobars in millibars
reduced to sea level
→ Mean surface winds

ACTUAL SURFACE TEMPERATURE : PRESSURE & WINDS
January

ACTUAL SURFACE TEMPERATURE : PRESSURE & WINDS
July

© Collins ◇ Longman Atlases

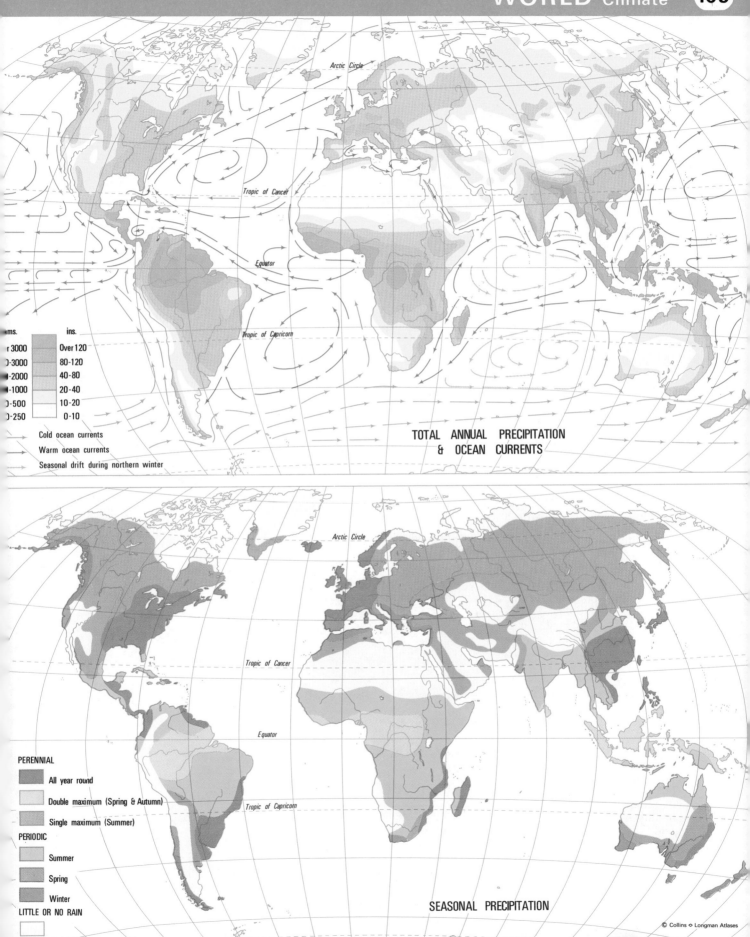

ms. **ins.**
r 3000	Over 120
0-3000	80-120
-2000	40-80
-1000	20-40
0-500	10-20
0-250	0-10

→ Cold ocean currents

→ Warm ocean currents

→ Seasonal drift during northern winter

TOTAL ANNUAL PRECIPITATION & OCEAN CURRENTS

Arctic Circle

Tropic of Cancer

Equator

Tropic of Capricorn

PERENNIAL

All year round

Double maximum (Spring & Autumn)

Single maximum (Summer)

PERIODIC

Summer

Spring

Winter

LITTLE OR NO RAIN

SEASONAL PRECIPITATION

© Collins ◊ Longman Atlases

Reindeer

Beef Wheat

Fruit

Beef Cattle

Dairy Cattle

Beef Cattle

Maize

Wheat

Sheep

Cotton

Fruit

Cotton

Sugar

Coffee Coffee

Coffee

Beef Cattle

Cocoa

Sheep

Cotton

Beef Cattle

Sugar

Beef Cattle

Cocoa

Sugar

Coffee

Coffee

Fruit

Maize

Wheat

Sheep

Dairy Cattle

Wheat

Fruit

Fruit

Fruit

Sheep

Sheep

Sheep

Cattle

Cattle

Came

Sh

Oil Palm

Coffee

Cocoa

Cocoa

Oil Palm

Coffee

Sh

Fr

Arctic Circle

R

Tropic of Cancer

Equator

Tropic of Capricorn

Scale 1:72 500 000

0   500   1000   1500   Miles

0   500   1000   1500   2000   Kms.

Winkel Projection

	Tundra and desert
	Forest
· · ·	Forest with small agricultural communities

© Collins ◇ Longman Atlases

Cattle

Wheat

Wheat

Maize

Beef Cattle

Sheep

Sheep

Cotton

Fruit

Fruit

Sheep

Wheat Sheep

Wheat

Yak

Wheat Cotton

Sheep

Reindeer

Fruit Tea

Rice

Tea

Tea

Rice

Fruit

Cotton

Rice

Camels

Rice

Cotton

Coffee

Sheep

Rice

Coffee

Tea

Rubber

Rice

Rubber

Coffee

Rice

Cattle

Tea Rice Coffee

Coffee

Tea

Cattle

Maize

Sugar

Sheep

Wheat

Beef Cattle

Fruit

Sheep

Fruit

Wheat

Fruit

Dairy Cattle

Sheep

Commercial farming: crops dominant

Commercial farming: animals dominant

Commercial farming: mixed farming and horticulture

Subsistence agriculture, crop based

Subsistence agriculture, animal based

Black names indicate main cash crops and stock, and red names indicate main subsistence crops and stock.

ARCTIC

GREENLAND
(Denmark)

Spitsbergen
(Norway)

Jan Mayen
(Norway)

Godthaab

Reykjavik ICELAND

Faroe Is.
(Den.)

NORWAY

SWEDEN

Hels

U.S.A.
ALASKA

Arctic Circle

Anchorage

CANADA

Edmonton

Calgary

Winnipeg

Vancouver
Seattle

Minneapolis St. Paul Toronto
Milwaukee Buffalo
Chicago
Detroit

Ottawa Quebec Montreal
Boston

Halifax

New York
Philadelphia
Washington

Salt Lake City Denver

San Francisco

UNITED STATES
OF AMERICA

St. Louis

Los Angeles

Dallas
New Orleans

Houston

Monterrey

Gulf of Miami
Mexico

Havana

Bermuda

BAHAMAS

CUBA

DOMINICAN
REPUBLIC

Oslo
Stockh

Copenha
Berlin POLA
Bonn E. GER
Prag
CZECH
Vienna
Belgrade

UNITED
KINGDOM
Glasgow
REPUBLIC
OF
IRELAND
London

DENMARK

Dublin NETH
BELG
WEST
L. GERMANY
Munich
SWITZ

Paris
FRANCE

Bordeaux Marseille

ANDORRA

Madrid

Rome
ITALY
ALBAN

Azores
(Port.)

PORTUGAL
Lisbon SPAIN

Algiers Tunis
TUNISIA

Ath

MEDITERRANE

Madeira
(Port.)

Rabat Morocco

Tripoli

LIBY

Tropic of Cancer

Mexico City

Revilla Gigedo Is.
(Mex.)

GUATEMALA HONDURAS
Guatemala City Tegucigalpa
EL SALVADOR NICARAGUA
Managua

San José Panama City
COSTA RICA

PANAMA

BELIZE

JAMAICA HAITI

Caribbean Sea

Caracas TRINIDAD

VENEZUELA

Georgetown

COLOMBIA Paramaribo
GUYANA Cayenne
SURINAM GUIANA
(Fr.)

Bogotá

Quito

ECUADOR
Guayaquil

Galapagos Is.
(Ecuador)

Equator

PACIFIC

OCEAN

P
E
R
U

Lima

Manaus

Belém

BRAZIL

Recife

Brasília

La Paz

BOLIVIA

Belo Horizonte

Rio de Janeiro
São Paulo

ATLANTIC

OCEAN

CAPE VERDE

El Aaiún
WESTERN
SAHARA

MAURITANIA

Nouakchott

Dakar SENEGAL
GAMBIA
GUINEA BISSAU

Conakry GUINEA
Freetown
SIERRA LEONE
Monrovia IVORY
LIBERIA COAST

ALGERIA

MALI

NIGER

Bamako

UPPER
VOLTA
Ouagadougou

Niamey

C
N'D

Abidjan Accra

GHANA
BENIN

NIGERIA

Lagos

CAMEROON

Bangui

EQUATORIAL
GUINEA
Libreville

Yaoundé

GABON

CONGO

Brazzaville

Kin

ANGOLA

Luanda

ANG

Ascension I.
(Br.)

St. Helena
(Br.)

SOUTH W
Windhoek

WALVIS BAY

AFRIC

(NAMIBI

Tropic of Capricorn

PARAGUAY

Asunción

Pôrto Alegre

Valparaíso
Santiago

Rosario
URUGUAY
Montevideo
Buenos Aires

Bahía Blanca

C
H
I
L
E

A
R
G
E
N
T
I
N
A

Juan Fernández Is.
(Chile)

Tristan da Cunha
(Br.)

Gough I.
(Br.)

Cape Town

Falkland Is.
(Br.)

South Georgia
(Br.)

A. : AUSTRIA
BELG. : BELGIUM
CZECH. : CZECHOSLOVAKIA
D. : DJIBOUTI
E. : EAST GERMANY
H. : HUNGARY
L. : LUXEMBOURG
MAL. : MALAWI
NETH. : NETHERLANDS
ROM. : ROMANIA
SWITZ. : SWITZERLAND
YUGO. : YUGOSLAVIA

CEAN

Arctic Circle

Aleutian Is.
(U.S.A.)

60° 80° 100° 120° 80° 140° 160° 180° 160°

◎ Arkhangel'sk

UNION OF SOVIET SOCIALIST REPUBLICS

ningrad

☒ Gorki ☒ Sverdlovsk ☒ Novosibirsk

☒ Moscow Omsk ◎

nsk

☒ Kiev ☒ Kharkov

Ulan Bator ☒

Odessa **MONGOLIA**

☒ Tashkent

charest Shenyang ☒ **NORTH**
KOREA

Black Sea ☒ Baku *Aral* Peking ☒ ☒ Pyongyang ◎ **JAPAN** 40°
180°

stanbul *Caspian* *Sea* **CHINA** ◎ Seoul ☒ Tokyo

☒ Ankara **SOUTH**
TURKEY **KOREA** ☒ Osaka

CYPRUS ☒ Tehran Nanking

LEBANON ☒ Baghdad Kabul ☒ Wuhan ☒ ☒ Shanghai **PACIFIC**
ISRAEL **IRAN** **AFGHANI-** Chungking ☒ Islamabad ☒ **STAN**

airo *JORDAN* **SYRIA** **IRAQ** Lahore ☒ **KASHMIR**

GYPT **KUWAIT** **PAKISTAN** Delhi ☒ **NEPAL**

BAHRAIN New Delhi Katmandu ◎ **BHUTAN** Taipei ☒ *Tropic of Cancer*

SAUDI **QATAR** Karachi ☒ Dacca ☒ Kwangchow ☒ **TAIWAN**

Riyadh ◎ **U. OF ARAB** ☒ Muscat Calcutta ☒ **(FORMOSA)**

ARABIA **EMIRATES** Ahmadabad ☒ **INDIA** **BANGLA-** **BURMA** ◎ Hanoi ◎ Victoria 20°

◎ Mecca **OMAN** **DESH** Hanoi **HONG KONG**

Bombay ☒ **(Br.)**

artoum Sana Vientiane ◎ *Mariana Is.*

DAN **SOUTHERN** ◎ Hyderabad Rangoon ☒ **LAOS** **(U.S.A.)**

YEMEN **YEMEN** Madras ☒ **THAI-** **VIETNAM** **OCEAN**

D. ◎ Aden *Andaman Is.* **LAND**

◎ Addis Ababa **(Ind.)** Bangkok ☒ ◎ Quezon City

ETHIOPIA *Lakshadweep Is.* **KAMPUCHEA** ◎ Manila **PHILIPPINES**

(Ind.) **SRI** Phnom ☒ Ho Chi

LANKA Penh ☒ Minh City

Colombo ◎ *Nicobar Is.* *Caroline Is.*

(Ind.) **(U.S.A.)**

◎ Mogadishu **MALDIVE** **BRUNEI**

UGANDA **SOMALI** **ISLANDS** Kuala Lumpur ◎ **MALAYSIA**

Kampala ◎ **REPUBLIC** **KENYA** ☒ Singapore *Equator* 0°

RWANDA ◎ Nairobi *SEYCHELLES* **SINGAPORE**

BURUNDI *Amirantes* **INDONESIA** **PAPUA**

TANZANIA **(Br.)** **NEW GUINEA**

◎ Dar es Salaam Jakarta ☒ ◎ Surabaya **SOLOMON**
IS

MAL. *Christmas I.*
(Austl.)

BIA *Lilongwe*

ury **MOCAMBIQUE** *Cocos Is.* **(Austl.)** *New Caledonia*

MBABWE **(Fr.)** 20°

◎ Pretoria **MADAGASCAR** **INDIAN OCEAN** *Tropic of Capricorn*

orone ◎ Maputo

SWAZILAND ◎ Tananarive

◎ Johannesburg *MAURITIUS*

A ◎ Durban **AUSTRALIA**

◎ Brisbane

Perth ◎

St. Paul *Amsterdam I.* ☒ Sydney
(Fr.) *(Fr.)* Adelaide ◎ ◎ Canberra

ce Edward Is. *Crozet Is.* ☒ Melbourne Auckland ◎
S. Africa) *(Fr.)* **NEW** 160° 180°
ZEALAND

Scale 1:72 500 000 Wellington ◎

0 500 1000 1500 2000 Miles

0 500 1000 1500 2000 2500 3000 Kms.

Kerguelen **Winkel Projection**
(Fr.)

40° 60° 80° 100° 120° 140° 160° 180°

Heard I. © Collins ◇ Longman Atlases
(Austl.)

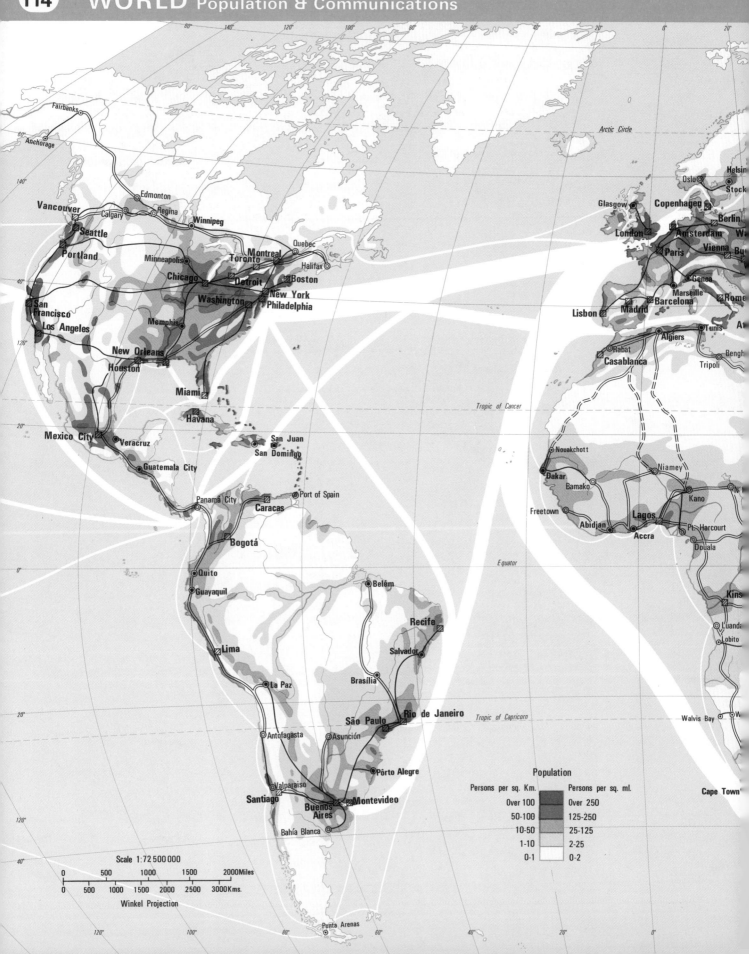

Fairbanks
Anchorage
Edmonton
Vancouver
Calgary
Regina
Winnipeg
Seattle
Portland
Minneapolis
Montreal
Quebec
Halifax
Chicago
Detroit
Boston
Washington
New York
Philadelphia
San Francisco
Los Angeles
Memphis
New Orleans
Houston
Miami
Havana
Mexico City
Veracruz
Guatemala City
San Juan
San Domingo
Port of Spain
Panamá City
Caracas
Bogotá
Quito
Guayaquil
Belém
Recife
Salvador
Lima
Brasília
La Paz
São Paulo
Rio de Janeiro
Antofagasta
Asunción
Pôrto Alegre
Valparaiso
Santiago
Buenos Aires
Montevideo
Bahía Blanca
Punta Arenas

Arctic Circle
Tropic of Cancer
Equator
Tropic of Capricorn

Oslo
Helsin
Stock
Glasgow
Copenhage
London
Berlin
Amsterdam
W
Paris
Vienna
Bu
Genoa
Marseille
Rome
Lisbon
Madrid
Barcelona
Tunis
A
Algiers
Rabat
Tripoli
Casablanca
Bengh
Nouakchott
Dakar
Bamako
Niamey
Freetown
Kano
N'
Abidjan
Lagos
Pt. Harcourt
Accra
Douala
Kins
Luanda
Lobito
Walvis Bay
W
Cape Town

Population

Persons per sq. Km.	Persons per sq. ml.
Over 100	Over 250
50-100	125-250
10-50	25-125
1-10	2-25
0-1	0-2

Scale 1:72 500 000

0   500   1000   1500   2000 Miles
0   500   1000   1500   2000   2500   3000 Kms.

Winkel Projection

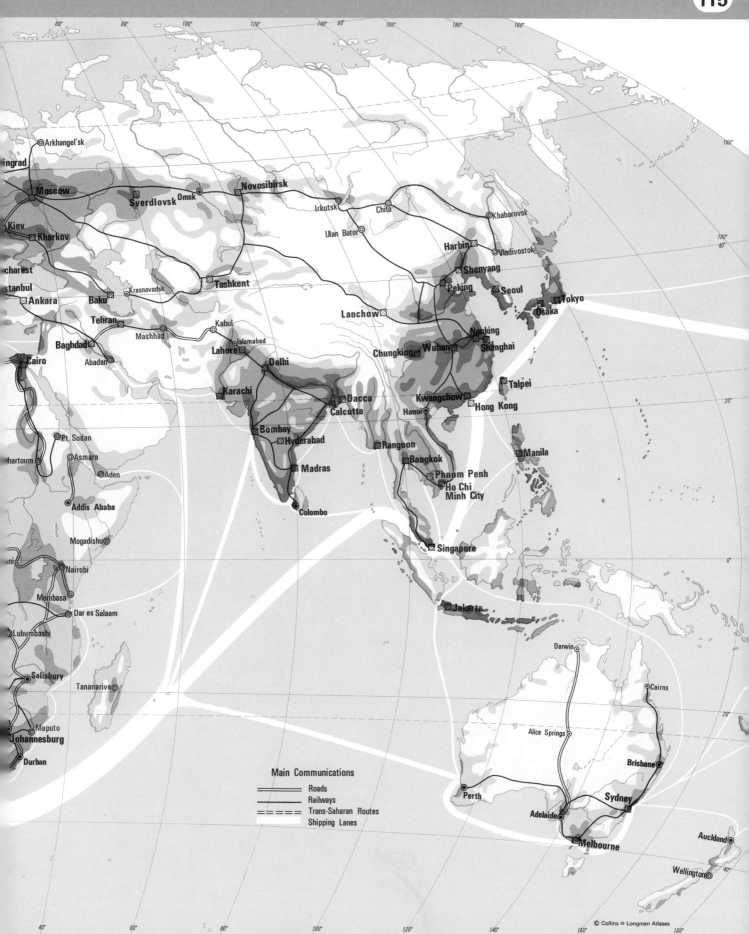

Main Communications

Roads
Railways
Trans-Saharan Routes
Shipping Lanes

© Collins ◇ Longman Atlases

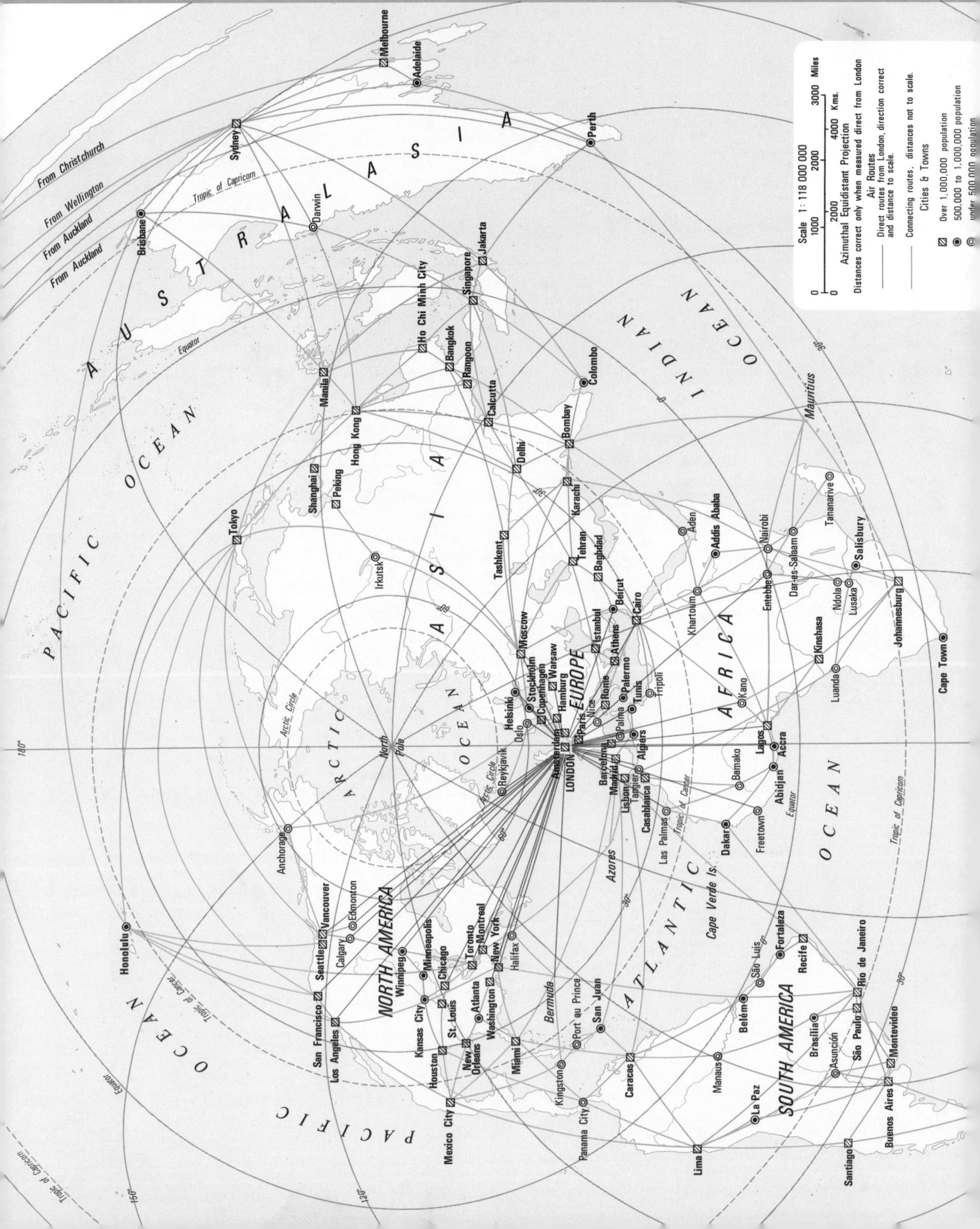

WORLD Airways

Scale 1 : 118 000 000

Azimuthal Equidistant Projection

Distances correct only when measured direct from London

Air Routes

Direct routes from London, direction correct and distance to scale.

Connecting routes, distances not to scale.

Cities & Towns

Over 1,000,000 population

500,000 to 1,000,000 population

under 500,000 population

Miles 3000

Kms. 4000

From Christchurch
From Wellington
From Auckland
From Auckland

Tropic of Capricorn

Equator

AUSTRALASIA

Melbourne
Adelaide
Perth
Sydney
Darwin
Brisbane
Jakarta
Singapore
Ho Chi Minh City
Bangkok
Rangoon
Manila
Calcutta
Colombo
Bombay
Hong Kong
Shanghai
Peking
Delhi
Tokyo
Irkutsk
Tashkent
Karachi

ASIA

Tehran
Baghdad
Beirut
Cairo
Aden
Addis Ababa
Nairobi
Dar-es-Salaam
Tananarive
Salisbury
Ndola
Lusaka
Khartoum
Entebbe

INDIAN OCEAN

Mauritius

Moscow
Istanbul
Athens
Rome
Palermo
Tunis
Nice
Tripoli
Warsaw
Hamburg
Stockholm
Copenhagen
Helsinki
Oslo
Reykjavik
Amsterdam
LONDON
Paris
Palma
Barcelona
Madrid
Algiers
Tangier
Lisbon
Casablanca

EUROPE

AFRICA

Kano
Lagos
Accra
Abidjan
Bamako
Freetown
Dakar
Kinshasa
Luanda
Johannesburg
Cape Town

Arctic Circle

North Pole

ARCTIC OCEAN

Anchorage

NORTH AMERICA

Vancouver
Seattle
Edmonton
Calgary
Winnipeg
Minneapolis
Chicago
Toronto
Montreal
New York
Halifax
San Francisco
Los Angeles
Kansas City
St. Louis
Atlanta
Washington
Houston
New Orleans
Miami
Mexico City
Panama City
Kingston
Port au Prince
San Juan
Bermuda

Honolulu

PACIFIC OCEAN

Tropic of Cancer

Equator

Tropic of Capricorn

ATLANTIC OCEAN

Azores
Cape Verde Is.
Las Palmas

SOUTH AMERICA

Caracas
Lima
La Paz
Manaus
Belém
São Luis
Fortaleza
Recife
Rio de Janeiro
São Paulo
Brasília
Asunción
Montevideo
Buenos Aires
Santiago

INDEX

All names in the atlas, except for some of those on the thematic maps, will be found in this index, printed in bold type. Each entry indicates the country or region of the world in which the name is located. This is followed by the number of the most appropriate page on which the name appears—generally the largest scale map. Lastly the latitude and longitude is given. Where the name applies to a very large area of the map these co- ordinates are sometimes omitted. For names that do apply to an area the reference is to the centre of the feature, which will usually also be the position of the name. In the case of rivers the mouth or confluence is always taken as the point of reference. Therefore it is necessary to follow the river upstream from this point to find its name on the map.

Towns listed in the index are not described as such unless the name could be misleading. Thus Whitley Bay is followed by 'town' in italic. Elsewhere, when the name itself does not indicate clearly what it is, a description is always added in italic immediately after. These descriptions have had to be abbreviated in many cases.

Abbreviations used in the index are explained below.

Abbreviations

Afghan.	Afghanistan	Neth.	Netherlands
Bangla.	Bangladesh	N. Ireland	Northern Ireland
b., **B.**	bay, Bay	Northants.	Northamptonshire
Beds.	Bedfordshire	Northum.	Northumberland
Berks.	Berkshire	N. Korea	North Korea
Bucks.	Buckinghamshire	N. Yorks.	North Yorkshire
Cambs.	Cambridgeshire	Notts.	Nottinghamshire
c., **C.**	cape, Cape	Oxon.	Oxfordshire
C.A.R.	Central African Republic	P.N.G.	Papua New Guinea
Czech.	Czechoslovakia	*pen.*, **Pen.**	peninsula, Peninsula
d.	internal division eg. county, region, state	Phil.	Philippines
Derbys.	Derbyshire	**Pt.**	Point
des.	desert	*r.*, **R.**	river, River
Dom. Rep.	Dominican Republic	Rep. of Ire.	Republic of Ireland
D. and G.	Dumfries and Galloway	R.S.A.	Republic of South Africa
E. Germany	Eastern Germany	**Resr.**	Reservoir
E. Sussex	East Sussex	Somali Rep.	Somali Republic
Equat. Guinea	Equatorial Guinea	**Sd.**	Sound
est.	estuary	S. Yemen	Southern Yemen
f.	physical feature eg. valley, plain, geographic district or region	S.G.	South Glamorgan
		S. Korea	South Korea
Game Res.	Game Reserve	S.W. Africa	South West Africa
Glos.	Gloucestershire	S. Yorks.	South Yorkshire
G.L.	Greater London	Staffs.	Staffordshire
G.M.	Greater Manchester	*str.*, **Str.**	strait, Strait
G.	Gulf	Strath.	Strathclyde
Hants.	Hampshire	Switz.	Switzerland
H. and W.	Hereford and Worcester	T. and W.	Tyne and Wear
Herts.	Hertfordshire	U.A.E.	Union of Arab Emirates
Humber.	Humberside	U.S.S.R.	Union of Soviet Socialist Republics
i., **I.**, *is.*, **Is.**	island, Island, islands, Islands	U.K.	United Kingdom
I.o.M.	Isle of Man	U.S.A.	United States of America
I.o.W.	Isle of Wight	U. Volta	Upper Volta
l., **L.**	lake, Lake	Warwicks.	Warwickshire
Lancs.	Lancashire	W. Germany	Western Germany
Leics.	Leicestershire	W.G.	West Glamorgan
Liech.	Liechtenstein	W. Isles	Western Isles
Lincs.	Lincolnshire	W. Midlands	West Midlands
Lux.	Luxembourg	W. Sussex	West Sussex
Mersey.	Merseyside	W. Yorks.	West Yorkshire
M.G.	Mid Glamorgan	Wilts.	Wiltshire
Mt.	Mount	Yugo.	Yugoslavia
mtn., **Mtn.**	mountain, Mountain		
mts., **Mts.**	mountains, Mountains		
Nat. Park	National Park		

A

Aa *r.* France **29** 51.00N 2.06E
Aachen W. Germany **45** 50.46N 6.06E
Aalen W. Germany **44** 48.50N 10.07E
Äänekoski Finland **46** 62.36N 25.44E
Aarau Switz. **44** 47.24N 8.04E
Aardenburg Neth. **45** 51.16N 3.26E
Aare *r.* Switz. **40** 47.03N 7.18E
Aarschot Belgium **45** 50.59N 4.50E
Aba Nigeria **71** 5.06N 7.21E
Abadan Iran **57** 30.21N 48.15E
Abadan I. Iran **57** 30.10N 48.30E
Abadeh Iran **57** 31.10N 52.40E
Abadla Algeria **68** 31.01N 2.45W
Abakaliki Nigeria **71** 6.17N 8.04E
Abakan U.S.S.R. **49** 53.43N 91.25E
Abaya, L. Ethiopia **69** 6.20N 38.00E
Abbeville France **40** 50.06N 1.51E
Abbeyfeale Rep. of Ire. **39** 52.23N 9.18W
Abbeyleix Rep. of Ire. **39** 52.55N 7.22W
Abbey Town England **32** 54.50N 3.18W
Abbotsbury England **28** 50.40N 2.36W
Abbots Langley England **27** 51.43N 0.25W
Abéché Chad **69** 13.49N 20.49E
Abengourou Ivory Coast **70** 6.42N 3.27W
Åbenrå Denmark **46** 55.03N 9.26E
Abeokuta Nigeria **71** 7.10N 3.26E
Aberayron Wales **30** 52.15N 4.16W
Abercarn Wales **31** 51.39N 3.09W
Aberdare Wales **31** 51.43N 3.27W
Aberdare Range *mts.* Kenya **73** 0.20S 36.40E
Aberdaron Wales **30** 52.48N 4.41W
Aberdeen Scotland **37** 57.08N 2.07W
Aberdeen S. Dak. U.S.A. **90** 45.28N 98.30W
Aberdeen Wash. U.S.A. **90** 46.58N 123.49W
Aberdovey Wales **30** 52.33N 4.03W
Aberfan Wales **31** 51.42N 3.20W
Aberfeldy Scotland **35** 56.37N 3.54W
Aberffraw Wales **30** 53.11N 4.28W
Aberfoyle Scotland **34** 56.11N 4.23W
Abergavenny Wales **30** 51.49N 3.01W
Abergele Wales **30** 53.17N 3.34W
Abernethy Scotland **35** 56.20N 3.19W
Aberporth Wales **30** 52.08N 4.33W
Abersoch Wales **30** 52.50N 4.31W
Abersychan Wales **28** 51.44N 3.03W
Abertillery Wales **31** 51.44N 3.09W
Aberystwyth Wales **30** 52.25N 4.06W
Ab-i-Diz *r.* Iran **57** 31.38N 48.54E
Abidjan Ivory Coast **70** 5.19N 4.01W
Abilene U.S.A. **90** 32.27N 99.45W
Abingdon England **28** 51.40N 1.17W
Abington Scotland **35** 55.29N 3.42W
Abitibi *r.* Canada **91** 51.15N 81.30W
Abitibi, L. Canada **95** 48.40N 79.35W
Abomey Benin **71** 7.14N 2.00E
Abou Deia Chad **71** 11.20N 19.20E
Aboyne Scotland **37** 57.05N 2.48W
Abqaiq Saudi Arabia **57** 25.55N 49.40E
Abrantes Portugal **41** 39.28N 8.12W
Abridge England **27** 51.40N 0.08E
Abu Dhabi U.A.E. **57** 24.27N 54.23E
Abu Hamed Sudan **69** 19.32N 33.20E
Abu Simbel Egypt **56** 22.18N 31.40E
Abu Tig Egypt **56** 27.06N 31.17E
Abu Zenima Egypt **56** 29.03N 33.06E
Acámbaro Mexico **96** 20.01N 101.42W
Acapulco Mexico **96** 16.51N 99.56W
Acarigua Venezuela **97** 9.35N 69.12W
Acatlán Mexico **96** 18.12N 98.02W
Accra Ghana **70** 5.33N 0.15W
Accrington England **32** 53.46N 2.22W
Achahoish Scotland **34** 55.57N 5.30W
à Chairn Bhain, Loch Scotland **36** 58.16N 5.05W
Achill Head Rep. of Ire. **38** 53.59N 10.15W
Achill I. Rep. of Ire. **38** 53.57N 10.00W
Achill Sound *town* Rep. of Ire. **38** 53.56N 9.56W
Achnasheen Scotland **36** 57.34N 5.05W
A'Chràlaig *mtn.* Scotland **36** 57.11N 5.09W
Acklin's I. Bahamas **97** 22.30N 74.10W
Ackworth Moor Top *town* England **33** 53.39N 1.20W
Aconcagua, Mt. S. America **106** 33.00S 70.00W
Acqui Italy **42** 44.41N 8.28E
Acton England **27** 51.31N 0.17W
Adamantina Brazil **103** 21.41S 51.04W
Adamawa Highlands Nigeria/Cameroon **71** 7.05N 12.00E
Adams, Mt. U.S.A. **90** 46.13N 121.29W
Adana Turkey **56** 37.00N 35.19E
Adapazari Turkey **56** 40.45N 30.23E
Adare Rep. of Ire. **39** 52.33N 8.48W
Adda *r.* Italy **40** 45.08N 9.55E
Ad Dahana *des.* Saudi Arabia **57** 26.00N 47.00E
Adderbury England **28** 52.01N 1.19W
Addis Ababa Ethiopia **69** 9.03N 38.42E

Ad Diwaniya Iraq **57** 31.59N 44.57E
Addlestone England **27** 51.22N 0.31W
Adelaide Australia **80** 34.56S 138.36E
Adélie Coast Antarctica **104** 80.00S 140.00E
Aden S. Yemen **69** 12.50N 45.00E
Aden, G. of Indian Oc. **69** 13.00N 50.00E
Adi *i.* Asia **61** 4.10S 133.10E
Adige *r.* Italy **42** 45.10N 12.20E
Adirondack Mts. U.S.A. **95** 44.00N 74.15W
Adiyaman Turkey **56** 37.46N 38.15E
Adlington England **32** 53.37N 2.36W
Admiralty Is. Pacific Oc. **61** 2.30S 147.20E
Adour *r.* France **40** 43.28N 1.35W
Adrano Italy **42** 37.39N 14.49E
Adrar des Iforas *mts.* Algeria **71** 20.00N 2.30E
Adraskand *r.* Afghan. **57** 33.17N 62.08E
Adrian U.S.A. **94** 41.55N 84.01W
Adriatic Sea Med. Sea **42** 42.30N 16.00E
Adur *r.* England **29** 50.50N 0.16W
Aduwa Ethiopia **69** 14.12N 38.56E
Adwick le Street England **33** 53.35N 1.12W
Aegean Sea Med. Sea **43** 39.00N 25.00E
Aeron *r.* Wales **30** 52.14N 4.16W
Afghanistan Asia **58** 34.00N 65.30E
Afif Saudi Arabia **56** 23.53N 42.59E
Afikpo Nigeria **71** 5.53N 7.55E
Afmadu Somali Rep. **73** 0.27N 42.05E
Africa **67**
Afyon Turkey **56** 38.46N 30.32E
Agadès Niger **71** 17.00N 7.56E
Agana Asia **61** 13.28N 144.45E
Agartala India **59** 23.49N 91.15E
Agboville Ivory Coast **70** 5.55N 4.15W
Agde France **41** 43.25N 3.30E
Agedabia Libya **68** 30.48N 20.15E
Agen France **40** 44.12N 0.38E
Agger *r.* W. Germany **45** 46.58N 7.06E
Aghada Rep. of Ire. **39** 51.50N 8.13W
Aghda Iran **57** 32.25N 33.38E
Aghleam Rep. of Ire. **38** 54.08N 10.06W
Agnew's Hill N. Ireland **34** 54.51N 5.59W
Agordat Ethiopia **69** 15.35N 37.55E
Agout *r.* France **41** 43.40N 1.40E
Agra India **58** 27.09N 78.00E
Agra *r.* Spain **41** 42.12N 1.43W
Agreda Spain **41** 41.51N 1.55W
Agri *r.* Italy **43** 40.13N 16.45E
Agri Turkey **56** 39.44N 43.04E
Agrigento Italy **42** 37.19N 13.36E
Agrihan *i.* Asia **61** 18.44N 145.39E
Aguascalientes Mexico **96** 21.51N 102.18W
Aguascalientes *d.* Mexico **96** 22.00N 102.00W
Agueda *r.* Spain **41** 41.00N 6.56W
Aguilar de Campóo Spain **40** 42.47N 4.15W
Aguilas Spain **41** 37.25N 1.35W
Agulhas, C. R.S.A. **74** 34.50S 20.00E
Ahaggar Mts. Algeria **71** 24.00N 5.50E
Ahar Iran **57** 38.25N 47.07E
Ahaus W. Germany **45** 52.04N 7.01E
Ahlen W. Germany **44** 51.46N 7.53E
Ahmadabad India **58** 23.03N 72.40E
Ahmednagar India **58** 19.08N 74.48E
Ahr *r.* W. Germany **45** 50.34N 7.16E
Ahwaz Iran **57** 31.17N 48.44E
Aigun China **63** 49.40N 127.10E
Ailette *r.* France **45** 49.35N 3.09E
Ailsa Craig *i.* Scotland **34** 55.15N 5.07W
Ain *r.* France **40** 45.47N 5.12E
Aïna *r.* Gabon **72** 0.38N 12.47E
Ain Beida Algeria **42** 35.50N 7.29E
Ain Salah Algeria **68** 27.12N 2.29E
Aïn Sefra Algeria **68** 32.45N 0.35W
Aïr *mts.* Niger **71** 18.30N 8.30E
Aird Brenish *c.* Scotland **36** 58.08N 7.08W
Airdrie Scotland **35** 55.52N 3.59W
Aire *r.* England **33** 53.42N 0.54W
Aire France **40** 43.39N 0.15W
Airedale *f.* England **32** 53.56N 1.54W
Aisne *r.* France **45** 49.27N 2.51E
Aitape P.N.G. **61** 3.10S 142.17E
Aith Scotland **36** 60.17N 1.23W
Aix-en-Provence France **40** 43.31N 5.27E
Aiyina *i.* Greece **43** 37.43N 23.30E
Ajaccio France **40** 41.55N 8.43E
Ajmer India **58** 26.29N 74.40E
Akbou Algeria **42** 36.26N 4.33E
Aketi Zaïre **72** 2.46N 23.51E
Akhaltsikhe U.S.S.R. **56** 41.37N 42.59E
Akhdar, Jebel *mts.* Libya **69** 32.10N 22.00E
Akhdar, Jebel *mts.* Oman **57** 23.10N 57.25E
Akhdar, Wadi *r.* Saudi Arabia **56** 28.30N 36.48E
Akhelóös *r.* Greece **43** 38.20N 21.04E
Akhisar Turkey **56** 38.54N 27.49E
Akimiski I. Canada **93** 53.00N 81.20W
Akita Japan **63** 39.44N 140.05E
Akjoujt Mauritania **70** 19.44N 14.26W

Akkajaure *l.* Sweden **46** 67.40N 17.30E
Akobo *r.* Sudan/Ethiopia **69** 8.30N 33.15E
Akola India **58** 20.40N 77.02E
Akpatok I. Canada **93** 60.30N 68.30W
Akron U.S.A. **94** 41.04N 81.31W
Aksaray Turkey **56** 38.22N 34.02E
Akşehir Turkey **56** 38.22N 31.24E
Aksu China **62** 42.10N 80.00E
Aktogay U.S.S.R. **62** 46.59N 79.42E
Aktyubinsk U.S.S.R. **48** 50.16N 57.13E
Akure Nigeria **71** 7.14N 5.08E
Akureyri Iceland **46** 65.41N 18.04W
Akuse Ghana **70** 6.04N 0.12E
Akyab Burma **59** 20.09N 92.55E
Alabama *d.* U.S.A. **91** 33.00N 87.00W
Alabama *r.* U.S.A. **91** 31.05N 87.55W
Alagez *mtn.* U.S.S.R. **57** 40.32N 44.11E
Al Ain, Wadi *r.* Oman **57** 22.18N 55.35E
Alakol, L. U.S.S.R. **62** 46.00N 81.40E
Alakurtti U.S.S.R. **46** 67.00N 30.23E
Alamagan *i.* Asia **61** 17.35N 145.50E
Alamosa U.S.A. **90** 37.28N 105.54W
Åland Is. Finland **46** 60.20N 20.00E
Alanya Turkey **56** 36.32N 32.02E
Alaşehir Turkey **43** 38.22N 28.29E
Alaska *d.* U.S.A. **92** 65.00N 153.00W
Alaska, G. of U.S.A. **92** 58.45N 145.00W
Alaska Pen. U.S.A. **92** 56.00N 160.00W
Alaska Range *mts.* U.S.A. **92** 62.10N 152.00W
Alazan *r.* U.S.S.R. **57** 41.06N 46.40E
Albacete Spain **41** 39.00N 1.52W
Alba Iulia Romania **43** 46.04N 23.33E
Albania Europe **43** 41.00N 20.00E
Albany Australia **79** 34.57S 117.54E
Albany *r.* Canada **91** 52.10N 82.00W
Albany Ga. U.S.A. **91** 31.37N 84.10W
Albany N.Y. U.S.A. **95** 42.40N 73.49W
Albany Oreg. U.S.A. **90** 44.38N 123.07W
Albemarle Sd. U.S.A. **91** 36.10N 76.00W
Alberche *r.* Spain **41** 40.00N 4.45W
Albert France **40** 50.00N 2.40E
Alberta *d.* Canada **92** 55.00N 115.00W
Albert Canal Belgium **45** 51.00N 5.15E
Albert Nile *r.* Uganda **73** 3.30N 32.00E
Albi France **40** 43.56N 2.08E
Alboran, Isleta de Spain **41** 35.55N 3.10W
Ålborg Denmark **46** 57.03N 9.56E
Albuquerque U.S.A. **90** 35.05N 106.38W
Alburquerque Spain **41** 39.13N 6.59W
Albury Australia **80** 36.03S 146.53E
Alcácer do Sal Portugal **41** 38.22N 8.30W
Alcalá de Chisvert Spain **41** 40.19N 0.13E
Alcalá de Henares Spain **41** 40.28N 3.22W
Alcalá la Real Spain **41** 37.28N 3.55W
Alcamo Italy **42** 37.59N 12.58E
Alcañiz Spain **41** 41.03N 0.09W
Alcaudete Spain **41** 37.35N 4.05W
Alcazar de San Juan Spain **41** 39.24N 3.12W
Alcazarquiver Morocco **41** 35.01N 5.54W
Alcester England **28** 52.13N 1.52W
Alcira Spain **41** 39.10N 0.27W
Alcoy Spain **41** 38.42N 0.29W
Alcubierre, Sierra de *mts.* Spain **41** 41.40N 0.20W
Alcudia Spain **41** 39.51N 3.09E
Aldabra Is. Indian Oc. **67** 9.00S 47.00E
Aldan U.S.S.R. **49** 58.44N 125.22E
Aldan *r.* U.S.S.R. **49** 63.30N 130.00E
Aldbourne England **28** 51.28N 1.38W
Aldbrough England **33** 53.50N 0.07W
Alde *r.* England **29** 52.02N 1.28E
Aldeburgh England **29** 52.09N 1.35E
Alderney *i.* Channel Is. **31** 49.42N 2.11W
Aldershot England **27** 51.15N 0.47W
Aldridge England **28** 52.36N 1.55W
Aldsworth England **28** 51.48N 1.46W
Alegrete Brazil **103** 29.45S 55.46W
Aleksandrovsk Sakhalinskiy U.S.S.R. **49** 50.55N 142.12E
Alençon France **40** 48.25N 0.05E
Aleppo Syria **56** 36.14N 37.10E
Aleria France **40** 42.05N 9.30E
Alès France **40** 44.08N 4.05E
Alessandria Italy **40** 44.55N 8.37E
Alesund Norway **46** 62.28N 6.11E
Aleutian Is. U.S.A. **54** 57.00N 180.00
Aleutian Range *mts.* U.S.A. **92** 58.00N 156.00W
Aleutian Trench Pacific Oc. **107** 50.00N 178.00E
Alexander Archipelago *is.* U.S.A. **92** 56.30N 134.30W
Alexander Bay *town* R.S.A. **74** 28.40S 16.30E
Alexandra New Zealand **82** 45.14S 169.26E
Alexandria Egypt **56** 31.13N 29.55E
Alexandria Scotland **34** 55.59N 4.35W
Alexandria La. U.S.A. **91** 31.19N 92.29W
Alexandria Va. U.S.A. **95** 38.49N 77.06W
Alexandroúpolis Greece **43** 40.50N 25.53E
Alfaro Spain **41** 42.11N 1.45W

For Khmer Republic *read* Kampuchea. *For* Malagasy Republic *read* Madagascar. *For* Rhodesia *read* Zimbabwe.

Alfiós to **Appleton** 119

Alfiós *r.* Greece **43** 37.37N 21.27E
Alford Scotland **37** 57.14N 2.42W
Alfreton England **33** 53.06N 1.22W
Algeciras Spain **41** 36.08N 5.27W
Alger *see* Algiers Algeria **41**
Algeria Africa **68** 28.00N 2.00E
Al Ghadaf, Wadi *r.* Iraq **56** 32.54N 43.33E
Alghero Italy **42** 40.33N 8.20E
Algiers Algeria **41** 36.50N 3.00E
Algoa B. R.S.A. **74** 33.56S 26.10E
Al Hamra *des.* U.A.E. **57** 22.45N 55.10E
Aliákmon *r.* Greece **43** 40.30N 22.38E
Alicante Spain **41** 38.21N 0.29W
Alice U.S.A. **90** 27.45N 98.06W
Alice Springs *town* Australia **79** 23.42S 133.52E
Aligarh India **58** 27.54N 78.04E
Aligudarz Iran **57** 33.25N 49.38E
Alima *r.* Congo **72** 1.36S 16.35E
Aling Kangri *mtn.* China **59** 32.51N 81.03E
Alingsås Sweden **46** 57.55N 12.30E
Aliquippa U.S.A. **94** 40.38N 80.16W
Aliwal North R.S.A. **74** 30.42S 26.43E
Al Jaub *f.* Saudi Arabia **57** 23.00N 50.00E
Al Jauf Saudi Arabia **56** 29.49N 39.52E
Al Jazi *des.* Iraq **56** 35.00N 41.00E
Al Khurr *r.* Iraq **56** 32.00N 44.15E
Alkmaar Neth. **45** 52.37N 4.44E
Al Kut Iraq **57** 32.30N 45.51E
Allagash *r.* U.S.A. **95** 47.08N 69.10W
Allahabad India **58** 25.57N 81.50E
Allakaket U.S.A. **92** 66.30N 152.45W
Allaqi, Wadi *r.* Egypt **56** 22.55N 33.02E
Allegheny *r.* U.S.A. **95** 40.26N 80.00W
Allegheny Mts. U.S.A. **95** 40.00N 79.00W
Allen *r.* England **35** 54.58N 2.18W
Allen, Lough Rep. of Ire. **38** 54 07N 8.04W
Allentown U.S.A. **95** 40.37N 75.30W
Alleppey India **58** 9.30N 76.22E
Aller *r.* W. Germany **44** 52.43N 9.38E
Alliance Nebr. U.S.A. **90** 42.08N 103.00W
Alliance Ohio U.S.A. **94** 40.56N 81.06W
Allier *r.* France **40** 46.58N 3.04E
Alloa Scotland **35** 56.07N 3.49W
Alma U.S.A. **94** 43.23N 84.40W
Alma-Ata U.S.S.R. **62** 43.19N 76.55E
Almadén Spain **41** 38.47N 4.50W
Al Maharadh *des.* Saudi Arabia **57** 20.00N 52.30E
Alma Hill U.S.A. **95** 42.03N 78.01W
Almansa Spain **41** 38.52N 1.06W
Almanzor, Pico de *mtn.* Spain **41** 40.20N 5.22W
Almanzora *r.* Spain **41** 37.16N 1.49W
Almazán Spain **41** 41.29N 2.31W
Almeirim Portugal **41** 39.12N 8.37W
Almelo Neth. **45** 52.21N 6.40E
Almeria Spain **41** 36.50N 2.26W
Älmhult Sweden **46** 56.32N 14.10E
Al Mira, Wadi *r.* Iraq **56** 32.27N 41.21E
Almond *r.* Scotland **35** 56.25N 3.28W
Almuñécar Spain **41** 36.44N 3.41W
Aln *r.* England **35** 55.23N 1.36W
Alness Scotland **37** 57.42N 4.15W
Alnwick England **35** 55.25N 1.41W
Alor *i.* Indonesia **61** 8.20S 124.30E
Alor Star Malaysia **60** 6.06N 100.23E
Alost Belgium **45** 50.57N 4.03E
Alpena U.S.A. **94** 45.04N 83.27W
Alpes Maritimes *mts.* France **40** 44.07N 7.08E
Alphen Neth. **45** 52.08N 4.40E
Alpine U.S.A. **90** 30.22N 103.40W
Alps *mts.* Europe **44** 47.00N 10.00E
Al Qurna Iraq **57** 31.00N 47.26E
Alsager England **32** 53.07N 2.20W
Alsásua Spain **41** 42.54N 2.10W
Alsh, Loch Scotland **36** 57.15N 5.36W
Al Shaab S. Yemen **69** 12.50N 44.56E
Alston England **32** 54.48N 2.26W
Alta Norway **46** 69.57N 23.10E
Alta *r.* Norway **46** 70.00N 23.15E
Altagracia Venezuela **97** 10.44N 71.30W
Altai China **62** 47.48N 88.07E
Altai *mts.* Mongolia **62** 46.30N 93.30E
Altaj Mongolia **62** 46.20N 97.00E
Altamaha *r.* U.S.A. **91** 31.15N 81.23W
Altamura Italy **43** 40.50N 16.32E
Altea Spain **41** 38.37N 0.03W
Altenburg E. Germany **44** 50.59N 12.27E
Altenkirchen W. Germany **45** 50.41N 7.40E
Al Tihama *des.* Saudi Arabia **56** 27.50N 35.30E
Altiplano Mexicano *mts.* N. America **106** 24.00N 105.00W
Altnaharra Scotland **37** 58.16N 4.26W
Alto Araguaia Brazil **103** 17.19S 53.10W
Alto Garcas Brazil **103** 16.57S 53.30W
Alto Molocue Moçambique **73** 15.38S 37.42E
Alton England **28** 51.08N 0.59W
Alton U.S.A. **94** 38.55N 90.10W
Altoona U.S.A. **95** 40.32N 78.23W
Altrincham England **32** 53.25N 2.21W
Altyn Tagh *mts.* China **62** 38.10N 87.50E
Al'Ula Saudi Arabia **56** 26.39N 37.58E
Alva Scotland **35** 56.09N 3.49W
Alva U.S.A. **90** 36.48N 98.40W
Alvarado Mexico **96** 18.49N 95.46W
Älvsbyn Sweden **46** 65.41N 21.00E
Al Wajh Saudi Arabia **56** 26.16N 36.28E
Al Wakrah Qatar **57** 25.09N 51.36E
Alwar India **58** 27.32N 76.35E
Alyaty U.S.S.R. **57** 39.59N 49.20E
Alyth Scotland **35** 56.38N 3.14W
Alzette *r.* Lux. **45** 49.52N 6.07E
Amadeus, L. Australia **79** 24.50S 131.00E
Amadi Sudan **73** 5.32N 30.20E
Amagasaki Japan **63** 34.42N 135.25E
Amami *i.* Japan **63** 28.20N 129.30E
Amara Iraq **57** 31.52N 47.50E
Amarillo U.S.A. **90** 35.14N 101.50W
Amaro, Monte *mtn.* Italy **42** 42.06N 14.04E
Amasya Turkey **56** 40.37N 35.50E
Amazon *r.* Brazil **102** 2.00S 52.00W
Ambala India **58** 30.19N 76.49E
Ambarchik U.S.S.R. **49** 69.39N 162.27E
Ambato-Boeni Malagasy Rep. **73** 16.30S 46.33E
Amberg W. Germany **44** 49.26N 11.52E
Ambergris Cay *i.* Belize **96** 18.00N 87.58W
Amberley England **29** 50.54N 0.33W
Amble England **35** 55.20N 1.34W
Ambleside England **32** 54.26N 2.58W
Ambon Indonesia **61** 4.50S 128.10E
Ambriz Angola **72** 7.54S 13.12E
Ambrizete Angola **72** 7.13S 12.56E
Ameland *i.* Neth. **45** 53.28N 5.48E
Amersfoort Neth. **45** 52.10N 5.23E
Amersham England **27** 51.40N 0.38W
Amesbury England **28** 51.10N 1.46W
Amga U.S.S.R. **49** 60.51N 131.59E
Amga *r.* U.S.S.R. **49** 62.40N 135.20E
Amgun *r.* U.S.S.R. **49** 53.10N 139.47E
Amherst U.S.A. **95** 43.00N 78.45W
Amiata *mtn.* Italy **42** 42.53N 11.37E
Amiens France **40** 49.54N 2.18E
Amirantes *is.* Indian Oc. **113** 6.00S 52.00E
Amlwch Wales **30** 53.24N 4.21W
Amman Jordan **56** 31.57N 35.56E
Ammanford Wales **31** 51.48N 4.00W
Amol Iran **57** 36.26N 52.24E
Amorgós *i.* Greece **43** 36.50N 25.55E
Amos Canada **95** 48.04N 78.08W
Amoy China **63** 24.26N 118.07E
Ampala Honduras **96** 13.16N 87.39W
Ampthill England **29** 52.03N 0.30W
Amraoti India **58** 20.58N 77.50E
Amritsar India **58** 31.35N 74.56E
Amroha India **58** 28.54N 78.14E
Amsterdam Neth. **45** 52.22N 4.54E
Amsterdam U.S.A. **95** 42.56N 74.12W
Amsterdam I. Indian Oc. **113** 37.00S 79.00E
Amu Darya *r.* U.S.S.R. **48** 43.50N 59.00E
Amundsen G. Canada **92** 70.30N 122.00W
Amundsen Sea Antarctica **106** 70.00S 116.00W
Amur *r.* U.S.S.R. **49** 53.17N 140.00E
Anabar *r.* U.S.S.R. **49** 72.40N 113.30E
Anadyr U.S.S.R. **49** 64.40N 177.32E
Anadyr *r.* U.S.S.R. **49** 65.00N 176.00E
Anadyr, G. of U.S.S.R. **49** 64.30N 177.50W
Anaiza Saudi Arabia **57** 26.05N 43.57E
Anambas Is. Indonesia **60** 3.00N 106.10E
Anambra *d.* Nigeria **71** 6.20N 7.25E
Anápolis Brazil **103** 16.19S 48.58W
Anar Iran **57** 30.54N 55.18E
Anatahan *i.* Asia **61** 16.22N 145.38E
Anatolia *f.* Turkey **56** 38.00N 35.00E
Anatuya Argentina **103** 28.26S 62.48W
Anchorage U.S.A. **92** 61.10N 150.00W
Ancona Italy **42** 43.37N 13.33E
Ancroft England **35** 55.42N 2.00W
Ancuabe Moçambique **73** 13.00S 39.50E
Andalsnes Norway **46** 62.33N 7.43E
Andaman Is. India **59** 12.00N 93.00E
Andaman Sea Indian Oc. **59** 11.15N 95.30E
Andara S.W. Africa **74** 18.04S 21.29E
Andernach W. Germany **45** 50.25N 7.24E
Anderson *r.* Canada **92** 69.45N 129.00W
Anderson U.S.A. **94** 40.05N 85.41W
Andes *mts.* S. America **106** 21.00S 68.00W
And Fjord *est.* Norway **46** 69.10N 16.20E
Andhra Pradesh *d.* India **59** 17.00N 79.00E
Andikíthira *i.* Greece **43** 35.52N 23.18E
Andizhan U.S.S.R. **62** 40.48N 72.23E
Andorra *town* Andorra **41** 42.29N 1.31E
Andorra Europe **41** 42.30N 1.32E
Andover England **28** 51.13N 1.29W
Andoy *i.* Norway **46** 69.00N 15.30E
Andreas I.o.M. **32** 54.22N 4.26W
Andreas, C. Cyprus **56** 35.40N 34.35E
Ándros *i.* Greece **56** 37.50N 24.50E
Andros I. Bahamas **91** 24.30N 78.00W
Andujar Spain **41** 38.02N 4.03W
Andulo Angola **72** 11.28S 16.43E
Anécho Togo **71** 6.17N 1.40E
Anegada *i.* Virgin Is. **97** 18.46N 64.24W
Aneiza, Jebel *mtn.* Asia **56** 32.15N 39.19E
Aneto, Pico de *mtn.* Spain **41** 42.40N 0.19E
Angara *r.* U.S.S.R. **49** 58.00N 93.00E
Angarsk U.S.S.R. **49** 52.31N 103.55E
Angaston Australia **80** 34.30S 139.03E
Ange Sweden **46** 62.31N 15.40E
Angel de la Guarda *i.* Mexico **90** 29.10N 113.20W
Angel Falls *f.* Venezuela **97** 5.55N 62.30W
Ängelholm Sweden **46** 56.15N 12.50E
Ångerman Sweden **46** 62.52N 17.45E
Angers France **40** 47.29N 0.32W
Angkor *ruins* Khmer Rep. **60** 13.26N 103.50E
Angle Wales **31** 51.40N 5.03W
Anglesey *i.* Wales **30** 53.16N 4.25W
Angmagssalik Greenland **93** 65.40N 38.00W
Ango Zaïre **72** 4.01N 25.52E
Angola Africa **72** 11.00S 18.00E
Angoulême France **40** 45.40N 0.10E
Anguilar de Campóo Spain **41** 42.55N 4.15W
Anguilla C. America **97** 18.14N 63.05W
Angumu Zaïre **73** 0.10S 27.38E
Anholt W. Germany **45** 51.51N 6.26E
Anhumas Brazil **103** 16.58S 54.43W
Anhwei *d.* China **63** 31.30N 116.45E
Aniak U.S.A. **92** 61.32N 159.40W
Anjouan *i.* Comoro Is. **73** 12.12S 44.28E
Ankara Turkey **56** 39.55N 32.50E
Anking China **63** 30.20N 116.50E
Ankober Ethiopia **69** 9.32N 39.43E
Annaba Algeria **42** 36.55N 7.47E
An Nafud *des.* Saudi Arabia **56** 28.40N 41.30E
An Najaf Iraq **57** 31.59N 44.19E
Annalee *r.* Rep. of Ire. **38** 54.02N 7.25W
Annam Highlands *mts.* Asia **60** 17.40N 105.30E
Annan Scotland **35** 54.59N 3.16W
Annan *r.* Scotland **35** 54.58N 3.16W
Annandale *f.* Scotland **35** 55.12N 3.25W
Annapolis U.S.A. **95** 38.59N 76.30W
Annapurna *mtn.* Nepal **58** 28.34N 83.50E
Ann Arbor U.S.A. **94** 42.18N 83.43W
An Nasiriya Iraq **57** 31.04N 46.16E
Annecy France **40** 45.54N 6.07E
Annfield Plain *town* England **32** 54.42N 1.45W
Annonay France **40** 45.15N 4.40E
Ansbach W. Germany **44** 49.18N 10.36E
Anshan China **63** 41.05N 122.58E
Anshun China **59** 26.02N 105.57E
Ansi China **62** 40.32N 95.57E
Anston England **33** 53.22N 1.13W
Anstruther Scotland **35** 56.14N 2.42W
Antakya Turkey **56** 36.12N 36.10E
Antalya Turkey **56** 36.53N 30.42E
Antalya, G. of Turkey **56** 36.38N 31.00E
Antarctica **104**
Antarctic Pen. Antarctica **106** 66.00S 65.00W
An Teallach *mtn.* Scotland **36** 57.48N 5.16W
Antequera Spain **41** 37.01N 4.34W
Anticosti I. Canada **93** 49.20N 63.00W
Antigo U.S.A. **94** 45.10N 89.10W
Antigua C. America **97** 17.09N 61.49W
Antigua Guatemala **96** 14.33N 90.42W
Anti-Lebanon *mts.* Lebanon **56** 34.00N 36.25E
Antofagasta Chile **102** 23.40S 70.23W
Antonio Enes Moçambique **73** 16.10S 39.57E
Antrim N. Ireland **34** 54.43N 6.14W
Antrim *d.* N. Ireland **34** 54.58N 6.20W
Antrim, Mts. of N. Ireland **34** 55.00N 6.10W
Antung China **63** 40.06N 124.25E
Antwerp Belgium **45** 51.13N 4.25E
Antwerp *d.* Belgium **45** 51.16N 4.45E
Anvik U.S.A. **92** 62.38N 160.20W
Anyang China **63** 36.04N 114.20E
Anzhero-Sudzhensk U.S.S.R. **48** 56.10N 86.10E
Aomori Japan **63** 40.50N 140.43E
Aosta Italy **40** 45.43N 7.19E
Apa *r.* Paraguay **103** 22.06S 58.00W
Apalachee B. U.S.A. **91** 29.30N 84.00W
Aparri Phil. **61** 18.22N 121.40E
Apatity U.S.S.R. **46** 67.32N 33.21E
Apeldoorn Neth. **45** 52.13N 5.57E
Apennines *mts.* Italy **42** 42.00N 13.30E
Apolda E. Germany **44** 51.02N 11.31E
Apostle Is. U.S.A. **94** 47.00N 90.30W
Appalachian Mts. U.S.A. **91** 39.30N 78.00W
Appennino Ligure *mts.* Italy **40** 44.33N 8.45E
Appingedam Neth. **45** 53.18N 6.52E
Appleby England **32** 54.35N 2.29W
Appleton U.S.A. **94** 44.17N 88.24W

For Khmer Republic *read* Kampuchea. *For* Malagasy Republic *read* Madagascar. *For* Rhodesia *read* Zimbabwe.

Apsheron Pen. to **Autun** 120

Apsheron Pen. U.S.S.R. **57** 40.28N 50.00E
Apure *r.* Venezuela **97** 7.44N 66.38W
Aqaba Jordan **56** 29.32N 35.00E
Aqaba, G. of Asia **56** 28.45N 34.45E
Aqlat as Suqur Saudi Arabia **56** 25.50N 42.12E
Aquidauana Brazil **103** 20.27S 55.45W
Aquila Mexico **96** 18.30N 103.50W
Arabia Asia **107** 25.00N 45.00E
Arabian Desert Egypt **56** 28.15N 31.55E
Arabian Sea Asia **58** 16.00N 65.00E
Aracaju Brazil **102** 10.54S 37.07W
Araçatuba Brazil **103** 21.12S 50.24W
Arad Romania **43** 46.12N 21.19E
Arafura Sea Austa. **61** 9.00S 135.00E
Aragon *r.* Spain **41** 42.20N 1.45W
Araguaia *r.* Brazil **102** 5.30S 48.20W
Araguari Brazil **103** 18.38S 48.13W
Arak Iran **57** 34.06N 49.44E
Arakan Yoma *mts.* Burma **59** 20.00N 94.00E
Aral Sea U.S.S.R. **48** 45.00N 60.00E
Aralsk U.S.S.R. **48** 46.56N 61.43E
Aranda de Duero Spain **41** 41.40N 3.41W
Aran Fawddwy *mtn.* Wales **30** 52.48N 3.42W
Aran I. Rep. of Ire. **38** 54.59N 8.27W
Aran Is. Rep. of Ire. **39** 53.07N 9.38W
Aranjuez Spain **41** 40.02N 3.37W
Araouane Mali **70** 18.53N 3.31W
Arapkir Turkey **56** 39.03N 38.29E
Arar, Wadi *r.* Iraq **56** 32.00N 42.30E
Ararat Australia **80** 37.20S 143.00E
Ararat, Mt. Turkey **57** 39.45N 44.15E
Aras *r. see* Araxes Turkey **56**
Arauca *r.* Venezuela **97** 7.20N 66.40W
Araxa Brazil **103** 19.37S 46.50W
Araxes *r.* U.S.S.R. **57** 40.00N 48.28E
Araya Pen. Venezuela **97** 10.30N 64.30W
Arbatax Italy **42** 39.56N 9.41E
Arbroath Scotland **37** 56.34N 2.35W
Arcachon France **40** 44.40N 1.11W
Archers Post Kenya **73** 0.42N 37.40E
Arcila Morocco **41** 35.28N 6.04W
Arctic Ocean 104
Arctic Red *r.* Canada **92** 67.26N 133.48W
Arda *r.* Greece **43** 41.39N 26.30E
Ardabil Iran **57** 38.15N 48.18E
Ardara Rep. of Ire. **38** 54.46N 8.25W
Ardèche *r.* France **40** 44.31N 4.40E
Ardee Rep. of Ire. **38** 53.51N 6.33W
Ardennes *mts.* Belgium **45** 50.10N 5.30E
Ardentinny Scotland **34** 56.03N 4.55W
Arderin *mtn.* Rep. of Ire. **39** 53.02N 7.40W
Ardfert Rep. of Ire. **39** 52.20N 9.48W
Ardglass N. Ireland **38** 54.16N 5.37W
Ardgour *f.* Scotland **36** 56.45N 5.20W
Ardila Spain **41** 38.10N 7.30W
Ardistan Iran **57** 33.22N 52.25E
Ardivachar Pt. Scotland **36** 57.23N 7.26W
Ardlamont Pt. Scotland **34** 55.49N 5.12W
Ardlui Scotland **34** 56.18N 4.43W
Ardmore Rep. of Ire. **39** 51.58N 7.43W
Ardmore Head Rep. of Ire. **39** 51.56N 7.43W
Ardmore Pt. Strath. Scotland **36** 56.39N 6.08W
Ardmore Pt. Strath. Scotland **34** 55.42N 6.01W
Ardnamurchan *f.* Scotland **36** 56.44N 6.00W
Ardnamurchan, Pt. of Scotland **36** 56.44N 6.14W
Ardnave Pt. Scotland **34** 55.54N 6.20W
Ardres France **29** 50.51N 1.59E
Ardrishaig Scotland **34** 56.00N 5.26W
Ardrossan Scotland **34** 55.38N 4.49W
Ards Pen. N. Ireland **38** 54.30N 5.30W
Ardvasar Scotland **36** 57.03N 5.54W
Arecibo Puerto Rico **97** 18.29N 66.44W
Arena, Pt. U.S.A. **90** 38.58N 123.44W
Arendal Norway **46** 58.27N 8.56E
Arequipa Peru **102** 16.25S 72.10W
Arès France **40** 44.47N 1.08W
Arezzo Italy **42** 43.27N 11.52E
Arfak *mtn.* Asia **61** 1.30S 133.50E
Arga *r.* Spain **40** 42.20N 1.44W
Arganda Spain **41** 40.19N 3.26W
Argens *r.* France **40** 43.10N 6.45E
Argentan France **40** 48.45N 0.01W
Argentina S. America **103** 33.30S 64.00W
Argenton France **40** 46.36N 1.30E
Argeş *r.* Romania **43** 44.13N 26.22E
Argos Greece **43** 37.37N 22.45E
Argun *r.* China **63** 53.30N 121.48E
Argyll *f.* Scotland **34** 56.12N 5.15W
Århus Denmark **46** 56.10N 10.13E
Ariano Italy **42** 41.04N 15.00E
Arica Chile **102** 18.30S 70.20W
Ariege *r.* France **41** 43.02N 1.40E
Arinagour Scotland **34** 56.37N 6.31W
Arisaig Scotland **36** 56.55N 5.51W
Arisaig, Sd. of Scotland **36** 56.51N 5.50W
Ariza Spain **41** 41.19N 2.03W
Arizona *d.* U.S.A. **90** 34.00N 112.00W
Arizpe Mexico **96** 30.20N 110.11W
Arjona Colombia **97** 10.14N 75.22W
Arkaig, Loch Scotland **36** 56.58N 5.08W
Arkansas *d.* U.S.A. **91** 35.00N 92.00W
Arkansas *r.* U.S.A. **91** 33.50N 91.00W
Arkansas City U.S.A. **91** 37.03N 97.02W
Arkhangel'sk U.S.S.R. **48** 64.32N 41.10E
Arklow Rep. of Ire. **39** 52.47N 6.10W
Arlberg Pass Austria **44** 47.00N 10.05E
Arles France **40** 43.41N 4.38E
Arlington U.S.A. **95** 38.52N 77.05W
Arlington Heights *town* U.S.A. **94** 42.06N 88.00W
Arlon Belgium **45** 49.41N 5.49E
Armadale Scotland **35** 55.54N 3.41W
Armagh N. Ireland **38** 54.21N 6.41W
Armagh *d.* N. Ireland **38** 54.16N 6.35W
Arma Plateau Saudi Arabia **57** 25.30N 46.30E
Armavir U.S.S.R. **47** 44.59N 41.10E
Armenia Soviet Socialist Republic *d.* U.S.S.R. **57** 40.00N 45.00E
Armentières France **45** 50.41N 2.53E
Armidale Australia **80** 30.32S 151.40E
Armoy N. Ireland **34** 55.07N 6.20W
Arnauti, C. Cyprus **56** 35.06N 32.17E
Arnhem Neth. **45** 52.00N 5.55E
Arnhem, C. Australia **79** 12.10S 137.00E
Arnisdale Scotland **36** 57.08N 5.34W
Arno *r.* Italy **42** 43.43N 10.17E
Arnold England **33** 53.00N 1.08W
Arnprior Canada **95** 45.26N 76.24W
Arnsberg W. Germany **45** 51.24N 8.03E
Arnside England **32** 54.12N 2.49W
Arnstadt E. Germany **44** 50.50N 10.57E
Arrah India **58** 25.34N 84.40E
Ar Ramadi Iraq **56** 33.27N 43.19E
Arra Mts. Rep. of Ire. **39** 52.50N 8.22W
Arran *i.* Scotland **34** 55.35N 5.14W
Arras France **45** 50.17N 2.46E
Arrochar Scotland **34** 56.12N 4.44W
Arrow, Lough Rep. of Ire. **38** 54.03N 8.20W
Ar Rutba Iraq **56** 33.03N 40.18E
Árta Greece **43** 39.10N 20.57E
Arthur's Pass *f.* New Zealand **82** 42.50S 171.45E
Artois *f.* France **45** 50.16N 2.50E
Artush China **62** 38.27N 77.16E
Artvin Turkey **56** 41.12N 41.48E
Arua Uganda **73** 3.02N 30.56E
Aruba *i.* Neth. Antilles **97** 12.30N 70.00W
Aru Is. Indonesia **61** 6.00S 134.30E
Arun *r.* England **28** 50.48N 0.32W
Arundel England **28** 50.52N 0.32W
Arusha Tanzania **73** 3.21S 36.40E
Arusha *d.* Tanzania **73** 4.00S 37.00E
Aruwimi *r.* Zaïre **72** 1.20N 23.36E
Arvagh Rep. of Ire. **38** 53.56N 7.35W
Arvidsjaur Sweden **46** 65.37N 19.10E
Arvika Sweden **46** 59.41N 12.38E
Arzamas U.S.S.R. **47** 55.24N 43.48E
Asahi daki *mtn.* Japan **63** 43.42N 142.54E
Asahigawa Japan **63** 43.50N 142.20E
Asansol India **58** 23.40N 87.00E
Ascension I. Atlantic Oc. **112** 8.00S 14.00W
Aschaffenburg W. Germany **44** 49.58N 9.10E
Aschendorf W. Germany **45** 53.03N 7.20E
Aschersleben E. Germany **44** 51.46N 11.28E
Ascoli Piceno Italy **42** 42.52N 13.36E
Aseda Sweden **46** 57.10N 15.20E
Ash England **27** 51.14N 0.44W
Ash *r.* England **27** 51.48N 0.00
Ashanti *d.* Ghana **70** 6.30N 1.30W
Ashbourne England **32** 53.02N 1.44W
Ashbourne Rep. of Ire. **38** 53.31N 6.25W
Ashburton *r.* Australia **79** 21.15S 115.00E
Ashburton England **31** 50.31N 3.45W
Ashburton New Zealand **82** 43.54S 171.46E
Ashby de la Zouch England **28** 52.45N 1.29W
Ashdown Forest England **29** 51.03N 0.05E
Asheville U.S.A. **91** 35.35N 82.35W
Ashford Kent England **29** 51.08N 0.53E
Ashford Surrey England **27** 51.26N 0.27W
Ashington England **35** 55.11N 1.34W
Ashkhabad U.S.S.R. **57** 37.58N 58.24E
Ashland Wisc. U.S.A. **94** 46.34N 90.45W
Ashland Ky. U.S.A. **91** 38.28N 82.40W
Ash Sham *des.* Saudi Arabia **56** 28.15N 43.05E
Ash Shama *des.* Saudi Arabia **56** 31.20N 38.00E
Ashtabula U.S.A. **94** 41.53N 80.47W
Ashtead England **27** 51.19N 0.18W
Ashton-in-Makerfield England **32** 53.29N 2.39W
Ashton-under-Lyne England **32** 53.30N 2.08W
Asia 54
Asinara *i.* Italy **42** 41.04N 8.18E
Asinara, G. of Med. Sea **42** 41.00N 8.32E
Asir *f.* Saudi Arabia **69** 19.00N 42.00E
Askeaton Rep. of Ire. **39** 52.36N 9.00W
Askern England **33** 53.37N 1.09W
Askersund Sweden **46** 58.55N 14.55E
Asmara Ethiopia **69** 15.20N 38.58E
Aspatria England **32** 54.45N 3.20W
Aspiring, Mt. New Zealand **82** 44.20S 168.45E
Assab Ethiopia **69** 13.01N 42.47E
Assam *d.* India **59** 26.30N 93.00E
Assen Neth. **45** 53.00N 6.34E
Assiniboine, Mt. Canada **90** 50.51N 115.39W
Assynt *f.* Scotland **36** 58.12N 5.08W
Assynt, L. Scotland **36** 58.11N 5.03W
Asti Italy **40** 44.55N 8.13E
Aston Clinton England **27** 51.54N 0.39W
Astorga Spain **41** 42.30N 6.02W
Astoria U.S.A. **90** 46.12N 123.50W
Astrakhan U.S.S.R. **48** 46.22N 48.00E
Asuncion *i.* Asia **61** 19.34N 145.24E
Asunción Paraguay **103** 25.15S 57.40W
Aswân Egypt **56** 24.05N 32.56E
Aswân High Dam Egypt **56** 23.59N 32.54E
Asyût Egypt **56** 27.14N 31.07E
Atakpamé Togo **71** 7.34N 1.14E
Atar Mauritania **70** 20.32N 13.08W
Atbara Sudan **69** 17.42N 34.00E
Atbara *r.* Sudan **69** 17.47N 34.00E
Atchafalaya B. U.S.A. **91** 29.30N 92.00W
Ath Belgium **45** 50.38N 3.45E
Athabasca Canada **92** 54.44N 113.15W
Athabasca *r.* Canada **92** 58.30N 111.00W
Athabasca, L. Canada **92** 59.30N 109.00W
Athboy Rep. of Ire. **38** 53.38N 6.56W
Athea Rep. of Ire. **39** 52.28N 9.19W
Athenry Rep. of Ire. **38** 53.18N 8.45W
Athens Greece **43** 37.59N 23.42E
Athens U.S.A. **94** 39.20N 82.06W
Atherstone England **28** 52.35N 1.32W
Atherton England **32** 53.32N 2.30W
Athleague Rep. of Ire. **38** 53.34N 8.16W
Athlone Rep. of Ire. **38** 53.26N 7.57W
Áthos, Mt. Greece **43** 40.09N 24.19E
Athy Rep. of Ire. **39** 53.00N 7.00W
Atikokan Canada **94** 48.45N 91.38W
Atkarsk U.S.S.R. **47** 51.55N 45.00E
Atlanta U.S.A. **91** 33.45N 84.23W
Atlantic City U.S.A. **95** 39.23N 74.27W
Atlantic Ocean 106
Atlas Mts. Africa **106** 33.00N 4.00W
Atouguia Portugal **41** 39.20N 9.20W
Åtran *r.* Sweden **46** 56.54N 12.30E
Atrato *r.* Colombia **97** 8.15N 76.58W
Atrek *r.* Asia **57** 37.23N 54.00E
Attleboro U.S.A. **95** 41.57N 71.16W
Attleborough England **29** 52.31N 1.01E
Attopeu Laos **60** 14.51N 106.56E
Atuel *r.* Argentina **103** 36.15S 66.45W
Atura Uganda **73** 2.09N 32.22E
Aubagne France **40** 43.17N 5.35E
Aube *r.* France **40** 48.30N 3.37E
Aubigny-sur-Nère France **40** 47.29N 2.26E
Aubin France **40** 44.32N 2.14E
Auburn U.S.A. **95** 42.57N 76.34W
Auch France **40** 43.40N 0.36E
Auchinleck Scotland **34** 55.28N 4.17W
Auchterarder Scotland **35** 56.18N 3.43W
Auchtermuchty Scotland **35** 56.17N 3.15W
Auckland New Zealand **82** 36.55S 174.45E
Aude *r.* France **40** 43.13N 2.20E
Audlem England **32** 52.59N 2.31W
Audruicq France **29** 50.52N 2.05E
Augher N. Ireland **38** 54.26N 7.09W
Aughnacloy N. Ireland **38** 54.25N 7.00W
Augrabies Falls *f.* R.S.A. **74** 28.30S 20.16E
Augsburg W. Germany **44** 48.21N 10.54E
Augusta Ga. U.S.A. **91** 33.29N 82.00W
Augusta Maine U.S.A. **95** 44.17N 69.50W
Aulne *r.* France **40** 48.30N 4.11W
Aultbea Scotland **36** 57.50N 5.35W
Aumâle France **40** 49.46N 1.45E
Aurangabad India **58** 19.52N 75.22E
Aurich W. Germany **45** 53.28N 7.29E
Aurillac France **40** 44.56N 2.26E
Aurora U.S.A. **94** 41.45N 88.20W
Au Sable *r.* U.S.A. **94** 44.25N 83.20W
Au Sable Pt. U.S.A. **94** 44.21N 83.20W
Auskerry *i.* Scotland **37** 59.02N 2.34W
Austin Minn. U.S.A. **94** 43.40N 92.58W
Austin Texas U.S.A. **90** 30.18N 97.47W
Australasia 107
Australia Austa. **79**
Australian Alps *mts.* Australia **80** 36.30S 148.45E
Australian Antarctic Territory Antarctica **104** 73.00S 90.00E
Australian Capital Territory *d.* Australia **80** 35.30S 149.00E
Austria Europe **44** 47.30N 14.00E
Autun France **40** 46.58N 4.18E

For Khmer Republic *read* Kampuchea. *For* Malagasy Republic *read* Madagascar. *For* Rhodesia *read* Zimbabwe.

Auxerre France **40** 47.48N 3.35E
Auzances France **40** 46.02N 2.29E
Avallon France **40** 47.30N 3.54E
Avanos Turkey **56** 38.44N 34.51E
Aveley England **27** 51.31N 0.15E
Avellaneda Argentina **103** 34.42S 58.20W
Avellino Italy **42** 40.55N 14.46E
Avesnes France **45** 50.08N 3.57E
Avesta Sweden **46** 60.09N 16.10E
Aveyron r. France **40** 44.09N 1.10E
Avezzano Italy **42** 42.03N 13.26E
Aviemore Scotland **37** 57.12N 3.50W
Aviero Portugal **41** 40.40N 8.35W
Avignon France **40** 43.56N 4.48E
Avila Spain **41** 40.39N 4.42W
Avon d. England **28** 51.35N 2.40W
Avon r. Avon England **28** 51.30N 2.43W
Avon r. Devon England **31** 50.17N 3.52W
Avon r. Dorset England **28** 50.43N 1.45W
Avon r. Glos. England **28** 52.00N 2.10W
Avon r. Scotland **37** 57.25N 3.23W
Avonmouth England **28** 51.30N 2.42W
Avranches France **40** 48.42N 1.21W
Awaso Ghana **70** 6.20N 2.22W
Awatera r. New Zealand **82** 41.37S 174.09E
Awe, Loch Scotland **34** 56.18N 5.24W
Axe r. Devon England **31** 50.42N 3.03W
Axe r. Somerset England **28** 51.18N 3.00W
Axel Heiberg I. Canada **93** 79.30N 90.00W
Axim Ghana **70** 4.53N 2.14W
Axminster England **28** 50.47N 3.01W
Ayaguz U.S.S.R. **62** 47.59N 80.27E
Ayan U.S.S.R. **49** 56.29N 138.00E
Aycliffe England **33** 54.36N 1.34W
Aydin Turkey **56** 37.52N 27.50E
Áyios Evstrátios i. Greece **43** 39.30N 25.00E
Aylesbury England **28** 51.48N 0.49W
Aylesham England **29** 51.14N 1.12E
Aylsham England **29** 52.48N 1.16E
Ayr Scotland **34** 55.28N 4.37W
Ayr r. Scotland **34** 55.28N 4.38W
Ayre, Pt. of I.o.M. **32** 54.25N 4.22W
Aysgarth England **32** 54.18N 2.00W
Ayutthaya Thailand **59** 14.25N 100.30E
Ayvalik Turkey **43** 39.19N 26.42E
Azamgarh India **58** 26.03N 83.10E
Azare Nigeria **71** 11.40N 10.08E
Azbine mts. see AïrNiger **71**
Azerbaijan Soviet Socialist Republic d. U.S.S.R. **57**
    40.10N 47.50E
Azores is. Atlantic Oc. **112** 39.00N 30.00W
Azov, Sea of U.S.S.R. **47** 46.00N 36.30E
Azua Dom. Rep. **97** 18.29N 70.44W
Azuaga Spain **41** 38.16N 5.40W
Azuero Pen. Panamá **97** 7.30N 80.30W
Azul Argentina **103** 36.46S 59.50W
Azurduy Bolivia **103** 20.00S 64.29W

B

Ba'albek Lebanon **56** 34.00N 36.12E
Baarle-Hertog Neth. **45** 51.26N 4.56E
Babar Is. Indonesia **61** 8.00S 129.30E
Babbacombe B. England **31** 50.30N 3.28W
Babol Iran **57** 36.32N 52.42E
Baboua C.A.R. **71** 5.49N 14.51E
Babuyan Is. Phil. **61** 19.20N 121.30E
Babylon ruins Iraq **57** 32.33N 44.25E
Bacau Romania **47** 46.32N 26.59E
Baccarat France **44** 48.27N 6.45E
Back r. Canada **93** 66.37N 96.00W
Backnang W. Germany **44** 48.57N 9.26E
Bacolod Phil. **61** 10.38N 122.58E
Bacton England **29** 52.50N 1.29E
Bacup England **32** 53.42N 2.12W
Badajoz Spain **41** 38.53N 6.58W
Badalona Spain **41** 41.27N 2.15E
Baden Austria **44** 48.01N 16.14E
Baden-Baden W. Germany **44** 48.45N 8.15E
Badenoch f. Scotland **37** 57.00N 4.10W
Badgastein Austria **44** 47.07N 13.09E
Bad Ischl Austria **44** 47.43N 13.38E
Bad Kreuznach W. Germany **45** 49.51N 7.52E
Baffin B. Canada **93** 74.00N 70.00W
Baffin I. Canada **93** 68.50N 70.00W
Bafia Cameroon **71** 4.39N 11.14E
Bafing r. Mali **70** 14.48N 12.00W
Bafoulabé Mali **70** 13.49N 10.50W
Bafq Iran **57** 31.35N 55.21E
Bafra Turkey **56** 41.34N 35.56E
Bafwasende Zaïre **73** 1.09N 27.12E
Bagamoyo Tanzania **73** 6.26S 38.55E
Bagé Brazil **103** 31.22S 54.06W

Baggy Pt. England **31** 51.08N 4.15W
Baghdad Iraq **57** 33.20N 44.26E
Baghelkhand f. India **58** 24.20N 82.00E
Bagh nam Faoileann str. Scotland **36** 57.23N 7.15W
Baghrash Köl l. China **62** 42.00N 87.00E
Bagoé r. Mali **70** 12.34N 6.30W
Bagshot England **27** 51.22N 0.42W
Baguio Phil. **61** 16.25N 120.37E
Bahama Is. C. America **106** 25.00N 77.00W
Bahamas C. America **97** 23.30N 75.00W
Bahao Kalat Iran **57** 25.42N 61.28E
Bahawalpur Pakistan **58** 29.24N 71.47E
Bahbah Algeria **41** 35.04N 3.05E
Bahía Blanca Argentina **103** 38.45S 62.15W
Bahraich India **58** 27.35N 81.36E
Bahrain Asia **57** 26.00N 50.35E
Bahramabad Iran **58** 30.24N 56.00E
Bahr Aouk r. C.A.R. **71** 8.50N 18.50E
Bahr el Ghazal r. Chad **71** 12.26N 15.25E
Bahr el Ghazal r. Sudan **69** 9.30N 31.30E
Bahr el Jebel r. Sudan **69** 9.30N 30.20E
Bahr Salamat r. Chad **71** 9.30N 18.10E
Baie Comeau Canada **91** 49.12N 68.10W
Baie St. Paul Canada **95** 47.27N 70.30W
Baikal, L. U.S.S.R. **82** 53.00N 108.00E
Bailieborough Rep. of Ire. **38** 53.55N 6.59W
Bailleul France **45** 50.44N 2.44E
Bain r. England **33** 53.05N 0.12W
Baing Indonesia **61** 10.15S 120.34E
Bairnsdale Australia **80** 37.51S 147.38E
Baise r. France **40** 44.15N 0.20E
Baja Hungary **43** 46.12N 18.58E
Bakali r. Zaïre **72** 3.58S 17.10E
Bakel Senegal **70** 14.54N 12.26W
Baker Mont. U.S.A. **90** 46.23N 104.16W
Baker Oreg. U.S.A. **90** 44.46N 117.50W
Baker, Mt. U.S.A. **90** 48.48N 121.10W
Bakersfield U.S.A. **90** 35.25N 119.00W
Bakewell England **32** 53.13N 1.40W
Baku U.S.S.R. **57** 40.22N 49.53E
Bala Wales **30** 52.54N 3.36W
Balabac Str. Asia **60** 7.30N 117.00E
Balallan Scotland **36** 58.25N 6.36W
Balama Moçambique **73** 13.19S 38.35E
Bala Murghab Afghan. **57** 35.34N 63.20E
Balashov U.S.S.R. **47** 51.30N 43.10E
Balasore India **59** 21.31N 86.59E
Balaton, L. Hungary **47** 46.55N 17.50E
Balboa Panama Canal Zone **97** 8.37N 79.33W
Balbriggan Rep. of Ire. **38** 53.36N 6.12W
Balchik Bulgaria **43** 43.24N 28.10E
Balclutha New Zealand **82** 46.16S 169.46E
Baldock England **29** 51.59N 0.11W
Balearic Is. Spain **41** 39.30N 2.30E
Balerno Scotland **35** 55.53N 3.10W
Baleshare i. Scotland **36** 57.32N 7.22W
Balfron Scotland **34** 56.04N 4.20W
Bali i. Indonesia **60** 8.30S 115.05E
Balikesir Turkey **43** 39.38N 27.51E
Balikpapan Indonesia **60** 1.15S 116.50E
Balkan Mts. Bulgaria **43** 42.50N 24.30E
Balkhan Range mts. U.S.S.R. **57** 39.38N 54.30E
Balkhash U.S.S.R. **62** 46.51N 75.00E
Balkhash, L. U.S.S.R. **62** 46.40N 75.00E
Balla Rep. of Ire. **38** 53.48N 9.08W
Ballachulish Scotland **34** 56.40N 5.08W
Ballagan Pt. Rep. of Ire. **38** 54.00N 6.07W
Ballaghaderreen Rep. of Ire. **38** 53.54N 8.36W
Ballantrae Scotland **34** 55.06N 5.01W
Ballarat Australia **80** 37.36S 143.58E
Ballater Scotland **37** 57.03N 3.03W
Ballenas B. Mexico **96** 26.40N 113.30W
Ballia India **58** 25.45N 84.09E
Ballickmoyler Rep. of Ire. **39** 52.52N 7.00W
Ballina Rep. of Ire. **38** 54.07N 9.10W
Ballinakill Rep. of Ire. **39** 52.53N 7.20W
Ballinamore Rep. of Ire. **38** 54.03N 7.50W
Ballinasloe Rep. of Ire. **38** 53.20N 8.15W
Ballincollig Rep. of Ire. **39** 51.53N 8.36W
Ballinderry r. N. Ireland **34** 54.40N 6.32W
Ballindine Rep. of Ire. **38** 53.40N 8.58W
Ballingarry Limerick Rep. of Ire. **39** 52.28N 8.51W
Ballingarry Tipperary Rep. of Ire. **39** 53.02N 8.02W
Ballingeary Rep. of Ire. **39** 51.50N 9.15W
Ballinhassig Rep. of Ire. **39** 51.48N 8.32W
Ballinlough Rep. of Ire. **38** 53.44N 8.40W
Ballinrobe Rep. of Ire. **38** 53.38N 9.15W
Ballinskelligs B. Rep. of Ire. **39** 51.48N 10.13W
Ballivor Rep. of Ire. **38** 53.31N 6.57W
Balloch Scotland **34** 56.00N 4.36W
Ballybay Rep. of Ire. **38** 54.08N 6.56W
Ballybunion Rep. of Ire. **39** 52.30N 9.40W
Ballycanew Rep. of Ire. **39** 52.36N 6.19W
Ballycarney Rep. of Ire. **39** 52.34N 6.35W
Ballycastle N. Ireland **34** 55.12N 6.15W
Ballyclare N. Ireland **34** 54.45N 6.00W

Ballyconnell Rep. of Ire. **38** 54.06N 7.37W
Ballydehob Rep. of Ire. **39** 51.34N 9.28W
Ballydonegan Rep. of Ire. **39** 51.38N 10.04W
Ballygar Rep. of Ire. **38** 53.32N 8.20W
Ballygawley N. Ireland **38** 54.28N 7.03W
Ballyhaunis Rep. of Ire. **38** 53.45N 8.47W
Ballyhoura Mts. Rep. of Ire. **39** 52.18N 8.31W
Ballyjamesduff Rep. of Ire. **38** 53.52N 7.47W
Ballykelly N. Ireland **34** 55.03N 7.00W
Ballymahon Rep. of Ire. **38** 53.33N 7.47W
Ballymena N. Ireland **34** 54.52N 6.17W
Ballymoe Rep. of Ire. **38** 53.41N 8.29W
Ballymoney N. Ireland **34** 55.04N 6.31W
Ballymore Rep. of Ire. **38** 53.30N 7.42W
Ballymote Rep. of Ire. **38** 54.06N 8.31W
Ballynahinch N. Ireland **38** 54.24N 5.53W
Ballynakill Harbour est. Rep. of Ire. **38** 53.34N 10.20W
Ballyquintin Pt. N. Ireland **38** 54.40N 5.30W
Ballyragget Rep. of Ire. **39** 52.47N 7.21W
Ballyshannon Rep. of Ire. **38** 54.30N 8.11W
Ballyvaughan Rep. of Ire. **39** 53.06N 9.09W
Ballyvourney Rep. of Ire. **39** 51.57N 9.10W
Ballywalter N. Ireland **34** 54.33N 5.30W
Balranald Australia **80** 34.37S 143.37E
Balsas r. Mexico **96** 18.10N 102.05W
Balta i. Scotland **36** 60.44N 0.46W
Baltasound Scotland **36** 60.45N 0.52W
Baltic Sea Europe **46** 56.30N 19.00E
Baltic Shield f. Europe **107** 63.00N 30.00E
Baltimore U.S.A. **95** 39.18N 76.38W
Baltinglass Rep. of Ire. **39** 52.56N 6.43W
Baltiysk U.S.S.R. **46** 54.41N 19.59E
Baluchistan f. Pakistan **58** 28.00N 66.00E
Bam Iran **57** 29.07N 58.20E
Bamako Mali **70** 12.40N 7.59W
Bamba Mali **70** 17.05N 1.23W
Ba-Mbassa r. Chad **71** 11.30N 15.30E
Bamberg W. Germany **44** 49.54N 10.53E
Bambesa Zaïre **72** 3.27N 25.43E
Bambili Zaïre **72** 3.34N 26.07E
Bamburgh England **35** 55.36N 1.41W
Bamenda Cameroon **71** 5.55N 10.09E
Bamenda Highlands Cameroon **71** 6.20N 10.20E
Bampton Devon England **28** 51.00N 3.29W
Bampton Oxon. England **28** 51.44N 1.33W
Bampur Iran **57** 27.13N 60.29E
Bampur r. Iran **57** 27.18N 59.02E
Banagher Rep. of Ire. **39** 53.12N 8.00W
Banalia Zaïre **72** 1.33N 25.23E
Banana Zaïre **72** 5.55S 12.27E
Banbasa Nepal **59** 29.00N 80.28E
Banbridge N. Ireland **38** 54.21N 6.17W
Banbury England **28** 52.04N 1.21W
Banchory Scotland **37** 57.03N 2.30W
Banda Gabon **72** 3.47S 11.04E
Banda India **58** 25.28N 80.25E
Banda i. Indonesia **61** 4.30S 129.55E
Banda Atjeh Indonesia **60** 5.35N 95.20E
Bandama r. Ivory Coast **70** 5.10N 4.59W
Bandar India **59** 16.13N 81.12E
Bandar Abbas Iran **57** 27.10N 56.15E
Bandar Dilam Iran **57** 30.05N 50.11E
Bandar-e-Lengeh Iran **57** 26.34N 54.53E
Bandar-e-Pahlavi Iran **57** 37.26N 49.29E
Bandar-e-Shah Iran **57** 36.55N 54.05E
Bandar Rig Iran **57** 29.30N 50.40E
Bandar Seri Begawan Brunei **60** 4.56N 114.58E
Bandar Shahpur Iran **57** 30.26N 49.03E
Banda Sea Indonesia **61** 5.00S 128.00E
Bandawe Malawi **73** 11.57S 34.11E
Bandirma Turkey **43** 40.22N 28.00E
Bandon Rep. of Ire. **39** 51.45N 8.45W
Bandon r. Rep. of Ire. **39** 51.43N 8.38W
Bandundu Zaïre **72** 3.20S 17.24E
Bandundu d. Zaïre **72** 4.00S 18.30E
Bandung Indonesia **60** 6.57S 107.34E
Banes Cuba **97** 20.59N 75.24W
Banff Canada **90** 51.10N 115.54W
Banff Scotland **37** 57.40N 2.31W
Bangalore India **58** 12.58N 77.35E
Bangangté Cameroon **72** 5.09N 10.29E
Bangassou C.A.R. **72** 4.41N 22.52E
Banggai Is. Indonesia **61** 1.30S 123.10E
Bangka i. Indonesia **60** 2.20S 106.10E
Bangkok Thailand **59** 13.45N 100.35E
Bangladesh Asia **58** 24.30N 90.00E
Bangor N. Ireland **34** 54.40N 5.41W
Bangor Rep. of Ire. **38** 54.09N 9.44W
Bangor U.S.A. **95** 44.49N 68.47W
Bangor Wales **30** 53.13N 4.09W
Bangui C.A.R. **71** 4.23N 18.37E
Bangweulu, L. Zambia **73** 11.15S 29.45E
Ban Hat Yai Thailand **60** 7.00N 100.28E
Ban Houei Sai Laos **59** 20.21N 100.26E
Bani r. Mali **70** 14.30N 4.15W
Banjak Is. Indonesia **60** 2.15N 97.10E

Banja Luka Yugo. **43** 44.47N 17.10E
Banjarmasin Indonesia **60** 3.22S 114.36E
Banjul Gambia **70** 13.28N 16.39W
Ban Kantang Thailand **59** 7.25N 99.30E
Bankfoot Scotland **35** 56.30N 3.32W
Banks I. Australia **61** 10.15S 142.15E
Banks I. Canada **92** 73.00N 122.00W
Banks Pen. New Zealand **82** 43.45S 173.10E
Banks Str. Australia **80** 40.37S 148.07E
Bankura India **58** 23.14N 87.05E
Ban Me Thuot Vietnam **60** 12.41N 108.02E
Bann *r.* N. Ireland **34** 55.10N 6.46W
Bann *r.* Rep. of Ire. **39** 52.33N 6.33W
Bannockburn Rhodesia **74** 20.16S 29.51E
Bannockburn Scotland **35** 56.06N 3.55W
Bannow B. Rep. of Ire. **39** 52.14N 6.48W
Bansha Rep. of Ire. **39** 52.26N 8.04W
Banstead England **27** 51.19N 0.12W
Bantry Rep. of Ire. **39** 51.41N 9.27W
Bantry B. Rep. of Ire. **39** 51.40N 9.40W
Banwy *r.* Wales **30** 52.41N 3.16W
Banyo Cameroon **71** 6.47N 11.50E
Banyuwangi Indonesia **60** 8.12S 114.22E
Baoulé *r.* Mali **70** 13.47N 10.45W
Bapaume France **45** 50.07N 2.51E
Bar Albania **43** 42.05N 19.06E
Bara Banki India **58** 26.56N 81.11E
Baracoa Cuba **97** 20.23N 74.31W
Baradine Australia **80** 30.56S 149.05E
Barahona Dom. Rep. **97** 18.13N 71.07W
Baranof I. U.S.A. **92** 57.05N 135.00W
Baranovichi U.S.S.R. **47** 53.09N 26.00E
Barbacena Brazil **103** 21.13S 43.47W
Barbados C. America **97** 13.20N 59.40W
Barbastro Spain **41** 42.02N 0.07E
Barberton R.S.A. **74** 25.48S 31.03E
Barberton U.S.A. **94** 41.02N 81.37W
Barbezieux France **40** 45.28N 0.09W
Barbuda C. America **97** 17.41N 61.48W
Barcaldine Australia **79** 23.31S 145.15E
Barcellona Italy **42** 38.10N 15.13E
Barcelona Spain **41** 41.25N 2.10E
Barcelona Venezuela **97** 10.08N 64.43W
Bardai Chad **71** 21.21N 16.56E
Bardera Somali Rep. **73** 2.18N 42.18E
Bardi India **58** 24.30N 82.28E
Bardia Libya **56** 31.44N 25.08E
Bardney England **33** 53.13N 0.19W
Bardsey *i.* Wales **30** 52.45N 4.48W
Bardsey Sd. Wales **30** 52.45N 4.48W
Bardu Norway **46** 68.54N 18.20E
Bareilly India **58** 28.20N 79.24E
Barents Sea Arctic Oc. **48** 73.00N 40.00E
Bari Italy **43** 41.08N 16.52E
Barika Algeria **42** 35.25N 5.19E
Barinas Venezuela **97** 8.36N 70.15W
Barisal Bangla. **58** 22.41N 90.20E
Barisan Range *mts.* Indonesia **60** 3.30S 102.30E
Barito *r.* Indonesia **60** 3.35S 114.35E
Bariz Kuh, Jebel *mts.* Iran **57** 28.40N 58.10E
Barking *d.* England **27** 51.32N 0.05E
Barkly West R.S.A. **74** 28.32S 24.32E
Barle *r.* England **31** 51.00N 3.31W
Bar-le-Duc France **40** 48.46N 5.10E
Barletta Italy **42** 41.20N 16.15E
Barmouth Wales **30** 52.44N 4.03W
Barnard Castle *town* England **32** 54.33N 1.55W
Barnaul U.S.S.R. **48** 53.21N 83.15E
Barnes England **27** 51.28N 0.15W
Barnet England **27** 51.39N 0.11W
Barneveld Neth. **45** 52.10N 5.39E
Barnoldswick England **32** 53.55N 2.11W
Barnsley England **33** 53.33N 1.29W
Barnstaple England **31** 51.05N 4.03W
Barnstaple B. England **31** 51.04N 4.20W
Baro Nigeria **71** 8.37N 6.19E
Baroda India **58** 22.19N 73.14E
Barquisimeto Venezuela **97** 10.03N 69.18W
Barra *i.* Scotland **36** 56.59N 7.28W
Barra, Sd. of Scotland **36** 57.04N 7.20W
Barra do Pirai Brazil **103** 22.30S 43.50W
Barra Head Scotland **36** 56.47N 7.36W
Barrancabermeja Colombia **97** 7.06N 73.54W
Barranquilla Colombia **97** 11.00N 74.50W
Barreiro Portugal **41** 38.40N 9.05W
Barrhead Scotland **34** 55.47N 4.24W
Barrie Canada **95** 44.22N 79.42W
Barrington, Mt. Australia **80** 32.03S 151.55E
Barrow *r.* Rep. of Ire. **39** 52.17N 7.00W
Barrow U.S.A. **92** 71.16N 156.50W
Barrow I. Australia **79** 21.40S 115.27E
Barrow-in-Furness England **32** 54.08N 3.15W
Barry Wales **31** 51.23N 3.19W
Barstow U.S.A. **90** 34.55N 117.01W
Bar-sur-Aube France **40** 48.14N 4.43E
Bartin Turkey **56** 41.37N 32.20E

Bartolomeu Dias Moçambique **74** 21.10S 35.09E
Barton on Sea England **28** 50.44N 1.40W
Barton-upon-Humber England **33** 53.41N 0.27W
Barvas Scotland **36** 58.21N 6.31W
Barwon *r.* Australia **80** 30.00S 148.03E
Basankusu Zaïre **72** 1.12N 19.50E
Basel Switz. **44** 47.33N 7.36E
Bashi Channel Asia **63** 21.40N 121.20E
Basilan *i.* Phil. **61** 6.40N 122.10E
Basildon England **27** 51.34N 0.25E
Basingstoke England **28** 51.15N 1.05W
Baskatong L. Canada **95** 46.50N 75.46W
Basoko Zaïre **72** 1.20N 23.36E
Basongo Zaïre **72** 4.23S 20.28E
Basra Iraq **57** 30.33N 47.50E
Bassein Burma **60** 16.45N 94.30E
Bass Rock *i.* Scotland **35** 56.05N 2.38W
Bass Str. Australia **80** 39.45S 146.00E
Bastak Iran **57** 27.15N 54.26E
Bastelica France **40** 42.00N 9.03E
Basti India **58** 26.48N 82.44E
Bastia France **40** 42.41N 9.26E
Bastogne Belgium **45** 50.00N 5.43E
Bas Zaïre *d.* Zaïre **72** 5.15S 14.00E
Bata Equat. Guinea **72** 1.51N 9.49E
Batabanó, G. of Cuba **96** 23.15N 82.30W
Batangas Phil. **61** 13.46N 121.01E
Batan Is. Phil. **61** 20.50N 121.55E
Batchawana Mtn. Canada **94** 46.54N 84.36W
Bath England **28** 51.22N 2.22W
Bath U.S.A. **95** 43.56N 69.50W
Batha *r.* Chad **71** 12.47N 17.34E
Batha, Wadi *r.* Oman **57** 20.01N 59.39E
Bathgate Scotland **35** 55.44N 3.38W
Bathurst Australia **80** 33.27S 149.35E
Bathurst Canada **91** 47.38N 65.40W
Bathurst, C. Canada **92** 70.30N 128.00W
Bathurst I. Australia **79** 11.45S 130.15E
Bathurst I. Canada **93** 76.00N 100.00W
Bathurst Inlet *town* Canada **92** 66.48N 108.00W
Batinah *f.* Oman **57** 24.25N 56.50E
Batjan *i.* Indonesia **61** 0.30S 127.30E
Batley England **32** 53.43N 1.38W
Batna Algeria **42** 35.35N 6.11E
Baton Rouge U.S.A. **91** 30.30N 91.10W
Batouri Cameroon **71** 4.26N 14.27E
Battambang Khmer Rep. **59** 13.06N 103.13E
Battersea England **27** 51.28N 0.10W
Batticaloa Sri Lanka **59** 7.43N 81.42E
Battle England **29** 50.55N 0.30E
Battle Creek *town* U.S.A. **94** 42.20N 85.10W
Battle Harbour Canada **93** 52.16N 55.36W
Battock, Mt. Scotland **37** 56.57N 2.44W
Batu Is. Indonesia **60** 0.30S 98.20E
Batumi U.S.S.R. **56** 41.37N 41.36E
Baturadja Indonesia **60** 4.10S 104.10E
Bauchi Nigeria **71** 10.16N 9.50E
Bauchi *d.* Nigeria **71** 10.40N 10.00E
Baugé France **40** 47.33N 0.06W
Bauld, C. Canada **93** 51.30N 55.45W
Bauru Brazil **103** 22.19S 49.07W
Bautzen E. Germany **44** 51.11N 14.29E
Bavay France **45** 50.18N 3.48E
Bawdsey England **29** 52.01N 1.27E
Bawean *i.* Indonesia **60** 5.50S 112.35E
Bawiti Egypt **56** 28.21N 28.51E
Bawtry England **33** 53.25N 1.01W
Bayamo Cuba **97** 20.23N 76.39W
Bayan Kara Shan *mts.* China **62** 34.00N 97.20E
Bayburt Turkey **56** 40.15N 40.16E
Bay City U.S.A. **94** 43.35N 83.52W
Baydaratskaya B. U.S.S.R. **48** 70.00N 66.00E
Bayeux France **40** 49.16N 0.42W
Bay Is. Honduras **96** 16.10N 86.30W
Bayonne France **40** 43.30N 1.28W
Bayonne U.S.A. **95** 40.39N 74.08W
Bayreuth W. Germany **44** 49.56N 11.35E
Baza Spain **41** 37.30N 2.45W
Bazman Kuh *mtn.* Iran **57** 28.06N 60.00E
Beachport Australia **80** 37.29S 140.01E
Beachy Head England **29** 50.43N 0.15E
Beacon Hill England **28** 51.12N 1.42W
Beacon Hill Wales **30** 52.23N 3.14W
Beaconsfield England **27** 51.37N 0.39W
Beaminster England **28** 50.48N 2.44W
Beare Green England **27** 51.10N 0.18W
Bear I. Rep. of Ire. **39** 51.38N 9.52W
Bearsden Scotland **34** 55.56N 4.20W
Bearsted England **27** 51.17N 0.35E
Beaufort Sea N. America **92** 72.00N 141.00W
Beaufort West R.S.A. **74** 32.21S 22.35E
Beauly Scotland **37** 57.29N 4.29W
Beauly *r.* Scotland **37** 57.29N 4.25W
Beauly Firth *est.* Scotland **37** 57.29N 4.20W
Beaumaris Wales **30** 53.16N 4.07W
Beaumont Belgium **45** 50.14N 4.16E

Beaumont U.S.A. **91** 30.04N 94.06W
Beaune France **40** 47.02N 4.50E
Beauvais France **40** 49.26N 2.05E
Beaver I. U.S.A. **94** 45.40N 85.35W
Beawar India **58** 26.02N 74.20E
Bebington England **32** 53.23N 3.01W
Beccles England **29** 52.27N 1.33E
Béchar Algeria **68** 31.35N 2.17W
Beckenham England **27** 51.24N 0.01W
Beckum W. Germany **45** 51.45N 8.02E
Bedale England **33** 54.18N 1.35W
Bédarieux France **40** 43.35N 3.10E
Beddgelert England **27** 51.22N 0.08W
Bedford England **29** 52.08N 0.29W
Bedford U.S.A. **94** 38.51N 86.30W
Bedford Levels *f.* England **29** 52.35N 0.08E
Bedfordshire *d.* England **29** 52.04N 0.28W
Bedlington England **35** 55.08N 1.34W
Bedwas Wales **31** 51.36N 3.10W
Bedwellty Wales **31** 51.42N 3.13W
Bedworth England **28** 52.28N 1.29W
Bee, Loch Scotland **36** 57.23N 7.22W
Beenoskee *mtn.* Rep. of Ire. **39** 52.47N 10.04W
Beersheba Israel **56** 31.15N 34.47E
Beeston England **33** 52.55N 1.11W
Beeville U.S.A. **90** 28.25N 97.47W
Befale Zaïre **72** 0.27N 21.01E
Beg, Lough N. Ireland **34** 54.47N 6.29W
Bega Australia **80** 36.41S 149.50E
Begna *r.* Norway **46** 60.06N 10.15E
Behbehan Iran **57** 30.35N 50.17E
Beida Libya **69** 32.50N 21.50E
Beilen Neth. **45** 52.51N 6.31E
Beinn à Ghlò *mtn.* Scotland **37** 56.50N 3.42W
Beinn an Tuirc *mtn.* Scotland **34** 55.24N 5.33W
Beinn Bheigeir *mtn.* Scotland **34** 55.44N 6.08W
Beinn Dearg *mtn.* Scotland **37** 57.47N 4.55W
Beinn Dhorain *mtn.* Scotland **37** 58.07N 3.50W
Beinn Mhor *mtn.* Scotland **36** 57.59N 6.40W
Beinn nam Bad Mor *mtn.* Scotland **37** 58.29N 3.43W
Beinn Resipol *mtn.* Scotland **36** 56.43N 6.38W
Beinn Sgritheall *mtn.* Scotland **36** 57.09N 5.34W
Beinn Tharsuinn *mtn.* Scotland **37** 57.47N 4.21W
Beira Moçambique **74** 19.49S 34.52E
Beirut Lebanon **56** 33.52N 35.30E
Beitbridge Rhodesia **74** 22.10S 30.01E
Beith Scotland **34** 55.45N 4.37W
Béja Tunisia **42** 36.44N 9.12E
Beja Portugal **41** 38.01N 7.52W
Bejaïa Algeria **42** 36.45N 5.05E
Béjar Spain **41** 40.24N 5.45W
Bejestan Iran **57** 34.32N 58.08E
Bela India **58** 25.55N 82.00E
Bela Pakistan **58** 26.12N 66.20E
Belalcázar Spain **41** 38.35N 5.10W
Belang Indonesia **61** 0.58N 124.56E
Bela Vista Brazil **103** 22.05S 56.22W
Bela Vista Moçambique **74** 26.20S 32.40E
Belaya *r.* U.S.S.R. **48** 55.40N 52.30E
Belcher Is. Canada **93** 56.00N 79.00W
Belcoo N. Ireland **38** 54.18N 7.53W
Belém Brazil **102** 1.27S 48.29W
Belen U.S.A. **90** 34.39N 106.48W
Belet Wen Somali Rep. **73** 4.38N 45.12E
Belfast N. Ireland **34** 54.36N 5.57W
Belfast Lough N. Ireland **34** 54.42N 5.45W
Belford England **35** 55.36N 1.48W
Belfort France **44** 47.38N 6.52E
Belgaum India **58** 15.54N 74.36E
Belgium Europe **45** 51.00N 4.30E
Belgorod U.S.S.R. **47** 50.38N 36.36E
Belgorod Dnestrovskiy U.S.S.R. **47** 46.10N 30.19E
Belgrade Yugo. **43** 44.49N 20.28E
Belikh *r.* Syria **56** 35.58N 39.05E
Belitung *i.* Indonesia **60** 3.00S 108.00E
Belize Belize **96** 17.29N 88.20W
Belize C. America **96** 17.00N 88.30W
Bellac France **40** 46.07N 1.04E
Bellary India **58** 15.11N 76.54E
Belleek N. Ireland **38** 54.29N 8.06W
Belle Île France **40** 47.20N 3.10W
Belle Isle Str. Canada **93** 50.45N 58.00W
Bellerive Australia **80** 42.52S 147.21E
Belleville Canada **95** 44.10N 77.22W
Belleville U.S.A. **94** 38.31N 89.59W
Bellingham England **35** 55.09N 2.15W
Bellingham U.S.A. **90** 48.45N 122.29W
Bellingshausen Sea Antarctica **106** 70.00S 84.00W
Bello Colombia **97** 6.20N 75.41W
Bell Rock *i. see* Inchcape Rock
Bell Ville Argentina **103** 32.35S 62.41W
Belmopan Belize **96** 17.25N 88.46W
Belmullet Rep. of Ire. **38** 54.14N 10.00W
Belo Horizonte Brazil **103** 19.45S 43.54W
Beloit U.S.A. **94** 42.31N 89.04W
Beloye, L. U.S.S.R. **47** 60.12N 37.45E

For Khmer Republic read Kampuchea. For Malagasy Republic read Madagascar. For Rhodesia read Zimbabwe.

Belozersk U.S.S.R. **47** 60.00N 37.49E
Belper England **33** 53.02N 1.29W
Beltra, Lough Rep. of Ire. **38** 53.56N 9.26W
Beltsy U.S.S.R. **47** 47.45N 27.59E
Belturbet Rep. of Ire. **38** 54.06N 7.27W
Belukha, Mt. U.S.S.R. **62** 49.46N 86.40E
Belvedere England **27** 51.30N 0.10E
Bembridge England **28** 50.41N 1.04W
Bemidji U.S.A. **91** 47.29N 94.52W
Ben Alder mtn. Scotland **37** 56.49N 4.28W
Benalla Australia **80** 36.35S 145.58E
Benavente Spain **41** 42.00N 5.40W
Ben Avon mtn. Scotland **37** 57.06N 3.27W
Benbane Head N. Ireland **34** 55.15N 6.29W
Benbecula i. Scotland **36** 57.26N 7.18W
Benbulbin mtn. Rep. of Ire. **38** 54.22N 8.28W
Ben Chonzie mtn. Scotland **35** 56.27N 4.00W
Ben Cruachan mtn. Scotland **34** 56.26N 5.18W
Bend U.S.A. **90** 44.04N 121.20W
Bendel d. Nigeria **71** 6.10N 6.00E
Bendigo Australia **80** 36.48S 144.21E
Beneraird mtn. Scotland **34** 55.04N 4.56W
Benevento Italy **42** 41.07N 14.46E
Bengal d. India **58** 23.00N 88.00E
Bengal, B. of Indian Oc. **59** 17.00N 89.00E
Benghazi Libya **68** 32.07N 20.05E
Bengkulu Indonesia **60** 3.46S 102.16E
Ben Griam More mtn. Scotland **37** 58.20N 4.02W
Benguela Angola **72** 12.34S 13.24E
Benguela d. Angola **72** 12.45S 14.00E
Ben Hee mtn. Scotland **37** 58.16N 4.41W
Ben Hiant mtn. Scotland **34** 56.42N 6.01W
Ben Hope mtn. Scotland **37** 58.24N 4.36W
Ben Horn mtn. Scotland **37** 58.07N 4.02W
Ben Hutig mtn. Scotland **37** 58.33N 4.31W
Beni d. Bolivia **103** 15.50S 65.00W
Beni Zaïre **73** 0.29N 29.27E
Benicarló Spain **41** 40.25N 0.25E
Benin Africa **71** 9.00N 2.30E
Benin, Bight of Africa **71** 5.30N 3.00E
Benin City Nigeria **71** 6.19N 5.41E
Beni-Saf Algeria **41** 35.28N 1.22W
Beni Suef Egypt **56** 29.05N 31.05E
Ben Klibreck mtn. Scotland **37** 58.15N 4.22W
Ben Lawers mtn. Scotland **34** 56.33N 4.14W
Benllech Wales **30** 53.18N 4.15W
Ben Lomond mtn. Scotland **34** 56.12N 4.38W
Ben Lomond mtn. Australia **80** 30.04S 151.43E
Ben Loyal mtn. Scotland **37** 58.24N 4.26W
Ben Lui mtn. Scotland **34** 56.23N 4.49W
Ben Macdhui mtn. Scotland **37** 57.04N 3.40W
Ben More mtn. Central Scotland **34** 56.23N 4.31W
Ben More mtn. Strath. Scotland **34** 56.26N 6.02W
Ben More Assynt mtn. Scotland **37** 58.07N 4.52W
Bennane Head Scotland **34** 55.08N 5.00W
Bennettsbridge Rep. of Ire. **39** 52.35N 7.11W
Ben Nevis mtn. Scotland **36** 56.48N 5.00W
Benoni R.S.A. **74** 26.12S 28.18E
Ben Rinnes mtn. Scotland **37** 57.24N 3.15W
Benton Harbor U.S.A. **94** 42.07N 86.27W
Benue d. Nigeria **71** 7.20N 8.00E
Benue r. Nigeria **71** 7.52N 6.45E
Ben Vorlich mtn. Scotland **34** 56.21N 4.13W
Benwee Head Rep. of Ire. **38** 54.21N 9.48W
Ben Wyvis mtn. Scotland **37** 57.40N 4.35W
Beragh N. Ireland **34** 54.34N 7.10W
Berat Albania **43** 40.42N 19.59E
Berbera Somali Rep. **69** 10.28N 45.02E
Berbérati C.A.R. **71** 4.19N 15.51E
Berchem Belgium **45** 50.48N 3.32E
Berdichev U.S.S.R. **47** 49.54N 28.39E
Berdyansk U.S.S.R. **47** 46.45N 36.47E
Berens r. Canada **91** 52.25N 97.00W
Berezniki U.S.S.R. **48** 59.26N 57.00E
Bergama Turkey **43** 39.08N 27.10E
Bergamo Italy **40** 45.42N 9.40E
Bergen Norway **46** 60.23N 5.20E
Bergen op Zoom Neth. **45** 51.30N 4.17E
Bergerac France **40** 44.50N 0.29E
Bergheim W. Germany **45** 50.58N 6.39E
Bergisch Gladbach W. Germany **45** 50.59N 7.10E
Berhampore India **58** 24.06N 88.18E
Berhampur India **59** 19.21N 84.51E
Bering Sea N. America/Asia **92** 65.00N 170.00W
Bering Str. U.S.S.R./U.S.A. **92** 65.00N 170.00W
Berkel r. Neth. **45** 52.10N 6.12E
Berkhamsted England **27** 51.46N 0.35W
Berkshire d. England **28** 51.25N 1.03W
Berkshire Downs hills England **28** 51.32N 1.36W
Berlin E. Germany **44** 52.32N 13.25E
Berlin U.S.A. **95** 44.27N 71.13W
Bermagui Australia **80** 36.28S 150.03E
Bermejo r. Argentina **103** 26.47S 58.30W
Bermondsey England **27** 51.30N 0.04W
Bermuda Atlantic Oc. **97** 32.18N 64.45W
Bernburg E. Germany **44** 51.49N 11.44E

Berne Switz. **44** 46.57N 7.26E
Berneray i. W. Isles Scotland **36** 56.47N 7.38W
Berneray i. W. Isles Scotland **36** 57.43N 7.11W
Bernina mtn. Italy/Switz. **42** 46.22N 9.57E
Bernkastel W. Germany **45** 49.55N 7.05E
Berri Australia **80** 34.17S 140.36E
Berriedale Scotland **37** 58.11N 3.30W
Berry Head England **31** 50.24N 3.28W
Bertnaghboy B. Rep. of Ire. **38** 53.23N 9.52W
Bertoua Cameroon **71** 4.34N 13.42E
Berwick-upon-Tweed England **35** 55.46N 2.00W
Berwyn mts. Wales **30** 52.55N 3.25W
Besalampy Malagasy Rep. **73** 16.53S 44.29E
Besançon France **44** 47.14N 6.02E
Bessarabia f. U.S.S.R. **47** 46.30N 28.40E
Betanzos Spain **41** 43.17N 8.13W
Bétaré Oya Cameroon **71** 5.34N 14.09E
Bethal R.S.A. **74** 26.27S 29.28E
Bethersden England **29** 51.08N 0.46E
Bethesda Wales **30** 53.11N 4.03W
Bethlehem R.S.A. **74** 28.15S 28.19E
Bethlehem U.S.A. **95** 40.36N 75.22W
Bethnal Green England **27** 51.32N 0.03W
Béthune France **45** 50.32N 2.38E
Bettyhill Scotland **37** 58.30N 4.14W
Betwa r. India **58** 25.48N 80.10E
Betws-y-Coed Wales **30** 53.05N 3.48W
Beult r. England **27** 51.13N 0.26E
Beverley England **33** 53.52N 0.26W
Beverly U.S.A. **95** 42.35N 70.52W
Beverwijk Neth. **45** 52.29N 4.40E
Bewcastle England **35** 55.03N 2.45W
Bewcastle Fells hills England **35** 55.05N 2.50W
Bewdley England **28** 52.23N 2.19W
Bexhill England **29** 50.51N 0.29E
Bexley England **27** 51.26N 0.10E
Beyla Guinea **70** 8.42N 8.39W
Beysehir L. Turkey **56** 37.47N 31.30E
Bezhetsk U.S.S.R. **47** 57.49N 36.40E
Bezhitsa U.S.S.R. **47** 53.19N 34.17E
Béziers France **40** 43.21N 3.13E
Bhagalpur India **58** 25.14N 85.59E
Bhamo Burma **59** 24.15N 97.15E
Bhatpara India **62** 22.51N 88.31E
Bhavnagar India **58** 21.46N 72.14E
Bhima r. India **58** 16.30N 77.10E
Bhind India **58** 26.33N 78.47E
Bhopal India **58** 23.17N 77.28E
Bhubaneswar India **59** 20.15N 85.50E
Bhuj India **58** 23.12N 69.54E
Bhutan Asia **58** 27.20N 90.30E
Biak i. Asia **61** 0.55S 136.00E
Białogard Poland **44** 54.00N 16.00E
Białystok Poland **47** 53.09N 23.10E
Biarritz France **40** 43.29N 1.33W
Bicester England **28** 51.53N 1.09W
Bickle Knob mtn. U.S.A. **95** 38.56N 79.44W
Bickley England **27** 51.24N 0.03E
Bida Nigeria **71** 9.06N 5.59E
Bidborough England **27** 51.11N 0.14E
Biddeford U.S.A. **95** 43.29N 70.27W
Biddulph England **32** 53.08N 2.11W
Bidean nam Bian mtn. Scotland **34** 56.39N 5.02W
Bideford England **31** 51.01N 4.13W
Bideford B. England **31** 51.04N 4.20W
Bié d. Angola **72** 12.30S 17.30E
Biel Switz. **44** 47.09N 7.16E
Bielefeld W. Germany **44** 52.02N 8.32E
Bié Plateau f. Angola **72** 13.00S 16.00E
Big Bald Mtn. Canada **95** 47.12N 66.25W
Bigbury B. England **31** 50.15N 3.56W
Biggar Scotland **35** 55.38N 3.31W
Biggin Hill town England **27** 51.19N 0.04E
Biggleswade England **29** 52.06N 0.16W
Big Horn r. U.S.A. **90** 46.05N 107.20W
Bignona Senegal **70** 12.48N 16.18W
Big Snowy Mtn. U.S.A. **90** 46.46N 109.31W
Big Spring town U.S.A. **90** 32.15N 101.30W
Bihać Yugo. **42** 44.49N 15.53E
Bihar India **58** 25.13N 85.31E
Bihar d. India **58** 24.35N 85.40E
Biharamulo Tanzania **73** 2.34S 31.20E
Bihor mtn. Romania **47** 46.26N 22.43E
Bijagos Archipelago is. Guinea Bissau **70** 11.30N 16.00W
Bijar Iran **57** 35.52N 47.39E
Bijawar India **58** 24.36N 79.30E
Bikaner India **58** 28.01N 73.22E
Bikin U.S.S.R. **63** 46.52N 134.15E
Bikoro Zaïre **72** 0.45S 18.09E
Bilaspur India **58** 22.03N 82.12E
Bilauktaung Range mts. Asia **60** 13.20N 99.30E
Bilbao Spain **41** 43.15N 2.56W
Bilecik Turkey **56** 40.10N 29.59E
Bili r. Zaïre **72** 4.09N 22.25E
Billericay England **27** 51.38N 0.25E
Billingham England **33** 54.36N 1.18W

Billings U.S.A. **90** 45.47N 108.30W
Billingshurst England **29** 51.02N 0.28W
Billington England **27** 51.54N 0.39W
Bill of Portland c. England **31** 50.32N 2.28W
Bilma Niger **71** 18.46N 12.50E
Biloxi U.S.A. **91** 30.30N 89.00W
Bima r. Zaïre **72** 3.24N 25.10E
Bina India **58** 24.09N 78.10E
Binaija mtn. Indonesia **61** 3.10S 129.30E
Binche Belgium **45** 50.25N 4.10E
Bindura Rhodesia **74** 17.20S 31.21E
Binga, Mt. Rhodesia **74** 19.47S 33.03E
Bingara Australia **80** 29.51S 150.38E
Bingen W. Germany **45** 49.58N 7.55E
Bingerville Ivory Coast **70** 5.20N 3.53W
Bingham England **33** 52.57N 0.57W
Binghamton U.S.A. **95** 42.06N 75.55W
Bingkor Malaysia **60** 5.26N 116.15E
Bingley England **32** 53.51N 1.50W
Bingöl Turkey **56** 38.54N 40.29E
Bingol Dağlari mtn. Turkey **56** 39.21N 41.22E
Binh Dinh Vietnam **60** 13.55N 109.07E
Binjai Indonesia **60** 3.37N 98.25E
Bintan i. Indonesia **60** 1.10N 104.30E
Bintulu Malaysia **60** 3.12N 113.01E
Birdum Australia **79** 15.38S 133.12E
Birecik Turkey **56** 37.03N 37.59E
Birhan mtn. Ethiopia **69** 11.00N 37.50E
Birjand Iran **57** 32.54N 59.10E
Birkenfeld W. Germany **45** 49.39N 7.10E
Birkenhead England **32** 53.24N 3.01W
Birket Qârûn l. Egypt **56** 29.30N 30.40E
Birmingham England **28** 52.30N 1.55W
Birmingham Ala. U.S.A. **91** 33.30N 86.55W
Birmingham Mich. U.S.A. **94** 42.33N 83.12W
Birnin Kebbi Nigeria **71** 12.30N 4.11E
Birni N'Konni Niger **71** 13.49N 5.19E
Birobidzhan U.S.S.R. **63** 48.49N 132.54E
Birq, Wadi r. Saudi Arabia **57** 24.08N 47.35E
Birr Rep. of Ire. **39** 53.06N 7.56W
Birreencorragh mtn. Rep. of Ire. **38** 53.59N 9.31W
Biscay, B. of France **40** 45.30N 4.00W
Bishop Auckland England **32** 54.40N 1.40W
Bishopbriggs Scotland **34** 55.55N 4.12W
Bishop's Castle England **28** 52.29N 3.00W
Bishop's Lydeard England **28** 51.04N 3.12W
Bishop's Stortford England **27** 51.53N 0.09E
Bishops Waltham England **28** 50.57N 1.13W
Bisina, L. Uganda **73** 1.35N 34.08E
Bisitun Iran **57** 34.22N 47.29E
Biskotasi L. Canada **94** 47.15N 82.15W
Biskra Algeria **42** 34.48N 5.40E
Bisley England **27** 51.20N 0.39W
Bismarck U.S.A. **90** 46.50N 100.48W
Bismarck Range mts. P.N.G. **61** 6.00S 145.00E
Bismarck Sea Pacific Oc. **61** 4.00S 146.30E
Bissau Guinea Bissau **70** 11.52N 15.39W
Bistrita r. Romania **47** 46.30N 26.54E
Bitburg W. Germany **45** 49.58N 6.31E
Bitlis Turkey **56** 38.23N 42.04E
Bitola Yugo. **43** 41.02N 21.21E
Bitterfontein R.S.A. **74** 31.03S 18.16E
Bitter Lakes Egypt **56** 30.20N 32.50E
Biu Nigeria **71** 10.36N 12.11E
Biumba Rwanda **73** 1.38S 30.02E
Biysk U.S.S.R. **48** 52.35N 85.16E
Bizerta Tunisia **42** 37.17N 9.51E
Black r. Vietnam **60** 21.20N 105.45E
Black r. Rep. of Ire. **38** 53.50N 7.51W
Black r. Ark. U.S.A. **91** 35.30N 91.20W
Black r. Wisc. U.S.A. **94** 43.55N 91.20W
Black Bull Head Rep. of Ire. **39** 51.35N 10.03W
Blackburn England **32** 53.44N 2.30W
Black Combe mtn. England **32** 54.15N 3.20W
Blackcraig Hill Scotland **34** 55.19N 4.08W
Black Down Hills England **28** 50.55N 3.10W
Blackford Scotland **35** 56.16N 3.48W
Black Forest f. W. Germany **44** 48.00N 7.45E
Black Head N. Ireland **34** 54.46N 5.41W
Black Head Rep. of Ire. **38** 53.09N 9.16W
Black Isle f. Scotland **37** 57.35N 4.15W
Blackmoor Vale f. England **28** 50.55N 2.25W
Black Mtn. Wales **30** 51.52N 3.50W
Black Mts. Wales **30** 51.52N 3.09W
Blackpool England **32** 53.48N 3.03W
Black River town Jamaica **97** 18.02N 77.52W
Blackrock Rep. of Ire. **38** 53.18N 6.13W
Black Rock Desert U.S.A. **90** 41.10N 118.45W
Black Sand Desert U.S.S.R. **57** 37.45N 60.00E
Black Sea Europe **47** 43.00N 35.00E
Blacksod B. Rep. of Ire. **38** 54.04N 10.00W
Black Volta r. Ghana/U. Volta **70** 8.14N 2.11W
Blackwater r. England **29** 51.43N 0.42E
Blackwater r. N. Ireland **34** 54.31N 6.36W
Blackwater Rep. of Ire. **39** 52.26N 6.20W
Blackwater r. Meath Rep. of Ire. **38** 53.39N 6.41W

For Khmer Republic *read* Kampuchea. For Malagasy Republic *read* Madagascar. For Rhodesia *read* Zimbabwe.

Blackwater to **Bream B.** 124

Blackwater *r.* Waterford Rep. of Ire. **39** 51.58N 7.52W
Blackwater Resr. Scotland **34** 56.43N 4.58W
Bladnoch *r.* Scotland **34** 54.52N 4.26W
Blaenau Ffestiniog Wales **30** 53.00N 3.57W
Blaenavon Wales **31** 51.46N 3.05W
Blagoevgrad Bulgaria **43** 42.02N 23.04E
Blagoveshchensk U.S.S.R. **63** 50.19N 127.30E
Blair Atholl Scotland **37** 56.46N 3.51W
Blairgowrie Scotland **35** 56.36N 3.21W
Blakeney Pt. England **33** 52.58N 0.57E
Blanc, Cap Mauritania **70** 20.44N 17.05W
Blanc, Mont Canada **95** 48.47N 66.51W
Blanc, Mont Europe **40** 45.50N 6.52E
Blanca, Bahía *b.* Argentina **103** 39.15S 61.00W
Blanchardstown Rep. of Ire. **38** 53.24N 6.23W
Blanche, L. Australia **80** 29.15S 139.40E
Blanco, C. Costa Rica **96** 9.36N 85.06W
Blanco, C. U.S.A. **90** 42.50N 124.29W
Blandford Forum England **28** 50.52N 2.10W
Blankenberge Belgium **45** 51.18N 3.08E
Blantyre Malaŵi **73** 15.46S 35.00E
Blarney Rep. of Ire. **39** 51.56N 8.34W
Blavet *r.* France **40** 47.43N 3.18W
Blaydon England **32** 54.58N 1.42W
Blaye France **40** 45.08N 0.40W
Bleaklow Hill England **32** 53.27N 1.50W
Blenheim New Zealand **82** 41.32S 173.58E
Blessington Rep. of Ire. **39** 53.11N 6.33W
Bletchley England **28** 51.59N 0.45W
Blida Algeria **41** 36.30N 2.50E
Blidworth England **33** 53.06N 1.07W
Blindley Heath England **27** 51.12N 0.04W
Blind River *town* Canada **94** 46.12N 82.59W
Blitta Togo **71** 8.23N 1.06E
Bloemfontein R.S.A. **74** 29.07S 26.14E
Blois France **40** 47.36N 1.20E
Bloody Foreland *c.* Rep. of Ire. **38** 55.09N 8.17W
Bloomington Ind. U.S.A. **94** 39.10N 86.31W
Bloomington Minn. U.S.A. **94** 44.48N 93.19W
Bloomsburg U.S.A. **95** 41.01N 76.27W
Bluefield U.S.A. **91** 37.14N 81.17W
Bluefields Nicaragua **96** 12.00N 83.49W
Blue Mts. Australia **80** 33.30S 150.15E
Blue Mts. U.S.A. **90** 45.00N 118.00W
Blue Nile *r.* Sudan **69** 15.45N 32.25E
Blue Stack Mts. Rep. of Ire. **38** 54.44N 8.09W
Bluff New Zealand **82** 46.38S 168.21E
Blumenau Brazil **103** 26.55S 49.07W
Blyth England **35** 55.07N 1.29W
Blyth *r.* Northum. England **35** 55.08N 1.29W
Blyth *r.* Suffolk England **29** 52.19N 1.36E
Blyth Bridge *town* Scotland **35** 55.42N 3.23W
Blyth Sands England **27** 51.28N 0.33E
Bo Sierra Leone **70** 7.58N 11.45W
Boardman U.S.A. **94** 41.02N 80.40W
Bobo-Dioulasso U. Volta **70** 11.11N 4.18W
Bobruysk U.S.S.R. **47** 53.08N 29.10E
Bocholt W. Germany **45** 51.49N 6.37E
Bochum W. Germany **45** 51.28N 7.11E
Boddam Scotland **37** 57.28N 1.48W
Bodélé Depression *f.* Chad **71** 16.50N 17.10E
Boden Sweden **46** 65.50N 21.44E
Bodenham England **28** 52.09N 2.41W
Bodmin England **31** 50.28N 4.44W
Bodmin Moor England **31** 50.35N 4.35W
Bodö Norway **46** 67.18N 14.26E
Boende Zaïre **72** 0.15S 20.49E
Boffa Guinea **70** 10.12N 14.02W
Bogan Gate *town* Australia **80** 33.08S 147.50E
Bogenfels S.W. Africa **74** 27.23S 15.22E
Boggabilla Australia **80** 28.36S 150.21E
Boggeragh Mts. Rep. of Ire. **39** 52.03N 8.53W
Boghari Algeria **41** 35.55N 2.47E
Bognor Regis England **28** 50.47N 0.40W
Bog of Allen *f.* Rep. of Ire. **38** 53.17N 7.00W
Bogong, Mt. Australia **80** 36.45S 147.21E
Bogor Indonesia **60** 6.34S 106.45E
Bogotá Colombia **102** 4.38N 74.05W
Bogra Bangla. **58** 24.52N 89.28E
Bogué Mauritania **70** 16.40N 14.10W
Bohain France **45** 49.59N 3.28E
Bohemian Forest *mts.* Czech. **44** 49.20N 13.10E
Bohol *i.* Phil. **61** 9.45N 124.10E
Boise U.S.A. **90** 43.38N 116.12W
Bojeador, C. Phil. **61** 18.30N 120.50E
Bojnurd Iran **57** 37.28N 57.20E
Boké Guinea **70** 10.57N 14.13W
Bokn Fjord *est.* Norway **46** 59.15N 5.50E
Bokoro Chad **71** 12.17N 17.04E
Bokungu Zaïre **72** 0.44S 22.28E
Bolamo Guinea Bissau **70** 11.35N 15.30W
Bolangir India **59** 20.41N 83.30E
Bolbec France **40** 49.34N 0.28E
Bole Ghana **70** 9.03N 2.23W
Bolgrad U.S.S.R. **43** 45.42N 28.40E
Bolivar Argentina **103** 36.15S 61.07W
Bolivar *mtn.* Venezuela **97** 7.27N 71.00W
Bolivia S. America **102** 17.00S 65.00W
Bollin *r.* England **32** 53.23N 2.29W
Bollnäs Sweden **46** 61.20N 16.25E
Bolmen *l.* Sweden **46** 57.00N 13.45E
Bolobo Zaïre **72** 2.10S 16.17E
Bologna Italy **42** 44.30N 11.20E
Bologoye U.S.S.R. **47** 57.58N 34.00E
Bolomba Zaïre **72** 0.30N 19.13E
Bolsena, Lago di *l.* Italy **42** 42.36N 11.55E
Bolshevik *i.* U.S.S.R. **49** 78.30N 102.00E
Bolshoi Lyakhovskiy *i.* U.S.S.R. **49** 73.30N 142.00E
Bolsover England **33** 53.14N 1.18W
Bolt Head *c.* England **31** 50.13N 3.48W
Bolton England **32** 53.35N 2.26W
Bolu Turkey **56** 40.45N 31.38E
Bolus Head Rep. of Ire. **39** 51.47N 10.20W
Bolvadin Turkey **56** 38.43N 31.02E
Bolzano Italy **44** 46.30N 11.20E
Boma Zaïre **72** 5.50S 13.03E
Bombala Australia **80** 36.55S 149.16E
Bombay India **58** 18.56N 72.51E
Bom Despacho Brazil **103** 19.46S 45.15W
Bomokandi *r.* Zaïre **73** 3.37N 26.09E
Bomongo Zaïre **72** 1.30N 18.21E
Bomu *r.* C.A.R. **72** 4.08N 22.25E
Bon, C. Tunisia **42** 37.05N 11.02E
Bonaire *i.* Neth. Antilles **97** 12.15N 68.27W
Bonar-Bridge *town* Scotland **37** 57.33N 4.21W
Bonavista Canada **93** 48.38N 53.08W
Bondo Zaïre **72** 3.47N 23.45E
Bondoukou Ivory Coast **70** 8.03N 2.15W
Bone, G. of Indonesia **61** 4.00S 120.50E
Bo'ness Scotland **35** 56.01N 3.36W
Bongandanga Zaïre **72** 1.28N 21.03E
Bonifacio France **42** 41.23N 9.10E
Bonifacio, Str. of Med. Sea **42** 41.18N 9.10E
Bonn W. Germany **45** 50.44N 7.06E
Bonny Nigeria **72** 4.25N 7.15E
Bonny, Bight of Africa **71** 2.58N 7.00E
Bonnyrigg Scotland **35** 55.52N 3.07W
Bontang Indonesia **60** 0.05N 117.31E
Boothia, G. of Canada **93** 70.00N 90.00W
Bootle Cumbria England **32** 54.17N 3.24W
Bootle Mersey. England **32** 53.28N 3.01W
Booué Gabon **72** 0.00 11.58E
Boppard W. Germany **45** 50.13N 7.35E
Borah Peak U.S.A. **90** 44.09N 113.47W
Borås Sweden **46** 57.44N 12.55E
Borazjan Iran **57** 29.14N 51.12E
Bordeaux France **40** 44.50N 0.34W
Borden I. Canada **92** 78.30N 111.00W
Borders *d.* Scotland **35** 55.30N 2.53W
Bordertown Australia **80** 36.18S 140.49E
Bordö *i.* Faroe Is. **46** 62.10N 7.13W
Bordon Camp England **28** 51.06N 0.52W
Borehamwood England **27** 51.40N 0.16W
Boreray *i.* Scotland **36** 57.43N 7.17W
Borgå Finland **46** 60.24N 25.40E
Borgefjell *mtn.* Norway **46** 65.15N 13.50E
Borger U.S.A. **90** 35.39N 101.24W
Borisoglebsk U.S.S.R. **47** 51.23N 42.02E
Borisov U.S.S.R. **47** 54.09N 28.30E
Borken W. Germany **45** 51.50N 6.52E
Borkum W. Germany **45** 53.34N 6.41E
Borkum *i.* W. Germany **45** 53.35N 6.45E
Borlänge Sweden **46** 60.29N 15.25E
Bormida *r.* Italy **40** 45.02N 8.43E
Borneo *i.* Asia **60** 1.00N 114.00E
Bornholm *i.* Denmark **46** 55.02N 15.00E
Borno *d.* Nigeria **71** 12.20N 12.40E
Boroughbridge England **33** 54.06N 1.23W
Borough Green England **27** 51.17N 0.19E
Borris-in-Ossory Rep. of Ire. **39** 52.56N 7.39W
Borrisokane Rep. of Ire. **39** 53.00N 8.08W
Borth Wales **30** 52.29N 4.03W
Borzya U.S.S.R. **63** 50.24N 116.35E
Bosa Italy **42** 40.18N 8.29E
Boscastle England **31** 50.42N 4.42W
Bosna *r.* Yugo. **43** 45.04N 18.27E
Bosobolo Zaïre **72** 4.11N 19.55E
Bosporus *str.* Turkey **43** 41.07N 29.04E
Bossangoa C.A.R. **71** 6.27N 17.21E
Bossembelé C.A.R. **72** 5.10N 17.44E
Bosso Niger **71** 13.43N 13.19E
Boston England **33** 52.59N 0.02W
Boston U.S.A. **95** 42.20N 71.05W
Botany B. Australia **80** 34.04S 151.08E
Botevgrad Bulgaria **43** 42.55N 23.57E
Bothnia, G. of Europe **46** 63.30N 20.30E
Botletle *r.* Botswana **74** 21.06S 24.47E
Botoşani Romania **47** 47.44N 26.41E
Botrange *mtn.* Belgium **45** 50.30N 6.04E
Botswana Africa **74** 22.00S 24.15E
Bottesford England **33** 52.56N 0.48W
Bottrop W. Germany **45** 51.31N 6.55E
Botucatu Brazil **103** 22.52S 48.30W
Bouaflé Ivory Coast **70** 7.01N 5.47W
Bouaké Ivory Coast **70** 7.42N 5.00W
Bouar C.A.R. **71** 5.58N 15.35E
Boufarik Algeria **41** 36.36N 2.54E
Boughton England **33** 53.13N 0.59W
Bougouni Mali **70** 11.25N 7.28W
Bouillon Belgium **40** 49.47N 5.04E
Bouira Algeria **41** 36.22N 3.55E
Boulder U.S.A. **90** 40.02N 105.16W
Boulogne France **40** 50.43N 1.37E
Boumba *r.* Cameroon **71** 2.00N 15.10E
Boumo Chad **71** 9.01N 16.24E
Bouna Ivory Coast **70** 9.19N 2.53W
Boundary Peak *mtn.* U.S.A. **90** 37.51N 118.23W
Boundiali Ivory Coast **70** 9.30N 6.31W
Bourem Mali **70** 16.59N 0.20W
Bourg France **40** 46.12N 5.13E
Bourganeuf France **40** 45.57N 1.44E
Bourges France **40** 47.05N 2.23E
Bourg Madame France **40** 42.26N 1.55E
Bourke Australia **80** 30.09S 145.59E
Bourne England **33** 52.46N 0.23W
Bourne *r.* England **28** 51.04N 1.47W
Bournebridge England **27** 51.37N 0.12E
Bourne End England **27** 51.34N 0.42W
Bournemouth England **28** 50.43N 1.53W
Bovingdon England **27** 51.44N 0.32W
Bowen Australia **79** 20.00S 148.15E
Bowes England **32** 54.31N 2.01W
Bowmore Scotland **34** 55.45N 6.17W
Bowness-on-Solway England **35** 54.57N 3.11W
Boxtel Neth. **45** 51.36N 5.20E
Boyle Rep. of Ire. **38** 53.58N 8.19W
Boyne *r.* Rep. of Ire. **38** 53.43N 6.17W
Boyoma Falls *f.* Zaïre **72** 0.18N 25.32E
Bozeman U.S.A. **90** 45.40N 111.00W
Braan *r.* Scotland **35** 56.34N 3.36W
Brabant *d.* Belgium **45** 50.47N 4.30E
Brac *i.* Yugo. **43** 43.20N 16.38E
Bracadale, Loch Scotland **36** 57.22N 6.30W
Bräcke Sweden **46** 62.44N 15.30E
Bracknell England **27** 51.26N 0.46W
Brad Romania **43** 46.06N 22.48E
Bradano *r.* Italy **43** 40.23N 16.52E
Bradford England **32** 53.47N 1.45W
Bradford-on-Avon England **28** 51.20N 2.15W
Bradwell-on-Sea England **29** 51.44N 0.55E
Bradworthy England **31** 50.54N 4.22W
Brae Scotland **36** 60.24N 1.21W
Braemar Scotland **37** 57.01N 3.24W
Braemar *f.* Scotland **37** 57.02N 3.24W
Braga Portugal **41** 41.32N 8.26W
Bragado Argentina **103** 35.10S 60.29W
Braganca Portugal **41** 41.47N 6.46W
Brahmaputra *r.* Asia **59** 23.50N 89.45E
Brăila Romania **43** 45.18N 27.58E
Brailsford England **32** 52.58N 1.35W
Brain *r.* England **27** 51.47N 0.40E
Braintree England **27** 51.53N 0.32E
Bramley England **27** 51.11N 0.35W
Brampton Canada **95** 43.41N 79.46W
Brampton England **35** 54.56N 2.43W
Brandberg *mtn.* S.W. Africa **74** 21.10S 14.33E
Brandenburg E. Germany **44** 52.25N 12.34E
Brandfort R.S.A. **74** 28.42S 26.28E
Brandon Canada **90** 49.50N 99.57W
Brandon Suffolk England **29** 52.27N 0.37E
Brandon Durham England **32** 54.46N 1.37W
Brandon B. Rep. of Ire. **39** 52.16N 10.05W
Brandon Hill Rep. of Ire. **39** 52.30N 7.00W
Brandon Mtn. Rep. of Ire. **39** 52.14N 10.15W
Brandon Pt. Rep. of Ire. **39** 52.17N 10.11W
Brantford Canada **94** 43.09N 80.17W
Brasília Brazil **103** 15.54S 47.50W
Braşov Romania **43** 45.40N 25.35E
Brass Nigeria **71** 4.20N 6.15E
Bratislava Czech. **47** 48.10N 17.10E
Bratsk U.S.S.R. **49** 56.20N 101.15E
Bratsk Resr. U.S.S.R. **49** 54.40N 103.00E
Brattleboro U.S.A. **95** 42.51N 72.36W
Braunschweig W. Germany **44** 52.15N 10.30E
Braunton England **31** 51.06N 4.09W
Brava Somali Rep. **73** 1.02N 44.02E
Brawley U.S.A. **90** 33.10N 115.30W
Bray *r.* England **31** 50.56N 3.54W
Bray Rep. of Ire. **39** 53.12N 6.07W
Bray Head Kerry Rep. of Ire. **39** 51.53N 10.26W
Bray Head Wicklow Rep. of Ire. **39** 53.11N 6.04W
Brazil S. America **103** 19.00S 50.00W
Brazilian Highlands Brazil **103** 17.02S 50.00W
Brazos *r.* U.S.A. **91** 28.55N 95.20W
Brazzaville Congo **72** 4.14S 15.10E
Breadalbane *f.* Scotland **34** 56.30N 4.20W
Breaksea Pt. Wales **31** 51.24N 3.25W
Bream B. New Zealand **82** 36.00S 174.30E

For Khmer Republic *read* Kampuchea. *For* Malagasy Republic *read* Madagascar. *For* Rhodesia *read* Zimbabwe.

Brechin to **Byfleet** 125

Brechin Scotland **35** 56.44N 2.40W
Breckland *f.* England **29** 52.28N 0.40E
Brecon Wales **30** 51.57N 3.23W
Brecon Beacons *mts.* Wales **30** 51.53N 3.27W
Breda Neth. **45** 51.35N 4.46E
Bredasdorp R.S.A. **74** 34.32S 20.02E
Brede *r.* England **29** 50.57N 0.44E
Bregenz Austria **44** 47.31N 9.46E
Breidha Fjördhur *est.* Iceland **46** 65.15N 23.00W
Bremen W. Germany **44** 53.05N 8.48E
Bremerhaven W. Germany **44** 53.33N 8.35E
Brendon Hills England **28** 51.05N 3.25W
Brenner Pass Austria/Italy **42** 47.00N 11.30E
Brent *d.* England **27** 51.33N 0.16W
Brenta *r.* Italy **42** 45.25N 12.15E
Brentford England **27** 51.30N 0.18W
Brentwood England **27** 51.38N 0.18E
Brescia Italy **42** 45.33N 10.12E
Breskens Neth. **45** 51.24N 3.34E
Bressanone Italy **44** 46.43N 11.40E
Bressay *i.* Scotland **36** 60.08N 1.05W
Bressay Sd. Scotland **36** 60.08N 1.10W
Bressuire France **40** 46.50N 0.28W
Brest France **40** 48.23N 4.30W
Brest U.S.S.R. **47** 52.08N 23.40E
Brest-Nantes Canal France **40** 47.55N 2.30W
Brett, C. New Zealand **82** 35.15S 174.20E
Brewarrina Australia **80** 29.57S 147.54E
Brewer U.S.A. **95** 44.48N 68.44W
Briançon France **40** 44.53N 6.39E
Bricket Wood *town* England **27** 51.42N 0.20W
Bride I.o.M. **32** 54.23N 4.24W
Bride *r.* Rep. of Ire. **39** 52.05N 7.52W
Bridgend Wales **31** 51.30N 3.35W
Bridge of Allan *town* Scotland **35** 56.09N 3.58W
Bridge of Cally *town* Scotland **35** 56.39N 3.25W
Bridge of Earn *town* Scotland **35** 56.24N 3.25W
Bridgeport U.S.A. **95** 41.12N 73.12W
Bridgetown Barbados **97** 13.06N 59.37W
Bridgetown Rep. of Ire. **39** 52.14N 6.33W
Bridgnorth England **28** 52.33N 2.25W
Bridgwater England **28** 51.08N 3.00W
Bridgwater B. England **28** 51.15N 3.10W
Bridlington England **33** 54.06N 0.11W
Bridlington B. England **33** 54.03N 0.10W
Bridport England **28** 50.43N 2.45W
Brienne-le-Château France **40** 48.24N 4.32E
Brienz Switz. **44** 46.46N 8.02E
Brierfield England **32** 53.49N 2.15W
Brig Switz. **40** 46.19N 8.00E
Brigg England **33** 53.33N 0.30W
Brighouse England **32** 53.42N 1.47W
Bright Australia **80** 36.42S 146.58E
Brightlingsea England **29** 51.49N 1.01E
Brighton England **29** 50.50N 0.09W
Brindisi Italy **43** 40.38N 17.57E
Brisbane Australia **80** 27.30S 153.00E
Bristol England **31** 51.26N 2.35W
Bristol B. U.S.A. **92** 58.00N 158.50W
Bristol Channel England/Wales **31** 51.17N 3.20W
British Antarctic Territory Antarctica **104** 70.00S 50.00W
British Columbia *d.* Canada **92** 55.00N 125.00W
British Isles Europe **106** 54.00N 5.00W
Briton Ferry *town* Wales **31** 51.37N 3.50W
Britstown R.S.A. **74** 30.36S 23.30E
Brive France **40** 45.09N 1.32E
Briviesca Spain **41** 42.33N 3.19W
Brixham England **31** 50.24N 3.31W
Brno Czech. **44** 49.11N 16.39E
Broad B. Scotland **36** 58.15N 6.15W
Broadback *r.* Canada **91** 51.15N 78.55W
Broadford Scotland **36** 57.14N 5.54W
Broad Haven *b.* Rep. of Ire. **38** 54.17N 9.53W
Broad Law *mtn.* Scotland **35** 55.30N 3.21W
Broadstairs England **29** 51.22N 1.27E
Broadstone England **28** 50.45N 2.00W
Broadway England **28** 52.02N 1.51W
Brocken *mtn.* E. Germany **44** 51.50N 10.50E
Brockenhurst England **28** 50.49N 1.34W
Brockham England **27** 51.13N 0.16W
Brockton U.S.A. **95** 42.06N 71.01W
Brockville Canada **95** 44.35N 75.44W
Brod Yugo. **43** 45.09N 18.02E
Brodick Scotland **34** 55.34N 5.09W
Brody U.S.S.R. **47** 50.05N 25.08E
Broken Hill *town* Australia **80** 31.57S 141.30E
Bromley England **27** 51.24N 0.02E
Bromley Common England **27** 51.23N 0.04E
Brompton England **27** 51.24N 0.35E
Bromsgrove England **28** 52.20N 2.03W
Bromyard England **28** 52.12N 2.30W
Brönderslev Denmark **46** 57.16N 9.58E
Brong-Ahafo *d.* Ghana **70** 7.45N 1.30W
Brookes Point *town* Phil. **60** 8.50N 117.52E
Brookmans Park *town* England **27** 51.43N 0.10W
Brooks Range *mts.* U.S.A. **92** 68.50N 152.00W
Brook Street England **27** 51.37N 0.17E
Broom, Loch Scotland **36** 57.52N 5.07W
Broome Australia **79** 17.58S 122.15E
Brora Scotland **37** 58.01N 3.52W
Brora *r.* Scotland **37** 58.00N 3.51W
Brosna *r.* Rep. of Ire. **39** 53.13N 7.58W
Brotton England **33** 54.34N 0.55W
Brough England **32** 54.32N 2.19W
Brough Head Scotland **37** 59.09N 3.19W
Brough Ness *c.* Scotland **37** 58.44N 2.57W
Broughton England **33** 54.26N 1.08W
Broughton Scotland **35** 55.37N 3.25W
Broughton in Furness England **32** 54.17N 3.12W
Brownhills England **28** 52.38N 1.57W
Brownsville U.S.A. **96** 25.54N 97.30W
Brown Willy *hill* England **31** 50.36N 4.36W
Broxbourne England **27** 51.45N 0.01W
Bruay-en-Artois France **45** 50.29N 2.36E
Bruchsal W. Germany **44** 49.07N 8.35E
Brue *r.* England **28** 51.13N 3.00W
Bruernish Pt. Scotland **36** 56.59N 7.22W
Bruges Belgium **45** 51.13N 3.14E
Brühl W. Germany **45** 50.50N 6.55E
Brunei Asia **60** 4.56N 114.58E
Brunner New Zealand **82** 42.28S 171.12E
Brunssun Neth. **45** 50.57N 5.59E
Brunswick U.S.A. **91** 31.09N 81.21W
Bruny I. Australia **80** 43.15S 147.16E
Bruree Rep. of Ire. **39** 52.25N 8.40W
Brussels Belgium **45** 50.50N 4.23E
Bruton England **28** 51.06N 2.28W
Bryansk U.S.S.R. **47** 53.15N 34.09E
Bryher *i.* England **31** 49.57N 6.21W
Bryn Brawd *mtn.* Wales **30** 52.08N 3.54W
Brynmawr Wales **31** 51.48N 3.10W
Bua *r.* Malaŵi **73** 12.42S 34.15E
Bubiyan I. Kuwait **57** 29.45N 48.15E
Bubye *r.* Rhodesia **74** 22.18S 31.00E
Bucaramanga Colombia **97** 7.08N 73.01W
Buchan *f.* Scotland **37** 57.34N 2.03W
Buchanan Liberia **70** 5.57N 10.02W
Buchan Ness *c.* Scotland **37** 57.28N 1.47W
Bucharest Romania **43** 44.25N 26.06E
Buckfastleigh England **31** 50.28N 3.47W
Buckhaven and Methil Scotland **35** 56.11N 3.03W
Buckhurst Hill England **27** 51.38N 0.03E
Buckie Scotland **37** 57.40N 2.58W
Buckingham England **28** 52.00N 0.59W
Buckinghamshire *d.* England **28** 51.50N 0.48W
Buckley Wales **30** 53.11N 3.04W
Buco Zau Angola **72** 4.46S 12.34E
Budapest Hungary **47** 47.30N 19.03E
Budaun India **58** 28.02N 79.07E
Buddon Ness *c.* Scotland **35** 56.29N 2.42W
Bude England **31** 50.49N 4.33W
Bude B. England **31** 50.50N 4.40W
Budjala Zaïre **72** 2.38N 19.48E
Budleigh Salterton England **28** 50.37N 3.19W
Buea Cameroon **71** 4.09N 9.13E
Buenos Aires Argentina **103** 34.40S 58.25W
Buenos Aires *d.* Argentina **103** 35.00S 61.00W
Buffalo N.Y. U.S.A. **95** 42.52N 78.55W
Buffalo Wyo. U.S.A. **90** 44.21N 106.40W
Bug *r.* Poland **47** 52.29N 21.11E
Bug *r.* U.S.S.R. **47** 46.55N 31.59E
Buggs Island *l.* U.S.A. **91** 36.35N 78.20W
Bugulma U.S.S.R. **48** 54.32N 52.46E
Buie, Loch Scotland **34** 56.20N 5.53W
Builth Wells Wales **30** 52.09N 3.24W
Buitenpost Neth. **45** 53.15N 6.09E
Bujumbura Burundi **73** 3.22S 29.21E
Bukama Zaïre **72** 9.16S 25.52E
Bukavu Zaïre **73** 2.30S 28.49E
Bukhara U.S.S.R. **57** 39.47N 64.26E
Bukittinggi Indonesia **60** 0.18S 100.20E
Bukoba Tanzania **73** 1.20S 31.49E
Bula Indonesia **61** 3.07S 130.27E
Bulagan Mongolia **62** 48.34N 103.12E
Bulan Phil. **61** 12.40N 123.53E
Bulandshahr India **58** 28.30N 77.49E
Bulawayo Rhodesia **74** 20.10S 28.43E
Bulgaria Europe **43** 42.30N 25.00E
Bulkington England **28** 52.29N 1.25W
Buller *r.* New Zealand **82** 41.45S 171.35E
Buller, Mt. Australia **80** 37.11S 146.26E
Bulloo *r.* Australia **80** 27.26S 144.06E
Bultfontein R.S.A. **74** 28.17S 26.10E
Bulun U.S.S.R. **49** 70.50N 127.20E
Bumba Zaïre **72** 2.15N 22.32E
Bum Tso *l.* China **59** 31.30N 91.10E
Bunbury Australia **79** 33.20S 115.34E
Buncrana Rep. of Ire. **38** 55.08N 7.27W
Bundaberg Australia **79** 24.50S 152.21E
Bunde W. Germany **45** 53.12N 7.16E
Bundelkhand *f.* India **58** 24.40N 80.00E
Bundoran Rep. of Ire. **38** 54.28N 8.17W
Bunessan Scotland **34** 56.18N 6.14W
Bungay England **29** 52.27N 1.26E
Bunguran *i.* Indonesia **60** 4.00N 108.20E
Bunguran Selatan *i.* Indonesia **60** 3.00N 108.50E
Buni Nigeria **71** 11.20N 11.59E
Bunia Zaïre **73** 1.30N 30.10E
Buntingford England **29** 51.57N 0.01W
Buol Indonesia **61** 1.12N 121.28E
Buqbuq Egypt **56** 31.30N 25.32E
Bura Coast Kenya **73** 3.30S 38.19E
Buraida Saudi Arabia **57** 26.18N 43.58E
Buraimi U.A.E. **57** 24.15N 55.45E
Burdur Turkey **56** 37.44N 30.17E
Burdwan India **58** 23.15N 87.52E
Bure *r.* England **29** 52.36N 1.44E
Bures England **29** 51.59N 0.46E
Burford England **28** 51.48N 1.38W
Burg E. Germany **44** 52.17N 11.51E
Burgan Kuwait **57** 29.00N 47.53E
Burgas Bulgaria **43** 42.30N 27.29E
Burgess Hill England **29** 50.57N 0.07W
Burghead Scotland **37** 57.42N 3.30W
Burgh Heath England **27** 51.18N 0.12W
Burgh le Marsh England **33** 53.10N 0.15E
Burgos Spain **41** 42.21N 3.41W
Burgsteinfurt W. Germany **45** 52.09N 7.21E
Burgsvik Sweden **46** 57.03N 18.19E
Burhanpur India **58** 21.18N 76.08E
Burias *i.* Phil. **61** 12.50N 123.10E
Burica, Punta Panamá **96** 8.05N 82.50W
Burley U.S.A. **90** 42.32N 113.48W
Burlington Canada **94** 43.19N 79.48W
Burlington Iowa U.S.A. **94** 40.50N 91.07W
Burlington Vt. U.S.A. **95** 44.28N 73.14W
Burma Asia **59** 21.00N 96.30E
Burnham England **27** 51.35N 0.39W
Burnham Beeches England **27** 51.33N 0.39W
Burnham Market England **33** 52.57N 0.43E
Burnham-on-Crouch England **29** 51.37N 0.50E
Burnham-on-Sea England **28** 51.15N 3.00W
Burnie Australia **80** 41.03S 145.55E
Burnley England **32** 53.47N 2.15W
Burntisland Scotland **35** 56.03N 3.15W
Burra Australia **80** 33.40S 138.57E
Burravoe Scotland **36** 60.23N 1.20W
Burray *i.* Scotland **37** 58.51N 2.54W
Burren Junction Australia **80** 30.08S 148.59E
Burriana Spain **41** 30.54N 0.05W
Burrinjuck Resr. Australia **80** 35.00S 148.40E
Burrow Head Scotland **34** 54.41N 4.24W
Burry Port Wales **31** 51.41N 4.17W
Bursa Turkey **43** 40.11N 29.04E
Burscough England **32** 53.37N 2.51W
Burton Agnes England **33** 54.04N 0.18W
Burton Latimer England **28** 52.23N 0.41W
Burton upon Trent England **32** 52.58N 1.39W
Buru *i.* Indonesia **61** 3.30S 126.30E
Burujird Iran **57** 33.54N 48.47E
Burullus, L. Egypt **56** 31.30N 30.45E
Burundi Africa **73** 3.00S 30.00E
Bururi Burundi **73** 3.58S 29.35E
Burwell Cambs. England **29** 52.17N 0.20E
Burwell Lincs. England **33** 53.19N 0.02E
Bury England **32** 53.36N 2.19W
Bury St. Edmunds England **29** 52.15N 0.42E
Bush *r.* N. Ireland **34** 55.13N 6.31W
Bushey England **27** 51.39N 0.22W
Bushire Iran **57** 28.57N 50.52E
Bushmanland *f.* R.S.A. **74** 29.20S 18.45E
Bushmills N. Ireland **34** 55.12N 6.32W
Bushy Park *f.* England **27** 51.25N 0.19W
Businga Zaïre **72** 3.16N 20.55E
Busira *r.* Zaïre **72** 0.05N 18.18E
Bussum Neth. **45** 52.17N 5.10E
Busu Djanoa Zaïre **72** 1.42N 21.23E
Buta Zaïre **72** 2.50N 24.50E
Butari Rwanda **73** 2.38S 29.43E
Bute *i.* Scotland **34** 55.51N 5.07W
Bute, Sd. of Scotland **34** 55.44N 5.10W
Butiaba Uganda **73** 1.48N 31.15E
Butser Hill England **28** 50.58N 0.58W
Butte U.S.A. **90** 46.00N 112.31W
Butterworth Malaysia **60** 5.24N 100.22E
Butterworth R.S.A. **74** 32.20S 28.09E
Buttevant Rep. of Ire. **39** 52.14N 8.41W
Butt of Lewis *c.* Scotland **36** 58.31N 6.15W
Butuan Phil. **61** 8.56N 125.31E
Butung *i.* Indonesia **61** 5.00S 122.50E
Buxton England **32** 53.16N 1.54W
Buy U.S.S.R. **47** 58.23N 41.27E
Buzău Romania **43** 45.10N 26.49E
Buzău *r.* Romania **43** 45.24N 27.48E
Buzi *r.* Moçambique **74** 19.52S 34.00E
Bydgoszcz Poland **47** 53.16N 17.33E
Byfield England **28** 52.10N 1.15W
Byfleet England **27** 51.20N 0.29W

For Khmer Republic *read* Kampuchea. *For* Malagasy Republic *read* Madagascar. *For* Rhodesia *read* Zimbabwe.

Bylot I. to **Carson City** 126

Bylot I. Canada **93** 73.00N 78.30W
Byrock Australia **80** 30.40S 146.25E
Byrranga Mts. U.S.S.R. **49** 74.50N 101.00E
Byske *r.* Sweden **46** 64.58N 21.10E

C

Cabanatuan Phil. **61** 15.30N 120.58E
Cabimas Venezuela **97** 10.26N 71.27W
Cabinda Angola **72** 5.34S 12.12E
Cabo Delgado *d.* Moçambique **73** 12.30S 39.00E
Cabonga Resr. Canada **95** 47.35N 76.40W
Cabora Bassa Dam Moçambique **73** 15.36S 32.41E
Cabot Str. Canada **93** 47.00N 59.00W
Cabrera *i.* Spain **41** 39.08N 2.56E
Cabrera, Sierra *mts.* Spain **41** 42.10N 6.30W
Cabriel *r.* Spain **41** 39.13N 1.07W
Caçador Brazil **103** 26.51S 50.54W
Čačak Yugo. **47** 43.45N 20.22E
Cáceres Brazil **103** 16.05S 57.40W
Cáceres Spain **41** 39.29N 6.23W
Cachimo *r.* Zaïre **72** 7.02S 21.13E
Cachoeira do Sul Brazil **103** 30.03S 52.52W
Cacin *r.* Spain **41** 37.10N 4.01W
Cacolo Angola **72** 10.09S 19.15E
Caconda Angola **72** 13.46S 15.06E
Cader Idris *mtn.* Wales **30** 52.40N 3.55W
Cadi, Sierra del *mts.* Spain **41** 42.12N 1.35E
Cadillac U.S.A. **94** 44.15N 85.23W
Cádiz Spain **41** 36.32N 6.18W
Cádiz, G. of Spain **41** 37.00N 7.10W
Caen France **40** 49.11N 0.22W
Caerleon Wales **31** 51.36N 2.57W
Caernarfon Wales **30** 53.08N 4.17W
Caernarfon B. Wales **30** 53.05N 4.25W
Caerphilly Wales **31** 51.34N 3.13W
Cagayan de Oro Phil. **61** 8.29N 124.40E
Cagliari Italy **42** 39.14N 9.07E
Cagliari, G. of Med. Sea **42** 39.07N 9.15E
Caguas Puerto Rico **97** 18.08N 66.00W
Caha Mts. Rep. of Ire. **39** 51.44N 9.45W
Caherciveen Rep. of Ire. **39** 51.56N 10.13W
Caher I. Rep. of Ire. **38** 53.43N 10.03W
Cahir Rep. of Ire. **39** 52.23N 7.56W
Cahore Pt. Rep. of Ire. **39** 52.34N 6.12W
Cahors France **40** 44.28N 0.26E
Caianda Angola **72** 11.02S 23.29E
Caibarién Cuba **97** 22.31N 79.28W
Caicos Is. C. America **97** 21.30N 72.00W
Cairn *r.* Scotland **35** 55.05N 3.38W
Cairn Gorm *mtn.* Scotland **37** 57.06N 3.39W
Cairngorms *mts.* Scotland **37** 57.04N 3.30W
Cairns Australia **79** 16.51S 145.43E
Cairnsmore of Carsphairn *mtn.* Scotland **34** 55.15N 4.12W
Cairn Table *mtn.* Scotland **35** 55.29N 4.02W
Cairo Egypt **56** 30.03N 31.15E
Cairo U.S.A. **91** 37.02N 89.02W
Caister-on-Sea England **29** 52.38N 1.43E
Caistor England **33** 53.29N 0.20W
Calabar Nigeria **72** 4.56N 8.22E
Calafat Romania **43** 43.59N 22.57E
Calahorra Spain **41** 41.19N 1.58W
Calais France **29** 50.57N 1.52E
Calais U.S.A. **95** 45.11N 67.16W
Calamar Colombia **97** 10.16N 74.55W
Calamian Group *is.* Phil. **61** 12.00N 120.05E
Calamocha Spain **41** 40.54N 1.18W
Calapan Phil. **61** 13.23N 121.10E
Călărăsi Romania **43** 44.11N 27.21E
Calatayud Spain **41** 41.21N 1.39W
Calbayog Phil. **61** 12.04N 124.58E
Calcutta India **58** 22.35N 88.21E
Caldas da Rainha Portugal **41** 39.24N 9.08W
Caldbeck England **32** 54.45N 3.03W
Caldew *r.* England **32** 54.54N 2.55W
Caldy *i.* Wales **31** 51.38N 4.43W
Caledon *r.* R.S.A. **74** 30.35S 26.00E
Calgary Canada **90** 51.05N 114.05W
Cali Colombia **102** 3.24N 76.30W
Caliente U.S.A. **90** 37.36N 114.31W
California *d.* U.S.A. **90** 37.00N 120.00W
California, G. of Mexico **90** 28.30N 112.30W
Callabonna *r.* Australia **80** 29.37S 140.08E
Callabonna, L. Australia **80** 29.47S 140.07E
Callan Rep. of Ire. **39** 52.33N 7.25W
Callander Scotland **34** 56.15N 4.13W
Callanish Scotland **36** 58.12N 6.45W
Callao Peru **102** 12.05S 77.08W
Callington England **31** 50.30N 4.19W
Calne England **28** 51.26N 2.00W
Caltagirone Italy **42** 37.14N 14.30E
Caltanissetta Italy **42** 37.30N 14.05E
Calulo Angola **72** 10.05S 14.56E
Calunga Cameia Angola **72** 11.30S 20.47E
Calvi France **40** 42.34N 8.44E
Calvinia R.S.A. **74** 31.25S 19.47E
Cam *r.* England **29** 52.34N 0.21E
Camabatela Angola **72** 8.20S 15.29E
Camagüey Cuba **97** 21.25N 77.55W
Camagüey *d.* Cuba **97** 21.30N 78.00W
Camagüey, Archipelago de Cuba **97** 22.30N 78.00W
Camapua Brazil **103** 18.34S 54.04W
Camarón, C. Honduras **96** 15.59N 85.00W
Camaross Rep. of Ire. **39** 52.22N 6.44W
Ca Mau, Pointe de *c.* Vietnam **60** 8.30N 104.35E
Cambay, G. of India **58** 20.30N 72.00E
Camberley England **27** 51.21N 0.45W
Camberwell England **27** 51.28N 0.05W
Camborne England **31** 50.12N 5.19W
Cambrai France **45** 50.11N 3.14E
Cambrian Mts. Wales **30** 52.33N 3.33W
Cambridge England **29** 52.13N 0.08E
Cambridge New Zealand **82** 37.53S 175.29E
Cambridge Mass. U.S.A. **95** 42.22N 71.06W
Cambridge Ohio U.S.A. **94** 40.02N 81.36W
Cambridge Bay *town* Canada **92** 69.09N 105.00W
Cambridgeshire *d.* England **29** 52.15N 0.05E
Camden Australia **80** 34.04S 150.40E
Camden *d.* England **27** 51.33N 0.10W
Camden U.S.A. **95** 39.52N 75.07W
Cameia Nat. Park Angola **72** 12.00S 21.30E
Camel *r.* England **31** 50.31N 4.50W
Camelford England **31** 50.37N 4.41W
Cameron Mts. New Zealand **82** 45.50S 167.00E
Cameroon Africa **71** 6.00N 12.30E
Cameroon, Mt. Cameroon **71** 4.20N 9.05E
Camiri Bolivia **103** 20.08S 63.33W
Campbell, C. New Zealand **82** 41.45S 174.15E
Campbellton Canada **95** 48.00N 66.41W
Campbelltown Australia **80** 34.04S 150.49E
Campbeltown Scotland **34** 55.25N 5.36W
Campeche Mexico **96** 19.50N 90.30W
Campeche *d.* Mexico **96** 19.00N 90.00W
Campeche B. Mexico **96** 19.30N 94.00W
Camperdown Australia **80** 38.15S 143.14E
Campinas Brazil **103** 22.54S 47.06W
Campina Verde Brazil **103** 19.36S 49.25W
Campine *f.* Belgium **45** 51.05N 5.00E
Campo Cameroon **71** 2.22N 9.50E
Campo *r.* Cameroon **72** 2.21N 9.51E
Campobasso Italy **42** 41.34N 14.39E
Campo Grande Brazil **103** 20.24S 54.35W
Campo Maior Portugal **41** 39.01N 7.04W
Campsie Fells *hills* Scotland **34** 56.02N 4.15W
Camrose Canada **92** 53.01N 112.48W
Can *r.* England **27** 51.44N 0.28E
Canada N. America **92** 60.00N 105.00W
Canadian *r.* U.S.A. **91** 35.20N 95.40W
Canadian Shield *f.* N. America **106** 50.00N 80.00W
Çanakkale Turkey **43** 40.09N 26.26E
Canal du Midi France **40** 43.18N 2.00E
Canarreos, Archipelago de los Cuba **96** 21.40N 82.30W
Canary Is. Atlantic Oc. **68** 29.00N 15.00W
Canberra Australia **80** 35.18S 149.08E
Candeleda Spain **41** 40.10N 5.14W
Canea Greece **43** 35.30N 24.02E
Canelones Uruguay **103** 34.32S 56.17W
Cangamba Angola **72** 13.40S 19.50E
Canglass Pt. Rep. of Ire. **39** 51.59N 10.15W
Çankiri Turkey **56** 40.35N 33.37E
Canna *i.* Scotland **36** 57.03N 6.30W
Canna, Sd. of Scotland **36** 57.03N 6.27W
Cannes France **40** 43.33N 7.00E
Cannich Scotland **37** 57.20N 4.45W
Cannock England **28** 52.42N 2.02W
Cannock Chase *f.* England **28** 52.45N 2.00W
Canonbie Scotland **35** 55.05N 2.56W
Canon City U.S.A. **90** 38.27N 105.14W
Cantabria, Sierra de *mts.* Spain **41** 42.40N 2.30W
Cantabrian Mts. Spain **41** 42.55N 5.10W
Canterbury England **29** 51.17N 1.05E
Canterbury Bight New Zealand **82** 44.15S 172.00E
Canton U.S.A. **94** 40.48N 81.23W
Canvey England **27** 51.32N 0.35E
Canvey Island England **27** 51.32N 0.34E
Cao Bang Vietnam **59** 22.37N 106.18E
Caoles Scotland **34** 56.32N 6.44W
Caolisport, Loch Scotland **34** 55.54N 5.38W
Cape Barren I. Australia **80** 40.22S 148.15E
Cape Breton I. Canada **93** 46.00N 61.00W
Cape Coast *town* Ghana **70** 5.10N 1.13W
Cape Johnson Depth Pacific Oc. **61** 10.20N 127.20E
Capel England **29** 51.08N 0.18W
Capelongo Angola **72** 14.55S 15.03E
Cape Matifou *town* Algeria **41** 36.51N 3.15E
Cape Province *d.* R.S.A. **74** 31.00S 22.00E
Cape Town R.S.A. **74** 33.56S 18.28E
Cape Verde Is. Atlantic Oc. **112** 17.00N 25.00W
Cap Haitien *town* Haiti **97** 19.47N 72.17W
Cappamore Rep. of Ire. **39** 52.37N 8.21W
Cappoquin Rep. of Ire. **39** 52.09N 7.52W
Capraia *i.* Italy **42** 43.03N 9.50E
Capreol Canada **94** 46.43N 80.56W
Caprera *i.* Italy **42** 41.48N 9.27E
Capri *i.* Italy **42** 40.33N 14.13E
Caprivi Strip *f.* S.W. Africa **74** 17.50S 22.50E
Caquengue Angola **72** 12.23S 22.31E
Cara *i.* Scotland **34** 55.58N 5.45W
Caracal Romania **43** 44.08N 24.18E
Caracas Venezuela **97** 10.35N 66.56W
Caragh, Lough Rep. of Ire. **39** 52.05N 9.51W
Caratasca Lagoon Honduras **96** 15.10N 89.00W
Caravaca Spain **41** 38.06N 1.51W
Carbonara, C. Italy **42** 39.06N 9.32E
Carbondale U.S.A. **95** 41.35N 75.31W
Carbost Scotland **36** 57.27N 6.18W
Carcassonne France **40** 43.13N 2.21E
Carcross Canada **92** 60.11N 134.41W
Cardenas Cuba **96** 23.02N 81.12W
Cardenete Spain **41** 39.46N 1.42W
Cardiff Wales **31** 51.28N 3.11W
Cardigan Wales **30** 52.06N 4.41W
Cardigan B. Wales **30** 52.30N 4.30W
Carentan France **40** 49.18N 1.14W
Carhaix France **40** 48.16N 3.35W
Carhué Argentina **103** 37.10S 62.45W
Caribbean Sea 97 15.00N 75.00W
Caribou U.S.A. **95** 46.52N 68.01W
Caribou Mtn. U.S.A. **95** 45.26N 70.38W
Caribou Mts. Canada **92** 58.30N 115.00W
Carignan France **45** 49.38N 5.10E
Caripito Venezuela **97** 10.07N 63.07W
Cark Mtn. Rep. of Ire. **38** 54.53N 7.53W
Carlingford Rep. of Ire. **38** 54.03N 6.12W
Carlingford Lough Rep. of Ire. **38** 54.03N 6.09W
Carlisle England **32** 54.54N 2.55W
Carlow Rep. of Ire. **39** 52.50N 6.46W
Carlow *d.* Rep. of Ire. **39** 52.43N 6.50W
Carloway Scotland **36** 58.17N 6.47W
Carlton England **33** 52.58N 1.06W
Carluke Scotland **35** 55.44N 3.51W
Carmacks Canada **92** 62.04N 136.21W
Carmarthen Wales **30** 51.52N 4.20W
Carmarthen B. Wales **31** 51.40N 4.30W
Carmel Head Wales **30** 53.24N 4.35W
Carmen Mexico **96** 18.38N 91.50W
Carmen de Patagones Argentina **103** 40.45S 63.00W
Carmen I. Mexico **96** 18.35N 91.40W
Carmona Spain **41** 37.28N 5.38W
Carmyllie Scotland **35** 56.36N 2.41W
Carnarvon R.S.A. **74** 30.59S 22.08E
Carndonagh Rep. of Ire. **34** 55.15N 7.15W
Carnedd y Filiast *mtn.* Wales **30** 52.56N 3.40W
Carnegie, L. Australia **79** 26.15S 123.00E
Carn Eige *mtn.* Scotland **36** 57.17N 5.07W
Carnew Rep. of Ire. **39** 52.43N 6.31W
Carnforth England **32** 54.08N 2.47W
Carnic Alps *mts.* Austria/Italy **42** 46.40N 12.48E
Car Nicobar *i.* India **60** 9.00N 92.30E
Carn Mòr *mtn.* Scotland **37** 57.14N 3.13W
Càrn na Loine *mtn.* Scotland **37** 57.24N 3.33W
Carnot C.A.R. **71** 4.59N 15.56E
Carnoustie Scotland **35** 56.30N 2.44W
Carnsore Pt. Rep. of Ire. **39** 52.10N 6.21W
Carnwath Scotland **35** 55.43N 3.37W
Carolina R.S.A. **74** 26.05S 30.07E
Caroline Is. Pacific Oc. **61** 7.50N 145.00E
Caroni *r.* Venezuela **97** 8.20N 62.45W
Carora Venezuela **97** 10.12N 70.07W
Carpathian Mts. Europe **47** 48.45N 23.45E
Carpentaria, G. of Australia **79** 14.00S 140.00E
Carpentras France **40** 44.03N 5.03E
Carpio Spain **41** 41.13N 5.07W
Carra, Lough Rep. of Ire. **38** 53.41N 9.15W
Carradale Scotland **34** 55.35N 5.28W
Carrara Italy **42** 44.04N 10.06E
Carrauntoohil *mtn.* Rep. of Ire. **39** 52.00N 9.45W
Carrbridge Scotland **37** 57.17N 3.49W
Carriacou *i.* Grenada **97** 12.30N 61.35W
Carrick *f.* Scotland **34** 55.12N 4.38W
Carrickfergus N. Ireland **34** 54.43N 5.49W
Carrick Forest *hills* Scotland **34** 55.11N 4.29W
Carrickmacross Rep. of Ire. **38** 53.58N 6.43W
Carrick-on-Shannon Rep. of Ire. **38** 53.57N 8.06W
Carrick-on-Suir Rep. of Ire. **39** 52.21N 7.26W
Carron *r.* Highland Scotland **36** 57.25N 5.27W
Carron *r.* Highland Scotland **37** 57.54N 4.23W
Carron, Loch Scotland **36** 57.23N 5.30W
Carrowkeel Rep. of Ire. **34** 55.07N 7.12W
Carrowmore Lough Rep. of Ire. **38** 54.11N 9.47W
Çarşamba Turkey **56** 41.13N 36.43E
Çarşamba *r.* Turkey **56** 37.52N 31.48E
Carse of Gowrie *f.* Scotland **35** 56.25N 3.15W
Carshalton England **27** 51.22N 0.10W
Carson City U.S.A. **90** 39.10N 119.46W

For Khmer Republic *read* Kampuchea. *For* Malagasy Republic *read* Madagascar. *For* Rhodesia *read* Zimbabwe.

Carsphairn to **Chihuahua** 127

Carsphairn Scotland **34** 55.13N 4.15W
Carstairs Scotland **35** 55.42N 3.41W
Cartagena Colombia **97** 10.24N 75.33W
Cartagena Spain **41** 37.36N 0.59W
Cartago Costa Rica **96** 9.50N 83.52W
Carúpano Venezuela **97** 10.39N 63.14W
Carvin France **45** 50.30N 2.58E
Cary *r.* England **28** 51.10N 3.00W
Casablanca Morocco **68** 33.39N 7.35W
Cascade Pt. New Zealand **82** 44.00S 168.20E
Cascade Range *mts.* U.S.A. **90** 44.00N 144.00W
Cascavel Brazil **103** 24.59S 53.29W
Caserta Italy **42** 41.06N 14.21E
Cashel Rep. of Ire. **39** 52.31N 7.54W
Casino Australia **80** 28.50S 153.02E
Caspe Spain **41** 41.14N 0.03W
Casper U.S.A. **90** 42.50N 106.20W
Caspian Depression *f.* U.S.S.R. **48** 47.00N 48.00E
Caspian Sea U.S.S.R. **48** 42.00N 51.00E
Cassai *r.* Angola **72** 10.38S 22.15E
Cassley *r.* Scotland **37** 57.58N 4.35W
Castaños Mexico **96** 26.48N 101.26W
Casteljaloux France **40** 44.19N 0.06W
Castellón de la Plana Spain **41** 39.59N 0.03W
Castelo Branco Portugal **41** 39.50N 7.30W
Casterton Australia **80** 37.35S 141.25E
Castlebar Rep. of Ire. **38** 53.52N 9.19W
Castlebay *town* Scotland **36** 56.58N 7.30W
Castlebellingham Rep. of Ire. **38** 53.53N 6.24W
Castleblayney Rep. of Ire. **38** 54.08N 6.46W
Castlebridge Rep. of Ire. **39** 52.23N 6.28W
Castle Cary England **28** 51.06N 2.31W
Castlecomer Rep. of Ire. **39** 52.48N 7.14W
Castledawson N. Ireland **34** 54.47N 6.35W
Castlederg N. Ireland **38** 54.42N 7.37W
Castledermot Rep. of Ire. **39** 52.54N 6.52W
Castle Douglas Scotland **35** 54.56N 3.56W
Castlefin Rep. of Ire. **38** 54.48N 7.41W
Castleford England **33** 53.43N 1.21W
Castlegregory Rep. of Ire. **39** 52.16N 10.01W
Castleisland *town* Rep. of Ire. **39** 52.13N 9.28W
Castlemaine Australia **80** 37.05S 144.19E
Castlemaine Rep. of Ire. **39** 52.10N 9.41W
Castlemaine Harbour *est.* Rep. of Ire. **39** 52.08N 9.50W
Castlepollard Rep. of Ire. **38** 53.41N 7.20W
Castlerea Rep. of Ire. **38** 53.45N 8.30W
Castlerock N. Ireland **34** 55.09N 6.47W
Castletown I.o.M. **32** 54.04N 4.38W
Castletownroche Rep. of Ire. **39** 52.10N 8.28W
Castletownshend Rep. of Ire. **39** 51.32N 9.12W
Castlewellan N. Ireland **38** 54.16N 5.57W
Castres France **40** 43.36N 2.14E
Castries St. Lucia **97** 14.01N 60.59W
Catalca Turkey **43** 41.09N 28.29E
Catamarca Argentina **103** 28.28S 65.46W
Catamarca *d.* Argentina **103** 27.40S 67.10W
Catanduanes *i.* Phil. **61** 13.45N 124.20E
Catanduva Brazil **103** 21.03S 49.00W
Catania Italy **42** 37.31N 15.05E
Catanzaro Italy **43** 38.55N 16.35E
Catarman Phil. **61** 12.28N 124.50E
Caterham England **29** 51.17N 0.04W
Catete Angola **72** 9.09S 13.40E
Catford England **27** 51.26N 0.00
Cat I. Bahamas **97** 24.30N 75.30W
Catoche, C. Mexico **96** 21.38N 87.08W
Catonsville U.S.A. **95** 39.17N 76.44W
Catskill Mts. U.S.A. **95** 42.15N 74.15W
Catterick England **32** 54.23N 1.38W
Cauca *r.* Colombia **97** 8.57N 74.30W
Caucasus Mts. U.S.S.R. **47** 43.00N 44.00E
Cauldcleuch Head *mtn.* Scotland **35** 55.18N 2.50W
Caungula Angola **72** 8.26S 18.35E
Caura *r.* Venezuela **97** 7.30N 65.00W
Causeway Rep. of Ire. **39** 52.25N 9.46W
Cavally *r.* Ivory Coast **70** 4.25N 7.39W
Cavan Rep. of Ire. **38** 54.00N 7.22W
Cavan *d.* Rep. of Ire. **38** 53.58N 7.10W
Cavite Phil. **61** 14.30N 120.54E
Cawood England **33** 53.50N 1.07W
Caxias do Sul Brazil **103** 29.14S 51.10W
Caxito Angola **72** 8.32S 13.38E
Cayenne French Guiana **102** 4.55N 52.18W
Cayman Brac *i.* Cayman Is. **97** 19.44N 79.48W
Cayman Is. C. America **97** 19.00N 81.00W
Cayuga L. U.S.A. **95** 42.40N 76.40W
Cazombo Angola **72** 11.54S 22.56E
Cebollera, Sierra de *mts.* Spain **41** 41.58N 2.30W
Cebu Phil. **61** 10.17N 123.56E
Cebu *i.* Phil. **61** 10.15N 123.45E
Cecina Italy **42** 43.18N 10.30E
Cedar *r.* U.S.A. **94** 41.10N 91.25W
Cedar City U.S.A. **90** 37.40N 113.04W
Cedar Falls *town* U.S.A. **94** 42.34N 92.26W
Cedar Rapids *town* U.S.A. **94** 41.59N 91.39W
Cedros I. Mexico **90** 28.15N 115.15W
Ceduna Australia **79** 32.07S 133.42E
Cefalù Italy **42** 38.01N 14.03E
Ceiriog *r.* Wales **30** 52.57N 3.01W
Cela Angola **72** 11.26S 15.05E
Celaya Mexico **96** 20.32N 100.48W
Celebes *i.* Indonesia **61** 2.00S 120.30E
Celebes Sea Indonesia **61** 3.00N 122.00E
Celje Yugo. **42** 46.15N 15.16E
Celle W. Germany **44** 52.37N 10.05E
Cemaes Bay *town* Wales **30** 53.24N 4.27W
Cemaes Head Wales **30** 52.08N 4.42W
Central *d.* Ghana **70** 5.30N 1.10W
Central *d.* Kenya **73** 0.30S 37.00E
Central *d.* Scotland **34** 56.10N 4.20W
Central, Cordillera *mts.* Bolivia **103** 19.00S 65.00W
Central African Republic Africa **68** 6.30N 20.00E
Centralia U.S.A. **94** 38.32N 89.08W
Central Russian Uplands U.S.S.R. **47** 53.00N 37.00E
Central Siberian Plateau *f.* U.S.S.R. **49** 66.00N 108.00E
Ceram *i.* Indonesia **61** 3.10S 129.30E
Ceram Sea Pacific Oc. **61** 2.50S 128.00E
Cerignola Italy **42** 41.17N 15.53E
Cernavodă Romania **43** 44.20N 28.02E
Cerne Abbas England **28** 50.49N 2.29W
Cervera Spain **41** 41.40N 1.16W
České Budějovice Czech. **44** 49.00N 14.30E
Cessnock Australia **80** 32.51S 151.21E
Cetinje Yugo. **43** 42.24N 18.55E
Ceuta Spain **41** 35.53N 5.19W
Cevennes *mts.* France **40** 44.25N 4.05E
Ceyhan *r.* Turkey **56** 36.54N 34.58E
Ceylon *i.* Asia **107** 7.00N 81.00E
Chacabuco Argentina **103** 34.40S 60.27W
Chaco *d.* Argentina **103** 26.30S 61.00W
Chad Africa **71** 15.00N 17.00E
Chad, L. Africa **71** 13.30N 14.00E
Chadwell St. Mary England **27** 51.29N 0.22E
Chagford England **31** 50.40N 3.50W
Chagos Archipelago Indian Oc. **55** 7.00S 72.00E
Chah Bahar Iran **57** 25.17N 60.41E
Chakansur Afghan. **57** 31.10N 62.02E
Chalfont St. Giles England **27** 51.39N 0.35W
Chalfont St. Peter England **27** 51.37N 0.33W
Challans France **40** 46.51N 1.52W
Challenger Depth Pacific Oc. **61** 11.19N 142.15E
Châlons-sur-Marne France **40** 48.58N 4.22E
Chalon-sur-Saône France **40** 46.47N 4.51E
Chamai Thailand **60** 8.10N 99.41E
Chambal *r.* India **58** 26.30N 79.20E
Chambéry France **40** 45.34N 5.55E
Chambeshi *r.* Zambia **73** 11.15S 30.37E
Chamo, L. Ethiopia **73** 4.45N 36.53E
Chamonix France **40** 45.55N 6.52E
Champ Iran **57** 26.40N 60.31E
Champaign U.S.A. **94** 40.07N 88.14W
Champlain, L. U.S.A. **95** 44.45N 73.20W
Chanchiang China **63** 21.05N 110.12E
Chanda India **59** 19.58N 79.21E
Chandeleur Is. U.S.A. **91** 29.50N 88.50W
Chandigarh India **58** 30.44N 76.54E
Changchow Fukien China **63** 24.31N 117.40E
Changchun China **63** 43.50N 125.20E
Changkiakow China **63** 41.00N 114.50E
Changsha China **63** 28.10N 113.00E
Changteh China **63** 29.03N 111.35E
Changting China **63** 25.47N 116.17E
Changtu China **62** 31.11N 97.18E
Channel Is. U.K. **31** 49.28N 2.13W
Chanthaburi Thailand **59** 12.38N 102.12E
Chaochow China **63** 23.43N 116.35E
Chao Phraya *r.* Thailand **59** 13.30N 100.25E
Chaotung China **59** 27.30N 103.40E
Chapala, Lago de Mexico **96** 20.00N 103.00W
Chapayevsk U.S.S.R. **47** 52.58N 49.44E
Chapel en le Frith England **32** 53.19N 1.54W
Chapel St. Leonards England **33** 53.14N 0.20E
Chapleau Canada **94** 47.50N 83.24W
Chapra India **58** 23.31N 88.40E
Charchan China **62** 38.08N 85.33E
Charchan *r.* China **62** 40.56N 86.27E
Chard England **28** 50.52N 2.59W
Chardzhou U.S.S.R. **57** 39.09N 63.34E
Chari *r.* Chad **71** 13.00N 14.30E
Charing England **29** 51.12N 0.49E
Charkhlik China **62** 39.00N 88.00E
Charleroi Belgium **45** 50.25N 4.27E
Charleston S.C. U.S.A. **91** 32.48N 79.58W
Charleston W. Va. U.S.A. **91** 38.23N 81.20W
Charlestown Rep. of Ire. **38** 53.57N 8.48W
Charlestown of Aberlour Scotland **37** 57.27N 3.14W
Charleville Australia **79** 26.25S 146.13E
Charleville-Mézières France **45** 49.46N 4.43E
Charlotte U.S.A. **91** 35.05N 80.50W
Charlottenburg W. Germany **44** 52.32N 13.18E
Charlottesville U.S.A. **91** 38.02N 78.29W
Charlottetown Canada **93** 46.14N 63.09W
Charlton Australia **80** 36.18S 143.27E
Charolles France **40** 46.26N 4.17E
Chartres France **40** 48.27N 1.30E
Chascomas Argentina **103** 35.34S 58.00W
Châteaubriant France **40** 47.43N 1.22W
Château du Loir France **40** 47.42N 0.25E
Châteaudun France **40** 48.04N 1.20E
Châteauroux France **40** 46.49N 1.41E
Château Thierry France **40** 49.03N 3.24E
Châtelet Belgium **45** 50.24N 4.32E
Châtellerault France **40** 46.49N 0.33E
Chatham Canada **94** 42.24N 82.11W
Chatham England **27** 51.23N 0.32E
Chatham Is. Pacific Oc. **107** 43.00S 176.00W
Châtillon-s-Seine France **40** 47.52N 4.35E
Chattahoochee *r.* U.S.A. **91** 29.45N 85.00W
Chattanooga U.S.A. **91** 35.01N 85.18W
Chatteris England **29** 52.27N 0.03E
Chauka *r.* India **58** 27.10N 81.28E
Chaumont France **40** 48.07N 5.08E
Chaves Portugal **41** 41.44N 7.28W
Cheadle England **32** 53.24N 2.13W
Cheam England **27** 51.22N 0.13W
Cheb Czech. **44** 50.04N 12.20E
Cheboksary U.S.S.R. **47** 56.08N 47.12E
Cheboygan U.S.A. **94** 45.40N 84.28W
Cheddar England **28** 51.16N 2.47W
Chekiang *d.* China **63** 29.15N 120.00E
Cheleken U.S.S.R. **57** 39.26N 53.11E
Chéliff *r.* Algeria **41** 36.15N 2.05E
Chelmer *r.* England **29** 51.43N 0.40E
Chelmsford England **27** 51.44N 0.28E
Cheltenham England **28** 51.53N 2.07W
Chelyabinsk U.S.S.R. **48** 55.10N 61.25E
Chelyuskin, C. U.S.S.R. **49** 77.20N 106.00E
Chemba Moçambique **73** 17.11S 34.53E
Chen, Mt. U.S.S.R. **49** 65.30N 141.20E
Chenab *r.* Asia **58** 29.26N 71.09E
Chengchow China **63** 34.35N 113.38E
Chengte China **63** 40.48N 118.06E
Chengtu China **62** 30.37N 104.06E
Chepstow Wales **31** 51.38N 2.40W
Cher *r.* France **40** 47.12N 2.04E
Cherbourg France **40** 49.38N 1.37W
Cherchel Algeria **41** 36.36N 2.11E
Cheremkhovo U.S.S.R. **49** 53.08N 103.01E
Cherepovets U.S.S.R. **47** 59.05N 37.55E
Cherkassy U.S.S.R. **47** 49.27N 32.04E
Cherkessk U.S.S.R. **47** 44.14N 42.05E
Chernigov U.S.S.R. **47** 51.30N 31.18E
Chernovtsy U.S.S.R. **47** 48.19N 25.52E
Chernyakhovsk U.S.S.R. **46** 54.36N 12.48E
Cherskogo Range *mts.* U.S.S.R. **49** 65.50N 143.00E
Chertsey England **27** 51.23N 0.27W
Chesapeake B. U.S.A. **91** 38.00N 76.00W
Chesham England **27** 51.43N 0.38W
Cheshire *d.* England **32** 53.14N 2.30W
Cheshunt England **27** 51.43N 0.02W
Chesil Beach *f.* England **28** 50.37N 2.33W
Chess *r.* England **27** 51.38N 0.28W
Chessington England **27** 51.21N 0.18W
Chester England **32** 53.12N 2.53W
Chester U.S.A. **95** 39.50N 75.23W
Chesterfield England **33** 53.14N 1.26W
Chesterfield Inlet *town* Canada **93** 63.00N 91.00W
Chester-le-Street England **33** 54.53N 1.34W
Chetumal Mexico **96** 18.30N 88.17W
Chetumal B. Mexico **96** 18.30N 88.00W
Chew *r.* England **28** 51.25N 2.30W
Chew Magna England **28** 51.21N 2.37W
Cheyenne U.S.A. **90** 41.08N 104.50W
Chhindwara India **58** 22.04N 78.58E
Chiang Mai Thailand **59** 18.48N 98.59E
Chiang Rai Thailand **59** 19.56N 99.51E
Chiapas *d.* Mexico **96** 16.30N 93.00W
Chiavari Italy **40** 44.19N 9.19E
Chibemba Angola **74** 15.43S 14.07E
Chibougamau Canada **91** 49.56N 74.24W
Chibuto Moçambique **74** 24.40S 33.33E
Chicago U.S.A. **94** 41.50N 87.45W
Chicago Heights *town* U.S.A. **94** 41.31N 87.39W
Chichagof I. U.S.A. **92** 57.55N 135.45W
Chichester England **28** 50.50N 0.47W
Chico U.S.A. **90** 39.46N 121.50W
Chicopee U.S.A. **95** 42.09N 72.37W
Chicoutimi-Jonquière Canada **95** 48.26N 71.06W
Chicualacuala Moçambique **74** 22.06S 31.42E
Chiddingstone Causeway *town* England **27** 51.12N 0.08E
Chidley, C. Canada **93** 60.30N 65.00W
Chiemsee *l.* W. Germany **44** 47.55N 12.30E
Chieti Italy **42** 42.22N 14.12E
Chigubo Moçambique **74** 22.38S 33.18E
Chigwell England **27** 51.38N 0.05E
Chihfeng China **63** 41.17N 118.56E
Chihli, G. of China **63** 38.30N 119.30E
Chihuahua Mexico **90** 28.40N 106.06W

For Khmer Republic *read* Kampuchea. *For* Malagasy Republic *read* Madagascar. *For* Rhodesia *read* Zimbabwe.

Chihuahua to **Colne** 128

Chihuahua *d.* Mexico **96** 28.40N 104.58W
Chikwawa Malaŵi **73** 16.00S 34.54E
Chil *r.* Iran **57** 25.12N 61.30E
Chilapa Mexico **96** 17.31N 99.27W
Chile S. America **102** 30.00S 71.00W
Chillicothe U.S.A. **94** 38.20N 83.00W
Chiloé I. Chile **102** 43.00S 74.00W
Chilpancingo Mexico **96** 17.33N 99.30W
Chiltern Hills England **27** 51.40N 0.53W
Chiltern Hundreds *hills* England **27** 51.37N 0.38W
Chilumba Malaŵi **73** 10.25S 34.18E
Chilung Taiwan **63** 25.10N 121.43E
Chilwa, L. Malaŵi **73** 15.15S 35.45E
Chimay Belgium **45** 50.03N 4.20E
Chimkent U.S.S.R. **62** 42.16N 69.05E
China Asia **62** 33.00N 103.00E
Chinandega Nicaragua **96** 12.35N 87.10W
Chinati Peak U.S.A. **90** 30.05N 104.30W
Chinchoua Gabon **72** 0.00 9.48E
Chinchow China **63** 41.07N 121.06E
Chindio Moçambique **73** 17.46S 35.23E
Chindwin *r.* Burma **62** 21.30N 95.12E
Chinga Moçambique **73** 15.14S 38.40E
Chingford England **27** 51.37N 0.00
Ching Hai *l.* China **62** 36.40N 100.00E
Chingola Zambia **73** 12.29S 27.53E
Chin Hills Burma **62** 22.40N 93.30E
Chinkiang China **63** 32.05N 119.30E
Chin Ling Shan *mts.* China **63** 33.40N 109.00E
Chinsali Zambia **73** 10.33S 32.05E
Chintheche Malaŵi **73** 11.50S 34.13E
Chipata Zambia **73** 13.37S 32.40E
Chipera Moçambique **73** 15.20S 32.35E
Chipinga Rhodesia **74** 20.12S 32.38E
Chippenham England **28** 51.27N 2.07W
Chippewa *r.* U.S.A. **94** 44.23N 92.05W
Chippewa Falls *town* U.S.A. **94** 44.56N 91.25W
Chipping Norton England **28** 51.56N 1.32W
Chipping Ongar England **27** 51.43N 0.15E
Chipping Sodbury England **28** 51.31N 2.23W
Chipstead England **27** 51.18N 0.10W
Chiquita, Mar *l.* Argentina **103** 30.50S 62.30W
Chir *r.* U.S.S.R. **47** 48.34N 42.53E
Chiredzi Rhodesia **74** 21.03S 31.39E
Chiredzi *r.* Rhodesia **74** 21.10S 31.50E
Chiriqui *mtn.* Panamá **96** 8.49N 82.38W
Chiriqui Lagoon Panamá **96** 9.00N 82.00W
Chirnside Scotland **35** 55.48N 2.12W
Chiromo Malaŵi **73** 16.28S 35.10E
Chirripo *mtn.* Costa Rica **96** 9.31N 83.30W
Chislehurst England **27** 51.25N 0.05E
Chistopol U.S.S.R. **47** 55.25N 50.38E
Chiswellgreen England **27** 51.43N 0.24W
Chiswick England **27** 51.29N 0.16W
Chita U.S.S.R. **63** 52.03N 113.35E
Chitipa Malaŵi **73** 9.41S 33.19E
Chitral Pakistan **58** 35.52N 71.58E
Chittagong Bangla. **59** 22.20N 91.48E
Chitterne England **28** 51.12N 2.01W
Chittoor India **59** 13.13N 79.06E
Chiumbe *r.* Zaïre **72** 6.37S 21.04E
Chiuta, L. Malaŵi/Moçambique **73** 14.45S 35.50E
Chivilcoy Argentina **103** 34.55S 60.03W
Chobe *r.* Botswana **72** 17.45S 25.12E
Chobham England **27** 51.21N 0.37W
Choele Choel Argentina **103** 39.16S 65.38W
Chojnice Poland **44** 53.42N 17.32E
Cholet France **40** 47.04N 0.53W
Cholon Vietnam **60** 10.45N 106.39E
Choluteca Honduras **96** 13.16N 87.11W
Choma Zambia **73** 16.51S 27.04E
Chomutov Czech. **44** 50.28N 13.25E
Chon Buri Thailand **59** 13.21N 101.01E
Chongjin N. Korea **63** 41.55N 129.50E
Chonju S. Korea **63** 35.50N 127.05E
Chorley England **32** 53.39N 2.39W
Chorleywood England **27** 51.40N 0.29W
Chorzów Poland **47** 50.19N 18.56E
Chota Nagpur *f.* India **58** 23.30N 84.00E
Chott Djerid *f.* Tunisia **68** 33.30N 8.30E
Chott ech Chergui *f.* Algeria **68** 34.00N 0.30E
Chott Melrhir *f.* Algeria **68** 34.15N 7.00E
Christchurch England **28** 50.44N 1.47W
Christchurch New Zealand **82** 43.33S 172.40E
Christianshaab Greenland **93** 68.50N 51.00W
Christmas I. Indian Oc. **60** 10.30S 105.40E
Christmas I. Pacific Oc. **106** 2.00N 157.00W
Chu *r.* U.S.S.R. **62** 42.30N 76.10E
Chuanchow China **63** 24.57N 118.36E
Chuckchee Pen. U.S.S.R. **49** 66.00N 174.30W
Chudleigh England **31** 50.35N 3.36W
Chudovo U.S.S.R. **47** 59.10N 31.41E
Chuhsien China **63** 28.57N 118.52E
Chuiquimula Guatemala **96** 15.52N 89.50W
Chukai Malaysia **60** 4.16N 103.24E
Chulmleigh England **31** 50.55N 3.52W
Chumphon Thailand **59** 10.35N 99.14E
Chuna *r.* U.S.S.R. **49** 58.00N 94.00E
Chungking China **62** 29.31N 106.35E
Chungtien China **59** 28.00N 99.30E
Chunya Tanzania **73** 8.31S 33.28E
Chuquisaca *d.* Bolivia **103** 21.00S 63.45W
Chur Switz. **44** 46.52N 9.32E
Churchill Canada **93** 58.45N 94.00W
Churchill *r.* Canada **93** 58.20N 94.15W
Churchill, C. Canada **93** 58.50N 93.00W
Churchill L. Canada **92** 56.00N 108.00W
Churchill Peak Canada **92** 58.10N 125.00W
Church Stoke Wales **30** 52.32N 3.04W
Church Stretton England **30** 52.32N 2.49W
Churn *r.* England **28** 51.38N 1.53W
Cicero U.S.A. **94** 41.50N 87.46W
Ciego de Avila Cuba **97** 21.51N 78.47W
Cienfuegos Cuba **97** 22.10N 80.27W
Cieza Spain **41** 38.14N 1.25W
Cifuentes Spain **41** 40.47N 2.37W
Cijara L. Spain **41** 39.20N 4.50W
Cilo, Mt. Turkey **57** 37.30N 44.00E
Cimarron *r.* U.S.A. **91** 36.15N 96.55W
Cimone, Monte *mtn.* Italy **42** 44.12N 10.42E
Cinca *r.* Spain **41** 41.22N 0.20W
Cincinnati U.S.A. **94** 39.10N 84.30W
Cinderford England **28** 51.49N 2.30W
Ciney Belgium **45** 50.17N 5.06E
Cinto, Mont *mtn.* France **40** 42.23N 8.57E
Cirebon Indonesia **60** 6.46S 108.33E
Cirencester England **28** 51.43N 1.59W
City of London England **27** 51.32N 0.06W
City of Westminster England **27** 51.30N 0.09W
Ciudad Bolívar Venezuela **97** 8.06N 63.36W
Ciudad Camargo Mexico **90** 27.41N 105.10W
Ciudadela Spain **41** 40.00N 3.50E
Ciudad Guerrero Mexico **90** 28.33N 107.28W
Ciudad Ixtepec Mexico **96** 16.32N 95.10W
Ciudad Juárez Mexico **90** 31.42N 106.29W
Ciudad Madera Mexico **96** 22.19N 95.50W
Ciudad Obregon Mexico **90** 27.28N 109.55W
Ciudad Real Spain **41** 38.59N 3.55W
Ciudad Rodrigo Spain **41** 40.36N 6.33W
Ciudad Victoria Mexico **96** 23.43N 99.10W
Civitavecchia Italy **42** 42.06N 11.48E
Civray France **40** 46.09N 0.18E
Civril Turkey **56** 38.18N 29.43E
Cizre Turkey **56** 37.21N 42.11E
Clackmannan Scotland **35** 56.06N 3.46W
Clacton on Sea England **29** 51.47N 1.10E
Clane Rep. of Ire. **38** 53.18N 6.42W
Clapham England **27** 51.27N 0.08W
Clara Rep. of Ire. **38** 53.21N 7.37W
Clare Australia **80** 33.50S 138.38E
Clare *d.* Rep. of Ire. **39** 52.52N 8.55W
Clare *r.* Rep. of Ire. **38** 53.17N 9.04W
Clare U.S.A. **94** 43.49N 84.47W
Clarecastle Rep. of Ire. **39** 52.49N 8.58W
Claregalway Rep. of Ire. **38** 53.21N 8.57W
Clare I. Rep. of Ire. **38** 53.48N 10.00W
Claremont U.S.A. **95** 43.23N 72.21W
Claremorris Rep. of Ire. **38** 53.44N 9.00W
Clarence *r.* New Zealand **82** 42.10S 173.55E
Clarke I. Australia **80** 40.30S 148.10E
Clarksburg U.S.A. **94** 39.16N 80.22W
Clatteringshaws Loch Scotland **34** 55.30N 4.25W
Claudy N. Ireland **34** 54.54N 7.09W
Clay Cross England **33** 53.11N 1.26W
Clay Head I.o.M. **32** 54.12N 4.23W
Clayton U.S.A. **90** 36.27N 103.12W
Clear, C. Rep. of Ire. **39** 51.25N 9.32W
Clear I. Rep. of Ire. **39** 51.26N 9.30W
Clearwater L. Canada **93** 56.10N 74.30W
Cleator Moor *town* England **32** 54.30N 3.32W
Clee Hills England **28** 52.25N 2.37W
Cleethorpes England **33** 53.33N 0.02W
Cleobury Mortimer England **28** 52.23N 2.28W
Clermont Ferrand France **40** 45.47N 3.05E
Clevedon England **28** 51.26N 2.52W
Cleveland *d.* England **33** 54.37N 1.08W
Cleveland *f.* England **33** 54.30N 0.55W
Cleveland U.S.A. **94** 41.30N 81.41W
Cleveland Heights *town* U.S.A. **94** 41.30N 81.35W
Cleveland Hills England **33** 54.25N 1.10W
Cleveleys England **32** 53.52N 3.01W
Clew B. Rep. of Ire. **38** 53.50N 9.47W
Cliffe England **27** 51.28N 0.30E
Clifton U.S.A. **95** 40.52N 74.09W
Clinton U.S.A. **94** 41.51N 90.12W
Clisham *mtn.* Scotland **36** 57.58N 6.50W
Clitheroe England **32** 53.52N 2.23W
Cloghan Rep. of Ire. **39** 53.13N 7.54W
Clogheen Rep. of Ire. **39** 52.16N 8.00W
Clogher Head Kerry Rep. of Ire. **39** 52.09N 10.28W
Clogher Head Louth Rep. of Ire. **38** 53.47N 6.14W
Clogh Mills N. Ireland **34** 55.00N 6.20W
Clonakilty Rep. of Ire. **39** 51.37N 8.54W
Clonakilty B. Rep. of Ire. **39** 51.35N 8.52W
Clones Rep. of Ire. **38** 54.11N 7.16W
Clonmany Rep. of Ire. **38** 55.16N 7.25W
Clonmel Rep. of Ire. **39** 52.21N 7.44W
Clonmellon Rep. of Ire. **38** 53.40N 7.02W
Clonroche Rep. of Ire. **39** 52.27N 6.45W
Cloppenburg W. Germany **45** 52.52N 8.02E
Cloquet U.S.A. **94** 46.40N 92.30W
Cloud Peak *mtn.* U.S.A. **90** 44.23N 107.11W
Cloughton England **33** 54.20N 0.27W
Clovelly England **31** 51.00N 4.25W
Clovis U.S.A. **90** 34.14N 103.13W
Clowne England **33** 53.18N 1.16W
Cluanie, Loch Scotland **36** 57.08N 5.05W
Cluj Romania **47** 46.47N 23.37E
Clun Forest *f.* England **28** 52.28N 3.10W
Clutha *r.* New Zealand **82** 46.18S 169.05E
Clwyd *d.* Wales **30** 53.07N 3.20W
Clwyd *r.* Wales **30** 53.19N 3.30W
Clwydian Range *mts.* Wales **30** 53.08N 3.15W
Clyde *r.* Scotland **34** 55.58N 4.53W
Clydebank Scotland **34** 55.53N 4.23W
Clydesdale *f.* Scotland **35** 55.41N 3.48W
Coahuila *d.* Mexico **96** 27.00N 103.00W
Coalville England **28** 52.43N 1.21W
Coast *d.* Kenya **73** 3.00S 39.30E
Coast *d.* Tanzania **73** 7.00S 39.00E
Coast Mts. Canada **92** 55.30N 128.00W
Coast Range *mts.* U.S.A. **90** 40.00N 123.00W
Coatbridge Scotland **35** 55.52N 4.02W
Coats I. Canada **93** 62.30N 83.00W
Coatzacoalcos Mexico **96** 18.10N 94.25W
Cobalt Canada **95** 47.24N 79.41W
Cobán Guatemala **96** 15.28N 90.20W
Cobar Australia **80** 31.32S 145.51E
Cobbin's Brook *r.* England **27** 51.40N 0.01W
Cobh Rep. of Ire. **39** 51.50N 8.18W
Cobham Kent England **27** 51.24N 0.25E
Cobham Surrey England **27** 51.20N 0.25W
Cobourg Canada **95** 43.58N 78.11W
Coburg W. Germany **44** 50.15N 10.58E
Cochabamba Bolivia **103** 17.26S 66.10W
Cochabamba *d.* Bolivia **103** 17.42S 65.00W
Cochin India **58** 9.56N 76.15E
Cochrane Canada **94** 49.04N 81.02W
Cockburn Australia **80** 32.05S 141.00E
Cockburnspath Scotland **35** 55.56N 2.22W
Cockermouth England **32** 54.40N 3.22W
Cockernhoe Green England **27** 51.55N 0.20W
Cockfosters England **27** 51.39N 0.09W
Coco *r.* Honduras **96** 14.58N 83.15W
Cocos Is. Indian Oc. **113** 13.00S 96.00E
Cod, C. U.S.A. **95** 42.08N 70.10W
Cod's Head Rep. of Ire. **39** 51.40N 10.06W
Coesfeld W. Germany **45** 51.55N 7.13E
Coevorden Neth. **45** 52.39N 6.45E
Coff's Harbour Australia **80** 30.19S 153.05E
Cofre de Perote *mtn.* Mexico **96** 19.30N 97.10W
Coggeshall England **29** 51.53N 0.41E
Coghinas *r.* Italy **42** 40.57N 8.50E
Cognac France **40** 45.42N 0.19W
Coiba I. Panamá **96** 8.30N 81.45W
Coigach *f.* Scotland **36** 58.00N 5.10W
Coimbatore India **58** 11.00N 76.57E
Coimbra Portugal **41** 40.12N 8.25W
Coin Spain **41** 36.40N 4.45W
Cojedes *r.* Venezuela **97** 7.35N 66.30W
Colac Australia **80** 38.22S 143.38E
Colchester England **29** 51.54N 0.55E
Coldblow England **27** 51.23N 0.11E
Cold Fell *mtn.* England **35** 54.54N 2.37W
Coldingham Scotland **35** 55.53N 2.10W
Coldstream Scotland **35** 55.39N 2.15W
Coleford England **28** 51.46N 2.38W
Coleman Canada **90** 49.38N 114.28W
Coleraine N. Ireland **34** 55.08N 6.40W
Colesberg R.S.A. **74** 30.44S 25.00E
Colgrave Sd. Scotland **36** 60.30N 0.58W
Colima Mexico **96** 18.00N 103.45W
Colima *d.* Mexico **96** 18.00N 103.45W
Colintraive Scotland **34** 55.56N 5.09W
Coll *i.* Scotland **34** 56.38N 6.34W
Collerina Australia **80** 29.22S 146.32E
Collier Law *mtn.* England **32** 54.45N 1.58W
Collier Row England **27** 51.36N 0.09E
Collier Street *town* England **27** 51.11N 0.27E
Collingwood Canada **94** 44.30N 80.14W
Collingwood New Zealand **82** 40.41S 172.41E
Collin Top *mtn.* N. Ireland **34** 54.58N 6.08W
Collon Rep. of Ire. **38** 53.47N 6.30W
Collooney Rep. of Ire. **38** 54.11N 8.29W
Colmar France **44** 48.05N 7.21E
Colmenar Viejo Spain **41** 40.39N 3.46W
Coln *r.* England **28** 51.41N 1.42W
Colne England **32** 53.51N 2.11W

For Khmer Republic *read* Kampuchea. *For* Malagasy Republic *read* Madagascar. *For* Rhodesia *read* Zimbabwe.

Colne to **Cruz del Eje** 129

Colne *r.* Bucks. England **27** 51.26N 0.32W
Colne *r.* Essex England **29** 51.50N 0.59E
Colnett, C. Mexico **90** 31.00N 116.20W
Colney Heath *town* England **27** 51.43N 0.14W
Cologne W. Germany **45** 50.56N 6.57E
Colombia S. America **97** 7.00N 74.00W
Colombo Sri Lanka **59** 6.55N 79.52E
Colón Panama Canal Zone **97** 9.21N 79.54W
Colonsay *i.* Scotland **34** 56.04N 6.13W
Colorado *r.* Argentina **103** 39.50S 62.02W
Colorado *r.* N. America **90** 32.00N 114.58W
Colorado *d.* U.S.A. **90** 39.00N 106.00W
Colorado *r.* Texas U.S.A. **91** 28.30N 96.00W
Colorado Plateau *f.* U.S.A. **90** 35.45N 112.00W
Colorado Springs *town* U.S.A. **90** 38.50N 104.40W
Colsterworth England **33** 52.48N 0.37W
Coltishall England **29** 52.44N 1.22E
Columbia U.S.A. **91** 34.00N 81.00W
Columbia *r.* U.S.A. **90** 46.10N 123.30W
Columbretes, Islas Spain **41** 39.50N 0.40E
Columbus Ga. U.S.A. **91** 32.28N 84.59W
Columbus Ohio U.S.A. **94** 39.59N 83.03W
Colville *r.* U.S.A. **92** 70.06N 151.30W
Colwyn Bay *town* Wales **30** 53.18N 3.43W
Comayagua Honduras **96** 14.30N 87.39W
Combe Martin England **31** 51.12N 4.02W
Comber N. Ireland **34** 54.33N 5.45W
Comeragh Mts. Rep. of Ire. **39** 52.17N 7.34W
Comilla Bangla. **59** 23.28N 91.10E
Commonwealth Territory *d.* Australia **80** 35.00S 151.00E
Como Italy **40** 45.48N 9.04E
Como, L. Italy **42** 46.05N 9.17E
Comodoro Rivadavia Argentina **102** 45.50S 67.30W
Comorin, C. India **58** 8.04N 77.35E
Comoro Is. Africa **73** 12.15S 44.00E
Comrie Scotland **35** 56.23N 4.00W
Cona *r.* Scotland **36** 56.46N 5.13W
Conakry Guinea **70** 9.30N 13.43W
Concarneau France **40** 47.53N 3.55W
Concepcion Argentina **103** 27.20S 65.35W
Concepción Chile **102** 36.50S 73.03W
Concepción Paraguay **103** 23.22S 57.26W
Conception, Pt. U.S.A. **90** 34.27N 120.26W
Conchos *r.* Mexico **90** 29.34N 104.30W
Concord U.S.A. **95** 43.13N 71.34W
Condobolin Australia **80** 33.03S 147.11E
Confolens France **40** 46.01N 0.40E
Congleton England **32** 53.10N 2.12W
Congo Africa **72** 1.00S 16.00E
Congo *r. see* ZaïreZaïre **72**
Congo Basin *f.* Africa **107** 0.30N 22.00E
Congresbury England **28** 51.20N 2.49W
Coningsby England **33** 53.07N 0.09W
Conisbrough England **33** 53.29N 1.12W
Coniston England **32** 54.22N 3.06W
Coniston Water *l.* England **32** 54.20N 3.05W
Conn, Lough Rep. of Ire. **38** 54.01N 9.15W
Connacht *d.* Rep. of Ire. **38** 53.45N 9.05W
Connah's Quay Wales **30** 53.13N 3.03W
Connecticut *d.* U.S.A. **95** 41.30N 72.50W
Connecticut *r.* U.S.A. **95** 41.20N 72.19W
Connel Scotland **34** 56.27N 5.24W
Connemara *f.* Rep. of Ire. **38** 53.32N 9.56W
Conon *r.* Scotland **37** 57.33N 4.33W
Conselheiro Lafaiete Brazil **103** 20.40S 43.48W
Consett England **32** 54.52N 1.50W
Con Son Is. Vietnam **60** 8.30N 106.30E
Constance, L. Europe **44** 47.40N 9.30E
Constanţa Romania **43** 44.10N 28.31E
Constantina Spain **41** 37.54N 5.36W
Constantine Algeria **42** 36.22N 6.38E
Constantine Mts. Algeria **42** 36.30N 6.35E
Conwy Wales **30** 53.17N 3.50W
Conwy *r.* Wales **30** 53.17N 3.49W
Conwy B. Wales **30** 53.19N 3.55W
Cooch Behar India **58** 26.18N 89.32E
Cook, Mt. New Zealand **82** 43.45S 170.12E
Cook Is. Pacific Oc. **106** 20.00S 157.00W
Cookstown N. Ireland **34** 54.39N 6.46W
Cook Str. New Zealand **82** 41.15S 174.30E
Cooktown Australia **79** 15.29S 145.15E
Coolah Australia **80** 31.48S 149.45E
Coolgreany Rep. of Ire. **39** 52.46N 6.15W
Cooma Australia **80** 36.15S 149.07E
Coomacarrea *mtn.* Rep. of Ire. **39** 51.58N 10.02W
Coomnadiha *mtn.* Rep. of Ire. **39** 51.46N 9.40W
Coonabarabran Australia **80** 31.16S 149.18E
Coonamble Australia **80** 30.55S 148.26E
Cooper Creek Australia **80** 28.36S 138.00E
Cootamundra Australia **80** 34.41S 148.03E
Cootehill Rep. of Ire. **38** 54.05N 7.05W
Copán *ruins* Guatemala **96** 14.52N 89.10W
Copeland I. N. Ireland **34** 54.40N 5.22W
Copenhagen Denmark **46** 55.43N 12.34E
Copinsay *i.* Scotland **37** 58.54N 2.41W
Copper Belt *f.* Zambia **73** 12.40S 28.00E
Coppermine *r.* Canada **92** 67.54N 115.10W
Coppermine *town* Canada **92** 67.49N 115.12W
Coquet *r.* England **35** 55.21N 1.35W
Coquet I. England **35** 55.20N 1.30W
Corabia Romania **43** 43.45N 24.29E
Coral Sea Pacific Oc. **79** 13.00S 148.00E
Corangamite, L. Australia **80** 38.10S 143.25E
Corbeil France **40** 48.37N 2.29E
Corbridge England **35** 54.58N 2.01W
Corby England **28** 52.29N 0.41W
Córdoba Argentina **103** 31.25S 64.11W
Córdoba *d.* Argentina **103** 32.00S 64.00W
Cordoba Mexico **96** 18.55N 96.55W
Cordoba Spain **41** 37.53N 4.46W
Córdoba, Sierras de *mts.* Argentina **103** 32.00S 64.10W
Corfu Greece **43** 39.37N 19.50E
Corfu *i.* Greece **43** 39.35N 19.50E
Corigliano Italy **43** 39.36N 16.31E
Corinna Australia **80** 41.38S 145.06E
Corinth Greece **43** 37.56N 22.55E
Corinth, G. of Greece **43** 38.15N 22.30E
Corinto Nicaragua **96** 12.29N 87.14W
Cork Rep. of Ire. **39** 51.54N 8.28W
Cork *d.* Rep. of Ire. **39** 52.00N 8.40W
Cork Harbour *est.* Rep. of Ire. **39** 51.50N 8.17W
Corner Brook *town* Canada **93** 48.58N 57.58W
Corning U.S.A. **95** 42.10N 77.04W
Corno, Monte *mtn.* Italy **42** 42.29N 13.33E
Cornwall Canada **95** 45.02N 74.45W
Cornwall *d.* England **31** 50.26N 4.40W
Cornwallis I. Canada **93** 75.00N 95.00W
Coro Venezuela **97** 11.27N 69.41W
Corofin Rep. of Ire. **39** 52.57N 9.04W
Coromandel New Zealand **82** 36.47S 175.32E
Coromandel Pen. New Zealand **82** 36.45S 175.30E
Coronation G. Canada **92** 68.00N 112.00W
Coronel Pringles Argentina **103** 37.56S 61.25W
Coronel Suárez Argentina **103** 37.30S 61.52W
Corowa Australia **80** 36.00S 146.20E
Corozal Belize **96** 18.23N 88.23W
Corpus Christi U.S.A. **91** 27.47N 97.26W
Corran Scotland **34** 56.43N 5.14W
Corraun Pen. Rep. of Ire. **38** 53.45N 9.52W
Corrib, Lough Rep. of Ire. **38** 53.26N 9.14W
Corrientes Argentina **103** 27.30S 58.48W
Corrientes *d.* Argentina **103** 29.00S 57.30W
Corringham England **27** 51.31N 0.28E
Corry U.S.A. **95** 41.56N 79.39W
Corryhabbie Hill Scotland **37** 57.21N 3.12W
Corryong Australia **80** 36.11S 147.58E
Corryvreckan, G. of Scotland **34** 56.09N 5.42W
Corse, Cap France **42** 43.00N 9.21E
Corsham England **28** 51.25N 2.11W
Corsica *i.* France **40** 42.00N 9.10E
Corte France **40** 42.18N 9.08E
Cortegana Spain **41** 37.55N 6.49W
Cortland U.S.A. **95** 42.36N 76.10W
Coruche Portugal **41** 38.58N 8.31W
Çorum Turkey **56** 40.31N 34.57E
Corumbá Brazil **103** 19.00S 57.25W
Corumbá *r.* Brazil **103** 18.15S 48.55W
Corve *r.* England **28** 52.22N 2.42W
Corwen Wales **30** 52.59N 3.23W
Cosenza Italy **42** 39.17N 16.14E
Coshocton U.S.A. **94** 40.16N 81.53W
Cosne France **40** 47.25N 2.55E
Costa Brava *d.* Spain **41** 41.30N 3.00E
Costa del Sol *d.* Spain **41** 36.30N 4.00W
Costa Rica C. America **96** 10.00N 84.00W
Costelloe Rep. of Ire. **38** 53.17N 9.33W
Côte d'Azur *f.* France **40** 43.20N 6.45E
Cothi *r.* Wales **30** 51.51N 4.10W
Cotonou Benin **71** 6.24N 2.31E
Cotswold Hills England **28** 51.50N 2.00W
Cottbus E. Germany **44** 51.43N 14.21E
Cottenham England **29** 52.18N 0.08E
Cottingham England **33** 53.17N 0.25W
Coucy France **45** 49.32N 3.20E
Coulagh B. Rep. of Ire. **39** 51.42N 10.00W
Coulonge *r.* Canada **95** 45.55N 76.52W
Coul Pt. Scotland **34** 55.47N 6.29W
Coulsdon England **27** 51.19N 0.07W
Council Bluffs U.S.A. **91** 41.14N 95.54W
Coupar Angus Scotland **35** 56.33N 3.17W
Courtmacsherry B. Rep. of Ire. **39** 51.37N 8.40W
Courtrai Belgium **45** 50.49N 3.17E
Coutances France **40** 49.03N 1.29W
Couvin Belgium **45** 50.03N 4.30E
Coventry England **28** 52.25N 1.31W
Cover *r.* England **32** 54.17N 1.47W
Covilhã Portugal **41** 40.17N 7.30W
Covington U.S.A. **94** 40.06N 84.21W
Cowal *f.* Scotland **34** 56.05N 5.05W
Cowal, L. Australia **80** 33.36S 147.22E
Cowan, L. Australia **79** 32.00S 122.00E
Cowbridge Wales **31** 51.28N 3.28W
Cowdenbeath Scotland **35** 56.07N 3.21W
Cowes England **28** 50.45N 1.18W
Cowra Australia **80** 33.50S 148.45E
Cox's Bazar Bangla. **59** 21.25N 91.59E
Cozumel I. Mexico **96** 20.30N 87.00W
Craboon Australia **80** 32.02S 149.29E
Cracow Poland **47** 50.03N 19.55E
Cradle Mtn. Australia **80** 41.40S 145.55E
Cradock R.S.A. **74** 32.10S 25.37E
Craigavon N. Ireland **38** 54.28N 6.25W
Craignish, Loch Scotland **34** 56.10N 5.32W
Crail Scotland **35** 56.16N 2.38W
Crailsheim W. Germany **44** 49.09N 10.06E
Craiova Romania **43** 44.18N 23.46E
Cramlington England **35** 55.06N 1.33W
Cranbourne England **27** 51.27N 0.42W
Cranbrook Canada **90** 49.29N 115.48W
Cranbrook England **29** 51.06N 0.33E
Cranham England **27** 51.33N 0.16E
Cranleigh England **29** 51.08N 0.29W
Cranston U.S.A. **95** 41.47N 71.27W
Crati *r.* Italy **43** 39.43N 16.29E
Craughwell Rep. of Ire. **39** 53.14N 8.44W
Crawford Scotland **35** 55.28N 3.39W
Crawley England **29** 51.07N 0.10W
Crays Hill *town* England **27** 51.36N 0.30E
Creach Bheinn *mtn.* Scotland **34** 56.40N 5.29W
Creag Meagaidh *mtn.* Scotland **37** 56.57N 4.38W
Credenhill England **28** 52.06N 2.49W
Crediton England **31** 50.47N 3.39W
Cree *r.* Scotland **34** 55.03N 4.35W
Creekmouth England **27** 51.32N 0.06E
Cree L. Canada **92** 57.20N 108.30W
Creeslough Rep. of Ire. **38** 55.07N 7.55W
Creetown Scotland **34** 54.54N 4.22W
Creggan N. Ireland **34** 54.45N 7.02W
Creil France **40** 49.16N 2.29E
Cremona Italy **42** 45.08N 10.03E
Cres *i.* Yugo. **42** 44.50N 14.20E
Crescent City U.S.A. **90** 41.46N 124.13W
Crest France **40** 44.44N 5.02E
Creston U.S.A. **91** 41.04N 94.20W
Creswell England **33** 53.16N 1.12W
Crete *i.* Greece **43** 35.15N 25.00E
Crete, Sea of Med. Sea **43** 36.00N 25.00E
Creus, Cabo Spain **41** 42.20N 3.19E
Creuse *r.* France **40** 47.00N 0.35E
Crewe England **32** 53.06N 2.28W
Crewkerne England **28** 50.53N 2.48W
Crianlarich Scotland **34** 56.23N 4.37W
Criccieth Wales **30** 52.55N 4.15W
Crickhowell Wales **30** 51.52N 3.08W
Cricklade England **28** 51.38N 1.50W
Crieff Scotland **35** 56.23N 3.52W
Criffel *mtn.* Scotland **35** 54.57N 3.38W
Crimea *pen.* U.S.S.R. **47** 45.30N 34.00E
Crinan Scotland **34** 56.06N 5.34W
Cristóbal Colón *mtn.* Colombia **97** 10.53N 73.48W
Crna *r.* Yugo. **43** 41.33N 21.58E
Croaghnameal *mtn.* Rep. of Ire. **38** 54.40N 7.57W
Crockham Hill *town* England **27** 51.14N 0.04E
Crocodile *r.* Transvaal R.S.A. **74** 24.11S 26.48E
Crohy Head Rep. of Ire. **38** 54.55N 8.28W
Cromarty Scotland **37** 57.40N 4.02W
Cromarty Firth *est.* Scotland **37** 57.41N 4.10W
Cromer England **33** 52.56N 1.18E
Cromwell New Zealand **82** 45.03S 169.14E
Crook England **32** 54.43N 1.45W
Crooked I. Bahamas **97** 22.45N 74.00W
Crookhaven Rep. of Ire. **39** 51.29N 9.45W
Croom Rep. of Ire. **39** 52.31N 8.43W
Crosby England **32** 53.30N 3.02W
Crosby I.o.M. **32** 54.11N 4.34W
Cross Fell *mtn.* England **32** 54.43N 2.28W
Cross Gates Wales **30** 52.17N 3.20W
Cross Hands Wales **31** 51.48N 4.05W
Crossmolina Rep. of Ire. **38** 54.06N 9.20W
Cross River *d.* Nigeria **71** 5.45N 8.25E
Crotone Italy **43** 39.05N 17.06E
Crouch *r.* England **29** 51.37N 0.34E
Crowborough England **29** 51.03N 0.09E
Crow Head Rep. of Ire. **39** 51.35N 10.10W
Crowland England **29** 52.41N 0.10W
Crowle England **33** 53.36N 0.49W
Crowlin Is. Scotland **36** 57.20N 5.50W
Crowsnest Pass Canada **90** 49.40N 114.41W
Croxley Green England **27** 51.39N 0.27W
Croyde England **31** 51.07N 4.13W
Croydon England **27** 51.23N 0.06W
Crozet Is. Indian Oc. **113** 46.27S 52.00E
Cruden B. Scotland **37** 57.24N 1.51W
Crumlin N. Ireland **34** 54.38N 6.13W
Crummock Water *l.* England **32** 54.33N 3.19W
Cruz, Cabo Cuba **97** 19.52N 77.44W
Cruz Alta Brazil **103** 28.38S 53.38W
Cruz del Eje Argentina **103** 30.44S 64.45W

For Khmer Republic *read* Kampuchea. *For* Malagasy Republic *read* Madagascar. *For* Rhodesia *read* Zimbabwe.

Cruzeiro to **Dessye** 130

Cruzeiro Brazil **103** 22.33S 44.59W
Crymmych Arms Wales **30** 51.59N 4.40W
Cuamba Moçambique **73** 14.48S 36.32E
Cuando *r.* Africa **74** 18.30S 23.32E
Cuando-Cubango *d.* Angola **72** 16.00S 20.00E
Cuangar Angola **74** 17.34S 18.39E
Cuango *r. see* Kwango Zaïre **72**
Cuanza *r.* Angola **72** 9.20S 13.09E
Cuanza Norte *d.* Angola **72** 8.45S 15.00E
Cuanza Sul *d.* Angola **72** 11.00S 15.00E
Cuba C. America **97** 22.00N 79.00W
Cubango *r. see* Okavango Angola **72**
Cubia *r.* Angola **72** 16.00S 21.46E
Cuchi *r.* Angola **72** 15.23S 17.12E
Cuckfield England **29** 51.00N 0.08W
Cuckmere *r.* England **29** 50.45N 0.09E
Cúcuta Colombia **97** 7.55N 72.31W
Cuddalore India **59** 11.43N 79.46E
Cuenca Spain **41** 40.04N 2.07W
Cuenca, Serrania de *mts.* Spain **41** 40.25N 2.00W
Cuernavaca Mexico **96** 18.57N 99.15W
Cuffley England **27** 51.42N 0.06W
Cuiabá Brazil **103** 15.32S 56.05W
Cuilcagh Mtn. Rep. of Ire. **38** 54.12N 7.50W
Cuillin Hills Scotland **36** 57.12N 6.13W
Cuilo *r. see* Kwilu Zaïre **72**
Cuito *r.* Angola **72** 18.01S 20.50E
Culdaff Rep. of Ire. **34** 55.17N 7.10W
Culemborg Neth. **45** 51.57N 5.14E
Culgoa *r.* Australia **80** 29.54S 145.31E
Cullen Scotland **37** 57.41N 2.50W
Cullera Spain **41** 39.10N 0.15W
Cullin, Lough Rep. of Ire. **38** 53.59N 9.19W
Cullompton England **28** 50.52N 3.23W
Culm *r.* England **28** 50.46N 3.30W
Culross Scotland **35** 56.03N 3.35W
Culvain *mtn.* Scotland **36** 56.57N 5.16W
Culzean B. Scotland **34** 55.21N 4.50W
Cumaná Venezuela **97** 10.29N 64.12W
Cumberland U.S.A. **95** 39.40N 78.47W
Cumberland *r.* U.S.A. **91** 37.16N 88.25W
Cumberland, L. U.S.A. **91** 37.00N 85.00W
Cumberland Sd. Canada **93** 65.00N 65.30W
Cumbernauld Scotland **35** 55.57N 4.00W
Cumbraes *is.* Scotland **34** 55.45N 4.57W
Cumbria *d.* England **32** 54.30N 3.00W
Cumbrian Mts. England **32** 54.32N 3.05W
Cuminestown Scotland **37** 57.32N 2.20W
Cumnock Scotland **34** 55.27N 4.15W
Cunene *r.* Angola **72** 17.15S 11.50E
Cúneo Italy **40** 44.22N 7.32E
Cunnamulla Australia **80** 28.04S 145.40E
Cunninghame *f.* Scotland **34** 55.40N 4.30W
Cupar Scotland **35** 56.19N 3.01W
Curaçao *i.* Neth. Antilles **97** 12.15N 69.00W
Curaco *r.* Argentina **103** 38.45S 65.10W
Curiapo Venezuela **97** 8.33N 61.05W
Curitiba Brazil **103** 25.24S 49.16W
Currane, Lough Rep. of Ire. **39** 51.50N 10.07W
Curuzú Cuatiá Argentina **103** 29.50S 58.05W
Curvelo Brazil **103** 18.45S 44.27W
Curwood, Mt. U.S.A. **94** 46.42N 88.14W
Cushendall N. Ireland **34** 55.06N 6.05W
Cushendun N. Ireland **34** 55.07N 6.03W
Cuttack India **59** 20.26N 85.56E
Cuxhaven W. Germany **44** 53.52N 8.42E
Cuyahoga Falls *town* U.S.A. **94** 41.08N 81.27W
Cuyuni *r.* Guyana **97** 6.10N 58.50W
Cuzco Peru **102** 13.42S 72.10W
Čvrsnica *mtn.* Yugo. **43** 43.35N 17.33E
Cwmbran Wales **31** 51.39N 3.01W
Cyclades *is.* Greece **43** 37.00N 25.00E
Cyprus Asia **56** 35.00N 33.00E
Cyrenaica *f.* Libya **69** 31.00N 22.10E
Czechoslovakia Europe **44** 49.30N 15.00E
Czestochowa Poland **47** 50.49N 19.07E

D

Dabakala Ivory Coast **70** 8.19N 4.24W
Dabola Guinea **70** 10.48N 11.02W
Dacca Bangla. **58** 23.42N 90.22E
Dachau W. Germany **44** 48.15N 11.26E
Dachstein *mtn.* Austria **44** 47.29N 13.36E
Daer Resr. Scotland **35** 55.21N 3.37W
Daet Phil. **61** 14.07N 122.58E
Dagana Senegal **70** 16.28N 15.35W
Dagenham England **27** 51.33N 0.08E
Dagupan Phil. **61** 16.02N 120.21E
Daingean Rep. of Ire. **39** 53.18N 7.19W
Dakar Senegal **70** 14.38N 17.27W
Dakhla Oasis Egypt **56** 25.30N 29.00E
Dal *r.* Sweden **46** 60.38N 17.05E
Da Lat Vietnam **60** 11.56N 108.25E
Dalbeattie Scotland **35** 54.55N 3.49W
Dalby Australia **80** 27.11S 151.12E
Dalkeith Scotland **35** 55.54N 3.04W
Dallas U.S.A. **91** 32.47N 96.48W
Dalmally Scotland **34** 56.25N 4.58W
Dalmatia *f.* Yugo. **43** 43.30N 17.00E
Dalmellington Scotland **34** 55.19N 4.24W
Dalnerechensk U.S.S.R. **63** 45.55N 133.45E
Daloa Ivory Coast **70** 6.56N 6.28W
Dalry D. and G. Scotland **34** 55.07N 4.10W
Dalry Strath. Scotland **34** 55.43N 4.43W
Daltonganj India **58** 24.02N 84.07E
Dalton-in-Furness England **32** 54.10N 3.11W
Dalwhinnie Scotland **37** 56.56N 4.15W
Dama, Wadi *r.* Saudi Arabia **56** 27.04N 35.48E
Daman India **58** 20.25N 72.58E
Damanhûr Egypt **56** 31.03N 30.28E
Damar *i.* Indonesia **61** 7.10S 128.30E
Damascus Syria **56** 33.30N 36.19E
Damaturu Nigeria **71** 11.49N 11.50E
Damba Angola **72** 6.44S 15.17E
Damghan Iran **57** 36.09N 54.22E
Damh, Loch Scotland **36** 57.29N 5.33W
Damietta Egypt **56** 31.26N 31.48E
Dammam Saudi Arabia **57** 26.23N 50.08E
Damodar *r.* India **58** 22.55N 88.30E
Dampier Str. Pacific Oc. **61** 0.30S 130.50E
Danakil *f.* Ethiopia **69** 13.00N 41.00E
Da Nang Vietnam **60** 16.04N 108.14E
Danbury England **27** 51.44N 0.33E
Danbury U.S.A. **95** 41.24N 73.26W
Dande *r.* Angola **72** 8.30S 13.23E
Dandenong Australia **80** 37.59S 145.14E
Danforth U.S.A. **95** 45.42N 67.52W
Danli Honduras **96** 14.02N 86.30W
Dannevirke New Zealand **82** 40.12S 176.08E
Danube *r.* Europe **43** 45.26N 29.38E
Danube, Mouths of the *f.* Romania **43** 45.05N 29.45E
Danville Ill. U.S.A. **94** 40.09N 87.37W
Danville Va. U.S.A. **91** 36.34N 79.25W
Daran Iran **57** 33.00N 50.27E
Darbhanga India **58** 26.10N 85.54E
Dardanelles *str.* Turkey **43** 40.15N 26.30E
Darent *r.* England **27** 51.29N 0.13E
Dar es Salaam Tanzania **73** 6.51S 39.18E
Dar es Salaam *d.* Tanzania **73** 6.45S 39.10E
Darfur *mts.* Sudan **69** 12.30N 24.00E
Dargaville New Zealand **82** 35.57S 173.53E
Darhan Suma Mongolia **62** 49.34N 106.23E
Darien, G. of Colombia **97** 9.20N 77.00W
Darjeeling India **58** 27.02N 88.20E
Darling *r.* Australia **80** 34.05S 141.57E
Darling Downs Australia **80** 28.00S 149.45E
Darlington England **33** 54.33N 1.33W
Darmstadt W. Germany **44** 49.52N 8.30E
Darreh Gaz Iran **57** 37.22N 59.08E
Dart *r.* England **31** 50.24N 3.41W
Dartford England **27** 51.27N 0.14E
Dartmoor Forest *hills* England **31** 50.33N 3.55W
Dartmouth England **31** 50.21N 3.35W
Darton England **33** 53.36N 1.32W
Dartry Mts. Rep. of Ire. **38** 54.23N 8.25W
Darvel Scotland **34** 55.37N 4.17W
Darvel B. Malaysia **60** 4.40N 118.30E
Darwen England **32** 53.42N 2.29W
Darwin Australia **79** 12.23S 130.44E
Dasht *r.* Pakistan **57** 25.07N 61.45E
Dasht-e-Kavir *des.* Iran **57** 34.40N 55.00E
Dasht-e-Lut *des.* Iran **57** 31.30N 58.00E
Dashtiari Iran **57** 25.29N 61.15E
Dasht-i-Margo *des.* Afghan. **57** 30.45N 63.00E
Dasht-i-Zirreh *des.* Afghan. **57** 30.00N 62.00E
Datchet England **27** 51.30N 0.35W
Datia India **58** 25.41N 78.28E
Daugavpils U.S.S.R. **46** 55.52N 26.31E
Daulatabad Iran **57** 28.19N 56.40E
Daun W. Germany **45** 50.11N 6.50E
Dauphin Canada **90** 51.09N 100.05W
Dauphiné, Alpes du *mts.* France **40** 44.35N 5.45E
Davangere India **58** 14.30N 75.52E
Davao Phil. **61** 7.05N 125.38E
Davao G. Phil. **61** 6.30N 126.00E
Davenport U.S.A. **94** 41.32N 90.36W
Daventry England **28** 52.16N 1.10W
David Panamá **96** 8.26N 82.26W
Davis, Mt. U.S.A. **95** 39.47N 79.11W
Davis Str. N. America **93** 66.00N 58.00W
Davos Switz. **44** 46.47N 9.50E
Dawa Palma *r.* Ethiopia **73** 4.10N 42.05E
Dawley England **28** 52.40N 2.29W
Dawlish England **28** 50.34N 3.28W
Dawna Range *mts.* Asia **60** 16.10N 98.30E
Dawros Head Rep. of Ire. **38** 54.50N 8.35W
Dawson Canada **92** 64.04N 139.24W
Dawson Creek *town* Canada **92** 55.44N 120.15W
Dax France **40** 43.43N 1.03W
Dayton U.S.A. **94** 39.45N 84.10W
Daytona Beach *town* U.S.A. **91** 29.11N 81.01W
De Aar R.S.A. **74** 30.39S 24.00E
Dead Sea Jordan **56** 31.25N 35.30E
Deal England **29** 51.13N 1.25E
Deán Funes Argentina **103** 30.25S 64.22W
Dearborn U.S.A. **94** 42.18N 83.14W
Death Valley *f.* U.S.A. **90** 36.00N 116.45W
Deauville France **40** 49.21N 0.04E
Deben *r.* England **29** 52.06N 1.20E
Debenham England **29** 52.14N 1.10E
Debrecen Hungary **47** 47.30N 21.37E
Decatur Ill. U.S.A. **94** 39.51N 88.57W
Decatur Ind. U.S.A. **94** 40.50N 84.57W
Deccan *f.* India **58** 18.30N 77.30E
Děčin Czech. **44** 50.48N 14.15E
Dedza Malaŵi **73** 14.20S 34.24E
Dee *r.* Rep. of Ire. **38** 53.52N 6.21W
Dee *r.* D. and G. Scotland **35** 54.50N 4.05W
Dee *r.* Grampian Scotland **37** 57.07N 2.04W
Dee *r.* Wales **30** 53.13N 3.05W
Deel *r.* Mayo Rep. of Ire. **38** 54.06N 9.17W
Deepcut England **27** 51.19N 0.40W
Deeping Fen *f.* England **29** 52.45N 0.15W
Defiance U.S.A. **94** 41.17N 84.21W
Deh Bid Iran **57** 30.38N 53.12E
Dehra Dun India **59** 30.19N 78.00E
Deinze Belgium **45** 50.59N 3.32E
Deir-ez-Zor Syria **56** 35.20N 40.08E
Dej Romania **47** 47.08N 23.55E
Dekese Zaïre **72** 3.25S 21.24E
Delano U.S.A. **90** 35.45N 119.16W
Delaware *d.* U.S.A. **95** 39.00N 75.30W
Delaware *r.* U.S.A. **95** 39.15N 75.20W
Delaware B. U.S.A. **95** 39.00N 75.05W
Delft Neth. **45** 52.01N 4.23E
Delfzijl Neth. **45** 53.20N 6.56E
Delgado, C. Moçambique **73** 10.45S 40.38E
Delhi India **58** 28.40N 77.14E
Delicias Mexico **90** 28.10N 105.30W
Dellys Algeria **41** 36.57N 3.55E
Delmenhorst W. Germany **44** 53.03N 8.37E
De Long Str. U.S.S.R. **49** 70.00N 178.00E
Del Rio U.S.A. **90** 29.23N 100.56W
Delta U.S.A. **90** 39.22N 112.35W
Delvin Rep. of Ire. **38** 53.37N 7.06W
Demavend *mtn.* Iran **57** 35.47N 52.04E
Demba Zaïre **72** 5.28S 22.14E
Demer *r.* Belgium **45** 50.59N 4.42E
Demirkazik *mtn.* Turkey **56** 37.50N 35.08E
Denbigh Wales **30** 53.11N 3.25W
Den Burg Neth. **45** 53.03N 4.47E
Denby Dale *town* England **32** 53.35N 1.40W
Dendermonde Belgium **45** 51.01N 4.07E
Dendre *r.* Belgium **45** 51.01N 4.07E
Denham England **27** 51.35N 0.31W
Den Helder Neth. **45** 52.58N 4.46E
Denia Spain **41** 38.51N 0.07E
Deniliquin Australia **80** 35.33S 144.58E
Denizli Turkey **56** 37.46N 29.05E
Denmark Europe **46** 56.00N 10.00E
Denmark Str. Greenland/Iceland **106** 66.00N 25.00W
Denny Scotland **35** 56.02N 3.55W
Den Oever Neth. **45** 52.56N 5.01E
Denpasar Indonesia **60** 8.40S 115.14E
Denver U.S.A. **90** 39.45N 104.58W
Deo *r.* Cameroon **71** 8.33N 12.45E
Deogarh India **59** 21.22N 84.45E
Depew U.S.A. **95** 42.54N 78.41W
Deptford England **27** 51.29N 0.03W
Dera Ismail Khan Pakistan **58** 31.51N 70.56E
Derbent U.S.S.R. **57** 42.03N 48.18E
Derby Australia **79** 17.19S 123.38E
Derby England **33** 52.55N 1.28W
Derbyshire *d.* England **33** 52.55N 1.28W
Derg *r.* N. Ireland **38** 54.44N 7.27W
Derg, Lough Donegal Rep. of Ire. **38** 54.37N 7.55W
Derg, Lough Tipperary Rep. of Ire. **39** 52.57N 8.18W
Derna Libya **69** 32.45N 22.39E
Derravaragh, Lough Rep. of Ire. **38** 53.39N 7.23W
Derry *r.* Rep. of Ire. **39** 52.41N 6.40W
Derrynasaggart Mts. Rep. of Ire. **39** 51.58N 9.15W
Derryveagh Mts. Rep. of Ire. **38** 55.00N 8.07W
Dersingham England **33** 52.51N 0.30E
Dervaig Scotland **34** 56.35N 6.11W
Derwent *r.* Australia **80** 42.45S 147.15E
Derwent *r.* Cumbria England **32** 54.38N 3.34W
Derwent *r.* Derbys. England **33** 52.52N 1.19W
Derwent *r.* N. Yorks. England **33** 53.44N 0.57W
Derwent *r.* T. and W. England **32** 54.58N 1.40W
Derwent Water *l.* England **32** 54.35N 3.09W
Desborough England **28** 52.27N 0.50W
Des Moines U.S.A. **91** 41.35N 93.35W
Desna *r.* U.S.S.R. **47** 50.32N 30.37E
Dessau E. Germany **44** 51.51N 12.15E
Dessye Ethiopa **69** 11.05N 39.40E

For Khmer Republic *read* Kampuchea. *For* Malagasy Republic *read* Madagascar. *For* Rhodesia *read* Zimbabwe.

Desvres to **Dunchurch** 131

Desvres France **29** 50.40N 1.50E
Detmold W. Germany **44** 51.56N 8.52E
Detroit U.S.A. **94** 42.23N 83.05W
Dett Rhodesia **74** 18.38S 26.50E
Deurne Belgium **45** 51.13N 4.26E
Deva Romania **43** 45.54N 22.55E
Deventer Neth. **45** 52.15N 6.10E
Deveron *r.* Scotland **37** 57.40N 2.30W
Devilsbit Mtn. Rep. of Ire. **39** 52.50N 7.55W
Devil's Bridge Wales **30** 52.23N 3.50W
Devils Lake *town* U.S.A. **90** 48.08N 98.50W
Devizes England **28** 51.21N 2.00W
Devon *d.* England **31** 50.50N 3.40W
Devon I. Canada **93** 75.00N 86.00W
Devonport Australia **80** 41.09S 146.16E
Devonport New Zealand **82** 36.49S 174.49E
Devrez *r.* Turkey **56** 41.07N 34.25E
Dewsbury England **32** 53.42N 1.38W
Dhahran Saudi Arabia **57** 26.18N 50.08E
Dhanbad India **58** 23.47N 86.32E
Dhaulagiri *mtn.* Nepal **58** 28.39N 83.28E
Dholpur India **58** 26.43N 77.54E
Dhubri India **58** 26.01N 90.00E
Dhulia India **58** 20.52N 74.50E
Dibaya Zaïre **72** 6.31S 22.57E
Dibbagh, Jebel *mtn.* Saudi Arabia **56** 27.51N 35.43E
Dibrugarh India **59** 27.29N 94.56E
Dickinson U.S.A. **90** 46.54N 102.48W
Didcot England **28** 51.36N 1.14W
Die France **40** 44.45N 5.23E
Diekirch Lux. **45** 49.52N 6.10E
Dieppe France **40** 49.55N 1.05E
Dieren Neth. **45** 52.03N 6.06E
Diest Belgium **45** 50.59N 5.03E
Dieuze France **44** 48.49N 6.43E
Digby Canada **91** 44.37N 65.47W
Digne France **40** 44.05N 6.14E
Digoel *r.* Indonesia **61** 7.10S 139.08E
Dijle *r.* Belgium **45** 51.02N 4.25E
Dijon France **40** 47.20N 5.02E
Dikili Turkey **43** 39.05N 26.52E
Dikwa Nigeria **71** 12.01N 13.55E
Dili Indonesia **61** 8.35S 125.35E
Dillon U.S.A. **90** 45.14N 112.38W
Dilolo Zaïre **72** 10.39S 22.20E
Dimbelenge Zaïre **72** 5.32S 23.04E
Dimbokro Ivory Coast **70** 6.43N 4.46W
Dîmbovita *r.* Romania **43** 44.13N 26.22E
Dimitrovgrad Bulgaria **43** 42.01N 25.34E
Dimitrovo Bulgaria **43** 42.35N 23.03E
Dinagat *i.* Phil. **61** 10.15N 125.30E
Dinajapur Bangla. **58** 25.38N 88.44E
Dinan France **40** 48.27N 2.02W
Dinant Belgium **45** 50.16N 4.55E
Dinaric Alps *mts.* Yugo. **43** 44.00N 16.30E
Dinas Head Wales **30** 52.03N 4.50W
Dinas Mawddwy Wales **30** 52.44N 3.41W
Dingle Rep. of Ire. **39** 52.09N 10.17W
Dingle B. Rep. of Ire. **39** 52.05N 10.12W
Dingwall Scotland **37** 57.35N 4.26W
Diourbel Senegal **70** 14.30N 16.10W
Dipolog Phil. **61** 8.34N 123.28E
Dippin Head Scotland **34** 55.27N 5.05W
Diredawa Ethiopia **69** 9.35N 41.50E
Dirranbandi Australia **80** 28.35S 148.10E
Disappointment, L. Australia **79** 23.30S 122.55E
Disaster B. Australia **80** 37.20S 149.58E
Disko I. Greenland **93** 69.45N 53.00W
Disna *r.* U.S.S.R. **46** 55.30N 28.20E
Diss England **29** 52.23N 1.06E
District of Columbia *d.* U.S.A. **95** 38.55N 77.00W
Ditchling Beacon *hill* England **29** 50.55N 0.08W
Diu India **58** 20.41N 71.03E
Divrigi Turkey **56** 39.23N 38.06E
Dixmude Belgium **45** 51.01N 2.52E
Dixon Entrance *str.* Canada **92** 54.10N 133.30W
Diyala *r.* Iraq **57** 33.13N 44.33E
Diyarbakir Turkey **56** 37.55N 40.14E
Dizful Iran **57** 32.24N 48.27E
Dja *r.* Cameroon **72** 1.38N 16.03E
Djado Niger **71** 21.00N 12.20E
Djado Plateau *f.* Niger **71** 22.00N 12.30E
Djailolo Indonesia **61** 1.05N 127.29E
Djajapura Indonesia **61** 2.28S 160.38E
Djajawidjaja Mts. Asia **61** 4.20S 139.10E
Djambala Congo **72** 2.33S 14.38E
Djelfa Algeria **68** 34.43N 3.14E
Djibouti Africa **69** 12.00N 42.50E
Djolu Zaïre **72** 0.35N 22.28E
Djouah *r.* Gabon **72** 1.16N 13.12E
Djougou Benin **71** 9.40N 1.47E
Djugu Zaïre **73** 1.55N 30.31E
Dneprodzerzhinsk U.S.S.R. **47** 48.30N 34.37E
Dnepropetrovsk U.S.S.R. **47** 48.29N 35.00E
Dnestr *r.* U.S.S.R. **47** 46.21N 30.20E
Dnieper *r.* U.S.S.R. **47** 46.30N 32.25E
Dno U.S.S.R. **47** 57.50N 30.00E
Döbeln E. Germany **44** 51.07N 13.07E
Doboj Yugo. **43** 44.44N 18.02E
Dobruja *f.* Romania **47** 44.30N 28.15E
Docking England **33** 52.55N 0.39E
Dodecanese *is.* Greece **43** 37.00N 27.00E
Dodge City U.S.A. **90** 37.45N 100.02W
Dodman Pt. England **31** 50.13N 4.48W
Dodoma Tanzania **73** 6.10S 35.40E
Dodoma *d.* Tanzania **73** 6.00S 36.00E
Doetinchem Neth. **45** 51.57N 6.17E
Dog L. Canada **94** 48.45N 89.30W
Doha Qatar **57** 25.15N 51.34E
Dokkum Neth. **45** 53.20N 6.00E
Dolbeau Canada **95** 48.52N 72.15W
Dôle France **40** 47.05N 5.30E
Dolgellau Wales **30** 52.44N 3.53W
Dolisie Congo **72** 4.09S 12.40E
Dollar Scotland **35** 56.09N 3.41W
Dollart *b.* W. Germany **45** 53.20N 7.10E
Dolo Ethiopia **73** 4.11N 42.03E
Dolomites *mts.* Italy **44** 46.25N 11.50E
Dolores Argentina **103** 36.23S 57.44W
Dolphin and Union Str. Canada **92** 69.20N 118.00W
Dombås Norway **46** 62.05N 9.07E
Dombe Grande Angola **72** 13.00S 13.06E
Dominica C. America **97** 15.30N 61.30W
Dominican Republic C. America **97** 18.00N 70.00W
Dommel *r.* Neth. **45** 51.44N 5.17E
Don *r.* England **33** 53.41N 0.50W
Don *r.* Scotland **37** 57.10N 2.05W
Don *r.* U.S.S.R. **47** 47.06N 39.16E
Donaghadee N. Ireland **34** 54.39N 5.33W
Donald Australia **80** 36.25S 143.04E
Donauworth W. Germany **44** 48.44N 10.48E
Don Benito Spain **41** 38.57N 5.52W
Doncaster England **33** 53.31N 1.09W
Dondo Angola **72** 9.40S 14.25E
Donegal Rep. of Ire. **38** 54.39N 8.06W
Donegal *d.* Rep. of Ire. **38** 54.52N 8.00W
Donegal B. Rep. of Ire. **38** 54.32N 8.18W
Donegal Pt. Rep. of Ire. **39** 52.43N 9.38W
Donets *r.* U.S.S.R. **47** 47.35N 40.55E
Donets Basin *f.* U.S.S.R. **47** 48.20N 38.15E
Donetsk U.S.S.R. **47** 48.00N 37.50E
Donga *r.* Nigeria **71** 8.20N 10.00E
Donggala Indonesia **60** 0.48S 119.45E
Dong Hoi Vietnam **60** 17.32N 106.35E
Dongkala Indonesia **61** 0.12N 120.07E
Dongola Sudan **69** 19.10N 30.27E
Dongou Congo **72** 2.05N 18.00E
Donington England **33** 52.55N 0.12W
Dooega Head Rep. of Ire. **38** 53.55N 10.03W
Doon *r.* Scotland **34** 55.26N 4.38W
Doon, Loch Scotland **34** 55.15N 4.23W
Doonbeg *r.* Rep. of Ire. **39** 52.44N 9.32W
Dora Baltea *r.* Italy **40** 45.08N 8.32E
Dora Riparia *r.* Italy **40** 45.07N 7.45E
Dorchester England **28** 50.52N 2.28W
Dordogne *r.* France **40** 45.03N 0.34W
Dordrecht Neth. **45** 51.48N 4.40E
Dordrecht R.S.A. **74** 31.22S 27.03E
Dore, Mont *mtn.* France **40** 45.32N 2.49E
Dores Scotland **37** 57.23N 4.20W
Dori U. Volta **70** 14.03N 0.02W
Dorking England **27** 51.14N 0.20W
Dormans Land *town* England **27** 51.10N 0.02E
Dornbirn Austria **44** 47.25N 9.46E
Dornie Scotland **36** 57.16N 5.31W
Dornoch Scotland **37** 57.52N 4.02W
Dornoch Firth *est.* Scotland **37** 57.50N 4.04W
Dornum W. Germany **45** 53.39N 7.26E
Dörpen W. Germany **45** 52.58N 7.20E
Dorset *d.* England **28** 50.48N 2.25W
Dorsten W. Germany **45** 51.38N 6.58E
Dortmund W. Germany **45** 51.32N 7.27E
Dortmund-Ems Canal W. Germany **45** 52.20N 7.30E
Doshakh *mtn.* Afghan. **57** 34.04N 61.28E
Dosso Niger **71** 13.03N 3.10E
Dothan U.S.A. **91** 31.12N 85.25W
Douai France **45** 50.22N 3.05E
Douala Cameroon **72** 4.05N 9.47E
Douarnenez France **40** 48.05N 4.20W
Doubs *r.* France **40** 46.57N 5.03E
Doubtless B. New Zealand **82** 35.10S 173.30E
Douentza Mali **70** 14.58N 2.48W
Dough Mtn. Rep. of Ire. **38** 54.20N 8.07W
Douglas I.o.M. **32** 54.09N 4.29W
Douglas Scotland **35** 55.33N 3.51W
Doulus Head Rep. of Ire. **39** 51.57N 10.19W
Doumé Cameroon **72** 4.16N 13.30E
Doumé *r.* Cameroon **72** 4.12N 14.35E
Doune Scotland **35** 56.11N 4.04W
Dounreay Scotland **37** 58.35N 3.42W
Douro *r.* Portugal **41** 41.10N 8.40W
Dove *r.* Derbys. England **32** 52.50N 1.35W
Dove *r.* N. Yorks. England **33** 54.11N 0.55W
Dover England **29** 51.07N 1.19E
Dover U.S.A. **95** 39.10N 75.32W
Dover, Str. of U.K./France **29** 51.00N 1.30E
Dovey *r.* Wales **30** 52.33N 3.56W
Dovrefjell *mts.* Norway **46** 62.05N 9.30E
Dowa Malaŵi **73** 13.40S 33.55E
Down *d.* N. Ireland **34** 54.20N 6.00W
Downham Market England **29** 52.36N 0.22E
Downpatrick N. Ireland **38** 54.21N 5.43W
Downpatrick Head Rep. of Ire. **38** 54.20N 9.22W
Downton England **28** 51.00N 1.44W
Dowra Rep. of Ire. **38** 54.11N 8.02W
Dra, Wadi Morocco **68** 28.40N 11.06W
Drachten Neth. **45** 53.05N 6.06E
Dragoman Pass Bulgaria/Yugo. **43** 42.56N 22.52E
Dragon's Mouth *str.* Trinidad **97** 11.20N 61.00W
Draguignan France **40** 43.32N 6.28E
Drakensberge *mts.* R.S.A. **74** 30.00S 29.00E
Dráma Greece **43** 41.09N 24.11E
Drammen Norway **46** 59.45N 10.15E
Draperstown N. Ireland **34** 54.48N 6.46W
Drau *r.* Austria **43** 46.20N 16.45E
Drava *r.* Yugo. **43** 45.34N 18.56E
Drenthe *d.* Neth. **45** 52.52N 6.30E
Dresden E. Germany **44** 51.03N 13.45E
Dreux France **40** 48.44N 1.23E
Drimnin Scotland **34** 56.37N 5.59W
Drin *r.* Albania **43** 41.45N 19.34E
Drina *r.* Yugo. **43** 44.53N 19.20E
Drogheda Rep. of Ire. **38** 53.43N 6.23W
Droichead Nua Rep. of Ire. **39** 53.11N 6.48W
Droitwich England **28** 52.16N 2.10W
Dromore Tyrone N. Ireland **38** 54.31N 7.28W
Dronfield England **33** 53.18N 1.29W
Dronne *r.* France **40** 44.55N 0.15W
Drumbeg Scotland **36** 58.14N 5.13W
Drumcollogher Rep. of Ire. **39** 52.20N 8.55W
Drumcondra Rep. of Ire. **38** 53.50N 6.40W
Drumheller Canada **90** 51.28N 112.40W
Drum Hills Rep. of Ire. **39** 52.03N 7.42W
Drumlish Rep. of Ire. **38** 53.50N 7.46W
Drummondville Canada **95** 45.52N 72.30W
Drummore Scotland **34** 54.41N 4.54W
Drumnadrochit Scotland **37** 57.20N 4.30W
Drumshanbo Rep. of Ire. **38** 54.03N 8.02W
Druz, Jebel ed *mts.* Syria **56** 32.42N 36.42E
Drymen Scotland **34** 56.04N 4.27W
Dschang Cameroon **72** 5.25N 10.02E
Dua *r.* Zaïre **72** 3.12N 20.55E
Duart Pt. Scotland **34** 56.27N 5.39W
Dubai U.A.E. **57** 25.13N 55.17E
Dubawnt *r.* Canada **93** 62.50N 102.00W
Dubawnt L. Canada **93** 62.50N 102.00W
Dubbo Australia **80** 32.16S 148.41E
Dubh Artach *i.* Scotland **34** 56.08N 6.38W
Dubica Yugo. **43** 45.11N 16.50E
Dublin Rep. of Ire. **38** 53.21N 6.18W
Dublin *d.* Rep. of Ire. **38** 53.20N 6.18W
Dublin B. Rep. of Ire. **38** 53.20N 6.09W
Du Bois U.S.A. **95** 41.06N 78.46W
Dubrovnik Yugo. **43** 42.40N 18.07E
Dubuque U.S.A. **94** 42.31N 90.41W
Duddington England **29** 52.36N 0.32W
Dudinka U.S.S.R. **49** 69.27N 86.13E
Dudley England **28** 52.30N 2.05W
Dudweiler W. Germany **44** 49.16N 7.03E
Duero *r. see* Douro Spain **41**
Duffield England **33** 52.59N 1.30W
Dufftown Scotland **37** 57.27N 3.09W
Dugi Otok *i.* Yugo. **42** 44.04N 15.00E
Duich, L. Scotland **36** 57.15N 5.30W
Duisburg W. Germany **45** 51.26N 6.45E
Duiveland *i.* Neth. **45** 51.39N 4.00E
Dukhan Qatar **57** 25.24N 50.47E
Dukhtaran *mtn.* Iran **57** 30.39N 60.38E
Dulawan Phil. **61** 7.02N 124.30E
Duleek Rep. of Ire. **38** 53.39N 6.24W
Dülmen W. Germany **45** 51.49N 7.17E
Duluth U.S.A. **94** 46.45N 92.10W
Dulverton England **31** 51.02N 3.33W
Dumbarton Scotland **34** 55.57N 4.35W
Dum-Dum India **58** 22.37N 88.25E
Dumfries Scotland **35** 55.04N 3.37W
Dumfries and Galloway *d.* Scotland **35** 55.05N 3.40W
Dumka India **58** 24.17N 87.15E
Dunany Pt. Rep. of Ire. **38** 53.51N 6.15W
Dunbar Scotland **35** 56.00N 2.31W
Dunbeath Scotland **37** 58.14N 3.26W
Dunbeg Rep. of Ire. **38** 55.04N 8.19W
Dunblane Scotland **35** 56.12N 3.59W
Dunboyne Rep. of Ire. **38** 53.26N 6.30W
Duncannon Rep. of Ire. **39** 52.14N 6.57W
Duncansby Head Scotland **37** 58.39N 3.01W
Dunchurch England **28** 52.21N 1.19W

For Khmer Republic *read* Kampuchea. *For* Malagasy Republic *read* Madagascar. *For* Rhodesia *read* Zimbabwe.

Dundalk to **El Paso** 132

Dundalk Rep. of Ire. **38** 54.01N 6.25W
Dundalk B. Rep. of Ire. **38** 53.55N 6.17W
Dundee R.S.A. **74** 28.10S 30.15E
Dundee Scotland **35** 56.28N 3.00W
Dundrum N. Ireland **38** 54.16N 5.51W
Dundrum Rep. of Ire. **38** 53.18N 6.16W
Dundrum B. N. Ireland **38** 54.12N 5.46W
Dunedin New Zealand **82** 45.52S 170.30E
Dunfermline Scotland **35** 56.04N 3.29W
Dungannon N. Ireland **34** 54.31N 6.47W
Dungarvan Rep. of Ire. **39** 52.06N 7.39W
Dungarvan Harbour *est.* Rep. of Ire. **39** 52.05N 7.36W
Dungeness *c.* England **29** 50.55N 0.58E
Dungiven N. Ireland **34** 54.56N 6.56W
Dungloe Rep. of Ire. **38** 54.57N 8.22W
Dungourney Rep. of Ire. **39** 51.58N 8.06W
Dungu Zaïre **73** 3.40N 28.40E
Dunholme England **33** 53.18N 0.29W
Dunipace Scotland **35** 56.02N 3.45W
Dunkeld Scotland **35** 56.34N 3.36W
Dunkirk France **29** 51.02N 2.23E
Dunkirk U.S.A. **95** 42.29N 79.21W
Dunkwa Central Ghana **70** 5.59N 1.45W
Dún Laoghaire Rep. of Ire. **38** 53.17N 6.09W
Dunlavin Rep. of Ire. **39** 53.04N 6.42W
Dunleer Rep. of Ire. **38** 53.49N 6.24W
Dunmahon Rep. of Ire. **39** 52.09N 7.23W
Dunmanus B. Rep. of Ire. **39** 51.33N 9.45W
Dunmanway Rep. of Ire. **39** 51.43N 9.08W
Dunmore Rep. of Ire. **38** 53.38N 8.45W
Dunmore East Rep. of Ire. **39** 52.10N 7.00W
Dunnet Scotland **37** 58.37N 3.21W
Dunnet B. Scotland **37** 58.38N 3.25W
Dunnet Head Scotland **37** 58.40N 3.23W
Dunoon Scotland **34** 55.57N 4.57W
Dun Rig *mtn.* Scotland **35** 55.34N 3.11W
Duns Scotland **35** 55.47N 2.20W
Dunscore Scotland **35** 55.08N 3.47W
Dunshaughlin Rep. of Ire. **38** 53.30N 6.34W
Dunstable England **29** 51.53N 0.32W
Dunster England **28** 51.11N 3.28W
Dunston Mts. New Zealand **82** 44.45S 169.45E
Dunvegan Scotland **36** 57.26N 6.35W
Dunvegan, Loch Scotland **36** 57.30N 6.40W
Dunvegan Head Scotland **36** 57.31N 6.43W
Duque de Bragança Angola **72** 9.06S 16.11E
Durance *r.* France **40** 43.55N 4.48E
Durango Mexico **96** 24.01N 104.00W
Durango *d.* Mexico **96** 24.01N 104.00W
Durazno Uruguay **103** 33.22S 56.31W
Durban R.S.A. **74** 29.53S 31.00E
Düren W. Germany **45** 50.48N 6.30E
Durham England **33** 54.47N 1.34W
Durham *d.* England **32** 54.42N 1.45W
Durlston Head *c.* England **28** 50.35N 1.58W
Durmitor *mtn.* Yugo. **43** 43.08N 19.03E
Durness Scotland **37** 58.33N 4.45W
Durrës Albania **43** 41.19N 19.27E
Durrow Rep. of Ire. **39** 52.51N 7.25W
Dursey Head Rep. of Ire. **39** 51.35N 10.15W
Dursey I. Rep. of Ire. **39** 51.36N 10.12W
Dursley England **28** 51.41N 2.21W
D'Urville I. New Zealand **82** 40.45S 173.50E
Dushanbe U.S.S.R. **62** 38.38N 68.51E
Düsseldorf W. Germany **45** 51.13N 6.47E
Dvina *r.* U.S.S.R. **46** 57.03N 24.00E
Dyce Scotland **37** 57.12N 2.11W
Dyer, C. Canada **93** 67.45N 61.45W
Dyérem *r.* Cameroon **71** 6.36N 13.10E
Dyfed *d.* Wales **30** 52.00N 4.17W
Dykh Tau *mtn.* U.S.S.R. **47** 43.04N 43.10E
Dymchurch England **29** 51.02N 1.00E
Dyulty *mtn.* U.S.S.R. **57** 41.55N 46.52E
Dzerzhinsk R.S.F.S.R. U.S.S.R. **47** 56.15N 43.30E
Dzerzhinsk White Russia S.S.R. U.S.S.R. **47** 53.40N 27.01E
Dzhambul U.S.S.R. **62** 42.50N 71.25E
Dzhankoi U.S.S.R. **47** 45.40N 34.30E
Dzhugdzhur Range *mts.* U.S.S.R. **49** 57.30N 138.00E
Dzungaria *f.* Asia **62** 44.20N 86.30E

E

Eabamet L. Canada **91** 51.20N 87.30W
Eagle Mtn. U.S.A. **94** 47.50N 90.42W
Eagle Pass *town* U.S.A. **90** 28.44N 100.31W
Eagles Hill Rep. of Ire. **39** 51.48N 10.04W
Ealing England **27** 51.31N 0.20W
Earby England **32** 53.55N 2.08W
Earn *r.* Scotland **35** 56.21N 3.18W
Earn, Loch Scotland **34** 56.23N 4.12W
Easington Durham England **33** 54.47N 1.21W
Easington Humber. England **33** 53.39N 0.08E
Easingwold England **33** 54.08N 1.11W
Easky Rep. of Ire. **38** 54.17N 8.58W
East Anglian Heights *hills* England **29** 52.03N 0.15E
East Barnet England **27** 51.39N 0.09W
Eastbourne England **29** 50.46N 0.18E
Eastbury England **27** 51.36N 0.24W
East C. New Zealand **82** 37.45S 178.30E
East Chicago U.S.A. **94** 41.40N 87.32W
East China Sea Asia **63** 29.00N 125.00E
Eastcote England **27** 51.35N 0.24W
East Dereham England **29** 52.40N 0.57E
Easter I. Pacific Oc. **106** 29.00S 99.00W
Eastern *d.* Ghana **70** 6.20N 0.45W
Eastern *d.* Kenya **73** 0.00 38.00E
Eastern Desert Egypt **56** 28.15N 31.55E
Eastern Ghats *mts.* India **59** 16.30N 80.30E
Eastern Hajar *mts.* Oman **57** 22.45N 58.45E
Eastern Sayan *mts.* U.S.S.R. **49** 53.30N 98.00E
Easter Ross *f.* Scotland **37** 57.46N 4.25W
East European Plain *f.* Europe **47** 57.30N 35.30E
East Flevoland *f.* Neth. **45** 52.30N 5.40E
East Frisian Is. W. Germany **45** 53.45N 7.00E
East Germany Europe **44** 52.15N 12.30E
East Grinstead England **29** 51.08N 0.01W
East Ham England **27** 51.32N 0.04E
East Hartford U.S.A. **95** 41.46N 72.38W
East Horsley England **27** 51.16N 0.26W
East Ilsley England **28** 51.33N 1.15W
Eastington England **28** 51.44N 2.19W
East Kilbride Scotland **34** 55.46N 4.09W
East Lansing U.S.A. **94** 42.45N 84.30W
Eastleigh England **28** 50.58N 1.21W
East Linton Scotland **35** 55.59N 2.39W
East Loch Roag Scotland **36** 58.16N 6.48W
East Loch Tarbert Scotland **36** 57.52N 6.43W
East London R.S.A. **74** 33.00S 27.54E
Eastmain Canada **93** 52.10N 78.30W
Eastmain *r.* Canada **93** 52.10N 78.30W
East Malaysia *d.* Malaysia **60** 4.00N 114.00E
East Markham England **33** 53.16N 0.53W
East Moor *hills* England **33** 53.10N 1.35W
Easton U.S.A. **95** 40.41N 75.13W
East Orange U.S.A. **95** 40.46N 74.14W
East Retford England **33** 53.19N 0.55W
East St. Louis U.S.A. **94** 38.34N 90.04W
East Schelde *est.* Neth. **45** 51.35N 3.57E
East Siberian Sea U.S.S.R. **49** 73.00N 160.00E
East Sussex *d.* England **29** 50.56N 0.12E
East Vlieland Neth. **45** 53.18N 5.04E
Eastwood England **33** 53.02N 1.17W
Eau Claire U.S.A. **94** 44.50N 91.30W
Eauripik *is.* Asia **61** 6.42N 143.04E
Ebbw Vale Wales **28** 51.47N 3.12W
Eberswalde E. Germany **44** 52.50N 13.50E
Ebi Nor *l.* China **62** 45.00N 83.00E
Ebola *r.* Zaïre **72** 3.12N 21.00E
Ebolowa Cameroon **72** 2.56N 11.11E
Ebro *r.* Spain **41** 42.50N 3.59W
Ecclefechan Scotland **35** 55.03N 3.18W
Eccles England **32** 53.29N 2.20W
Eccleshall England **32** 52.52N 2.14W
Echternach Lux. **45** 49.49N 6.25E
Echuca Australia **80** 36.10S 144.20E
Ecija Spain **41** 37.33N 5.04W
Ecuador S. America **102** 2.00S 79.00W
Edam Neth. **45** 52.30N 5.02E
Eday *i.* Scotland **37** 59.11N 2.47W
Ed Damer Sudan **69** 17.37N 33.59E
Eddleston Scotland **35** 55.43N 3.13W
Eddrachillis B. Scotland **36** 58.17N 5.15W
Eddystone *i.* England **31** 50.12N 4.15W
Eddystone Pt. Australia **80** 40.58S 148.12E
Ede Neth. **45** 52.03N 5.40E
Edea Cameroon **72** 3.47N 10.15E
Eden Australia **80** 37.04S 149.54E
Eden *r.* Cumbria England **35** 54.57N 3.02W
Eden *r.* Kent England **27** 51.12N 0.10E
Eden *r.* Scotland **35** 56.22N 2.52W
Edenbridge England **27** 51.12N 0.04E
Edenderry Rep. of Ire. **38** 53.21N 7.05W
Eden Park England **27** 51.23N 0.01W
Ederny N. Ireland **38** 54.32N 7.40W
Edge Hill England **28** 52.08N 1.30W
Edgeworthstown Rep. of Ire. **38** 53.42N 7.38W
Edgware England **27** 51.37N 0.17W
Edhessa Greece **43** 40.47N 22.03E
Edinburgh Scotland **35** 55.57N 3.13W
Edirne Turkey **43** 41.40N 26.35E
Edmonton Canada **92** 53.34N 113.25W
Edmonton England **27** 51.37N 0.02W
Edmundston Canada **95** 47.22N 68.20W
Edremit Turkey **43** 39.35N 27.02E
Edsin Gol *r.* China **62** 42.15N 101.03E
Edwards Plateau *f.* U.S.A. **90** 30.30N 100.30W
Edzell Scotland **37** 56.49N 2.40W
Eeklo Belgium **45** 51.11N 3.34E
Effingham U.S.A. **94** 39.07N 88.33W
Egersund Norway **46** 58.27N 6.01E
Egham England **27** 51.26N 0.34W
Egilsay *i.* Scotland **37** 59.09N 2.56W
Eglington N. Ireland **34** 55.03N 7.10W
Egmont, Mt. New Zealand **82** 39.20S 174.05E
Egremont England **32** 54.28N 3.33W
Eğridir Turkey **56** 37.52N 30.51E
Eğridir L. Turkey **56** 38.04N 30.55E
Egypt Africa **56** 27.00N 29.00E
Eibar Spain **41** 43.11N 2.28W
Eifel *f.* W. Germany **45** 50.10N 6.45E
Eigg *i.* Scotland **36** 56.53N 6.09W
Eigg, Sd. of Scotland **36** 56.51N 6.11W
Eighty Mile Beach *f.* Australia **79** 19.00S 121.00E
Eil, Loch Scotland **36** 56.51N 5.12W
Eilat Israel **56** 29.33N 34.56E
Eildon Resr. Australia **80** 37.10S 146.00E
Eindhoven Neth. **45** 51.26N 5.30E
Eisenach E. Germany **44** 50.59N 10.19E
Eisenhut *mtn.* Austria **44** 47.00N 13.45E
Eisenhüttenstadt E. Germany **44** 52.09N 14.41E
Eishort, Loch Scotland **36** 57.09N 5.58W
Eisleben E. Germany **44** 51.32N 11.33E
Eitorf W. Germany **45** 50.46N 7.27E
Ekeia *r.* Congo **72** 1.40N 16.05E
Eksjo Sweden **46** 57.40N 15.00E
El Aaiún W. Sahara **68** 27.10N 13.11W
El Agheila Libya **68** 30.15N 19.12E
El Alamein Egypt **56** 30.50N 28.57E
Elands *r.* Transvaal R.S.A. **74** 24.55S 29.20E
El'Arish Egypt **56** 31.08N 33.48E
El'Arish, Wadi *r.* Egypt **56** 31.09N 33.49E
El Asnam Algeria **41** 36.20N 1.30E
Elâziğ Turkey **56** 38.41N 39.14E
Elba *i.* Italy **42** 42.47N 10.17E
El Banco Colombia **97** 9.04N 73.59W
Elbasan Albania **43** 41.07N 20.04E
Elbe *r.* W. Germany **44** 53.33N 10.00E
Elbert, Mt. U.S.A. **90** 39.05N 106.27W
Elbeuf France **40** 49.17N 1.01E
Elbistan Turkey **56** 38.14N 37.11E
Elbląg Poland **47** 54.10N 19.25E
Elbrus *mtn.* U.S.S.R. **47** 43.21N 42.29E
Elburg Neth. **45** 52.27N 5.50E
Elburz Mts. Iran **57** 36.00N 52.30E
El Cardon Venezuela **97** 11.24N 70.09W
Elche Spain **41** 38.16N 0.41W
Elde *r.* E. Germany **44** 53.17N 12.40E
Eldorado Argentina **103** 26.28S 54.43W
Eldoret Kenya **73** 0.31N 35.17E
Electrostal U.S.S.R. **47** 55.46N 38.30E
Elephant Butte Resr. U.S.A. **90** 33.25N 107.10W
El Escorial Spain **41** 40.34N 4.08W
Eleuthera I. Bahamas **97** 25.00N 76.00W
El Faiyûm Egypt **56** 29.19N 30.50E
El Fasher Sudan **69** 13.37N 25.22E
El Fekka, Wadi *r.* Tunisia **42** 35.25N 9.40E
El Ferrol Spain **41** 43.29N 8.14W
Elgin Scotland **37** 57.39N 3.20W
Elgin U.S.A. **94** 42.03N 88.19W
El Giza Egypt **56** 30.01N 31.12E
Elgol Scotland **36** 57.09N 6.07W
El Goléa Algeria **68** 30.35N 2.51E
Elgon, Mt. Kenya/Uganda **73** 1.07N 34.35E
El Hamad *des.* Asia **56** 31.45N 39.00E
El Hatob, Wadi *r.* Tunisia **42** 35.25N 9.40E
Elie and Earlsferry Scotland **35** 56.11N 2.50W
Elista U.S.S.R. **47** 46.18N 44.14E
Elizabeth U.S.A. **95** 40.40N 74.13W
El Jauf Libya **69** 24.09N 23.19E
El Khârga Egypt **56** 25.27N 30.32E
Elkhart U.S.A. **94** 41.52N 85.56W
Elkhovo Bulgaria **43** 42.10N 26.35E
Elkins U.S.A. **94** 38.56N 79.53W
Elk Lake *town* Canada **94** 47.44N 80.21W
Elko U.S.A. **90** 40.50N 115.46W
Elland England **32** 53.41N 1.49W
Ellen *r.* England **32** 54.42N 3.30W
Ellen, Mt. U.S.A. **90** 38.06N 110.50W
Ellesmere England **32** 52.55N 2.53W
Ellesmere I. Canada **93** 78.00N 82.00W
Ellesmere Port England **32** 53.17N 2.55W
Ellon Scotland **37** 57.22N 2.05W
El Loz, Jebel *mtn.* Saudi Arabia **56** 28.40N 35.20E
Ellsworth U.S.A. **95** 44.34N 68.24W
El Mahalla el Kubra Egypt **56** 30.59N 31.12E
Elmali Turkey **56** 36.43N 29.56E
El Mansûra Egypt **56** 31.03N 31.23E
El Minya Egypt **56** 28.06N 30.45E
Elmira U.S.A. **95** 42.06N 76.50W
Elmshorn W. Germany **44** 53.46N 9.40E
El Muglad Sudan **69** 11.01N 27.50E
El Natrûn, Wadi *f.* Egypt **56** 30.25N 30.18E
El Obeid Sudan **69** 13.11N 30.10E
Eloy U.S.A. **90** 32.45N 111.33W
El Paso U.S.A. **90** 31.45N 106.30W

For Khmer Republic *read* Kampuchea. *For* Malagasy Republic *read* Madagascar. *For* Rhodesia *read* Zimbabwe.

Elphin Rep. of Ire. **38** 53.50N 8.11W
El Qantara Egypt **56** 30.52N 32.20E
El Qasr Egypt **56** 25.43N 28.54E
El Qatrun Libya **68** 24.55N 14.38E
El Real Panamá **97** 8.06N 77.42W
El Salvador C. America **96** 13.30N 89.00W
Elstead England **27** 51.11N 0.43W
Elstree England **27** 51.39N 0.18W
Eltham England **27** 51.27N 0.04E
El Tigre Venezuela **97** 8.44N 64.18W
El Tîh, Plateau of Egypt **56** 28.50N 34.00E
Elvas Portugal **41** 38.53N 7.10W
Elverum Norway **46** 60.54N 11.33E
El Wak Kenya **73** 2.45N 40.52E
Elwy r. Wales **30** 53.17N 3.27W
Ely England **29** 52.24N 0.16E
Ely U.S.A. **94** 47.53N 91.52W
Elyria U.S.A. **94** 41.22N 82.06W
Emba r. U.S.S.R. **48** 46.40N 53.30E
Embarcación Argentina **103** 23.15S 64.05W
Embleton England **35** 55.30N 1.37W
Embu Kenya **73** 0.32S 37.28E
Emden W. Germany **45** 53.23N 7.13E
Emerson Canada **91** 49.00N 97.11W
Emi Koussi mtn. Chad **71** 19.58N 18.30E
Emlagh Pt. Rep. of Ire. **38** 53.46N 9.45W
Emly Rep. of Ire. **39** 52.28N 8.21W
Emmeloord Neth. **45** 52.43N 5.46E
Emmen Neth. **45** 52.48N 6.55E
Emmerich W. Germany **45** 51.49N 6.16E
Emory Peak U.S.A. **90** 29.15N 103.19W
Empangeni R.S.A. **74** 28.45S 31.54E
Empedrado Argentina **103** 27.59S 58.47W
Emporia U.S.A. **91** 38.24N 96.10W
Ems r. W. Germany **45** 53.14N 7.25E
Ems-Jade Canal W. Germany **45** 53.28N 7.40E
Emyvale Rep. of Ire. **38** 54.20N 6.59W
Enard B. Scotland **36** 58.05N 5.20W
Encarnación Paraguay **103** 27.20S 55.50W
Enchi Ghana **70** 5.53N 2.48W
Ende Indonesia **61** 8.51S 121.40E
Endicott Mts. U.S.A. **92** 68.00N 152.00W
Enfida Tunisia **42** 36.08N 10.22E
Enfield England **27** 51.40N 0.05W
Enfield Rep. of Ire. **38** 53.25N 6.52W
Engaño, C. Phil. **61** 18.30N 122.20E
Engels U.S.S.R. **47** 51.30N 46.07E
Enggano i. Indonesia **60** 5.20S 102.15E
Enghien Belgium **45** 50.42N 4.02E
Englefield Green England **27** 51.26N 0.36W
English Bazar India **58** 25.00N 88.12E
English Channel France/U.K. **40** 50.15N 1.00W
Enkeldoorn Rhodesia **74** 19.01S 30.53E
Enkhuizen Neth. **45** 52.42N 5.17E
Enköping Sweden **46** 59.38N 17.07E
Enna Italy **42** 37.34N 14.15E
En Nahud Sudan **69** 12.41N 28.28E
Ennell, Lough Rep. of Ire. **38** 53.28N 7.25W
Ennerdale Water l. England **32** 54.31N 3.21W
Ennis Rep. of Ire. **39** 52.51N 9.00W
Enniscorthy Rep. of Ire. **39** 52.30N 6.35W
Enniskean Rep. of Ire. **39** 51.45N 8.55W
Enniskerry Rep. of Ire. **39** 53.11N 6.12W
Enniskillen N. Ireland **38** 54.21N 7.40W
Ennistymon Rep. of Ire. **39** 52.56N 9.18W
Enns r. Austria **44** 48.14N 14.22E
Enrick r. Scotland **37** 57.20N 4.28W
Enschede Neth. **45** 52.13N 6.54E
Ensenada Mexico **90** 31.53N 116.35W
Entebbe Uganda **73** 0.08N 32.29E
Entre Rios d. Argentina **103** 31.50S 59.00W
Entre-Rios Moçambique **73** 14.55S 37.09E
Enugu Nigeria **71** 6.20N 7.29E
Epe Neth. **45** 52.21N 5.59E
Epernay France **40** 49.02N 3.58E
Épinal France **44** 48.10N 6.28E
Eport, Loch Scotland **36** 57.30N 7.10W
Epping England **27** 51.42N 0.07E
Epping Forest f. England **27** 51.39N 0.03E
Epping Green England **27** 51.43N 0.06E
Epsom England **27** 51.20N 0.16W
Epworth England **33** 53.30N 0.50W
Equateur d. Zaïre **72** 0.00 21.00E
Equatorial Guinea Africa **72** 2.00N 10.00E
Erbil Iraq **57** 36.12N 44.01E
Erciyaş, Mt. Turkey **56** 38.33N 35.25E
Erdre r. France **40** 47.27N 1.34W
Erebus, Mt. Antarctica **104** 77.40S 167.20E
Ereğli Konya Turkey **56** 37.30N 34.02E
Ereğli Zonguldak Turkey **56** 41.17N 31.26E
Erexim Brazil **103** 27.35S 52.15W
Erft r. W. Germany **45** 51.12N 6.45E
Erfurt E. Germany **44** 50.58N 11.02E
Ergani Turkey **56** 38.17N 39.44E
Ergene r. Turkey **43** 41.02N 26.22E
Erhlien China **63** 43.50N 112.00E

Eriboll, Loch Scotland **37** 58.28N 4.41W
Ericht, Loch Scotland **37** 56.52N 4.20W
Erie U.S.A. **94** 42.07N 80.05W
Erie, L. Canada/U.S.A. **94** 42.15N 81.00W
Erigavo Somali Rep. **69** 10.40N 47.20E
Eriskay i. Scotland **36** 57.04N 7.17W
Erisort, Loch Scotland **36** 58.06N 6.30W
Erith England **27** 51.29N 0.11E
Erkelenz W. Germany **45** 51.05N 6.18E
Erlangen W. Germany **44** 49.36N 11.02E
Ermelo Neth. **45** 52.19N 5.38E
Ermelo R.S.A. **74** 26.32S 29.59E
Erne r. Rep. of Ire. **38** 54.30N 8.17W
Er Rahad Sudan **69** 12.42N 30.33E
Errigal Mtn. Rep. of Ire. **38** 55.02N 8.08W
Erris Head Rep. of Ire. **38** 54.19N 10.00W
Er Roseires Sudan **69** 11.52N 34.23E
Erskine Scotland **34** 55.53N 4.27W
Erzincan Turkey **56** 39.44N 39.30E
Erzurum Turkey **56** 39.57N 41.17E
Esbjerg Denmark **46** 55.28N 8.28E
Escanaba U.S.A. **94** 45.47N 87.04W
Esch Lux. **45** 49.31N 5.59E
Eschweiler W. Germany **45** 50.49N 6.16E
Escondido r. Nicaragua **96** 11.58N 83.45W
Escuintla Guatemala **96** 14.18N 90.47W
Esha Ness c. Scotland **36** 60.29N 1.37W
Esher England **27** 51.23N 0.22W
Eshowe R.S.A. **74** 28.54S 31.28E
Esk r. Cumbria England **32** 54.20N 3.24W
Esk r. Cumbria England **32** 54.58N 3.02W
Esk r. N. Yorks. England **33** 54.29N 0.37W
Eskdale f. Scotland **35** 55.13N 3.08W
Eskilstuna Sweden **46** 59.22N 16.31E
Eskimo Point town Canada **93** 61.10N 94.15W
Eskişehir Turkey **56** 39.46N 30.30E
Esla r. Spain **41** 41.50N 5.48W
Esperance Australia **79** 33.49S 121.52E
Esperanza Argentina **103** 31.29S 61.00W
Espungabera Moçambique **74** 20.28S 32.47E
Essen W. Germany **45** 51.27N 6.57E
Essendon England **27** 51.46N 0.09W
Essequibo r. Guyana **97** 6.30N 58.40W
Essex d. England **27** 51.46N 0.30E
Esslingen W. Germany **44** 48.45N 9.19E
Estats, Pic d' mtn. Spain **40** 42.40N 1.23E
Estepona Spain **41** 36.26N 5.09W
Estevan Canada **90** 49.09N 103.00W
Eston England **33** 54.34N 1.07W
Estonia Soviet Socialist Republic d. U.S.S.R. **46** 58.45N 25.30E
Estrêla, Serra da mts. Portugal **41** 40.20N 7.40W
Estremoz Portugal **41** 38.50N 7.35W
Etah India **58** 27.33N 78.39E
Etaples France **40** 50.31N 1.39E
Etawah India **58** 26.40N 79.20E
Ethiopia Africa **69** 10.00N 39.00E
Ethiopian Highlands Ethiopia **69** 10.00N 37.00E
Etive, Loch Scotland **34** 56.27N 5.15W
Etna, Mt. Italy **42** 37.43N 14.59E
Etobicoke Canada **94** 43.38N 79.30W
Eton England **27** 51.31N 0.37W
Etosha Game Res. S.W. Africa **74** 18.45S 14.55E
Etosha Pan f. S.W. Africa **74** 18.50S 16.30E
Ettelbrück Lux. **45** 49.51N 6.06E
Ettrick r. Scotland **35** 55.36N 2.49W
Ettrick Forest f. Scotland **35** 55.30N 3.00W
Ettrick Pen mtn. Scotland **35** 55.21N 3.16W
Et Tubeiq, Jebel mts. Saudi Arabia **56** 29.30N 37.15E
Euboea i. Greece **43** 38.30N 23.50E
Euclid U.S.A. **94** 41.34N 81.33W
Eufaula Resr. U.S.A. **91** 35.15N 95.35W
Eugene U.S.A. **90** 44.03N 123.07W
Eugenia, Punta c. Mexico **90** 27.50N 115.50W
Eupen Belgium **45** 50.38N 6.04E
Euphrates r. Asia **57** 31.00N 47.27E
Eureka U.S.A. **90** 40.49N 124.10W
Euroa Australia **80** 36.46S 145.35E
Europa, Picos de mts. Spain **41** 43.10N 4.40W
Europe **18**
Europoort Neth. **45** 51.56N 4.08E
Euskirchen W. Germany **45** 50.40N 6.47E
Evale Angola **72** 16.24S 15.50E
Evans, L. Canada **91** 50.55N 77.00W
Evanston U.S.A. **94** 42.02N 87.41W
Evansville U.S.A. **91** 38.02N 87.24W
Evanton Scotland **37** 57.39N 4.21W
Evenlode r. England **28** 51.46N 1.21W
Everard, C. Australia **80** 37.50S 149.16E
Evercreech England **28** 51.08N 2.30W
Everest, Mt. Asia **58** 27.59N 86.56E
Evesham England **28** 52.06N 1.57W
Evje Norway **46** 58.36N 7.51E
Evora Portugal **41** 38.34N 7.54W
Evreux France **40** 49.03N 1.11E
Ewe, Loch Scotland **36** 57.48N 5.38W

Ewell England **27** 51.21N 0.15W
Exe r. England **31** 50.40N 3.28W
Exeter England **31** 50.43N 3.31W
Exmoor Forest hills England **31** 51.08N 3.45W
Exmouth England **28** 50.37N 3.24W
Exuma Is. Bahamas **97** 24.00N 76.00W
Eyasi, L. Tanzania **73** 3.40S 35.00E
Eye England **29** 52.19N 1.09E
Eyemouth Scotland **35** 55.52N 2.05W
Eygurande France **40** 45.40N 2.26E
Eynhallow Sd. Scotland **37** 59.08N 3.05W
Eynort, Loch Scotland **36** 57.13N 7.15W
Eynsford England **27** 51.22N 0.14E
Eyre, L. Australia **79** 28.30S 137.25E
Eyrecourt Rep. of Ire. **39** 53.11N 8.08W

F

Fåborg Denmark **46** 55.06N 10.15E
Fada-N'Gourma U. Volta **70** 12.03N 0.22E
Faenza Italy **42** 44.17N 11.52E
Fagernes Norway **46** 60.59N 9.17E
Fagersta Sweden **46** 59.59N 15.49E
Fairbanks U.S.A. **92** 64.50N 147.50W
Fairborn U.S.A. **94** 39.48N 84.03W
Fairbourne Wales **30** 52.42N 4.03W
Fairfield U.S.A. **95** 41.09N 73.15W
Fair Head N. Ireland **34** 55.13N 6.09W
Fair Isle Scotland **36** 59.32N 1.38W
Fairlie New Zealand **82** 44.05S 170.50E
Fairmont U.S.A. **94** 39.28N 80.08W
Fairweather, Mt. U.S.A. **92** 59.00N 137.30W
Faizabad Afghan. **62** 36.17N 64.49E
Faizabad India **58** 26.46N 82.08E
Fajr, Wadi r. Saudi Arabia **56** 30.00N 38.25E
Fakenham England **33** 52.50N 0.51E
Fakfak Asia **61** 2.55S 132.17E
Fal r. England **31** 50.14N 4.58W
Falaise France **40** 48.54N 0.11W
Falcarragh Rep. of Ire. **38** 55.08N 8.06W
Falcone, C. Italy **42** 40.57N 8.12E
Falcon Resr. U.S.A. **96** 26.46N 98.55W
Falémé r. Senegal **70** 14.55N 12.00W
Falkenberg Sweden **46** 56.54N 12.30E
Falkirk Scotland **35** 56.00N 3.48W
Falkland Scotland **35** 56.15N 3.13W
Falkland Is. S. America **102** 52.00S 60.00W
Fall River town U.S.A. **95** 41.42N 71.08W
Falmouth England **31** 50.09N 5.05W
Falmouth B. England **31** 50.06N 5.05W
False B. R.S.A. **74** 34.20S 18.30E
Falster i. Denmark **44** 54.30N 12.00E
Falun Sweden **46** 60.37N 15.40E
Famagusta Cyprus **56** 35.07N 33.57E
Fanad Head Rep. of Ire. **38** 55.17N 7.38W
Fannich, Loch Scotland **36** 57.38N 5.00W
Fao Iraq **57** 29.57N 48.30E
Faradje Zaïre **73** 3.45N 29.43E
Farafra Oasis Egypt **56** 27.00N 28.20E
Farah Afghan. **57** 32.23N 62.07E
Farah r. Afghan. **57** 31.25N 61.30E
Farallon de Medinilla i. Asia **61** 16.01N 146.04E
Farallon de Pajaros i. Asia **61** 20.33N 144.59E
Faranah Guinea **70** 10.01N 10.47W
Faraulep is. Asia **61** 8.36N 144.33E
Farcet Fen England **29** 52.32N 0.11W
Fareham England **28** 50.52N 1.11W
Farewell, C. Greenland **93** 60.00N 44.20W
Farewell, C. New Zealand **82** 40.30S 172.35E
Farewell Spit f. New Zealand **82** 40.30S 173.00E
Fargo U.S.A. **91** 46.52N 96.59W
Farim Guinea Bissau **70** 12.30N 15.09W
Faringdon England **28** 51.39N 1.34W
Farnborough Hants. England **27** 51.17N 0.46W
Farnborough Kent England **27** 51.22N 0.05E
Farncombe England **27** 51.12N 0.37W
Farndon England **32** 53.06N 2.53W
Farne Is. England **35** 55.38N 1.36W
Farnham Canada **95** 45.17N 72.59W
Farnham England **28** 51.13N 0.49W
Farningham England **27** 51.23N 0.15E
Farnworth England **32** 53.33N 2.33W
Faro Portugal **41** 37.01N 7.56W
Faroe Is. Europe **46** 62.00N 7.00W
Fårösund Sweden **46** 57.51N 19.05E
Farrar r. Scotland **37** 57.25N 4.39W
Farrukhabad India **58** 27.23N 79.35E
Fársala Greece **43** 39.17N 22.22E
Farsi Afghan. **57** 33.47N 63.12E
Farsund Norway **46** 58.05N 6.49E
Fasa Iran **57** 28.55N 53.38E
Fashven mtn. Scotland **37** 58.34N 4.54W
Fastnet Rock i. Rep. of Ire. **39** 51.23N 9.37W
Fastov U.S.S.R. **47** 50.08N 29.59E

For Khmer Republic read Kampuchea. For Malagasy Republic read Madagascar. For Rhodesia read Zimbabwe.

Fatehpur India **58** 25.56N 80.55E
Fathpur India **58** 25.29N 79.00E
Fatshan China **63** 23.03N 113.08E
Fauldhouse Scotland **35** 55.49N 3.41W
Fauquembergues France **29** 50.35N 2.06E
Faurei Romania **43** 45.04N 27.15E
Faüske Norway **46** 67.17N 15.25E
Faversham England **29** 51.18N 0.54E
Favignana *i.* Italy **42** 37.57N 12.19E
Fawley England **28** 50.49N 1.20W
Faxa Flói *b.* Iceland **46** 64.30N 22.50W
Faxe *r.* Sweden **46** 63.15N 17.15E
Fayetteville U.S.A. **91** 35.03N 78.53W
Fdérik Mauritania **68** 22.30N 12.30W
Fear, C. U.S.A. **91** 33.51N 77.59W
Fécamp France **40** 49.45N 0.23E
Federal Capital Territory *d.* Nigeria **71** 8.50N 7.00E
Federal District *d.* Brazil **103** 15.50S 47.40W
Federal District *d.* Mexico **96** 19.20N 99.10W
Fedorovka U.S.S.R. **47** 47.07N 35.19E
Feeagh, Lough Rep. of Ire. **38** 53.56N 9.35W
Fehmarn *i.* W. Germany **44** 54.30N 11.05E
Feilding New Zealand **82** 40.10S 175.25E
Feira Zambia **73** 15.30S 30.27E
Felanitx Spain **41** 39.27N 3.08E
Feldkirch Austria **44** 47.15N 9.38E
Felixstowe England **29** 51.58N 1.20E
Felsted England **27** 51.52N 0.25E
Feltham England **27** 51.27N 0.25W
Felton England **35** 55.18N 1.42W
Femunden *l.* Norway **46** 62.05N 11.55E
Fengkieh China **63** 31.00N 109.30E
Fenit Rep. of Ire. **39** 52.17N 9.51W
Fenyang China **63** 37.14N 111.43E
Feodosiya U.S.S.R. **47** 45.03N 35.23E
Fer, Cap de Algeria **42** 37.07N 7.10E
Ferbane Rep. of Ire. **39** 53.16N 7.50W
Ferdaus Iran **57** 34.00N 58.10E
Fergus Falls *town* U.S.A. **91** 46.18N 96.00W
Ferkéssédougou Ivory Coast **70** 9.30N 5.10W
Fermanagh *d.* N. Ireland **38** 54.21N 7.40W
Fermoselle Spain **41** 41.19N 6.24W
Fermoy Rep. of Ire. **39** 52.08N 8.17W
Ferndown England **28** 50.48N 1.55W
Ferness Scotland **37** 57.28N 3.45W
Ferns Rep. of Ire. **39** 52.35N 6.31W
Ferozepore India **58** 30.55N 74.38E
Ferrara Italy **42** 44.49N 11.38E
Ferret, Cap France **40** 44.42N 1.16W
Feshi Zaïre **72** 6.08S 18.12E
Fetcham England **27** 51.17N 0.22W
Fethard Tipperary Rep. of Ire. **39** 52.28N 7.42W
Fethard Wexford Rep. of Ire. **39** 52.12N 6.51W
Fethiye Turkey **56** 36.37N 29.06E
Fetlar *i.* Scotland **36** 60.37N 0.52W
Fettercairn Scotland **37** 56.51N 2.35W
Fevzipaşa Turkey **56** 37.07N 36.38E
Fez Morocco **68** 34.05N 5.00W
Ffestiniog Wales **30** 52.58N 3.56W
Ffostrasol Wales **30** 52.06N 4.23W
Fife *d.* Scotland **35** 56.10N 3.10W
Fife Ness *c.* Scotland **35** 56.17N 2.36W
Figeac France **40** 44.32N 2.01E
Figueira da Foz Portugal **41** 40.09N 8.51W
Figueras Spain **41** 42.16N 2.57E
Fiji Is. Pacific Oc. **107** 17.00S 178.00E
Filabusi Rhodesia **74** 20.34S 29.20E
Filey England **33** 54.13N 0.18W
Fimi *r.* Zaïre **72** 3.00S 17.00E
Finchley England **27** 51.37N 0.11W
Findhorn Scotland **37** 57.39N 3.37W
Findhorn *r.* Scotland **37** 57.38N 3.37W
Findlay U.S.A. **94** 41.02N 83.40W
Finisterre, C. Spain **41** 42.54N 9.16W
Finland Europe **46** 64.30N 27.00E
Finland, G. of Finland/U.S.S.R. **46** 60.00N 26.50E
Finlay *r.* Canada **92** 56.30N 124.40W
Finn *r.* Rep. of Ire. **38** 54.50N 7.30W
Finsbury England **27** 51.32N 0.06W
Finschhafen P.N.G. **61** 6.35S 147.51E
Fintona N. Ireland **38** 54.31N 7.19W
Fionn Loch Scotland **36** 57.45N 5.27W
Fionnphort Scotland **34** 56.19N 6.23W
Firozabad India **58** 27.09N 78.24E
Firth of Clyde *est.* Scotland **34** 55.35N 4.53W
Firth of Forth *est.* Scotland **35** 56.05N 3.00W
Firth of Lorne *est.* Scotland **34** 56.20N 5.40W
Firth of Tay *est.* Scotland **35** 56.24N 3.08W
Firuzabad Iran **57** 28.50N 52.35E
Fisher Str. Canada **93** 63.00N 84.00W
Fishguard Wales **30** 51.59N 4.59W
Fishguard B. Wales **30** 52.06N 4.44W
Fitchburg U.S.A. **95** 42.35N 71.50W
Fitful Head Scotland **36** 59.55N 1.23W
Fittri, L. Chad **71** 12.50N 17.30E
Fizi Zaïre **73** 4.18S 28.56E

Flackwell Heath England **27** 51.36N 0.43W
Flagstaff U.S.A. **90** 35.12N 111.38W
Flåm Norway **46** 60.51N 7.08E
Flamborough England **33** 54.07N 0.07W
Flamborough Head England **33** 54.06N 0.05W
Flaming Gorge Resr. U.S.A. **90** 41.10N 109.30W
Flanders *f.* Belgium **45** 50.52N 3.00E
Flanders East *d.* Belgium **45** 51.00N 3.45E
Flanders West *d.* Belgium **45** 51.00N 3.00E
Flathead L. U.S.A. **90** 47.50N 114.05W
Flat Holm *i.* England **28** 51.23N 3.08W
Flattery, C. U.S.A. **90** 48.23N 124.43W
Fleet England **28** 51.16N 0.50W
Fleet *r.* Scotland **37** 57.57N 4.05W
Fleetwood England **32** 53.55N 3.01W
Flekkefjord *town* Norway **46** 58.17N 6.40E
Flen Sweden **46** 59.04N 16.39E
Flensburg W. Germany **44** 54.47N 9.27E
Flers France **40** 48.45N 0.34W
Flimby England **32** 54.42N 3.31W
Flinders *r.* Australia **79** 17.30S 140.45E
Flinders I. Australia **80** 40.00S 148.00E
Flinders Range *mts.* Australia **80** 31.00S 138.30E
Flin Flon Canada **93** 54.47N 101.51W
Flint U.S.A. **94** 43.03N 83.40W
Flint *r.* U.S.A. **91** 30.52N 84.35W
Flint Wales **30** 53.15N 3.07W
Flitwick England **29** 51.59N 0.30W
Flora Norway **46** 61.45N 4.55E
Florence Italy **42** 43.46N 11.15E
Florence U.S.A. **91** 34.12N 79.44W
Florenville Belgium **45** 49.42N 5.19E
Flores *i.* Indonesia **61** 8.40S 121.20E
Flores Sea Indonesia **61** 7.00S 121.00E
Florianópolis Brazil **103** 27.35S 48.31W
Florida Uruguay **103** 34.04S 56.14W
Florida *d.* U.S.A. **91** 29.00N 82.00W
Florida, Straits of U.S.A. **97** 24.00N 81.00W
Florida Keys *is.* U.S.A. **96** 24.30N 81.00W
Florina Greece **43** 40.48N 21.25E
Florissant U.S.A. **94** 38.49N 90.24W
Flotta *i.* Scotland **37** 58.49N 3.07W
Flushing Neth. **45** 51.27N 3.35E
Fly *r.* P.N.G. **61** 8.22S 142.23E
Fochabers Scotland **37** 57.37N 3.07W
Focşani Romania **43** 45.40N 27.12E
Foggia Italy **42** 41.28N 15.33E
Foinaven *mtn.* Scotland **37** 58.24N 4.53W
Foix France **40** 42.57N 1.35E
Folda *est.* Norway **46** 64.45N 11.20E
Foligno Italy **42** 42.56N 12.43E
Folkestone England **29** 51.05N 1.11E
Folkingham England **33** 52.54N 0.24W
Fond du Lac Canada **92** 59.20N 107.09W
Fond du Lac U.S.A. **94** 43.48N 88.27W
Fonseca, G. of Honduras **96** 13.10N 87.30W
Fontainebleau France **40** 48.24N 2.42E
Fontenay France **40** 46.28N 0.48W
Foochow China **63** 26.01N 119.20E
Forbes Australia **80** 33.24S 148.03E
Ford U.S.A. **94** 45.10N 5.26W
Fordingbridge England **28** 50.56N 1.48W
Forécariah Guinea **70** 9.28N 13.06W
Forel, Mt. Greenland **93** 67.00N 37.00W
Foreland *c.* England **28** 50.42N 1.06W
Foreland Pt. England **31** 51.15N 3.47W
Forest of Atholl *f.* Scotland **37** 56.50N 3.58W
Forest of Bowland *hills* England **32** 53.57N 2.30W
Forest of Dean *f.* England **28** 51.48N 2.32W
Forest of Rossendale *f.* England **32** 53.43N 2.15W
Forest Row England **29** 51.06N 0.03E
Forfar Scotland **35** 56.38N 2.54W
Forli Italy **42** 44.13N 12.02E
Forlorn Pt. Rep. of Ire. **39** 52.10N 6.35W
Formartine *f.* Scotland **37** 57.21N 2.12W
Formby England **32** 53.34N 3.04W
Formby Pt. England **32** 53.34N 3.07W
Formentera *i.* Spain **41** 38.41N 1.30E
Formiga Brazil **103** 20.30S 45.27W
Formosa *d.* Argentina **103** 25.00S 60.00W
Formosa *town* Argentina **103** 26.06S 58.14W
Formosa *i.* Asia **107** 23.00N 121.00E
Formosa *see* Taiwan Asia **63**
Formosa Brazil **103** 15.30S 47.22W
Formosa Str. Asia **63** 25.00N 120.00E
Forres Scotland **37** 57.37N 3.38W
Forssa Finland **46** 60.49N 23.40E
Forst E. Germany **44** 51.46N 14.39E
Forster Australia **80** 32.11S 152.30E
Fort Albany Canada **93** 52.15N 81.35W
Fortaleza Brazil **102** 3.45S 38.35W
Fort Augustus Scotland **37** 57.09N 4.41W
Fort Beaufort R.S.A. **74** 32.47S 26.38E
Fort Chimo Canada **93** 58.10N 68.15W
Fort Chipewyan Canada **92** 58.46N 111.09W
Fort Collins U.S.A. **90** 40.35N 105.05W

Fort Crampel C.A.R. **71** 7.00N 19.10E
Fort-Dauphin Malagasy Rep. **67** 25.01S 47.00E
Fort-de-France Martinique **97** 14.36N 61.05W
Fort de Possel C.A.R. **72** 5.03N 19.14E
Fort Frances Canada **94** 48.37N 93.23W
Fort George Canada **93** 53.50N 79.01W
Fort George *r.* Canada **93** 53.50N 79.00W
Fort Good Hope Canada **92** 66.16N 128.37W
Forth Scotland **35** 55.46N 3.42W
Forth *r.* Scotland **35** 56.06N 3.48W
Fort Lauderdale U.S.A. **91** 26.08N 80.08W
Fort Liard Canada **92** 60.14N 123.28W
Fort Madison U.S.A. **94** 40.38N 91.21W
Fort Maguire Malaŵi **73** 13.38S 34.59E
Fort McPherson Canada **92** 67.29N 134.50W
Fort Myers U.S.A. **91** 26.39N 81.51W
Fort Nelson Canada **92** 58.48N 122.44W
Fort Norman Canada **92** 64.55N 125.29W
Fort Peck Dam U.S.A. **90** 47.55N 106.15W
Fort Peck Resr. U.S.A. **90** 47.55N 107.00W
Fort Polignac Algeria **68** 26.20N 8.20E
Fort Portal Uganda **73** 0.40N 30.17E
Fort Randall U.S.A. **92** 55.10N 162.47W
Fort Reliance Canada **92** 62.45N 109.08W
Fort Resolution Canada **92** 61.10N 113.39W
Fortrose Scotland **37** 57.34N 4.09W
Fort Rousset Congo **72** 0.30S 15.48E
Fort Rupert Canada **93** 51.30N 79.45W
Fort St. John Canada **92** 56.14N 120.55W
Fort Scott U.S.A. **91** 37.52N 94.43W
Fort Severn Canada **93** 56.00N 87.40W
Fort Shevchenko U.S.S.R. **48** 44.31N 50.15E
Fort Sibut C.A.R. **71** 5.46N 19.06E
Fort Simpson Canada **92** 61.46N 121.15W
Fort Smith U.S.A. **91** 35.22N 94.27W
Fortune *i.* Bahamas **97** 22.30N 74.15W
Fortuneswell England **28** 50.33N 2.27W
Fort Vermilion Canada **92** 58.22N 115.59W
Fort Victoria Rhodesia **74** 20.10S 30.49E
Fort Wayne U.S.A. **94** 41.05N 85.08W
Fort William Scotland **36** 56.49N 5.07W
Fort Worth U.S.A. **91** 32.45N 97.20W
Fort Yukon U.S.A. **92** 66.35N 145.20W
Fostoria U.S.A. **94** 41.10N 83.25W
Fougamou Gabon **72** 1.10S 10.31E
Fougères France **40** 48.21N 1.12W
Foula *i.* Scotland **36** 60.08N 2.05W
Foulness I. England **29** 51.35N 0.55E
Foulness Pt. England **29** 51.37N 1.00E
Foulwind, C. New Zealand **82** 41.45S 171.30E
Foumban Cameroon **72** 5.43N 10.50E
Four Elms England **27** 51.14N 0.07E
Foveaux Str. New Zealand **82** 46.40S 168.00E
Fowey England **31** 50.20N 4.39W
Fowey *r.* England **31** 50.22N 4.40W
Fox *r.* U.S.A. **94** 41.19N 88.59W
Foxe Basin *b.* Canada **93** 67.30N 79.00W
Foxe Channel Canada **93** 65.00N 80.00W
Foxford Rep. of Ire. **38** 53.58N 9.08W
Foxton New Zealand **82** 40.27S 175.18E
Foyle *r.* N. Ireland **38** 55.00N 7.20W
Foyle, Lough N. Ireland **34** 55.05N 7.10W
Foz do Iguaçu Brazil **103** 25.33S 54.31W
Framingham U.S.A. **95** 42.18N 71.25W
Framlingham England **29** 52.14N 1.20E
Franca Brazil **103** 20.33S 47.27W
France Europe **40** 47.00N 2.00E
Franceville Gabon **72** 1.38S 13.31E
Francistown Botswana **74** 21.11S 27.32E
Frankfort R.S.A. **74** 27.16S 28.30E
Frankfort U.S.A. **91** 38.11N 84.53W
Frankfurt E. Germany **44** 52.20N 14.32E
Frankfurt W. Germany **44** 50.06N 8.41E
Franklin *d.* Canada **93** 73.00N 100.00W
Franklin U.S.A. **94** 39.29N 86.02W
Franklin D. Roosevelt L. U.S.A. **90** 47.55N.118.20W
Frank Saale *r.* W. Germany **40** 50.00N 8.21E
Franz Canada **94** 48.28N 84.25W
Franz Josef Land *is.* U.S.S.R. **48** 81.00N 54.00E
Fraser *r.* Canada **90** 49.05N 123.00W
Fraserburg R.S.A. **74** 31.55S 21.31E
Fraserburgh Scotland **37** 57.42N 2.00W
Fray Bentos Uruguay **103** 33.10S 58.20W
Fredericia Denmark **46** 55.34N 9.47E
Frederick U.S.A. **95** 39.25N 77.25W
Fredericksburg U.S.A. **91** 38.18N 77.30W
Fredericton Canada **95** 45.57N 66.40W
Frederikshaab Greenland **93** 62.05N 49.30W
Frederikshavn Denmark **46** 57.28N 10.33E
Fredrikstad Norway **46** 59.15N 10.55E
Freeport Bahamas **97** 26.40N 78.30W
Freeport U.S.A. **94** 42.17N 89.38W
Freetown Sierra Leone **70** 8.30N 13.17W
Freiburg W. Germany **44** 48.00N 7.52E
Freilingen W. Germany **45** 50.33N 7.50E
Freising W. Germany **44** 48.24N 11.45E

For Khmer Republic read Kampuchea. For Malagasy Republic read Madagascar. For Rhodesia read Zimbabwe.

Freital E. Germany **44** 51.00N 13.40E
Fréjus France **40** 43.26N 6.44E
Fremantle Australia **79** 32.07S 115.44E
French Cays *is.* Bahamas **97** 21.31N 72.14W
Frenchman's Cap *mtn.* Australia **80** 42.27S 145.54E
French Territory of Afars and Issas
   see Djibouti Africa **69**
Frenda Algeria **41** 35.04N 1.03E
Freshford Rep. of Ire. **39** 52.44N 7.23W
Fresno U.S.A. **90** 36.41N 119.57W
Freycinet Pen. Australia **80** 42.10S 148.18E
Frias Argentina **103** 28.35S 65.06W
Fribourg Switz. **44** 46.50N 7.10E
Friedrichshafen W. Germany **44** 47.39N 9.29E
Friern Barnet England **27** 51.37N 0.09W
Friesland *d.* Neth. **45** 53.05N 5.45E
Friesoythe W. Germany **45** 53.02N 7.52E
Frimley England **27** 51.19N 0.44W
Frinton England **29** 51.50N 1.16E
Frisa, Loch Scotland **34** 56.33N 6.05W
Frobisher B. Canada **93** 63.00N 66.45W
Frobisher Bay *town* Canada **93** 63.45N 68.30W
Frodsham England **32** 53.17N 2.45W
Fro Havet *est.* Norway **46** 63.55N 9.05E
Frome England **28** 51.16N 2.17W
Frome *r.* England **28** 50.41N 2.05W
Frome, L. Australia **80** 30.45S 139.45E
Frosinone Italy **42** 41.36N 13.21E
Fröya *i.* Norway **46** 63.45N 8.30E
Frunze U.S.S.R. **62** 42.53N 74.46E
Fuchin China **63** 47.15N 131.59E
Fuchow China **63** 28.03N 116.15E
Fuday *i.* Scotland **36** 57.03N 7.23W
Fuerte *r.* Mexico **90** 25.42N 109.20W
Fuerteventura *i.* Canary Is. **68** 28.20N 14.10W
Fujiyama *mtn.* Japan **63** 35.20N 138.30E
Fukien *d.* China **63** 26.30N 118.00E
Fukuoka Japan **63** 33.39N 130.21E
Fulda W. Germany **44** 50.35N 9.41E
Fulham England **27** 51.29N 0.13W
Fumay France **45** 49.59N 4.42E
Fundy, B. of N.America **91** 44.30N 66.30W
Funen *i.* Denmark **46** 55.15N 10.30E
Funzie Scotland **36** 60.35N 0.48W
Furancungo Moçambique **73** 14.51S 33.38E
Furnas Resr. Brazil **103** 21.00S 46.00W
Furneaux Group *is.* Australia **80** 40.15S 148.15E
Furnes Belgium **45** 51.04N 2.40E
Fürstenau W. Germany **45** 52.32N 7.41E
Fürstenwalde E. Germany **44** 52.22N 14.04E
Fürth W. Germany **44** 49.28N 11.00E
Fushun China **63** 41.51N 123.53E
Fussen W. Germany **44** 47.35N 10.43E
Futa Jalon *f.* Guinea **70** 11.30N 12.30W
Fuyu China **63** 45.12N 124.49E
Fyfield England **27** 51.45N 0.16E
Fyne, Loch Scotland **34** 55.55N 5.23W
Fyvie Scotland **37** 57.26N 2.24W

G

Gabela Angola **72** 10.52S 14.24E
Gabes Tunisia **68** 33.52N 10.06E
Gabes, G. of Tunisia **68** 34.00N 11.00E
Gabon Africa **72** 0.00 12.00E
Gabon *r.* Gabon **72** 0.15N 10.00E
Gaborone Botswana **74** 24.45S 25.55E
Gabriel, Mt. Rep. of Ire. **39** 51.34N 9.34W
Gach Saran Iran **57** 30.13N 50.49E
Gadsden U.S.A. **91** 34.00N 86.00W
Gaeta Italy **42** 41.13N 13.35E
Gaeta, G. of Med. Sea **42** 41.05N 13.30E
Gaferut *i.* Asia **61** 9.14N 145.23E
Gagnoa Ivory Coast **70** 6.04N 5.55W
Gagnon Canada **93** 51.56N 68.16W
Gago Coutinho Angola **72** 14.02S 21.35E
Gaillac France **40** 43.54N 1.53E
Gainesville U.S.A. **91** 29.37N 82.31W
Gainford England **32** 54.34N 1.44W
Gainsborough England **33** 53.23N 0.46W
Gairdner, L. Australia **79** 31.30S 136.00E
Gairloch Scotland **36** 57.43N 5.40W
Gairloch, Loch Scotland **36** 57.43N 5.43W
Gairsay *i.* Scotland **37** 59.05N 2.58W
Galala Plateau Egypt **56** 29.00N 32.10E
Galana *r.* Kenya **73** 3.12S 40.09E
Galangue Angola **72** 13.40S 16.00E
Galapagos Is. Ecuador **102** 0.20S 91.00W
Galashiels Scotland **35** 55.37N 2.49W
Galati Romania **43** 45.27N 27.59E
Galena U.S.A. **94** 64.43N 157.00W
Galesburg U.S.A. **94** 40.58N 90.22W
Galey *r.* Rep. of Ire. **39** 52.26N 9.37W

Galita *i.* Tunisia **42** 37.31N 8.55E
Gallan Head Scotland **36** 58.14N 7.01W
Galle Sri Lanka **59** 6.01N 80.13E
Gállego *r.* Spain **41** 41.40N 0.55W
Galley Head Rep. of Ire. **39** 51.32N 8.57W
Gallinas, C. Colombia **102** 12.20N 71.30W
Gallipoli Italy **43** 40.02N 18.01E
Gallipoli Turkey **43** 40.25N 26.31E
Gällivare Sweden **46** 67.10N 20.40E
Galloway *f.* Scotland **34** 55.00N 4.28W
Gallup U.S.A. **90** 35.32N 108.46W
Galong Australia **80** 34.37S 148.34E
Galston Scotland **34** 55.36N 4.23W
Galt Canada **94** 43.21N 80.19W
Galtby Finland **46** 60.08N 21.33E
Galtymore *mtn.* Rep. of Ire. **39** 52.22N 8.13W
Galty Mts. Rep. of Ire. **39** 52.20N 8.10W
Galveston U.S.A. **91** 29.17N 94.48W
Galveston B. U.S.A. **91** 29.40N 94.40W
Galvez Argentina **103** 32.03S 61.14W
Galway Rep. of Ire. **38** 53.17N 9.04W
Galway *d.* Rep. of Ire. **38** 53.25N 9.00W
Galway B. Rep. of Ire. **39** 53.12N 9.07W
Gambia Africa **70** 13.10N 16.00W
Gambia *r.* Gambia **70** 13.28N 15.55W
Gamboma Congo **72** 1.50S 15.58E
Ganale Dorya *r.* Ethiopia **73** 4.13N 42.04E
Gandajika Zaïre **72** 6.46S 23.58E
Gandak *r.* India **58** 25.35N 85.20E
Gander Canada **93** 48.58N 54.34W
Gandia Spain **41** 38.59N 0.11W
Ganges *r.* India **58** 23.30N 90.25E
Ganges, Mouths of the India/Bangla. **58** 22.00N 89.35E
Gangtok India **58** 27.20N 88.39E
Gannat France **40** 46.06N 3.11E
Gannett Peak *mtn.* U.S.A. **90** 43.10N 109.38W
Gao Mali **70** 16.19N 0.09W
Gaoual Guinea **70** 11.44N 13.14W
Gap France **40** 44.33N 6.05E
Gara, Lough Rep. of Ire. **38** 53.57N 8.27W
Gard *r.* France **40** 43.52N 4.40E
Garda, L. Italy **42** 45.40N 10.40E
Gar Dzong China **59** 32.10N 79.59E
Garelochhead Scotland **34** 56.05N 4.49W
Garforth England **33** 53.48N 1.22W
Garies R.S.A. **74** 30.30S 18.00E
Garioch *f.* Scotland **37** 57.18N 2.30W
Garissa Kenya **73** 0.27S 39.49E
Garlieston Scotland **34** 54.46N 4.22W
Garmisch Partenkirchen W. Germany **44** 47.30N 11.05E
Garmouth Scotland **37** 57.40N 3.07W
Garmsar Iran **57** 35.15N 52.21E
Garo Hills India **58** 25.30N 90.30E
Garonne *r.* France **40** 45.00N 0.37W
Garoua Cameroon **71** 9.17N 13.22E
Garrison Resr. U.S.A. **90** 47.30N 102.20W
Garroch Head Scotland **34** 55.43N 5.02W
Garron Pt. N. Ireland **34** 55.03N 5.57W
Garry, Loch Scotland **37** 57.05N 4.55W
Garry L. Canada **93** 66.00N 100.00W
Garstang England **32** 53.53N 2.47W
Garth Wales **30** 52.08N 3.32W
Garthorpe England **33** 53.40N 0.42W
Gartok China **62** 32.00N 80.20E
Garvagh N. Ireland **34** 54.58N 6.42W
Garvão Portugal **41** 37.42N 8.21W
Garve Scotland **37** 57.37N 4.41W
Garvellachs *i.* Scotland **34** 56.15N 5.45W
Garvie Mts. New Zealand **82** 45.15S 169.00E
Garwah India **58** 24.11N 83.47E
Gary U.S.A. **94** 41.34N 87.20W
Gascony, G. of France **40** 44.00N 2.40W
Gascoyne *r.* Australia **79** 25.00S 113.40E
Gaspé Canada **93** 48.50N 64.30W
Gaspé Pen. Canada **95** 48.30N 66.45W
Gata, C. Cyprus **56** 34.33N 33.03E
Gata, Cabo de Spain **41** 36.45N 2.11W
Gata, Sierra de *mts.* Spain **41** 40.20N 6.30W
Gatehouse of Fleet Scotland **34** 54.53N 4.12W
Gateshead England **32** 54.57N 1.35W
Gatineau *r.* Canada **95** 45.25N 75.43W
Gatooma Rhodesia **74** 18.16S 29.55E
Gatun L. Canal Zone **97** 9.20N 80.00W
Gauhati India **59** 26.05N 91.55E
Gauja *r.* U.S.S.R. **46** 57.10N 24.17E
Gavá Spain **41** 41.18N 2.00E
Gävle Sweden **46** 60.41N 17.10E
Gawler Australia **80** 34.38S 138.44E
Gaya India **58** 24.48N 85.00E
Gaya Niger **71** 11.53N 3.31E
Gaydon England **28** 52.11N 1.27W
Gaza Egypt **56** 31.30N 34.28E
Gaza *d.* Moçambique **74** 23.30S 33.00E
Gaziantep Turkey **56** 37.04N 37.21E
Gdańsk Poland **46** 54.22N 18.38E
Gdańsk, G. of Poland **47** 54.45N 19.15E

Gdov U.S.S.R. **46** 58.48N 27.52E
Gdynia Poland **46** 54.31N 18.30E
Geal Chàrn *mtn.* Scotland **37** 57.06N 3.30W
Gebze Turkey **56** 40.48N 29.26E
Gediz *r.* Turkey **43** 38.37N 26.47E
Gedser Denmark **44** 54.35N 11.57E
Geel Belgium **45** 51.10N 5.00E
Geelong Australia **80** 38.10S 144.26E
Geh Iran **57** 26.14N 60.15E
Geidam Nigeria **71** 12.55N 11.55E
Geilenkirchen W. Germany **45** 50.58N 6.08E
Gelderland *d.* Neth. **45** 52.05N 6.00E
Geldern W. Germany **45** 51.31N 6.19E
Geleen Neth. **45** 50.58N 5.51E
Gelligaer Wales **31** 51.40N 3.18W
Gelsenkirchen W. Germany **45** 51.30N 7.05E
Gemas Malaysia **60** 2.35N 102.35E
Gembloux Belgium **45** 50.34N 4.42E
Gemena Zaïre **72** 3.14N 19.48E
Gemlik Turkey **56** 40.26N 29.10E
Geneina Sudan **69** 13.27N 22.30E
General Acha Argentina **103** 37.25S 64.38W
General Alvear Argentina **103** 34.59S 67.40W
Geneva Switz. **44** 46.13N 6.09E
Geneva, L. Switz. **44** 46.30N 6.30E
Genichesk U.S.S.R. **47** 46.10N 34.49E
Genil *r.* Spain **41** 37.42N 5.20W
Genk Belgium **44** 50.58N 5.30E
Genoa Italy **40** 44.24N 8.54E
Genoa, G. of Italy **40** 44.12N 8.55E
Gent Belgium **45** 51.02N 3.42E
George *r.* Canada **93** 58.30N 66.00W
George R.S.A. **74** 33.57S 22.28E
George, L. Australia **80** 35.07S 149.22E
George, L. Uganda **73** 0.00 30.10E
George, L. U.S.A. **95** 43.30N 73.30W
George Town Australia **80** 41.04S 146.48E
Georgetown Cayman Is. **96** 19.20N 81.23W
Georgetown Guyana **102** 6.46N 58.10W
George Town Malaysia **60** 5.30N 100.16E
Georgia *d.* U.S.A. **91** 33.00N 83.00W
Georgia, Str. of Canada **90** 49.15N 123.45W
Georgian B. Canada **94** 45.15N 80.45W
Georgia Soviet Socialist Republic *d.* U.S.S.R. **56** 42.00N 43.30E
Gera E. Germany **44** 50.51N 12.11E
Geraardsbergen Belgium **45** 50.47N 3.53E
Geraldton Australia **79** 28.49S 114.36E
Germiston R.S.A. **74** 26.15S 28.10E
Gerona Spain **41** 41.59N 2.49E
Gerrards Cross England **27** 51.35N 0.34W
Getafe Spain **41** 40.18N 3.44W
Gete *r.* Belgium **45** 50.58N 5.07E
Geyve Turkey **56** 40.32N 30.18E
Gezira *f.* Sudan **69** 14.30N 33.00E
Ghadames Libya **68** 30.10N 9.30E
Ghaghara *r.* India **58** 25.45N 84.50E
Ghana Africa **70** 8.00N 1.00W
Ghanzi Botswana **74** 21.34S 21.42E
Ghardaïa Algeria **68** 32.20N 3.40E
Ghat Libya **68** 24.59N 10.11E
Ghazaouet Algeria **41** 35.10N 1.50W
Ghaziabad India **58** 28.37N 77.30E
Ghazipur India **58** 25.36N 83.36E
Ghurian Afghan. **57** 34.20N 61.25E
Gialo Libya **69** 29.00N 21.30E
Giant's Causeway *f.* N. Ireland **34** 55.14N 6.32W
Gibraltar Europe **41** 36.07N 5.22W
Gibraltar, Str. of Africa/Europe **41** 36.00N 5.25W
Gibraltar Pt. England **33** 53.05N 0.20E
Giessen W. Germany **44** 50.35N 8.42E
Gieten Neth. **45** 53.01N 6.45E
Gifford Scotland **35** 55.55N 2.45W
Gifu Japan **63** 35.27N 136.46E
Gigha *i.* Scotland **34** 55.41N 5.44W
Gigha, Sd. of Scotland **34** 55.40N 5.41W
Giglio *i.* Italy **42** 42.21N 10.53E
Gijón Spain **41** 43.32N 5.40W
Gila *r.* U.S.A. **90** 32.45N 114.30W
Gilbert Is. Pacific Oc. **107** 2.00S 175.00E
Gilé Moçambique **73** 16.10S 38.17E
Gilehdar Iran **57** 27.36N 52.42E
Gilgandra Australia **80** 31.42S 148.40E
Gilgil Kenya **73** 0.29S 36.19E
Gilgit Jammu and Kashmir **58** 35.54N 74.20E
Gilgunnia Australia **80** 32.25S 146.04E
Gill, Lough Rep. of Ire. **38** 54.15N 8.14W
Gillingham Dorset England **28** 51.02N 2.17W
Gillingham Kent England **27** 51.24N 0.33E
Gilsland England **35** 54.59N 2.34W
Gimbala, Jebel *mtn.* Sudan **69** 13.00N 24.20E
Ginz *r.* W. Germany **44** 48.28N 10.18E
Gippsland *f.* Australia **80** 37.40S 147.00E
Giresun Turkey **56** 40.55N 38.25E
Giri *r.* Zaïre **72** 0.30N 17.58E
Gironde *r.* France **40** 45.35N 1.00W

Girvan Scotland **34** 55.15N 4.51W
Gisborne New Zealand **82** 38.41S 178.02E
Gitega Burundi **73** 3.25S 29.58E
Giurgiu Romania **43** 43.52N 25.58E
Givet France **45** 50.08N 4.49E
Gizhiga U.S.S.R. **49** 62.00N 160.34E
Gizhiga G. U.S.S.R. **49** 61.00N 158.00E
Gjövik Norway **46** 60.47N 10.41E
Glacier Peak mtn. U.S.A. **90** 48.07N 121.06W
Glamis Scotland **35** 56.37N 3.01W
Glan r. W. Germany **45** 49.46N 7.43E
Glanamman Wales **31** 51.49N 3.54W
Glanaruddery Mts. Rep. of Ire. **39** 52.19N 9.27W
Glandorf W. Germany **45** 52.05N 8.00E
Glanton England **35** 55.25N 1.53W
Glasgow Scotland **34** 55.52N 4.15W
Glasgow U.S.A. **90** 48.12N 106.37W
Glas Maol mtn. Scotland **37** 56.52N 3.22W
Glass, Loch Scotland **37** 57.43N 4.30W
Glasson England **32** 54.00N 2.49W
Glastonbury England **28** 51.09N 2.42W
Glazov U.S.S.R. **47** 58.09N 52.42E
Glen r. England **29** 52.50N 0.06W
Glen Affric f. Scotland **36** 57.15N 5.03W
Glen Almond f. Scotland **35** 56.28N 3.48W
Glenanane Rep. of Ire. **38** 53.37N 9.40W
Glénans, Îles de France **40** 47.43N 3.57W
Glenarm N. Ireland **34** 54.57N 5.58W
Glen Cannich f. Scotland **36** 57.19N 5.03W
Glen Clova f. Scotland **37** 56.48N 3.01W
Glen Coe f. Scotland **34** 56.40N 5.03W
Glendive U.S.A. **90** 47.08N 104.42W
Glen Dochart f. Scotland **34** 56.25N 4.30W
Glen Dye f. Scotland **37** 56.58N 2.34W
Glenelg Scotland **36** 57.13N 5.37W
Glenelly r. N. Ireland **34** 54.45N 7.19W
Glen Esk f. Scotland **37** 56.53N 2.46W
Glen Etive f. Scotland **34** 56.37N 5.01W
Glenfinnan Scotland **36** 56.53N 5.27W
Glengarriff Rep. of Ire. **39** 51.45N 9.33W
Glen Garry f. Highland Scotland **36** 57.03N 5.04W
Glen Garry f. Tayside Scotland **37** 56.47N 4.02W
Glengormley N. Ireland **34** 54.40N 5.59W
Glen Head Rep. of Ire. **38** 54.44N 8.46W
Glen Innes Australia **80** 29.42S 151.45E
Glen Kinglass f. Scotland **34** 56.29N 5.03W
Glenluce Scotland **34** 54.53N 4.48W
Glen Lyon f. Scotland **34** 56.36N 4.15W
Glen Mòr f. Scotland **37** 57.15N 4.30W
Glen More f. Scotland **34** 56.25N 5.48W
Glennagalliagh mtn. Rep. of Ire. **39** 52.49N 8.32W
Glen Orchy f. Scotland **34** 56.28N 4.50W
Glen Orrin f. Scotland **37** 57.30N 4.45W
Glen Prosen f. Scotland **37** 56.45N 3.05W
Glenrothes Scotland **35** 56.12N 3.10W
Glen Roy f. Scotland **37** 56.58N 4.47W
Glens Falls town U.S.A. **95** 43.17N 73.41W
Glenshaw U.S.A. **94** 40.31N 79.57W
Glenshee f. Scotland **37** 56.45N 3.25W
Glen Spean f. Scotland **37** 56.53N 4.40W
Glenties Rep. of Ire. **38** 54.47N 8.17W
Glen Tilt f. Scotland **37** 56.50N 3.45W
Glenwhappen Rig mtn. Scotland **35** 55.33N 3.30W
Glin Rep. of Ire. **39** 52.34N 9.17W
Glittertind mtn. Norway **46** 61.30N 8.20E
Głogów Poland **44** 51.40N 16.06E
Glomma r. Norway **46** 59.15N 10.55E
Glossop England **32** 53.27N 1.56W
Gloucester England **28** 51.52N 2.15W
Gloucester U.S.A. **95** 42.37N 70.41W
Gloucestershire d. England **28** 51.45N 2.00W
Glyncorrwg Wales **31** 51.40N 3.39W
Glyn Neath Wales **31** 51.45N 3.37W
Gmünd Austria **44** 48.47N 14.59E
Gmunden Austria **44** 47.56N 13.48E
Gniezno Poland **47** 52.32N 17.32E
Goa d. India **58** 15.30N 74.00E
Goalpara India **58** 26.10N 90.38E
Goat Fell mtn. Scotland **34** 55.37N 5.12W
Gobabis S.W. Africa **74** 22.30S 18.58E
Gobi des. Asia **62** 43.30N 103.30E
Godalming England **27** 51.11N 0.37W
Godavari r. India **59** 16.40N 82.15E
Goderich Canada **94** 43.43N 81.43W
Godhavn Greenland **93** 69.20N 53.30W
Godhra India **58** 22.49N 73.40E
Godmanchester England **29** 52.19N 0.11W
Godrevy Pt. England **31** 51.15N 5.25W
Godstone England **27** 51.15N 0.04W
Godthaab Greenland **93** 64.10N 51.40W
Gogra r. see Ghaghara India **58**
Goiandira Brazil **103** 18.06S 48.07W
Goiânia Brazil **103** 16.43S 49.18W
Goiás Brazil **103** 15.57S 50.07W
Goiás d. Brazil **103** 16.00S 50.10W
Göksun Turkey **56** 38.03N 36.30E

Gol Norway **46** 60.43N 8.55E
Gola I. Rep. of Ire. **38** 55.05N 8.21W
Golden Canada **90** 51.19N 116.58W
Golden Rep. of Ire. **39** 52.30N 7.59W
Golden B. New Zealand **82** 40.45S 172.50E
Golden Vale f. Rep. of Ire. **39** 52.30N 8.07W
Golders Green England **27** 51.35N 0.12W
Golfito Costa Rica **96** 8.42N 83.10W
Golspie Scotland **37** 57.58N 3.58W
Golyshi U.S.S.R. **47** 58.26N 45.28E
Goma Zaïre **73** 1.37S 29.10E
Gombe Nigeria **71** 10.17N 11.20E
Gombe r. Tanzania **73** 4.43S 31.30E
Gomel U.S.S.R. **47** 52.25N 31.00E
Gómez Palacio Mexico **96** 25.39N 103.30W
Gomshall England **27** 51.13N 0.25W
Gonaives Haiti **97** 19.29N 72.42W
Gonâve, G. of Haiti **97** 19.20N 73.00W
Gonâve I. Haiti **97** 18.50N 73.00W
Gonbad-e-Kavus Iran **57** 37.15N 55.11E
Gonda India **58** 27.08N 81.58E
Gondar Ethiopia **69** 12.39N 37.29E
Gongola d. Nigeria **71** 8.40N 11.30E
Gongola r. Nigeria **71** 9.30N 12.06E
Good Hope, C. of R.S.A. **74** 34.20S 18.25E
Goodooga Australia **80** 29.08S 147.30E
Goodwin Sands f. England **29** 51.16N 1.31E
Goole England **33** 53.42N 0.52W
Goondiwindi Australia **80** 28.30S 150.17E
Goose L. U.S.A. **90** 41.55N 120.25W
Göppingen W. Germany **44** 48.43N 9.39E
Gorakhpur India **58** 26.45N 83.23E
Gordon Scotland **35** 55.41N 2.34W
Gore New Zealand **82** 46.06S 168.58E
Gorebridge Scotland **35** 55.51N 3.02W
Gorey Rep. of Ire. **39** 52.40N 6.19W
Gorgan Iran **57** 36.50N 54.29E
Gorgan r. Iran **57** 37.00N 54.00E
Gori U.S.S.R. **57** 41.59N 44.05E
Gorinchem Neth. **45** 51.50N 4.59E
Goring England **28** 51.32N 1.08W
Gorizia Italy **42** 45.58N 13.37E
Gorki U.S.S.R. **47** 56.20N 44.00E
Görlitz E. Germany **44** 51.09N 15.00E
Gorlovka U.S.S.R. **47** 48.17N 38.05E
Gorm, Loch Scotland **34** 55.48N 6.25W
Gorongosa r. Moçambique **74** 20.29S 34.36E
Gorontalo Indonesia **61** 0.33N 123.05E
Gorseinon Wales **31** 51.40N 4.03W
Gort Rep. of Ire. **39** 53.04N 8.49W
Gortin N. Ireland **38** 54.43N 7.15W
Gorzów Wielkopolski Poland **44** 52.42N 15.12E
Gosford Australia **80** 33.25S 151.18E
Gosforth England **35** 55.02N 1.35W
Goslar W. Germany **44** 51.54N 10.25E
Gospić Yugo. **42** 4.34N 15.23E
Gosport England **28** 50.48N 1.08W
Göta Canal Sweden **46** 57.50N 11.50E
Göteborg Sweden **46** 57.45N 12.00E
Gotha E. Germany **44** 50.57N 10.43E
Gotland i. Sweden **46** 57.30N 18.30E
Göttingen W. Germany **44** 51.32N 9.57E
Gouda Neth. **45** 52.01N 4.43E
Gough I. Atlantic Oc. **112** 41.00S 10.00W
Gouin Resr. Canada **95** 48.40N 74.45W
Goulburn Australia **80** 34.47S 149.43E
Goundam Mali **70** 17.27N 3.39W
Gourdon France **40** 44.45N 1.22E
Gouré Niger **71** 13.59N 10.15E
Gourma-Rarous Mali **70** 16.58N 1.50W
Gournay France **40** 49.29N 1.44E
Gourock Scotland **34** 55.58N 4.49W
Gourock Range mts. Australia **80** 35.45S 149.25E
Gower pen. Wales **31** 51.37N 4.10W
Gowna, Lough Rep. of Ire. **38** 53.50N 7.34W
Gowran Rep. of Ire. **39** 52.38N 7.04W
Gozo i. Malta **42** 36.03N 14.16E
Gracias á Dios, Cabo c. Honduras/Nicaragua **96** 15.00N 83.10W
Grafton Australia **80** 29.40S 152.56E
Grafton U.S.A. **91** 48.28N 97.25W
Grahamstown R.S.A. **74** 33.19S 26.32E
Graiguenamanagh Rep. of Ire. **39** 52.33N 6.57W
Grain England **29** 51.28N 0.43E
Grampian d. Scotland **37** 57.22N 2.35W
Grampian Highlands Scotland **37** 56.55N 4.00W
Grampound England **31** 50.18N 4.54W
Granada Nicaragua **96** 11.58N 85.59W
Granada Spain **41** 37.10N 3.35W
Granard Rep. of Ire. **38** 53.47N 7.30W
Granby Canada **95** 45.23N 72.44W
Gran Canaria i. Canary Is. **68** 28.00N 15.30W
Gran Chaco f. S. America **103** 23.20S 60.00W
Grand r. Canada **94** 42.53N 79.35W
Grand Bahama I. Bahamas **97** 26.35N 78.00W
Grand Bassam Ivory Coast **70** 5.14N 3.45W

Grand Canal Rep. of Ire. **38** 53.21N 6.14W
Grand Canyon f. U.S.A. **90** 36.15N 113.00W
Grand Canyon town U.S.A. **90** 36.04N 112.07W
Grand Cayman i. Cayman Is. **96** 19.20N 81.30W
Grande r. Brazil **103** 20.00S 51.00W
Grande Comore i. Comoro Is. **73** 11.35S 43.20E
Grande I. Brazil **103** 23.15S 44.30W
Grande Prairie town Canada **92** 55.10N 118.52W
Grand Falls town New Brunswick Canada **95** 47.02N 67.46W
Grand Falls town Newfoundland Canada **93** 48.57N 55.40W
Grand Forks U.S.A. **91** 47.57N 97.05W
Grand Fort Philippe France **29** 51.00N 2.06E
Grand Island town U.S.A. **90** 40.56N 98.21W
Grand Junction U.S.A. **90** 39.04N 108.33W
Grand Manan I. Canada **95** 44.45N 66.45W
Grand Marais U.S.A. **94** 47.45N 90.20W
Grândola Portugal **41** 38.10N 8.34W
Grand Rapids town Mich. U.S.A. **94** 42.57N 85.40W
Grand Rapids town Minn. U.S.A. **94** 47.13N 93.31W
Grand Teton mtn. U.S.A. **90** 43.45N 110.50W
Grand Union Canal England **27** 52.37N 0.30W
Graney, Lough Rep. of Ire. **39** 52.59N 8.40W
Grangemouth Scotland **35** 56.01N 3.44W
Grange-over-Sands England **32** 54.12N 2.55W
Granite Peak mtn. U.S.A. **90** 45.10N 109.50W
Grankulla Finland **46** 60.12N 24.45E
Granóllers Spain **41** 41.37N 2.18E
Gran Paradiso mtn. Italy **42** 45.31N 7.15E
Gran Pilastro mtn. Italy **44** 46.58N 11.44E
Grantham England **33** 52.55N 0.39W
Grantown-on-Spey Scotland **37** 57.20N 3.38W
Grants Pass U.S.A. **90** 42.26N 123.20W
Granville France **40** 48.50N 1.35W
Graskop R.S.A. **74** 24.55S 30.50E
Grasse France **40** 43.40N 6.56E
Grave Neth. **45** 51.45N 5.45E
Grave, Pointe de France **40** 45.35N 1.04W
Gravelines France **29** 50.59N 2.08E
Gravesend England **27** 51.27N 0.24E
Gravir Scotland **36** 58.03N 6.26W
Gray France **40** 47.27N 5.35E
Grayling U.S.A. **94** 44.40N 84.43W
Grays England **27** 51.29N 0.20E
Graz Austria **44** 47.05N 15.22E
Great Abaco I. Bahamas **97** 26.30N 77.00W
Great Artesian Basin f. Australia **79** 26.30S 143.02E
Great Australian Bight Australia **79** 33.20S 130.00E
Great Baddow England **27** 51.43N 0.29E
Great Bardfield England **29** 51.57N 0.26E
Great Barrier I. New Zealand **82** 36.15S 175.30E
Great Barrier Reef f. Australia **79** 16.30S 146.30E
Great Basin f. U.S.A. **90** 39.00N 115.30W
Great Bear L. Canada **92** 66.00N 120.00W
Great Bend town U.S.A. **90** 38.22N 98.47W
Great Bernera i. Scotland **36** 58.13N 6.50W
Great Blasket I. Rep. of Ire. **39** 52.05N 10.32W
Great Bookham England **27** 51.16N 0.20W
Great Chesterford England **29** 52.04N 0.11E
Great Coates England **33** 53.34N 0.05W
Great Coco i. Burma **60** 14.10N 93.25E
Great Dividing Range mts. Australia **80** 33.00S 151.00E
Great Driffield England **33** 54.01N 0.26W
Great Dunmow England **27** 51.53N 0.22E
Great Eccleston England **32** 53.51N 2.52W
Greater Antilles is. C. America **97** 17.00N 70.00W
Greater London d. England **27** 51.31N 0.06W
Greater Manchester d. England **32** 53.30N 2.18W
Great Exuma I. Bahamas **97** 23.00N 76.00W
Great Falls town U.S.A. **90** 47.30N 111.16W
Great Fish r. S.W. Africa **74** 28.07S 17.10E
Great Harwood England **32** 53.48N 2.24W
Great Inagua I. Bahamas **97** 21.00N 73.20W
Great Irgiz r. U.S.S.R. **47** 52.00N 47.20E
Great Karas Mts. S.W. Africa **74** 27.30S 18.45E
Great Karroo f. R.S.A. **74** 32.50S 22.30E
Great Khingan Shan mts. China **63** 50.00N 122.10E
Great L. Australia **80** 41.50S 146.43E
Great Lakes N. America **106** 47.00N 83.00W
Great Malvern England **28** 52.07N 2.19W
Great Missenden England **27** 51.43N 0.43W
Great Nama Land f. S.W. Africa **74** 25.30S 17.30E
Great Nicobar i. India **59** 7.00N 93.50E
Great Ormes Head Wales **30** 53.20N 3.52W
Great Ouse r. England **33** 52.47N 0.23E
Great Plains f. N. America **106** 45.00N 107.00W
Great Rift Valley f. Africa **107** 7.00S 33.00E
Great Ruaha r. Tanzania **73** 7.55S 37.52E
Great St. Bernard Pass Italy/Switz. **40** 45.52N 7.11E
Great Salt L. U.S.A. **90** 41.10N 112.40W
Great Sandy Desert Australia **107** 22.00S 125.00E
Great Sandy Desert Saudi Arabia **56** 28.40N 41.30E
Great Shelford England **29** 52.09N 0.08E
Great Shunner Fell mtn. England **32** 54.22N 2.12W
Great Skellig i. Rep. of Ire. **39** 51.46N 10.33W

Great Slave L. Canada 92 61.30N 114.20W
Great Stour r. England 29 51.19N 1.15E
Great Torrington England 31 50.57N 4.09W
Great Whale r. Canada 93 55.28N 77.45W
Great Whernside mtn. England 32 54.09N 1.59W
Great Yarmouth England 29 52.40N 1.45E
Great Zab r. Iraq 57 35.37N 43.20E
Gredos, Sierra de mts. Spain 41 40.18N 5.20W
Greece Europe 43 39.00N 22.00E
Greece U.S.A. 95 43.14N 77.38W
Greeley U.S.A. 90 40.26N 104.43W
Green r. U.S.A. 90 38.20N 109.53W
Green B. U.S.A. 94 45.00N 87.30W
Green Bay town U.S.A. 94 44.32N 88.00W
Greencastle Rep. of Ire. 34 55.12N 6.59W
Greenhithe England 27 51.28N 0.17E
Greenland N. America 93 68.00N 45.00W
Greenlaw Scotland 35 55.43N 2.28W
Green Lowther mtn. Scotland 35 55.23N 3.45W
Green Mts. U.S.A. 95 43.30N 73.00W
Greenock Scotland 34 55.57N 4.45W
Greenore Pt. Rep. of Ire. 39 52.14N 6.19W
Greensboro U.S.A. 91 36.03N 79.50W
Greenstone Pt. Scotland 36 57.55N 5.37W
Greenville Liberia 70 5.01N 9.03W
Greenville Maine U.S.A. 95 45.28N 69.36W
Greenville Miss. U.S.A. 91 33.23N 91.03W
Greenville S.C. U.S.A. 91 34.52N 82.25W
Greenwich d. England 27 51.28N 0.00
Greenwich U.S.A. 95 41.02N 73.37W
Gregory, L. Australia 80 28.55S 139.00E
Greifswald E. Germany 44 54.06N 13.24E
Greiz E. Germany 44 50.40N 12.11E
Grenå Denmark 46 56.25N 10.53E
Grenada C. America 97 12.15N 61.45W
Grenade France 40 43.47N 1.10E
Grenoble France 40 45.11N 5.43E
Greta r. England 32 54.09N 2.37W
Gretna Scotland 35 55.00N 3.04W
Grey r. New Zealand 82 42.28S 171.13E
Greyabbey N. Ireland 34 54.32N 5.35W
Greymouth New Zealand 82 42.28S 171.12E
Grey Range mts. Australia 80 28.30S 142.15E
Greystones Rep. of Ire. 39 53.09N 6.04W
Gribbin Head England 31 50.19N 4.41W
Griffith Australia 80 34.18S 146.04E
Grim, C. Australia 80 40.45S 144.45E
Griminish Pt. Scotland 36 57.40N 7.29W
Grimsay i. Scotland 36 57.29N 7.14W
Grimsby England 33 53.35N 0.05W
Grimsvötn mtn. Iceland 46 64.30N 17.10W
Griqualand East f. R.S.A. 74 30.30S 29.00E
Griqualand West f. R.S.A. 74 28.55S 22.50E
Gris Nez, Cap France 29 50.52N 1.35E
Grodno U.S.S.R. 47 53.40N 23.50E
Groenlo Neth. 45 52.02N 6.36E
Groix, Île de France 40 47.38N 3.26N
Gröningen Neth. 45 53.13N 6.35E
Gröningen d. Neth. 45 53.15N 6.45E
Groomsport N. Ireland 34 54.41N 5.37W
Groot r. Cape Province R.S.A. 74 33.57S 25.00E
Groote Eylandt i. Australia 79 14.00S 136.30E
Grootfontein S.W. Africa 74 19.32S 18.05E
Grootlaagte r. Botswana 74 20.50S 22.05E
Grosnez Pt. Channel Is. 31 49.15N 2.15W
Grossenbrode W. Germany 44 54.23N 11.07E
Grosseto Italy 42 42.46N 11.08E
Gross Glockner mtn. Austria 44 47.05N 12.50E
Grote Nete r. Belgium 45 51.07N 4.20E
Groundhog r. Canada 94 48.45N 82.00W
Grove Park England 27 51.24N 0.03E
Groznyy U.S.S.R. 47 43.21N 45.42E
Grumeti r. Tanzania 73 2.05S 33.45E
Gruting Voe b. Scotland 36 60.12N 1.32W
Guadalajara Mexico 96 20.30N 103.20W
Guadalajara Spain 41 40.37N 3.10W
Guadalete r. Spain 41 36.37N 6.15W
Guadalmena r. Spain 41 38.00N 3.50W
Guadalquivir r. Spain 41 36.50N 6.20W
Guadalupe Mexico 96 25.41N 100.15W
Guadalupe, Sierra de mts. Spain 41 39.30N 5.25W
Guadalupe I. Mexico 90 29.00N 118.25W
Guadarrama r. Spain 41 39.55N 4.10W
Guadarrama, Sierra de mts. Spain 41 41.00N 3.50W
Guadeloupe C. America 97 16.20N 61.40W
Guadiana r. Spain 41 37.10N 8.36W
Guadix Spain 41 37.19N 3.08W
Guaira Falls f. Brazil 103 24.00S 54.10W
Guajira Pen. Colombia 97 12.00N 72.00W
Gualeguay Argentina 103 33.10S 59.14W
Guam i. Pacific Oc. 61 13.30N 144.40E
Guanajuato Mexico 96 21.00N 101.16W
Guanajuato d. Mexico 96 21.01N 101.00W
Guanare r. Venezuela 97 8.20N 67.50W
Guane Cuba 96 22.13N 84.07W
Guantánamo Cuba 97 20.09N 75.14W

Guarapuava Brazil 103 25.22S 51.28W
Guaratingueta Brazil 103 22.49S 45.09W
Guarda Portugal 41 40.32N 7.17W
Guardafui, C. Somali Rep. 69 12.00N 51.30E
Guardo Spain 41 42.47N 4.50W
Guatemala C. America 96 15.40N 90.00W
Guatemala City Guatemala 96 14.38N 90.22W
Guaxupe Brazil 103 21.17S 46.44W
Guayaquil Ecuador 102 2.13S 80.05W
Guaymas Mexico 90 27.59N 110.54W
Gubin Poland 44 51.59N 14.42E
Gudermes U.S.S.R. 47 43.22N 46.06E
Guebwiller France 44 47.55N 7.13E
Guecho Spain 41 43.21N 3.01W
Guelph Canada 94 43.34N 80.16W
Guéret France 40 46.10N 1.52E
Guernsey i. Channel Is. 31 49.27N 2.35W
Guerrero d. Mexico 96 18.00N 100.00W
Guguan i. Asia 61 17.20N 145.51E
Guiana S. America 102 3.00N 53.00W
Guiana Highlands S. America 106 4.00N 60.00W
Guildford England 27 51.14N 0.35W
Guildtown Scotland 35 56.28N 3.25W
Guilherne Capelo Ihe Angola 72 5.11S 12.10E
Guinea Africa 70 10.30N 11.30W
Guinea, G. of Africa 71 3.00N 3.00E
Guinea Bissau Africa 70 11.30N 15.00W
Güines Cuba 96 22.50N 82.02W
Guînes France 29 50.51N 1.52E
Guingamp France 40 48.34N 3.09W
Guisborough England 33 54.32N 1.02W
Guise France 45 49.54N 3.39E
Guiseley England 32 53.53N 1.42W
Gujarat d. India 58 22.45N 71.30E
Gujranwala Pakistan 58 32.06N 74.11E
Gulbarga India 58 17.22N 76.47E
Gulbin Ka r. Nigeria 71 11.35N 4.10E
Gulgong Australia 80 32.20S 149.49E
Gullane Scotland 35 56.02N 2.49W
Gulpaigan Iran 57 33.23N 50.18E
Gulu Uganda 73 2.46N 32.21E
Guma China 62 37.30N 78.20E
Gümüşane Turkey 56 40.26N 39.26E
Guna India 58 24.39N 77.18E
Gundagai Australia 80 35.07S 148.05E
Gungu Zaïre 72 5.43S 19.20E
Gunnedah Australia 80 30.59S 150.15E
Guntersville L. U.S.A. 91 34.35N 86.00W
Guntur India 59 16.20N 80.27E
Gunung Balu mtn. Indonesia 60 3.00N 116.00E
Gurnard's Head c. England 31 50.12N 5.35W
Gürün Turkey 56 38.44N 37.15E
Guryev U.S.S.R. 48 47.00N 52.00E
Gusau Nigeria 71 12.12N 6.40E
Güstrow E. Germany 44 53.48N 12.11E
Gütersloh W. Germany 44 51.54N 8.22E
Guyana S. America 97 6.00N 60.00W
Guyhirn England 29 52.37N 0.05E
Gwabegar Australia 80 30.34S 149.00E
Gwadar Pakistan 57 25.09N 62.21E
Gwai Rhodesia 74 19.15S 27.42E
Gwai r. Rhodesia 74 18.00S 26.47E
Gwalior India 58 26.12N 78.09E
Gwanda Rhodesia 74 20.59S 29.00E
Gwatar Iran 57 25.10N 61.31E
Gweebarra B. Rep. of Ire. 38 54.52N 8.28W
Gwelo Rhodesia 74 19.25S 29.50E
Gwent d. Wales 31 51.44N 3.00W
Gwynedd d. Wales 30 53.00N 4.00W
Gyangtse China 59 29.00N 89.40E
Gydanskiy Pen. U.S.S.R. 48 70.00N 78.30E
Györ Hungary 47 47.41N 17.40E

H

Haapajärvi Finland 46 63.45N 25.20E
Haapamäki Finland 46 62.15N 24.25E
Haapsalu U.S.S.R. 46 58.58N 23.32E
Haarlem Neth. 45 52.22N 4.38E
Habbaniya Iraq 56 33.22N 43.35E
Hachinohe Japan 63 40.30N 141.30E
Hacketstown Rep. of Ire. 39 52.52N 6.35W
Hackney d. England 27 51.33N 0.03W
Haddington Scotland 35 55.57N 2.47W
Hadejia Nigeria 71 12.30N 10.03E
Hadejia r. Nigeria 71 12.47N 10.44E
Haderslev Denmark 46 55.15N 9.30E
Hadfield England 32 53.28N 1.59W
Hadhramaut d. S. Yemen 69 16.30N 49.30E
Hadleigh England 29 52.03N 0.58E
Hafar Saudi Arabia 57 28.28N 46.00E
Hafnarfjördhur Iceland 46 64.04N 21.58W
Haft Kel Iran 57 31.28N 49.35E

Hagen W. Germany 45 51.22N 7.27E
Hagerstown U.S.A. 95 33.39N 77.44W
Ha Giang Vietnam 59 22.50N 104.58E
Hags Head Rep. of Ire. 39 52.56N 9.29W
Haifa Israel 56 32.49N 34.59E
Haikow China 63 20.05N 110.25E
Hail Saudi Arabia 56 27.31N 41.45E
Hailar China 63 49.15N 119.41E
Hailsham England 29 50.52N 0.17E
Hailun China 63 47.29N 126.58E
Hailuoto i. Finland 46 65.00N 24.50E
Hainan i. China 60 18.30N 109.40E
Hainaut d. Belgium 45 50.30N 3.45E
Haines U.S.A. 92 59.11N 135.23W
Haiphong Vietnam 59 20.50N 106.41E
Haiti C. America 97 19.00N 73.00W
Hakari Turkey 57 37.36N 43.45E
Hakodate Japan 63 41.46N 140.44E
Halberstadt E. Germany 44 51.54N 11.04E
Halden Norway 46 59.08N 11.13E
Halesowen England 28 52.27N 2.02W
Halesworth England 29 52.21N 1.30E
Haliburton Highlands Canada 95 45.10N 78.30W
Halifax Canada 93 44.38N 63.35W
Halifax England 32 53.43N 1.51W
Halil r. Iran 58 27.35N 58.44E
Halkett, C. U.S.A. 92 71.00N 152.00W
Halkirk Scotland 37 58.30N 3.30W
Halladale r. Scotland 37 58.34N 3.54W
Halle Belgium 45 50.45N 4.14E
Halle E. Germany 44 51.28N 11.58E
Hallow England 28 52.14N 2.15W
Hallsberg Sweden 46 59.05N 15.07E
Hall's Creek town Australia 79 18.17S 127.44E
Hallstavik Sweden 46 60.06N 18.42E
Halmahera i. Indonesia 61 0.45N 128.00E
Halmstad Sweden 46 56.41N 12.55E
Hälsingborg Sweden 46 56.05N 12.45E
Halstead England 29 51.57N 0.39E
Haltern W. Germany 45 51.45N 7.10E
Haltia Tunturi mtn. Norway 46 69.20N 21.10E
Haltwhistle England 35 54.58N 2.27W
Ham Scotland 36 6.08N 2.04W
Hama Syria 56 35.09N 36.44E
Hamadán Iran 57 34.47N 48.33E
Hamamatsu Japan 63 34.42N 137.42E
Hamar Norway 46 60.47N 10.55E
Hamata, Gebel mtn. Egypt 56 24.11N 35.01E
Hamble England 28 50.52N 1.19W
Hambleton England 33 53.46N 1.11W
Hambleton Hills England 33 54.15N 1.11W
Hamborn W. Germany 45 51.29N 6.46E
Hamburg W. Germany 44 53.33N 10.00E
Hamdh, Wadi r. Saudi Arabia 56 25.49N 36.37E
Hämeenlinna Finland 46 61.00N 24.25E
Hameln W. Germany 44 52.06N 9.21E
Hamersley Range mts. Australia 79 22.00S 118.00E
Hami China 62 42.40N 93.30E
Hamilton Australia 80 37.45S 142.04E
Hamilton Bermuda 97 32.18N 64.48W
Hamilton Canada 94 43.15N 79.50W
Hamilton r. Canada 93 53.20N 60.00W
Hamilton New Zealand 82 37.46S 175.18E
Hamilton Scotland 35 55.46N 4.10W
Hamilton U.S.A. 94 39.23N 84.33W
Hamina Finland 46 60.33N 27.15E
Hamirpur India 58 25.57N 80.08E
Hamm W. Germany 45 51.40N 7.49E
Hammerfest Norway 46 70.40N 23.44E
Hammond U.S.A. 94 39.48N 88.37W
Hamoir Belgium 45 50.25N 5.32E
Hampshire d. England 28 51.03N 1.20W
Hampshire Downs hills England 28 51.18N 1.25W
Hampstead England 27 51.33N 0.11W
Hampton England 27 51.25N 0.22W
Hamrin, Jabal mts. Iraq 57 34.40N 44.10E
Hamstreet England 29 51.03N 0.52E
Hamun-i-Sabari l. Iran 57 31.24N 61.16E
Hanakiya Saudi Arabia 56 24.53N 40.30E
Hanang mtn. Tanzania 73 4.30S 35.21E
Hanau W. Germany 44 50.08N 8.56E
Hanchung China 59 33.10N 107.02E
Hancock U.S.A. 94 47.08N 88.34W
Handa i. Scotland 36 58.23N 5.12W
Handeni Tanzania 73 5.25S 38.04E
Hangchow China 63 30.10N 120.07E
Hangö Finland 46 59.50N 23.00E
Han Kiang r. China 63 30.45N 114.24E
Hanmer Springs town New Zealand 82 42.34S 172.46E
Hannibal U.S.A. 94 39.41N 91.20W
Hanningfield Water England 27 51.38N 0.28E
Hannover W. Germany 44 52.23N 9.44E
Hannut Belgium 45 50.40N 5.05E
Hanoi Vietnam 59 21.01N 105.52E
Hanover R.S.A. 74 31.05S 24.27E

For Khmer Republic read Kampuchea. For Malagasy Republic read Madagascar. For Rhodesia read Zimbabwe.

Hanworth to **Holstebro** 138

Hanworth England **27** 51.26N 0.23W
Haparanda Sweden **46** 65.50N 24.10E
Haradh Saudi Arabia **57** 24.12N 49.08E
Harar Ethiopia **69** 9.20N 42.10E
Harbin China **63** 45.45N 126.41E
Harburg W. Germany **44** 53.27N 9.58E
Hardanger Fjord *est.* Norway **46** 60.15N 6.25E
Hardanger Vidda *f.* Norway **46** 60.20N 8.00E
Harderwijk Neth. **45** 52.21N 5.37E
Harding R.S.A. **74** 30.36S 29.55E
Hardoi India **58** 27.23N 80.06E
Harefield England **27** 51.36N 0.28W
Haren W. Germany **45** 52.48N 7.15E
Hargeisa Somali Rep. **69** 9.31N 44.02E
Hari *r.* Afghan. **57** 35.42N 61.12E
Hari *r.* Indonesia **60** 1.00S 104.15E
Haringey *d.* England **27** 51.36N 0.06W
Harlech Wales **30** 52.52N 4.08W
Harleston England **29** 52.25N 1.18E
Harlingen Neth. **45** 53.10N 5.25E
Harlington England **27** 51.29N 0.25W
Harlow England **27** 51.47N 0.08E
Harmerhill England **32** 52.48N 2.45W
Harney Basin *f.* U.S.A. **90** 43.20N 119.00W
Härnösand Sweden **46** 62.37N 17.55E
Harold Hill England **27** 51.36N 0.12E
Haroldswick Scotland **36** 60.47N 0.50W
Harold Wood England **27** 51.35N 0.12E
Harpenden England **27** 51.49N 0.22W
Harricanaw *r.* Canada **91** 51.05N 79.45W
Harris *i.* Scotland **36** 57.50N 6.55W
Harris, Sd. of Scotland **36** 57.43N 7.05W
Harrisburg U.S.A. **95** 40.17N 76.54W
Harrismith R.S.A. **74** 28.16S 29.08E
Harrison, C. Canada **93** 55.00N 58.00W
Harrogate England **33** 53.59N 1.32W
Harrow England **27** 51.35N 0.21W
Harrow on the Hill England **27** 51.34N 0.21W
Harstad Norway **46** 68.48N 16.30E
Hartford U.S.A. **95** 41.45N 72.42W
Hartington England **32** 53.08N 1.49W
Hartland England **31** 50.59N 4.29W
Hartland Pt. England **31** 51.01N 4.32W
Hartlepool England **33** 54.42N 1.11W
Hartley England **27** 51.23N 0.18E
Hartley Rhodesia **74** 18.04S 30.06E
Harud *r.* Afghan. **57** 31.36N 61.12E
Harvey U.S.A. **94** 41.38N 87.40W
Harwich England **29** 51.56N 1.18E
Haryana *d.* India **58** 29.15N 76.00E
Harz Mts. E. Germany/W. Germany **44** 51.40N 10.55E
Hasa Oasis Saudi Arabia **57** 25.37N 49.40E
Hase *r.* W. Germany **45** 52.42N 7.17E
Hashtrud Iran **57** 37.29N 47.05E
Haslemere England **28** 51.05N 0.41W
Haslingden England **32** 53.43N 2.20W
Hasselt Belgium **45** 50.56N 5.20E
Hassi Messaoud Algeria **68** 31.53N 5.43E
Hässleholm Sweden **46** 56.09N 13.45E
Hastings England **29** 50.51N 0.36E
Hastings New Zealand **82** 39.39S 176.52E
Hastings U.S.A. **94** 44.43N 92.50W
Hatfield Australia **80** 33.53S 143.47E
Hatfield England **27** 51.46N 0.13W
Hatherleigh England **31** 50.49N 4.04W
Hathersage England **32** 53.20N 1.39W
Hathras India **58** 27.36N 78.02E
Hatteras, C. U.S.A. **91** 35.14N 75.31W
Hattiesburg U.S.A. **91** 31.25N 89.19W
Hatton England **32** 52.52N 1.40W
Haugesund Norway **46** 59.25N 5.16E
Hauki Vesi *l.* Finland **46** 62.10N 28.30E
Hauraki G. New Zealand **82** 36.30S 175.00E
Hauran, Wadi *r.* Iraq **56** 33.57N 42.35E
Haut Zaïre *d.* Zaïre **73** 2.00N 27.00E
Havana Cuba **96** 23.07N 82.25W
Havana *d.* Cuba **96** 23.07N 82.25W
Havant England **28** 50.51N 0.59W
Havel *r.* E. Germany **44** 52.51N 11.57E
Haverfordwest Wales **31** 51.48N 4.59W
Haverhill England **29** 52.06N 0.27E
Haverhill U.S.A. **95** 42.47N 71.07W
Havering England **27** 51.34N 0.14E
Havlickuv Brod Czech. **44** 49.38N 15.35E
Havre U.S.A. **90** 48.34N 109.45W
Havre de Grace U.S.A. **95** 39.33N 76.06W
Hawaii *d.* U.S.A. **90** 21.00N 156.00W
Hawaii *i.* Hawaii U.S.A. **90** 19.30N 155.30W
Hawaiian Is. U.S.A. **90** 21.00N 157.00W
Hawea, L. New Zealand **82** 44.30S 169.15E
Hawera New Zealand **82** 39.35S 174.19E
Hawes England **32** 54.18N 2.12W
Hawes Water *l.* England **32** 54.30N 2.45W
Hawick Scotland **35** 55.25N 2.47W
Hawke, C. Australia **80** 32.12S 152.33E
Hawke B. New Zealand **82** 39.18S 177.15E
Hawkhurst England **29** 51.02N 0.31E
Hawthorne U.S.A. **90** 38.13N 118.37W
Hay Australia **80** 34.31S 144.31E
Haydon Bridge England **35** 54.58N 2.14W
Hayes *r.* Canada **93** 57.00N 92.30W
Hayes England **27** 51.31N 0.25W
Hayle England **31** 50.12N 5.25W
Hay-on-Wye Wales **30** 52.04N 3.09W
Hay River *town* Canada **92** 60.51N 115.42W
Haywards Heath *f.* England **29** 51.00N 0.05W
Hazaribagh India **58** 24.00N 85.23E
Hazelton Canada **92** 55.16N 127.18W
Hazlemere England **27** 51.39N 0.42W
Hazleton U.S.A. **95** 40.58N 75.59W
Heacham England **33** 52.55N 0.30E
Headcorn England **27** 51.11N 0.37E
Headford Rep. of Ire. **38** 53.28N 9.08W
Heads of Ayr *c.* Scotland **34** 55.26N 4.42W
Heanor England **33** 53.01N 1.20W
Heard I. Indian Oc. **113** 53.07S 73.20E
Hearst Canada **94** 49.42N 83.40W
Heath End England **28** 51.21N 1.08W
Heathfield England **29** 50.58N 0.18E
Hebden Bridge *town* England **32** 53.45N 2.00W
Hebel Australia **80** 28.55S 147.49E
Hebrides *is.* U.K. **18** 58.00N 7.00W
Hebron Jordan **56** 31.32N 35.06E
Hecate Str. Canada **92** 53.00N 131.00W
Hechtel Belgium **45** 51.07N 5.22E
Heckington England **33** 52.59N 0.18W
Hedon England **33** 53.44N 0.11W
Heemstede Neth. **45** 52.21N 4.38E
Heerde Neth. **45** 52.23N 6.02E
Heerenveen Neth. **45** 52.57N 5.55E
Heerlen Neth. **45** 50.53N 5.59E
Heidelberg W. Germany **44** 49.25N 8.42E
Heidenheim W. Germany **44** 48.41N 10.10E
Heilbron R.S.A. **74** 27.17S 27.58E
Heilbronn W. Germany **44** 49.08N 9.14E
Heilungkiang *d.* China **63** 47.00N 109.00E
Heinola Finland **46** 61.13N 26.05E
Heinsberg W. Germany **45** 51.04N 6.06E
Hejaz *f.* Saudi Arabia **56** 26.00N 37.30E
Hekla, Mt. Iceland **46** 64.00N 19.45W
Helena U.S.A. **90** 46.35N 112.00W
Helen Reef *i.* Asia **61** 2.43N 131.46E
Helensburgh Scotland **34** 56.01N 4.44W
Helensville New Zealand **82** 36.40S 174.28E
Heligoland *i.* W. Germany **44** 54.10N 7.51E
Heligoland B. W. Germany **44** 54.00N 8.15E
Heliopolis Egypt **56** 30.06N 31.20E
Hellendoorn Neth. **45** 52.24N 6.29E
Hellevoetsluis Neth. **45** 51.49N 4.08E
Hellifield England **32** 54.00N 2.13W
Hellín Spain **41** 38.31N 1.43W
Helmand *r.* Asia **58** 31.10N 61.20E
Helmond Neth. **45** 51.28N 5.40E
Helmsdale Scotland **37** 58.07N 3.40W
Helmsley England **33** 54.15N 1.20W
Helmstedt W. Germany **44** 52.14N 11.01E
Helsingör Denmark **46** 56.03N 12.38E
Helsinki Finland **46** 60.08N 25.00E
Helston England **31** 50.07N 5.17W
Helvellyn *mtn.* England **32** 54.31N 3.00W
Helvick Head Rep. of Ire. **39** 52.03N 7.32W
Helwân Egypt **56** 29.51N 31.20E
Hemel Hempstead England **27** 51.46N 0.28W
Hempstead U.S.A. **95** 40.42N 73.37W
Hemsworth England **33** 53.37N 1.21W
Henares *r.* Spain **41** 40.26N 3.35W
Hendaye France **40** 43.22N 1.46W
Hendon England **27** 51.35N 0.14W
Hendrik Verwoerd Dam R.S.A. **74** 31.00S 26.00E
Henfield England **29** 50.56N 0.17W
Hengelo Neth. **45** 52.16N 6.46E
Henley-on-Thames England **28** 51.32N 0.53W
Henrietta Maria, C. Canada **93** 55.00N 82.15W
Henrique de Carvalho Angola **72** 9.38S 20.20E
Henty Australia **80** 35.30S 147.03E
Henzada Burma **59** 17.38N 95.35E
Herat Afghan. **57** 34.21N 62.10E
Herauabad Iran **57** 37.36N 48.36E
Hérault *r.* France **40** 43.17N 3.28E
Hereford England **28** 52.04N 2.43W
Hereford and Worcester *d.* England **28** 52.08N 2.30W
Herford W. Germany **44** 52.07N 8.40E
Herma Ness *c.* Scotland **36** 60.50N 0.54W
Hermidale Australia **80** 31.33S 146.44E
Hermon, Mt. Lebanon **56** 33.24N 35.52E
Hermosillo Mexico **90** 29.15N 110.59W
Herne W. Germany **45** 51.32N 7.12E
Herne Bay *town* England **29** 51.23N 1.10E
Herning Denmark **46** 56.08N 9.00E
Heron Bay *town* Canada **94** 48.41N 86.26W
Herrick Australia **80** 41.04S 147.53E
Herstal Belgium **45** 50.14N 5.38E
Hertford England **27** 51.48N 0.05W
Hertfordshire *d.* England **29** 51.51N 0.05W
Hesbaye *f.* Belgium **45** 50.32N 5.07E
Hessle England **33** 53.44N 0.28W
Heston England **27** 51.29N 0.23W
Heswall England **30** 53.20N 3.06W
Hetton-le-Hole England **33** 54.19N 1.26W
Hexham England **35** 54.58N 2.06W
Hextable England **27** 51.25N 0.12E
Heysham England **32** 54.03N 2.53W
Heywood England **32** 53.36N 2.13W
Hidalgo *d.* Mexico **96** 20.50N 98.30W
Hidalgo Sabinas Mexico **96** 26.33N 100.10W
Hieradhsvotn *r.* Iceland **46** 65.45N 18.50W
Higham England **27** 51.25N 0.29E
Higham Ferrers England **28** 52.18N 0.36W
High Atlas *mts.* Morocco **68** 32.00N 5.50W
High Bentham England **32** 54.08N 2.31W
Highland *d.* Scotland **36** 57.42N 5.00W
High Peak *mtn.* England **32** 53.22N 1.48W
High Willhays *mtn.* England **31** 50.41N 4.00W
Highworth England **28** 51.38N 1.42W
High Wycombe England **27** 51.38N 0.46W
Hiiumaa *i.* U.S.S.R. **46** 58.50N 22.30E
Hikurangi *mtn.* New Zealand **82** 37.50S 178.10E
Hildesheim W. Germany **44** 52.09N 9.58E
Hilla Iraq **57** 32.28N 44.29E
Hillingdon England **27** 51.32N 0.27W
Hill of Fare Scotland **37** 57.06N 2.33W
Hill of Fearn *town* Scotland **37** 57.47N 3.57W
Hillston Australia **80** 33.30S 145.33E
Hillswick Scotland **36** 60.28N 1.30W
Hilo Hawaii U.S.A. **90** 19.42N 155.04W
Hilpsford Pt. England **32** 54.02N 3.10W
Hilversum Neth. **45** 52.14N 5.12E
Himachal Pradesh *d.* India **58** 31.45N 77.30E
Himalaya *mts.* Asia **58** 29.00N 84.00E
Hinckley England **28** 52.33N 1.21W
Hindhead England **28** 51.06N 0.42W
Hindmarsh, L. Australia **80** 36.03S 141.53E
Hindu Kush *mts.* Asia **58** 36.40N 70.00E
Hingol *r.* Pakistan **58** 25.25N 65.32E
Hinnoy *i.* Norway **46** 68.30N 16.00E
Hirakud Resr. India **59** 21.32N 83.55E
Hirgis Nur *l.* Mongolia **62** 49.20N 93.40E
Hiroshima Japan **63** 34.23N 132.27E
Hirson France **45** 49.56N 4.05E
Hirwaun Wales **31** 51.43N 3.30W
Hispaniola *i.* C. America **97** 19.00N 71.00W
Histon England **29** 52.15N 0.05E
Hit Iraq **56** 33.38N 42.50E
Hitchin England **29** 51.57N 0.16W
Hitra *i.* Norway **46** 63.30N 8.50E
Hjälmaren *l.* Sweden **46** 59.10N 15.45E
Hjörring Denmark **46** 57.28N 9.59E
Hlotse Lesotho **74** 28.52S 28.03E
Ho Ghana **70** 6.38N 0.38E
Hoarusib *r.* S.W. Africa **74** 19.05S 12.36E
Hobart Australia **80** 42.54S 147.18E
Hobro Denmark **46** 56.39N 9.49E
Ho Chi Minh City Vietnam **60** 10.46N 106.43E
Hochschwab *mts.* Austria **44** 47.37N 15.08E
Hochwan China **59** 30.00N 106.15E
Hockley Heath England **28** 52.21N 1.46W
Hodder *r.* England **32** 53.50N 2.26W
Hoddesdon England **27** 51.46N 0.01W
Hodeida Yemen **69** 14.50N 42.58E
Hódmezövásárhely Hungary **43** 46.26N 20.21E
Hodnet England **32** 52.51N 2.35W
Hoehuetenango Guatemala **96** 15.19N 91.26W
Hof W. Germany **44** 50.19N 11.56E
Hofei China **63** 31.55N 117.18E
Hofn Iceland **46** 64.16N 15.10W
Hofors Sweden **46** 60.34N 16.17E
Hofsjökull *mtn.* Iceland **46** 64.50N 19.00W
Hofuf Saudi Arabia **57** 25.20N 49.34E
Hog's Back *hill* England **27** 51.14N 0.39W
Hog's Head Rep. of Ire. **39** 51.47N 10.13W
Hoima Uganda **73** 1.25N 31.22E
Hokitika New Zealand **82** 42.42S 170.59E
Hokkaido *i.* Japan **63** 43.30N 143.20E
Hokow China **59** 22.39N 103.57E
Holbeach England **33** 52.48N 0.01E
Holbrook Australia **80** 35.46S 147.20E
Holbrook U.S.A. **90** 34.58N 110.00W
Holderness *f.* England **33** 53.45N 0.05W
Holguín Cuba **97** 20.54N 76.15W
Holkham B. England **33** 53.00N 0.45E
Holland U.S.A. **94** 42.46N 86.06W
Holland Fen *f.* England **33** 53.02N 0.12W
Hollesley B. England **29** 52.02N 1.33E
Holmes Chapel England **32** 53.13N 2.21W
Holme upon Spalding Moor England **33** 53.50N 0.47W
Holmfirth England **32** 53.34N 1.48W
Holstebro Denmark **46** 56.22N 8.38E

For Khmer Republic *read* Kampuchea. *For* Malagasy Republic *read* Madagascar. *For* Rhodesia *read* Zimbabwe.

Holsworthy to **Indore** 139

Holsworthy England **31** 50.48N 4.21W
Holt England **33** 52.55N 1.04E
Holten Neth. **45** 52.18N 6.26E
Holwerd Neth. **45** 53.22N 5.54E
Holyhead Wales **30** 53.18N 4.38W
Holyhead B. Wales **30** 53.22N 4.40W
Holy I. England **35** 55.41N 1.47W
Holy I. Scotland **34** 55.32N 5.04W
Holy I. Wales **30** 53.15N 4.38W
Holyoke U.S.A. **95** 42.12N 72.37W
Holywell Wales **30** 53.17N 3.13W
Holywood N. Ireland **34** 54.38N 5.50W
Home B. Canada **93** 69.00N 66.00W
Homer U.S.A. **92** 59.40N 151.37W
Homer Tunnel New Zealand **82** 44.40S 168.15E
Homoine Moçambique **74** 23.45S 35.09E
Homs Syria **56** 34.44N 36.43E
Honan *d.* China **63** 33.45N 113.00E
Hondo *r.* Mexico **96** 18.33N 88.22W
Honduras C. America **96** 14.30N 87.00W
Honduras, G. of Carib. Sea **96** 16.20N 87.30W
Hönefoss Norway **46** 60.10N 10.16E
Honfleur France **40** 49.25N 0.14E
Hong Kong Asia **60** 22.30N 114.10E
Honiton England **28** 50.48N 3.13W
Honolulu Hawaii U.S.A. **90** 21.19N 157.50W
Honshu *i.* Japan **63** 36.00N 138.00E
Hoogeveen Neth. **45** 52.44N 6.29E
Hoogezand Neth. **45** 53.10N 6.47E
Hoogstade Belgium **45** 50.59N 2.42E
Hook England **28** 51.17N 0.55W
Hook Head Rep. of Ire. **39** 52.07N 6.55W
Hook of Holland Neth. **45** 51.59N 4.08E
Hoopstad R.S.A. **74** 27.50S 25.55E
Hoorn Neth. **45** 52.38N 5.03E
Hoover Dam U.S.A. **90** 36.01N 114.45W
Hope, Loch Scotland **37** 58.27N 4.38W
Hopedale Canada **93** 55.30N 60.10W
Hopeh *d.* China **63** 39.20N 117.15E
Hopetoun Australia **80** 35.43S 142.20E
Hopetown R.S.A. **74** 29.37S 24.05E
Hor Al Hammar *l.* Iraq **57** 30.50N 47.00E
Hor Auda *l.* Iraq **57** 31.36N 46.53E
Horbury England **33** 53.41N 1.33W
Horde W. Germany **45** 51.29N 7.30E
Horley England **27** 51.11N 0.11W
Hormuz, Str. of Asia **57** 26.35N 56.20E
Horn, C. S. America **106** 55.00S 67.00W
Hornavan *l.* Sweden **46** 66.15N 17.40E
Horncastle England **33** 53.13N 0.08W
Hornchurch England **27** 51.34N 0.13E
Horn Head Rep. of Ire. **38** 55.13N 7.59W
Hornsea England **33** 53.55N 0.10W
Hornsey England **27** 51.35N 0.08W
Hor Sanniya *l.* Iraq **57** 31.52N 46.50E
Horsell England **27** 51.20N 0.35W
Horsens Denmark **46** 55.53N 9.53E
Horsforth England **33** 53.50N 1.39W
Horsham Australia **80** 36.45S 142.15E
Horsham England **29** 51.04N 0.20W
Horten Norway **46** 59.25N 10.30E
Horton *r.* Canada **92** 70.00N 127.00W
Horton Bucks. England **27** 51.53N 0.40W
Horton Surrey England **27** 51.21N 0.18W
Horwich England **32** 53.37N 2.33W
Hose Range *mts.* Malaysia **60** 1.30N 114.10E
Hoshangabad India **58** 22.44N 77.45E
Hoshiarpur India **58** 31.30N 75.59E
Hospital *town* Rep. of Ire. **39** 52.29N 8.26W
Hospitalet Spain **41** 41.20N 2.06E
Hotazel R.S.A. **74** 27.18S 22.54E
Hoting Sweden **46** 64.08N 16.15E
Houghton-le-Spring England **33** 54.51N 1.28W
Houlton U.S.A. **95** 46.09N 67.50W
Houndé U. Volta **70** 11.34N 3.31W
Hounslow England **27** 51.29N 0.22W
Hourn, Loch Scotland **36** 57.06N 5.33W
Houston U.S.A. **91** 29.45N 95.25W
Hovd Mongolia **62** 46.40N 90.45E
Hove England **29** 50.50N 0.10W
Hoveton England **29** 52.45N 1.23E
Hovingham England **33** 54.10N 0.59W
Howden England **33** 53.45N 0.52W
Howe, C. Australia **80** 37.30S 149.59E
Howitt, Mt. Australia **80** 37.15S 146.40E
Howmore Scotland **36** 57.18N 7.23W
Howrah India **58** 22.35N 88.20E
Howth Rep. of Ire. **38** 53.23N 6.06W
Hoy *i.* Scotland **37** 58.51N 3.17W
Hoyerswerda E. Germany **44** 51.28N 14.17E
Hoylake England **32** 53.24N 3.11W
Hoy Sd. Scotland **37** 58.55N 3.20W
Hradec Králové Czech. **44** 50.13N 15.50E
Hsiapachen China **62** 40.52N 107.04E
Huab *r.* S.W. Africa **74** 20.45S 13.27E
Huajuápam Mexico **96** 17.50N 97.48W
Hualien Taiwan **63** 24.00N 121.39E
Huambo *d.* Angola **72** 12.30S 15.45E
Huambo Angola **72** 12.47S 15.44E
Hubli India **58** 15.20N 75.14E
Hucknall England **33** 53.03N 1.12W
Hucqueliers France **29** 50.34N 1.55E
Huddersfield England **32** 53.38N 1.49W
Hudiksvall Sweden **46** 61.45N 17.10E
Hudson *r.* U.S.A. **95** 40.45N 74.00W
Hudson B. Canada **93** 58.00N 86.00W
Hudson Str. Canada **93** 62.00N 70.00W
Hué Vietnam **60** 16.28N 107.35E
Huelva Spain **41** 37.15N 6.56W
Huelva *r.* Spain **41** 37.25N 6.00W
Huércal Overa Spain **41** 37.23N 1.56W
Huesca Spain **41** 42.02N 0.25W
Hughenden Australia **79** 20.50S 144.10E
Hugh Town England **31** 49.55N 6.19W
Huhehot China **63** 40.49N 111.37E
Huiarau Range *mts.* New Zealand **82** 38.20S 177.15E
Huila *d.* Angola **72** 15.30S 15.30E
Huixtla Mexico **96** 15.09N 92.30W
Hull Canada **95** 45.26N 75.45W
Hull *r.* England **33** 53.44N 0.23W
Hullbridge England **27** 51.37N 0.36E
Hultsfred Sweden **46** 57.30N 15.50E
Hulun Chih *l.* China **63** 49.00N 117.20E
Humansdorp R.S.A. **74** 34.01S 24.45E
Humber *r.* England **33** 53.40N 0.12W
Humberside *d.* England **33** 53.48N 0.35W
Hume, L. Australia **80** 36.05S 147.10E
Humphreys Peak *mtn.* U.S.A. **90** 35.21N 111.41W
Hun Libya **68** 29.06N 15.57E
Húna Flói *b.* Iceland **46** 65.45N 20.50W
Hunan *d.* China **63** 27.30N 111.30E
Hungary Europe **47** 47.30N 19.00E
Hungerford Australia **80** 29.00S 144.26E
Hungerford England **28** 51.25N 1.30W
Hungnam N. Korea **63** 39.49N 127.40E
Hungshui Ho *r.* China **63** 23.20N 110.04E
Hunse *r.* Neth. **45** 53.20N 6.18E
Hunsrück *mts.* W. Germany **45** 49.44N 7.05E
Hunstanton England **33** 52.57N 0.30E
Hunte *r.* W. Germany **44** 52.30N 8.19E
Hunter Mtn. U.S.A. **95** 42.10N 74.14W
Huntingdon England **29** 52.20N 0.11W
Huntly New Zealand **82** 37.35S 175.10E
Huntly Scotland **37** 57.27N 2.47W
Huntsville Canada **95** 45.20N 79.14W
Huntsville U.S.A. **91** 30.43N 95.34W
Hunyani *r.* Moçambique **74** 15.35S 30.30E
Huon Pen. P.N.G. **61** 6.00S 147.00E
Hupeh *d.* China **63** 31.15N 112.15E
Hurd, C. Canada **94** 45.14N 81.44W
Hurghada Egypt **56** 27.17N 33.47E
Hurliness Scotland **37** 58.47N 3.13W
Huron U.S.A. **90** 44.22N 98.12W
Huron, L. Canada/U.S.A. **94** 45.00N 82.30W
Hursley England **28** 51.01N 1.23W
Hurst Green England **27** 51.14N 0.00
Husavik Iceland **46** 66.03N 17.17W
Husbands Bosworth England **28** 52.27N 1.03W
Huskvarna Sweden **46** 57.47N 14.15E
Husum W. Germany **44** 54.29N 9.04E
Hutchinson U.S.A. **90** 38.03N 97.56W
Hutt New Zealand **82** 41.12S 174.54E
Hutton Cranswick England **33** 53.57N 0.27W
Huy Belgium **45** 50.31N 5.14E
Hvar *i.* Yugo. **43** 43.10N 16.45E
Hvita *r.* Iceland **46** 64.33N 21.45W
Hwaian Kiangsu China **63** 33.30N 119.20E
Hwai Ho *r.* China **63** 32.58N 118.18E
Hwang Ho *r.* China **63** 37.55N 118.46E
Hwangkang China **63** 30.40N 114.50E
Hwangshih China **63** 30.13N 115.05E
Hyde England **32** 53.26N 2.06W
Hyde Park *f.* England **27** 51.31N 0.12W
Hyderabad India **59** 17.22N 78.26E
Hyderabad Pakistan **58** 25.23N 68.24E
Hyères France **40** 43.07N 6.08E
Hyères, Îles d' France **40** 43.01N 6.25E
Hyndman Peak U.S.A. **90** 43.46N 113.55W
Hynish Scotland **34** 56.26N 6.55W
Hynish B. Scotland **34** 56.28N 6.52W
Hythe Hants. England **28** 50.51N 1.24W
Hythe Kent England **29** 51.04N 1.05E
Hyvinkää Finland **46** 60.37N 24.50E

I

Ialomita *r.* Romania **43** 44.41N 27.52E
Iar Connacht *f.* Rep. of Ire. **38** 53.21N 9.22W
Iaşi Romania **47** 47.09N 27.38E
Ibadan Nigeria **71** 7.23N 3.56E
Ibar *r.* Yugo. **43** 43.44N 20.44E
Ibbenbüren W. Germany **45** 52.17N 7.44E
Ibi Nigeria **71** 8.11N 9.44E
Ibina *r.* Zaïre **73** 1.00N 28.40E
Ibiza Spain **41** 38.55N 1.30E
Ibiza *i. see* Iviza Spain **41**
Ibstock England **28** 52.42N 1.23W
Iceland Europe **46** 64.45N 18.00W
Ichang China **63** 30.43N 111.22E
Ickenham England **27** 51.34N 0.26W
Idah Nigeria **71** 7.05N 6.45E
Idaho *d.* U.S.A. **90** 45.00N 115.00W
Idaho Falls *town* U.S.A. **90** 43.30N 112.01W
Idar W. Germany **45** 49.43N 7.19E
Idfu Egypt **56** 24.58N 32.50E
Ídhi *mtn.* Greece **43** 35.13N 24.45E
Idi Amin Dada, L. Uganda/Zaïre **73** 0.30S 29.30E
Idiofa Zaïre **72** 4.58S 19.38E
Idrigill Pt. Scotland **36** 57.20N 6.35W
Iesi Italy **42** 43.32N 13.15E
Ifalik *is.* Asia **61** 7.15N 144.27E
Ife Western Nigeria **71** 7.33N 4.34E
Ighil Izane Algeria **41** 35.45N 0.30E
Iglésias Italy **42** 39.18N 8.32E
Iğneada, C. Turkey **43** 41.50N 28.05E
Igoumenitsa Greece **43** 39.32N 20.14E
Iguaçu *r.* Brazil **103** 25.33S 54.35W
Iguala Mexico **96** 18.21N 99.31W
Igualada Spain **41** 41.35N 1.37E
Iguape Brazil **103** 24.44S 47.31W
Ii *r.* Finland **46** 65.17N 25.15E
Iisalmi Finland **46** 63.34N 27.08E
Ijebu Ode Nigeria **71** 6.47N 3.54E
IJmuiden Neth. **45** 52.28N 4.37E
IJssel *r.* Overijssel Neth. **45** 52.34N 5.50E
IJssel *r.* South Holland Neth. **45** 51.54N 4.32E
IJsselmeer *l.* Neth. **45** 52.45N 5.20E
Ijzer *r.* Belgium **45** 51.09N 2.44E
Ikaría *i.* Greece **43** 37.35N 26.10E
Ikela Zaïre **72** 1.06S 23.04E
Ikelemba Congo **72** 1.15N 16.38E
Ikelemba *r.* Zaïre **72** 0.08N 18.19E
Ikomba Tanzania **73** 9.09S 32.20E
Ikopa *r.* Malagasy Rep. **73** 16.00S 46.22E
Ilagan Phil. **61** 17.07N 121.53E
Ilam Iran **57** 33.27N 46.27E
Ilan China **63** 46.22N 129.31E
Ilaro Nigeria **71** 6.53N 3.03E
Ilchester England **28** 51.00N 2.41W
Ilebo Zaïre **72** 4.20S 20.35E
Ilen *r.* Rep. of Ire. **39** 51.53N 9.20W
Ilesha Western Nigeria **71** 7.39N 4.38E
Ilford England **27** 51.33N 0.06E
Ilfracombe England **31** 51.13N 4.08W
Ili *r.* U.S.S.R. **62** 45.00N 74.20E
Iligan Phil. **61** 8.12N 124.13E
Ilkeston England **33** 52.59N 1.19W
Ilkley England **32** 53.56N 1.49W
Iller *r.* W. Germany **40** 48.29N 10.03E
Illescas Uruguay **103** 33.34S 55.20W
Illinois *d.* U.S.A. **94** 40.15N 89.15W
Illinois *r.* U.S.A. **94** 38.56N 90.27W
Ilminster England **28** 50.55N 2.56W
Iloilo Phil. **61** 10.45N 122.33E
Ilorin Nigeria **71** 8.32N 4.34E
Imala Moçambique **73** 14.39S 39.34E
Imandra, L. U.S.S.R. **46** 67.30N 32.45E
Imatra Finland **46** 61.14N 28.50E
Immingham England **33** 53.37N 0.12W
Imo *d.* Nigeria **71** 5.30N 7.20E
Imperia Italy **40** 43.53N 8.00E
Imperial Dam U.S.A. **90** 33.01N 114.25W
Impfondo Congo **72** 1.36N 17.58E
Imphal India **59** 24.47N 93.55E
Imroz *i.* Turkey **43** 40.10N 25.51E
Ina *r.* Poland **44** 53.32N 14.38E
Inari *l.* Finland **46** 69.00N 28.00E
Inca Spain **41** 39.43N 2.54E
Incesu Turkey **56** 38.39N 35.12E
Inchard, Loch Scotland **36** 58.27N 5.05W
Inchcape *i.* Scotland **35** 56.27N 2.24W
Inchfree B. Rep. of Ire. **38** 55.03N 8.23W
Inchkeith *i.* Scotland **35** 56.02N 3.08W
Inchnadamph Scotland **36** 58.08N 4.58W
Inchon S. Korea **63** 37.30N 126.38E
Indaal, Loch Scotland **34** 55.45N 6.20W
Indals *r.* Sweden **46** 62.30N 17.20E
Inderagiri *r.* Indonesia **60** 0.30S 103.08E
India Asia **59** 23.00N 78.30E
Indiana *d.* U.S.A. **94** 40.00N 86.05W
Indianapolis U.S.A. **94** 39.45N 86.10W
Indian Harbour Canada **93** 54.25N 57.20W
Indian Ocean **107**
Indigirka *r.* U.S.S.R. **49** 71.00N 148.45E
Indonesia Asia **60** 6.00S 118.00E
Indore India **58** 22.42N 75.54E

For Khmer Republic *read* Kampuchea. *For* Malagasy Republic *read* Madagascar. *For* Rhodesia *read* Zimbabwe.

Indravati to **João de Almeida** 140

Indravati *r.* India **59** 18.45N 80.16E
Indre *r.* France **40** 47.16N 0.06W
Indus *r.* Pakistan **58** 24.00N 67.33E
Inebolu Turkey **56** 41.57N 33.45E
Infiesto Spain **41** 43.21N 5.21W
Ingatestone England **27** 51.41N 0.22E
Ingende Zaïre **72** 0.17S 18.58E
Ingham Australia **79** 18.35S 146.12E
Ingleborough *mtn.* England **32** 54.10N 2.23W
Ingleton England **32** 54.09N 2.29W
Ingolstadt W. Germany **44** 48.46N 11.27E
Inhambane Moçambique **74** 23.51S 35.29E
Inhambane *d.* Moçambique **74** 22.20S 34.00E
Inharrime Moçambique **74** 24.29S 35.01E
Inishark *i.* Rep. of Ire. **38** 53.37N 10.18W
Inishbofin *i.* Donegal Rep. of Ire. **38** 55.10N 8.10W
Inishbofin *i.* Galway Rep. of Ire. **38** 53.38N 10.14W
Inisheer *i.* Rep. of Ire. **39** 53.04N 9.32W
Inishkea *i.* Rep. of Ire. **38** 54.08N 10.13W
Inishmaan *i.* Rep. of Ire. **39** 53.06N 9.36W
Inishmore *i.* Rep. of Ire. **39** 53.08N 9.43W
Inishmurray *i.* Rep. of Ire. **38** 54.26N 8.40W
Inishowen Head Rep. of Ire. **34** 55.09N 6.56W
Inishowen Pen. Rep. of Ire. **34** 55.08N 7.20W
Inishturk *i.* Rep. of Ire. **38** 53.43N 10.08W
Inishvickillane *i.* Rep. of Ire. **39** 52.02N 10.36W
Inn *r.* Europe **44** 48.33N 13.26E
Innellan Scotland **34** 55.54N 4.58W
Inner Hebrides *is.* Scotland **36** 56.50N 6.45W
Innerleithen Scotland **35** 55.37N 3.04W
Inner Mongolia *d.* China **63** 41.30N 112.00E
Inner Sd. Scotland **36** 57.30N 5.55W
Innsbruck Austria **44** 46.17N 11.25E
Inny *r.* England **31** 50.35N 4.17W
Inny *r.* Rep. of Ire. **39** 51.51N 10.10W
Inongo Zaïre **72** 1.55S 18.20E
Inowrocław Poland **47** 52.49N 18.12E
Insch Scotland **37** 57.21N 2.36W
Interlaken Switz. **44** 46.42N 7.52E
International Falls *town* U.S.A. **94** 48.38N 93.26W
Inuvik Canada **92** 68.16N 133.40W
Inveraray Scotland **34** 56.24N 5.05W
Inver B. Rep. of Ire. **38** 54.36N 8.20W
Inverbervie Scotland **37** 56.51N 2.17W
Invercargill New Zealand **82** 46.26S 168.21E
Inverell Australia **80** 29.46S 151.10E
Invergordon Scotland **37** 57.42N 4.10W
Inverie Scotland **36** 57.03N 5.41W
Inverkeithing Scotland **35** 56.02N 3.25W
Invermoriston Scotland **37** 57.13N 4.38W
Inverness Scotland **37** 57.27N 4.15W
Inverurie Scotland **37** 57.17N 2.23W
Inyangani *mtn.* Rhodesia **74** 18.18S 32.54E
Inyonga Tanzania **73** 6.43S 32.02E
Inzia *r.* Zaïre **72** 3.47S 17.57E
Ioánnina Greece **43** 39.39N 20.49E
Iona *i.* Scotland **34** 56.20N 6.25W
Iona, Sd. of Scotland **34** 56.19N 6.24W
Ionian Is. Greece **43** 38.45N 20.00E
Ionian Sea Med. Sea **43** 38.30N 18.45E
Ios *i.* Greece **43** 36.42N 25.20E
Iowa *d.* U.S.A. **91** 42.00N 93.00W
Iowa City U.S.A. **94** 41.39N 91.31W
Iping China **58** 28.50N 104.35E
Ipoh Malaysia **60** 4.36N 101.02E
Ipswich Australia **80** 27.38S 152.40E
Ipswich England **29** 52.04N 1.09E
Iquique Chile **102** 20.15S 70.00W
Iquitos Peru **102** 3.51S 73.30W
Iráklion Greece **43** 35.20N 25.08E
Iran Asia **57** 32.00N 54.30E
Iranian Plateau *f.* Asia **107** 33.00N 55.00E
Iran Range *mts.* Malaysia **60** 3.20N 115.00E
Iranshar Iran **57** 27.14N 60.42E
Irapuato Mexico **96** 20.40N 101.40W
Iraq Asia **56** 33.00N 44.00E
Irazu *mtn.* Costa Rica **96** 9.59N 83.52W
Ireland's Eye *i.* Rep. of Ire. **38** 53.25N 6.05W
Irian Jaya *d.* Indonesia **61** 4.00S 138.00E
Iringa Tanzania **73** 7.49S 35.39E
Iringa *d.* Tanzania **73** 8.30S 35.00E
Iriomote *i.* Japan **63** 24.30N 124.00E
Irish Sea U.K./Rep. of Ire. **38** 53.30N 5.40W
Irkutsk U.S.S.R. **62** 52.18N 104.15E
Iron-Bridge England **28** 52.38N 2.30W
Irondequoit U.S.A. **95** 43.12N 77.36W
Iron Gate *f.* Romania/Yugo. **43** 44.40N 22.30E
Iron Mountain *town* U.S.A. **94** 45.51N 88.05W
Iron Mts. Rep. of Ire. **38** 54.10N 7.56W
Iron River *town* U.S.A. **94** 46.05N 88.38W
Ironwood U.S.A. **94** 46.25N 90.08W
Iroquois Falls *town* Canada **94** 48.47N 80.41W
Irrawaddy *r.* Burma **59** 17.45N 95.25E
Irrawaddy Delta Burma **59** 16.30N 95.20E
Irthing *r.* England **35** 54.55N 2.50W
Irthlingborough England **28** 52.20N 0.37W
Irtysh *r.* U.S.S.R. **48** 61.00N 68.40E
Irumu Zaïre **73** 1.29N 29.48E
Irun Spain **41** 43.20N 1.48W
Irvine Scotland **34** 55.37N 4.40W
Irvine *r.* Scotland **34** 55.37N 4.41W
Irvine B. Scotland **34** 55.36N 4.42W
Irvinestown N. Ireland **38** 54.29N 7.40W
Irvington U.S.A. **95** 40.43N 74.15W
Isabelia, Cordillera *mts.* Nicaragua **96** 13.30N 85.00W
Isafjördhur Iceland **46** 66.05N 23.06W
Isangi Zaïre **72** 0.48N 24.03E
Isar *r.* W. Germany **44** 48.48N 12.57E
Ischia *i.* Italy **42** 40.43N 13.54E
Iscia Baidoa Somali Rep. **73** 3.08N 43.34E
Isère *r.* France **40** 45.02N 4.54E
Iserlohn W. Germany **45** 51.23N 7.42E
Isfahan Iran **57** 32.42N 51.40E
Isfandaqeh Iran **57** 28.39N 57.13E
Ishim *r.* U.S.S.R. **48** 57.50N 71.00E
Ishqanan Iran **57** 27.10N 53.38E
Isiolo Kenya **73** 0.20N 37.36E
Isiro Zaïre **73** 2.50N 27.40E
Iskenderun Turkey **56** 36.37N 36.08E
Iskenderun, G. of Turkey **56** 36.40N 35.50E
Iskilip Turkey **56** 40.45N 34.28E
Iskŭr *r.* Bulgaria **43** 43.42N 24.27E
Isla *r.* Scotland **37** 56.32N 3.22W
Islamabad Pakistan **58** 33.40N 73.08E
Island Magee *pen.* N. Ireland **34** 54.48N 5.44W
Islands, B. of New Zealand **82** 35.15S 174.15E
Islay *i.* Scotland **34** 55.45N 6.20W
Islay, Sd. of Scotland **34** 55.50N 6.06W
Isle *r.* France **40** 45.02N 0.08W
Isle of Axholme *f.* England **33** 53.32N 0.50W
Isle of Ely *f.* England **29** 52.25N 0.11E
Isle of Man U.K. **32** 54.15N 4.30W
Isle of Oxney *f.* England **29** 51.02N 0.44E
Isle of Portland *f.* England **28** 50.32N 2.25W
Isle of Purbeck *f.* England **28** 50.40N 2.05W
Isle of Thanet *f.* England **29** 51.22N 1.20E
Isle of Whithorn *town* Scotland **34** 54.43N 4.22W
Isle of Wight *d.* England **28** 50.40N 1.17W
Isleworth England **27** 51.28N 0.20W
Islington *d.* England **27** 51.33N 0.06W
Ismâ'ilîa Egypt **56** 30.36N 32.15E
Isna Egypt **56** 25.16N 32.30E
Isoka Zambia **73** 10.06S 32.39E
Isparta Turkey **56** 37.46N 30.32E
Israel Asia **56** 32.00N 34.50E
Isser *r.* Algeria **41** 36.20N 3.28E
Issoire France **40** 45.33N 3.15E
Is-sur-Tille France **40** 47.30N 5.10E
Issyk Kul *l.* U.S.S.R. **62** 43.30N 77.20E
Istanbul Turkey **43** 41.02N 28.58E
Istehbanat Iran **57** 29.05N 54.03E
Isthmus of Kra Thailand **59** 10.10N 99.00E
Istra *pen.* Yugo. **42** 45.12N 13.55E
Itajaí Brazil **103** 26.50S 48.39W
Italy Europe **42** 43.00N 12.00E
Itapeva Brazil **103** 23.59S 48.59W
Itaqui Brazil **103** 29.07S 56.33W
Itchen *r.* England **28** 50.55N 1.23W
Iterup *i.* U.S.S.R. **63** 44.00N 147.30E
Ithaca U.S.A. **95** 42.26N 76.30W
Ithon *r.* Wales **30** 52.12N 3.26W
Itimbiri *r.* Zaïre **72** 2.02N 22.47E
Ituri *r.* Zaïre **73** 1.45N 27.06E
Itzehoe W. Germany **44** 53.56N 9.32E
Ivai *r.* Brazil **103** 23.20S 53.40W
Ivalo Finland **46** 68.41N 27.30E
Ivalo *r.* Finland **46** 68.45N 27.36E
Ivanhoe Australia **80** 32.56S 144.22E
Ivano-Frankovsk U.S.S.R. **47** 48.55N 24.42E
Ivanovo U.S.S.R. **47** 57.00N 41.00E
Iver England **27** 51.31N 0.30W
Ivigtut Greenland **93** 61.10N 48.00W
Ivindo Gabon **72** 0.02S 12.13E
Ivinghoe England **27** 51.51N 0.39W
Iviza *i.* Spain **41** 39.00N 1.23E
Ivory Coast Africa **70** 8.00N 5.30W
Ivrea Italy **40** 45.28N 7.52E
Ivybridge England **31** 50.24N 3.56W
Iwo Nigeria **71** 7.38N 4.11E
Ixworth England **29** 52.18N 0.50E
Izabal, L. Guatemala **96** 15.30N 89.00W
Izhevsk U.S.S.R. **48** 56.49N 53.11E
Izmail U.S.S.R. **43** 45.20N 28.50E
Izmir Turkey **43** 38.24N 27.09E
Izmir, G. of Med. Sea **43** 38.30N 26.45E
Izmit Turkey **56** 40.48N 29.55E
Izozog Marshes *f.* Bolivia **103** 18.30S 62.05W

J

Jabalón *r.* Spain **41** 38.55N 4.07W
Jabalpur India **58** 23.10N 79.59E
Jablonec nad Nisou Czech. **44** 50.44N 15.10E
Jabrin Oasis Saudi Arabia **57** 23.15N 49.15E
Jaca Spain **41** 42.34N 0.33W
Jackson Mich. U.S.A. **94** 42.15N 84.24W
Jackson Miss. U.S.A. **91** 32.20N 90.11W
Jacksonville Fla. U.S.A. **91** 30.20N 81.40W
Jacksonville Ill. U.S.A. **94** 39.44N 90.14W
Jacobabad Pakistan **58** 28.16N 68.30E
Jacques-Cartier Canada **95** 45.31N 73.31W
Jade B. W. Germany **45** 53.30N 8.12E
Jaén Spain **41** 37.46N 3.48W
Jaffa, C. Australia **80** 36.58S 139.39E
Jaffna Sri Lanka **59** 9.38N 80.02E
Jafura *des.* Saudi Arabia **57** 24.40N 50.20E
Jagdalpur India **59** 19.04N 82.05E
Jaghbub Libya **56** 29.42N 24.38E
Jaguarao Brazil **103** 32.30S 53.25W
Jahara Kuwait **57** 29.20N 47.41E
Jahrom Iran **57** 28.30N 53.30E
Jaipur India **58** 26.53N 75.50E
Jakarta Indonesia **60** 6.08S 106.45E
Jakobstad Finland **46** 63.41N 22.40E
Jalapa Mexico **96** 19.45N 96.48W
Jalgaon India **58** 21.01N 75.39E
Jalisco *d.* Mexico **96** 21.00N 103.00W
Jalna India **58** 19.50N 75.58E
Jalón *r.* Spain **41** 41.47N 1.02W
Jalpaiguri India **58** 26.30N 88.50E
Jamaica C. America **97** 18.00N 77.00W
Jamalpur Bangla. **58** 24.54N 89.57E
Jamalpur India **58** 25.19N 86.30E
Jamdena *i.* Asia **61** 7.30S 131.00E
James *r.* U.S.A. **91** 42.50N 97.15W
James B. Canada **91** 52.00N 80.00W
Jamestown Australia **80** 33.12S 138.38E
Jamestown N. Dak. U.S.A. **90** 46.54N 98.42W
Jamestown N.Y. U.S.A. **95** 42.05N 79.15W
Jammu and Kashmir *d.* Pakistan **58** 36.00N 75.00W
Jammu and Kashmir *d.* India **58** 33.30N 76.00W
Jamnagar India **58** 22.28N 70.06E
Jämsänkoski Finland **46** 61.54N 25.10E
Jamshedpur India **58** 22.47N 86.12E
Janda, Lago de Spain **41** 36.15N 5.50W
Jandula *r.* Spain **41** 38.08N 4.08W
Janesville U.S.A. **94** 42.42N 89.02W
Jan Mayen *i.* Arctic Oc. **112** 71.00N 9.00W
Japan Asia **63** 36.00N 136.00E
Japan, Sea of Asia **63** 40.00N 135.00E
Japan Trench Pacific Oc. **107** 30.00N 142.00E
Japen *i.* Indonesia **61** 1.45S 136.10E
Jarama *r.* Spain **41** 40.27N 3.32W
Jardines de la Reina *is.* Cuba **97** 20.30N 79.00W
Jarrahi *r.* Iran **57** 30.40N 48.23E
Jarrow England **33** 54.59N 1.28W
Järvenpää Finland **46** 60.29N 25.06E
Jashpurnagur India **58** 22.52N 84.14E
Jask Iran **57** 25.40N 57.45E
Jasper Canada **92** 52.55N 118.05W
Jataí Brazil **103** 17.58S 51.45W
Játiva Spain **41** 39.00N 0.32W
Jau Brazil **103** 22.11S 48.35W
Jaunpur India **58** 25.44N 82.41E
Java *i.* Indonesia **60** 7.30S 110.00E
Java Sea Indonesia **60** 5.00S 111.00E
Jebba Nigeria **71** 9.11N 4.49E
Jedburgh Scotland **35** 55.29N 2.33W
Jefferson, Mt. U.S.A. **90** 38.47N 116.58W
Jefferson City U.S.A. **94** 38.33N 92.10W
Jelenia Góra Poland **44** 50.55N 15.45E
Jelgava U.S.S.R. **46** 56.39N 23.40E
Jena E. Germany **44** 50.56N 11.35E
Jérémie Haiti **97** 18.40N 74.09W
Jerez de la Frontera Spain **41** 36.41N 6.08W
Jericho Jordan **56** 31.51N 35.27E
Jerilderie Australia **80** 35.23S 145.41E
Jersey *i.* Channel Is. **31** 49.13N 2.08W
Jersey City U.S.A. **95** 40.44N 74.04W
Jerusalem Israel/Jordan **56** 31.47N 35.13E
Jessore Bangla. **58** 23.10N 89.12E
Jever W. Germany **45** 53.34N 7.54E
Jeypore India **59** 18.51N 82.41E
Jhansi India **58** 25.27N 78.34E
Jhelum *r.* Pakistan **58** 31.04N 72.10E
Jihlava Czech. **44** 49.24N 15.35E
Jimma Ethiopia **69** 7.39N 36.47E
Jinja Uganda **73** 0.27N 33.10E
Jinotepe Nicaragua **96** 11.50N 86.10W
Jiu *r.* Romania **43** 43.44N 23.52E
Jizl, Wadi *r.* Saudi Arabia **56** 25.37N 38.20E
Joaçiba Brazil **103** 27.05S 51.31W
João de Almeida Angola **72** 15.10S 13.32E

For Khmer Republic *read* Kampuchea. *For* Malagasy Republic *read* Madagascar. *For* Rhodesia *read* Zimbabwe.

For Khmer Republic *read* Kampuchea. *For* Malagasy Republic *read* Madagascar. *For* Rhodesia *read* Zimbabwe.

Kasese to **Killybegs** 142

Kasese Uganda **73** 0.07N 30.06E
Kashan Iran **57** 33.59N 51.31E
Kashgar China **62** 39.29N 76.02E
Kashing China **63** 30.40N 120.50E
Kashmar Iran **57** 35.12N 58.26E
Kaskaskia U.S.A. **94** 38.30N 89.15W
Kasongo Zaïre **73** 4.32S 26.33E
Kasongo-Lunda Zaïre **72** 6.30S 16.47E
Kásos *i.* Greece **56** 35.22N 26.57E
Kassala Sudan **69** 15.24N 36.30E
Kassel W. Germany **44** 51.18N 9.30E
Kasserine Tunisia **42** 35.15N 8.44E
Kastamonu Turkey **56** 41.22N 33.47E
Kastellorizon *i.* Greece **56** 36.08N 29.32E
Kastoria Greece **43** 40.32N 21.15E
Kasungu Malaŵi **73** 13.04S 33.29E
Kataba Zambia **72** 16.12S 25.05E
Katahdin, Mt. U.S.A. **95** 45.55N 68.57W
Katako Kombe Zaïre **72** 3.27S 24.21E
Katete Zambia **73** 14.08S 31.50E
Katha Burma **59** 24.11N 96.20E
Katherina, Gebel *mtn.* Egypt **56** 28.30N 33.57E
Katherine Australia **79** 14.29S 132.20E
Kati Mali **70** 12.41N 8.04W
Katihar India **58** 25.33N 87.34E
Katima Rapids *f.* Zambia **72** 17.15S 24.20E
Katmandu Nepal **58** 27.42N 85.19E
Katonga *r.* Uganda **73** 0.03N 30.15E
Katoomba Australia **80** 33.42S 150.23E
Katowice Poland **47** 50.15N 18.59E
Katrine, Loch Scotland **34** 56.15N 4.30W
Katrineholm Sweden **46** 58.59N 16.15E
Katsina Nigeria **71** 13.00N 7.32E
Katsina Ala Nigeria **71** 7.10N 9.30E
Katsina Ala *r.* Nigeria **71** 7.50N 8.58E
Kattegat *str.* Denmark/Sweden **46** 57.00N 11.20E
Katwijk aan Zee Neth. **45** 52.13N 4.27E
Kauai *i.* Hawaii U.S.A. **90** 22.05N 159.30W
Kaufbeuren W. Germany **44** 47.53N 10.37E
Kauhajoki Finland **46** 62.26N 21.10E
Kauhava Finland **46** 63.06N 23.05E
Kaunas U.S.S.R. **46** 54.52N 23.55E
Kaura Namoda Nigeria **71** 12.39N 6.38E
Kavali India **59** 14.55N 80.01E
Kavála Greece **43** 40.56N 24.24E
Kawambwa Zambia **73** 9.47S 29.10E
Kawasaki Japan **63** 35.32N 139.41E
Kawimbe Zambia **73** 8.50S 31.31E
Kawthoolei *d.* Burma **59** 19.00N 96.30E
Kayah Burma **62** 18.20N 97.00E
Kayes Mali **70** 14.26N 11.28W
Kayseri Turkey **56** 38.42N 35.28E
Kazachye U.S.S.R. **49** 70.46N 136.15E
Kazakhstan Soviet Socialist Republic *d.* U.S.S.R. **47** 48.00N 48.00E
Kazan U.S.S.R. **47** 55.45N 49.10E
Kazanlŭk Bulgaria **43** 42.38N 25.26E
Kazarun Iran **57** 29.35N 51.39E
Kazbek *mtn.* U.S.S.R. **47** 42.42N 44.30E
Kazumba Zaïre **72** 6.30S 22.02E
Kéa *i.* Greece **43** 37.36N 24.20E
Keady N. Ireland **38** 54.15N 6.43W
Keal, Loch na Scotland **34** 56.28N 6.04W
Kearney U.S.A. **90** 40.42N 99.04W
Kebbi *r.* Nigeria **68** 11.22N 4.10E
Kebnekaise *mtn.* Sweden **46** 67.55N 18.30E
Kebock Head Scotland **36** 58.02N 6.22W
Kecskemet Hungary **47** 46.56N 19.43E
Kediri Indonesia **60** 7.55S 112.01E
Kédougou Senegal **70** 12.35N 12.09W
Keele Peak *mtn.* Canada **92** 63.15N 129.50W
Keen, Mt. Scotland **37** 56.58N 2.56W
Keene U.S.A. **95** 42.55N 72.17W
Keeper Hill Rep. of Ire. **39** 52.45N 8.17W
Keetmanshoop S.W. Africa **74** 26.36S 18.08E
Keewatin Canada **91** 49.46N 94.30W
Keewatin *d.* Canada **93** 67.00N 90.00W
Kefallinía *i.* Greece **43** 38.15N 20.33E
Keflavik Iceland **46** 64.01N 22.35W
Kei *r.* R.S.A. **74** 32.40S 28.22E
Keighley England **32** 53.52N 1.54W
Keitele *l.* Finland **46** 62.59N 26.00E
Keith Scotland **37** 57.32N 2.57W
Kelberg W. Germany **45** 50.17N 6.56E
Kelkit *r.* Turkey **56** 40.46N 36.32E
Kelloselkä Finland **46** 66.55N 28.50E
Kells Kilkenny Rep. of Ire. **39** 52.32N 7.18W
Kells Meath Rep. of Ire. **38** 53.44N 6.53W
Kelowna Canada **90** 49.50N 119.29W
Kelsall England **32** 53.14N 2.44W
Kelso Scotland **35** 55.36N 2.26W
Kelvedon England **29** 51.50N 0.43E
Kelvedon Hatch England **27** 51.40N 0.16E
Kemaliye Turkey **56** 39.16N 38.29E
Kemerovo U.S.S.R. **48** 55.25N 86.10E
Kemi Finland **46** 65.45N 24.12E
Kemi *r.* Finland **46** 55.47N 24.28E
Kemijärvi Finland **46** 66.40N 27.21E
Kempsey Australia **80** 31.05S 152.50E
Kempston England **29** 52.07N 0.30W
Kempt, L. Canada **95** 47.30N 74.15W
Kempten W. Germany **44** 47.44N 10.19E
Kemsing England **27** 51.18N 0.14E
Ken, Loch Scotland **35** 55.02N 4.04W
Kendal Australia **80** 31.28S 152.40E
Kendal England **32** 54.19N 2.44W
Kendari Indonesia **61** 3.57S 122.36E
Kenema Sierra Leone **70** 7.57N 11.11W
Kenge Zaïre **72** 4.56S 17.04E
Kengtung Burma **59** 21.16N 99.39E
Kenhardt R.S.A. **74** 29.19S 21.08E
Kenilworth England **28** 52.22N 1.35W
Kenmare Rep. of Ire. **39** 51.53N 9.36W
Kenmare *r.* Rep. of Ire. **39** 51.47N 9.52W
Kenmore Scotland **35** 56.35N 4.00W
Kennebec *r.* U.S.A. **95** 43.55N 69.49W
Kennedy, C. U.S.A. **91** 28.28N 80.28W
Kennet *r.* England **28** 51.28N 0.57W
Kennington England **29** 51.10N 0.54E
Kenogamissi L. Canada **94** 48.10N 81.35W
Keno Hill *town* Canada **92** 63.58N 135.22W
Kenora Canada **91** 49.47N 94.26W
Kenosha U.S.A. **94** 42.34N 87.50W
Kensington and Chelsea *d.* England **27** 51.29N 0.12W
Kent *d.* England **29** 51.12N 0.40E
Kentford England **29** 52.16N 0.30E
Kentucky *d.* U.S.A. **91** 38.00N 85.00W
Kentucky L. U.S.A. **91** 36.15N 88.00W
Kenya Africa **73** 1.00N 38.00E
Kenya, Mt. Kenya **73** 0.10S 37.19E
Kerala *d.* India **58** 10.30N 76.30E
Kerang Australia **80** 35.42S 143.59E
Kerch U.S.S.R. **47** 45.22N 36.27E
Kerch Str. U.S.S.R. **47** 45.15N 36.35E
Kerguelen *i.* Indian Oc. **113** 49.30S 69.30E
Kericho Kenya **73** 0.22S 35.19E
Kerintji *mtn.* Indonesia **60** 1.45S 101.20E
Kerkrade Neth. **45** 50.52N 6.02E
Kerloch *mtn.* Scotland **37** 56.59N 2.30W
Kermadec Trench Pacific Oc. **107** 33.00S 176.00W
Kermān Iran **57** 30.18N 57.05E
Kermānshāhān Iran **57** 34.19N 47.04E
Kerme, G. of Turkey **43** 36.52N 27.53E
Kerpen W. Germany **45** 50.52N 6.42E
Kerrera *i.* Scotland **34** 56.24N 5.33W
Kerry *d.* Rep. of Ire. **39** 52.07N 9.35W
Kerry Head Rep. of Ire. **39** 52.24N 9.56W
Kerulen *r.* Mongolia **63** 48.45N 117.00E
Keşan Turkey **43** 40.50N 26.39E
Kessingland England **29** 52.25N 1.41E
Keswick England **32** 54.35N 3.09W
Ketapang Indonesia **60** 1.50S 110.02E
Ketchikan U.S.A. **92** 55.25N 131.40W
Kete Krachi Ghana **70** 7.50N 0.03W
Kettering England **28** 52.24N 0.44W
Kettering U.S.A. **94** 39.42N 84.11W
Kew England **27** 51.29N 0.18W
Keweenaw B. U.S.A. **94** 47.00N 88.15W
Keweenaw Pt. U.S.A. **94** 47.23N 87.42W
Key, Lough Rep. of Ire. **38** 54.00N 8.15W
Keyingham England **33** 53.42N 0.07W
Keynsham England **28** 51.25N 2.30W
Key West U.S.A. **96** 24.34N 81.48W
Keyworth England **33** 52.52N 1.08W
Khabarovsk U.S.S.R. **63** 48.32N 135.08E
Khabur *r.* Syria **56** 35.07N 40.30E
Khaburah Oman **57** 23.58N 57.10E
Khairpur Pakistan **58** 27.30N 68.50E
Khalkidhiki *pen.* Greece **56** 40.30N 23.25E
Khalkis Greece **43** 38.27N 23.36E
Khanaqin Iraq **57** 34.22N 45.22E
Khandwa India **58** 21.49N 76.23E
Khanka, L. U.S.S.R. **63** 45.00N 132.30E
Khanty-Mansiysk U.S.S.R. **48** 61.00N 69.00E
Khanu Iran **57** 27.55N 57.45E
Kharagpur India **58** 22.23N 87.22E
Kharan *r.* Iran **57** 27.37N 58.48E
Kharga Oasis Egypt **56** 25.00N 30.40E
Kharkov U.S.S.R. **47** 50.00N 36.15E
Kharovsk U.S.S.R. **47** 59.67N 40.07E
Khartoum Sudan **69** 15.33N 32.35E
Khash *r.* Afghan. **57** 31.12N 62.00E
Khaskovo Bulgaria **43** 41.57N 25.33E
Khatanga U.S.S.R. **49** 71.50N 102.31E
Khatangskiy G. U.S.S.R. **49** 75.00N 112.10E
Khemmarat Thailand **59** 16.04N 105.10E
Khenifra Morocco **68** 33.00N 5.40W
Kherson U.S.S.R. **47** 46.39N 32.38E
Khíos Greece **56** 38.23N 26.07E
Khíos *i.* Greece **43** 38.23N 26.04E
Khirsan *r.* Iran **57** 31.29N 48.53E
Khiva U.S.S.R. **57** 41.25N 60.49E
Khmelnitskiy U.S.S.R. **47** 49.25N 26.49E
Khmer Republic Asia **60** 12.00N 105.00E
Khöbsögöl Dalai *l.* Mongolia **62** 51.00N 100.30E
Khoi Iran **57** 38.32N 45.02E
Khomas-Hochland *mts.* S.W. Africa **74** 22.45S 16.20E
Khoper *r.* U.S.S.R. **47** 49.35N 42.17E
Khor Qatar **57** 25.39N 51.32E
Khorramabad Iran **57** 33.29N 48.21E
Khorramshahr Iran **57** 30.26N 48.09E
Khotan China **62** 37.07N 79.57E
Khotin U.S.S.R. **47** 48.30N 26.31E
Khulna Bangla. **58** 22.49N 89.34E
Khunsar Iran **57** 33.12N 50.20E
Khur Iran **57** 33.47N 55.06E
Khurmuj Iran **57** 28.40N 51.20E
Khwash Iran **57** 28.14N 61.15E
Khyber Pass Asia **58** 34.06N 71.05E
Kialing Kiang *r.* China **59** 29.33N 106.30E
Kian China **63** 27.08N 115.00E
Kiangling China **63** 30.20N 112.20E
Kiangsi *d.* China **63** 27.25N 115.20E
Kiangsu *d.* China **63** 34.00N 119.00E
Kibali *r.* Zaïre **73** 3.37N 28.38E
Kibombo Zaïre **72** 3.58S 25.57E
Kibondo Tanzania **73** 3.35S 30.41E
Kibungu Rwanda **73** 2.10S 30.31E
Kibwezi Kenya **73** 2.28S 37.57E
Kicking Horse Pass Canada **90** 51.28N 116.23W
Kidal Mali **71** 18.27N 1.25E
Kidan *des.* Saudi Arabia **57** 22.20N 54.20E
Kidderminster England **28** 52.24N 2.13W
Kidsgrove England **32** 53.06N 2.15W
Kidwelly Wales **31** 51.44N 4.20W
Kiel W. Germany **44** 54.20N 10.08E
Kiel B. W. Germany **44** 54.30N 10.30E
Kiel Canal W. Germany **44** 53.54N 9.12E
Kielder Forest *hills* England **35** 55.15N 2.30W
Kienshui China **59** 23.57N 102.45E
Kienyang Fukien China **63** 27.20N 117.50E
Kiev U.S.S.R. **47** 50.28N 30.29E
Kiffa Mauritania **70** 16.38N 11.28W
Kigali Rwanda **73** 1.59S 30.05E
Kigoma Tanzania **73** 4.52S 29.36E
Kigoma *d.* Tanzania **73** 4.45S 30.00E
Kigosi *r.* Tanzania **73** 4.37S 31.29E
Kikinda Yugo. **43** 45.51N 20.30E
Kikori P.N.G. **61** 7.25S 144.13E
Kikwit Zaïre **72** 5.02S 18.51E
Kil Sweden **46** 59.30N 13.20E
Kilbaha Rep. of Ire. **39** 52.35N 9.52W
Kilbeggan Rep. of Ire. **38** 53.22N 7.31W
Kilberry Head Scotland **34** 55.47N 5.38W
Kilbirnie Scotland **34** 55.45N 4.41W
Kilbrannan Sd. Scotland **34** 55.37N 5.25W
Kilchrenan Scotland **34** 56.21N 5.11W
Kilcock Rep. of Ire. **38** 53.25N 6.43W
Kilcreggan Scotland **34** 55.59N 4.50W
Kilcrohane Rep. of Ire. **39** 51.35N 9.42W
Kilcullen Rep. of Ire. **39** 53.08N 6.46W
Kildare Rep. of Ire. **39** 53.10N 6.55W
Kildare *d.* Rep. of Ire. **39** 53.10N 6.50W
Kildonan Rhodesia **74** 17.15S 30.44E
Kildorrery Rep. of Ire. **39** 52.14N 8.26W
Kilfinan Scotland **34** 55.58N 5.18W
Kilfinane Rep. of Ire. **39** 52.21N 8.28W
Kilgarvan Rep. of Ire. **39** 51.54N 9.28W
Kilifi Kenya **73** 3.30S 39.50E
Kilimanjaro *d.* Tanzania **73** 3.45S 37.40E
Kilimanjaro *mtn.* Tanzania **73** 3.02S 37.20E
Kilis Turkey **56** 36.43N 37.07E
Kilkee Rep. of Ire. **39** 52.41N 9.40W
Kilkeel N. Ireland **38** 54.04N 6.00W
Kilkelly Rep. of Ire. **38** 53.52N 8.52W
Kilkenny Rep. of Ire. **39** 52.39N 7.16W
Kilkenny *d.* Rep. of Ire. **39** 52.35N 7.15W
Kilkhampton England **31** 50.53N 4.29W
Kilkieran B. Rep. of Ire. **38** 53.20N 9.42W
Kilkis Greece **43** 40.59N 22.51E
Killala Rep. of Ire. **38** 54.13N 9.14W
Killala B. Rep. of Ire. **38** 54.15N 9.10W
Killaloe Rep. of Ire. **39** 52.47N 8.28W
Killamarsh England **33** 53.19N 1.19W
Killard Pt. N. Ireland **38** 54.41N 5.31W
Killarney Rep. of Ire. **39** 52.04N 9.32W
Killary Harbour *est.* Rep. of Ire. **38** 53.38N 9.56W
Killchianaig Scotland **34** 56.01N 5.47W
Killeagh Rep. of Ire. **39** 51.56N 8.00W
Killearn Scotland **34** 56.03N 4.22W
Killeshandra Rep. of Ire. **38** 54.01N 7.33W
Killin Scotland **34** 56.29N 4.19W
Killington Mtn. U.S.A. **95** 43.36N 72.49W
Killingworth England **35** 55.02N 1.32W
Killíni *mtn.* Greece **43** 37.56N 22.22E
Killorglin Rep. of Ire. **39** 52.07N 9.45W
Killucan Rep. of Ire. **38** 53.30N 7.09W
Killybegs Rep. of Ire. **38** 54.38N 8.27W

For Khmer Republic *read* Kampuchea. *For* Malagasy Republic *read* Madagascar. *For* Rhodesia *read* Zimbabwe.

For Khmer Republic read Kampuchea. *For Malagasy Republic read* Madagascar. *For Rhodesia read* Zimbabwe.

L

For Khmer Republic read Kampuchea. For Malagasy Republic read Madagascar. For Rhodesia read Zimbabwe.

Lamego to **Lichfield**

145

Lamego Portugal **41** 41.05N 7.49W
Lameroo Australia **80** 35.20S 140.33E
Lamía Greece **43** 38.53N 22.25E
Lamlash Scotland **34** 55.32N 5.08W
Lammermuir *f.* Scotland **35** 55.50N 2.25W
Lammermuir Hills Scotland **35** 55.51N 2.40W
Lamotrek *i.* Asia **61** 7.28N 146.23E
Lampedusa *i.* Italy **42** 35.30N 12.35E
Lampeter Wales **30** 52.06N 4.06W
Lampione *i.* Italy **42** 35.33N 12.18E
Lamu Kenya **73** 2.20S 40.54E
La Nao, Cabo de Spain **41** 38.42N 0.15E
Lanark Scotland **35** 55.41N 3.47W
Lancashire *d.* England **32** 53.53N 2.30W
Lancaster England **32** 54.03N 2.48W
Lancaster U.S.A. **95** 40.01N 76.19W
Lancaster Sd. Canada **93** 74.00N 85.00W
Lanchow China **62** 36.01N 103.45E
Landau W. Germany **44** 49.12N 8.07E
Landeck Austria **44** 47.09N 10.35E
Land's End *c.* England **31** 50.03N 5.45W
Landshut W. Germany **44** 48.31N 12.10E
Landskrona Sweden **46** 55.53N 12.50E
Lanesborough Rep. of Ire. **38** 53.40N 8.00W
Langanes *c.* Iceland **46** 66.30N 14.30W
Langavat, Loch Scotland **36** 58.04N 6.45W
Langeland *i.* Denmark **44** 54.50N 10.50E
Langeoog *i.* W. Germany **45** 53.46N 7.30E
Langholm Scotland **35** 55.09N 3.00W
Langkawi *i.* Malaysia **60** 6.20N 99.30E
Langness *c.* I.o.M. **32** 54.03N 4.37W
Langon France **40** 44.33N 0.14W
Langöy *i.* Norway **46** 68.50N 15.00E
Langport England **28** 51.02N 2.51W
Langres France **40** 47.53N 5.20E
Langsa Indonesia **60** 4.28N 97.59E
Långseleån *r.* Sweden **46** 63.30N 16.53E
Lang Son Vietnam **60** 21.50N 106.55E
Langstrothdale Chase *hills* England **32** 54.13N 2.15W
Lannion France **40** 48.44N 3.27W
Lansing U.S.A. **94** 42.44N 84.34W
Lanzarote *i.* Canary Is. **68** 29.00N 13.55W
Laoag Phil. **61** 18.14N 120.36E
Laois *d.* Rep. of Ire. **39** 53.00N 7.20W
Laokay Vietnam **59** 22.30N 104.00E
Laon France **45** 49.34N 3.37E
Laos Asia **60** 19.00N 104.00E
La Palma *i.* Canary Is. **68** 28.50N 18.00W
La Palma Spain **41** 37.23N 6.33W
La Pampa *d.* Argentina **103** 37.30S 65.50W
La Paz Argentina **103** 30.45S 59.36W
La Paz Bolivia **102** 16.30S 68.10W
La Peña, Sierra de *mts.* Spain **41** 42.30N 0.50W
La Perouse Str. U.S.S.R. **49** 45.50N 142.30E
Lapford England **31** 50.52N 3.49W
Lapland *f.* Sweden/Finland **46** 68.10N 24.00E
La Plata Argentina **103** 34.58S 57.55W
La Plata, Rio de *est.* S. America **103** 35.15S 56.45W
Lappa Järvi *l.* Finland **46** 63.05N 23.30E
Lappeenranta Finland **46** 61.04N 28.05E
Laptev Sea U.S.S.R. **49** 74.30N 125.00E
L'Aquila Italy **42** 42.22N 13.25E
Lar Iran **57** 27.37N 54.16E
Larache Morocco **41** 35.12N 6.10W
Laramie U.S.A. **90** 41.20N 105.38W
Larbert Scotland **35** 56.02N 3.51W
Larch *r.* Canada **93** 57.40N 69.30W
Laredo U.S.A. **90** 27.32N 99.22W
Largo Ward Scotland **35** 56.15N 2.52W
Largs Scotland **34** 55.48N 4.52W
La Rioja Argentina **103** 29.26S 66.50W
La Rioja *d.* Argentina **103** 29.40S 67.00W
Lárisa Greece **43** 39.36N 22.24E
Lark *r.* England **29** 52.26N 0.20E
Larkhall Scotland **35** 55.45N 3.59W
Lar Koh *mtn.* Afghan. **57** 32.25N 62.36E
Larnaca Cyprus **56** 34.54N 33.39E
Larne N. Ireland **34** 54.51N 5.49W
Larne Lough N. Ireland **34** 54.50N 5.47W
La Roche Belgium **45** 50.11N 5.35E
La Rochelle France **40** 46.10N 1.10W
La Roche-sur-Yon France **40** 46.40N 1.25W
La Rocque Pt. Channel Is. **31** 49.09N 2.05W
La Roda Spain **41** 39.13N 2.10W
La Romana Dom. Rep. **97** 18.27N 68.57W
La Ronge Canada **92** 55.07N 105.18W
Larvik Norway **46** 59.04N 10.02E
La Sagra *mtn.* Spain **41** 37.58N 2.35W
La Salle U.S.A. **94** 41.20N 89.06W
Las Cruces U.S.A. **90** 32.18N 106.47W
La Seine, Baie de France **40** 49.40N 0.30W
Las Flores Argentina **103** 36.03S 59.08W
Lashio Burma **59** 22.58N 97.48E
Las Palmas Canary Is. **68** 28.08N 15.27W
Las Perlas, Archipelago de Panamá **97** 8.45N 79.30W
La Spezia Italy **40** 44.07N 9.49E
Lastoursville Gabon **72** 0.50S 12.47E
Lastovo *i.* Yugo. **43** 42.45N 16.52E
Las Vegas U.S.A. **90** 36.10N 115.10W
Las Villas *d.* Cuba **97** 22.00N 80.00W
Latakia Syria **56** 35.31N 35.47E
La Tuque Canada **95** 47.26N 72.47W
Latvia Soviet Socialist Republic *d.* U.S.S.R. **46** 57.00N 25.00E
Lauchhammer E. Germany **44** 51.30N 13.48E
Lauder Scotland **35** 55.43N 2.45W
Lauderdale *f.* Scotland **35** 55.43N 2.42W
Laugharne Wales **31** 51.45N 4.28W
Launceston Australia **80** 41.25S 147.07E
Launceston England **31** 50.38N 4.21W
Laune *r.* Rep. of Ire. **39** 52.08N 9.45W
Laurel U.S.A. **95** 38.22N 75.34W
Laurencekirk Scotland **37** 56.50N 2.29W
Laurencetown Rep. of Ire. **39** 53.15N 8.12W
Laurentides Mts. Canada **95** 47.40N 71.40W
Lauritsala Finland **46** 61.05N 28.20E
Lausanne Switz. **44** 46.32N 6.39E
Laut *i.* Indonesia **60** 3.45S 116.20E
Lauterecken W. Germany **45** 49.39N 7.36E
Lavagh More *mtn.* Rep. of Ire. **38** 54.45N 8.07W
Laval Canada **95** 45.33N 73.44W
Laval France **40** 48.04N 0.45W
La Vega Dom. Rep. **97** 19.15N 70.33W
Lavernock Pt. Wales **31** 51.25N 3.10W
Lavras Brazil **103** 21.15S 44.59W
Lawers Scotland **34** 56.32N 4.10W
Lawra Ghana **70** 10.40N 2.49W
Lawrence U.S.A. **95** 42.41N 71.12W
Lawrenceville U.S.A. **94** 38.44N 87.42W
Laxey I.o.M. **32** 54.14N 4.24W
Laxford, Loch Scotland **36** 58.25N 5.06W
Lea *r.* England **27** 51.30N 0.00
Leach *r.* England **28** 51.41N 1.39W
Leadburn Scotland **35** 55.47N 3.14W
Leader *r.* Scotland **35** 55.37N 2.40W
Leadhills Scotland **35** 55.25N 3.46W
Leaf *r.* Canada **93** 58.47N 70.06W
Leamington Canada **94** 42.03N 82.35W
Leane, Lough Rep. of Ire. **39** 52.03N 9.35W
Leatherhead England **27** 51.18N 0.20W
Lebanon Asia **56** 34.00N 36.00E
Lebanon N.H. U.S.A. **95** 43.39N 72.17W
Lebanon Penn. U.S.A. **95** 40.21N 76.25W
Lebork Poland **46** 54.32N 17.43E
Lebrija Spain **41** 36.55N 6.10W
Le Cateau France **45** 50.07N 3.33E
Lecce Italy **43** 40.21N 18.11E
Lech *r.* W. Germany **44** 48.45N 10.51E
Le Chesne France **45** 49.31N 4.46E
Lechlade England **28** 51.42N 1.40W
Le Creusot France **40** 46.48N 4.27E
Lectoure France **40** 43.56N 0.38E
Ledbury England **28** 52.03N 2.25W
Ledesma Spain **41** 41.05N 6.00W
Lee *r.* Rep. of Ire. **39** 51.53N 8.25W
Leech L. U.S.A. **91** 47.10N 94.30W
Leeds England **33** 53.48N 1.34W
Leek England **32** 53.07N 2.02W
Leer W. Germany **45** 53.14N 7.27E
Leeton Australia **80** 34.33S 146.24E
Leeuwarden Neth. **45** 53.12N 5.48E
Leeuwin, C. Australia **79** 34.00S 115.00E
Leeward Is. C. America **97** 18.00N 61.00W
Legaspi Phil. **61** 13.10N 123.45E
Legges Tor *mtn.* Australia **80** 41.32S 147.41E
Leghorn Italy **42** 43.33N 10.18E
Leipzig E. Germany **48** 51.20N 12.20E
Legnica Poland **44** 51.12N 16.10E
Leh Jammu and Kashmir **58** 34.09N 77.35E
Le Havre France **40** 49.30N 0.06E
Leicester England **28** 52.39N 1.09W
Leicestershire *d.* England **28** 52.29N 1.10W
Leiden Neth. **45** 52.10N 4.30E
Leie *r.* Belgium **45** 51.03N 3.44E
Leigh G.M. England **32** 53.30N 2.33W
Leigh Kent England **27** 51.12N 0.13E
Leigh Creek *town* Australia **80** 30.31S 138.25E
Leighlinbridge Rep. of Ire. **39** 52.44N 6.59W
Leighton Buzzard England **28** 51.55N 0.39W
Leinster *d.* Rep. of Ire. **39** 53.05N 7.00W
Leinster, Mt. Rep. of Ire. **39** 52.38N 6.47W
Leipzig E. Germany **44** 51.20N 12.20E
Leiston England **29** 52.13N 1.35E
Leith Scotland **35** 55.59N 2.09W
Leith Hill England **27** 51.11N 0.21W
Leitrim *d.* Rep. of Ire. **38** 54.08N 8.00W
Leixlip Rep. of Ire. **38** 53.22N 6.31W
Lek *r.* Neth. **45** 51.55N 4.29E
Le Kef Algeria **42** 36.10N 8.40E
Lelystad Neth. **45** 52.32N 5.29E
Le Mans France **40** 48.01N 0.10E
Lemmer Neth. **45** 52.50N 5.43E
Lemmon U.S.A. **90** 45.56N 102.00W
Len *r.* England **27** 51.16N 0.31E
Lena *r.* U.S.S.R. **49** 72.00N 127.10E
Lenadoon Pt. Rep. of Ire. **38** 54.18N 9.04W
Lengerich W. Germany **45** 52.12N 7.52E
Lengoue *r.* Congo **72** 1.15S 16.42E
Lenina, Peak *mtn.* U.S.S.R. **62** 40.14N 69.40E
Leninabad U.S.S.R. **62** 40.14N 69.40E
Leninakan U.S.S.R. **57** 40.47N 43.49E
Leningrad U.S.S.R. **47** 59.55N 30.25E
Leninogorsk U.S.S.R. **48** 50.23N 83.32E
Leninsk Kuznetskiy U.S.S.R. **48** 54.44N 86.13E
Lenkoran U.S.S.R. **57** 38.45N 48.50E
Lenne *r.* W. Germany **45** 51.24N 7.30E
Lennoxtown Scotland **34** 55.59N 4.12W
Lens France **45** 50.26N 2.50E
Leoben Austria **44** 47.23N 15.06E
Leominster England **28** 52.15N 2.43W
Leominster U.S.A. **95** 42.31N 71.45W
León Mexico **96** 21.10N 101.42W
León Nicaragua **96** 12.24N 86.52W
Léon Spain **41** 42.35N 5.34W
Le Puy France **40** 45.03N 3.54E
Le Quesnoy France **45** 50.15N 3.39E
Lérida Spain **41** 41.37N 0.38E
Lerma Spain **41** 42.02N 3.46W
Lerwick Scotland **36** 60.09N 1.09W
Les Cayes Haiti **97** 18.15N 73.46W
Les Ecréhou *is.* Channel Is. **31** 49.17N 1.56W
Les Ecrins *mtn.* France **40** 44.50N 6.20E
Leskovac Yugo. **43** 43.00N 21.56E
Leslie Scotland **35** 56.13N 3.13W
Lesmahagow Scotland **35** 55.38N 3.54W
Lesotho Africa **74** 29.00S 28.00E
Les Sables d'Olonne France **40** 46.30N 1.47W
Lesser Antilles *is.* C. America **97** 13.00N 65.00W
Lesser Slave L. Canada **92** 55.30N 115.00W
Lesser Sunda Is. Indonesia **60** 8.30S 118.00E
Lessines Belgium **45** 50.43N 3.50E
Lésvos *i.* Greece **43** 39.10N 26.16E
Leszno Poland **44** 51.51N 16.35E
Letchworth England **29** 51.58N 0.13W
Lethbridge Canada **90** 49.43N 112.48W
Leti Is. Indonesia **61** 8.20S 128.00E
Le Tréport France **40** 50.04N 1.22E
Letterkenny Rep. of Ire. **38** 54.56N 7.45W
Leuser *mtn.* Indonesia **60** 3.50N 97.10E
Leuze Belgium **45** 50.36N 3.37E
Leven England **33** 53.54N 0.18W
Leven Scotland **35** 56.12N 3.00W
Leven, Loch Scotland **35** 56.13N 3.23W
Lévêque, C. Australia **79** 16.25S 123.00E
Leverburgh Scotland **36** 57.46N 7.00W
Le Verdon France **40** 45.33N 1.04W
Leverkusen W. Germany **45** 51.02N 6.59E
Levin New Zealand **82** 40.37S 175.18E
Levis Canada **95** 46.47N 71.12W
Levittown U.S.A. **95** 40.10N 74.50W
Levkás *i.* Greece **43** 38.44N 20.37E
Lew *r.* England **31** 50.50N 4.05W
Lewes England **29** 50.53N 0.02E
Lewis *i.* Scotland **36** 58.10N 6.40W
Lewisham *d.* England **27** 51.27N 0.01W
Lewis Pass *f.* New Zealand **82** 42.30S 172.15E
Lewistown Maine U.S.A. **95** 44.05N 70.15W
Lewistown Penn. U.S.A. **95** 40.37N 77.36W
Lexington U.S.A. **91** 38.02N 84.30W
Leyburn England **32** 54.19N 1.50W
Leydsdorp R.S.A. **74** 23.59S 30.30E
Leyland England **32** 53.41N 2.42W
Leysdown-on-Sea England **29** 51.23N 0.57E
Leyte *i.* Phil. **61** 10.40N 124.50E
Leyton England **27** 51.34N 0.01W
Lezignan France **40** 43.12N 2.46E
Lhasa China **59** 29.41N 91.10E
Lhokseumawe Indonesia **60** 5.09N 97.09E
Liane *r.* France **29** 50.43N 1.35E
Liaocheng China **63** 36.29N 115.55E
Liaoning *d.* China **63** 41.30N 123.00E
Liaotung B. China **63** 40.20N 121.00E
Liaotung Pen. China **63** 40.00N 122.50E
Liaoyuan China **63** 42.53N 125.10E
Liard *r.* Canada **92** 61.56N 120.35W
Libenge Zaïre **72** 3.39N 18.39E
Liberal U.S.A. **90** 37.03N 100.56W
Liberec Czech. **44** 50.48N 15.05E
Liberia Africa **70** 6.30N 9.30W
Liberia Costa Rica **96** 10.39N 85.28W
Libourne France **40** 44.55N 0.14W
Libreville Gabon **72** 0.25N 9.30E
Libya Africa **68** 26.30N 17.00E
Libyan Desert Africa **69** 25.00N 26.10E
Libyan Plateau Africa **56** 30.45N 26.00E
Licata Italy **42** 37.07N 13.58E
Lichanga Moçambique **73** 13.09S 35.17E
Lichfield England **28** 52.40N 1.50W

For Khmer Republic *read* Kampuchea. *For* Malagasy Republic *read* Madagascar. *For* Rhodesia *read* Zimbabwe.

Lichtenburg to **Loralai** 146

Lichtenburg R.S.A. **74** 26.09S 26.11E
Liddel Water *r.* England **35** 54.58N 3.00W
Liddesdale *f.* Scotland **35** 55.10N 2.50W
Lidköping Sweden **46** 58.30N 13.10E
Liechtenstein Europe **44** 47.08N 9.35E
Liège Belgium **45** 50.38N 5.35E
Liège *d.* Belgium **45** 50.32N 5.35E
Lieksa Finland **46** 63.13N 30.01E
Lienyunkang China **63** 34.42N 119.28E
Lienz Austria **44** 46.51N 12.50E
Liepāja U.S.S.R. **46** 56.30N 21.00E
Lier Belgium **45** 51.08N 4.35E
Liévin France **45** 50.27N 2.49E
Lièvre, R. du Canada **95** 45.29N 75.33W
Liffey *r.* Rep. of Ire. **38** 53.21N 6.14W
Lifford Rep. of Ire. **38** 54.50N 7.31W
Lightning Ridge *town* Australia **80** 29.25S 147.59E
Lightwater England **27** 51.21N 0.37W
Ligurian Sea Med. Sea **42** 43.30N 9.00E
Lihue Hawaii U.S.A. **90** 21.59N 159.23W
Likasi Zaïre **73** 10.58S 26.50E
Likiang China **59** 26.50N 100.15E
Likona *r.* Congo **72** 0.11N 16.25E
Likouala *r.* Congo **72** 0.51S 17.17E
Lille France **45** 50.39N 3.05E
Lillehammer Norway **46** 61.06N 10.27E
Lillers France **45** 50.34N 2.29E
Lilleström Norway **46** 59.58N 11.05E
Lilongwe Malaŵi **73** 13.58S 33.49E
Lim *r.* Yugo. **43** 43.45N 19.13E
Lima Peru **102** 12.06S 76.03W
Lima *r.* Portugal **41** 41.40N 8.50W
Lima U.S.A. **94** 40.43N 84.06W
Limassol Cyprus **56** 34.40N 33.03E
Limavady N. Ireland **34** 55.03N 6.57W
Limbourg Belgium **45** 50.36N 5.57E
Limbourg *d.* Belgium **45** 51.00N 5.30E
Limburg *d.* Neth. **45** 51.15N 5.45E
Limeira Brazil **103** 22.34S 47.25W
Limerick Rep. of Ire. **39** 52.40N 8.37W
Limerick *d.* Rep. of Ire. **39** 52.40N 8.37W
Lim Fjord *est.* Denmark **46** 56.55N 9.10E
Límnos *i.* Greece **43** 39.55N 25.14E
Limoges France **40** 45.50N 1.15E
Límon Costa Rica **96** 10.00N 83.01W
Limpopo *r.* Moçambique **74** 25.14S 33.33E
Limpsfield England **27** 51.16N 0.02E
Lina Saudi Arabia **57** 28.48N 43.45E
Linares Mexico **96** 24.54N 99.38W
Linares Spain **41** 38.05N 3.38W
Lincoln England **33** 53.14N 0.32W
Lincoln Maine U.S.A. **95** 45.23N 68.30W
Lincoln Nebr. U.S.A. **91** 40.49N 96.41W
Lincoln Edge *hills* England **33** 53.13N 0.31W
Lincolnshire *d.* England **33** 53.14N 0.32W
Lincoln Wolds *hills* England **33** 53.22N 0.08W
Lindau W. Germany **44** 47.33N 9.41E
Lindenborg Denmark **46** 55.56N 10.03E
Lindesnes *c.* Norway **46** 58.00N 7.05E
Lindi Tanzania **73** 10.00S 39.41E
Lindi *r.* Zaïre **72** 0.30N 25.06E
Lindos Greece **43** 36.05N 28.02E
Lingen W. Germany **45** 52.32N 7.19E
Lingfield England **27** 51.11N 0.01W
Lingga *i.* Indonesia **60** 0.20S 104.30E
Linguère Senegal **70** 15.22N 15.11W
Linköping Sweden **46** 58.25N 15.35E
Linlithgow Scotland **35** 55.58N 3.36W
Linney Head Wales **31** 51.37N 5.05W
Linnhe, Loch Scotland **34** 56.35N 5.25W
Linosa *i.* Italy **42** 35.52N 12.50E
Linsia China **62** 35.31N 103.08E
Linslade England **28** 51.55N 0.40W
Lintan China **62** 34.39N 103.40E
Linton England **29** 52.06N 0.19E
Linxe France **40** 43.56N 1.10W
Linz Austria **44** 48.19N 14.18E
Lions, G. of France **40** 43.12N 4.15E
Liouesso Congo **72** 1.12N 15.47E
Lipari Is. Italy **42** 38.35N 14.45E
Lipetsk U.S.S.R. **47** 52.37N 39.36E
Liphook England **28** 51.05N 0.49W
Lippe *r.* W. Germany **45** 51.38N 6.37E
Lippstadt W. Germany **44** 51.41N 8.20E
Lira Uganda **73** 2.15N 32.55E
Lisala Zaïre **72** 2.13N 21.37E
Lisboa *see* Lisbon Portugal **41**
Lisbon Portugal **41** 38.44N 9.08W
Lisburn N. Ireland **38** 54.30N 6.03W
Lisburne, C. U.S.A. **92** 69.00N 165.50W
Liscannor B. Rep. of Ire. **39** 52.55N 9.24W
Lishui China **63** 28.30N 119.59E
Liskeard England **31** 50.27N 4.29W
Liski U.S.S.R. **47** 51.00N 39.30E
Lismore Australia **80** 28.48S 153.17E
Lismore Rep. of Ire. **39** 52.08N 7.57W
Lismore *i.* Scotland **34** 56.31N 5.30W
Lisnaskea N. Ireland **38** 54.16N 7.28W
Liss England **28** 51.03N 0.53W
Listowel Rep. of Ire. **39** 52.27N 9.30W
Litang *r.* China **59** 28.09N 101.30E
Lithgow Australia **80** 33.30S 150.09E
Lithuania Soviet Socialist Republic *d.* U.S.S.R. **46** 55.00N 23.50E
Little Andaman *i.* India **59** 10.50N 92.38E
Little Cayman *i.* Cayman Is. **97** 19.40N 80.00W
Little Chalfont England **27** 51.39N 0.33W
Little Coco *i.* Burma **60** 13.50N 93.10E
Little Current *town* Canada **94** 45.57N 81.56W
Little Fen *f.* England **29** 52.18N 0.30E
Little Grand Rapids *town* Canada **91** 52.00N 95.01W
Littlehampton England **29** 50.48N 0.32W
Little Inagua *i.* Bahamas **97** 21.30N 73.00W
Little Karroo *f.* R.S.A. **74** 33.40S 21.30E
Little Khingan Shan *mts.* China **63** 48.40N 128.30E
Little Loch Broom *l.* Scotland **36** 57.53N 5.20W
Little Nicobar *i.* Asia **60** 8.00N 93.30E
Little Ouse *r.* England **29** 52.34N 0.20E
Littleport England **29** 52.27N 0.18E
Little Rock *town* U.S.A. **91** 34.42N 92.17W
Little St. Bernard Pass France/Italy **42** 45.40N 6.53E
Little Thurrock England **27** 51.28N 0.20E
Littleton Rep. of Ire. **39** 52.39N 7.44W
Little Zab *r.* Iraq **57** 35.15N 43.27E
Liuchow China **63** 24.17N 109.15E
Livermore, Mt. U.S.A. **90** 30.39N 104.11W
Liverpool Canada **93** 44.03N 64.43W
Liverpool England **32** 53.25N 3.00W
Liverpool B. England **32** 53.30N 3.10W
Liverpool Plains *f.* Australia **80** 31.20S 150.00E
Liverpool Range *mts.* Australia **80** 31.45S 150.45E
Livingston Scotland **35** 55.54N 3.31W
Livingstone Zambia **72** 17.40S 25.50E
Livingstonia Malaŵi **73** 10.35S 34.10E
Livonia U.S.A. **94** 42.25N 83.23W
Livramento Brazil **103** 30.52S 55.30W
Liwale Tanzania **73** 9.47S 38.00E
Lizard England **31** 49.58N 5.12W
Lizard Pt. England **31** 49.57N 5.15W
Ljubljana Yugo. **44** 46.04N 14.28E
Ljungan *r.* Sweden **46** 62.20N 17.19E
Ljungby Sweden **46** 56.49N 13.55E
Ljusdal Sweden **46** 61.49N 16.09E
Ljusnan *r.* Sweden **46** 61.15N 17.08E
Ljusnarsberg Sweden **46** 59.48N 14.57E
Llanbedr Wales **30** 52.40N 4.07W
Llanberis Wales **30** 53.07N 4.07W
Llanbister Wales **30** 52.22N 3.19W
Llandeilo Wales **30** 51.54N 4.00W
Llandovery Wales **30** 51.59N 3.49W
Llandrillo Wales **30** 52.55N 3.25W
Llandrindod Wells Wales **30** 52.15N 3.23W
Llandudno Wales **30** 53.19N 3.49W
Llandyssul Wales **30** 52.03N 4.20W
Llanelli Wales **31** 51.41N 4.11W
Llanerchymedd Wales **30** 53.20N 4.22W
Llanes Spain **41** 43.25N 4.45W
Llanfair-ar-y-bryn Wales **30** 52.04N 3.43W
Llanfair Caereinion Wales **30** 52.39N 3.20W
Llanfairfechan Wales **30** 53.15N 3.58W
Llanfihangel-Ystrad Wales **30** 52.11N 4.11W
Llanfyllin Wales **30** 52.47N 3.17W
Llangadfan Wales **30** 52.41N 3.28W
Llangadog Wales **30** 51.56N 3.53W
Llangefni Wales **30** 53.15N 4.20W
Llangollen Wales **30** 52.58N 3.10W
Llangynog Wales **30** 52.50N 3.24W
Llanidloes Wales **30** 52.28N 3.31W
Llanos *f.* Venezuela **97** 8.30N 67.00W
Llanrhystyd Wales **30** 52.19N 4.09W
Llanrwst Wales **30** 53.08N 3.48W
Llantrisant Wales **31** 51.33N 3.23W
Llantwit Major Wales **31** 51.24N 3.29W
Llanuwchllyn Wales **30** 52.52N 3.41W
Llanwrtyd Wells Wales **30** 52.06N 3.39W
Llanybyther Wales **30** 52.04N 4.10W
Llerena Spain **41** 38.14N 6.00W
Lleyn Pen. Wales **30** 52.50N 4.35W
Lloydminster Canada **92** 53.18N 110.00W
Loange *r.* Zaïre **72** 4.18S 20.05E
Loanhead Scotland **35** 55.53N 3.09W
Lobatse Botswana **74** 25.11S 25.40E
Lobaye *r.* C.A.R. **71** 3.40N 18.35E
Loberia Argentina **103** 38.08S 58.48W
Lobito Angola **72** 12.20S 13.34E
Lobos Argentina **103** 35.11S 59.08W
Locarno Switz. **44** 46.10N 8.48E
Lochaber *f.* Scotland **37** 56.55N 4.55W
Lochailort Scotland **36** 56.50N 5.40W
Lochaline Scotland **34** 56.32N 5.47W
Lochboisdale *town* Scotland **36** 57.09N 7.19W
Lochbuie Scotland **34** 56.22N 5.52W
Lochcarron Scotland **36** 57.25N 5.36W
Lochdonhead Scotland **34** 56.26N 5.41W
Lochearnhead Scotland **34** 56.23N 4.17W
Lochem Neth. **45** 52.10N 6.25E
Loches France **40** 47.08N 1.00E
Lochgelly Scotland **35** 56.08N 3.19W
Lochgilphead Scotland **34** 56.02N 5.26W
Lochgoilhead Scotland **34** 56.10N 4.54W
Lochinver Scotland **36** 58.09N 5.15W
Lochmaben Scotland **35** 55.08N 3.27W
Lochmaddy *town* Scotland **36** 57.36N 7.10W
Lochnagar *mtn.* Scotland **37** 56.57N 3.15W
Lochranza Scotland **34** 55.42N 5.18W
Lochwinnoch Scotland **34** 55.48N 4.38W
Lochy *r.* Scotland **36** 56.50N 5.05W
Lochy, Loch Scotland **37** 56.58N 4.55W
Lockerbie Scotland **35** 55.07N 3.21W
Lockport U.S.A. **95** 43.11N 78.39W
Loc Ninh Vietnam **60** 11.55N 106.35E
Loddon *r.* England **28** 51.30N 0.53W
Lodja Zaïre **72** 3.29S 23.33E
Lodwar Kenya **73** 3.06N 35.38E
Łódź Poland **47** 51.49N 19.28E
Lofoten *is.* Norway **46** 68.15N 13.50E
Loftus England **33** 54.33N 0.52W
Logan, Mt. Canada **92** 60.45N 140.00W
Logansport U.S.A. **94** 40.45N 86.25W
Logone *r.* Cameroon/Chad **71** 12.10N 15.00E
Logroño Spain **41** 42.28N 2.26W
Loimaa Finland **46** 60.50N 23.05E
Loir *r.* France **40** 47.29N 0.32E
Loire *r.* France **40** 47.18N 2.00W
Loja Spain **41** 37.10N 4.09W
Loje *r.* Angola **72** 7.52S 13.08E
Loka Sudan **73** 4.18N 31.00E
Lokeren Belgium **45** 51.06N 3.59E
Lokitaung Kenya **73** 4.15N 35.45E
Lokoja Nigeria **71** 7.49N 6.44E
Lokolo *r.* Zaïre **72** 0.45S 19.36E
Lokoro *r.* Zaïre **72** 1.40S 18.29E
Lolland *i.* Denmark **44** 54.50N 11.30E
Lom Bulgaria **43** 43.49N 23.13E
Lomami *r.* Zaïre **72** 0.45N 24.10E
Lombok *i.* Indonesia **60** 8.30S 116.20E
Lomé Togo **71** 6.10N 1.21E
Lomela Zaïre **72** 2.15S 23.15E
Lomela *r.* Zaïre **72** 0.14S 20.45E
Lomié Cameroon **71** 3.09N 13.35E
Lomond, Loch Scotland **34** 56.07N 4.36W
Łomża Poland **47** 53.11N 22.04E
London Canada **94** 42.58N 81.15W
London England **27** 51.32N 0.06W
London Colney England **27** 51.44N 0.18W
Londonderry N. Ireland **34** 55.00N 7.21W
Londonderry *d.* N. Ireland **34** 55.00N 7.00W
Londonderry, C. Australia **79** 13.58S 126.55E
Long, Loch Scotland **34** 56.05N 4.52W
Longa *r.* Angola **72** 16.15S 19.07E
Longa *i.* Scotland **36** 57.44N 5.48W
Long Beach *town* U.S.A. **90** 33.57N 118.15W
Long Bennington England **33** 52.59N 0.45W
Longbenton England **35** 55.02N 1.33W
Long Branch U.S.A. **95** 40.17N 73.59W
Long Ditton England **27** 51.23N 0.20W
Long Eaton England **33** 52.54N 1.16W
Longford Australia **80** 41.25S 147.02E
Longford Rep. of Ire. **38** 53.44N 7.48W
Longford *d.* Rep. of Ire. **38** 53.42N 7.45W
Longhorsley England **35** 55.15N 1.46W
Longhoughton England **35** 55.26N 1.36W
Long I. Bahamas **97** 23.00N 75.00W
Long I. U.S.A. **95** 40.50N 73.20W
Long L. Canada **94** 49.40N 86.45W
Longlac *town* Canada **91** 49.47N 86.34W
Long Mtn. England **28** 52.40N 3.05W
Longniddry Scotland **35** 55.58N 2.53W
Long Pt. Canada **94** 42.33N 80.04W
Long Pt. New Zealand **82** 46.35S 169.35E
Longridge England **32** 53.50N 2.37W
Longs Peak U.S.A. **90** 40.16N 105.37W
Long Sutton England **33** 52.47N 0.09E
Longtown England **35** 55.01N 2.58W
Longwy France **45** 49.32N 5.46E
Long Xuyen Vietnam **60** 10.23N 105.25E
Löningen W. Germany **45** 52.44N 7.46E
Looe England **31** 50.51N 4.26W
Lookout, C. U.S.A. **91** 34.34N 76.34W
Loolmalasin *mtn.* Tanzania **73** 3.00S 35.45E
Loop Head Rep. of Ire. **39** 52.33N 9.56W
Lopari *r.* Zaïre **72** 1.20N 20.22E
Lopez, C. Gabon **72** 0.36S 8.40E
Lopi Congo **72** 2.57N 2.47E
Lop Nor *l.* China **62** 40.30N 90.30E
Lopp Havet *est.* Norway **46** 70.30N 21.00E
Lorain U.S.A. **94** 41.28N 82.11W
Loralai Pakistan **58** 30.20N 68.41E

For Khmer Republic *read* Kampuchea. *For* Malagasy Republic *read* Madagascar. *For* Rhodesia *read* Zimbabwe.

Lorca Spain 41 37.40N 1.41W
Lordsburg U.S.A. 90 32.22N 108.43W
Lorient France 40 47.45N 3.21W
Lörrach W. Germany 44 47.37N 7.40E
Los Angeles U.S.A. 90 34.00N 118.17W
Los Blancos Spain 41 37.37N 0.48W
Loshan China 59 29.34N 103.42E
Lošinj i. Yugo. 42 44.36N 14.20E
Los Libres, Punta de c. Argentina 103 29.40S 57.06W
Los Roques i. Venezuela 97 12.00N 67.00W
Lossie r. Scotland 37 57.43N 3.18W
Lossiemouth Scotland 37 57.43N 3.18W
Lostwithiel England 31 50.24N 4.41W
Lot r. France 40 44.17N 0.22E
Lothian d. Scotland 35 55.50N 3.00W
Lotoi r. Zaïre 72 1.30S 18.30E
Lotsani r. Botswana 74 22.41S 28.06E
Lotschberg Tunnel Switz. 44 46.25N 7.53E
Lotta r. U.S.S.R. 46 68.36N 31.06E
Lotuke mtn. Sudan 73 4.10N 33.46E
Loudéac France 40 48.11N 2.45W
Loudima Congo 72 4.06S 13.05E
Louga Senegal 70 15.37N 16.13W
Loughborough England 33 52.47N 1.11W
Loughor r. Wales 31 51.41N 4.04W
Loughrea Rep. of Ire. 39 53.12N 8.35W
Loughros More B. Rep. of Ire. 38 54.48N 8.32W
Loughton England 27 51.39N 0.03E
Louisburgh Rep. of Ire. 38 53.46N 9.49W
Louisiana d. U.S.A. 91 31.00N 92.30W
Louis Trichardt R.S.A. 74 23.01S 29.43E
Louisville U.S.A. 91 38.13N 85.45W
Lourdes France 40 43.06N 0.02W
Louth Australia 80 30.34S 145.09E
Louth England 33 53.23N 0.00
Louth d. Rep. of Ire. 38 53.55N 6.30W
Louvain Belgium 45 50.53N 4.45E
Lovat r. U.S.S.R. 47 58.06N 31.37E
Lovech Bulgaria 43 43.08N 24.44E
Lovoi r. Zaïre 73 8.14S 26.40E
Lovua r. Zaïre 72 6.08S 20.35E
Lowa r. Kivu Zaïre 72 1.25S 25.55E
Lowell U.S.A. 95 42.38N 71.19W
Lower California pen. Mexico 90 30.00N 115.00W
Lower Egypt f. Egypt 56 30.30N 31.00E
Lower Lough Erne N. Ireland 38 54.28N 7.48W
Lower Nazeing England 27 51.43N 0.03E
Lower Tunguska r. U.S.S.R. 49 65.50N 88.00E
Lowestoft England 29 52.29N 1.44E
Lowick England 35 55.39N 1.58W
Lowicz Poland 47 52.06N 19.55E
Lowther Hills Scotland 35 55.20N 3.40W
Loxton Australia 80 34.38S 140.38E
Loyal, Loch Scotland 37 58.23N 4.21W
Lua r. Zaïre 72 2.45N 18.28E
Lualaba r. Zaïre 72 0.18N 25.32E
Luama r. Zaïre 73 4.45S 26.55E
Luanchimo r. Zaïre 72 6.32S 20.57E
Luanda Angola 72 8.50S 13.20E
Luanda d. Angola 72 9.00S 13.30E
Luando Game Res. Angola 72 11.00S 17.45E
Luang Prabang Laos 60 19.53N 102.10E
Luangwa r. Central Zambia 73 15.32S 30.28E
Luanshya Zambia 73 13.09S 28.24E
Luapula r. Zambia 73 9.25S 28.36E
Luarca Spain 41 43.33N 6.31W
Lubango Angola 72 14.52S 13.30E
Lubbock U.S.A. 90 33.35N 101.53W
Lübeck W. Germany 44 53.52N 10.40E
Lübeck B. W. Germany 44 54.05N 11.00E
Lubefu r. Zaïre 72 4.05S 23.00E
Lubilash r. Zaïre 72 4.59S 23.25E
Lublin Poland 47 51.18N 22.31E
Lubny U.S.S.R. 47 50.01N 33.00E
Lubudi Zaïre 72 9.57S 25.59E
Lubudi r. Kasai Occidental Zaïre 72 4.00S 21.23E
Lubudi r. Shaba Zaïre 72 9.13S 25.40E
Lubumbashi Zaïre 73 11.44S 27.29E
Lubutu Zaïre 73 0.48S 26.19E
Lucan Rep. of Ire. 38 53.21N 6.27W
Luce, Water of r. Scotland 34 54.52N 4.49W
Luce B. Scotland 34 54.45N 4.47W
Lucena Spain 41 37.25N 4.29W
Lučenec Czech. 47 48.20N 19.40E
Lucero Mexico 90 30.50N 106.30W
Luchow China 59 28.25N 105.20E
Luckenwalde E. Germany 44 52.05N 13.11E
Lucknow India 58 26.50N 80.54E
Lüdenscheid W. Germany 45 51.13N 7.36E
Ludgate Canada 94 45.54N 80.32W
Ludgershall England 28 51.15N 1.38W
Ludhiana India 58 30.56N 75.52E
Lüdinghausen W. Germany 45 51.46N 7.27E
Ludington U.S.A. 94 43.58N 86.27W
Ludlow England 28 52.23N 2.42W

Ludvika Sweden 46 60.08N 15.14E
Ludwigshafen W. Germany 44 49.29N 8.27E
Luebo Zaïre 72 5.16S 21.27E
Luena r. Angola 72 12.30S 22.37E
Luena Zambia 73 10.40S 30.21E
Luena r. Western Zambia 72 14.47S 23.05E
Luengue r. Angola 72 16.58S 21.15E
Luenha r. Moçambique 74 16.29S 33.40E
Lufira r. Zaïre 73 8.15S 26.30E
Lufkin U.S.A. 91 31.21N 94.47W
Luga U.S.S.R. 47 58.42N 29.49E
Luga r. U.S.S.R. 46 59.40N 28.15E
Lugano Switz. 40 46.01N 8.57E
Lugenda r. Moçambique 73 11.23S 38.30E
Lugg r. England 28 52.01N 2.38W
Lugh Ganana Somali Rep. 73 3.49N 42.34E
Lugnaquilla Mtn. Rep. of Ire. 39 52.58N 6.28W
Lugo Spain 41 43.00N 7.33W
Lugoj Romania 43 45.42N 21.56E
Luiana Angola 72 17.08S 22.59E
Luiana r. Angola 72 17.28S 23.02E
Luichart, Loch Scotland 37 57.36N 4.45W
Luichow Pen. China 63 20.40N 109.30E
Luilaka r. Zaïre 72 0.15S 19.00E
Luilu r. Zaïre 72 6.22S 23.53E
Luing i. Scotland 34 56.14N 5.38W
Luiro r. Finland 46 67.22N 27.30E
Luisa Zaïre 72 7.15S 22.27E
Lukala Zaïre 72 5.23S 13.02E
Lukanga Swamp f. Zambia 73 14.15S 27.30E
Lukenie r. Zaïre 72 2.43S 18.12E
Lukuga r. Zaïre 73 5.37S 26.58E
Lukula r. Zaïre 72 4.15S 17.59E
Luleå Sweden 46 65.35N 22.10E
Luleburgaz Turkey 43 41.25N 27.23E
Lulonga r. Zaïre 72 0.42N 18.26E
Lulua r. Zaïre 72 5.03S 21.07E
Lumsden New Zealand 82 45.45S 168.27E
Lumsden Scotland 37 57.17N 2.53W
Lunan B. Scotland 35 56.38N 2.30W
Lund Sweden 46 55.42N 13.10E
Lunda d. Angola 72 9.30S 20.00E
Lundazi Zambia 73 12.19S 33.11E
Lundi r. Rhodesia 74 21.16S 32.20E
Lundy i. England 31 51.10N 4.41W
Lune r. England 32 54.03N 2.49W
Lüneburg W. Germany 44 53.15N 10.24E
Lunga r. Zambia 73 14.28S 26.27E
Lungsi China 62 35.00N 105.00E
Lungwebungu r. Zambia 72 14.20S 23.15E
Luninets U.S.S.R. 47 52.18N 26.50E
Lunna Ness c. Scotland 36 60.27N 1.03W
Luofo Zaïre 73 0.12S 29.15E
Luque Paraguay 103 25.15S 57.32W
Lure France 44 47.42N 6.30E
Lurgan N. Ireland 38 54.28N 6.21W
Lurio Moçambique 73 13.30S 40.30E
Lurio r. Moçambique 73 13.32S 40.31E
Lusaka Zambia 73 15.20S 28.14E
Lusambo Zaïre 72 4.59S 23.26E
Lushoto Tanzania 73 4.48S 38.20E
Lusiti r. Moçambique 74 20.00S 33.51E
Lusk Rep. of Ire. 38 53.32N 6.12W
Lusk U.S.A. 90 42.47N 104.26W
Luss Scotland 34 56.06N 4.38W
Lüta China 63 38.53N 121.37E
Lutfabad U.S.S.R. 57 37.32N 59.17E
Luton England 27 51.53N 0.25W
Lutterworth England 28 52.28N 1.12W
Luvua r. Zaïre 73 6.45S 27.00E
Luwegu r. Tanzania 73 8.30S 37.28E
Luwingu Zambia 73 10.13S 30.05E
Luxembourg d. Belgium 45 49.58N 5.30E
Luxembourg Europe 45 49.50N 6.15E
Luxembourg town Lux. 45 49.37N 6.08E
Luxor Egypt 56 24.41N 32.24E
Luzern Switz. 44 47.03N 8.17E
Luzon i. Phil. 61 17.50N 121.00E
Luzon Str. Pacific Oc. 61 20.20N 122.00E
Lvov U.S.S.R. 47 49.50N 24.00E
Lyallpur Pakistan 58 31.25N 73.09E
Lybster Scotland 37 58.18N 3.18W
Lycksele Sweden 46 64.34N 18.40E
Lyd r. England 31 50.38N 4.18W
Lydd England 29 50.57N 0.56E
Lydda Israel 56 31.57N 34.54E
Lydenburg R.S.A. 74 25.10S 30.29E
Lydney England 28 51.43N 2.32W
Lyell, Mt. U.S.A. 90 37.45N 119.18W
Lyme B. England 28 50.40N 2.55W
Lyme Regis England 28 50.44N 2.57W
Lyminge England 29 51.07N 1.06E
Lymington England 28 50.46N 1.32W
Lympstone England 28 50.39N 3.25W
Lyndhurst England 28 50.53N 1.33W
Lynher r. England 31 50.23N 4.18W

Lynn U.S.A. 95 42.29N 70.57W
Lynn Lake town Canada 93 56.51N 101.01W
Lynton England 31 51.14N 3.50W
Lyon France 40 45.46N 4.50E
Lyon r. Scotland 35 56.37N 3.59W
Lyon Mtn. U.S.A. 95 4444N 73.56W
Lysekil Sweden 46 58.16N 11.26E
Lytham St. Anne's England 32 53.45N 3.01W
Lyubertsy U.S.S.R. 47 55.38N 37.58E

M

Maamakeogh mtn. Rep. of Ire. 38 54.17N 9.29W
Maamtrasna mtn. Rep. of Ire. 38 53.37N 9.35W
Maamturk Mts. Rep. of Ire. 38 53.32N 9.42W
Ma'an Jordan 56 30.11N 35.43E
Maas r. Neth. 45 51.44N 4.42E
Maaseik Belgium 45 51.08N 5.48E
Maastricht Neth. 45 50.51N 5.42E
Mablethorpe England 33 53.21N 0.14E
Macao Asia 60 22.13N 113.36E
Macclesfield England 32 53.16N 2.09W
Macdonnell Ranges mts. Australia 79 23.30S 132.00E
Macduff Scotland 37 57.40N 2.29W
Maceió Brazil 102 9.34S 35.47W
Macenta Guinea 70 8.31N 9.32W
Macerata Italy 42 43.18N 13.30E
Macgillycuddy's Reeks mts. Rep. of Ire. 39 52.00N 9.43W
Macheke Rhodesia 74 18.05S 31.51E
Machrihanish Scotland 34 55.25N 5.44W
Machynlleth Wales 30 52.35N 3.51W
Mackay Australia 79 21.10S 149.10E
Mackay, L. Australia 79 22.30S 128.58E
Mackenzie d. Canada 92 65.00N 115.00W
Mackenzie r. Canada 92 69.20N 134.00W
Mackenzie King I. Canada 92 77.30N 112.00W
Mackenzie Mts. Canada 92 64.00N 130.00W
Mackinaw City U.S.A. 94 45.47N 84.43W
Mackinnon Road town Kenya 73 3.50S 39.03E
Maclean Australia 80 29.27S 153.14E
Maclear R.S.A. 74 31.05S 28.22E
Macleod's Tables mtn. Scotland 36 57.25N 6.45W
Macloutsie r. Botswana 74 22.15S 29.00E
Macnean, Lough N. Ireland 38 54.19N 7.56W
Macomer Italy 42 40.16N 8.45E
Mâcon France 40 46.18N 4.50E
Macon U.S.A. 91 32.47N 83.37W
Macpherson Range mts. Australia 80 28.15S 153.00E
Macquarie r. Australia 80 41.08S 146.52E
Macroom Rep. of Ire. 39 51.54N 8.58W
Madang P.N.G. 61 5.14S 145.45E
Madawaska r. Canada 95 45.35N 76.25W
Madeira i. Atlantic Oc. 68 32.45N 17.00W
Madeira r. Brazil 102 3.50S 58.30W
Madhya Pradesh d. India 59 23.00N 79.30E
Madison Fla. U.S.A. 91 30.29N 83.39W
Madison Wisc. U.S.A. 94 43.04N 89.22W
Madiun Indonesia 60 7.37S 111.33E
Mado Gashi Kenya 73 0.40N 39.11E
Madras India 59 13.05N 80.18E
Madre, Sierra mts. Mexico 96 16.00N 93.00W
Madre del Sur, Sierra mts. Mexico 96 17.00N 100.00W
Madre Lagoon Mexico 96 25.00N 97.30W
Madre Occidental, Sierra mts. Mexico 96 24.00N 103.00W
Madre Oriental, Sierra mts. Mexico 96 24.00N 99.00W
Madrid Spain 41 40.25N 3.43W
Madukani Tanzania 73 3.57S 35.49E
Madura i. Indonesia 60 7.00S 113.30E
Madurai India 59 9.55N 78.07E
Maesteg Wales 31 51.36N 3.40W
Maestra, Sierra mts. Cuba 97 20.10N 76.30W
Mafeking R.S.A. 74 25.53S 25.39E
Mafeteng Lesotho 74 29.49S 27.14E
Mafia I. Tanzania 73 7.50S 39.50E
Mafraq Jordan 56 32.20N 36.12E
Magadan U.S.S.R. 49 59.38N 150.50E
Magadi Kenya 73 1.53S 36.18E
Magangue Colombia 97 9.14N 74.46W
Magas Iran 57 27.08N 61.36E
Magburaka Sierra Leone 70 8.44N 11.57W
Magdalena r. Colombia 97 10.56N 74.58W
Magdalena Mexico 90 30.38N 110.59W
Magdeburg E. Germany 44 52.08N 11.36E
Mageröya i. Norway 46 71.00N 25.50E
Maggiore, L. Italy 40 45.57N 8.37E
Maghera N. Ireland 34 54.51N 6.41W
Magherafelt N. Ireland 34 54.45N 6.38W
Maghull England 32 53.31N 2.56W
Magnitogorsk U.S.S.R. 48 53.28N 59.06E
Magude Moçambique 74 25.02S 32.40E
Magué Moçambique 73 15.46S 31.42E

For Khmer Republic read Kampuchea. For Malagasy Republic read Madagascar. For Rhodesia read Zimbabwe.

Magwe Burma **59** 20.10N 95.00E
Mahabad Iran **57** 36.44N 45.44E
Mahaddei Wen Somali Rep. **73** 2.58N 45.32E
Mahagi Zaïre **73** 2.16N 30.59E
Mahalapye Botswana **74** 23.05S 26.51E
Mahallat Iran **57** 33.54N 50.28E
Mahanadi r. India **59** 20.17N 86.43E
Maharashtra d. India **58** 20.00N 77.00E
Mahdia Tunisia **42** 35.28N 11.01E
Mahenge Tanzania **73** 8.46S 36.38E
Mahia Pen. New Zealand **82** 37.10S 178.30E
Mahón Spain **41** 39.55N 4.18E
Maidenhead England **27** 51.32N 0.44W
Maiden Newton England **28** 50.46N 2.35W
Maidens Scotland **34** 55.20N 4.49W
Maidstone England **27** 51.17N 0.32E
Maiduguri Nigeria **71** 11.53N 13.16E
Maihar India **58** 24.14N 80.50E
Maiko r. Zaïre **72** 0.15N 25.35E
Main r. N. Ireland **34** 54.43N 6.19W
Main r. W. Germany **44** 50.00N 8.19E
Main Barrier Range mts. Australia **80** 31.25S 141.25E
Mai Ndombe l. Zaïre **72** 2.00S 18.20E
Maine r. Rep. of Ire. **39** 52.09N 9.44W
Maine d. U.S.A. **95** 45.00N 69.00W
Mainland i. Orkney Is. Scotland **37** 59.00N 3.10W
Mainland i. Shetland Is. Scotland **37** 60.15N 1.22W
Mainpuri India **58** 27.14N 79.01E
Mainz W. Germany **44** 50.00N 8.16E
Maipu Argentina **103** 36.52S 57.52W
Maitland Australia **80** 32.33S 151.33E
Maja i. Indonesia **60** 1.05S 109.25E
Majene Indonesia **60** 3.33S 118.59E
Majma'a Saudi Arabia **57** 25.52N 45.25E
Majorca i. Spain **41** 39.35N 3.00E
Majuba Hill R.S.A. **74** 27.30S 29.50E
Majunga Malagasy Rep. **73** 15.50S 46.20E
Makarikari Salt Pan f. Botswana **74** 20.50S 25.45E
Makassar Str. Indonesia **60** 3.00S 118.00E
Makeni Sierra Leone **70** 8.57N 12.02W
Makeyevka U.S.S.R. **47** 48.01N 38.00E
Makó Hungary **43** 46.13N 20.30E
Makokou Gabon **72** 0.38N 12.47E
Makoua Congo **72** 0.01S 15.40E
Makran f. Asia **57** 26.30N 61.20E
Makurdi Nigeria **71** 7.44N 8.35E
Malabo Equat. Guinea **71** 3.45N 8.48E
Malacca Malaysia **60** 2.14N 102.14E
Malacca, Straits of Indian Oc. **60** 3.00N 100.30E
Málaga Colombia **97** 6.44N 72.45W
Málaga Spain **41** 36.43N 4.25W
Malagasy Republic Africa **73** 17.00S 46.00E
Malahide Rep. of Ire. **38** 53.27N 6.10W
Malakal Sudan **69** 9.31N 31.40E
Malakand Pakistan **58** 34.34N 71.57E
Malang Indonesia **60** 7.59S 112.45E
Malanje Angola **72** 9.36S 16.21E
Malanje d. Angola **72** 9.00S 17.00E
Mälaren l. Sweden **46** 59.30N 17.00E
Malatya Turkey **56** 38.22N 38.18E
Malaŵi Africa **73** 12.00S 34.00E
Malaŵi, L. Africa **73** 12.00S 34.30E
Malayer Iran **57** 34.19N 48.51E
Malaysia Asia **60** 5.00N 110.00E
Malbork Poland **47** 54.02N 19.01E
Malden England **27** 51.23N 0.15W
Malden U.S.A. **95** 42.24N 71.04W
Maldive Is. Indian Oc. **58** 6.20N 73.00E
Maldon England **29** 51.43N 0.41E
Maldonado Uruguay **103** 34.57S 54.59W
Maléa, C. Greece **43** 36.27N 23.11E
Malebo Pool f. Zaïre **72** 4.15S 15.25E
Malegaon India **58** 20.32N 74.38E
Mali Africa **70** 17.30N 2.30E
Malili Indonesia **61** 2.38S 121.06E
Malin Rep. of Ire. **34** 55.18N 7.15W
Malindi Kenya **73** 3.14S 40.08E
Malines Belgium **45** 51.01N 4.28E
Malin Head Rep. of Ire. **38** 55.23N 7.24W
Malin More Rep. of Ire. **38** 54.42N 8.48W
Mallacoota Australia **80** 37.34S 149.43E
Mallaig Scotland **36** 57.00N 5.50W
Mallawi Egypt **56** 27.44N 30.50E
Mallorca i. see MajorcaSpain **41**
Mallow Rep. of Ire. **39** 52.08N 8.39W
Malmédy Belgium **45** 50.25N 6.02E
Malmesbury England **28** 51.35N 2.05W
Malmesbury R.S.A. **74** 33.28S 18.43E
Malmö Sweden **46** 55.35N 13.00E
Malone U.S.A. **95** 44.52N 74.19W
Malonga Zaïre **72** 10.26S 23.10E
Malta Europe **42** 35.55N 14.25E
Malta i. Malta **42** 35.55N 14.25E
Malta Channel Med. Sea **42** 36.20N 14.45E
Maltby England **33** 53.25N 1.12W

Malton England **33** 54.09N 0.48W
Maluku d. Indonesia **61** 4.00S 129.00E
Malvern Hills England **28** 52.05N 2.16W
Mambasa Zaïre **73** 1.20N 29.05E
Mamberamo r. Asia **61** 1.45S 137.25E
Mambéré r. C.A.R. **71** 3.30N 16.08E
Mambilima Falls town Zambia **73** 10.32S 28.45E
Mamfe Cameroon **71** 5.46N 9.18E
Mamou Guinea **70** 10.24N 12.05W
Mamudju Indonesia **60** 2.41S 118.55E
Man Ivory Coast **70** 7.31N 7.37W
Manacle Pt. England **31** 50.04N 5.05W
Manacor Spain **41** 39.32N 3.12E
Manado Indonesia **61** 1.30N 124.58E
Managua Nicaragua **96** 12.06N 86.18W
Managua, L. Nicaragua **96** 12.10N 86.30W
Manama Bahrain **57** 26.12N 50.36E
Manapouri New Zealand **82** 45.35S 167.38E
Manapouri, L. New Zealand **82** 45.30S 167.00E
Manastir Turkey **56** 37.33N 31.37E
Manaus Brazil **102** 3.06S 60.00W
Manchester England **32** 53.30N 2.15W
Manchester Conn. U.S.A. **95** 41.47N 72.31W
Manchester N.H. U.S.A. **95** 42.59N 71.28W
Manchuria f. China **63** 46.00N 125.00E
Manchurian Plain f. Asia **107** 42.00N 122.00E
Mand r. Iran **57** 28.09N 51.16E
Manda Iringa Tanzania **73** 10.30S 34.37E
Mandal Norway **46** 58.02N 7.30E
Mandala Peak Asia **61** 4.45S 140.15E
Mandalay Burma **59** 21.57N 96.04E
Mandal Gobi Mongolia **62** 45.40N 106.10E
Mandara Mts. Nigeria/Cameroon **71** 10.30N 13.30E
Mandla India **58** 22.35N 80.28E
Manfredonia Italy **42** 41.38N 15.54E
Mangalia Romania **43** 43.48N 28.30E
Mangalore India **58** 12.54N 74.51E
Mangerton Mtn. Rep. of Ire. **39** 51.58N 9.30W
Mangochi Malaŵi **73** 14.29S 35.15E
Mangotsfield England **28** 51.29N 2.29W
Mangueira L. Brazil **103** 33.15S 52.50W
Mangyai China **62** 37.52N 91.26E
Mangyshlak Pen. U.S.S.R. **48** 44.00N 52.30E
Manhiça Moçambique **74** 25.23S 32.49E
Maniamba Moçambique **73** 12.30S 35.05E
Manica e Sofala d. Moçambique **74** 17.30S 34.00E
Manicouagan r. Canada **93** 49.00N 68.13W
Manila Phil. **61** 14.36N 120.59E
Maninga r. Zambia **73** 13.28S 24.25E
Manipur d. India **59** 25.00N 93.40E
Manisa Turkey **43** 38.37N 27.28E
Manistee r. U.S.A. **94** 44.17N 85.45W
Manistique U.S.A. **94** 45.58N 86.17W
Manitoba d. Canada **93** 54.00N 96.00W
Manitoba, L. Canada **90** 51.35N 99.00W
Manitou Is. U.S.A. **94** 45.05N 86.05W
Manitoulin I. Canada **94** 45.50N 82.15W
Manitowoc U.S.A. **94** 44.04N 87.40W
Maniwaki Canada **95** 46.22N 75.58W
Manizales Colombia **102** 5.30N 75.38W
Manjil Iran **57** 36.44N 49.29E
Mankono Ivory Coast **70** 8.01N 6.09W
Manly Australia **80** 33.47S 151.17E
Mannar, G. of India/Sri Lanka **59** 8.20N 79.00E
Mannheim W. Germany **44** 49.30N 8.28E
Mannin B. Rep. of Ire. **38** 53.28N 10.06W
Manningtree England **29** 51.56N 1.03E
Mannu r. Italy **42** 39.16N 9.00E
Manokwari Asia **61** 0.53S 134.05E
Manono Zaïre **73** 7.18S 27.24E
Manorhamilton Rep. of Ire. **38** 54.18N 8.10W
Manosque France **40** 43.50N 5.47E
Manresa Spain **41** 41.43N 1.50E
Mansa Zambia **73** 11.10S 28.52E
Mansel I. Canada **93** 62.00N 80.00W
Mansfield Australia **80** 37.04S 146.04E
Mansfield England **33** 53.08N 1.12W
Mansfield U.S.A. **94** 40.46N 82.31W
Mänttä Finland **46** 62.00N 24.40E
Mantua Italy **42** 45.09N 10.47E
Manukau Harbour New Zealand **82** 37.10S 174.00E
Manus i. Pacific Oc. **61** 2.00S 147.00E
Manyara, L. Tanzania **73** 3.40S 35.50E
Manych r. U.S.S.R. **47** 47.14N 40.20E
Manych Gudilo, L. U.S.S.R. **47** 46.20N 42.45E
Manyoni Tanzania **73** 5.46S 34.50E
Manzala, L. Egypt **56** 31.20N 32.00E
Manzanares Spain **41** 39.00N 3.23W
Manzanillo Cuba **97** 20.21N 77.21W
Manzini Swaziland **74** 26.30S 31.22E
Maoke Range mts. Indonesia **61** 4.00S 137.30E
Mapai Moçambique **74** 22.51S 32.00E
Mapia Is. Asia **61** 1.00N 134.15E
Maputo Moçambique **74** 25.58S 32.35E
Maputo d. Moçambique **74** 26.00S 32.30E
Ma'qala Saudi Arabia **57** 26.29N 47.20E

Maquela do Zombo Angola **72** 6.06S 15.12E
Maquinchao Argentina **103** 41.19S 68.47W
Mar f. Scotland **37** 57.07N 3.03W
Mar, Serra do mts. Brazil **103** 28.00S 49.30W
Mara d. Tanzania **73** 1.45S 34.30E
Mara r. Tanzania **73** 1.30S 33.52E
Maracaibo Venezuela **97** 10.44N 71.37W
Maracaibo, L. Venezuela **97** 10.00N 71.30W
Maracaju Brazil **103** 21.38S 55.10W
Maracaju, Serra de mts. Brazil **103** 21.00S 55.05W
Maracay Venezuela **97** 10.20N 67.28W
Maradi Niger **71** 13.29N 7.10E
Maragheh Iran **57** 37.25N 46.13E
Maralal Kenya **73** 1.15N 36.48E
Marand Iran **57** 38.25N 45.50E
Marandellas Rhodesia **74** 18.05S 31.42E
Marapi mtn. Indonesia **60** 0.20S 100.45E
Maraş Turkey **56** 37.34N 36.54E
Marathon Greece **43** 38.10N 23.59E
Marazion England **31** 50.08N 5.29W
Marbella Spain **41** 36.31N 4.53W
Marble Bar Australia **79** 21.16S 119.45E
Marburg W. Germany **44** 50.49N 8.36E
March England **29** 52.33N 0.05E
Marche Belgium **45** 50.13N 5.21E
Marchena Spain **41** 37.20N 5.24W
Marcy, Mt. U.S.A. **95** 44.07N 73.56W
Mar del Plata Argentina **103** 38.00S 57.32W
Marden England **27** 51.11N 0.30E
Mardin Turkey **56** 37.19N 40.43E
Maree, Loch Scotland **36** 57.41N 5.28W
Marettimo i. Italy **42** 37.58N 12.05E
Margarita I. Venezuela **97** 11.00N 64.00W
Margate England **29** 51.23N 1.24E
Mariana Is. Asia **61** 15.00N 145.00E
Marianao Cuba **96** 23.03N 82.29W
Marianas Trench Pacific Oc. **107** 19.00N 146.00E
Maribor Yugo. **44** 46.35N 15.40E
Marico r. Botswana **74** 24.15S 26.48E
Maridi Sudan **73** 4.55N 29.30E
Marie Galante i. Guadeloupe **97** 16.00N 61.15W
Mariehamn Finland **46** 60.05N 19.55E
Mariental S.W. Africa **74** 24.36S 17.59E
Mariestad Sweden **46** 58.44N 13.50E
Mariga r. Nigeria **71** 9.37N 5.55E
Marinette U.S.A. **94** 45.06N 87.38W
Maringá Brazil **103** 23.36S 52.02W
Maringa r. Zaïre **72** 1.13N 19.50E
Maringue Moçambique **74** 17.55S 34.24E
Marinha Grande Portugal **41** 39.45N 8.55W
Marion Ind. U.S.A. **94** 40.33N 85.40W
Marion Ohio U.S.A. **94** 40.35N 83.08W
Mariscal Estigarribia Paraguay **103** 22.03S 60.35W
Maritsa r. Turkey **43** 41.00N 26.15E
Markaryd Sweden **46** 56.26N 13.35E
Markerwaard f. Neth. **45** 52.30N 5.15E
Market Deeping England **29** 52.40N 0.20W
Market Drayton England **32** 52.55N 2.30W
Market Harborough England **28** 52.29N 0.55W
Market Rasen England **33** 53.24N 0.20W
Market Weighton England **33** 53.52N 0.04W
Markha r. U.S.S.R. **49** 63.37N 119.00E
Markinch Scotland **35** 56.12N 3.09W
Markyate England **27** 51.51N 0.28W
Marlborough England **28** 51.26N 1.44W
Marlborough Downs hills England **28** 51.28N 1.48W
Marle France **45** 49.44N 3.47E
Marlow England **27** 51.35N 0.48W
Marlpit Hill town England **27** 51.13N 0.04E
Marmagao India **58** 15.26N 73.50E
Marmara i. Turkey **43** 40.38N 27.37E
Marmara, Sea of Turkey **43** 40.45N 28.15E
Marmaris Turkey **43** 36.50N 28.17E
Marne r. France **40** 48.50N 2.25E
Maroua Cameroon **71** 10.35N 14.20E
Marovoay Malagasy Rep. **73** 16.05S 46.35E
Marple England **32** 53.23N 2.05W
Marquesas Is. Pacific Oc. **106** 9.00S 139.00W
Marquette U.S.A. **94** 46.33N 87.23W
Marquise France **29** 50.48N 1.42E
Marrakesh Morocco **68** 31.49N 8.00W
Marrawah Australia **80** 40.57S 144.44E
Marrupa Moçambique **73** 13.10S 37.30E
Marsabit Kenya **73** 2.20N 37.59E
Marsala Italy **42** 37.48N 12.27E
Marsden England **32** 53.36N 1.55W
Marseille France **40** 43.18N 5.22E
Marshall Is. Pacific Oc. **107** 8.00N 172.00E
Marshfield England **28** 51.28N 2.19W
Marshfield U.S.A. **94** 44.40N 90.11W
Marshland Fen f. England **29** 52.40N 0.18E
Marske-by-the-Sea England **33** 54.35N 1.00W
Martaban, G. of Burma **59** 15.10N 96.30E
Martelange Belgium **45** 49.50N 5.44E
Martés, Sierra mts. Spain **41** 39.10N 1.00W
Martha's Vineyard i. U.S.A. **95** 41.25N 70.35W

For Khmer Republic read Kampuchea. For Malagasy Republic read Madagascar. For Rhodesia read Zimbabwe.

Martigny to **Mexico** 149

Martigny Switz. **44** 46.07N 7.05E
Martinique C. America **97** 14.40N 61.00W
Martin Pt. U.S.A. **92** 70.10N 143.50W
Martinsburg U.S.A. **95** 39.28N 77.59W
Marton New Zealand **82** 40.04S 175.25E
Maruchak Afghan. **57** 35.50N 63.08E
Marum Neth. **45** 53.06N 6.16E
Marvejols France **40** 44.33N 3.18E
Mary U.S.S.R. **69** 37.42N 61.54E
Maryborough Australia **80** 37.05S 143.47E
Maryland *d.* U.S.A. **91** 39.00N 76.30W
Maryport England **32** 54.43N 3.30W
Masai Steppe *f.* Tanzania **73** 4.30S 37.00E
Masaka Uganda **73** 0.20S 31.46E
Masan S. Korea **63** 35.10N 128.35E
Masasi Tanzania **73** 10.43S 38.48E
Masbate *i.* Phil. **61** 12.00N 123.30E
Mascara Algeria **41** 35.20N 0.09E
Maseru Lesotho **74** 29.19S 27.29E
Masham England **32** 54.15N 1.40W
Mashhad Iran **57** 36.16N 59.34E
Mashonaland *f.* Rhodesia **74** 18.20S 32.00E
Masi-Manimba Zaïre **72** 4.47S 17.54E
Masindi Uganda **73** 1.41N 31.45E
Masira I. Oman **58** 20.30N 58.50E
Masjid-i-Sulaiman Iran **57** 31.59N 49.18E
Mask, Lough Rep. of Ire. **38** 53.38N 9.22W
Mason City U.S.A. **91** 43.10N 93.10W
Massa Italy **42** 44.02N 10.09E
Massachusetts *d.* U.S.A. **95** 43.00N 72.25W
Massangena Moçambique **74** 21.31S 33.03E
Massawa Ethiopia **69** 15.36N 39.29E
Massif Central *mts.* France **40** 45.00N 3.30E
Massif de l'Ouarsenis *mts.* Algeria **41** 35.55N 1.40E
Massillon U.S.A. **94** 40.48N 81.32W
Massinga Moçambique **74** 23.20S 35.25E
Masterton New Zealand **82** 40.57S 175.39E
Masurian Lakes Poland **47** 54.00N 21.45E
Matabeleland *f.* Rhodesia **74** 19.30S 28.15E
Matadi Zaïre **72** 5.50S 13.36E
Matagorda B. U.S.A. **91** 28.30N 96.20W
Matakana I. New Zealand **82** 37.35S 176.15E
Matam Senegal **70** 15.40N 13.18W
Matamoros Mexico **96** 25.33N 103.15W
Matandu *r.* Tanzania **73** 8.44S 39.22E
Matane Canada **95** 48.50N 67.13W
Matanzas Cuba **96** 23.04N 81.35W
Matanzas *d.* Cuba **96** 23.04N 81.35W
Matapan, C. Greece **43** 36.22N 22.28E
Mataró Spain **41** 41.32N 2.72E
Matatiele R.S.A. **74** 30.20S 28.49E
Mataura *r.* New Zealand **82** 46.34S 168.45E
Matawin *r.* Canada **95** 46.56N 72.55W
Matehuala Mexico **96** 23.40N 100.40W
Matera Italy **43** 40.41N 16.36E
Mateur Tunisia **42** 37.02N 9.39E
Mathews Peak *mtn.* Kenya **73** 1.18N 37.20E
Mathura India **58** 27.30N 77.42E
Matlock England **33** 53.08N 1.32W
Mato Grosso *d.* Brazil **103** 19.00S 55.00W
Matope Malaŵi **73** 15.20S 34.57E
Matopo Hills Rhodesia **74** 20.45S 28.30E
Matrah Oman **57** 23.37N 58.33E
Matruh Egypt **56** 31.21N 27.15E
Matsu Is. Taiwan **63** 26.12N 120.00E
Matsuyama Japan **63** 33.50N 132.47E
Mattagami *r.* Canada **94** 49.45N 82.00W
Mattawa Canada **95** 46.19N 58.42W
Matterhorn *mtn.* Switz. **40** 45.58N 7.38E
Maturín Venezuela **97** 9.45N 61.16W
Maubeuge France **45** 50.17N 3.58E
Mauchline Scotland **34** 55.31N 4.23W
Maude Australia **80** 34.27S 144.21E
Mauganj India **58** 24.40N 81.53E
Maughold Head I.o.M. **32** 54.18N 4.19W
Maui *i.* Hawaii U.S.A. **90** 20.45N 156.15W
Maumee *r.* U.S.A. **94** 41.34N 83.41W
Maumere Indonesia **61** 8.35S 122.13E
Maun Botswana **74** 19.52S 23.40E
Mauritania Africa **70** 20.00N 10.00E
Mauritius Indian Oc. **113** 20.10S 58.00E
Mavinga Angola **72** 15.47S 20.21E
Mavuradonha Mts. Rhodesia **74** 16.30S 31.30E
Mawlaik Burma **59** 23.40N 94.26E
May, C. U.S.A. **95** 38.55N 74.55W
May, Isle of Scotland **35** 56.12N 2.32W
Maya Spain **41** 43.12N 1.29W
Mayaguana I. Bahamas **97** 22.30N 73.00W
Mayaguez Puerto Rico **97** 18.13N 67.09W
Mayamey Iran **57** 36.27N 55.40E
Maya Mts. Belize **96** 16.30N 89.00W
Maybole Scotland **34** 55.21N 4.41W
Maydena Australia **80** 42.48S 146.30E
Mayen W. Germany **45** 50.19N 7.14E
Mayenne France **40** 48.18N 0.37W
Mayenne *r.* France **40** 48.18N 0.37W
Mayfield England **29** 51.01N 0.17E
Maykop U.S.S.R. **47** 44.37N 40.48E
Maymyo Burma **59** 22.05N 96.33E
Maynooth Rep. of Ire. **38** 53.23N 6.37W
Mayo *d.* Rep. of Ire. **38** 53.47N 9.07W
Mayo Daga Nigeria **71** 6.59N 11.25E
Mayo Landing Canada **92** 63.45N 135.45W
Mayor I. New Zealand **82** 37.15S 176.15E
Mayotte, Île *i.* Comoro Is. **73** 12.50S 45.10E
Mayoumba Gabon **72** 3.23S 10.38E
Mazabuka Zambia **73** 15.50S 27.47E
Mazatenango Guatemala **96** 14.31N 91.30W
Mažeikiai U.S.S.R. **46** 56.06N 23.06E
Mazoe *r.* Moçambique **73** 16.22S 33.38E
Mazoe Rhodesia **74** 17.30S 31.03E
Mbabane Swaziland **74** 26.20S 31.08E
M'Baere *r.* C.A.R. **72** 3.45N 17.35E
M'Baiki C.A.R. **71** 3.53N 18.01E
Mbala Zambia **73** 8.50S 31.24E
Mbale Uganda **73** 1.04N 34.12E
Mbamba Bay *town* Tanzania **73** 11.18S 34.50E
Mbandaka Zaïre **72** 0.03N 18.21E
M'Bangé Cameroon **72** 4.32N 9.31E
Mbarara Uganda **73** 0.36S 30.40E
Mbeya Tanzania **73** 8.54S 33.29E
Mbeya *d.* Tanzania **73** 8.30S 32.30E
Mbinda Congo **72** 2.11S 12.55E
M'bridge *r.* Angola **72** 7.12S 12.55E
Mbuji Mayi Zaïre **72** 6.08S 23.39E
Mbulamuti Uganda **73** 0.50N 33.05E
McClintock Channel Canada **93** 71.20N 102.00W
McClure Str. Canada **92** 74.30N 116.00W
McConaughy, L. U.S.A. **90** 41.20N 102.00W
McCook U.S.A **90** 40.15N 100.45W
McGrath U.S.A. **92** 62.58N 155.40W
Mchinja Tanzania **73** 9.44S 39.45E
Mchinji Malaŵi **73** 13.48S 32.55E
McKeesport U.S.A. **94** 40.21N 79.52W
McKinley, Mt. U.S.A. **92** 63.00N 151.00W
McMurray Canada **92** 56.45N 111.27W
McSwyne's B. Rep. of Ire. **38** 54.36N 8.26W
Mead, L. U.S.A. **90** 36.10N 114.25W
Meadville U.S.A. **94** 41.38N 80.10W
Mealasta *i.* Scotland **36** 58.05N 7.07W
Meath *d.* Rep. of Ire. **38** 53.32N 6.40W
Meaux France **40** 48.58N 2.54E
Mecca Saudi Arabia **69** 21.26N 39.49E
Meconta Moçambique **73** 15.00S 39.50E
Medan Indonesia **60** 3.35N 98.39E
Médéa Algeria **41** 36.15N 2.48E
Mededsiz *mtn.* Turkey **56** 37.33N 34.38E
Medellín Colombia **97** 6.15N 75.36W
Medenine Tunisia **68** 33.24N 10.25E
Méderdra Mauritania **70** 17.02N 15.41W
Medford U.S.A. **95** 42.25N 71.05W
Medicine Hat Canada **90** 50.03N 110.41W
Medina Saudi Arabia **56** 24.30N 39.35E
Medina del Campo Spain **41** 41.20N 4.55W
Medina de Rioseco Spain **41** 41.53N 5.03W
Mediterranean Sea **68** 37.00N 15.00E
Medjerda, Wadi *r.* Algeria **42** 37.07N 10.12E
Medjerda Mts. Algeria **42** 36.35N 8.20E
Medveditsa *r.* U.S.S.R. **47** 49.35N 42.45E
Medway *r.* England **27** 51.24N 0.31E
Meekatharra Australia **79** 26.35S 118.30E
Meerut India **58** 29.00N 77.42E
Mega Ethiopia **69** 4.02N 38.19E
Megantic Canada **95** 45.34N 70.53W
Megantic Mtn. Canada **95** 45.27N 71.09W
Mégara Greece **43** 38.00N 23.21E
Meghalaya *d.* India **58** 25.30N 91.00E
Meiktila Burma **59** 20.53N 95.54E
Meiningen E. Germany **44** 50.34N 10.25E
Meissala Chad **71** 8.20N 17.40E
Meissen E. Germany **44** 51.10N 13.28E
Meknès Morocco **68** 33.53N 5.37W
Mekong *r.* Asia **60** 10.00N 106.20E
Mekong Delta Vietnam **60** 10.00N 106.20E
Mekongga *mtn.* Indonesia **61** 3.39S 121.15E
Mékrou *r.* Benin **71** 12.20N 2.47E
Melbourn England **29** 52.05N 0.01E
Melbourne Australia **80** 37.45S 144.58E
Melbourne England **33** 52.50N 1.25W
Melfi Chad **71** 11.04N 18.03E
Melfi Italy **42** 40.59N 15.39E
Melilla Spain **41** 35.17N 2.57W
Melitopol U.S.S.R. **47** 46.51N 35.22E
Melksham England **28** 51.22N 2.09W
Mellerud Sweden **46** 58.42N 12.27E
Melmore Pt. Rep. of Ire. **38** 55.15N 7.49W
Melo Uruguay **103** 32.22S 54.10W
Melrose Scotland **35** 55.36N 2.43W
Melsetter Rhodesia **74** 19.48S 32.50E
Meltham England **32** 53.36N 1.52W
Melton Mowbray England **28** 52.46N 0.53W
Melun France **40** 48.32N 2.40E
Melvaig Scotland **36** 57.48N 5.49W
Melville Canada **90** 50.57N 102.49W
Melville, C. Australia **79** 14.02S 144.30E
Melville I. Australia **79** 11.30S 131.00E
Melville I. Canada **92** 75.30N 110.00W
Melville Pen. Canada **93** 68.00N 84.00W
Melvin, Lough N. Ireland **38** 54.26N 8.12W
Memba Moçambique **73** 14.16S 40.30E
Memel *see* Klaipeda U.S.S.R. **47**
Memmingen W. Germany **44** 47.59N 10.11E
Memphis U.S.A. **91** 35.05N 90.00W
Memphis *ruins* Egypt **56** 29.52N 31.12E
Menai Bridge *town* Wales **30** 53.14N 4.11W
Menai Str. Wales **30** 53.17N 4.20W
Mendawai *r.* Indonesia **60** 3.17S 113.20E
Mende France **40** 44.32N 3.30E
Menderes *r.* Turkey **43** 37.30N 27.05E
Mendip Hills England **28** 51.15N 2.40W
Mendocino, C. U.S.A. **90** 40.26N 124.24W
Mendoza Argentina **102** 34.00S 68.52W
Mendoza *d.* Argentina **103** 34.00S 67.40W
Mengtsz China **59** 23.20N 103.21E
Menin Belgium **45** 50.48N 3.07E
Menindee Australia **80** 32.23S 142.30E
Menjapa *mtn.* Indonesia **60** 1.00N 116.20E
Menongue Angola **72** 14.40S 17.41E
Menorca *i. see* MinorcaSpain **41**
Mentawai Is. Indonesia **60** 2.50S 99.00E
Menteith, L. of Scotland **34** 56.10N 4.18W
Menton France **40** 43.47N 7.30E
Mentor U.S.A. **94** 41.42N 81.22W
Meon *r.* England **28** 50.49N 1.15W
Meopham Station England **27** 51.23N 0.22E
Meppel Neth. **45** 52.42N 6.12E
Meppen W. Germany **45** 52.42N 7.17E
Merano Italy **44** 46.41N 11.10E
Merauke Indonesia **61** 8.30S 140.22E
Merca Somali Rep. **73** 1.42N 44.47E
Merced U.S.A. **90** 37.17N 120.29W
Mercedes Buenos Aires Argentina **103** 34.42S 59.30W
Mercedes Corrientes Argentina **103** 29.15S 58.05W
Mercedes San Luis Argentina **103** 33.43S 65.29W
Mercedes Uruguay **103** 33.16S 58.05W
Mere England **28** 51.05N 2.16W
Mergui Burma **59** 12.26N 98.34E
Mergui Archipelago *is.* Burma **59** 11.30N 98.15E
Meribah Australia **80** 34.42S 140.53E
Mérida Mexico **96** 20.59N 89.39W
Mérida Spain **41** 38.55N 6.20W
Mérida Venezuela **97** 8.24N 71.08W
Mérida, Cordillera de *mts.* Venezuela **97** 8.00N 71.30W
Meriden U.S.A. **95** 41.32N 72.48W
Meridian U.S.A. **91** 32.21N 88.42W
Merir *i.* Asia **61** 4.19N 132.18E
Merksem Belgium **45** 51.14N 4.25E
Merowe Sudan **69** 18.30N 31.49E
Merrick *mtn.* Scotland **34** 55.08N 4.29W
Merrygoen Australia **80** 31.51S 149.16E
Merse *f.* Scotland **35** 55.45N 2.15W
Mersea I. England **29** 51.47N 0.58E
Merseburg E. Germany **44** 51.22N 12.00E
Mersey *r.* England **32** 53.22N 2.37W
Merseyside *d.* England **32** 53.28N 3.00W
Mersin Turkey **56** 36.47N 34.37E
Mersing Malaysia **60** 2.25N 103.50E
Merstham England **27** 51.16N 0.09W
Merthyr Tydfil Wales **31** 51.45N 3.23W
Mértola Portugal **41** 37.38N 7.40W
Merton *d.* England **27** 51.25N 0.12W
Meru *mtn.* Tanzania **73** 3.15S 36.44E
Merzifon Turkey **56** 40.52N 35.28E
Merzig W. Germany **45** 49.26N 6.39E
Mesolóngion Greece **43** 38.23N 21.23E
Mesopotamia *f.* Iraq **57** 33.30N 44.30E
Messalo *r.* Moçambique **73** 11.38S 40.27E
Messina Italy **42** 38.13N 15.34E
Messina R.S.A. **74** 22.23S 30.00E
Messina, G. of Med. Sea **43** 36.50N 22.05E
Messina, Str. of Med. Sea **42** 38.10N 15.35E
Mesta *r.* Greece **43** 40.51N 24.48E
Meta *r.* Venezuela **97** 6.10N 67.30W
Metan Argentina **103** 25.30S 64.50W
Metheringham England **33** 53.09N 0.22W
Methven Scotland **35** 56.25N 3.37W
Methwold England **29** 52.30N 0.33E
Metković Yugo. **43** 43.03N 17.38E
Metz France **40** 49.07N 6.11E
Meulaboh Indonesia **60** 4.10N 96.09E
Meuse *r. see* Maas Belgium **45**
Mevagissey England **31** 50.16N 4.48W
Mevatanana Malagasy Rep. **73** 17.06S 46.45E
Mexborough England **33** 53.29N 1.18W
Mexicali Mexico **90** 32.26N 115.30W
Mexico C. America **89** 20.00N 100.00W
Mexico *d.* Mexico **96** 19.45N 99.30W
Mexico U.S.A. **94** 39.10N 91.53W

For Khmer Republic *read* Kampuchea. *For* Malagasy Republic *read* Madagascar. *For* Rhodesia *read* Zimbabwe.

Mexico, G. of to **Montpellier** 150

Mexico, G. of N. America **96** 25.00N 90.00W
Mexico City Mexico **96** 19.25N 99.10W
Meyadin Syria **56** 35.01N 40.28E
Mezen U.S.S.R. **48** 65.50N 44.20E
Mezenc, Mt. France **40** 44.54N 4.11E
Miami U.S.A. **91** 25.45N 80.10W
Miami *r.* U.S.A. **94** 39.07N 84.43W
Mianduab Iran **57** 36.57N 46.06E
Mianeh Iran **57** 37.23N 47.45E
Mianwali Pakistan **58** 32.32N 71.33E
Michigan *d.* U.S.A. **94** 44.50N 85.20W
Michigan, L. U.S.A. **94** 44.00N 87.00W
Michigan City U.S.A. **94** 41.43N 86.54W
Michipicoten Harbour *town* Canada **94** 47.57N 84.55W
Michipicoten I. Canada **94** 47.45N 85.45W
Michoacan *d.* Mexico **96** 19.20N 101.00W
Michurinsk U.S.S.R. **47** 52.54N 40.30E
Middelburg Neth. **45** 51.30N 3.36E
Middelburg Cape Province R.S.A. **74** 31.30S 25.00E
Middelburg Transvaal R.S.A. **74** 25.47S 29.28E
Middlesbrough England **33** 54.34N 1.13W
Middleton England **32** 53.33N 2.12W
Middleton in Teesdale England **32** 54.38N 2.05W
Middleton on the Wolds England **33** 53.56N 0.35W
Middletown U.S.A. **94** 39.31N 84.13W
Middlewich England **32** 53.12N 2.28W
Mid Glamorgan *d.* Wales **31** 51.38N 3.25W
Midhurst England **28** 50.59N 0.44W
Midi, Canal du France **41** 43.18N 2.00W
Midland Canada **94** 44.45N 79.53W
Midland U.S.A. **94** 43.38N 84.14W
Midleton Rep. of Ire. **39** 51.55N 8.10W
Midsomer Norton England **28** 51.17N 2.29W
Midye Turkey **43** 41.37N 28.07E
Mid Yell Scotland **36** 60.31N 1.03W
Mienning China **59** 24.00N 100.10E
Mieres Spain **41** 43.15N 5.46W
Mijares *r.* Spain **41** 39.58N 0.01W
Mikhaylovka U.S.S.R. **47** 50.05N 43.15E
Mikindani Tanzania **73** 10.16S 40.05E
Mikkeli Finland **46** 61.44N 27.15E
Mikumi Tanzania **73** 7.22S 37.00E
Milan Italy **40** 45.28N 9.10E
Milange Moçambique **73** 16.09S 35.44E
Milâs Turkey **43** 37.18N 27.48E
Milborne Port England **28** 50.58N 2.28W
Mildenhall England **29** 52.20N 0.30E
Mildura Australia **80** 34.14S 142.13E
Miles City U.S.A. **90** 46.24N 105.48W
Milford England **27** 51.10N 0.40W
Milford U.S.A. **95** 41.13N 73.04W
Milford Haven *b.* Wales **31** 51.42N 5.05W
Milford Haven *town* Wales **31** 51.43N 5.02W
Milford on Sea England **28** 50.44N 1.36W
Milford Sound *town* New Zealand **82** 44.41S 167.56E
Miliana Algeria **41** 36.20N 2.15E
Milk *r.* U.S.A. **90** 47.55N 106.15W
Millau France **40** 44.06N 3.05E
Mille Lacs, Lac des Canada **94** 48.50N 90.30W
Mille Lacs L. U.S.A. **91** 46.15N 93.40W
Millerovo U.S.S.R. **47** 48.55N 40.25E
Milleur Pt. Scotland **34** 55.01N 5.07W
Mill Hill *town* England **27** 51.37N 0.14W
Millicent Australia **80** 37.36S 140.22E
Millom England **32** 54.13N 3.16W
Millport Scotland **34** 55.45N 4.56W
Millstreet Rep. of Ire. **39** 52.04N 9.05W
Milnathort Scotland **35** 56.14N 3.26W
Milngavie Scotland **34** 55.57N 4.19W
Milnthorpe England **32** 54.14N 2.47W
Milo *r.* Guinea **70** 11.05N 9.05W
Milos *i.* Greece **43** 36.40N 24.26E
Milparinka Australia **80** 29.45S 141.55E
Milton New Zealand **82** 46.08S 169.59E
Milton Abbot England **31** 50.35N 4.16W
Milton Keynes England **28** 52.03N 0.42W
Miltown Malbay Rep. of Ire. **39** 52.51N 9.25W
Milverton England **28** 51.02N 3.15W
Milwaukee U.S.A. **94** 43.03N 87.56W
Minab Iran **57** 27.07N 57.05E
Minas Uruguay **103** 34.20S 55.15W
Mina Saud Kuwait **57** 28.48N 48.24E
Minas Gerais Brazil **103** 18.00S 45.00W
Minatitlán Mexico **96** 17.59N 94.32W
Mindanao *i.* Phil. **61** 7.30N 125.00E
Minden W. Germany **44** 52.18N 8.54E
Mindoro *i.* Phil. **61** 13.00N 121.00E
Mindoro Str. Pacific Oc. **61** 12.30N 120.10E
Mindra, Mt. Romania **43** 45.20N 23.32E
Minehead England **28** 51.12N 3.29W
Mine Head Rep. of Ire. **39** 51.59N 7.35W
Minginish *f.* Scotland **36** 57.15N 6.20W
Mingulay *i.* Scotland **36** 56.48N 7.37W
Minna Nigeria **71** 9.39N 6.32E
Minneapolis U.S.A. **94** 45.00N 93.15W
Minnesota *d.* U.S.A. **91** 46.00N 95.00W
Miño *r.* Spain **41** 42.50N 8.52W
Minorca *i.* Spain **41** 40.00N 4.00E
Minot U.S.A. **90** 48.16N 101.19W
Minsk U.S.S.R. **46** 53.51N 27.30E
Minster England **29** 51.25N 0.50E
Minsterley England **28** 52.38N 2.56W
Mintlaw Scotland **37** 57.31N 2.00W
Minya Konka *mtn.* China **59** 29.30N 101.30E
Miraj India **58** 16.51N 74.42E
Miranda Brazil **103** 20.10S 56.19W
Miranda de Ebro Spain **41** 42.41N 2.57W
Miranda do Douro Portugal **41** 41.30N 6.16W
Mirande France **40** 43.31N 0.25E
Mirandela Portugal **41** 41.28N 7.10W
Mirecourt France **44** 48.18N 6.08E
Miri Malaysia **60** 4.28N 114.00E
Mirim, L. Brazil **103** 33.10S 53.30W
Mirpur Khas Pakistan **58** 25.33N 69.05E
Mirzapur India **58** 25.09N 82.34E
Misbourne *r.* England **27** 51.33N 0.29W
Mishawaka U.S.A. **94** 41.38N 86.10W
Misiones *d.* Argentina **103** 27.00S 54.30W
Miskolc Hungary **47** 48.07N 20.47E
Misoöl *i.* Indonesia **61** 1.50S 130.10E
Missinaibi *r.* Canada **91** 50.50N 81.12W
Mississauga Canada **95** 43.35N 79.37W
Mississippi *d.* U.S.A. **91** 33.00N 90.00W
Mississippi *r.* U.S.A. **94** 28.55N 89.05W
Mississippi Delta U.S.A. **91** 29.00N 89.10W
Missoula U.S.A. **90** 46.52N 114.00W
Missouri *d.* U.S.A. **94** 39.45N 91.30W
Missouri *r.* U.S.A. **94** 38.40N 90.20W
Mistassini, L. Canada **91** 50.45N 73.40W
Misurata Libya **68** 32.24N 15.04E
Mitcham England **27** 51.24N 0.09W
Mitchell *r.* Australia **79** 15.12S 141.40E
Mitchell U.S.A. **90** 43.40N 98.01W
Mitchell, Mt. U.S.A. **91** 35.57N 82.16W
Mitchelstown Rep. of Ire. **39** 52.16N 8.17W
Mitilíni Greece **43** 39.06N 26.34E
Mittelland Canal W. Germany **45** 52.24N 7.52E
Mitumba Mts. Zaïre **73** 3.00S 28.30E
Mitwaba Zaïre **73** 8.32S 27.20E
Mitzic Gabon **72** 0.48N 11.30E
Miyako *i.* Japan **63** 24.45N 125.25E
Mizen Head Rep. of Ire. **39** 51.27N 9.50W
Mjölby Sweden **46** 58.19N 15.10E
Mjösa *l.* Norway **46** 60.50N 10.50E
Mkushi Zambia **73** 13.40S 29.26E
Mladá Boleslav Czech. **44** 50.26N 14.55E
Mljet *i.* Yugo. **43** 42.45N 17.30E
Moamba Moçambique **74** 25.35S 32.13E
Moanda Gabon **72** 1.25S 13.18E
Moate Rep. of Ire. **38** 53.24N 7.45W
Moatize Moçambique **73** 16.04S 33.40E
Moba Zaïre **73** 7.03S 29.42E
Mobaye C.A.R. **72** 4.21N 21.10E
Mobile U.S.A. **91** 30.40N 88.05W
Mobile B. U.S.A. **91** 30.30N 87.50W
Mobridge U.S.A. **90** 45.31N 100.25W
Mobutu, L. Uganda/Zaïre **73** 1.45N 31.00E
Moçambique Africa **74** 21.00S 34.00E
Moçambique *d.* Moçambique **73** 15.00S 39.00E
Moçambique *town* Moçambique **73** 15.00S 40.47E
Moçambique Channel Indian Oc. **73** 16.00S 42.30E
Moçâmedes Angola **72** 15.10S 12.10E
Moçâmedes *d.* Angola **72** 15.00S 12.30E
Mocimboa da Praia Moçambique **73** 11.19S 40.19E
Mocuba Moçambique **73** 16.52S 37.02E
Modane France **40** 45.12N 6.40E
Modbury England **31** 50.21N 3.53W
Modder *r.* R.S.A. **74** 29.03S 23.56E
Modena Italy **42** 44.39N 10.55E
Módica Italy **42** 36.51N 14.51E
Moffat Scotland **35** 55.20N 3.27W
Mogadishu Somali Rep. **73** 2.02N 45.21E
Mogaung Burma **59** 25.20N 97.00E
Moghan Steppe *f.* U.S.S.R. **57** 39.40N 48.30E
Mogilev U.S.S.R. **47** 53.54N 30.20E
Mogincual Moçambique **73** 15.33S 40.29E
Mogok Burma **59** 23.00N 96.40E
Mogomo Moçambique **73** 15.25S 36.45E
Mohaka *r.* New Zealand **82** 39.07S 177.10E
Mohammadia Algeria **41** 35.35N 0.05E
Mohawk *r.* U.S.A. **95** 42.50N 73.40W
Mohéli *i.* Comoro Is. **73** 12.22S 43.45E
Mohill Rep. of Ire. **38** 53.55N 7.53W
Mohoro Tanzania **73** 8.09S 39.07E
Moidart *f.* Scotland **36** 56.48N 5.40W
Mo-i-Rana Norway **46** 66.20N 14.12E
Moisie *r.* Canada **93** 50.15N 66.00W
Moissac France **40** 44.07N 1.05E
Moji das Cruzes Brazil **103** 23.33S 46.14W
Mokpo S. Korea **63** 34.50N 126.25E
Mold Wales **30** 53.10N 3.08W
Moldavia Soviet Socialist Republic *d.* U.S.S.R. **47** 47.30N 28.30E
Molde Norway **46** 62.44N 7.08E
Mole *r.* Devon England **31** 50.59N 3.53W
Mole *r.* Surrey England **27** 51.24N 0.20W
Molepolole Botswana **74** 24.25S 25.30E
Molfetta Italy **43** 41.12N 16.36E
Molina de Aragón Spain **41** 40.50N 1.54W
Moline U.S.A. **94** 41.31N 90.26W
Moliro Zaïre **73** 8.11S 30.29E
Mölndal Sweden **47** 57.40N 12.00E
Molodechno U.S.S.R. **46** 54.16N 26.50E
Molokai *i.* Hawaii U.S.A. **90** 21.20N 157.00W
Molong Australia **80** 33.08S 148.53E
Molopo *r.* R.S.A. **74** 28.30S 20.07E
Molteno R.S.A. **74** 31.24S 26.22E
Moluccas *is.* Indonesia **61** 4.00S 128.00E
Molucca Sea Pacific Oc. **61** 2.00N 126.30E
Moma Moçambique **73** 16.40S 39.10E
Mombasa Kenya **73** 4.04S 39.40E
Mön *i.* Denmark **44** 54.58N 12.20E
Mona *i.* Puerto Rico **97** 18.06N 67.54W
Monach, Sd. of *str.* Scotland **36** 57.34N 7.35W
Monach Is. Scotland **36** 57.32N 7.38W
Monaco Europe **40** 43.40N 7.25E
Monadhliath Mts. Scotland **37** 57.09N 4.08W
Monaghan Rep. of Ire. **38** 54.15N 6.58W
Monaghan *d.* Rep. of Ire. **38** 54.10N 7.00W
Monar, Loch Scotland **36** 57.25N 5.05W
Monasterevan Rep. of Ire. **39** 53.09N 7.05W
Monastir Tunisia **42** 35.35N 10.50E
Monavullagh Mts. Rep. of Ire. **39** 52.14N 7.37W
Monchegorsk U.S.S.R. **46** 67.55N 33.01E
Mönchen-Gladbach W. Germany **45** 51.12N 6.25E
Monclova Mexico **90** 26.55N 101.20W
Moncton Canada **91** 46.10N 64.50W
Mondovi Italy **40** 44.24N 7.48E
Moneygall Rep. of Ire. **39** 52.53N 7.58W
Moneymore N. Ireland **34** 54.42N 6.40W
Monforte Spain **41** 42.32N 7.30W
Monga Zaïre **72** 4.10N 23.00E
Mongala *r.* Zaïre **72** 1.58N 19.55E
Mongalla Sudan **73** 5.12N 31.42E
Monghyr India **58** 25.24N 86.29E
Mongolia Asia **62** 46.30N 104.00E
Mongu Zambia **72** 15.10S 23.09E
Moniaive Scotland **35** 55.12N 3.55W
Monifieth Scotland **35** 56.29N 2.50W
Monkoto Zaïre **72** 1.39S 20.41E
Monmouth Wales **31** 51.48N 2.43W
Monnow *r.* England **28** 51.49N 2.42W
Monongahela *r.* U.S.A. **94** 40.26N 80.00W
Monopoli Italy **43** 40.56N 17.19E
Monroe La. U.S.A. **91** 32.31N 92.06W
Monroe Mich. U.S.A. **94** 41.56N 83.21W
Monrovia Liberia **70** 6.20N 10.46W
Mons Belgium **45** 50.27N 3.57E
Montalbán Spain **41** 40.50N 0.48W
Montana *d.* U.S.A. **90** 47.00N 110.00W
Montargis France **40** 48.00N 2.44E
Montauban France **40** 44.01N 1.20E
Montauk Pt. U.S.A. **95** 41.04N 71.51W
Mont-aux-Sources *mtn.* Lesotho **74** 28.50S 28.50E
Montbéliard France **44** 47.31N 6.48E
Montbrison France **40** 45.37N 4.04E
Montcalm, L. China **59** 34.30N 89.00E
Mont Cenis Pass France **40** 45.15N 6.55E
Montcornet France **45** 49.41N 4.01E
Mont de Marsan *town* France **40** 43.54N 0.30W
Monte Carlo Monaco **40** 43.44N 7.25E
Montecristo *i.* Italy **42** 42.20N 10.19E
Montego Bay *town* Jamaica **97** 18.27N 77.56W
Montélimar France **40** 44.33N 4.45E
Monterey U.S.A. **90** 36.35N 121.55W
Monterey B. U.S.A. **90** 36.45N 122.00W
Montería Colombia **97** 8.45N 75.54W
Montero Bolivia **103** 17.20S 63.15W
Monterrey Mexico **96** 25.40N 100.20W
Monte Santu, C. Italy **42** 40.05N 9.44E
Montes Claros Brazil **103** 16.45S 43.52W
Monte Verde Angola **72** 8.45S 16.50E
Montevideo Uruguay **103** 34.55S 56.10W
Montfort-sur-Meu France **40** 48.08N 1.57W
Montgomery U.S.A. **91** 32.22N 86.20W
Montgomery Wales **30** 52.34N 3.09W
Montijo Portugal **41** 38.42N 8.59W
Montijo Dam Spain **41** 38.52N 6.20W
Mont Joli Canada **95** 48.34N 68.05W
Mont Laurier *town* Canada **95** 46.33N 75.31W
Montluçon France **40** 46.20N 2.36E
Montmagny Canada **95** 46.58N 70.34W
Montmédy France **45** 49.31N 5.21E
Montmorillon France **40** 46.26N 0.52E
Montoro Spain **41** 38.02N 4.23W
Montpelier U.S.A. **95** 44.16N 72.34W
Montpellier France **40** 43.36N 3.53E

For Khmer Republic *read* Kampuchea. *For* Malagasy Republic *read* Madagascar. *For* Rhodesia *read* Zimbabwe.

Montreal Canada **95** 45.30N 73.36W
Montreal r. Canada **94** 47.13N 84.40W
Montrejeau France **40** 43.05N 0.33E
Montreuil France **40** 50.28N 1.46E
Montreux Switz. **44** 46.27N 6.55E
Montrose Scotland **35** 56.43N 2.29W
Montrose U.S.A. **90** 38.29N 107.53W
Montsant, Sierra de mts. Spain **41** 41.20N 1.00E
Montserrat i. C. America **97** 16.45N 62.14W
Monywa Burma **59** 22.07N 95.11E
Monza Italy **40** 45.35N 9.16E
Monze Zambia **73** 16.16S 27.28E
Monzón Spain **41** 41.52N 0.10E
Moore, L. Australia **79** 29.30S 117.30E
Moorfoot Hills Scotland **35** 55.43N 3.03W
Moorhead U.S.A. **91** 46.51N 96.44W
Moosehead L. U.S.A. **95** 45.45N 69.45W
Moose Jaw Canada **90** 50.23N 105.35W
Moosonee Canada **91** 51.18N 80.40W
Mopti Mali **70** 14.29N 4.10W
Mora Sweden **46** 61.00N 14.30E
Moradabad India **58** 28.50N 78.45E
Morar, Loch Scotland **36** 56.56N 5.40W
Morava r. Yugo. **43** 44.43N 21.02E
Moravian Heights mts. Czech. **44** 49.30N 15.45E
Moray Firth est. Scotland **37** 57.35N 4.00W
Morcenx France **40** 44.02N 0.55W
Morden Canada **93** 49.15N 98.10W
Morden England **27** 51.23N 0.12W
More, Loch Scotland **37** 58.23N 4.51W
Morecambe England **32** 54.03N 2.52W
Morecambe B. England **32** 54.05N 3.00W
Moree Australia **80** 29.29S 149.53E
Morelia Mexico **96** 19.40N 101.11W
Morella Spain **41** 40.37N 0.06W
Morelos d. Mexico **96** 18.40N 99.00W
Morena, Sierra mts. Spain **41** 38.10N 5.00W
Moretonhampstead England **31** 50.39N 3.45W
Morez France **40** 46.31N 6.02E
Morgan Australia **80** 34.02S 139.40E
Morgan City U.S.A. **91** 29.41N 91.13W
Morie, Loch Scotland **37** 57.44N 4.27W
Morioka Japan **63** 39.43N 141.08E
Morkalla Australia **80** 34.22S 141.10E
Morlaix France **40** 48.35N 3.50W
Morley England **33** 53.45N 1.36W
Morocco Africa **68** 31.00N 5.00W
Moro G. Phil. **61** 6.30N 123.20E
Morogoro Tanzania **73** 6.47S 37.40E
Morogoro d. Tanzania **73** 8.30S 37.00E
Morón Cuba **97** 22.08N 78.39W
Mörön Mongolia **62** 49.36N 100.08E
Moroni Comoro Is. **73** 11.40S 43.19E
Morotai i. Indonesia **61** 2.10N 128.30E
Moroto Uganda **73** 2.32N 34.41E
Morpeth England **35** 55.10N 1.40W
Morsbach W. Germany **45** 50.52N 7.44E
Mortagne France **40** 48.32N 0.33E
Morte Pt. England **31** 51.12N 4.13W
Mortimer Common England **28** 51.22N 1.05W
Moruya Australia **80** 35.56S 150.06E
Morven mtn. Scotland **37** 58.13N 3.42W
Morvern f. Scotland **36** 56.37N 5.45W
Morwell Australia **80** 38.14S 146.25E
Moscow U.S.S.R. **47** 55.45N 37.42E
Mosel r. W. Germany **45** 50.23N 7.37E
Moselle r. see Mosel France/Lux. **45**
Moshi Tanzania **73** 3.20S 37.21E
Mosjöen Norway **46** 65.50N 13.10E
Moskog Norway **46** 61.30N 5.59E
Moskva r. U.S.S.R. **47** 55.08N 38.50E
Mosquitia Plain Honduras **96** 15.00N 89.00W
Mosquito Coast f. Nicaragua **96** 13.00N 84.00W
Mosquitos, G. of Panamá **96** 9.00N 81.00W
Moss Norway **46** 59.26N 10.41E
Mossbank Scotland **36** 60.27N 1.10W
Mossel Bay town R.S.A. **74** 34.12S 22.08E
Mossgiel Australia **80** 33.18S 144.05E
Mossuma r. Zambia **72** 15.11S 23.05E
Moss Vale town Australia **80** 34.33S 150.20E
Most Czech. **44** 50.31N 13.39E
Mostaganem Algeria **41** 35.54N 0.05E
Mostar Yugo. **43** 43.20N 17.50E
Mosul Iraq **56** 36.21N 43.08E
Motagua r. Guatemala **96** 15.56N 87.45W
Motala Sweden **46** 58.34N 15.05E
Motherwell Scotland **35** 55.48N 4.00W
Motu r. New Zealand **82** 37.52S 177.37E
Motueka New Zealand **82** 41.08S 173.01E
Mouila Gabon **72** 1.50S 11.02E
Moulamein Australia **80** 35.03S 144.05E
Moulins France **40** 46.34N 3.20E
Moulmein Burma **59** 16.30N 97.40E
Mountain Ash Wales **31** 51.42N 3.22W
Mount Bellew town Rep. of Ire. **38** 53.28N 8.30W
Mount Darwin town Rhodesia **74** 16.45S 31.39E

Mount Fletcher town R.S.A. **74** 30.41S 28.30E
Mount Gambier town Australia **80** 37.51S 140.50E
Mount Hagen town P.N.G. **61** 5.54S 144.13E
Mount Isa town Australia **79** 20.50S 139.29E
Mount Lebanon town U.S.A. **94** 40.52N 80.04W
Mountmellick Rep. of Ire. **39** 53.08N 7.21W
Mountnessing England **27** 51.40N 0.21E
Mountrath Rep. of Ire. **39** 53.00N 7.30W
Mount's B. England **31** 50.05N 5.25W
Mourne r. N. Ireland **38** 54.50N 7.29W
Mourne Mts. N. Ireland **38** 54.10N 6.02W
Moussoro Chad **71** 13.41N 16.31E
Moville Rep. of Ire. **34** 55.11N 7.03W
Moxico Angola **72** 11.50S 20.05E
Moxico d. Angola **72** 13.00S 21.00E
Moy N. Ireland **38** 54.27N 6.43W
Moy r. Rep. of Ire. **38** 54.10N 9.09W
Moyale Kenya **73** 3.31N 39.04E
Moyowosi r. Tanzania **73** 4.59S 30.58E
Mozdok U.S.S.R. **47** 43.45N 44.43E
Mozyr U.S.S.R. **47** 52.02N 29.10E
M'Pama r. Congo **72** 0.59S 15.40E
Mpanda Tanzania **73** 6.21S 31.01E
Mpika Zambia **73** 11.52S 31.30E
Mporokoso Zambia **73** 9.22S 30.06E
M'Pouya Congo **72** 2.38S 16.08E
Mpwapwa Tanzania **73** 6.23S 36.38E
Mrewa Rhodesia **74** 17.35S 31.45E
Msaken Tunisia **42** 35.42N 10.33E
Msta r. U.S.S.R. **47** 58.28N 31.20E
Mtakuja Tanzania **73** 7.21S 30.37E
Mtsensk U.S.S.R. **47** 53.18N 36.35E
Mt. Vernon town U.S.A. **95** 40.55N 73.51W
Mtwara Tanzania **73** 10.17S 40.11E
Mtwara d. Tanzania **73** 10.00S 38.30E
Muang Khon Kaen Thailand **59** 16.25N 102.50E
Muang Lampang Thailand **59** 18.16N 99.30E
Muang Nan Thailand **59** 18.52N 100.42E
Muang Phitsanulok Thailand **59** 16.50N 100.15E
Muang Phrae Thailand **59** 18.07N 100.09E
Muara Indonesia **60** 0.32S 101.20E
Mubende Uganda **73** 0.30N 31.24E
Mubi Nigeria **71** 10.16N 13.17E
Much Hadham England **27** 51.52N 0.04E
Muchinga Mts. Zambia **73** 12.15S 31.00E
Much Wenlock England **28** 52.36N 2.34W
Muck i. Scotland **36** 56.50N 6.14W
Muckish Mtn. Rep. of Ire. **38** 55.06N 7.59W
Muckle Roe i. Scotland **36** 60.22N 1.26W
Muckle Skerry i. Scotland **37** 58.41N 2.53W
Muckno Lough Rep. of Ire. **38** 54.07N 6.43W
Mucojo Moçambique **73** 12.05S 40.26E
Mudgee Australia **80** 32.37S 149.36E
Mudhnib Saudi Arabia **57** 25.52N 44.15E
Muff Rep. of Ire. **34** 55.04N 7.16W
Mufulira Zambia **73** 12.30S 28.12E
Mugia Spain **41** 43.06N 9.14W
Muğla Turkey **43** 37.12N 28.22E
Muharraq Bahrain **57** 26.16N 50.38E
Mühlhausen E. Germany **44** 51.12N 10.27E
Muine Bheag town Rep. of Ire. **39** 52.42N 6.58W
Muirkirk Scotland **35** 55.31N 4.04W
Muir of Ord f. Scotland **37** 57.31N 4.28W
Mukachevo U.S.S.R. **47** 48.26N 22.45E
Mukah Malaysia **60** 2.56N 112.02E
Mukalla S. Yemen **69** 14.34N 49.09E
Mulanje Mts. Malaŵi **73** 15.57S 35.33E
Mulgrave Is. Australia **61** 10.05S 142.00E
Mulhacén mtn. Spain **41** 37.04N 3.22W
Mülheim Nordrhein-Westfalen W. Germany **45** 51.25N 6.50E
Mülheim Nordrhein-Westfalen W. Germany **45** 50.58N 7.00E
Mulhouse France **44** 47.45N 7.21E
Mull i. Scotland **34** 56.28N 5.56W
Mull, Sd. of str. Scotland **34** 56.32N 5.55W
Mullaghanattin mtn. Rep. of Ire. **39** 51.56N 9.51W
Mullaghareirk Mts. Rep. of Ire. **39** 52.19N 9.06W
Mullaghcarn mtn. N. Ireland **38** 54.40N 7.14W
Mullaghcleevaun mtn. Rep. of Ire. **39** 53.06N 6.25W
Mullaghmore mtn. N. Ireland **34** 54.51N 6.51W
Mullaley Australia **80** 31.06S 149.55E
Mullardoch, Loch Scotland **36** 57.19N 5.04W
Mullet Pen. Rep. of Ire. **38** 54.12N 10.04W
Mull Head Orkney Is. Scotland **37** 59.23N 2.53W
Mull Head Orkney Is. Scotland **38** 58.58N 2.42W
Mullinavat Rep. of Ire. **39** 52.22N 7.11W
Mullingar Rep. of Ire. **38** 53.31N 7.21W
Mullion England **31** 50.01N 5.15W
Mull of Galloway c. Scotland **34** 54.39N 4.52W
Mull of Kintyre c. Scotland **34** 55.17N 5.45W
Mull of Oa c. Scotland **34** 55.36N 6.20W
Mulobezi Zambia **72** 16.45S 25.11E
Mulroy B. Rep. of Ire. **38** 55.15N 7.46W
Multan Pakistan **58** 30.10N 71.36E
Multyfarnham Rep. of Ire. **38** 53.37N 7.25W

Mumbles Head Wales **31** 51.35N 3.58W
Mumbwa Zambia **73** 14.57S 27.01E
Muna i. Indonesia **61** 5.00S 122.30E
München see Munich W. Germany **44**
Muncie U.S.A. **94** 40.11N 85.22W
Mundesley England **33** 52.53N 1.24E
Mundo r. Spain **41** 38.20N 1.50W
Mungari Moçambique **73** 17.12S 33.35E
Mungbere Zaïre **73** 2.40N 28.25E
Mungindi Australia **80** 28.58S 148.56E
Mungret Rep. of Ire. **39** 52.38N 8.42W
Munich W. Germany **44** 48.08N 11.35E
Munising U.S.A. **94** 46.24N 86.40W
Munku Sardyk mtn. Mongolia **49** 51.45N 100.30E
Munster d. Rep. of Ire. **39** 52.10N 8.25W
Münster W. Germany **45** 51.58N 7.37E
Muntok Indonesia **60** 2.04S 105.12E
Muonio Finland **46** 67.52N 23.45E
Muonio r. Sweden/Finland **46** 67.13N 23.30E
Mur r. Austria **44** 46.40N 16.03E
Mura r. Yugo. **44** 46.18N 16.53E
Muranga Kenya **73** 0.43S 37.10E
Murchison r. Australia **79** 27.30S 114.10E
Murcia Spain **41** 37.59N 1.08W
Mures r. Romania **43** 46.16N 20.10E
Muret France **40** 43.28N 1.19E
Murghab r. Afghan. **58** 36.50N 63.00E
Müritz, L. E. Germany **44** 52.25N 12.45E
Murjo mtn. Indonesia **60** 6.30S 110.55E
Murle Ethiopia **73** 5.11N 36.09E
Murmansk U.S.S.R. **46** 68.59N 33.08E
Muroran Japan **63** 42.21N 140.59E
Murray r. Australia **80** 35.23S 139.20E
Murray Bridge town Australia **80** 35.10S 139.17E
Murrumbidgee r. Australia **80** 34.38S 143.10E
Murrurundi Australia **80** 31.47S 150.51E
Murtoa Australia **80** 36.40S 142.31E
Murud, Mt. Malaysia **60** 3.45N 115.30E
Murwara India **58** 23.49N 80.28E
Murwillumbah Australia **80** 28.20S 153.24E
Murzuq Libya **68** 25.56N 13.57E
Muş Turkey **56** 38.45N 41.30E
Musala mtn. Bulgaria **43** 42.11N 23.35E
Muscat Oman **57** 23.36N 58.37E
Musgrave Ranges mts. Australia **79** 26.30S 131.10E
Musheramore mtn. Rep. of Ire. **39** 52.01N 8.58W
Mushie Zaïre **72** 2.59S 16.55E
Musi r. Indonesia **60** 2.20S 104.57E
Muskegon U.S.A. **94** 43.13N 86.15W
Muskegon r. U.S.A. **94** 43.13N 86.20W
Muskingum r. U.S.A. **94** 39.25N 81.25W
Muskogee U.S.A. **91** 35.45N 95.21W
Musoma Tanzania **73** 1.31S 33.48E
Musselburgh Scotland **35** 55.57N 3.04W
Mussende Angola **72** 10.33S 16.02E
Mustang Nepal **59** 29.10N 83.55E
Mustjala U.S.S.R. **46** 58.30N 22.10E
Muswellbrook Australia **80** 32.17S 150.55E
Mut Turkey **56** 36.38N 33.27E
Mutankiang China **63** 44.36N 129.42E
Muwai Hakran Saudi Arabia **56** 22.41N 41.37E
Muxima Angola **72** 9.33S 13.58E
Muyinga Burundi **73** 2.48S 30.21E
Muzaffarnagar India **58** 29.28N 77.42E
Muzaffarpur India **58** 26.07N 85.23E
Mwanza Tanzania **73** 2.30S 32.54E
Mwanza d. Tanzania **73** 3.00S 32.30E
Mwanza Zaïre **73** 7.51S 26.43E
Mwaya Mbeya Tanzania **73** 9.33S 33.56E
Mweelrea Mts. Rep. of Ire. **38** 53.40N 9.52W
Mweka Zaïre **72** 4.51S 21.34E
Mwene Ditu Zaïre **72** 7.04S 23.27E
Mweru, L. Zaïre/Zambia **73** 9.00S 28.40E
Mwinilunga Zambia **72** 11.44S 24.24E
Myanaung Burma **59** 18.25N 95.10E
Myingyan Burma **59** 21.25N 95.20E
Myitkyina Burma **59** 25.24N 97.25E
Mymensingh Bangla. **58** 24.45N 90.23E
Mynydd Bach mts. Wales **30** 52.18N 4.03W
Mynydd Eppynt mts. Wales **30** 52.06N 3.30W
Mynydd Prescelly mts. Wales **30** 51.58N 4.47W
Myrdal Norway **46** 60.44N 7.08E
Mysen Norway **46** 59.33N 11.20E
Mysore India **58** 12.18N 76.37E
My Tho Vietnam **60** 10.21N 106.21E
Mytishchi U.S.S.R. **47** 55.54N 37.47E
Mzimba Malaŵi **73** 12.00S 33.39E

N

Naas Rep. of Ire. **39** 53.13N 6.41W
Nabeul Tunisia **42** 36.28N 10.44E
Nacala Moçambique **73** 14.30S 40.37E
Nachingwea Tanzania **73** 10.21S 38.46E

For Khmer Republic read Kampuchea. For Malagasy Republic read Madagascar. For Rhodesia read Zimbabwe.

Nadder to **Newport** 152

Nadder *r.* England **28** 51.05N 1.52W
Naestved Denmark **46** 55.14N 11.47E
Naft Safid Iran **57** 31.38N 49.20E
Naga Phil. **61** 13.36N 123.12E
Nagaland *d.* India **59** 26.10N 94.30E
Nagappattinam India **59** 10.45N 79.50E
Nagasaki Japan **63** 32.45N 129.52E
Nagercoil India **58** 8.11N 77.30E
Nag' Hammadi Egypt **56** 26.04N 32.13E
Nagishot Sudan **73** 4.18N 33.32E
Nagles Mts. Rep. of Ire. **39** 52.06N 8.26W
Nagoya Japan **63** 35.08N 136.53E
Nagpur India **59** 21.10N 79.12E
Nagykanizsa Hungary **43** 46.27N 17.01E
Naha Japan **63** 26.10N 127.40E
Nahavand Iran **57** 34.13N 48.23E
Nahe *r.* W. Germany **45** 49.58N 7.54E
Nahr Ouassel *r.* Algeria **41** 35.30N 2.03E
Nailsworth England **28** 51.41N 2.12W
Nain Canada **93** 56.30N 61.45W
Nain Iran **57** 32.52N 53.05E
Nairn Scotland **37** 57.35N 3.52W
Nairn *r.* Scotland **37** 57.35N 3.51W
Nairobi Kenya **73** 1.17S 36.50E
Naivasha Kenya **73** 0.44S 36.26E
Nakhichevan U.S.S.R. **57** 39.12N 45.24E
Nakhon Phanom Thailand **60** 17.22N 104.45E
Nakhon Ratchasima Thailand **59** 14.59N 102.12E
Nakhon Sawan Thailand **59** 15.35N 100.10E
Nakhon Si Thammarat Thailand **59** 8.29N 100.00E
Naknek U.S.A. **92** 58.45N 157.00W
Nakskov Denmark **44** 54.50N 11.10E
Nakuru Kenya **73** 0.16S 36.04E
Nakusimi *r.* Canada **94** 49.55N 82.00W
Nalchik U.S.S.R. **47** 43.31N 43.38E
Nalon *r.* Spain **41** 43.35N 6.06W
Nalut Libya **68** 31.53N 10.59E
Namaki *r.* Iran **57** 31.02N 55.20E
Namanga Kenya **73** 2.33S 36.48E
Namangan U.S.S.R. **62** 40.59N 71.41E
Namapa Moçambique **73** 13.48S 39.44E
Namaponda Moçambique **73** 15.51S 39.52E
Namarroi Moçambique **73** 15.58S 36.55E
Namcha Barwa *mtn.* China **59** 29.30N 95.10E
Nam Dinh Vietnam **60** 20.25N 106.12E
Nametil Moçambique **73** 15.41S 39.30E
Namibia *see* South West Africa Africa **74**
Namib Desert S.W. Africa **74** 23.30S 15.00E
Namlea Indonesia **61** 3.15S 127.07E
Nampo N. Korea **63** 38.40N 125.30E
Nampula Moçambique **73** 15.09S 39.14E
Namsos Norway **46** 64.28N 11.30E
Nam Tso *l.* China **59** 30.40N 90.30E
Namur Belgium **45** 50.28N 4.52E
Namur *d.* Belgium **45** 50.20N 4.45E
Namurro Moçambique **73** 16.57S 39.06E
Namutoni S.W. Africa **74** 18.49S 16.55E
Namwala Zambia **73** 15.44S 26.25E
Nana Candundo Angola **72** 11.28S 23.01E
Nanaimo Canada **90** 49.08N 123.58W
Nanchang China **63** 28.38N 115.56E
Nanchung China **62** 30.54N 106.06E
Nancy France **44** 48.42N 6.12E
Nanda Devi *mtn.* India **59** 30.21N 79.50E
Nander India **58** 19.11N 77.21E
Nandewar Range *mts.* Australia **80** 30.20S 150.45E
Nanga Parbat *mtn.* Kashmir **58** 35.10N 74.35E
Nanking China **63** 32.00N 118.40E
Nan Ling *mts.* China **63** 25.20N 110.30E
Nanning China **60** 22.50N 108.19E
Nanping China **63** 26.40N 118.07E
Nan Shan *mts.* China **62** 38.30N 99.20E
Nanshan Is. Asia **60** 10.30N 116.00E
Nantaise *r.* France **40** 47.12N 1.35W
Nantes France **40** 47.14N 1.35W
Nantucket I. U.S.A. **95** 41.16N 70.00W
Nantucket Sd. U.S.A. **95** 41.30N 70.15W
Nantung China **63** 32.05N 120.59E
Nantwich England **32** 53.05N 2.31W
Nanyuki Kenya **73** 0.01N 37.03E
Napier New Zealand **82** 39.29S 176.58E
Naples Italy **42** 40.50N 14.14E
Naples, G. of Med. Sea **42** 40.42N 14.15E
Nar *r.* England **29** 52.45N 0.24E
Nara Mali **70** 15.13N 7.20W
Naracoorte Australia **80** 36.58S 140.46E
Narayanganj Bangla. **58** 23.36N 90.28E
Narbada *r. see* NarmadaIndia **58**
Narberth Wales **31** 51.48N 4.45W
Narbonne France **40** 43.11N 3.00E
Nare Head England **31** 50.12N 4.55W
Nares Str. Canada **93** 78.30N 75.00W
Narmada *r.* India **58** 21.40N 73.00E
Narodnaya *mtn.* U.S.S.R. **48** 65.00N 61.00E
Narok Kenya **73** 1.04S 35.54E
Narooma Australia **80** 36.15S 150.06E
Narrabri Australia **80** 30.20S 149.49E
Narrandera Australia **80** 34.36S 146.34E
Narran L. Australia **80** 29.40S 147.25E
Narromine Australia **80** 32.17S 148.20E
Narsimhapur India **58** 22.58N 79.15E
Narva U.S.S.R. **46** 59.22N 28.17E
Narva *r.* U.S.S.R. **46** 59.30N 28.00E
Narvik Norway **46** 68.26N 17.25E
Naryan Mar U.S.S.R. **48** 67.37N 53.02E
Nasarawa Nigeria **71** 8.35N 7.44E
Nash Pt. Wales **31** 51.25N 3.35W
Nashua U.S.A. **95** 42.44N 71.28W
Nashville U.S.A. **91** 36.10N 86.50W
Nasik India **58** 20.00N 73.52E
Nasratabad Iran **57** 29.54N 59.58E
Nassau Bahamas **97** 25.03N 77.20W
Nasser, L. Egypt **56** 22.40N 32.00E
Nässjö Sweden **46** 57.39N 14.40E
Natal Brazil **102** 5.46S 35.15W
Natal Indonesia **60** 0.35N 99.07E
Natal *d.* R.S.A. **74** 28.30S 31.00E
Natanz Iran **57** 33.30N 51.57E
Natchez U.S.A. **91** 31.22N 91.24W
Natitingou Benin **71** 10.17N 1.19E
Natron, L. Tanzania **73** 2.18S 36.05E
Naumburg E. Germany **44** 51.09N 11.48E
Nava *r.* Zaïre **73** 1.45N 27.06E
Navalmoral de la Mata Spain **41** 39.54N 5.33W
Navan Rep. of Ire. **38** 53.39N 6.42W
Nave *i.* Scotland **34** 55.55N 6.20W
Navenby England **33** 53.07N 0.32W
Naver *r.* Scotland **37** 58.32N 4.14W
Naver, Loch Scotland **37** 58.17N 4.20W
Návpaktos Greece **43** 38.24N 21.49E
Návplion Greece **43** 37.33N 22.47E
Navrongo Ghana **70** 10.51N 1.03W
Náxos *i.* Greece **43** 37.03N 25.30E
Nayarit *d.* Mexico **96** 21.30N 104.00W
Nayland England **29** 51.59N 0.52E
Nazareth Israel **56** 32.41N 35.16E
Nazas *r.* Mexico **96** 25.34N 103.25W
Nazilli Turkey **56** 37.55N 28.20E
N'Dendé Gabon **72** 2.20S 11.23E
N'Djamena Chad **71** 12.10N 14.59E
Ndjolé Gabon **72** 0.07S 10.45E
Ndola Zambia **73** 13.00S 28.35E
Neagh, Lough N. Ireland **34** 54.36N 6.25W
Neath Wales **31** 51.39N 3.49W
Neath *r.* Wales **31** 51.39N 3.50W
Nebit Dag U.S.S.R. **57** 39.31N 54.24E
Nebraska *d.* U.S.A. **90** 41.30N 100.00W
Nebrodi Mts. Italy **42** 37.53N 14.32E
Neches *r.* U.S.A. **91** 29.55N 93.50W
Neckar *r.* W. Germany **44** 49.32N 8.26E
Necochea Argentina **103** 38.31S 58.46W
Necuto Angola **72** 4.55S 12.38E
Needham Market England **29** 52.09N 1.02E
Needles U.S.A. **90** 34.51N 114.36W
Neerpelt Belgium **45** 51.13N 5.28E
Nefyn Wales **30** 52.55N 4.31W
Negaunee U.S.A. **94** 46.31N 87.37W
Negev *des.* Israel **56** 30.42N 34.55E
Negoiu *mtn.* Romania **43** 45.36N 24.32E
Negotin Yugo. **43** 44.14N 22.33E
Negrais, C. Burma **59** 16.00N 94.30E
Negro *r.* Argentina **103** 41.00S 62.48W
Negro *r.* Brazil **102** 3.30S 60.05W
Negro *r.* Uruguay **103** 33.27S 58.20W
Negros *i.* Phil. **61** 10.00N 123.00E
Neisse *r.* Poland/E. Germany **44** 52.05N 14.42E
Nejd *d.* Saudi Arabia **56** 25.00N 45.00E
Neksö Denmark **46** 55.04N 15.09E
Nellore India **59** 14.29N 80.00E
Nelson Canada **90** 49.29N 117.17W
Nelson England **32** 53.50N 2.14W
Nelson *r.* Canada **93** 57.00N 93.20W
Nelson New Zealand **82** 41.18S 173.17E
Nelson U.S.A. **90** 35.30N 113.16W
Nelson, C. Australia **80** 38.27S 141.35E
Nelspruit R.S.A. **74** 25.30S 30.58E
Néma Mauritania **70** 16.32N 7.12W
Neman *r.* U.S.S.R. **46** 55.23N 21.15E
Nemours France **40** 48.16N 2.41E
Nenagh Rep. of Ire. **39** 52.52N 8.13W
Nenana U.S.A. **92** 64.35N 149.20W
Nene *r.* England **33** 52.49N 0.12E
Nepal Asia **58** 28.00N 84.30E
Nephin *mtn.* Rep. of Ire. **38** 54.01N 9.23W
Nephin Beg *mtn.* Rep. of Ire. **38** 54.02N 9.38W
Nephin Beg Range *mts.* Rep. of Ire. **38** 54.00N 9.37W
Nera *r.* Italy **42** 42.33N 12.43E
Neretva *r.* Yugo. **43** 43.02N 17.28E
Neriquinha Angola **72** 15.50S 21.40E
Nero Deep Pacific Oc. **61** 12.40N 145.50E
Nes Neth. **45** 53.27N 5.46E
Ness *f.* Scotland **36** 58.26N 6.15W
Ness, Loch Scotland **37** 57.16N 4.30W
Neston England **30** 53.17N 3.03W
Netherlands Europe **45** 52.00N 5.30E
Nether Stowey England **28** 51.10N 3.10W
Neto *r.* Italy **43** 39.12N 17.08E
Neubrandenburg E. Germany **44** 53.33N 13.16E
Neuchâtel Switz. **44** 47.00N 6.56E
Neuchâtel, Lac de Switz. **44** 46.55N 6.55E
Neuenhaus W. Germany **45** 52.30N 6.58E
Neufchâteau Belgium **45** 49.51N 5.26E
Neufchâtel France **40** 49.44N 1.26E
Neumünster W. Germany **44** 54.06N 9.59E
Neuquén Argentina **103** 38.55S 68.55W
Neuse *r.* U.S.A. **91** 35.04N 77.04W
Neusiedler, L. Austria **44** 47.52N 16.45E
Neuss W. Germany **45** 51.12N 6.42E
Neustrelitz E. Germany **44** 53.22N 13.05E
Neutral Territory Asia **57** 29.05N 45.40E
Neuwied W. Germany **45** 50.26N 7.28E
Nevada *d.* U.S.A. **90** 39.00N 117.00W
Nevada, Sierra *mts.* Spain **41** 37.04N 3.20W
Nevada, Sierra *mts.* U.S.A. **90** 37.30N 119.00W
Nevada de Cocuy, Sierra *mts.* Colombia **97** 6.15N 72.00W
Nevada de Santa Marta, Sierra *mts.* Colombia **97** 11.00N 73.30W
Nevel U.S.S.R. **47** 56.00N 29.59E
Nevers France **40** 47.00N 3.09E
Nevertire Australia **80** 31.52S 147.47E
Nevis *i.* C. America **97** 17.11N 62.35W
Nevis, Loch Scotland **36** 56.59N 5.40W
Nevşehir Turkey **56** 38.38N 34.43E
New Addington England **27** 51.21N 0.00
New Alresford England **28** 51.06N 1.10W
Newark N.J. U.S.A. **95** 40.44N 74.11W
Newark Ohio U.S.A. **94** 40.03N 82.25W
Newark-on-Trent England **33** 53.06N 0.48W
New Bedford U.S.A. **95** 41.38N 70.55W
New Bern U.S.A. **91** 35.05N 77.04W
Newberry U.S.A. **94** 46.22N 85.30W
Newbiggin-by-the-Sea England **35** 55.11N 1.30W
Newbridge on Wye Wales **30** 52.13N 3.27W
New Britain *i.* P.N.G. **79** 6.00S 150.00E
New Britain U.S.A. **95** 41.40N 72.47W
New Brunswick *d.* Canada **93** 47.00N 66.00W
New Brunswick U.S.A. **95** 40.29N 74.27W
Newburgh Fife Scotland **35** 56.21N 3.15W
Newburgh Grampian Scotland **37** 57.19N 2.01W
Newburgh U.S.A. **95** 41.30N 74.00W
Newbury England **28** 51.24N 1.19W
New Caledonia *i.* Pacific Oc. **107** 22.00S 165.00E
Newcastle Australia **80** 32.55S 151.46E
Newcastle N. Ireland **38** 54.13N 5.53W
New Castle U.S.A. **94** 41.00N 80.22W
Newcastle U.S.A. **90** 43.52N 104.14W
Newcastle Emlyn Wales **30** 52.02N 4.29W
Newcastleton Scotland **35** 55.21N 2.49W
Newcastle-under-Lyme England **32** 53.02N 2.15W
Newcastle upon Tyne England **35** 54.58N 1.36W
Newcastle West Rep. of Ire. **39** 52.26N 9.04W
New Cumnock Scotland **34** 55.24N 4.11W
New Deer Scotland **37** 57.31N 2.11W
New Delhi India **58** 28.37N 77.13E
New England Range *mts.* Australia **80** 30.00S 152.00E
Newent England **28** 51.56N 2.24W
New Forest *f.* England **28** 50.50N 1.35W
Newfoundland *d.* Canada **93** 55.00N 60.00W
Newfoundland *i.* Canada **93** 48.30N 56.00W
New Galloway Scotland **34** 55.05N 4.09W
New Guinea *i.* Austa. **61** 5.00S 140.00E
Newham *d.* England **27** 51.32N 0.03E
New Hampshire *d.* U.S.A. **95** 43.50N 71.45W
New Hanover *i.* Pacific Oc. **79** 2.00S 150.00E
Newhaven England **29** 50.47N 0.04E
New Haven U.S.A. **95** 41.18N 72.55W
New Hebrides *is. see* **Vanuatu**
New Holland England **33** 53.42N 0.22W
New Hythe England **27** 51.18N 0.27E
New Ireland *i.* P.N.G. **79** 2.30S 151.30E
New Jersey *d.* U.S.A. **95** 39.50N 74.45W
New London U.S.A. **95** 41.21N 72.06W
Newmarket England **29** 52.15N 0.23E
Newmarket Rep. of Ire. **39** 52.13N 9.00W
Newmarket-on-Fergus Rep. of Ire. **39** 52.46N 8.55W
New Mexico *d.* U.S.A **90** 34.00N 106.00W
New Mills England **32** 53.23N 2.00W
Newmilns Scotland **34** 55.37N 4.20W
Newnham England **28** 51.48N 2.27W
New Norfolk Australia **80** 42.46S 147.02E
New Orleans U.S.A. **91** 30.00N 90.03W
New Pitsligo Scotland **37** 57.35N 2.12W
New Plymouth New Zealand **82** 39.03S 174.04E
Newport Essex England **29** 51.58N 0.13E
Newport Hants. England **28** 50.43N 1.18W
Newport Salop England **30** 52.47N 2.22W
Newport Mayo Rep. of Ire. **38** 53.53N 9.34W
Newport Tipperary Rep. of Ire. **39** 52.42N 8.25W

Newport Ky. U.S.A. **94** 39.05N 84.27W
Newport R.I. U.S.A. **95** 41.30N 71.19W
Newport Dyfed Wales **30** 52.01N 4.51W
Newport Gwent Wales **31** 51.34N 2.59W
Newport News U.S.A. **91** 36.59N 76.26W
Newport-on-Tay Scotland **35** 56.27N 2.56W
Newport Pagnell England **28** 52.05N 0.42W
New Providence i. Bahamas **97** 25.03N 77.25W
Newquay England **31** 50.24N 5.06W
New Quay Wales **30** 52.13N 4.22W
New Radnor Wales **30** 52.15N 3.10W
New Rochelle U.S.A. **95** 40.55N 73.47W
New Romney England **29** 50.59N 0.58E
New Ross Rep. of Ire. **39** 52.24N 6.57W
Newry N. Ireland **38** 54.11N 6.21W
New Scone Scotland **35** 56.25N 3.25W
New Siberian Is. U.S.S.R. **49** 76.00N 144.00E
New South Wales d. Australia **80** 33.45S 147.00E
Newton Abbot England **31** 50.32N 3.37W
Newton-le-Willows England **32** 53.28N 2.38W
Newton Mearns Scotland **34** 55.46N 4.18W
Newtonmore Scotland **37** 57.04N 4.08W
Newton Stewart Scotland **34** 54.57N 4.29W
Newtown Rep. of Ire. **39** 52.20N 8.48W
Newtown Wales **30** 52.31N 3.19W
Newtownabbey N. Ireland **34** 54.39N 5.57W
Newtownards N. Ireland **34** 54.35N 5.41W
Newtown Butler N. Ireland **38** 54.12N 7.22W
Newtown Cunningham Rep. of Ire. **38** 54.59N 7.31W
Newtown Forbes Rep. of Ire. **38** 53.45N 7.50W
Newtown Hamilton N. Ireland **38** 54.12N 6.36W
Newtown Mount Kennedy Rep. of Ire. **39** 53.06N 6.07W
Newtownstewart N. Ireland **38** 54.43N 7.25W
New York U.S.A. **95** 40.40N 73.50W
New York d. U.S.A. **95** 42.50N 75.50W
New Zealand Austa. **82** 41.00S 175.00E
Neyland Wales **31** 51.43N 4.58W
Nezhin U.S.S.R. **47** 51.03N 31.54E
Ngambwe Rapids f. Zambia **72** 17.08S 24.10E
Ngami, L. Botswana **74** 20.25S 23.00E
Ngamiland f. Botswana **74** 20.00S 22.30E
N'Gao Congo **72** 2.28S 15.40E
Ngaoundéré Cameroon **71** 7.20N 13.35E
Ngaruroro r. New Zealand **82** 39.34S 176.54E
Ngauruhoe mtn. New Zealand **82** 37.10S 175.35E
Ngong Kenya **73** 1.22S 36.40E
Ngonye Falls f. Zambia **72** 16.35S 23.39E
Ngorongoro Crater f. Tanzania **73** 3.13S 35.32E
Ngozi Burundi **73** 2.52S 29.50E
Nguigmi Niger **71** 14.00N 13.11E
Nguru North-Eastern Nigeria **71** 12.53N 10.30E
Nhamacurra Moçambique **73** 17.35S 37.00E
Nhanduge r. Moçambique **74** 19.45S 34.40E
Nha Trang Vietnam **60** 12.15N 109.10E
Nhill Australia **80** 36.20S 141.40E
Niagara Falls town U.S.A. **95** 43.06N 79.04W
Niamey Niger **71** 13.32N 2.05E
Niangara Zaïre **73** 3.47N 27.54E
Niapa mtn. Indonesia **60** 2.45N 117.30E
Nias i. Indonesia **60** 1.05N 97.30E
Niassa d. Moçambique **73** 13.00S 36.30E
Nicaragua C. America **96** 13.00N 85.00W
Nicaragua, L. Nicaragua **96** 11.30N 85.30W
Nicastro Italy **42** 38.58N 16.16E
Nice France **40** 43.42N 7.16E
Nicobar Is. India **59** 8.00N 94.00E
Nicosia Cyprus **56** 35.11N 33.23E
Nicoya, G. of Costa Rica **96** 9.30N 85.00W
Nicoya Pen. Costa Rica **96** 10.30N 85.30W
Nidd r. England **33** 54.01N 1.12W
Nidderdale f. England **32** 54.07N 1.50W
Nidelva r. Norway **46** 58.26N 8.44E
Niers r. Neth. **45** 51.43N 5.56E
Nieuwpoort Belgium **45** 51.08N 2.45E
Niğde Turkey **56** 37.58N 34.42E
Niger Africa **68** 17.00N 9.30E
Niger d. Nigeria **71** 9.50N 6.00E
Niger r. Nigeria **71** 4.15N 6.05E
Niger Delta Nigeria **71** 4.00N 6.10E
Nigeria Africa **71** 9.00N 9.00E
Niigata Japan **63** 37.58N 139.02E
Nijmegen Neth. **45** 51.50N 5.52E
Nikel U.S.S.R. **46** 69.20N 29.44E
Nikiniki Indonesia **61** 9.49S 124.29E
Nikki Benin **71** 9.55N 3.18E
Nikolayev U.S.S.R. **47** 46.57N 32.00E
Nikolayevsk-na-Amur U.S.S.R. **49** 53.20N 140.44E
Niksar Turkey **56** 40.35N 36.59E
Nikšić Yugo. **43** 42.48N 18.56E
Nila i. Indonesia **61** 6.45S 129.30E
Nile r. Egypt **56** 31.30N 30.25E
Nile Delta Egypt **56** 31.00N 31.00E
Niles U.S.A. **94** 41.11N 80.46W
Nilgiri Hills India **58** 11.30N 77.30E
Nimba, Mt. Guinea **70** 7.35N 8.28W
Nîmes France **42** 43.50N 4.21E

Nimmitabel Australia **80** 36.32S 149.19E
Nimule Sudan **73** 3.35N 32.04E
Ninety Mile Beach f. Australia **80** 38.07S 147.30E
Ninety Mile Beach f. New Zealand **82** 34.45S 173.00E
Nineveh ruins Iraq **56** 36.24N 43.08E
Ningpo China **63** 29.54N 121.33E
Ningsia Hui d. China **59** 34.00N 104.30E
Ningwu China **63** 39.00N 112.19E
Ninove Belgium **45** 50.50N 4.02E
Niobrara r. U.S.A. **90** 42.45N 98.10W
Nioro Mali **70** 15.12N 9.35W
Niort France **40** 46.19N 0.27W
Nipigon Canada **94** 49.02N 88.26W
Nipigon, L. Canada **94** 49.40N 88.30W
Nipissing, L. Canada **94** 46.15N 79.45W
Niriz Iran **57** 29.12N 54.17E
Niš Yugo. **43** 43.20N 21.54E
Nishapur Iran **57** 36.13N 58.49E
Niterói Brazil **103** 22.54S 43.06W
Nith r. Scotland **35** 55.00N 3.35W
Nithsdale f. Scotland **35** 55.15N 3.48W
Niut mtn. Indonesia **60** 1.00N 110.00E
Nivelles Belgium **45** 50.36N 4.20E
Nizamabad India **59** 18.40N 78.05E
Nizhneudinsk U.S.S.R. **49** 54.55N 99.00E
Nizhniy Tagil U.S.S.R. **48** 58.00N 60.00E
Njombe Tanzania **73** 9.20S 34.47E
Njombe r. Tanzania **73** 7.02S 35.55E
Njoro Tanzania **73** 5.16S 36.30E
Nkhata Bay town Malaŵi **73** 11.37S 34.20E
Nkhotakota Malaŵi **73** 12.55S 34.19E
Nkongsamba Cameroon **71** 4.59N 9.53E
Nkungwe Mt. Tanzania **73** 6.15S 29.54E
Nogales Mexico **90** 31.20N 111.00W
Nogent le Rotrou France **40** 48.19N 0.50E
Noguera Ribagorzana r. Spain **41** 41.27N 0.25E
Noirmoutier, Île de i. France **40** 47.00N 2.15W
Nokia Finland **46** 61.29N 23.31E
Nola C.A.R. **71** 3.28N 16.08E
Noma Omuramba r. Botswana **74** 19.20S 22.05E
Nome U.S.A. **92** 64.30N 165.30W
Nong Khai Thailand **59** 17.50N 102.46E
Nongoma R.S.A. **74** 27.54S 31.40E
Noord Brabant d. Neth. **45** 51.37N 5.00E
Noorvik U.S.A. **92** 66.50N 161.14W
Noranda Canada **95** 48.16N 79.03W
Nord d. France **29** 50.49N 2.21E
Norddeich W. Germany **45** 53.35N 7.10E
Norden W. Germany **45** 53.34N 7.13E
Nordenham W. Germany **45** 53.30N 8.29E
Norderney i. W. Germany **45** 53.45N 7.15E
Nord Fjord est. Norway **46** 61.50N 6.00E
Nordhausen E. Germany **44** 51.31N 10.48E
Nordhorn W. Germany **45** 52.27N 7.05E
Nordvik U.S.S.R. **49** 73.40N 110.50E
Nore r. Rep. of Ire. **39** 52.25N 6.58W
Norfolk d. England **29** 52.39N 1.00E
Norfolk U.S.A. **91** 36.54N 76.18W
Norfolk Broads f. England **29** 52.43N 1.35E
Norham England **35** 55.43N 2.10W
Norilsk U.S.S.R. **49** 69.21N 88.02E
Normandie, Collines de hills France **40** 48.50N 0.40W
Normandy England **27** 51.15N 0.38W
Normanton Australia **79** 17.40S 141.05E
Normanton England **33** 53.41N 1.26W
Norman Wells Canada **92** 65.19N 126.46W
Nörresundby Denmark **46** 57.05N 9.52E
Norris L. U.S.A. **91** 36.20N 83.55W
Norristown U.S.A. **95** 40.07N 75.20W
Norrköping Sweden **46** 58.35N 16.10E
Norrtälje Sweden **46** 59.46N 18.43E
Norte, Punta c. Argentina **103** 36.08S 56.50W
Northallerton England **33** 54.20N 1.26W
Northam England **31** 51.02N 4.13W
North America **89**
Northampton England **28** 52.14N 0.54W
Northampton U.S.A. **95** 42.19N 72.38W
Northamptonshire d. England **28** 52.18N 0.55W
Northaw England **27** 51.43N 0.09W
North Ballachulish Scotland **36** 56.42N 5.11W
North Battleford Canada **92** 52.47N 108.19W
North Bay town Canada **95** 46.20N 79.28W
North Bend U.S.A. **90** 43.26N 124.14W
North Berwick Scotland **35** 56.04N 2.43W
North Beveland f. Neth. **45** 51.35N 3.45E
North C. New Zealand **82** 34.28S 173.00E
North C. Norway **46** 71.10N 25.45E
North Canadian r. U.S.A. **91** 35.30N 95.45W
North Carolina d. U.S.A. **91** 35.30N 79.00W
North Channel Canada **94** 46.05N 83.00W
North Channel U.K. **34** 55.15N 5.52W
North Chicago U.S.A. **94** 42.18N 87.52W
North China Plain f. China **63** 34.30N 117.00E
North Dakota d. U.S.A. **90** 47.00N 100.00W
North Donets r. U.S.S.R. **47** 49.08N 37.28E
North Dorset Downs hills England **28** 50.46N 2.25W

North Downs hills England **29** 51.18N 0.40E
North Dvina r. U.S.S.R. **48** 64.40N 40.50E
North Eastern d. Kenya **73** 1.00N 40.00E
North East Polder f. Neth. **45** 52.45N 5.45E
Northern d. Ghana **70** 9.00N 1.30W
Northern Ireland U.K. **38** 54.40N 6.45W
Northern Territory d. Australia **79** 20.00S 133.00E
North Esk r. Scotland **37** 56.45N 2.25W
North European Plain f. Europe **107** 56.00N 27.00E
Northfleet England **27** 51.27N 0.20E
North Foreland c. England **29** 51.23N 1.26E
North Frisian Is. W. Germany **44** 54.30N 8.00E
North Harris f. Scotland **36** 57.58N 6.52W
North Holland d. Neth. **45** 52.37N 4.50E
North Horr Kenya **73** 3.19N 37.00E
North I. New Zealand **82** 39.00S 175.00E
Northiam England **29** 50.59N 0.39E
North Korea Asia **63** 40.00N 128.00E
North Kyme England **33** 53.04N 0.17W
Northleach England **28** 51.49N 1.50W
North Platte U.S.A. **90** 41.09N 100.45W
North Platte r. U.S.A. **90** 41.09N 100.55W
North Pt. U.S.A. **94** 45.02N 83.17W
North Ronaldsay i. Scotland **37** 59.23N 2.26W
North Ronaldsay Firth est. Scotland **37** 59.20N 2.25W
North Sd. Rep. of Ire. **39** 53.11N 9.34W
North Sea Europe **18** 56.00N 5.00E
North Somercotes England **33** 53.28N 0.08E
North Sporades is. Greece **43** 39.00N 24.00E
North Taranaki Bight b. New Zealand **82** 38.45S 174.15E
North Tawton England **31** 50.48N 3.55W
North Tidworth England **28** 51.14N 1.40W
North Tolsta Scotland **36** 58.20N 6.13W
North Truchas Peak mtn. U.S.A. **90** 35.58N 105.48W
North Tyne r. England **35** 54.59N 2.08W
North Uist i. Scotland **36** 57.35N 7.20W
Northumberland d. England **35** 55.12N 2.00W
North Walsham England **29** 52.49N 1.22E
Northway U.S.A. **92** 62.58N 142.00W
North Weald Bassett England **27** 51.42N 0.12E
North West Highlands Scotland **36** 57.30N 5.15W
North West River town Canada **93** 53.30N 60.10W
Northwest Territories d. Canada **93** 66.00N 95.00W
Northwich England **32** 53.16N 2.30W
Northwood England **27** 51.36N 0.25W
North York Canada **95** 43.44N 79.26W
North York Moors hills England **33** 54.21N 0.50W
North Yorkshire d. England **33** 54.14N 1.14W
Norton England **33** 54.08N 0.47W
Norton de Matos Angola **72** 12.20S 14.45E
Norton Sound b. U.S.A. **92** 63.50N 164.00W
Norwalk U.S.A. **95** 41.07N 73.25W
Norway Europe **46** 65.00N 13.00E
Norway House town Canada **93** 53.59N 97.50W
Norwegian Sea Europe **54** 65.00N 5.00E
Norwich England **29** 52.38N 1.17E
Norwich U.S.A. **95** 41.32N 72.05W
Noss, I. of Scotland **36** 60.08N 1.01W
Noss Head Scotland **37** 58.28N 3.03W
Nossob r. R.S.A./Botswana **74** 26.54S 20.39E
Noteć r. Poland **44** 52.44N 15.26E
Nottingham England **33** 52.57N 1.10W
Nottinghamshire d. England **33** 53.10N 1.00W
Notwani r. Botswana **74** 23.14S 27.30E
Nouadhibou Mauritania **70** 20.54N 17.01W
Nouakchott Mauritania **68** 18.09N 15.58W
Nouvelle Anvers Zaïre **72** 1.38N 19.10E
Nova Gaia Angola **72** 10.09S 17.35E
Nova Lima Brazil **103** 20.00S 43.51W
Novara Italy **40** 45.27N 8.37E
Nova Scotia d. Canada **93** 45.00N 64.00W
Nova Sofala Moçambique **74** 20.09S 34.42E
Novaya Ladoga U.S.S.R. **47** 60.09N 32.15E
Novaya Siberia i. U.S.S.R. **49** 75.20N 148.00E
Novaya Zemlya i. U.S.S.R. **48** 74.00N 56.00E
Novelda Spain **41** 38.24N 0.45W
Novgorod U.S.S.R. **47** 58.30N 31.20E
Novi-Ligure Italy **40** 44.46N 8.47E
Novi Pazar Yugo. **43** 43.08N 20.28E
Novi Sad Yugo. **43** 45.16N 19.52E
Novocherkassk U.S.S.R. **47** 47.25N 40.05E
Novograd Volynskiy U.S.S.R. **47** 50.34N 27.32E
Novogrudok U.S.S.R. **47** 53.35N 25.50E
Novo Hamburgo Brazil **103** 29.37S 51.07W
Novokazalinsk U.S.S.R. **48** 45.48N 62.06E
Novokuznetsk U.S.S.R. **48** 53.45N 87.12E
Novomoskovsk U.S.S.R. **47** 54.06N 38.15E
Novo Redondo Angola **72** 11.11S 13.52E
Novorossiysk U.S.S.R. **47** 44.44N 37.46E
Novoshakhtinsk U.S.S.R. **47** 47.46N 39.55E
Novosibirsk U.S.S.R. **48** 55.04N 82.55E
Novy Port U.S.S.R. **48** 67.38N 72.33E
Nowa Ruda Poland **44** 50.34N 16.30E
Nowa Sól Poland **44** 51.49N 15.41E
Nowgong India **59** 26.20N 92.41E

For Khmer Republic read Kampuchea. For Malagasy Republic read Madagascar. For Rhodesia read Zimbabwe.

Nowra to **Oshawa** 154

Nowra Australia **80** 34.54S 150.36E
Nowy Sącz Poland **47** 49.39N 20.40E
Noyon France **45** 49.35N 3.00E
Nsanje Malaŵi **73** 16.55S 35.12E
Nsukka Nigeria **71** 6.51N 7.29E
Ntcheu Malaŵi **73** 14.50S 34.45E
Nuanetsi *r.* Moçambique **74** 22.42S 31.45E
Nuanetsi Rhodesia **74** 21.22S 30.45E
Nubian Desert Sudan **69** 21.00N 34.00E
Nudushan Iran **57** 32.03N 53.33E
Nueces *r.* U.S.A. **91** 27.55N 97.30W
Nueva Gerona Cuba **96** 21.53N 82.49W
Nuevitas Cuba **97** 21.34N 77.18W
Nuevo Laredo Mexico **90** 27.30N 99.30W
Nuevo Leon *d.* Mexico **96** 26.00N 99.00W
Nukha U.S.S.R. **57** 41.12N 47.10E
Nullarbor Plain *f.* Australia **79** 31.30S 128.00E
Nuneaton England **28** 52.32N 1.29W
Nungo Moçambique **73** 13.25S 37.45E
Nunivak I. U.S.A. **92** 60.00N 166.30W
Nunkiang China **63** 49.10N 125.15E
Nuqra Saudi Arabia **56** 25.35N 41.28E
Nure *r.* Italy **40** 45.06N 9.50E
Nurmes Finland **46** 63.32N 29.10E
Nürnberg W. Germany **44** 49.27N 11.05E
Nusaybin Turkey **56** 37.05N 41.11E
Nuweveld Mts. R.S.A. **74** 32.00S 21.50E
Nyahururu Kenya **73** 0.04N 36.22E
Nyakanazi Tanzania **73** 3.05S 31.16E
Nyala Sudan **69** 12.01N 24.50E
Nyamandhlovu Rhodesia **74** 19.50S 28.15E
Nyanga *r.* Gabon **72** 3.00S 10.17E
Nyanza *d.* Kenya **73** 0.30S 34.30E
Nyanza Rwanda **73** 2.20S 29.42E
Nyasa, L. *see* Malaŵi, L. Africa **73**
Nybro Sweden **46** 56.44N 15.55E
Nyeri Kenya **73** 0.22S 36.56E
Nyika Plateau *f.* Malaŵi **73** 10.25S 33.50E
Nyiru, Mt. Kenya **73** 2.06N 36.44E
Nyköbing Falster Denmark **44** 54.47N 11.53E
Nyköbing Thisted Denmark **46** 56.49N 8.50E
Nyköping Sweden **46** 58.45N 17.03E
Nylstroom R.S.A. **74** 24.42S 28.20E
Nymagee Australia **80** 32.05S 146.20E
Nynäshamn Sweden **46** 58.54N 17.55E
Nyngan Australia **80** 31.34S 147.14E
Nyong *r.* Cameroon **71** 3.15N 9.55E
Nyons France **40** 44.22N 5.08E
Nyunzu Zaïre **73** 5.55S 28.00E
Nzega Tanzania **73** 4.13S 33.09E
N'zérékoré Guinea **70** 7.49N 8.48W

O

Oadby England **28** 52.37N 1.07W
Oahe Resr. U.S.A. **90** 45.45N 100.20W
Oahu *i.* Hawaii U.S.A. **90** 21.30N 158.00W
Oakengates England **28** 52.42N 2.29W
Oakham England **28** 52.40N 0.43W
Oakland U.S.A. **90** 37.50N 122.15W
Oak Lawn U.S.A. **94** 41.42N 87.45W
Oak Park *town* U.S.A. **94** 41.52N 87.47W
Oakville Canada **95** 43.27N 79.41W
Oamaru New Zealand **82** 45.07S 170.58E
Oasis *d.* Algeria **71** 22.00N 6.00E
Oaxaca Mexico **96** 17.05N 96.41W
Oaxaca *d.* Mexico **96** 17.30N 97.00W
Ob *r.* U.S.S.R. **48** 66.50N 69.00E
Ob, G. of U.S.S.R. **48** 68.30N 74.00E
Oba Canada **94** 49.04N 84.07W
Oban Scotland **34** 56.26N 5.28W
Obbia Somali Rep. **69** 5.20N 48.30E
Oberhausen W. Germany **45** 51.28N 6.51E
Obi *i.* Indonesia **61** 1.45S 127.30E
Obo C.A.R. **73** 5.18N 26.28E
Obuasi Ghana **70** 6.15N 1.36W
Ocaña Spain **41** 39.57N 3.30W
Occidental, Cordillera *mts.* Colombia **97** 7.00N 76.15W
Ochil Hills Scotland **35** 56.16N 3.25W
Ock *r.* England **28** 51.40N 1.18W
Ocotlán Mexico **96** 20.21N 102.42W
October Revolution *i.* U.S.S.R. **49** 79.30N 96.00E
Ocua Moçambique **73** 13.37S 39.42E
Oda Ghana **70** 5.55N 0.56W
Odádhahraun *mts.* Iceland **46** 65.00N 17.30W
Odda Norway **46** 60.03N 6.45E
Oddur Somali Rep. **73** 4.11N 43.52E
Ödemis Turkey **43** 38.12N 28.00E
Odense Denmark **46** 55.24N 10.25E
Odenwald *mts.* W. Germany **44** 49.40N 9.20E
Oder *r.* Europe **44** 53.30N 14.36E
Odessa U.S.A. **90** 31.50N 102.23W
Odessa U.S.S.R. **47** 46.30N 30.46E
Odienné Ivory Coast **70** 9.36N 7.32W
Odorhei Romania **43** 46.18N 25.18E
Odzi *r.* Rhodesia **74** 19.49S 32.15E
Ofanto *r.* Italy **42** 41.22N 16.12E
Offaly *d.* Rep. of Ire. **39** 53.15N 7.30W
Offenbach W. Germany **44** 50.06N 8.46E
Offenburg W. Germany **44** 48.29N 7.57E
Ogbomosho Nigeria **71** 8.05N 4.11E
Ogden U.S.A. **90** 41.14N 111.59W
Ogdensburg U.S.A. **95** 44.42N 75.31W
Ogeechee *r.* U.S.A. **91** 32.54N 81.05W
Ognon *r.* France **40** 47.20N 5.37E
Ogoja Nigeria **71** 6.40N 8.45E
Ogoki *r.* Canada **91** 51.00N 84.30W
Ogosta *r.* Bulgaria **43** 43.44N 23.51E
Ogowe *r.* Gabon **72** 1.00S 9.05E
Ogulin Yugo. **42** 45.17N 15.14E
Ogun *d.* Nigeria **71** 6.50N 3.20E
Ohakune New Zealand **82** 39.24S 175.25E
Ohio *d.* U.S.A. **94** 40.10N 82.20W
Ohio *r.* U.S.A. **94** 37.07N 89.10W
Ohře *r.* Czech. **44** 50.32N 14.08E
Ohrid Yugo. **43** 41.06N 20.48E
Ohridsko, L. Albania/Yugo. **43** 41.00N 20.43E
Oich *r.* Scotland **37** 57.04N 4.46W
Oich, Loch Scotland **37** 57.04N 4.46W
Oil City U.S.A. **95** 41.26N 79.44W
Oise *r.* France **40** 49.00N 2.10E
Ojocaliente Mexico **96** 22.35N 102.18W
Ojo de Agua Argentina **103** 29.30S 63.44W
Oka *r.* U.S.S.R. **47** 56.09N 43.00E
Okahandja S.W. Africa **74** 21.59S 16.58E
Okaihau New Zealand **82** 35.18S 173.47E
Okanogan *r.* U.S.A. **90** 47.45N 120.05W
Okavango *r.* Botswana **74** 18.30S 22.04E
Okavango Basin *f.* Botswana **74** 19.30S 23.00E
Okayama Japan **63** 34.40N 133.54E
Okeechobee, L. U.S.A. **91** 27.00N 80.45W
Okeefenoke Swamp *f.* U.S.A. **91** 30.40N 82.40W
Okehampton England **31** 50.44N 4.01W
Okement *r.* England **31** 50.50N 4.04W
Okere *r.* Uganda **73** 1.37N 33.53E
Okha India **58** 22.29N 69.09E
Okha U.S.S.R. **49** 53.35N 142.50E
Okhotsk U.S.S.R. **49** 59.20N 143.15E
Okhotsk, Sea of U.S.S.R. **49** 55.00N 150.00E
Oki gunto *is.* Japan **63** 36.30N 133.20E
Okinawa *i.* Japan **63** 26.30N 128.00E
Okipoko *r.* S.W. Africa **74** 18.40S 16.03E
Okitipupa Nigeria **71** 6.31N 4.50E
Oklahoma *d.* U.S.A. **91** 35.00N 97.00W
Oklahoma City U.S.A. **91** 35.28N 97.33W
Öland *i.* Sweden **46** 56.50N 16.50E
Olary Australia **80** 32.18S 140.19E
Olavarria Argentina **103** 36.57S 60.20W
Olbia Italy **42** 40.55N 9.29E
Old Crow Canada **92** 67.34N 139.43W
Oldenburg Niedersachsen West W. Germany **45** 53.08N 8.13E
Oldenburg Schleswig Holstein W. Germany **44** 54.17N 10.52E
Oldenzaal Neth. **45** 52.19N 6.55E
Old Fletton England **29** 52.34N 0.14W
Oldham England **32** 53.33N 2.08W
Old Head of Kinsale *c.* Rep. of Ire. **39** 51.37N 8.33W
Oldmeldrum Scotland **37** 57.20N 2.20W
Old Rhine *r.* Neth. **45** 52.14N 4.26E
Old Windsor England **27** 51.28N 0.35W
Olean U.S.A. **95** 42.05N 78.26W
Olekma *r.* U.S.S.R. **49** 60.20N 120.30E
Olekminsk U.S.S.R. **49** 60.25N 120.00E
Olenek U.S.S.R. **49** 68.38N 112.15E
Olenek *r.* U.S.S.R. **49** 73.00N 120.00E
Olenekskiy G. U.S.S.R. **49** 74.00N 120.00E
Oléron, Île d' *i.* France **40** 45.55N 1.16W
Olga U.S.S.R. **63** 43.46N 135.14E
Olhão Portugal **41** 37.01N 7.50W
Olifants *r.* Cape Province R.S.A. **74** 31.43S 18.10E
Olifants *r.* Transvaal R.S.A. **74** 24.08S 32.40E
Olifants *r.* S.W. Africa **74** 25.28S 19.23E
Olivares Spain **41** 39.45N 2.21W
Olney England **28** 52.09N 0.42W
Ölögey Mongolia **62** 48.54N 90.00E
Olomouc Czech. **47** 49.38N 17.15E
Oloron France **40** 43.12N 0.35W
Olot Spain **41** 42.11N 2.30E
Olpe W. Germany **45** 51.02N 7.52E
Olsztyn Poland **47** 53.48N 20.29E
Oltenița Romania **43** 44.05N 26.31E
Oltet *r.* Romania **43** 44.13N 24.28E
Olympus, Mt. Cyprus **56** 34.55N 32.52E
Olympus, Mt. Greece **43** 40.04N 22.20E
Omagh N. Ireland **38** 54.36N 7.20W
Omaha U.S.A. **91** 41.15N 96.00W
Oman Asia **58** 22.30N 57.30E
Oman, G. of Asia **57** 25.00N 58.00E
Omarama New Zealand **82** 44.29S 169.59E
Omaruru S.W. Africa **74** 21.28S 15.56E
Ombrone *r.* Italy **42** 42.40N 11.00E
Omdurman Sudan **69** 15.37N 32.59E
Ommen Neth. **45** 52.32N 6.25E
Omolon *r.* U.S.S.R. **49** 68.50N 158.30E
Omsk U.S.S.R. **48** 55.00N 73.22E
Omuramba Omatako *r.* S.W. Africa **74** 17.59S 20.32E
Omuta Japan **63** 33.02N 130.26E
Oña Spain **41** 42.44N 3.25W
Onda Spain **41** 39.58N 0.16W
Ondangua S.W. Africa **74** 17.59S 16.02E
Ondo *d.* Nigeria **70** 7.10N 5.20E
Onega, L. U.S.S.R. **48** 62.00N 35.30E
Oneida L. U.S.A. **95** 43.13N 75.55W
Oneonta U.S.A. **95** 42.28N 75.04W
Onitsha Nigeria **71** 6.10N 6.47E
Onslow Village England **27** 51.14N 0.36W
Onstwedde Neth. **45** 53.04N 7.02E
Ontario *d.* Canada **94** 47.00N 80.40W
Ontario, L. N. America **95** 43.40N 78.00W
Ontonagon U.S.A. **94** 46.52N 89.18W
Oosterhout Neth. **45** 51.38N 4.50E
Oosthuizen Neth. **45** 52.33N 5.00E
Oostmalle Belgium **45** 51.18N 4.45E
Opala Zaïre **72** 0.42S 24.15E
Opole Poland **47** 50.40N 17.56E
Oporto Portugal **41** 41.09N 8.37W
Opotiki New Zealand **82** 38.00S 177.18E
Opunake New Zealand **82** 39.27S 173.52E
Oradea Romania **47** 47.03N 21.55E
Orai India **58** 26.00N 79.26E
Oran Algeria **41** 35.45N 0.38W
Orán Argentina **103** 23.07S 64.16W
Orange Australia **80** 33.19S 149.10E
Orange France **40** 44.08N 4.48E
Orange *r.* R.S.A. **74** 28.43S 16.30E
Orangeburg U.S.A. **91** 33.28N 80.53W
Orange Free State *d.* R.S.A. **74** 29.00S 26.30E
Oranjemond S.W. Africa **74** 28.38S 16.24E
Oranmore Rep. of Ire. **39** 53.17N 8.52W
Orbost Australia **80** 37.42S 148.30E
Orchies France **45** 50.28N 3.15E
Orchila *i.* Venezuela **97** 11.52N 66.10W
Orchy *r.* Scotland **34** 56.25N 5.02W
Ord *r.* Australia **79** 15.30S 128.30E
Ordu Turkey **56** 41.00N 37.52E
Orduna Spain **41** 43.00N 3.00W
Ordzhonikidze U.S.S.R. **47** 43.02N 44.43E
Örebro Sweden **46** 59.17N 15.13E
Oregon *d.* U.S.A. **90** 44.00N 120.00W
Öregrund Sweden **46** 60.20N 18.30E
Orekhovo Zuyevo U.S.S.R. **47** 55.47N 39.00E
Orel U.S.S.R. **47** 52.58N 36.04E
Ore Mts. E. Germany **44** 50.30N 12.50E
Orenburg U.S.S.R. **48** 51.50N 55.00E
Orense Spain **41** 42.20N 7.52W
Ore Sund *str.* Denmark **46** 56.00N 12.30E
Oreti *r.* New Zealand **82** 46.27S 168.14E
Orford England **29** 52.06N 1.31E
Orford Ness *c.* England **29** 52.05N 1.36E
Oriental, Cordillera *mts.* Bolivia **103** 17.00S 65.00W
Oriental, Cordillera *mts.* Colombia **97** 6.30N 74.30W
Oriente *d.* Cuba **97** 20.30N 75.30W
Orihuela Spain **41** 38.05N 0.56W
Orinoco *r.* Venezuela **97** 9.00N 61.30W
Orinoco Delta *f.* Venezuela **97** 9.00N 61.30W
Orissa *d.* India **59** 20.15N 84.00E
Oristano Italy **42** 39.53N 8.36E
Oristano, G. of Med. Sea **42** 39.50N 8.30E
Ori Vesi *l.* Finland **46** 62.20N 29.30E
Orizaba Mexico **96** 18.51N 97.08W
Orkney Is. *d.* Scotland **37** 59.00N 3.00W
Orlando U.S.A. **91** 28.33N 81.21W
Orléans France **40** 47.54N 1.54E
Ormiston Scotland **35** 55.55N 2.56W
Ormskirk England **32** 53.35N 2.53W
Orne *r.* France **40** 49.17N 0.10W
Ornsay *i.* Scotland **36** 57.08N 5.49W
Ornsköldsvik Sweden **46** 63.19N 18.45E
Oromocto Canada **95** 45.50N 66.28W
Oronsay *i.* Scotland **34** 56.01N 6.14W
Orosei Italy **42** 40.23N 9.40E
Orosei, G. of Med. Sea **42** 40.15N 9.45E
Oroville U.S.A. **90** 48.57N 119.27W
Orpington England **27** 51.23N 0.06E
Orrin *r.* Scotland **37** 57.33N 4.29W
Orsett England **27** 51.31N 0.23E
Orsha U.S.S.R. **47** 54.30N 30.23E
Orsk U.S.S.R. **48** 51.13N 58.35E
Orşova Romania **43** 44.42N 22.22E
Orthez France **40** 43.29N 0.46W
Ortles *mtn.* Italy **44** 46.30N 10.30E
Oryakhovo Bulgaria **43** 43.42N 23.58E
Osaka Japan **63** 34.40N 135.30E
Osa Pen. Costa Rica **96** 8.20N 83.30W
Oshawa Canada **95** 43.53N 78.51W

For Khmer Republic *read* Kampuchea. *For* Malagasy Republic *read* Madagascar. *For* Rhodesia *read* Zimbabwe.

Oshkosh to **Patrington** 155

Oshkosh U.S.A. **94** 44.01N 88.32W
Oshogbo Nigeria **71** 7.50N 4.35E
Oshwe Zaïre **72** 3.27S 19.32E
Osijek Yugo. **43** 45.35N 18.43E
Oskarshamn Sweden **46** 57.16N 16.25E
Oskol *r.* U.S.S.R. **47** 49.08N 37.10E
Oslo Norway **46** 59.56N 10.45E
Oslo Fjord *est.* Norway **46** 59.30N 10.30E
Osmancik Turkey **56** 40.58N 34.50E
Osmaniye Turkey **56** 37.04N 36.15E
Osnabrück W. Germany **45** 52.17N 8.03E
Osorno Spain **41** 42.24N 4.22W
Oss Neth. **45** 51.46N 5.31E
Ossa *mtn.* Greece **43** 39.47N 22.41E
Ossa, Mt. Australia **80** 41.52S 146.04E
Osse *r.* Nigeria **71** 5.55N 5.15E
Ossett England **33** 53.40N 1.35W
Ostashkov U.S.S.R. **47** 57.09N 33.10E
Oste *r.* W. Germany **44** 53.10N 9.40E
Ostend Belgium **45** 51.13N 2.55E
Österdal *r.* Sweden **46** 61.03N 14.30E
Österö *i.* Faroe Is. **46** 62.10N 7.00W
Östersund Sweden **46** 63.10N 14.40E
Östhammar Sweden **46** 60.15N 18.25E
Ostrava Czech. **47** 49.50N 18.15E
Ostrov U.S.S.R. **46** 57.22N 28.22E
Ostrów Mazowiecka Poland **47** 52.50N 21.51E
Osüm *r.* Bulgaria **43** 43.41N 24.51E
Osumi gunto *is.* Japan **63** 30.30N 130.40E
Osuna Spain **41** 37.14N 5.06W
Oswego U.S.A. **95** 43.27N 76.31W
Oswestry England **30** 52.52N 3.03W
Otago Pen. New Zealand **82** 45.48S 170.45E
Otaru Japan **63** 43.14N 140.59E
Otavi S.W. Africa **74** 19.39S 17.20E
Otford England **27** 51.19N 0.12E
Oti *r.* Ghana **70** 8.43N 0.10E
Otjiwarongo S.W. Africa **74** 20.29S 16.36E
Otley England **32** 53.54N 1.41W
Otra *r.* Norway **46** 58.10N 8.00E
Otranto Italy **43** 40.09N 18.30E
Otranto, Str. of Med. Sea **43** 40.10N 19.00E
Otta Norway **46** 61.46N 9.33E
Ottawa Canada **95** 45.25N 75.43W
Ottawa *r.* Canada **95** 45.23N 73.55W
Ottawa Is. Canada **93** 59.50N 80.00W
Otter *r.* England **31** 50.38N 3.19W
Otterburn England **35** 55.14N 2.10W
Ottery St. Mary England **31** 50.45N 3.16W
Ottumwa U.S.A. **94** 41.02N 92.26W
Otway, C. Australia **80** 38.51S 143.34E
Ouachita *r.* U.S.A. **91** 33.10N 92.10W
Ouachita Mts. U.S.A. **91** 34.40N 94.30W
Ouagadougou U. Volta **70** 12.20N 1.40W
Ouahigouya U. Volta **70** 13.31N 2.21W
Ouargla Algeria **68** 32.00N 5.16E
Oudenarde Belgium **45** 50.50N 3.37E
Oudtshoorn R.S.A. **74** 33.35S 22.12E
Ouerk *r.* Algeria **41** 35.15N 2.15E
Ouessant, Île d' *i.* France **40** 48.28N 5.05W
Ouesso Congo **72** 1.38N 16.03E
Ouezzane Morocco **41** 34.52N 5.35W
Oughter, Lough Rep. of Ire. **38** 54.01N 7.28W
Oughterard Rep. of Ire. **38** 53.27N 9.22W
Ouham *r.* Chad **71** 9.15N 18.13E
Oujda Morocco **68** 34.41N 1.45W
Oulu Finland **46** 65.02N 25.27E
Oulu *r.* Finland **46** 65.04N 25.23E
Oulu Järvi *l.* Finland **46** 64.30N 27.00E
Ounas *r.* Finland **46** 66.33N 25.37E
Oundle England **29** 52.28N 0.28W
Our *r.* Lux. **45** 49.53N 6.16E
Ourinhos Brazil **103** 23.00S 49.54W
Ourthe *r.* Belgium **45** 50.38N 5.36E
Ouse *r.* E. Sussex England **29** 50.46N 0.03E
Ouse *r.* Humber. England **33** 53.41N 0.42W
Outer Hebrides *is.* Scotland **36** 57.40N 7.35W
Outjo S.W. Africa **74** 20.08S 16.08E
Out Skerries *is.* Scotland **36** 60.20N 0.45W
Outwell England **29** 52.36N 0.15E
Ouyen Australia **80** 35.06S 142.22E
Ovambo *f.* S.W. Africa **74** 17.45S 16.00E
Overath W. Germany **45** 50.56N 7.18E
Overflakkee *i.* Neth. **45** 51.45N 4.08E
Overijssel *d.* Neth. **45** 52.25N 6.30E
Overton England **28** 51.15N 1.15W
Overton Wales **30** 52.58N 2.56W
Overuman *l.* Sweden **46** 66.06N 14.40E
Oviedo Spain **41** 43.21N 5.50W
Owel, Lough Rep. of Ire. **38** 53.34N 7.24W
Owen Falls Dam Uganda **73** 0.30N 33.07E
Oweniny *r.* Rep. of Ire. **38** 54.08N 9.51W
Owenkillew *r.* N. Ireland **34** 54.43N 7.23W
Owen Sound *town* Canada **94** 44.34N 80.56W
Owen Stanley Range *mts.* P.N.G. **79** 9.30S 148.00E
Owerri Nigeria **71** 5.29N 7.02E
Owo Nigeria **71** 7.10N 5.39E
Owosso U.S.A. **94** 43.00N 84.11W
Oxelösund Sweden **46** 58.40N 17.10E
Oxford England **28** 51.45N 1.15W
Oxfordshire *d.* England **28** 51.46N 1.10W
Oxley Australia **80** 34.11S 144.10E
Oxley's Peak *mtn.* Australia **80** 31.48S 150.17E
Oxshott England **27** 51.19N 0.20W
Oxted England **27** 51.16N 0.01E
Oykel *r.* Scotland **37** 57.53N 4.21W
Oykel Bridge *town* Scotland **37** 57.57N 4.44W
Oymyakon U.S.S.R. **49** 63.30N 142.44E
Oyo Nigeria **71** 7.50N 3.55E
Oyo *d.* Nigeria **71** 8.10N 3.40E
Oyster B. Australia **80** 42.10S 148.10E
Ozamiz Phil. **61** 8.09N 123.59E
Ozark Plateau U.S.A. **91** 36.00N 93.35W

P

Paan China **59** 30.02N 99.01E
Paarl R.S.A. **74** 33.45S 18.58E
Pabbay *i.* W. Isles Scotland **36** 57.46N 7.14W
Pabbay *i.* W. Isles Scotland **36** 56.51N 7.35W
Pabna Bangla. **58** 24.00N 89.15E
Pachuca Mexico **96** 20.10N 98.44W
Pacific Ocean 106
Padang Indonesia **60** 0.55S 100.21E
Paddington England **27** 51.31N 0.12W
Paddock Wood England **29** 51.11N 0.23E
Paderborn W. Germany **44** 51.43N 8.44E
Padre I. U.S.A. **91** 27.00N 97.20W
Padstow England **31** 50.33N 4.57W
Padua Italy **42** 45.27N 11.52E
Pag *i.* Yugo. **42** 44.28N 15.00E
Pagai Selatan *i.* Indonesia **60** 3.00S 100.30E
Pagai Utara *i.* Indonesia **60** 2.40S 100.10E
Pagan *i.* Asia **61** 18.08N 145.46E
Pager *r.* Uganda **73** 3.05N 32.28E
Pahala Hawaii U.S.A. **90** 19.12N 155.28W
Paible Scotland **36** 57.35N 7.27W
Paijänne *l.* Finland **46** 61.30N 25.30E
Paimboeuf France **40** 47.14N 2.01W
Painesville U.S.A. **94** 41.43N 81.15W
Painswick England **28** 51.47N 2.11W
Paisley Scotland **34** 55.50N 4.26W
Pakanbaru Indonesia **60** 0.33N 101.20E
Pakhoi China **60** 21.39N 109.10E
Pakistan Asia **58** 30.00N 70.00E
Pak Lay Laos **60** 18.10N 101.24E
Pakse Laos **60** 15.05N 105.50E
Pakwach Uganda **73** 2.27N 31.18E
Palana U.S.S.R. **49** 59.05N 159.59E
Palapye Botswana **74** 22.37S 27.06E
Palau Is. Asia **61** 7.00N 134.25E
Palawan *i.* Phil. **60** 9.30N 118.30E
Paldiski U.S.S.R. **47** 59.22N 24.08E
Palembang Indonesia **60** 2.59S 104.50E
Palencia Spain **41** 42.01N 4.34W
Palenque Mexico **96** 17.32N 91.59W
Palermo Italy **42** 38.09N 13.22E
Palit, C. Albania **43** 41.24N 19.23E
Palk Str. India/Sri Lanka **59** 10.00N 79.40E
Pallaskenry Rep. of Ire. **39** 52.39N 8.52W
Palliser, C. New Zealand **82** 41.35S 175.15E
Palma Moçambique **73** 10.48S 40.25E
Palma Spain **41** 39.36N 2.39E
Palma, B. of Spain **41** 39.30N 2.40E
Palma del Rio Spain **41** 37.43N 5.17W
Palmas, C. Liberia **70** 4.30N 7.55W
Palmas, G. of Med. Sea **42** 39.00N 8.30E
Palmeirinhas, Punta das Angola **72** 9.09S 12.58E
Palmerston New Zealand **82** 45.30S 170.42E
Palmerston North New Zealand **82** 40.20S 175.39E
Palmi Italy **42** 38.22N 15.50E
Palm Springs *town* U.S.A. **90** 33.49N 116.34W
Palmyra Syria **56** 34.36N 38.15E
Palmyras Pt. India **59** 20.40N 87.00E
Paloh Indonesia **60** 1.46N 109.17E
Palopo Indonesia **61** 3.01S 120.12E
Pamekasan Indonesia **60** 7.11S 113.50E
Pamiers France **40** 43.07N 1.36E
Pamirs *mts.* U.S.S.R. **62** 37.50N 73.30E
Pampa U.S.A. **90** 35.32N 100.58W
Pampas *f.* Argentina **103** 34.00S 64.00W
Pamplona Colombia **97** 7.24N 72.38W
Pamplona Spain **41** 42.49N 1.39W
Panama C. America **97** 9.00N 80.00W
Panamá, G. of Panama **97** 8.30N 79.00W
Panama Canal Zone C. America **97** 9.10N 79.55W
Panamá City Panama **97** 8.57N 79.30W
Panama City U.S.A. **91** 30.10N 85.41W
Panay *i.* Phil. **61** 11.10N 122.30E
Panevežys U.S.S.R. **46** 55.44N 24.24E
Pangani Tanga Tanzania **73** 5.21S 39.00E
Pangi Zaïre **73** 3.10S 26.38E
Pangkalpinang Indonesia **60** 2.05S 106.09E
Pangnirtung Canada **93** 66.05N 65.45W
Pantano del Esla *l.* Spain **41** 41.40N 5.50W
Pantelleria *i.* Italy **42** 36.48N 12.00E
Paoki China **62** 34.23N 107.16E
Páola Italy **42** 39.21N 16.03E
Paoshan China **59** 25.07N 99.08E
Paoting China **63** 38.54N 115.26E
Paotow China **63** 40.38N 109.59E
Papa Stour *i.* Scotland **36** 60.20N 1.42W
Papa Westray *i.* Scotland **37** 59.22N 2.54W
Papenburg W. Germany **45** 53.05N 7.25E
Paphos Cyprus **56** 34.45N 32.25E
Paps of Jura *mts.* Scotland **34** 55.55N 6.00W
Papua, G. of P.N.G. **61** 8.50S 145.00E
Papua New Guinea Austa. **61** 6.00S 143.00E
Paracatu Brazil **103** 17.14S 46.52W
Paracatu *r.* Brazil **103** 16.30S 45.10W
Paracel Is. Asia **60** 16.20N 112.00E
Paragua *r.* Venezuela **97** 6.45N 63.00W
Paraguaná Pen. Venezuela **97** 12.00N 70.00W
Paraguarí Paraguay **103** 25.36S 57.06W
Paraguay *r.* Argentina **103** 27.30S 58.50W
Paraguay S. America **103** 23.00S 57.00W
Parakou Benin **71** 9.23N 2.40E
Paramaribo Surinam **102** 5.52N 55.14W
Paraná Argentina **103** 31.45S 60.30W
Paraná *r.* Argentina **103** 34.00S 58.30W
Paraná *d.* Brazil **103** 24.30S 52.00W
Paranaguá Brazil **103** 25.32S 48.36W
Paranaiba *r.* Brazil **103** 20.00S 51.00W
Paranapanema *r.* Brazil **103** 22.30S 53.03W
Paranapiacaba, Serra *mts.* Brazil **103** 24.30S 49.15W
Parana Plateau Paraguay **103** 24.32S 55.00W
Pardo *r.* Brazil **103** 20.10S 48.30W
Pardubice Czech. **44** 50.03N 15.45E
Parece Vela *i.* Asia **61** 20.24N 136.02E
Parepare Indonesia **60** 4.03S 119.40E
Paria, G. of Venezuela **97** 10.30N 62.00W
Pariaman Indonesia **60** 0.36S 100.09E
Paria Pen. Venezuela **97** 10.45N 62.30W
Paris France **40** 48.52N 2.20E
Park *f.* Scotland **36** 58.05N 6.32W
Parkano Finland **46** 62.03N 23.00E
Parker Dam U.S.A. **90** 34.25N 114.05W
Parkersburg U.S.A. **94** 39.17N 81.33W
Parkes Australia **80** 33.10S 148.13E
Park Falls *town* U.S.A. **94** 45.57N 90.28W
Park Forest *town* U.S.A. **94** 41.28N 87.40W
Parkville U.S.A. **95** 39.23N 76.32W
Parma Italy **42** 44.48N 10.18E
Parma U.S.A. **94** 41.24N 81.44W
Parnassos *mtn.* Greece **43** 38.33N 22.35E
Pärnu U.S.S.R. **46** 58.28N 24.30E
Pärnu *r.* U.S.S.R. **46** 58.23N 24.32E
Paroo *r.* Australia **80** 31.30S 143.34E
Paropamisus Mts. Afghan. **57** 34.30N 63.30E
Páros *i.* Greece **43** 37.04N 25.11E
Parral Mexico **90** 26.58N 105.40W
Parramatta Australia **80** 33.50S 150.57E
Parrett *r.* England **28** 51.10N 3.00W
Parry, C. Greenland **93** 76.50N 71.00W
Parry Is. Canada **93** 76.00N 102.00W
Parry Sound *town* Canada **94** 45.21N 80.03W
Parseta *r.* Poland **44** 54.12N 15.33E
Partabpur India **58** 23.28N 83.15E
Parthenay France **40** 46.39N 0.14W
Partry Mts. Rep. of Ire. **38** 53.40N 9.30W
Parys R.S.A. **74** 26.55S 27.28E
Pasadena U.S.A. **90** 34.10N 118.09W
Pas de Calais *d.* France **29** 50.30N 2.30E
Paso de los Toros *town* Uruguay **103** 32.45S 56.47W
Passage East *town* Rep. of Ire. **39** 52.14N 7.00W
Passage West *town* Rep. of Ire. **39** 51.52N 8.20W
Passau W. Germany **44** 48.35N 13.28E
Passero, C. Italy **42** 36.40N 15.08E
Pass of Thermopylae Greece **43** 38.47N 22.34E
Passo Fundo Brazil **103** 28.16S 52.20W
Pasvik *r.* Norway **46** 69.45N 30.00E
Patagonia *f.* Argentina **103** 40.20S 67.00W
Pate I. Kenya **73** 2.08S 41.02E
Pateley Bridge *town* England **32** 54.05N 1.45W
Paterson U.S.A. **95** 40.55N 74.10W
Pathari India **58** 23.56N 78.12E
Pathfinder Resr. U.S.A. **90** 42.25N 106.55W
Patiala India **58** 30.21N 76.27E
Patkai Hills Burma **59** 26.30N 95.40E
Patna India **58** 25.37N 85.12E
Patna Scotland **34** 55.22N 4.30W
Patos, L. Brazil **103** 31.00S 51.10W
Pátras Greece **43** 38.15N 21.45E
Patras, G. of Med. Sea **43** 38.15N 21.35E
Patrickswell Rep. of Ire. **39** 52.36N 8.43W
Patrington England **33** 53.41N 0.02W

For Khmer Republic *read* Kampuchea. *For* Malagasy Republic *read* Madagascar. *For* Rhodesia *read* Zimbabwe.

Patuca to **Pontoise** 156

Patuca *r.* Honduras **96** 30.48N 84.25W
Pau France **40** 43.18N 0.22W
Pauillac France **40** 45.12N 0.44W
Pavia Italy **40** 45.12N 9.09E
Pavlodar U.S.S.R. **48** 52.21N 76.59E
Pavlograd U.S.S.R. **47** 48.34N 35.50E
Pawtucket U.S.A. **95** 41.53N 71.23W
Payne *r.* Canada **93** 60.00N 69.45W
Paysandú Uruguay **103** 32.21S 58.05W
Peace *r.* Canada **92** 59.00N 111.26W
Peace River *town* Canada **92** 56.15N 117.18W
Peace River Resr. Canada **92** 55.00N 126.00W
Peaked Mtn. Canada **95** 46.34N 68.49W
Peak Hill *town* Australia **80** 32.47S 148.13E
Peale, Mt. U.S.A. **90** 38.26N 109.14W
Pearl *r.* U.S.A. **91** 30.15N 89.25W
Pebane Moçambique **73** 17.14S 38.10E
Pec Yugo. **43** 42.40N 20.17E
Pechenga U.S.S.R. **46** 69.28N 31.04E
Pechora *r.* U.S.S.R. **48** 68.10N 54.00E
Pechora G. U.S.S.R. **48** 69.00N 56.00E
Pecos U.S.A. **96** 31.25N 103.30W
Pecos *r.* U.S.A. **90** 29.45N 101.25W
Pécs Hungary **43** 46.05N 18.14E
Pedro J. Caballero Paraguay **103** 22.30S 55.44W
Peebinga Australia **80** 34.55S 140.57E
Peebles Scotland **35** 55.39N 3.12W
Peel *r.* Canada **92** 68.13N 135.00W
Peel I.o.M. **32** 54.14N 4.42W
Peel *f.* Neth. **45** 51.30N 5.50E
Peel Fell *mtn.* England/Scotland **35** 55.17N 2.35W
Peene *r.* E. Germany **44** 53.53N 13.49E
Pegasus B. New Zealand **82** 43.15S 173.00E
Pegu Burma **59** 17.18N 96.31E
Pegu Yoma *mts.* Burma **59** 18.40N 96.00E
Pegwell B. England **29** 51.18N 1.25E
Pehan China **63** 48.17N 126.33E
Pehuajó Argentina **103** 35.50S 61.50W
Peipus, L. U.S.S.R. **46** 58.30N 27.30E
Pekalongan Indonesia **60** 6.54S 109.37E
Pekin U.S.A. **94** 40.34N 89.40W
Peking China **63** 39.55N 116.25E
Pelat, Mont *mtn.* France **40** 44.17N 6.41E
Pelee, Pt. Canada **94** 41.45N 82.09W
Peleng *i.* Indonesia **61** 1.30S 123.10E
Pelly *r.* Canada **92** 62.50N 137.35W
Pelotas Brazil **103** 31.45S 52.20W
Pematangsiantar Indonesia **60** 2.59N 99.01E
Pemba Moçambique **73** 13.02S 40.30E
Pemba I. Tanzania **73** 5.10S 39.45E
Pembridge England **28** 52.13N 2.54W
Pembroke Canada **95** 45.49N 77.08W
Pembroke Wales **31** 51.41N 4.57W
Penang I. Malaysia **60** 5.30N 100.10E
Peñaranda de Bracamonte Spain **41** 40.54N 5.13W
Penarth Wales **31** 51.26N 3.11W
Peñas, Cabo de Spain **41** 43.42N 5.52W
Pende *r.* Chad **71** 7.30N 16.20E
Pendembu Eastern Sierra Leone **70** 8.09N 10.42W
Pendine Wales **31** 51.44N 4.33W
Pendle Hill England **32** 53.52N 2.18W
Penganga *r.* India **59** 18.52N 79.56E
Penge England **27** 51.25N 0.04W
Pengpu China **63** 32.56N 117.27E
Penicuik Scotland **35** 55.49N 3.13W
Penistone England **32** 53.31N 1.38W
Penki China **63** 41.21N 123.45E
Penmaenmawr Wales **30** 53.16N 3.54W
Pennsylvania *d.* U.S.A. **95** 41.00N 75.45W
Penny Highland Canada **93** 67.10N 66.50W
Penobscot *r.* U.S.A. **95** 44.34N 68.48W
Penola Australia **80** 37.23S 140.21E
Penonomé Panamá **97** 8.30N 80.20W
Penrhyndeudraeth Wales **30** 52.56N 4.04W
Penrith Australia **80** 33.47S 150.44E
Penrith England **32** 54.40N 2.45W
Penryn England **31** 50.10N 5.07W
Pensacola U.S.A. **91** 30.30N 87.12W
Penticton Canada **90** 49.29N 119.38W
Pentire Pt. England **31** 50.35N 4.55W
Pentland Firth *str.* Scotland **37** 58.40N 3.00W
Pentland Hills Scotland **35** 55.50N 3.20W
Pen-y-ghent *mtn.* England **32** 54.10N 2.14W
Pen-y-groes Wales **30** 53.03N 4.18W
Penza U.S.S.R. **47** 53.11N 45.00E
Penzance England **31** 50.07N 5.32W
Penzhina, G. of U.S.S.R. **49** 61.00N 163.00E
Peoria U.S.A. **94** 40.43N 89.38W
Perekop U.S.S.R. **47** 46.10N 33.42E
Pergamino Argentina **103** 33.55S 60.32W
Peribonca *r.* Canada **91** 48.50N 72.00W
Périgueux France **40** 45.12N 0.44E
Perija, Sierra de *mts.* Venezuela **97** 9.00N 73.00W
Perim *i.* Asia **69** 12.40N 43.24E
Perm U.S.S.R. **48** 58.01N 56.10E
Pernik *see* Dimitrovo Bulgaria **43**
Péronne France **45** 49.56N 2.57E
Perpignan France **40** 42.42N 2.54E
Perranporth England **31** 50.21N 5.09W
Persepolis *ruins* Iran **57** 29.55N 53.00E
Pershore England **28** 52.07N 2.04W
Persian G. Asia **57** 27.00N 50.00E
Perth Australia **79** 31.58S 115.49E
Perth Scotland **35** 56.24N 3.28W
Perth Amboy U.S.A. **95** 40.32N 74.17W
Peru S. America **102** 10.00S 75.00W
Peru U.S.A. **94** 40.45N 86.04W
Peru-Chile Trench Pacific Oc. **106** 24.00S 74.00W
Perugia Italy **42** 43.06N 12.24E
Péruwelz Belgium **45** 50.32N 3.36E
Pésaro Italy **42** 43.54N 12.54E
Pescara Italy **42** 42.27N 14.13E
Pescara *r.* Italy **42** 42.28N 14.13E
Peshawar Pakistan **58** 34.01N 71.40E
Petatlán Mexico **96** 17.31N 101.16W
Petauke Zambia **73** 14.16S 31.21E
Peterborough Australia **80** 33.00S 138.51E
Peterborough Canada **95** 44.19N 78.20W
Peterborough England **29** 52.35N 0.14W
Peterhead Scotland **37** 57.30N 1.46W
Peterlee England **35** 54.45N 1.18W
Petersfield England **28** 51.00N 0.56W
Petra *ruins* Jordan **56** 30.19N 35.26E
Petrich Bulgaria **43** 41.25N 23.13E
Petropavlovsk U.S.S.R. **48** 54.53N 69.13E
Petropavlovsk Kamchatskiy U.S.S.R. **49** 53.03N 158.43E
Petrópolis Brazil **103** 22.30S 43.06W
Petrovsk Zabaykal'skiy U.S.S.R. **49** 51.20N 108.55E
Petrozavodsk U.S.S.R. **48** 61.46N 34.19E
Petworth England **28** 50.59N 0.37W
Pewsey England **28** 51.20N 1.46W
Pézenas France **40** 43.28N 3.25E
Pforzheim W. Germany **44** 48.53N 8.41E
Phan Rang Vietnam **60** 11.35N 109.00E
Phet Buri Thailand **59** 13.01N 99.55E
Philadelphia U.S.A. **95** 40.00N 75.10W
Philippeville Belgium **45** 50.12N 4.32E
Philippine Is. Asia **107** 10.00N 124.00E
Philippines Asia **61** 13.00N 123.00E
Philippine Trench Pacific Oc. **61** 8.45N 127.20E
Philipstown R.S.A. **74** 30.26S 24.28E
Phnom Penh Khmer Rep. **59** 11.35N 104.55E
Phoenix U.S.A. **90** 33.30N 111.55W
Phong Saly Laos **60** 21.40N 102.06E
Phukao Miang *mtn.* Thailand **59** 16.50N 101.00E
Phuket Thailand **59** 8.00N 98.28E
Phuket *i.* Thailand **60** 8.10N 98.20E
Phu Quoc *i.* Khmer Rep. **60** 10.10N 104.00E
Piacenza Italy **42** 45.03N 9.42E
Piangil Australia **80** 35.04S 143.20E
Pianosa *i.* Italy **42** 42.35N 10.05E
Piave *r.* Italy **42** 45.33N 12.45E
Pic *r.* Canada **94** 48.35N 86.17W
Picardy *f.* France **45** 49.47N 2.45E
Pickering England **33** 54.15N 0.46W
Pickwick L. U.S.A. **91** 35.00N 88.10W
Picton Canada **95** 44.01N 77.09W
Picton New Zealand **82** 41.17S 174.02E
Picton, Mt. Australia **80** 43.10S 146.30E
Piedras Negras Mexico **90** 28.40N 100.32W
Pieksämäki Finland **46** 62.18N 27.10E
Pielinen *l.* Finland **46** 63.20N 29.50E
Pierowall Scotland **37** 59.19N 3.00W
Pierre U.S.A. **90** 44.23N 100.20W
Pietermaritzburg R.S.A. **74** 29.36S 30.24E
Pietersburg R.S.A. **74** 23.54S 29.23E
Piet Retief R.S.A. **74** 27.00S 30.49E
Pigailoe *i.* Asia **61** 8.08N 146.40E
Pikes Peak U.S.A. **90** 38.50N 105.03W
Piketberg R.S.A. **74** 32.55S 18.45E
Piła Poland **44** 53.09N 16.44E
Pilcomayo *r.* Argentina/Paraguay **103** 25.15S 57.43W
Pilgrim's Hatch England **27** 51.37N 0.16E
Pilibhit India **58** 28.37N 79.48E
Pílos Greece **43** 36.55N 21.40E
Pinarbaşi Turkey **56** 38.43N 36.23E
Pinar del Rio Cuba **96** 22.24N 83.42W
Pinar del Rio *d.* Cuba **96** 22.30N 83.30W
Pindus Mts. Albania/Greece **43** 39.40N 21.00E
Pine Bluff U.S.A. **91** 34.13N 92.00W
Pines, I. of Cuba **96** 21.40N 82.40W
Ping *r.* Thailand **59** 15.45N 100.10E
Pingliang China **62** 35.25N 107.14E
Pini *i.* Indonesia **60** 0.10N 98.30E
Pinios *r.* Greece **43** 37.51N 22.37E
Pinnaroo Australia **80** 35.18S 140.54E
Pinner England **27** 51.36N 0.23W
Pinsk U.S.S.R. **47** 52.08N 26.01E
Pinto Argentina **103** 29.09S 62.38W
Piombino Italy **42** 42.56N 10.30E
Piqua U.S.A. **94** 40.08N 84.14W
Piquiri *r.* Brazil **103** 24.00S 54.00W
Piraeus Greece **43** 37.56N 23.38E
Pirapora Brazil **103** 17.20S 44.54W
Pirbright England **27** 51.18N 0.39W
Pírgos Greece **43** 37.42N 21.27E
Pirmasens W. Germany **44** 49.12N 7.37E
Pirna E. Germany **44** 50.58N 13.58E
Pirot Yugo. **43** 43.10N 22.32E
Pisa Italy **42** 43.43N 10.24E
Pisciotta Italy **42** 40.08N 15.12E
Pisek Czech. **44** 49.19N 14.10E
Pisuerga *r.* Spain **41** 41.35N 5.40W
Pita Guinea **70** 11.05N 12.15W
Pitea Sweden **46** 65.19N 21.30E
Piteşti Romania **43** 44.52N 24.51E
Pitlochry Scotland **37** 56.43N 3.45W
Pittenweem Scotland **35** 56.13N 2.44W
Pittsburgh U.S.A. **94** 40.26N 80.00W
Pittsfield U.S.A. **95** 42.27N 73.15W
Plain of Bornu *f.* Nigeria **71** 12.30N 13.00E
Plains of Ellertrin *f.* Rep. of Ire. **38** 53.37N 9.11W
Plains of Mayo *f.* Rep. of Ire. **38** 53.46N 9.05W
Plasencia Spain **41** 40.02N 6.05W
Platani *r.* Italy **42** 37.24N 13.15E
Plate, R. *see* la Plata, Rio de Argentina **103**
Plateau *d.* Nigeria **71** 8.50N 9.00E
Platí, C. Greece **43** 40.26N 23.59E
Platinum U.S.A. **92** 59.00N 161.50W
Platte *r.* U.S.A. **91** 41.05N 96.50W
Plattsburgh U.S.A. **95** 44.42N 73.29W
Plauen E. Germany **44** 50.29N 12.08E
Plenty, B. of New Zealand **82** 37.40S 176.50E
Pleven Bulgaria **43** 43.25N 24.39E
Pljevlja Yugo. **43** 43.22N 19.22E
Ploeşti Romania **43** 44.57N 26.02E
Plomb du Cantal *mtn.* France **40** 45.04N 2.45E
Plombières France **44** 47.58N 6.28E
Ploudalmézeau France **40** 48.33N 4.39W
Plovdiv Bulgaria **43** 42.09N 24.45E
Plumtree Rhodesia **74** 20.30S 27.50E
Plym *r.* England **31** 50.21N 4.06W
Plymouth England **31** 50.23N 4.09W
Plymouth Ind. U.S.A. **94** 41.20N 86.19W
Plymouth Mass. U.S.A. **95** 41.58N 70.40W
Plympton England **31** 50.24N 4.02W
Plzeň Czech. **44** 49.45N 13.22E
Po *r.* Italy **42** 44.51N 12.30E
Pô U. Volta **70** 11.11N 1.10W
Pobé Benin **71** 7.00N 2.56E
Pobeda, Mt. U.S.S.R. **49** 65.20N 145.50E
Pobedy *mtn.* China **62** 42.09N 80.12E
Pobla de Segur Spain **41** 42.15N 0.58E
Pocatello U.S.A. **90** 42.53N 112.26W
Pocklington England **33** 53.56N 0.48W
Podolsk U.S.S.R. **47** 55.23N 37.32E
Podor Senegal **70** 16.35N 15.02W
Pods Brook *r.* England **27** 51.52N 0.33E
Pofadder R.S.A. **74** 29.09S 19.25E
Poh Indonesia **61** 1.00S 122.50E
Pohsien China **63** 33.40N 115.50E
Pointe-à-Pitre Guadeloupe **97** 16.14N 61.32W
Pointe Noire *town* Congo **72** 4.46S 11.53E
Poitiers France **40** 46.35N 0.20E
Pokhara Nepal **58** 28.14N 83.58E
Poko Zaïre **73** 3.08N 26.51E
Pokotu China **63** 48.45N 121.58E
Poland Europe **47** 52.30N 19.00E
Polatli Turkey **56** 39.34N 32.08E
Polden Hills England **28** 51.07N 2.50W
Polegate England **29** 50.49N 0.15E
Policastro, G. of Med. Sea **42** 40.00N 15.35E
Poligny France **40** 46.50N 4.42E
Pollina *mtn.* Italy **42** 39.53N 16.11E
Pollnalaght *mtn.* N. Ireland **38** 54.34N 7.27W
Polperro England **31** 50.19N 4.31W
Poltava U.S.S.R. **47** 49.35N 34.35E
Pombal Portugal **41** 39.55N 8.38W
Ponce Puerto Rico **97** 18.00N 66.40W
Pondicherry India **59** 11.59N 79.50E
Pond Inlet *str.* Canada **93** 72.30N 75.00W
Ponferrada Spain **41** 42.32N 6.31W
Pongola *r.* Moçambique **74** 26.13S 32.38E
Ponta Grossa Brazil **103** 25.00S 50.09W
Pont-à-Mousson France **44** 48.55N 6.03E
Ponta Pora Brazil **103** 22.27S 55.39W
Pontardawe Wales **31** 51.44N 3.51W
Pontardulais Wales **31** 51.42N 4.03W
Pontchartrain, L. U.S.A. **96** 30.50N 90.00W
Pontefract England **33** 53.42N 1.19W
Ponteland England **35** 55.03N 1.43W
Ponterwyd Wales **30** 52.25N 3.50W
Pontevedra Spain **41** 42.25N 8.39W
Pontiac U.S.A. **94** 42.39N 83.18W
Pontianak Indonesia **60** 0.05S 109.16E
Pontine Is. Italy **42** 40.56N 12.58E
Pontine Mts. Turkey **56** 40.32N 38.00E
Pontoise France **40** 49.03N 2.05E

For Khmer Republic *read* Kampuchea. *For* Malagasy Republic *read* Madagascar. *For* Rhodesia *read* Zimbabwe.

Pontrilas England **28** 51.56N 2.53W
Pontypool Wales **31** 51.42N 3.01W
Pontypridd Wales **28** 51.36N 3.21W
Poole England **28** 50.42N 2.02W
Poole B. England **28** 50.40N 1.55W
Poolewe Scotland **36** 57.45N 5.37W
Pooley Bridge *town* England **32** 54.37N 2.49W
Poona India **58** 18.34N 73.58E
Poperinge Belgium **45** 50.51N 2.44E
Poplar England **27** 51.31N 0.01E
Poplar Bluff U.S.A. **91** 36.40N 90.25W
Popocatépetl *mtn.* Mexico **96** 19.02N 98.38W
Popokabaka Zaïre **72** 5.41S 16.40E
Porahat India **58** 22.35N 85.27E
Porbandar India **58** 21.40N 69.40E
Porcupine *r.* U.S.A. **92** 66.25N 145.20W
Pori Finland **46** 61.28N 21.45E
Porkkala Finland **46** 60.00N 24.25E
Porlamar Venezuela **97** 11.01N 63.54W
Porlock England **31** 51.14N 3.36W
Pornic France **40** 47.07N 2.05W
Poronaysk U.S.S.R. **49** 49.13N 142.55E
Porsanger *est.* Norway **46** 70.30N 25.45E
Porsgrunn Norway **46** 59.10N 9.40E
Porsuk *r.* Turkey **56** 39.41N 31.56E
Port Adelaide Australia **80** 34.52S 138.30E
Portadown N. Ireland **38** 54.25N 6.27W
Portaferry N. Ireland **38** 54.23N 5.33W
Portage U.S.A. **94** 43.33N 89.29W
Portage la Prairie *town* Canada **90** 50.01N 98.20W
Portalegre Portugal **41** 39.17N 7.25W
Port Alfred R.S.A. **74** 33.36S 26.54E
Port Angeles U.S.A. **90** 48.06N 123.26W
Port Antonio Jamaica **97** 18.10N 76.27W
Portarlington Rep. of Ire. **39** 53.10N 7.12W
Port Arthur Australia **80** 43.08S 147.50E
Port Arthur U.S.A. **91** 29.55N 93.56W
Port Askaig Scotland **34** 55.51N 6.07W
Port Augusta Australia **79** 32.30S 137.46E
Port-au-Prince Haiti **97** 18.33N 72.20W
Port Austin U.S.A. **94** 44.04N 82.59W
Port aux Basques Canada **93** 47.35N 59.10W
Port Bannatyne Scotland **34** 55.52N 5.04W
Port Blair India **59** 11.40N 92.30E
Port Bou Spain **41** 42.25N 3.09E
Port Bouet Ivory Coast **70** 5.14N 3.58W
Port Burwell Canada **94** 42.39N 80.47W
Port Cartier Canada **93** 50.03N 66.46W
Port Charlotte Scotland **34** 55.44N 6.23W
Port Dinorwic Wales **30** 53.11N 4.12W
Port Elizabeth R.S.A. **74** 33.58S 25.36E
Port Ellen Scotland **34** 55.38N 6.12W
Port Erin I.o.M. **32** 54.05N 4.45W
Port-Eynon Wales **31** 51.33N 4.13W
Port Gentil Gabon **72** 0.40S 8.46E
Port Glasgow Scotland **34** 55.56N 4.40W
Portglenone N. Ireland **34** 54.52N 6.30W
Port Harcourt Nigeria **71** 4.43N 7.05E
Port Harrison Canada **93** 58.25N 78.18W
Porthcawl Wales **31** 51.28N 3.42W
Port Hedland Australia **79** 20.24S 118.36E
Porthmadog Wales **30** 52.55N 4.08W
Port Huron U.S.A. **94** 42.59N 82.28W
Portimão Portugal **41** 37.08N 8.32W
Port Isaac B. England **31** 50.36N 4.50W
Portishead England **28** 51.29N 2.46W
Portiţei Mouth *f.* Romania **43** 44.40N 29.00E
Port Kelang Malaysia **60** 2.57N 101.24E
Port Kembla Australia **80** 34.30S 150.54E
Portknockie Scotland **37** 57.42N 2.52W
Portland Australia **80** 38.21S 141.38E
Portland Ind. U.S.A. **94** 40.25N 84.58W
Portland Maine U.S.A. **95** 43.41N 70.18W
Portland Oreg. U.S.A. **90** 45.32N 122.40W
Portland, C. Australia **80** 40.43S 148.08E
Portland, I. of England **31** 50.32N 2.25W
Port Laoise Rep. of Ire. **39** 53.03N 7.20W
Port Logan Scotland **34** 54.43N 4.57W
Port Loko Sierra Leone **70** 8.50N 12.50W
Port Macquarie Australia **80** 31.28S 152.25E
Portmahomack Scotland **37** 57.49N 3.50W
Portmarnock Rep. of Ire. **38** 53.25N 6.09W
Port Moresby P.N.G. **61** 9.30S 147.07E
Portnacroish Scotland **36** 56.25N 5.22W
Portnaguiran Scotland **36** 58.15N 6.10W
Portnahaven Scotland **34** 55.41N 6.31W
Port Nelson Canada **93** 57.10N 92.35W
Port Nolloth R.S.A. **74** 29.17S 16.51E
Port-Nouveau Québec Canada **93** 58.35N 65.59W
Pôrto *see* Oporto Portugal **41**
Pôrto Alegre Brazil **103** 30.03S 51.10W
Porto Alexandre Angola **72** 15.55S 11.51E
Porto Amboim Angola **72** 10.45S 13.43E
Port of Ness Scotland **36** 58.30N 6.13W
Port of Spain Trinidad **97** 10.38N 61.31W
Pörtom Finland **46** 62.44N 21.35E

Porton England **28** 51.08N 1.44W
Porto-Novo Benin **71** 6.30N 2.47E
Porto Torres Italy **42** 40.49N 8.24E
Porto Vecchio France **40** 41.35N 9.16E
Portpatrick Scotland **34** 54.51N 5.07W
Port Phillip B. Australia **80** 38.05S 144.50E
Port Pirie Australia **80** 33.11S 138.01E
Portreath England **31** 50.15N 5.17W
Portree Scotland **36** 57.24N 6.12W
Portrush N. Ireland **34** 55.12N 6.40W
Port Safâga Egypt **56** 26.45N 33.55E
Port Said Egypt **56** 31.17N 32.18E
Port St. Johns R.S.A. **74** 31.37S 29.32E
Port St. Louis France **40** 43.25N 4.40E
Port Shepstone R.S.A. **74** 30.44S 30.28E
Portskerra Scotland **37** 58.33N 3.55W
Portsmouth England **28** 50.48N 1.06W
Portsmouth N.H. U.S.A. **95** 43.03N 70.47W
Portsmouth Ohio U.S.A. **94** 38.45N 82.59W
Portsoy Scotland **37** 57.41N 2.41W
Portstewart N. Ireland **34** 55.11N 6.43W
Port Sudan Sudan **69** 19.39N 37.01E
Port Talbot Wales **31** 51.35N 3.48W
Portugal Europe **41** 39.30N 8.05W
Portugalia Angola **72** 7.25S 20.43E
Portumna Rep. of Ire. **39** 53.06N 8.14W
Port Vendres France **40** 42.31N 3.06E
Port Victoria Kenya **73** 0.07N 34.00E
Port William Scotland **34** 54.46N 4.35W
Porz W. Germany **45** 50.53N 7.05E
Posadas Argentina **103** 27.25S 55.48W
Poso Indonesia **61** 1.23S 120.45E
Postmasburg R.S.A. **74** 28.20S 23.05E
Potchefstroom R.S.A. **74** 26.42S 27.06E
Potenza Italy **42** 40.40N 15.47E
Potgietersrus R.S.A. **74** 24.15S 28.55E
Poti U.S.S.R. **47** 42.11N 41.41E
Potiskum Nigeria **71** 11.40N 11.03E
Potomac *r.* U.S.A. **95** 38.35N 77.00W
Potosí Bolivia **103** 19.34S 65.45W
Potosi *d.* Bolivia **103** 21.50S 66.00W
Potsdam E. Germany **44** 52.24N 13.04E
Potters Bar England **27** 51.42N 0.11W
Potter Street England **27** 51.46N 0.08E
Pottstown U.S.A. **95** 40.15N 75.38W
Pottsville U.S.A. **95** 40.41N 76.13W
Poughkeepsie U.S.A. **95** 41.43N 73.56W
Póvoa de Varzim Portugal **41** 41.22N 8.46W
Povorino U.S.S.R. **47** 51.12N 42.15E
Powder *r.* U.S.A. **90** 46.40N 105.15W
Powell, L. U.S.A. **90** 37.30N 110.45W
Powys *d.* Wales **30** 52.26N 3.26W
Poyang Hu *l.* China **63** 29.05N 116.20E
Poyntzpass N. Ireland **38** 54.16N 6.23W
Požarevac Yugo. **43** 44.38N 21.12E
Poza Rica Mexico **96** 20.34N 97.26W
Poznań Poland **44** 52.25N 16.53E
Pozoblanco Spain **41** 38.23N 4.51W
Prachuap Khiri Khan Thailand **59** 11.50N 99.49E
Prades France **40** 42.38N 2.25E
Prague Czech. **44** 50.05N 14.25E
Praha *see* Prague Czech. **44**
Prato Italy **42** 43.52N 10.50E
Pratt's Bottom England **27** 51.21N 0.06E
Prawle Pt. England **31** 50.12N 3.43W
Preesall England **32** 53.55N 2.58W
Preparis *i.* Burma **60** 14.40N 93.40E
Prescot England **32** 53.27N 2.49W
Prescott U.S.A. **90** 34.34N 112.28W
Presidente Epitácio Brazil **103** 21.56S 52.07W
Presidente Prudente Brazil **103** 22.09S 51.24W
Prespa, L. Albania/Greece/Yugo. **43** 40.53N 21.02E
Presque Isle *town* U.S.A. **95** 46.42N 68.01W
Prestatyn Wales **30** 53.20N 3.24W
Prestea Ghana **70** 5.26N 2.07W
Presteigne Wales **30** 52.17N 3.00W
Preston England **32** 53.46N 2.42W
Prestonpans Scotland **35** 55.57N 3.00W
Prestwick Scotland **34** 55.30N 4.36W
Prestwood England **27** 51.42N 0.43W
Pretoria R.S.A. **74** 25.45S 28.12E
Préveza Greece **43** 38.58N 20.43E
Příbram Czech. **44** 49.42N 14.00E
Prieska R.S.A. **74** 29.40S 22.45E
Prikumsk U.S.S.R. **47** 44.46N 44.10E
Prilep Yugo. **43** 41.20N 21.32E
Priluki U.S.S.R. **47** 50.35N 32.24E
Primorsk U.S.S.R. **46** 60.18N 28.35E
Prince Albert Canada **92** 53.13N 105.45W
Prince Albert R.S.A. **74** 33.15S 22.03E
Prince Alfred C. Canada **92** 74.30N 125.00W
Prince Charles I. Canada **93** 67.50N 76.00W
Prince Edward I. Canada **93** 46.15N 64.00W
Prince Edward Is. Indian Oc. **107** 47.00S 37.00E
Prince Edward Island *d.* Canada **93** 46.15N 63.10W

Prince George Canada **92** 53.55N 122.49W
Prince of Wales, C. U.S.A. **92** 66.00N 168.30W
Prince of Wales I. Australia **61** 10.55S 142.05E
Prince of Wales I. Canada **93** 73.00N 99.00W
Prince of Wales I. U.S.A. **92** 55.00N 132.30W
Prince Patrick I. Canada **92** 77.00N 120.00W
Prince Rupert Canada **92** 54.09N 130.20W
Princes Risborough England **28** 51.43N 0.50W
Princeton U.S.A. **94** 38.21N 87.33W
Princetown England **31** 50.33N 4.00W
Principe *i.* Africa **71** 1.37N 7.27E
Prinzapolca Nicaragua **96** 13.19N 83.35W
Pripet *r.* U.S.S.R. **47** 51.08N 30.30E
Pripet Marshes *f.* U.S.S.R. **47** 52.15N 28.00E
Priština Yugo. **43** 42.39N 21.10E
Prizren Yugo. **43** 42.13N 20.42E
Progreso Mexico **96** 21.20N 89.40W
Prokopyevsk U.S.S.R. **48** 53.55N 86.45E
Prome Burma **59** 18.50N 95.14E
Providence U.S.A. **95** 41.50N 71.25W
Provideniya U.S.S.R. **92** 64.30N 173.11W
Provins France **40** 48.34N 3.18E
Provo U.S.A. **90** 40.15N 111.40W
Prudhoe England **35** 54.58N 1.51W
Prüm W. Germany **45** 50.12N 6.25E
Prüm *r.* W. Germany **45** 49.50N 6.29E
Prut *r.* Romania/U.S.S.R. **43** 45.29N 28.14E
Przemyśl Poland **47** 49.48N 22.48E
Przhevalsk U.S.S.R. **62** 42.31N 78.22E
Psará *i.* Greece **43** 38.34N 25.35E
Psel *r.* U.S.S.R. **47** 49.03N 33.26E
Pskov U.S.S.R. **46** 57.48N 28.00E
Pskov, L. U.S.S.R. **47** 58.00N 28.00E
Pucallpa Peru **102** 7.06S 75.36W
Puddletown England **28** 50.45N 2.21W
Pudsey England **32** 53.47N 1.40W
Puebla Mexico **96** 19.03N 98.10W
Puebla *d.* Mexico **96** 18.30N 98.00W
Pueblo U.S.A. **90** 38.17N 104.38W
Puente Genil Spain **41** 37.24N 4.46W
Puerto Armuelles Panamá **96** 8.19N 82.15W
Puerto Barrios Guatemala **96** 15.41N 88.32W
Puerto Cabello Venezuela **97** 10.29N 68.02W
Puerto Cabezas Nicaragua **96** 14.02N 83.24W
Puerto Carreño Colombia **97** 6.00N 67.35W
Puerto Cortes Honduras **96** 15.50N 87.55W
Puerto de Santa Maria Spain **41** 36.36N 6.14W
Puerto Ibicuy Argentina **103** 33.44S 59.10W
Puerto Juárez Mexico **96** 21.26N 86.51W
Puerto la Cruz Venezuela **97** 10.14N 64.40W
Puertollano Spain **41** 38.41N 4.07W
Puerto Montt Chile **102** 41.28S 73.04W
Puerto Penasco Mexicó **90** 31.20N 113.35W
Puerto Pinasco Paraguay **103** 22.36S 57.53W
Puerto Plata Dom. Rep. **97** 19.48N 70.41W
Puerto Princesa Phil. **60** 9.46N 118.45E
Puerto Quepos Costa Rica **96** 9.28N 84.10W
Puerto Rico C. America **97** 18.20N 66.30W
Puerto Rico Trench Atlantic Oc. **97** 19.50N 66.00W
Puerto Sastre Paraguay **103** 22.02S 58.00W
Puerto Suárez Bolivia **103** 18.59S 57.46W
Puffin I. Rep. of Ire. **39** 51.50N 10.25W
Puffin I. Wales **30** 53.18N 4.04W
Pujehun Sierra Leone **70** 7.23N 11.44W
Pukaki, L. New Zealand **82** 44.00S 170.10E
Pukekohe New Zealand **82** 37.12S 174.56E
Pula Yugo. **42** 44.52N 13.53E
Pulaski U.S.A. **95** 43.34N 76.06W
Pulborough England **29** 50.58N 0.30W
Pulog, Mt. Phil. **61** 16.50N 120.50E
Pułtusk Poland **47** 52.42N 21.02E
Pulvar *r.* Iran **57** 29.50N 52.47E
Pumlumon Fawr *mtn.* Wales **30** 52.28N 3.47W
Pumpsaint Wales **30** 52.03N 3.58W
Punjab *d.* India **58** 30.30N 75.15E
Punta Alta *town* Argentina **103** 38.50S 62.00W
Punta Arenas *town* Chile **102** 53.10S 70.56W
Punta Gorda *town* Belize **96** 16.10N 88.45W
Puntarenas Costa Rica **96** 10.00N 84.50W
Pur *r.* U.S.S.R. **48** 67.30N 75.30E
Purfleet England **27** 51.29N 0.15E
Puri India **59** 19.49N 85.54E
Purley England **27** 51.21N 0.07W
Purnea India **58** 25.47N 87.28E
Pursat Khmer Rep. **59** 12.33N 103.55E
Purulia India **58** 23.20N 86.24E
Puru Vesi *l.* Finland **46** 62.00N 29.50E
Pusan S. Korea **63** 35.05N 129.02E
Pushkin U.S.S.R. **47** 59.43N 30.22E
Pustoshka U.S.S.R. **47** 56.20N 29.20E
Putao Burma **59** 27.22N 97.27E
Putien China **63** 25.32N 119.02E
Putjak Djaja *mtn.* Indonesia **61** 4.00S 137.15E
Putney England **27** 51.28N 0.14W
Putoran Mts. U.S.S.R. **49** 68.30N 96.00E
Puttalam Sri Lanka **59** 8.02N 79.50E

Puula Vesi to **Resolute** 158

Puula Vesi *l.* Finland **46** 63.45N 25.25E
Puy de Dôme *mtn.* France **40** 45.46N 2.56E
Puysegur Pt. New Zealand **82** 46.10S 166.35E
Pweto Zaïre **73** 8.27S 28.52E
Pwllheli Wales **30** 52.53N 4.25W
Pya, L. U.S.S.R. **46** 66.00N 31.00E
Pyasina *r.* U.S.S.R. **49** 73.10N 84.55E
Pyatigorsk U.S.S.R. **47** 44.04N 43.06E
Pyha *r.* Finland **46** 64.30N 24.20E
Pyhä-järvi *l.* Finland **46** 61.00N 22.10E
Pyhajoki Finland **46** 64.28N 24.15E
Pyinmana Burma **59** 19.45N 96.12E
Pyongyang N. Korea **63** 39.00N 125.47E
Pyramid L. U.S.A. **90** 40.00N 119.35W
Pyrénées *mts.* France/Spain **40** 42.40N 0.30E
Pytalovo U.S.S.R. **46** 57.30N 27.57E

Q

Qara Egypt **56** 29.38N 26.30E
Qasr Farafra Egypt **56** 27.05N 28.00E
Qasrqand Iran **57** 26.13N 60.37E
Qatar Asia **57** 25.20N 51.10E
Qatif Saudi Arabia **57** 26.31N 5.00E
Qattara Depression *f.* Egypt **56** 29.40N 27.30E
Qayen Iran **57** 33.44N 59.07E
Qazvin Iran **57** 36.16N 50.00E
Qena Egypt **56** 26.08N 32.42E
Qena, Wadi *r.* Egypt **56** 26.07N 32.42E
Qishm Iran **57** 26.58N 57.17E
Qishm *i.* Iran **57** 26.48N 55.48E
Qishn S. Yemen **58** 15.25N 51.40E
Qizil Uzun *r.* Iran **57** 36.44N 49.27E
Qom Iran **57** 34.40N 50.57E
Quang Ngai Vietnam **60** 15.09N 108.50E
Quang Tri Vietnam **60** 16.46N 107.11E
Quantock Hills England **28** 51.06N 3.12W
Qu'Appelle *r.* Canada **90** 49.40N 99.40W
Quchan Iran **57** 37.04N 58.29E
Queanbeyan Australia **80** 35.24S 149.17E
Quebec Canada **95** 46.50N 71.15W
Quebec *d.* Canada **93** 51.00N 70.00W
Quebrabasa Gorge *f.* Moçambique **73** 15.34S 33.00E
Quedlinburg E. Germany **44** 51.48N 11.09E
Queenborough England **29** 51.24N 0.46E
Queen Charlotte Is. Canada **92** 53.00N 132.30W
Queen Charlotte Str. Canada **92** 51.00N 129.00W
Queen Elizabeth Is. Canada **93** 78.30N 99.00W
Queen Maud G. Canada **93** 68.30N 99.00W
Queen Maud Land Antarctica **104** 74.00S 10.00E
Queensberry *mtn.* Scotland **35** 55.16N 3.36W
Queensferry Scotland **35** 56.01N 3.24W
Queensland *d.* Australia **79** 23.30S 144.00E
Queenstown Australia **80** 42.07S 145.33E
Queenstown New Zealand **82** 45.03S 168.41E
Queenstown R.S.A. **74** 31.54S 26.53E
Quela Angola **72** 9.18S 17.05E
Quelimane Moçambique **73** 17.53S 36.57E
Quelpart *i.* S. Korea **63** 33.20N 126.30E
Que Que Rhodesia **74** 18.55S 29.51E
Querétaro Mexico **96** 20.38N 100.23W
Querétaro *d.* Mexico **96** 21.03N 100.00W
Quesnel Canada **92** 53.03N 122.31W
Quetta Pakistan **58** 30.15N 67.00E
Quezaltenango Guatemala **96** 14.50N 91.30W
Quezon City Phil. **61** 14.59N 121.01E
Qufa *des.* U.A.E. **57** 23.30N 53.30E
Quibala Angola **72** 10.48S 14.56E
Quibaxi Angola **72** 8.34S 14.37E
Quiberon France **40** 47.29N 3.07W
Quicama Nat. Park Angola **72** 9.40S 13.30E
Quilengues Angola **72** 14.09S 14.04E
Quill Lakes Canada **90** 51.50N 104.10W
Quimbele Angola **72** 6.29S 16.25E
Quimilí Argentina **103** 27.35S 62.25W
Quimper France **40** 48.00N 4.06W
Quimperlé France **40** 47.52N 3.33W
Quincy Ill. U.S.A. **94** 39.55N 91.22W
Quincy Mass. U.S.A. **95** 42.14N 71.00W
Quintana Roo *d.* Mexico **96** 19.00N 88.00W
Quinto Spain **41** 41.25N 0.30W
Quirigua *ruins* Guatemala **96** 15.20N 89.25W
Quirindi Australia **80** 31.32S 150.44E
Quissanga Moçambique **73** 12.24S 40.33E
Quissico Moçambique **74** 24.42S 34.44E
Quito Ecuador **102** 0.14S 78.30W
Quoich, Loch Scotland **36** 57.04N 5.15W
Quorn Australia **80** 32.20S 138.02E
Quoyness Scotland **37** 58.54N 3.17W
Quseir Egypt **56** 26.04N 34.15E
Qutur Iran **57** 38.28N 44.25E

R

Raalte Neth. **45** 52.22N 6.17E
Raasay *i.* Scotland **36** 57.25N 6.05W
Raasay, Sd. of Scotland **36** 57.25N 6.05W
Raba Indonesia **60** 8.27S 118.45E
Rabat Morocco **68** 34.02N 6.51W
Racine U.S.A. **94** 42.42N 87.50W
Radcliffe England **32** 53.35N 2.19W
Radebeul E. Germany **44** 51.06N 13.41E
Radhwa, Jebel *mtn.* Saudi Arabia **56** 24.36N 38.18E
Radlett England **27** 51.42N 0.20W
Radom Poland **47** 51.26N 21.10E
Radomir Bulgaria **43** 42.32N 22.56E
Radstock England **28** 51.17N 2.25W
Rae Bareli India **58** 26.14N 81.14E
Rafaela Argentina **103** 31.16S 61.44W
Rafai C.A.R. **72** 4.56N 23.55E
Rafsanjan Iran **57** 30.24N 56.00E
Raglan Wales **31** 51.46N 2.51W
Ragusa Italy **42** 36.56N 14.44E
Rahbur Iran **57** 29.18N 56.56E
Raichur India **58** 16.15N 77.20E
Raiganj India **58** 25.38N 88.11E
Raigarh India **58** 21.53N 83.28E
Rainford England **32** 53.30N 2.48W
Rainham G.L. England **27** 51.31N 0.12E
Rainham Kent England **27** 51.23N 0.36E
Rainier, Mt. U.S.A. **90** 46.52N 121.45W
Rainy L. Canada **94** 48.40N 93.15W
Raipur India **59** 21.16N 81.42E
Raja *mtn.* Indonesia **60** 0.45S 112.45E
Rajahmundry India **59** 17.01N 81.52E
Rajang *r.* Malaysia **60** 2.10N 112.45E
Rajapalaiyam India **58** 9.26N 77.36E
Rajasthan *d.* India **58** 27.00N 74.00E
Rajgarh India **58** 24.01N 76.42E
Rajkot India **58** 22.18N 70.53E
Rajshahi Bangla. **58** 24.24N 88.40E
Rakaia *r.* New Zealand **82** 43.52S 172.13E
Rakvere U.S.S.R. **46** 59.22N 26.28E
Raleigh U.S.A. **91** 35.46N 78.39W
Rama Nicaragua **96** 12.09N 84.15W
Ramah Saudi Arabia **57** 25.33N 47.08E
Rame Head England **31** 50.18N 4.13W
Ramelton Rep. of Ire. **38** 55.02N 7.40W
Ramhormoz Iran **57** 31.14N 49.37E
Ramillies Belgium **45** 50.39N 4.56E
Ramishk Iran **57** 26.52N 58.46E
Râmnicu Sarat Romania **43** 45.24N 27.06E
Ramor, Lough Rep. of Ire. **38** 53.49N 7.05W
Rampur India **58** 28.48N 79.03E
Ramree I. Burma **59** 19.10N 93.40E
Ramsar Iran **57** 36.54N 50.41E
Ramsbottom England **32** 53.38N 2.20W
Ramsey England **29** 52.27N 0.06W
Ramsey I.o.M. **32** 54.19N 4.23W
Ramsey *i.* Wales **30** 51.53N 5.21W
Ramsey B. I.o.M. **32** 54.20N 4.20W
Ramsgate England **29** 51.20N 1.25E
Ranchi India **58** 23.22N 85.20E
Randalstown N. Ireland **34** 54.45N 6.20W
Randers Denmark **46** 56.28N 10.03E
Ranfurly New Zealand **82** 45.08S 170.08E
Rangiora New Zealand **82** 43.18S 172.38E
Rangitaiki *r.* New Zealand **82** 37.55S 176.50E
Rangoon Burma **59** 16.45N 96.20E
Rangpur Bangla. **58** 25.45N 89.21E
Rannoch, Loch Scotland **37** 56.41N 4.20W
Rannoch Moor *f.* Scotland **37** 56.38N 4.40W
Rann of Kutch *f.* India **58** 23.50N 69.50E
Ranobe *r.* Malagasy Rep. **73** 17.20S 44.05E
Rantauparapat Indonesia **60** 2.05N 99.46E
Rantekombola *mtn.* Indonesia **60** 3.30S 119.58E
Rapallo Italy **40** 44.20N 9.14E
Rapid City U.S.A. **90** 44.06N 103.14W
Raqqa Syria **56** 35.57N 39.03E
Ras al Hadd *c.* Oman **57** 22.32N 59.49E
Ras Banas *c.* Egypt **56** 23.54N 35.48E
Ras Dashan *mtn.* Ethiopia **69** 13.20N 38.10E
Rasht Iran **57** 37.18N 49.38E
Ras Madraka *c.* Oman **58** 19.00N 57.55E
Ras Muhammad *c.* Egypt **56** 27.42N 34.13E
Rass Saudi Arabia **56** 25.54N 43.30E
Ras Tanura *c.* Saudi Arabia **57** 26.40N 50.10E
Rastatt W. Germany **44** 48.51N 8.13E
Rathangan Rep. of Ire. **39** 53.13N 7.00W
Rathcoole Rep. of Ire. **38** 53.17N 6.30W
Rathcormack Rep. of Ire. **39** 52.05N 8.18W
Rathdowney Rep. of Ire. **39** 52.51N 7.36W
Rathdrum Rep. of Ire. **39** 52.56N 6.15W
Rathenow E. Germany **44** 52.37N 12.21E
Rathfriland N. Ireland **38** 54.14N 6.10W
Rathkeale Rep. of Ire. **39** 52.30N 8.57W
Rathlin I. N. Ireland **34** 55.17N 6.15W
Rathlin Sd. N. Ireland **34** 55.15N 6.15W
Rath Luirc Rep. of Ire. **39** 52.21N 8.41W
Rathmore Rep. of Ire. **39** 52.05N 9.12W
Rathmullen Rep. of Ire. **38** 55.06N 7.32W
Rathnew Rep. of Ire. **39** 53.01N 6.07W
Rathvilly Rep. of Ire. **39** 52.52N 6.43W
Ratlam India **58** 23.18N 75.06E
Raton U.S.A. **90** 36.54N 104.27W
Rattray Head Scotland **37** 57.37N 1.50W
Rättvik Sweden **46** 60.56N 15.10E
Rauch Argentina **103** 36.45S 59.05W
Raukumara Range *mts.* New Zealand **82** 38.00S 177.45E
Rauma Finland **46** 61.09N 21.30E
Raunds England **29** 52.21N 0.33W
Ravar Iran **57** 31.14N 56.51E
Ravenna Italy **42** 44.25N 12.12E
Ravensburg W. Germany **44** 47.47N 9.37E
Ravi *r.* Pakistan **58** 30.30N 72.13E
Rawalpindi Pakistan **58** 33.40N 73.08E
Rawlinna Australia **79** 31.00S 125.21E
Rawlins U.S.A. **90** 41.46N 107.16W
Rawmarsh England **33** 53.27N 1.20W
Rawtenstall England **32** 53.42N 2.18W
Rayen Iran **57** 29.34N 57.26E
Rayleigh England **27** 51.36N 0.36E
Razan Iran **57** 35.22N 49.02E
Razgrad Bulgaria **43** 43.32N 26.30E
Ré, Ile de *i.* France **40** 46.10N 1.26W
Reading England **28** 51.27N 0.57W
Reading U.S.A. **95** 40.20N 75.55W
Reay Forest *f.* Scotland **37** 58.17N 4.48W
Recife Brazil **102** 8.06S 35.34W
Recklinghausen W. Germany **45** 51.36N 7.11E
Reconquista Argentina **103** 29.08S 59.38W
Recreo Argentina **103** 29.18S 65.05W
Red *r.* Canada **91** 50.30N 96.50W
Red *r.* Vietnam **62** 20.15N 106.25E
Red *r.* U.S.A. **91** 31.10N 92.00W
Red B. N. Ireland **34** 55.04N 6.02W
Red Bluff U.S.A. **90** 40.11N 122.16W
Redbourn England **27** 51.48N 0.24W
Redbridge England **27** 51.35N 0.06E
Redcar England **33** 54.37N 1.04W
Red Deer Canada **92** 52.15N 113.48W
Red Deer *r.* Canada **90** 50.55N 110.00W
Redding U.S.A. **90** 40.35N 122.24W
Redditch England **28** 52.18N 1.57W
Rede *r.* England **35** 55.08N 2.13W
Redhill England **27** 51.14N 0.11W
Red L. U.S.A. **91** 48.00N 95.00W
Red Lake *town* Canada **91** 50.59N 93.40W
Redpoint Scotland **36** 57.39N 5.49W
Redruth England **31** 50.14N 5.14W
Red Sea Africa/Asia **69** 20.00N 39.00E
Red Tower Pass Romania **43** 45.37N 24.17E
Red Volta *r.* Ghana **70** 10.32N 0.31W
Red Wharf B. Wales **30** 53.20N 4.10W
Ree, Lough Rep. of Ire. **38** 53.31N 7.58W
Reedham England **29** 52.34N 1.33E
Reefton New Zealand **82** 42.05S 171.51E
Rega *r.* Poland **44** 54.10N 15.18E
Regen *r.* W. Germany **44** 49.02N 12.03E
Regensburg W. Germany **44** 49.01N 12.07E
Reggan Algeria **68** 26.30N 0.30E
Reggio Calabria Italy **42** 38.07N 15.38E
Reggio Emilia-Romagnaltaly **42** 44.40N 10.37E
Regina Canada **90** 50.30N 104.38W
Rehoboth S.W. Africa **74** 23.18S 17.03E
Reigate England **27** 51.14N 0.13W
Reims France **40** 49.15N 4.02E
Reindeer L. Canada **92** 57.00N 102.20W
Reinosa Mexico **96** 26.09N 97.10W
Reinosa Spain **41** 43.01N 4.09W
Reiss Scotland **37** 58.28N 3.09W
Rembang Indonesia **60** 6.45S 111.22E
Remich Lux. **45** 49.34N 6.23E
Remscheid W. Germany **45** 51.10N 7.11E
Renaix Belgium **45** 50.45N 3.36E
Rendsburg W. Germany **44** 54.19N 9.39E
Renfrew Canada **95** 45.28N 76.44W
Renfrew Scotland **34** 55.52N 4.23W
Rengat Indonesia **60** 0.26S 102.35E
Reni U.S.S.R. **43** 45.28N 28.17E
Renish Pt. Scotland **36** 57.43N 6.58W
Renkum Neth. **45** 51.59N 5.46E
Renmark Australia **80** 34.10S 140.45E
Rennes France **40** 48.06N 1.40W
Reno *r.* Italy **42** 44.36N 12.17E
Reno U.S.A. **90** 39.32N 119.49W
Renvyle Pt. Rep. of Ire. **38** 53.37N 10.04W
Republican *r.* U.S.A. **91** 39.05N 94.50W
Republic of Ireland Europe **39** 53.00N 8.00W
Republic of South Africa Africa **74** 28.30S 24.50E
Requena Spain **41** 39.29N 1.08W
Resistencia Argentina **103** 27.28S 59.00W
Resolute Canada **93** 74.40N 95.00W

For Khmer Republic *read* Kampuchea. *For* Malagasy Republic *read* Madagascar. *For* Rhodesia *read* Zimbabwe.

Resolution I. to **Rush** 159

Resolution I. New Zealand **82** 45.40S 166.30E
Resort, Loch Scotland **36** 58.03N 6.56W
Rethel France **45** 49.31N 4.22E
Réthimnon Greece **43** 35.22N 24.29E
Réunion *i.* Indian Oc. **107** 22.00S 55.00E
Reus Spain **41** 41.10N 1.06E
Reutlingen W. Germany **44** 48.30N 9.13E
Revelstoke Canada **90** 51.00N 118.12W
Revilla Gigedo Is. Mexico **89** 19.00N 111.00W
Revue *r.* Moçambique **74** 19.58S 34.40E
Rewa India **58** 24.32N 81.18E
Reykjavik Iceland **46** 64.09N 21.58W
Rezaiyeh Iran **57** 37.32N 45.02E
Rēzekne U.S.S.R. **46** 56.30N 27.22E
Rhayader Wales **30** 52.19N 3.30W
Rheden Neth. **45** 52.01N 6.02E
Rheine W. Germany **45** 52.17N 7.26E
Rhenen Neth. **45** 51.58N 5.34E
Rheydt W. Germany **45** 51.10N 6.25E
Rhine *r.* Europe **45** 51.53N 6.03E
Rhinelander U.S.A. **94** 45.39N 89.23W
Rhinns of Kells *hills* Scotland **34** 55.08N 4.21W
Rhinns Pt. Scotland **34** 55.40N 6.29W
Rhino Camp *town* Uganda **73** 2.58N 31.20E
Rhode Island *d.* U.S.A. **95** 43.30N 71.35W
Rhodes Greece **43** 36.24N 28.15E
Rhodes *i.* Greece **43** 36.12N 28.00E
Rhodesia Africa **74** 18.55S 30.00E
Rhodope Mts. Bulgaria **43** 41.35N 24.35E
Rhondda Wales **31** 51.39N 3.30W
Rhondda Valley *f.* Wales **31** 51.38N 3.29W
Rhône *r.* France **40** 43.25N 4.45E
Rhosllanerchrugog Wales **30** 53.03N 3.04W
Rhosneigr Wales **30** 53.14N 4.31W
Rhum *i.* Scotland **36** 57.00N 6.20W
Rhum, Sd. of *str.* Scotland **36** 56.57N 6.15W
Rhyddhywel *mtn.* Wales **30** 52.25N 3.27W
Rhyl Wales **30** 53.19N 3.29W
Riau Is. Indonesia **60** 0.50N 104.00E
Rib *r.* England **27** 51.48N 0.04W
Ribadeo Spain **41** 43.32N 7.04W
Ribauè Moçambique **73** 14.57S 38.27E
Ribble *r.* England **32** 53.45N 2.44W
Ribblesdale *f.* England **32** 54.03N 2.17W
Ribeirão Prêto Brazil **103** 21.09S 47.48W
Riberac France **40** 45.14N 0.22E
Riccall England **33** 53.50N 1.04W
Richelieu *r.* Canada **95** 46.02N 73.03W
Richfield U.S.A. **94** 44.51N 93.17W
Richland U.S.A. **90** 46.20N 119.17W
Richmond England **32** 54.24N 1.43W
Richmond Cape Province R.S.A. **74** 31.25S 23.57E
Richmond Ind. U.S.A. **94** 39.50N 84.51W
Richmond Va. U.S.A. **91** 37.34N 77.27W
Richmond Park *f.* England **27** 51.26N 0.13W
Richmond-upon-Thames England **27** 51.26N 0.17W
Rickmansworth England **27** 51.39N 0.29W
Ridderkirk Neth. **45** 51.53N 4.39E
Riesa E. Germany **44** 51.18N 13.18E
Rieti Italy **42** 42.24N 12.53E
Rift Valley *d.* Kenya **73** 1.00N 36.00E
Riga U.S.S.R. **46** 56.53N 24.08E
Riga, G. of U.S.S.R. **46** 57.30N 23.50E
Rigan Iran **57** 28.40N 58.58E
Rigmati Iran **57** 27.40N 58.11E
Rihand Dam India **58** 24.09N 83.02E
Riihimaki Finland **46** 60.45N 24.45E
Rijeka Yugo. **42** 45.20N 14.25E
Rijswijk Neth. **45** 52.03N 4.22E
Rima, Wadi *r.* Saudi Arabia **56** 26.10N 44.00E
Rimini Italy **42** 44.01N 12.34E
Rimouski Canada **95** 48.27N 68.32W
Ringköbing Denmark **46** 56.06N 8.15E
Ringvassöy *i.* Norway **46** 70.00N 19.00E
Ringwood England **28** 50.50N 1.48W
Rinrawros Pt. Rep. of Ire. **38** 55.01N 8.34W
Rio Claro *town* Brazil **103** 22.19S 47.35W
Rio de Janeiro *town* Brazil **103** 22.53S 43.17W
Rio Grande *town* Brazil **103** 32.03S 52.08W
Rio Grande *r.* Mexico/U.S.A. **96** 25.55N 97.08W
Río Grande *r.* Nicaragua **96** 12.48N 83.30W
Rio Grande do Sul *d.* Brazil **103** 30.15S 53.30W
Riohacha Colombia **97** 11.34N 72.58W
Rio Negro *d.* Argentina **103** 41.15S 67.15W
Riosucio Colombia **97** 7.25N 77.05W
Rio Verde *town* Brazil **103** 17.50S 50.55W
Ripley Derbys. England **33** 53.03N 1.24W
Ripley Surrey England **27** 51.18N 0.29W
Ripon England **33** 54.08N 1.31W
Risca Wales **31** 51.36N 3.06W
Risha, Wadi *r.* Saudi Arabia **57** 25.40N 44.08E
Risor Norway **46** 58.44N 9.15E
Ristikent U.S.S.R. **46** 68.40N 31.47E
Rivas Nicaragua **96** 11.26N 85.50W
Riverhead England **27** 51.17N 0.11E
Riverina *f.* Australia **80** 35.00S 146.00E
Rivers *d.* Nigeria **71** 4.45N 6.35E
Riversdale R.S.A. **74** 34.05S 21.14E
Rivière-du-Loup *town* Canada **95** 47.49N 69.32W
Riyadh Saudi Arabia **57** 24.39N 46.44E
Rize Turkey **56** 41.03N 40.31E
Rizzuto, C. Italy **43** 38.53N 17.06E
Rjukan Norway **46** 59.54N 8.33E
Roanne France **40** 46.02N 4.05E
Roanoke *r.* U.S.A. **91** 36.00N 76.35W
Roaringwater B. Rep. of Ire. **39** 51.32N 9.26W
Robertson R.S.A. **74** 33.48S 19.53E
Roberval Canada **95** 48.31N 72.16W
Robin Hood's Bay *town* England **33** 54.26N 0.31W
Robinvale Australia **80** 34.37S 142.50E
Roboré Bolivia **103** 18.20S 59.45W
Robson, Mt. Canada **92** 53.00N 121.00W
Roca, Cabo de Portugal **41** 38.40N 9.31W
Roçadas Angola **72** 16.31S 15.00E
Roccella Italy **43** 38.19N 16.24E
Rocha Uruguay **103** 34.30S 54.22W
Rochdale England **32** 53.36N 2.10W
Rochechouart France **40** 45.49N 0.50E
Rochefort Belgium **45** 50.10N 5.13E
Rochefort France **40** 45.57N 0.58W
Rochester Kent England **27** 51.22N 0.30E
Rochester Northum. England **35** 55.16N 2.16W
Rochester Minn. U.S.A. **94** 44.01N 92.27W
Rochester N.Y. U.S.A. **95** 43.12N 77.37W
Rochfort Bridge Rep. of Ire. **38** 53.25N 7.19W
Rock *r.* U.S.A. **94** 41.30N 90.35W
Rockford U.S.A. **94** 42.16N 89.06W
Rockhampton Australia **79** 23.22S 150.32E
Rockingham Forest *f.* England **28** 52.30N 0.35W
Rock Island *town* U.S.A. **94** 41.30N 90.34W
Rockland U.S.A. **95** 44.06N 69.08W
Rocklands Resr. Australia **80** 37.13S 141.52E
Rock Springs *town* U.S.A. **90** 41.35N 109.13W
Rockville U.S.A. **95** 39.05N 77.10W
Rocky Mts. N. America **92** 50.00N 114.00W
Rocroi France **45** 49.56N 4.31E
Rodel Scotland **36** 57.44N 6.58W
Roden *r.* England **32** 52.42N 2.36W
Rodez France **40** 44.21N 2.34E
Roding *r.* England **27** 51.31N 0.05E
Rodonit, C. Albania **43** 41.34N 19.25E
Roe *r.* N. Ireland **34** 55.06N 7.00W
Roermond Neth. **45** 51.12N 6.00E
Rogan's Seat *mtn.* England **32** 54.25N 2.05W
Rogers City U.S.A. **94** 45.24N 83.50W
Rokan *r.* Indonesia **60** 2.00N 101.00E
Rokel *r.* Sierra Leone **70** 8.36N 12.55W
Rolla U.S.A. **91** 37.56N 91.55W
Roma *i.* Indonesia **61** 7.45S 127.20E
Romain, C. U.S.A. **91** 33.01N 71.23W
Romaine *r.* Canada **93** 50.20N 63.45W
Romania Europe **47** 46.30N 24.00E
Romano, C. U.S.A. **91** 25.50N 81.42W
Romans France **40** 45.03N 5.03E
Rome Italy **42** 41.54N 12.29E
Rome U.S.A. **95** 43.13N 75.28W
Romford England **27** 51.35N 0.11E
Romilly France **40** 48.31N 3.44E
Romney Marsh *f.* England **29** 51.03N 0.55E
Romorantin France **40** 47.22N 1.44E
Romsey England **28** 51.00N 1.29W
Rona *i.* Scotland **36** 57.33N 5.58W
Ronas Hill Scotland **36** 60.32N 1.26W
Ronas Voe *b.* Scotland **36** 60.31N 1.29W
Ronay *i.* Scotland **36** 57.29N 7.10W
Ronda Spain **41** 36.45N 5.10W
Rönne Denmark **46** 55.07N 14.43E
Roof Butte *mtn.* U.S.A. **90** 36.29N 109.05W
Roosendaal Neth. **45** 51.32N 4.28E
Roper *r.* Australia **79** 14.40S 135.30E
Roque Sáenz Peña Argentina **103** 26.50S 60.28W
Rora Head Scotland **37** 58.52N 3.26W
Röros Norway **46** 62.35N 11.23E
Rosa, Monte Italy/Switz. **40** 45.56N 7.51E
Rosario Argentina **103** 33.00S 60.40W
Rosario Paraguay **103** 24.28S 57.13W
Rosario Uruguay **103** 34.20S 57.26W
Roscommon Rep. of Ire. **38** 53.38N 8.13W
Roscommon *d.* Rep. of Ire. **38** 53.38N 8.11W
Roscrea Rep. of Ire. **39** 52.57N 7.49W
Roseau Dominica **97** 15.18N 61.23W
Roseburg U.S.A. **90** 43.13N 123.21W
Rosehearty Scotland **37** 57.42N 2.07W
Rosenheim W. Germany **44** 47.51N 12.09E
Rosetown Canada **92** 51.34N 107.59W
Rosetta Egypt **56** 31.25N 30.25E
Roseville U.S.A. **94** 44.59N 93.11W
Rosières France **45** 49.49N 2.43E
Roskilde Denmark **46** 55.39N 12.07E
Roslags-Näsby Sweden **46** 59.01N 18.02E
Roslavl U.S.S.R. **47** 53.55N 32.53E
Ross New Zealand **82** 42.54S 170.48E
Rossall Pt. England **32** 53.55N 3.03W
Ross Dependency Antarctica **104** 75.00S 170.00W
Rosses B. Rep. of Ire. **38** 55.01N 8.29W
Rosskeeragh Pt. Rep. of Ire. **38** 54.21N 8.41W
Rosslare Rep. of Ire. **39** 52.17N 6.23W
Rosslea N. Ireland **38** 54.15N 7.12W
Ross of Mull *pen.* Scotland **34** 56.19N 6.10W
Ross-on-Wye England **28** 51.55N 2.36W
Ross Sea Antarctica **107** 73.00S 179.00E
Rostock E. Germany **44** 54.06N 12.09E
Rostov R.S.F.S.R. U.S.S.R. **47** 47.15N 39.45E
Rostov R.S.F.S.R. U.S.S.R. **47** 57.11N 39.23E
Rösvatn *l.* Norway **46** 65.50N 14.00E
Rosyth Scotland **35** 56.03N 3.26W
Rota *i.* Asia **61** 14.10N 145.15E
Rothbury England **35** 55.19N 1.54W
Rothbury Forest *f.* England **35** 55.18N 1.52W
Rother *r.* E. Sussex England **29** 50.56N 0.46E
Rother *r.* W. Sussex England **29** 50.57N 0.32W
Rotherham England **33** 53.26N 1.21W
Rothes Scotland **37** 57.31N 3.13W
Rothesay Scotland **34** 55.50N 5.03W
Rothwell Northants. England **28** 52.25N 0.48W
Rothwell W. Yorks. England **33** 53.46N 1.29W
Roti *i.* Indonesia **61** 10.30S 123.10E
Roto Australia **80** 33.04S 145.27E
Rotorua New Zealand **82** 38.07S 176.17E
Rotorua, L. New Zealand **82** 38.00S 176.00E
Rotterdam Neth. **45** 51.55N 4.29E
Roubaix France **45** 50.42N 3.10E
Rouen France **40** 49.26N 1.05E
Roulers Belgium **45** 50.57N 3.06E
Round Mt. Australia **80** 30.26S 152.15E
Roundup U.S.A. **90** 46.27N 108.34W
Rousay *i.* Scotland **37** 59.10N 3.02W
Rouyn Canada **95** 48.15N 79.00W
Rovaniemi Finland **46** 66.29N 25.40E
Rovinj Yugo. **42** 45.06N 13.39E
Roxburgh New Zealand **82** 45.34S 169.21E
Roxburgh Scotland **35** 55.34N 2.23W
Royale, I. U.S.A. **94** 48.00N 88.45W
Royal Leamington Spa England **28** 52.18N 1.32W
Royal Tunbridge Wells England **29** 51.07N 0.16E
Roydon England **27** 51.46N 0.03E
Roye France **45** 49.42N 2.48E
Royston Herts. England **29** 52.03N 0.01W
Royston S. Yorks. England **33** 53.37N 1.27W
Rozel Channel Is. **31** 49.19N 2.03W
Rtishchevo U.S.S.R. **47** 52.16N 43.45E
Ruabon Wales **30** 53.00N 3.03W
Ruahine Range *mts.* New Zealand **82** 40.00S 176.00E
Ruapehu *mtn.* New Zealand **82** 39.20S 175.30E
Ruapuke I. New Zealand **82** 46.45S 168.30E
Rub al Khali *des.* Saudi Arabia **58** 20.20N 52.30E
Rubha A'Mhàil *c.* Scotland **34** 55.57N 6.08W
Rubha Ardvule *c.* Scotland **36** 57.15N 7.28W
Rubha Coigeach *c.* Scotland **36** 58.06N 5.25W
Rubha Hunish *c.* Scotland **36** 57.42N 6.21W
Rubh'an Dunain *c.* Scotland **36** 57.09N 6.19W
Rubha Réidh *c.* Scotland **36** 57.51N 5.49W
Rubi *r.* Zaïre **72** 2.50N 24.06E
Rudan *r.* Iran **57** 27.02N 56.53E
Rudbar Afghan. **57** 30.10N 62.38E
Ruddstadt E. Germany **44** 50.44N 11.20E
Rud-i-Pusht *r.* Iran **57** 29.09N 58.09E
Rud-i-Shur *r.* Kermā n Iran **57** 31.14N 55.29E
Rud-i-Shur *r.* Khorā sā n Iran **57** 34.05N 60.22E
Rudok China **62** 33.30N 79.40E
Ruffec France **40** 46.02N 0.12E
Rufford England **32** 53.38N 2.50W
Rufiji *r.* Tanzania **73** 8.02S 39.19E
Rufino Argentina **103** 34.16S 62.45W
Rufisque Senegal **70** 14.43N 17.16W
Rugby England **28** 52.23N 1.16W
Rugby U.S.A. **90** 48.24N 99.59W
Rugeley England **32** 52.47N 1.56W
Rügen *i.* E. Germany **44** 54.30N 13.30E
Ruhr *f.* W. Germany **45** 51.22N 7.26E
Ruhr *r.* W. Germany **45** 51.27N 6.41E
Ruislip England **27** 51.35N 0.25W
Rukwa *d.* Tanzania **73** 7.05S 31.25E
Rukwa, L. Tanzania **73** 8.00S 32.20E
Ruma Yugo. **43** 44.59N 19.51E
Rum Cay *i.* Bahamas **97** 23.41N 74.53W
Rumney Wales **31** 51.32N 3.07W
Rump Mtn. U.S.A. **95** 45.12N 71.04W
Runabay Head N. Ireland **34** 55.09N 6.02W
Runcorn England **32** 53.20N 2.44W
Rungwa Singida Tanzania **73** 6.57S 33.35E
Rungwa *r.* Tanzania **73** 7.38S 31.55E
Rungwe Mt. Tanzania **73** 9.10S 33.40E
Rupert *r.* Canada **91** 51.25N 78.45W
Rur *r.* Neth. **45** 51.12N 5.58E
Rusape Rhodesia **74** 18.35S 32.08E
Ruse Bulgaria **43** 43.50N 25.59E
Rush Rep. of Ire. **38** 53.32N 6.06W

For Khmer Republic *read* Kampuchea. *For* Malagasy Republic *read* Madagascar. *For* Rhodesia *read* Zimbabwe.

Rushden England **28** 52.17N 0.37W
Russian Soviet Federal Socialist Republic d. U.S.S.R. **48**
 62.00N 80.00E
Rustenburg R.S.A. **74** 25.40S 27.15E
Rutana Burundi **73** 3.58S 30.00E
Rütenbrock W. Germany **45** 52.51N 7.06E
Ruteng Indonesia **61** 8.35S 120.28E
Rutherglen Scotland **34** 55.49N 4.12W
Ruthin Wales **30** 53.07N 3.18W
Rutland U.S.A. **95** 43.37N 72.59W
Rutshuru Zaïre **73** 1.10S 29.26E
Ruvu Coast Tanzania **73** 6.50S 38.42E
Ruvuma r. Moçambique/Tanzania **73** 10.30S 40.30E
Ruvuma d. Tanzania **73** 10.45S 36.15E
Ruwandiz Iraq **57** 36.38N 44.32E
Ruwenzori Range mts. Uganda/Zaïre **73** 0.30N 30.00E
Ruyigi Burundi **73** 3.26S 30.14E
Rwanda Africa **73** 2.00S 30.00E
Ryan, Loch Scotland **34** 54.56N 5.02W
Ryazan U.S.S.R. **47** 54.37N 39.43E
Ryazhsk U.S.S.R. **47** 53.40N 40.07E
Rybachi Pen. U.S.S.R. **46** 69.45N 32.30E
Rybinsk U.S.S.R. **47** 58.01N 38.52E
Rybinsk Resr. U.S.S.R. **47** 58.30N 38.25E
Ryde England **28** 50.44N 1.09W
Ryder's Hill England **31** 50.31N 3.53W
Rye England **29** 50.57N 0.46E
Rye r. England **33** 54.10N 0.44W
Rye B. England **29** 50.53N 0.48E
Ryton England **35** 54.59N 1.47W
Ryukyu Is. Japan **63** 26.30N 125.00E
Rzeszów Poland **47** 50.04N 22.00E
Rzhev U.S.S.R. **47** 56.15N 34.18E

S

Saale r. E. Germany **44** 51.58N 11.53E
Saar r. W. Germany **45** 49.43N 6.34E
Saarbrücken W. Germany **44** 49.15N 6.58E
Saarburg W. Germany **45** 49.36N 6.33E
Saaremaa i. U.S.S.R. **46** 58.30N 22.30E
Saarijärvi Finland **46** 62.44N 25.15E
Saarlouis W. Germany **44** 49.19N 6.45E
Saba i. Neth. Antilles **96** 17.42N 63.26W
Šabac Yugo. **43** 44.45N 19.41E
Sabadell Spain **41** 41.33N 2.07E
Sabana, Archipelago de Cuba **97** 23.30N 80.00W
Sabi r. Rhodesia **74** 21.16S 32.20E
Sabinas Mexico **90** 26.33N 101.10W
Sabinas r. Mexico **96** 27.31N 100.40W
Sabine r. U.S.A. **91** 29.40N 93.50W
Sable, C. Canada **93** 43.30N 65.50W
Sable, C. U.S.A. **96** 25.05N 81.10W
Sable I. Canada **93** 44.00N 60.00W
Sabzawar Afghan. **57** 33.18N 62.05E
Sabzawar Iran **57** 36.13N 57.38E
Sacedón Spain **41** 40.29N 2.44W
Sacquoy Head Scotland **37** 59.12N 3.05W
Sacramento U.S.A. **90** 38.32N 121.30W
Sacramento r. U.S.A. **90** 38.05N 122.00W
Sádaba Spain **41** 42.19N 1.10W
Sadani Tanzania **73** 6.00S 38.40E
Saddle Head Rep. of Ire. **38** 54.02N 10.12W
Saddleworth Moor hills England **32** 53.32N 1.55W
Sadiya India **59** 27.49N 95.38E
Safaha des. Saudi Arabia **56** 26.30N 39.30E
Safaniya Saudi Arabia **57** 28.00N 48.48E
Safed Koh mtn. Afghan. **57** 34.15N 63.30E
Säffle Sweden **46** 59.08N 12.55E
Saffron Walden England **29** 52.02N 0.15E
Safi Morocco **68** 32.20N 9.17W
Safonovo U.S.S.R. **47** 55.08N 33.16E
Sagaing Burma **59** 22.00N 96.00E
Sagar India **58** 23.50N 78.44E
Saginaw U.S.A. **94** 43.25N 83.54W
Saginaw B. U.S.A. **94** 44.00N 83.30W
Sagua la Grande Cuba **97** 22.55N 80.05W
Saguenay r. Canada **95** 48.10N 69.43W
Sagunto Spain **41** 39.40N 0.17W
Sahagún Spain **41** 42.23N 5.02W
Sahara des. Africa **68** 18.00N 12.00E
Saharan Atlas mts. Algeria **68** 34.20N 2.00E
Saharanpur India **58** 29.58N 77.33E
Sahba, Wadi r. Saudi Arabia **57** 23.48N 49.50E
Saida Algeria **41** 34.50N 0.10E
Saidabad Iran **57** 29.28N 55.43E
Saidpur Bangla. **58** 25.48N 89.00E
Saimaa l. Finland **46** 61.20N 28.00E
Saimbeyli Turkey **56** 38.07N 36.08E
Saindak Pakistan **57** 29.16N 61.36E
St. Abb's Head Scotland **35** 55.54N 2.07W
St. Agnes England **31** 50.18N 5.13W
St. Agnes i. England **31** 49.53N 6.20W

St. Albans England **27** 51.46N 0.21W
St. Alban's Head England **28** 50.35N 2.04W
St. Aldhelm's Head England **28** 50.35N 2.04W
St. Amand France **45** 50.27N 3.26E
St. Amand-Mt. Rond town France **40** 46.43N 2.29E
St. André, Cap Malagasy Rep. **73** 16.10S 44.27E
St. Andrews Canada **95** 45.05N 67.04W
St. Andrews Scotland **35** 56.20N 2.48W
St. Andrews B. Scotland **35** 56.23N 2.43W
St. Ann's Bay town Jamaica **97** 18.26N 77.12W
St. Ann's Head Wales **31** 51.41N 5.11W
St. Anthony Canada **93** 51.24N 55.37W
St. Arnaud Australia **80** 36.40S 143.20E
St. Aubin Channel Is. **31** 49.12N 2.10W
St. Augustine U.S.A. **91** 29.54N 81.19W
St. Austell England **31** 50.20N 4.48W
St. Austell B. England **31** 50.16N 4.43W
St. Barthélemy C. America **97** 17.55N 62.50W
St. Bees England **32** 54.29N 3.36W
St. Bees Head England **32** 54.31N 3.39W
St. Blazey England **31** 50.22N 4.48W
St. Boniface Canada **91** 49.58N 97.07W
St. Boswells Scotland **35** 55.35N 2.40W
St. Brides B. Wales **30** 51.48N 5.03W
St. Brieuc France **40** 48.31N 2.45W
St. Catherines Canada **95** 43.10N 79.15W
St. Catherine's Pt. England **28** 50.34N 1.18W
St. Céré France **40** 44.52N 1.53E
St. Christophe i. Malagasy Rep. **73** 17.06S 42.53E
St. Clair, L. Canada **94** 42.25N 82.35W
St. Clears Wales **30** 51.48N 4.30W
St. Cloud U.S.A. **91** 45.34N 94.10W
St. Columb Major England **31** 50.26N 4.56W
St. Croix r. U.S.A. **94** 44.43N 92.47W
St. Croix i. Virgin Is. **97** 17.45N 64.35W
St. David's Wales **30** 51.54N 5.16W
St. David's Head Wales **30** 51.55N 5.19W
St. Denis France **40** 48.56N 2.21E
St. Dié France **44** 48.17N 6.57E
St. Dizier France **40** 48.38N 4.58E
St. Elias, Mt. U.S.A. **92** 60.20N 139.00W
Saintes France **40** 45.44N 0.38W
St. Etienne France **40** 45.26N 4.26E
Saintfield N. Ireland **38** 54.28N 5.50W
St. Fillans Scotland **34** 56.24N 4.07W
St. Finan's B. Rep. of Ire. **39** 51.49N 10.21W
St. Flour France **40** 45.02N 3.05E
St. Gallen Switz. **44** 47.25N 9.23E
St. Gaudens France **40** 43.07N 0.44E
St. George Australia **80** 28.03S 148.30E
St. George's Grenada **97** 12.04N 61.44W
St. George's Channel Rep. of Ire./U.K. **39** 51.30N 6.20W
St. Germain France **40** 48.53N 2.04E
St. Gheorghe's Mouth est. Romania **43** 44.51N 29.37E
St. Gilles-sur-Vie France **40** 46.42N 1.56W
St. Girons France **40** 42.59N 1.08E
St. Gotthard Pass Switz. **44** 46.30N 8.55E
St. Govan's Head Wales **31** 51.36N 4.55W
St. Helena i. Atlantic Oc. **112** 16.00S 6.00W
St. Helena B. R.S.A. **74** 32.35S 18.00E
St. Helens England **32** 53.28N 2.43W
St. Helens U.S.A. **90** 45.51N 122.50W
St. Helier Channel Is. **31** 49.12N 2.07W
St. Hubert Belgium **45** 50.02N 5.22E
St. Hyacinthe Canada **95** 45.38N 72.57W
St. Ives Cambs. England **29** 52.20N 0.05W
St. Ives Cornwall England **31** 50.13N 5.29W
St. Ives B. England **31** 50.14N 5.26W
St. Jean Pied de Port France **40** 43.10N 1.14W
St. Jérôme Canada **95** 45.47N 74.01W
St. John Canada **91** 45.16N 66.03W
St. John r. Canada **93** 45.30N 66.05W
St. John, L. Canada **95** 48.40N 72.00W
St. John's Antigua **97** 17.07N 61.51W
St. John's Canada **93** 47.34N 52.41W
St. John's Pt. N. Ireland **38** 54.14N 5.39W
St. John's Pt. Rep. of Ire. **38** 54.34N 8.28W
St. Joseph U.S.A. **91** 39.45N 94.51W
St. Joseph, L. Canada **91** 51.00N 91.05W
St. Just England **31** 50.07N 5.41W
St. Keverne England **31** 50.03N 5.05W
St. Kitts i. C. America **97** 17.25N 62.45W
St. Lawrence r. Canada **95** 48.45N 68.30W
St. Lawrence, G. of Canada **93** 48.00N 52.00W
St. Lawrence I. U.S.A. **92** 63.00N 170.00W
St. Leonard Canada **95** 47.10N 67.55W
St. Lô France **40** 49.07N 1.05W
St. Louis Senegal **70** 16.01N 16.30W
St. Louis U.S.A. **94** 38.40N 90.15W
St. Lucia C. America **97** 14.05N 61.00W
St. Magnus B. Scotland **36** 60.25N 1.35W
St. Maixent France **40** 46.25N 0.12W
St. Malo France **40** 48.39N 2.00W
St. Malo, Golfe de France **40** 49.20N 2.00W
St. Marc Haiti **97** 19.08N 72.41W
St. Margaret's at Cliffe England **29** 51.10N 1.23E
St. Margaret's Hope Scotland **37** 58.49N 2.57W

St. Martin Channel Is. **31** 49.27N 2.34W
St. Martin C. America **97** 18.05N 63.05W
St. Martin's i. England **31** 49.57N 6.16W
St. Mary Channel Is. **31** 49.14N 2.10W
St. Marys Australia **80** 41.33S 148.12E
St. Mary's i. England **31** 49.55N 6.16W
St. Mary's Scotland **37** 58.54N 2.55W
St. Mary's Loch Scotland **35** 55.29N 3.12W
St. Maurice r. Canada **95** 46.20N 72.30W
St. Mawes England **31** 50.10N 5.01W
St. Moritz Switz. **44** 46.30N 9.51E
St. Nazaire France **40** 47.17N 2.12W
St. Neots England **29** 52.14N 0.16W
St. Nicolas Belgium **45** 51.10N 4.09E
St. Ninian's I. Scotland **36** 59.58N 1.21W
St. Omer France **29** 50.45N 2.15E
St. Pancras England **27** 51.32N 0.08W
St. Paul France **40** 42.49N 2.29E
St. Paul i. Indian Oc. **113** 38.44S 77.30E
St. Paul U.S.A. **94** 45.00N 93.10W
St. Paul's Cray England **27** 51.24N 0.06E
St. Peter Port Channel Is. **31** 49.27N 2.32W
St. Petersburg U.S.A. **91** 27.45N 82.40W
St. Pierre-Miquelon i. N. America **93** 47.00N 56.15W
St. Pölten Austria **44** 48.13N 15.37E
St. Quentin France **45** 49.51N 3.17E
St. Sampson Channel Is. **31** 49.29N 2.31W
St. Stephen Canada **95** 45.12N 67.18W
St. Thomas Canada **94** 42.46N 81.12W
St. Thomas i. Virgin Is. **97** 18.22N 64.57W
St. Trond Belgium **45** 50.49N 5.11E
St. Tropez France **40** 43.16N 6.39E
St. Vallier France **40** 45.11N 4.49E
St. Vincent C. America **97** 13.10N 61.15W
St. Vincent, C. Portugal **41** 37.01N 8.59W
St. Vith Belgium **45** 50.15N 6.08E
St. Wendel W. Germany **45** 49.27N 7.10E
St. Yrieix France **40** 45.31N 1.12E
Saipan i. Asia **61** 15.12N 145.43E
Sakaka Saudi Arabia **56** 29.59N 40.12E
Sakania Zaïre **73** 12.44S 28.34E
Sakarya r. Turkey **56** 41.08N 30.36E
Sakété Benin **71** 6.45N 2.45E
Sakhalin i. U.S.S.R. **63** 50.00N 143.00E
Sakrivier R.S.A. **74** 30.50S 20.26E
Sakti India **58** 22.02N 82.56E
Sal r. U.S.S.R. **47** 47.33N 40.40E
Sala Sweden **46** 59.55N 16.38E
Salado r. La Pampa Argentina **103** 36.15S 66.45W
Salado r. Santa Fé Argentina **102** 32.00S 61.00W
Salado r. Mexico **96** 26.46N 98.55W
Salala Oman **58** 17.00N 54.04E
Salamanca Spain **41** 40.58N 5.40W
Salbris France **40** 47.26N 2.03E
Saldanha B. R.S.A. **74** 33.00S 17.56E
Sale Australia **80** 38.06S 147.06E
Sale England **32** 53.26N 2.19W
Salekhard U.S.S.R. **48** 66.33N 66.35E
Salem India **59** 11.38N 78.08E
Salem U.S.A. **94** 38.37N 88.58W
Salen Highland Scotland **34** 56.43N 5.46W
Salen Strath. Scotland **34** 56.31N 5.56W
Salerno Italy **42** 40.41N 14.45E
Salerno, G. of Med. Sea **42** 40.30N 14.45E
Salford England **32** 53.30N 2.17W
Salfords England **27** 51.12N 0.12W
Salima Malaŵi **73** 13.45S 34.29E
Salina Cruz Mexico **96** 16.11N 95.12W
Salins France **40** 46.56N 4.53E
Salisbury Rhodesia **74** 17.43S 31.05E
Salisbury England **28** 51.04N 1.48W
Salisbury U.S.A. **91** 38.22N 75.37W
Salisbury Plain f. England **28** 51.15N 1.55W
Salmon r. U.S.A. **90** 45.50N 116.50W
Salmon River Mts. U.S.A. **90** 44.30N 114.30W
Salo Finland **46** 60.23N 23.10E
Salobreña Spain **41** 36.45N 3.35W
Salon France **40** 43.38N 5.06E
Salonga r. Zaïre **72** 0.09S 19.52E
Salop d. England **28** 52.35N 2.40W
Salsk U.S.S.R. **47** 46.30N 41.33E
Salso r. Italy **42** 37.07N 13.57E
Salt Jordan **56** 32.03N 35.44E
Salta Argentina **103** 24.46S 65.28W
Salta d. Argentina **103** 25.05S 65.00W
Saltash England **31** 50.25N 4.13W
Saltburn-by-the-Sea England **33** 54.35N 0.58W
Saltcoats Scotland **34** 55.37N 4.47W
Saltee Is. Rep. of Ire. **39** 52.08N 6.36W
Saltfleet England **33** 53.25N 0.11E
Saltillo Mexico **96** 25.30N 101.00W
Salt Lake City U.S.A. **90** 40.45N 111.55W
Salto Uruguay **103** 31.27S 57.50W
Salton Sea l. U.S.A. **90** 33.25N 115.45W
Salûm Egypt **56** 31.31N 25.09E

For Khmer Republic read Kampuchea. For Malagasy Republic read Madagascar. For Rhodesia read Zimbabwe.

Salvador to **Schwecht** 161

Salvador Brazil **102** 12.58S 38.20W
Salwa Qatar **57** 24.44N 50.50E
Salween *r.* Burma **59** 16.30N 97.33E
Salyany U.S.S.R. **57** 39.36N 48.59E
Salzach *r.* Austria **44** 48.35N 13.30E
Salzburg Austria **44** 47.54N 13.03E
Salzgitter W. Germany **44** 52.02N 10.22E
Samana Dom. Rep. **97** 19.14N 69.20W
Samana Cay *i.* Bahamas **97** 23.05N 73.45W
Samar *i.* Phil. **61** 11.45N 125.15E
Samarinda Indonesia **60** 0.30S 117.09E
Samarkand U.S.S.R. **48** 39.40N 66.57E
Samarra Iraq **57** 34.13N 43.52E
Samawa Iraq **57** 31.18N 45.18E
Sambalpur India **59** 21.28N 84.04E
Samborombon Bay Argentina **103** 36.00S 56.50W
Sambre *r.* Belgium **45** 50.29N 4.52E
Same Tanzania **73** 4.10S 37.43E
Samer France **29** 50.38N 1.45E
Samirum Iran **57** 31.31N 52.10E
Sam Neua Laos **60** 20.25N 104.04E
Samoa Is. Pacific Oc. **107** 13.00S 171.00W
Sámos *i.* Greece **43** 37.44N 26.45E
Samothráki *i.* Greece **43** 40.26N 25.35E
Sampit Indonesia **60** 2.34S 112.59E
Samsun Turkey **56** 41.17N 36.22E
San Mali **70** 13.21N 4.57W
Sana Yemen **69** 16.02N 49.44E
Sana *r.* Yugo. **42** 45.03N 16.22E
Sanaga *r.* Cameroon **71** 3.35N 9.40E
Sanandaj Iran **57** 35.18N 47.01E
San Antonio U.S.A. **90** 29.25N 98.30W
San Antonio, C. Cuba **96** 21.50N 84.57W
San Antonio, Punta *c.* Mexico **90** 29.45N 115.41W
San Antonio Oeste Argentina **103** 40.45S 65.05W
San Bernardino U.S.A. **90** 34.07N 117.18W
San Blas, C. U.S.A. **91** 29.40N 85.25W
San Carlos Phil. **61** 15.59N 120.22E
San Cristóbal Argentina **103** 30.20S 61.14W
San Cristóbal Dom. Rep. **97** 18.27N 70.07W
San Cristóbal Venezuela **97** 7.46N 72.15W
Sancti Spíritus Cuba **97** 21.55N 79.28W
Sanda *i.* Scotland **34** 55.17N 5.34W
Sandakan Malaysia **60** 5.52N 118.04E
Sanday *i.* Scotland **37** 59.15N 2.33W
Sanday Sd. Scotland **37** 59.11N 2.35W
Sandbach England **32** 53.09N 2.23W
Sandbank Scotland **34** 55.59N 4.58W
Sanderstead England **27** 51.21N 0.05W
Sandgate Australia **80** 27.18S 153.00E
Sandgate England **29** 51.05N 1.09E
San Diego U.S.A. **90** 32.45N 117.10W
Sandling England **27** 51.18N 0.33E
Sandnes Norway **46** 58.51N 5.45E
Sandness Scotland **36** 60.18N 1.38W
Sandö *i.* Faroe Is. **46** 61.50N 6.45W
Sandoa Zaïre **72** 9.41S 22.56E
Sandoway Burma **59** 18.28N 94.20E
Sandown England **28** 50.39N 1.09W
Sandpoint U.S.A. **90** 48.17N 116.34W
Sandray *i.* Scotland **36** 56.53N 7.31W
Sandringham England **33** 52.50N 0.30E
Sandusky U.S.A. **94** 41.27N 82.42W
Sandviken Sweden **46** 60.38N 16.50E
Sandwich England **29** 51.16N 1.21E
Sandwick Scotland **36** 60.00N 1.14W
Sandy England **29** 52.08N 0.18W
Sandy L. Canada **91** 53.00N 93.00W
San Felipe Mexico **90** 31.03N 114.52W
San Felipe Venezuela **97** 10.25N 68.40W
San Felíu de Guixols Spain **41** 41.47N 3.02E
San Félix Venezuela **97** 8.22N 62.37W
San Fernando Phil. **61** 16.39N 120.19E
San Fernando Spain **41** 36.28N 6.12W
San Fernando Trinidad **97** 10.16N 61.28W
San Fernando Venezuela **97** 7.53N 67.15W
San Francisco Argentina **103** 31.29S 62.06W
San Francisco U.S.A. **90** 37.45N 122.27W
San Francisco de Macorís Dom. Rep. **97** 19.19N 70.15W
Sangerhausen E. Germany **44** 51.29N 11.18E
Sangha *r.* Congo **72** 1.10S 16.47E
Sangi *i.* Indonesia **61** 3.30N 125.30E
Sangihe Is. Indonesia **61** 2.45N 125.20E
Sangkan Ho *r.* China **63** 40.23N 115.18E
Sangonera *r.* Spain **41** 37.58N 1.04W
San Javier Bolivia **103** 16.22S 62.38W
San Jorge *r.* Colombia **97** 9.10N 74.40W
San Jorge, G. of Spain **41** 40.50N 1.10E
San José Costa Rica **96** 9.59N 84.04W
San José Guatemala **96** 13.58N 90.50W
San José Uruguay **103** 34.20S 56.42W
San Jose U.S.A. **90** 37.20N 121.55W
San José de Chiquitos Bolivia **103** 17.53S 60.45W
San Juan *r.* Costa Rica **96** 10.50N 83.40W
San Juan Puerto Rico **97** 18.29N 66.08W
San Juan *r.* U.S.A. **90** 37.20N 110.05W
San Juan del Norte Nicaragua **96** 10.58N 83.40W
San Juan de los Morros Venezuela **97** 9.53N 67.23W
San Juan Mts. U.S.A. **90** 37.30N 107.00W
Sankuru *r.* Zaïre **72** 4.20S 20.27E
San Leonardo Spain **41** 41.49N 3.04W
Sanlúcar de Barrameda Spain **41** 36.46N 6.21W
San Lucas, C. N. America **106** 22.50N 110.00W
San Luis Argentina **103** 33.20S 66.23W
San Luis *d.* Argentina **103** 33.00S 66.10W
San Luis Cuba **97** 20.13N 75.50W
San Luis Obispo U.S.A. **90** 35.16N 120.40W
San Luis Potosí Mexico **96** 22.10N 101.00W
San Luis Potosí *d.* Mexico **96** 23.00N 100.00W
San Marino Europe **42** 43.55N 12.27E
San Marino *town* San Marino **42** 43.55N 12.27E
San Matias, G. of Argentina **103** 41.30S 64.00W
San Miguel El Salvador **96** 13.28N 88.10W
San Miguel de Tucumán Argentina **103** 26.47S 65.15W
San Nicolás Argentina **103** 33.25S 60.15W
San Pablo Phil. **61** 13.58N 121.10E
San Pedro Argentina **103** 24.30S 65.00W
San Pedro Dom. Rep. **97** 18.30N 69.18W
San Pedro Mexico **96** 24.50N 102.59W
San Pedro Paraguay **103** 24.08S 57.08W
San Pedro, Punta *c.* Costa Rica **96** 8.30N 83.30W
San Pedro, Sierra de *mts.* Spain **41** 39.20N 6.20W
San Pedro Sula Honduras **96** 15.26N 88.01W
San Pietro *i.* Italy **42** 39.09N 8.16E
Sanquhar Scotland **35** 55.22N 3.56W
San Remo Italy **40** 43.48N 7.46E
San Salvador *i.* Bahamas **97** 24.00N 74.32W
San Salvador El Salvador **96** 13.40N 89.10W
San Salvador de Jujuy Argentina **103** 24.10S 65.18W
Sansanné-Mango Togo **70** 10.23N 0.30E
San Sebastián Spain **41** 43.19N 1.59W
San Severo Italy **42** 41.40N 15.24E
Santa Ana El Salvador **96** 14.00N 79.31W
Santa Barbara U.S.A. **90** 34.25N 119.41W
Santa Catarina *d.* Brazil **103** 27.00S 52.00W
Santa Clara Cuba **97** 22.25N 79.58W
Santa Cruz Bolivia **103** 17.45S 63.14W
Santa Cruz *d.* Bolivia **103** 17.45S 62.00W
Santa Elena, C. Costa Rica **96** 10.54N 85.56W
Santa Fé Argentina **103** 31.38S 60.43W
Santa Fé *d.* Argentina **103** 31.00S 61.00W
Santa Fe U.S.A. **90** 35.41N 105.57W
Santa María Brazil **103** 29.40S 53.47W
Santa Maria U.S.A. **90** 34.56N 120.25W
Santa Maria di Leuca, C. Italy **43** 39.47N 18.24E
Santa Marta Colombia **97** 11.18N 74.10W
Santander Spain **41** 43.28N 3.48W
Santañy Spain **41** 39.20N 3.07E
Santarém Portugal **41** 39.14N 8.40W
Santa Rosa Honduras **96** 14.47N 88.46W
Santa Rosa de Toay Argentina **103** 36.36S 64.15W
Santa Rosalia Mexico **90** 27.20N 112.20W
Santiago Chile **102** 34.00S 70.40W
Santiago Dom. Rep. **97** 19.30N 70.42W
Santiago Panamá **96** 8.08N 80.59W
Santiago de Compostela Spain **41** 42.52N 8.33W
Santiago de Cuba Cuba **97** 20.00N 75.49W
Santiago del Estero Argentina **103** 27.48S 64.15W
Santiago del Estero *d.* Argentina **103** 28.00S 63.50W
Santo André Brazil **103** 23.39S 46.29W
Santo Antonio do Zaire Angola **72** 6.12S 12.25E
Santo Domingo Dom. Rep. **97** 18.30N 69.57W
Santoña Spain **41** 43.27N 3.26W
Santos Brazil **103** 23.56S 46.22W
Santo Tomé Argentina **103** 28.31S 56.03W
San Vicente El Salvador **96** 13.38N 88.42W
Sanza Pombo Angola **72** 7.20S 16.12E
São Borja Brazil **103** 28.35S 56.01W
São Carlos Brazil **103** 22.02S 47.53W
São Francisco *r.* Brazil **102** 10.10S 36.10W
São Francisco do Sul Brazil **103** 26.17S 48.39W
São Luís Brazil **102** 2.44S 44.16W
Saona *i.* Dom. Rep. **97** 18.09N 68.42W
Saône *r.* France **40** 45.46N 4.52E
São Paulo Brazil **103** 23.33S 46.39W
São Paulo *d.* Brazil **103** 22.05S 48.00W
São Roque, C. S. America **106** 5.00S 35.00W
São Salvador do Congo Angola **72** 6.18S 14.16E
São Sebastião I. Brazil **103** 24.00S 45.25W
São Tomé *i.* Africa **72** 0.20N 6.30E
Saoura *d.* Algeria **70** 22.50N 0.10W
Sapporo Japan **63** 43.05N 141.21E
Sapri Italy **42** 40.04N 15.38E
Saqqiz Iran **57** 36.14N 46.15E
Sarab Iran **57** 37.56N 47.35E
Sara Buri Thailand **60** 14.32N 100.53E
Sarajevo Yugo. **43** 43.52N 18.26E
Sarangarh India **59** 21.38N 83.09E
Saransk U.S.S.R. **47** 54.12N 45.10E
Saratov U.S.S.R. **47** 51.30N 45.55E
Saratov Resr. U.S.S.R. **47** 51.00N 46.00E
Sarbaz Iran **57** 26.39N 61.20E
Sardinia *i.* Italy **42** 40.00N 9.00E
Sarek *mtn.* Sweden **46** 67.10N 17.45E
Sarh Chad **71** 9.08N 18.22E
Sari Iran **57** 36.33N 53.06E
Sarigan *i.* Asia **61** 16.43N 145.47E
Sark *i.* Channel Is. **31** 49.26N 2.22W
Sarmi Asia **61** 1.51S 138.45E
Särna Sweden **46** 61.40N 13.10E
Sarnia Canada **94** 42.57N 82.24W
Sarny U.S.S.R. **47** 51.21N 26.31E
Saros, G. of Turkey **43** 40.32N 26.25E
Sarpsborg Norway **46** 59.17N 11.06E
Sarre *r. see* Saar France **44**
Sarrebourg France **44** 48.43N 7.03E
Sarria Spain **41** 42.47N 7.25W
Sartène France **42** 41.38N 8.48E
Sarthe *r.* France **40** 47.29N 0.30W
Sarur Oman **57** 23.25N 58.10E
Sasaram India **58** 24.58N 84.01E
Sasebo Japan **63** 33.10N 129.42E
Saskatchewan *d.* Canada **92** 55.00N 105.00W
Saskatchewan *r.* Canada **93** 53.25N 100.15W
Saskatoon Canada **90** 52.10N 106.40W
Sasovo U.S.S.R. **47** 54.21N 41.58E
Sassandra Ivory Coast **70** 4.58N 6.08W
Sassandra *r.* Ivory Coast **70** 5.00N 6.04W
Sássari Italy **42** 40.43N 8.33E
Sassnitz E. Germany **44** 54.32N 13.40E
Sasyk, L. U.S.S.R. **43** 45.38N 29.38E
Satadougou Mali **70** 12.30N 11.30W
Satara India **58** 17.43N 74.05E
Satna India **58** 24.33N 80.50E
Satpura Range *mts.* India **58** 21.50N 76.00E
Satu Mare Romania **47** 47.48N 22.52E
Sauda Norway **46** 59.38N 6.23E
Saudi Arabia Asia **56** 26.00N 44.00E
Saulieu France **40** 47.17N 4.14E
Sault Sainte Marie Canada **94** 46.32N 84.20W
Sault Sainte Marie U.S.A. **94** 46.29N 84.22W
Saumur France **40** 47.16N 0.05W
Saundersfoot Wales **31** 51.43N 4.42W
Sava *r.* Yugo. **43** 44.50N 20.26E
Savannah U.S.A. **91** 32.09N 81.01W
Savannah *r.* U.S.A. **91** 32.10N 81.00W
Savannakhet Laos **60** 16.34N 104.55E
Savé Benin **71** 8.04N 2.37E
Save *r.* France **41** 43.30N 0.55E
Save *r.* Moçambique **74** 21.00S 35.01E
Saveh Iran **57** 35.00N 50.25E
Savona Italy **40** 44.18N 8.28E
Savonlinna Finland **46** 61.52N 28.51E
Savu Sea Pacific Oc. **61** 9.30S 122.30E
Sawbridgeworth England **27** 51.50N 0.09E
Sawston England **29** 52.07N 0.11E
Sawu *i.* Indonesia **61** 10.30S 121.50E
Saxmundham England **29** 52.13N 1.29E
Saxthorpe England **29** 52.50N 1.09E
Sayan Mts. U.S.S.R. **62** 51.30N 102.00E
Sayn Shand Mongolia **63** 44.58N 110.10E
Sayula Mexico **96** 19.52N 103.36W
Sázava *r.* Czech. **44** 49.53N 14.21E
Sbeitla Tunisia **42** 35.16N 9.10E
Scafell Pike *mtn.* England **32** 54.27N 3.12W
Scalasaig Scotland **34** 56.04N 6.12W
Scalby England **33** 54.18N 0.26W
Scalloway Scotland **36** 60.08N 1.17W
Scalpay *i.* Highland Scotland **36** 57.18N 5.58W
Scalpay *i.* W. Isles Scotland **36** 57.52N 6.40W
Scammon Bay *town* U.S.A. **92** 61.50N 165.35W
Scandinavia *f.* Europe **107** 65.00N 18.00E
Scapa Flow *str.* Scotland **37** 58.53N 3.05W
Scarba *i.* Scotland **34** 56.11N 5.42W
Scarborough Canada **95** 43.44N 79.16W
Scarborough England **33** 54.17N 0.24W
Scariff I. Rep. of Ire. **39** 51.43N 10.16W
Scarinish Scotland **34** 56.30N 6.48W
Scarp *i.* Scotland **36** 58.02N 7.07W
Scavaig, Loch Scotland **36** 57.10N 6.08W
Schaffhausen Switz. **44** 47.42N 8.38E
Schagen Neth. **45** 52.47N 4.47E
Schefferville Canada **93** 54.50N 67.00W
Schelde *r.* Belgium **45** 51.13N 4.25E
Schenectady U.S.A. **95** 42.28N 73.57W
Scheveningen Neth. **45** 52.07N 4.16E
Schiedam Neth. **45** 51.55N 4.25E
Schiehallion *mtn.* Scotland **35** 56.40N 4.08W
Schiermonnikoog *i.* Neth. **45** 53.28N 6.15E
Schleiden W. Germany **45** 50.32N 6.29E
Schleswig W. Germany **44** 54.32N 9.34E
Schönebeck E. Germany **44** 52.01N 11.45E
Schouten Is. Indonesia **61** 0.45S 135.50E
Schouwen *i.* Neth. **45** 51.42N 3.45E
Schwäbish Hall W. Germany **44** 49.07N 9.45E
Schwandorf W. Germany **44** 49.20N 12.07E
Schwaner Mts. Indonesia **60** 0.45S 113.20E
Schwecht E. Germany **44** 53.04N 14.17E

For Khmer Republic *read* Kampuchea. *For* Malagasy Republic *read* Madagascar. *For* Rhodesia *read* Zimbabwe.

Schweinfurt to **Sibu** 162

Schweinfurt W. Germany **44** 50.03N 10.16E
Schwelm W. Germany **45** 51.17N 7.18E
Schwenningen W. Germany **44** 48.03N 8.32E
Schwerin E. Germany **44** 53.38N 11.25E
Sciacca Italy **42** 37.31N 13.05E
Scilly, Isles of England **31** 49.55N 6.20W
Scioto *r.* U.S.A. **94** 38.43N 83.00W
Scone Australia **80** 32.01S 150.53E
Scottsbluff U.S.A. **90** 41.52N 103.40W
Scottsdale Australia **80** 41.09S 147.31E
Scourie Scotland **36** 58.20N 5.08W
Scranton U.S.A. **95** 41.25N 75.40W
Scridain, Loch Scotland **34** 56.22N 6.06W
Scunthorpe England **33** 53.35N 0.38W
Seaford England **29** 50.46N 0.08E
Seaham England **33** 54.52N 1.21W
Seahouses England **35** 55.35N 1.38W
Seal *r.* Canada **93** 59.00N 95.00W
Sea Lake *town* Australia **80** 35.31S 142.54E
Seamill Scotland **34** 55.41N 4.52W
Seascale England **32** 54.24N 3.29W
Seaton Cumbria England **32** 54.41N 3.31W
Seaton Devon England **28** 50.43N 3.05W
Seaton Delaval England **35** 55.05N 1.31W
Seattle U.S.A. **90** 47.35N 122.20W
Sebago L. U.S.A. **95** 43.37N 71.20W
Sebastian Vizcaino B. Mexico **90** 28.20N 114.45W
Sebha Libya **68** 27.04N 14.25E
Sebinkarahisar Turkey **56** 40.19N 38.25E
Séda *r.* Portugal **41** 38.55N 7.30W
Sedan France **45** 49.42N 4.57E
Sedbergh England **32** 54.20N 2.31W
Sedgefield England **33** 54.40N 1.27W
Sédhiou Senegal **70** 12.44N 15.30W
Sefadu Sierra Leone **70** 8.41N 10.55W
Ségou Mali **70** 13.28N 6.18W
Segovia Spain **41** 40.57N 4.07W
Segre *r.* Spain **41** 41.25N 0.21E
Séguéla Ivory Coast **70** 7.58N 6.44W
Segura *r.* Spain **41** 38.07N 0.14W
Segura, Sierra de *mts.* Spain **41** 38.00N 2.50W
Sehkuheh Iran **57** 30.45N 61.29E
Seil *i.* Scotland **34** 56.18N 5.33W
Seiland Norway **46** 70.30N 23.00E
Seinäjoki Finland **46** 62.45N 22.55E
Seine *r.* France **40** 49.28N 0.25E
Seistan *f.* Iran **57** 31.00N 61.15E
Sekondi-Takoradi Ghana **70** 4.57N 1.44W
Selaru *i.* Asia **61** 8.15S 131.00E
Selby England **33** 53.47N 1.05W
Sele *r.* Italy **42** 40.30N 14.50E
Selenga *r.* U.S.S.R. **62** 52.20N 106.20E
Sélestat France **44** 48.16N 7.28E
Selkirk Scotland **35** 55.33N 2.51W
Selkirk Mts. Canada/U.S.A. **90** 50.00N 116.30W
Selsdon England **27** 51.21N 0.03W
Selsey England **28** 50.44N 0.47W
Selsey Bill *c.* England **28** 50.44N 0.47W
Selukwe Rhodesia **74** 19.40S 30.00E
Selvas *f.* S. America **106** 7.00S 66.00W
Selwyn Mts. Canada **92** 63.00N 130.00W
Seman *r.* Albania **43** 40.53N 19.25E
Semarang Indonesia **60** 6.58S 110.29E
Seminoe Resr. U.S.A. **90** 42.05N 106.50W
Semipalatinsk U.S.S.R. **48** 50.26N 80.16E
Semliki *r.* Zaïre **73** 1.12N 30.27E
Semmering Pass Austria **44** 47.40N 16.00E
Semnan Iran **57** 35.31N 53.24E
Semois *r.* France **45** 49.53N 4.45E
Semu *r.* Tanzania **73** 3.57S 34.20E
Senanga Zambia **72** 15.52S 23.19E
Send England **27** 51.17N 0.33W
Sendai Japan **63** 38.16N 140.52E
Seneca L. U.S.A. **95** 42.35N 77.07W
Senegal Africa **70** 14.30N 14.30W
Sénégal *r.* Senegal/Mauritania **70** 16.00N 16.28W
Senekal R.S.A. **74** 28.19S 27.38E
Senigallia Italy **42** 43.42N 13.14E
Senja *i.* Norway **46** 69.20N 17.30E
Senlis France **40** 49.12N 2.35E
Sennar Sudan **69** 13.31N 33.38E
Sennen England **31** 50.04N 5.42W
Senneterre Canada **95** 48.24N 77.16W
Sennybridge Wales **30** 51.57N 3.35W
Sens France **40** 48.12N 3.18E
Sentery Zaïre **72** 5.19S 25.43E
Seoul S. Korea **63** 37.30N 127.00E
Sepik *r.* P.N.G. **61** 3.54S 144.30E
Sept Îles *town* Canada **93** 50.13N 66.22W
Seraing Belgium **45** 50.37N 5.33E
Serengeti Nat. Park Tanzania **73** 2.30S 35.00E
Serengeti Plain *f.* Tanzania **73** 3.00S 35.00E
Serenje Zambia **73** 13.12S 30.50E
Sérevac France **42** 44.20N 3.05E
Sergach U.S.S.R. **47** 55.32N 45.27E
Sermate *i.* Indonesia **61** 8.30S 129.00E
Serov U.S.S.R. **48** 59.22N 60.32E
Serowe Botswana **74** 22.25S 26.44E
Serpa Portugal **41** 37.56N 7.36W
Serpent's Mouth *str.* Venezuela **97** 9.50N 61.00W
Serpukhov U.S.S.R. **47** 54.53N 37.25E
Sérrai Greece **43** 41.04N 23.32E
Serrat, C. Tunisia **42** 37.15N 9.12E
Serre *r.* France **45** 49.40N 3.22E
Sese Is. Uganda **73** 0.20S 32.30E
Sesheke Zambia **72** 17.14S 24.22E
Sesimbra Portugal **41** 38.26N 9.06W
Sète France **40** 43.25N 3.43E
Sete Lagoas Brazil **103** 19.29S 44.15W
Sétif Algeria **42** 36.10N 5.26E
Setté Cama Gabon **72** 2.32S 9.46E
Settle England **32** 54.05N 2.18W
Setúbal Portugal **41** 38.31N 8.54W
Setúbal, B. of Portugal **41** 38.20N 9.00W
Seul, Lac *l.* Canada **91** 50.25N 92.15W
Sevan, L. U.S.S.R. **57** 40.22N 45.20E
Sevastopol' U.S.S.R. **47** 44.36N 33.31E
Seven Heads *c.* Rep. of Ire. **39** 51.34N 8.43W
Seven Kings England **27** 51.34N 0.06E
Sevenoaks England **27** 51.16N 0.12E
Séverac France **40** 44.20N 3.05E
Severn *r.* Canada **93** 56.00N 87.40W
Severn *r.* England **28** 51.50N 2.21W
Severnaya Zemlya *is.* U.S.S.R. **49** 80.00N 96.00E
Seville Spain **41** 37.24N 5.59W
Sèvre Niortaise *r.* France **40** 46.35N 1.05W
Sewa *r.* Sierra Leone **70** 7.15N 12.08W
Seward U.S.A. **92** 60.05N 149.34W
Seward Pen. U.S.A. **92** 65.00N 164.10W
Seychelles *is.* Indian Oc. **55** 5.00S 55.00E
Seydhisfjördhur Iceland **46** 65.16N 14.02W
Seymour U.S.A. **94** 38.57N 85.55W
Sézanne France **40** 48.44N 3.44E
Sfântu Gheorghe Romania **43** 45.52N 25.50E
Sfax Tunisia **68** 34.45N 10.43E
'sGravenhage *see* The Hague Neth. **45**
Sgurr Mòr *mtn.* Scotland **36** 57.41N 5.01W
Sgurr na Lapaich *mtn.* Scotland **36** 57.22N 5.04W
Shaba *d.* Zaïre **73** 8.00S 27.00E
Shabani Rhodesia **74** 20.20S 30.05E
Shabunda Zaïre **73** 2.42S 27.20E
Shaftesbury England **28** 51.00N 2.12W
Shahabad Iran **57** 34.08N 46.35E
Shah Dad Iran **57** 30.27N 57.44E
Shahdol India **58** 23.10N 81.26E
Shahjahanpur India **58** 27.53N 79.55E
Shahpur Iran **57** 38.13N 44.50E
Shahreza Iran **57** 32.00N 51.52E
Shahr-i-Babak Iran **57** 30.08N 55.04E
Shahr Kord Iran **57** 32.40N 50.52E
Shahrud Iran **57** 36.25N 55.00E
Shahsawar Iran **57** 36.49N 50.54E
Shaib al Qur *r.* Saudi Arabia **56** 31.02N 42.00E
Shakhty U.S.S.R. **47** 47.43N 40.16E
Shalford England **27** 51.13N 0.35W
Sham, Jebel *mtn.* Oman **57** 23.14N 57.17E
Shamiya Desert Iraq **57** 30.30N 45.30E
Shamley Green England **27** 51.11N 0.30W
Shamva Rhodesia **74** 17.20S 31.38E
Shanghai China **63** 31.13N 121.25E
Shanklin England **28** 50.39N 1.09W
Shannon *r.* Rep. of Ire. **38** 52.39N 8.43W
Shannon, Mouth of the *est.* Rep. of Ire. **39** 52.29N 9.57W
Shansi *d.* China **63** 36.45N 112.00E
Shan State *d.* Burma **59** 21.30N 98.00E
Shantar Is. U.S.S.R. **49** 55.00N 138.00E
Shantung *d.* China **63** 35.45N 117.30E
Shantung Pen. China **63** 37.00N 121.30E
Shaohing China **63** 30.02N 120.35E
Shaoyang China **63** 27.43N 111.24E
Shap England **32** 54.32N 2.40W
Shapinsay *i.* Scotland **37** 59.03N 2.51W
Shapinsay Sd. Scotland **37** 59.01N 2.55W
Shapur *ruins* Iran **57** 29.42N 51.30E
Shaqra Saudi Arabia **57** 25.17N 45.14E
Sharjah U.A.E. **57** 25.20N 55.26E
Sharon U.S.A. **94** 41.16N 80.30W
Shashi *r.* Botswana **74** 22.10S 29.15E
Shasi China **63** 30.16N 112.20E
Shasta, Mt. U.S.A. **90** 41.35N 122.12W
Shatt al Arab *r.* Iraq **57** 30.00N 48.30E
Shawano U.S.A. **94** 44.46N 88.38W
Shawinigan Canada **95** 46.33N 72.45W
Shebelle *r.* Somali Rep. **73** 0.30N 43.10E
Sheboygan U.S.A. **94** 43.46N 87.44W
Shebshi Mts. Nigeria **71** 8.30N 11.45E
Sheeffry Hills Rep. of Ire. **38** 53.41N 9.42W
Sheelin, Lough Rep. of Ire. **38** 53.48N 7.20W
Sheep Haven *b.* Rep. of Ire. **38** 55.12N 7.52W
Sheep's Head Rep. of Ire. **39** 51.33N 9.52W
Sheerness England **29** 51.26N 0.47E
Sheffield England **33** 53.23N 1.28W
Shefford England **29** 52.02N 0.20W
Shehy Mts. Rep. of Ire. **39** 51.47N 9.15W
Shelag *r.* Afghan. **57** 30.18N 61.02E
Shelby U.S.A. **90** 48.30N 111.52W
Shelikof Str. U.S.A. **92** 58.00N 153.45W
Shellharbour Australia **80** 34.35S 150.52E
Shëngjin Albania **43** 41.49N 19.33E
Shenley England **27** 51.43N 0.17W
Shensi *d.* China **63** 35.00N 109.00E
Shenyang China **63** 41.50N 123.26E
Shepparton Australia **80** 36.25S 145.26E
Shepperton England **27** 51.23N 0.28W
Sheppey, Isle of England **29** 51.24N 0.50E
Shepshed England **33** 52.46N 1.17W
Shepton Mallet England **28** 51.11N 2.31W
Shepway England **27** 51.15N 0.33E
Sherborne England **28** 50.56N 2.31W
Sherbro I. Sierra Leone **70** 7.30N 12.50W
Sherbrooke Canada **95** 45.24N 71.54W
Shere England **27** 51.13N 0.28W
Sheridan U.S.A. **90** 44.48N 107.05W
Sheringham England **33** 52.56N 1.11E
Sherkin I. Rep. of Ire. **39** 51.28N 9.25W
Sherman U.S.A. **91** 33.39N 96.35W
Sherridon Canada **93** 57.07N 101.05W
'sHertogenbosch Neth. **45** 51.42N 5.19E
Sherwood Forest *f.* England **33** 53.10N 1.05W
Shetland Is. *d.* Scotland **36** 60.20N 1.15W
Shevchenko U.S.S.R. **48** 43.40N 51.20E
Shiant Is. Scotland **36** 57.54N 6.20W
Shiel, Loch Scotland **36** 56.48N 5.33W
Shiel Bridge *town* Scotland **36** 57.12N 5.26W
Shieldaig Scotland **36** 57.31N 5.40W
Shifnal England **28** 52.40N 2.23W
Shigatse China **59** 29.18N 88.50E
Shihkiachwang China **63** 38.04N 114.28E
Shihtsien China **63** 27.30N 108.20E
Shikarpur Pakistan **58** 27.58N 68.42E
Shikoku *i.* Japan **63** 33.30N 133.30E
Shilbottle England **35** 55.22N 1.43W
Shildon England **32** 54.37N 1.39W
Shilka U.S.S.R. **63** 51.55N 116.01E
Shilka *r.* U.S.S.R. **63** 53.20N 121.10E
Shillong India **59** 25.34N 91.53E
Shimoga India **58** 13.56N 75.31E
Shimonoseki Japan **63** 33.59N 130.58E
Shin, Loch Scotland **37** 58.06N 4.32W
Shinyanga Tanzania **73** 3.40S 33.20E
Shinyanga *d.* Tanzania **73** 3.30S 33.00E
Shipka Pass Bulgaria **43** 42.45N 25.25E
Shipley England **32** 53.50N 1.47W
Shipston on Stour England **28** 52.04N 1.38W
Shipton England **33** 54.01N 1.09W
Shirak Steppe *f.* U.S.S.R. **57** 41.40N 46.20E
Shiraz Iran **57** 29.36N 52.33E
Shire *r.* Moçambique **73** 17.46S 35.20E
Shir Kuh *mtn.* Iran **57** 31.38N 54.07E
Shiukwan China **63** 24.54N 113.33E
Shivpuri India **58** 25.26N 77.39E
Shizuoka Japan **63** 34.59N 138.24E
Shkodër Albania **43** 42.03N 19.30E
Shkoder, L. Albania/Yugo. **43** 42.10N 19.18E
Shoeburyness England **29** 51.31N 0.49E
Sholapur India **58** 17.43N 75.56E
Shoreditch England **27** 51.32N 0.05W
Shoreham-by-Sea England **29** 50.50N 0.17W
Shostka U.S.S.R. **47** 51.53N 33.30E
Shotts Scotland **35** 55.49N 3.48W
Shreveport U.S.A. **91** 32.30N 93.46W
Shrewsbury England **28** 52.42N 2.45W
Shrewton England **28** 51.11N 1.55W
Shu'aiba Iraq **57** 30.30N 47.40E
Shumagin Is. U.S.A. **92** 55.00N 160.00W
Shur *r.* Iran **57** 28.00N 55.45E
Shurab *r.* Iran **57** 31.30N 55.18E
Shushtar Iran **57** 32.04N 48.53E
Shuya U.S.S.R. **47** 56.49N 41.23E
Shwebo Burma **59** 22.35N 95.42E
Sialkot Pakistan **58** 32.29N 74.35E
Siam, G. of Asia **59** 10.30N 101.00E
Sian China **63** 34.16N 108.54E
Siangfan China **63** 32.20N 112.05E
Siang Kiang *r.* Kwangsi-Chuang China **63** 23.25N 110.00E
Siangtan China **63** 27.55N 112.47E
Siangyang China **63** 32.00N 112.00E
Siargao *i.* Phil. **61** 9.55N 126.05E
Šiauliai U.S.S.R. **46** 55.51N 23.20E
Šibenik Yugo. **42** 43.45N 15.55E
Siberia *d.* Asia **107** 62.00N 104.00E
Siberut *i.* Indonesia **60** 1.30S 99.00E
Sibi Pakistan **58** 29.31N 67.54E
Sibiti Congo **72** 3.40S 13.24E
Sibiti *r.* Tanzania **73** 3.47S 34.45E
Sibiu Romania **43** 45.47N 24.09E
Sibolga Indonesia **60** 1.42N 98.48E
Sibu Malaysia **60** 2.18N 111.49E

For Khmer Republic *read* Kampuchea. *For* Malagasy Republic *read* Madagascar. *For* Rhodesia *read* Zimbabwe.

Sichang China 59 28.00N 102.10E	Sitapur India 58 27.33N 80.40E	Slyne Head Rep. of Ire. 38 53.25N 10.12W
Sicily i. Italy 42 37.30N 14.00E	Sitka U.S.A. 92 57.05N 135.20W	Slyudyanka U.S.S.R. 62 51.40N 103.40E
Sidcup England 27 51.26N 0.07E	Sittang r. Burma 59 17.30N 96.53E	Smithfield R.S.A. 74 30.13S 26.32E
Sidi Barrani Egypt 56 31.38N 25.58E	Sittard Neth. 45 51.00N 5.52E	Smith's Falls town Canada 95 44.54N 76.01W
Sidi-bel-Abbès Algeria 41 35.15N 0.39W	Sittingbourne England 29 51.20N 0.43E	Smöla i. Norway 46 63.20N 8.00E
Sidlaw Hills Scotland 35 56.31N 3.10W	Sivas Turkey 56 39.44N 37.01E	Smolensk U.S.S.R. 47 54.49N 32.04E
Sidmouth England 28 50.40N 3.13W	Sivrihisar Turkey 56 39.29N 31.32E	Smólikas mtn. Greece 43 40.06N 20.55E
Sidon Lebanon 56 33.32N 35.22E	Siwa Egypt 56 29.11N 25.31E	Smolyan Bulgaria 43 41.34N 24.45E
Siedlce Poland 47 52.10N 22.18E	Siwa Oasis Egypt 56 29.10N 25.45E	Smorgon U.S.S.R. 47 54.28N 27.20E
Sieg r. W. Germany 45 50.49N 7.11E	Sixmilebridge town Rep. of Ire. 39 52.45N 8.47W	Snaefell mtn. I.o.M. 32 54.16N 4.28W
Siegburg W. Germany 45 50.48N 7.13E	Sixmilecross N. Ireland 34 54.34N 7.08W	Snaith England 33 53.42N 1.01W
Siegen W. Germany 45 50.52N 8.02E	Skagen Denmark 46 57.44N 10.37E	Snake r. Idaho U.S.A. 90 43.50N 117.05W
Siena Italy 42 43.19N 11.20E	Skagerrak str. Denmark/Norway 46 57.45N 8.55E	Snake r. Wash. U.S.A. 90 46.15N 119.00W
Sierra Blanca mtn. U.S.A. 90 33.23N 105.49W	Skagway U.S.A. 92 59.23N 135.20W	Snåsa Norway 46 64.15N 12.23E
Sierra Leone Africa 70 9.00N 12.00W	Skaill Scotland 37 58.56N 2.43W	Snåsavatn l. Norway 46 64.10N 12.00E
Sighişoara Romania 43 46.13N 24.49E	Skalintyy mtn. U.S.S.R. 49 56.00N 130.40E	Sneek Neth. 45 53.03N 5.40E
Sighty Crag mtn. England 35 55.07N 2.38W	Skara Sweden 46 58.23N 13.25E	Sneem Rep. of Ire. 39 51.50N 9.54W
Siglufjördhur Iceland 46 66.09N 18.55W	Skaw Taing c. Scotland 36 60.23N 0.56W	Sneeuwberg mtn. R.S.A. 74 32.20S 19.10E
Signy France 45 49.42N 4.25E	Skeena r. Canada 92 54.10N 129.08W	Snizort, Loch Scotland 36 57.35N 6.30W
Sigüenza Spain 41 41.04N 2.38W	Skegness England 33 53.09N 0.20E	Snodland England 27 51.20N 0.27E
Siguiri Guinea 70 11.28N 9.07W	Skellefte r. Sweden 46 64.44N 21.07E	Snöhetta mtn. Norway 46 62.15N 9.05E
Siirt Turkey 56 37.56N 41.56E	Skellefteå Sweden 46 64.45N 21.00E	Snook Pt. England 35 55.31N 1.35W
Sikar India 58 27.33N 75.12E	Skelmersdale England 32 53.34N 2.49W	Snowdon mtn. Wales 30 53.05N 4.05W
Sikasso Mali 70 11.18N 5.38W	Skelmorlie Scotland 34 55.51N 4.52W	Snowy r. Australia 80 37.49S 148.30E
Sikhote-Alin Range mts. U.S.S.R. 63 45.20N 136.50E	Skene Sweden 46 57.30N 12.35E	Snowy Mtn. U.S.A. 95 43.42N 74.23W
Si Kiang r. China 63 22.23N 113.20E	Skerries Rep. of Ire. 38 53.35N 6.07W	Snowy Mts. Australia 80 36.25S 145.15E
Sikkim d. India 58 27.30N 88.30E	Skerryvore i. Scotland 34 56.20N 7.05W	Soalala Malagasy Rep. 73 16.08S 45.21E
Sil r. Spain 41 42.24N 7.15W	Skhiza i. Greece 43 36.42N 21.45E	Soar r. England 33 52.52N 1.17W
Silchar India 59 24.49N 92.47E	Ski Norway 46 59.43N 10.52E	Soay i. Scotland 36 57.09N 6.13W
Sileby England 28 52.44N 1.06W	Skibbereen Rep. of Ire. 39 51.34N 9.16W	Soay Sd. str. Scotland 36 57.09N 6.16W
Silesian Plateau f. Poland 47 50.30N 20.00E	Skiddaw mtn. England 32 54.40N 3.09W	Sobat r. Sudan/Ethiopia 69 9.30N 31.30E
Silgarhi Nepal 59 29.14N 80.58E	Skien Norway 46 59.14N 9.37E	Sobernheim W. Germany 45 49.47N 7.40E
Silifke Turkey 56 36.22N 33.57E	Skikda Algeria 42 36.53N 6.54E	Sochi U.S.S.R. 47 43.35N 39.46E
Siliguri India 58 26.42N 88.30E	Skipness Scotland 34 56.45N 5.22W	Society Is. Pacific Oc. 106 17.00S 150.00W
Silistra Bulgaria 43 44.07N 27.17E	Skipton England 32 53.57N 2.01W	Socotra i. Indian Oc. 69 12.30N 54.00E
Siljan l. Sweden 46 60.50N 14.40E	Skíros i. Greece 43 38.50N 24.33E	Sodankylä Finland 46 67.21N 26.31E
Silkeborg Denmark 46 56.10N 9.39E	Skjálfanda Fljót r. Iceland 46 65.55N 17.30W	Söderhamn Sweden 46 61.19N 17.10E
Silloth England 35 54.53N 3.25W	Skokholm i. Wales 31 51.42N 5.17W	Södertälje Sweden 46 59.11N 17.39E
Silsden England 32 53.55N 1.55W	Skokie U.S.A. 94 42.01N 87.45W	Soest W. Germany 45 51.34N 8.06E
Silver City U.S.A. 90 32.47N 108.16W	Skomer i. Wales 31 51.45N 5.18W	Sofia Bulgaria 43 42.41N 23.19E
Silver End England 27 51.51N 0.38E	Skopje Yugo. 43 41.58N 21.27E	Sogne Fjord est. Norway 46 61.10N 5.50E
Silvermines Rep. of Ire. 39 52.48N 8.15W	Skövde Sweden 46 58.24N 13.52E	Sögüt Turkey 56 40.02N 30.10E
Silvermines Mts. Rep. of Ire. 39 52.46N 8.17W	Skovorodino U.S.S.R. 49 54.00N 123.53E	Sohag Egypt 56 26.33N 31.42E
Silver Spring town U.S.A. 95 39.00N 77.01W	Skreia Norway 46 60.38N 10.57E	Soham England 29 52.20N 0.20E
Silverstone England 28 52.05N 1.03W	Skull Rep. of Ire. 39 51.32N 9.33W	Sohar Oman 57 24.23N 56.43E
Silverton England 28 50.49N 3.29W	Skye i. Scotland 36 57.20N 6.15W	Soignies Belgium 45 50.35N 4.04E
Simanggang Malaysia 60 1.10N 111.32E	Slagelse Denmark 46 55.24N 11.23E	Soissons France 40 49.23N 3.20E
Simard, L. Canada 95 47.37N 78.40W	Slaidburn England 32 53.57N 2.28W	Söke Turkey 43 37.46N 27.26E
Simav r. Turkey 43 40.24N 28.31E	Slamat mtn. Indonesia 60 7.10S 109.10E	Sokodé Togo 71 8.59N 1.11E
Simcoe, L. Canada 95 44.25N 79.20W	Slane Rep. of Ire. 38 53.43N 6.33W	Sokol U.S.S.R. 47 59.28N 40.04E
Simeulue i. Indonesia 60 2.30N 96.00E	Slaney r. Rep. of Ire. 39 52.21N 6.30W	Sokolo Mali 70 14.53N 6.11W
Simferopol' U.S.S.R. 47 44.57N 34.05E	Slantsy U.S.S.R. 46 59.09N 28.09E	Sokoto Nigeria 71 13.02N 5.15E
Simiyu r. Tanzania 73 2.32S 33.25E	Slapin, Loch Scotland 36 57.11N 6.01W	Sokoto d. Nigeria 71 11.50N 5.05E
Simla India 58 31.07N 77.09E	Slatina Romania 43 44.26N 24.23E	Sokoto r. Nigeria 71 13.05N 5.13E
Simmern W. Germany 45 49.59N 7.32E	Slave r. Canada 92 51.10N 113.30W	Soledad Colombia 97 10.54N 74.58W
Simo r. Finland 46 65.38N 24.57E	Slavgorod R.S.F.S.R. U.S.S.R. 48 53.01N 78.37E	Solihull England 28 52.26N 1.47W
Simonsbath England 31 51.07N 3.45W	Slavgorod W.R.S.S.R. U.S.S.R. 47 53.25N 31.00E	Solingen W. Germany 45 51.10N 7.05E
Simonstown R.S.A. 74 34.12S 18.26E	Slavyansk U.S.S.R. 47 48.51N 37.36E	Sollas Scotland 36 57.39N 7.22W
Simplon Pass Switz. 40 46.15N 8.03E	Sleaford England 33 53.00N 0.22W	Sollefteå Sweden 46 63.09N 17.15E
Simplon Tunnel Italy/Switz. 44 46.20N 8.05E	Slea Head Rep. of Ire. 39 52.05N 10.27W	Soller Spain 41 39.47N 2.41E
Simrishamn Sweden 46 55.35N 14.20E	Sleat, Pt. of Scotland 36 57.01N 6.01W	Solling mtn. W. Germany 44 51.45N 9.30E
Sinai pen. Egypt 56 29.00N 34.00E	Sleat, Sd. of str. Scotland 36 57.05N 5.48W	Solomon Is. Austa. 113 10.00S 160.00E
Sinclair's B. Scotland 37 58.30N 3.07W	Sledmere England 33 54.04N 0.35W	Solomon Sea Austa. 79 7.00S 150.00E
Sines Portugal 41 37.58N 8.52W	Sleetmute U.S.A. 92 61.40N 157.11W	Solta i. Yugo. 42 43.23N 16.17E
Singapore Asia 60 1.20N 103.45E	Sleights England 33 54.26N 0.40W	Solway Firth est. England/Scotland 32 54.50N 3.30W
Singapore town Singapore 60 1.20N 103.45E	Sliabh Gaoil mtn. Scotland 34 55.54N 5.30W	Solwezi Zambia 73 12.11S 26.23E
Singaraja Indonesia 60 8.06S 115.07E	Slide Mtn. U.S.A. 95 42.00N 74.23W	Soma Turkey 43 39.11N 27.36E
Singen W. Germany 44 47.45N 8.50E	Sliedrecht Neth. 45 51.48N 4.46E	Somabula Rhodesia 74 19.40S 29.38E
Singida Tanzania 73 4.45S 34.42E	Slieveardagh Hills Rep. of Ire. 39 52.39N 7.32W	Somali Republic Africa 69 5.30N 47.00E
Singida d. Tanzania 73 6.00S 34.30E	Slieve Aughty mtn. Rep. of Ire. 39 53.05N 8.37W	Sombor Yugo. 43 45.48N 19.08E
Singitikos G. Med. Sea 43 40.12N 24.00E	Slieve Aughty Mts. Rep. of Ire. 39 53.05N 8.31W	Somerset d. England 28 51.09N 3.00W
Singkep i. Indonesia 60 0.30S 104.20E	Slieve Bernagh mts. Rep. of Ire. 39 52.48N 8.35W	Somerset East R.S.A. 74 32.44S 25.35E
Sinhailien China 63 34.37N 119.10E	Slieve Bloom Mts. Rep. of Ire. 39 53.03N 7.35W	Somerset I. Canada 93 73.00N 93.30W
Sining China 62 36.35N 101.55E	Slieve Callan mtn. Rep. of Ire. 39 52.51N 9.18W	Somerton England 28 51.03N 2.44W
Sinj Yugo. 43 43.42N 16.38E	Slieve Donard mtn. N. Ireland 38 54.11N 5.56W	Somes r. Hungary 47 48.40N 22.30E
Sinkiang-Uighur d. China 62 41.15N 87.00E	Slieve Felim Mts. Rep. of Ire. 39 52.40N 8.16W	Somme r. France 40 50.01N 1.40E
Sinoia Rhodesia 74 17.21S 30.13E	Slieve Fyagh mtn. Rep. of Ire. 38 54.12N 9.42W	Son r. India 58 25.55N 84.55E
Sinop Turkey 56 42.02N 35.09E	Slieve Gamph mts. Rep. of Ire. 38 54.06N 8.52W	Sönderborg Denmark 44 54.55N 9.48E
Sint Eustatius i. Neth. Antilles 97 17.33N 63.00W	Slievekimalta mtn. Rep. of Ire. 39 52.45N 8.17W	Sondrio Italy 44 46.11N 9.52E
Sinu r. Colombia 97 9.25N 76.00W	Slieve Mish mts. Rep. of Ire. 39 52.12N 9.48W	Songea Tanzania 73 10.42S 35.39E
Sioux City U.S.A. 91 42.30N 96.28W	Slieve Miskish mts. Rep. of Ire. 39 51.41N 9.56W	Songkhla Thailand 59 7.13N 100.37E
Sioux Falls town U.S.A. 91 43.34N 96.42W	Slievemore mtn. Rep. of Ire. 38 54.01N 10.04W	Songololo Zaïre 72 5.40S 14.05E
Sioux Lookout town Canada 91 50.07N 91.54W	Slieve Na Calliagh mtn. Rep. of Ire. 38 53.45N 7.06W	Sonneberg E. Germany 44 50.22N 11.10E
Sipolilo Rhodesia 74 16.43S 30.43E	Slievenamon mtn. Rep. of Ire. 39 52.25N 7.34W	Sonora r. Mexico 90 28.45N 111.55W
Sipora i. Indonesia 60 2.10S 99.40E	Slieve Snaght mtn. Donegal Rep. of Ire. 38 55.12N 7.20W	Sonsorol i. Asia 61 5.20N 132.13E
Sira r. Norway 46 58.13N 6.13E	Sligachan Scotland 36 57.17N 6.10W	Soochow China 63 31.21N 120.40E
Siracusa Italy 42 37.05N 15.17E	Sligo Rep. of Ire. 38 54.17N 8.28W	Sorel Canada 95 46.03N 73.06W
Siret r. Romania 43 45.28N 27.56E	Sligo d. Rep. of Ire. 38 54.10N 8.35W	Soria Spain 41 41.46N 2.28W
Sirhan, Wadi f. Saudi Arabia 56 31.00N 37.30E	Sligo B. Rep. of Ire. 38 54.18N 8.40W	Sorisdale Scotland 34 56.40N 6.28W
Sirra, Wadi r. Saudi Arabia 57 23.10N 44.22E	Slioch mtn. Scotland 36 57.40N 5.20W	Sor Kvalöy i. Norway 46 69.45N 18.20E
Sirte Libya 68 31.10N 16.39E	Sliven Bulgaria 43 42.41N 26.19E	Sorocaba Brazil 103 23.30S 47.32W
Sirte, G. of Libya 68 31.45N 17.50E	Slobodskoy U.S.S.R. 46 58.42N 50.10E	Sorol i. Asia 61 8.09N 140.25E
Sisak Yugo. 42 45.30N 16.21E	Slough England 27 51.30N 0.35W	Sorong Asia 61 0.50S 131.17E
Sishen R.S.A. 74 27.47S 23.00E	Sluch r. U.S.S.R. 47 52.05N 27.52E	Soroti Uganda 73 1.40N 33.37E
Sisophon Khmer Rep. 59 13.37N 102.58E	Sluis Neth. 45 51.18N 3.23E	Söröya i. Norway 46 70.30N 22.30E
Sisteron France 40 44.16N 5.56E	Słupsk Poland 44 54.28N 17.00E	Sorraia r. Portugal 41 39.00N 8.51W

For Khmer Republic read Kampuchea. *For Malagasy Republic read* Madagascar. *For Rhodesia read* Zimbabwe.

Sorsele to **Stronsay Firth** 164

Sorsele Sweden **46** 65.32N 17.34E
Sortavala U.S.S.R. **46** 61.40N 30.40E
Sotik Kenya **73** 0.40S 35.08E
Sotra *i.* Norway **46** 60.20N 5.00E
Souk Ahras Algeria **42** 36.14N 7.59E
Soure Portugal **41** 40.04N 8.38W
Souris *r.* U.S.A. **90** 49.38N 99.35W
Sousse Tunisia **42** 35.48N 10.38E
Soustons France **40** 43.45N 1.19W
Southall England **27** 51.31N 0.23W
Southam England **28** 52.16N 1.24W
South America 102
Southampton England **28** 50.54N 1.23W
Southampton I. Canada **93** 64.30N 84.00W
Southampton Water *est.* England **28** 50.52N 1.21W
South Atlantic Ocean 102
South Australia *d.* Australia **79** 29.00S 135.00E
South Barrule *mtn.* I.o.M. **32** 54.09N 4.41W
South Bend U.S.A. **94** 41.40N 86.15W
South Benfleet England **27** 51.33N 0.34E
South Beveland *f.* Neth. **45** 51.30N 3.50E
Southborough England **29** 51.10N 0.15E
South Brent England **31** 50.26N 3.50W
South Carolina *d.* U.S.A. **91** 34.00N 81.00W
South Cave England **33** 53.46N 0.37W
South Cerney England **28** 51.40N 1.55W
South China Sea Asia **60** 12.30N 115.00E
South Dakota *d.* U.S.A. **90** 44.30N 100.00W
South Dorset Downs *hills* England **28** 50.40N 2.25W
South Downs *hills* England **28** 50.04N 0.34W
South East C. Australia **80** 43.38S 146.48E
Southend Scotland **34** 55.19N 5.38W
Southend-on-Sea England **29** 51.32N 0.43E
Southern Alps *mts.* New Zealand **82** 43.20S 170.45E
Southern Lueti *r.* Zambia **74** 16.16S 23.15E
Southern Uplands *hills* Scotland **35** 55.30N 3.30W
Southern Yemen Asia **69** 16.00N 49.30E
South Esk *r.* Scotland **35** 56.43N 2.32W
South Flevoland *f.* Neth. **45** 52.22N 5.22E
South Foreland *c.* England **29** 51.08N 1.24E
Southgate England **27** 51.38N 0.07W
South Georgia *i.* Atlantic Oc. **106** 54.00S 37.00W
South Glamorgan *d.* Wales **31** 51.27N 3.22W
South-haa Scotland **36** 60.34N 1.17W
South Harris *f.* Scotland **36** 57.49N 6.55W
South Haven U.S.A. **94** 42.25N 86.16W
South Hayling England **28** 50.47N 0.56W
South Holland *d.* Neth. **45** 52.00N 4.30E
South Hornchurch England **27** 51.32N 0.13E
South Horr Kenya **73** 2.10N 36.45E
South I. New Zealand **82** 43.00S 171.00E
South Kirby England **33** 53.35N 1.25W
South Korea Asia **63** 36.00N 128.00E
Southland *f.* New Zealand **82** 45.40S 167.15E
Southminster England **29** 51.40N 0.51E
South Molton England **31** 51.01N 3.50W
South Nahanni *r.* Canada **92** 61.00N 123.20W
South Norwood England **27** 51.24N 0.04W
South Nutfield England **27** 51.14N 0.06W
South Ockendon England **27** 51.32N 0.18E
South Oxhey England **27** 51.38N 0.24W
Southport Australia **80** 27.58S 153.20E
Southport England **32** 53.38N 3.01W
South Ronaldsay *i.* Scotland **37** 58.47N 2.56W
South Saskatchewan *r.* Canada **90** 50.45N 108.30W
South Sd. Rep. of Ire. **39** 53.03N 9.28W
South Shetland Is. Antarctica **106** 62.00S 60.00W
South Shields England **33** 55.00N 1.24W
South Tyne *r.* England **35** 54.59N 2.08W
South Uist *i.* Scotland **36** 57.15N 7.20W
South Walls *i.* Scotland **37** 58.45N 3.07W
Southwark *d.* England **27** 51.30N 0.06W
Southwell England **33** 53.05N 0.58W
South West Africa Africa **74** 22.30S 17.00E
South West C. Australia **80** 43.32S 145.59E
Southwest C. New Zealand **82** 47.15S 167.30E
Southwick England **29** 50.50N 0.14W
Southwold England **29** 52.19N 1.41E
South Woodham Ferrers England **27** 51.39N 0.36E
South Yorkshire *d.* England **33** 53.28N 1.25W
Soutpansberge *mts.* R.S.A. **74** 22.50S 29.30E
Sovetsk U.S.S.R. **46** 55.02N 21.50E
Sovetskaya Gavan U.S.S.R. **49** 48.57N 140.16E
Spa Belgium **45** 50.29N 5.52E
Spain Europe **41** 40.00N 4.00W
Spalding Australia **80** 33.29S 138.40E
Spalding England **33** 52.47N 0.09W
Spandau W. Germany **44** 52.32N 13.13E
Spanish Sahara Africa **70** 2.30N 14.30E
Sparta U.S.A. **94** 43.57N 90.50W
Spárti Greece **43** 37.04N 22.28E
Spartivento, C. Calabria Italy **42** 37.55N 16.04E
Spartivento, C. Sardinia Italy **42** 38.53N 8.51E
Spátha, C. Greece **43** 35.42N 23.43E
Spean Bridge *town* Scotland **37** 56.53N 4.54W
Speke G. Tanzania **73** 2.20S 33.30E
Spence Bay *town* Canada **93** 69.30N 93.20W
Spencer G. Australia **79** 34.30S 136.10E
Spennymoor *town* England **33** 54.43N 1.35W
Spenser Mts. New Zealand **82** 42.15S 172.45E
Sperrin Mts. N. Ireland **34** 54.49N 7.06W
Spey *r.* Scotland **37** 57.40N 3.06W
Spey B. Scotland **37** 57.42N 3.04W
Speyer W. Germany **44** 49.18N 8.26E
Spiekeroog *i.* W. Germany **45** 53.48N 7.45E
Spilsby England **33** 53.10N 0.06E
Spithead *str.* England **28** 50.45N 1.05W
Spitsbergen *is.* Europe **54** 78.00N 17.00E
Spittal Austria **44** 46.48N 13.30E
Split Yugo. **43** 43.32N 16.27E
Spokane U.S.A. **90** 47.40N 117.25W
Spooner U.S.A. **94** 45.50N 91.53W
Spratly I. Asia **60** 8.45N 111.54E
Spree *r.* E. Germany **44** 52.32N 13.15E
Springbok R.S.A. **74** 29.43S 17.55E
Springfield Ill. U.S.A. **94** 39.49N 89.39W
Springfield Mass. U.S.A. **95** 42.07N 72.35W
Springfield Miss. U.S.A. **91** 37.11N 93.19W
Springfield Ohio U.S.A. **94** 39.55N 83.48W
Springfontein R.S.A. **74** 30.16S 25.42E
Springs *town* R.S.A. **74** 26.15S 28.26E
Spurn Head England **33** 53.35N 0.08E
Sredne Kolymskaya U.S.S.R. **49** 67.27N 153.35E
Sri Lanka Asia **59** 7.30N 80.50E
Srinagar Jammu and Kashmir **58** 34.08N 74.50E
Stack's Mts. Rep. of Ire. **39** 52.18N 9.36W
Stadskanaal Neth. **45** 53.02N 6.55E
Stadtkyll W. Germany **45** 50.21N 6.32E
Staffa *i.* Scotland **34** 56.26N 6.21W
Staffin Scotland **36** 57.38N 6.13W
Stafford England **32** 52.49N 2.09W
Staffordshire *d.* England **28** 52.40N 1.57W
Staines England **27** 51.26N 0.31W
Stainforth England **33** 53.37N 1.01W
Stalbridge England **28** 50.57N 2.22W
Stalham England **29** 52.46N 1.31E
Stamford England **29** 52.39N 0.29W
Stamford U.S.A. **95** 41.03N 73.32W
Stamford Bridge *town* England **33** 53.59N 0.53W
Standerton R.S.A. **74** 26.57S 29.14E
Standon England **27** 51.53N 0.02E
Stanford le Hope England **27** 51.31N 0.26E
Stanger R.S.A. **74** 29.20S 31.18E
Stanhope England **32** 54.45N 2.00W
Stanley Australia **80** 40.46S 145.20E
Stanley England **32** 54.53N 1.42W
Stanley Scotland **35** 56.29N 3.28W
Stanmore England **27** 51.38N 0.19W
Stanovoy Range *mts.* U.S.S.R. **49** 56.00N 125.40E
Stanstead Abbots England **27** 51.47N 0.01E
Stansted Mountfitchet England **27** 51.55N 0.12E
Stanthorpe Australia **80** 28.37S 151.52E
Stapleford England **33** 52.56N 1.16W
Staraya Russa U.S.S.R. **47** 58.00N 31.22E
Stara Zagora Bulgaria **43** 42.26N 25.37E
Stargard Poland **44** 53.21N 15.01E
Start B. England **31** 50.17N 3.35W
Start Pt. England **31** 50.13N 3.38W
Start Pt. Scotland **37** 59.17N 2.24W
State College U.S.A. **95** 40.48N 77.52W
Staunton England **28** 51.58N 2.19W
Stavanger Norway **46** 58.58N 5.45E
Staveley England **33** 53.16N 1.20W
Stavelot Belgium **45** 50.23N 5.54E
Staveren Neth. **45** 52.53N 5.21E
Stavropol' U.S.S.R. **47** 45.03N 41.59E
Stavropol Highlands U.S.S.R. **47** 45.00N 42.30E
Stawell Australia **80** 37.06S 142.52E
Staxton England **33** 54.11N 0.26W
Steelpoort R.S.A. **74** 24.48S 30.11E
Steenbergen Neth. **45** 51.36N 4.19E
Steenvorde France **45** 50.49N 2.35E
Steenwijk Neth. **45** 52.47N 6.07E
Steep Holm *i.* England **28** 51.20N 3.06W
Steeping *r.* England **33** 53.06N 0.19E
Steinkjer Norway **46** 64.00N 11.30E
Stellenbosch R.S.A. **74** 33.56S 18.51E
Stenay France **45** 49.29N 5.12E
Stendal E. Germany **44** 52.36N 11.52E
Stepanakert U.S.S.R. **57** 39.48N 46.45E
Stepney England **27** 51.31N 0.04W
Sterling U.S.A. **90** 40.37N 103.13W
Sterling Heights *town* U.S.A. **94** 44.08N 83.52W
Steubenville U.S.A. **94** 40.22N 80.39W
Stevenage England **29** 51.54N 0.11W
Stevenston Scotland **34** 55.39N 4.45W
Stewart Canada **92** 55.56N 130.01W
Stewart I. New Zealand **82** 47.00S 168.00E
Stewarton Scotland **34** 55.41N 4.31W
Stewartstown N. Ireland **34** 54.35N 6.42W
Steyning England **29** 50.54N 0.19W
Steyr Austria **44** 48.04N 14.25E
Stikine *r.* Canada **92** 56.45N 132.30W
Stikine Mts. Canada **92** 59.00N 129.00W
Stilton England **29** 52.29N 0.17W
Stinchar *r.* Scotland **34** 55.06N 5.00W
Stirling Scotland **35** 56.07N 3.57W
Stjördalshalsen Norway **46** 63.30N 10.59E
Stock England **27** 51.40N 0.26E
Stockbridge England **28** 51.07N 1.30W
Stockholm Sweden **46** 59.20N 18.05E
Stockport England **32** 53.25N 2.11W
Stocksbridge England **33** 53.30N 1.36W
Stockton U.S.A. **90** 37.59N 121.20W
Stockton-on-Tees England **33** 54.34N 1.20W
Stoer Scotland **36** 58.12N 5.20W
Stoer, Pt. of Scotland **36** 58.16N 5.23W
Stoke D'Abernon England **27** 51.19N 0.22W
Stoke Newington England **27** 51.34N 0.04W
Stoke-on-Trent England **32** 53.01N 2.11W
Stokesley England **33** 54.27N 1.12W
Stone Kent England **27** 51.27N 0.17E
Stone Staffs. England **32** 52.55N 2.10W
Stonehaven Scotland **37** 56.58N 2.13W
Stony Stratford England **28** 52.04N 0.51W
Stony Tunguska *r.* U.S.S.R. **49** 61.40N 90.00E
Stopsley England **27** 51.54N 0.24W
Stora Lule *r.* Sweden **46** 65.40N 21.48E
Stora Lulevatten *l.* Sweden **46** 67.00N 19.30E
Storavan *l.* Sweden **46** 65.45N 18.10E
Storby Finland **46** 60.14N 19.36E
Stord *i.* Norway **46** 59.50N 5.25E
Store Baelt *str.* Denmark **46** 55.30N 11.00E
Stören Norway **46** 63.03N 10.16E
Stornoway Scotland **36** 58.12N 6.23W
Storsjön *l.* Sweden **46** 63.10N 14.20E
Storuman Sweden **46** 65.05N 17.10E
Storuman *l.* Sweden **46** 65.14N 16.50E
Stotfold England **29** 52.02N 0.13W
Stoughton England **27** 51.15N 0.36W
Stour *r.* Dorset England **28** 50.43N 1.47W
Stour *r.* Kent England **29** 51.19N 1.22E
Stour *r.* Suffolk England **29** 51.56N 1.03E
Stourbridge England **28** 52.28N 2.08W
Stourport-on-Severn England **28** 52.21N 2.16W
Stow Scotland **35** 55.42N 2.52W
Stowmarket England **29** 52.11N 1.00E
Stow on the Wold England **28** 51.55N 1.42W
Strabane N. Ireland **38** 54.50N 7.30W
Strachur Scotland **34** 56.10N 5.04W
Stradbally Laois Rep. of Ire. **39** 53.01N 7.09W
Stradbally Waterford Rep. of Ire. **39** 52.08N 7.29W
Strahan Australia **80** 42.08S 145.21E
Stralsund E. Germany **44** 54.18N 13.06E
Strangford Lough N. Ireland **38** 54.28N 5.35W
Stranorlar Rep. of Ire. **38** 54.48N 7.48W
Stranraer Scotland **34** 54.54N 5.02W
Strasbourg France **44** 48.35N 7.45E
Stratford Canada **94** 43.22N 81.00W
Stratford New Zealand **82** 39.20S 174.18E
Stratford-upon-Avon England **28** 52.12N 1.42W
Strathallan *f.* Scotland **35** 56.14N 3.52W
Strathardle *f.* Scotland **35** 56.42N 3.28W
Strathaven *town* Scotland **35** 55.41N 4.05W
Strath Avon *f.* Scotland **37** 57.21N 3.21W
Strathbogie *f.* Scotland **37** 57.25N 2.55W
Strathclyde *d.* Scotland **34** 55.45N 4.45W
Strathdearn *f.* Scotland **37** 57.17N 4.00W
Strathearn *f.* Scotland **35** 56.20N 3.45W
Strathglass *f.* Scotland **37** 57.25N 4.38W
Strath Halladale *f.* Scotland **37** 58.27N 3.53W
Strath More *f.* Highland Scotland **37** 58.25N 4.38W
Strathmore *f.* Tayside Scotland **37** 56.44N 2.45W
Strathnairn *f.* Scotland **37** 57.23N 4.10W
Strathnaver *f.* Scotland **37** 58.24N 4.12W
Strath of Kildonan *f.* Scotland **37** 58.09N 3.50W
Strathpeffer *town* Scotland **37** 57.34N 4.33W
Strathspey *f.* Scotland **37** 57.25N 3.25W
Strath Tay *f.* Scotland **35** 56.38N 3.41W
Strathy Pt. Scotland **37** 58.35N 4.01W
Stratton England **31** 50.49N 4.31W
Straubing W. Germany **44** 48.53N 12.35E
Straumnes *c.* Iceland **46** 66.30N 23.05W
Streatham England **27** 51.26N 0.07W
Streek Head Rep. of Ire. **39** 51.29N 9.43W
Street England **28** 51.07N 2.43W
Strichen Scotland **37** 57.35N 2.05W
Striven, Loch Scotland **34** 55.57N 5.05W
Strokestown Rep. of Ire. **38** 53.46N 8.08W
Stroma *i.* Scotland **37** 58.41N 3.09W
Stromboli *i.* Italy **42** 38.48N 15.14E
Stromeferry Scotland **36** 57.21N 5.34W
Stromness Scotland **37** 58.57N 3.18W
Strömö *i.* Faroe Is. **46** 62.08N 7.00W
Strömstad Sweden **46** 58.56N 11.11E
Ströms Vattudal *l.* Sweden **46** 63.55N 15.30E
Stronsay *i.* Scotland **37** 59.07N 2.36W
Stronsay Firth *est.* Scotland **37** 59.05N 2.45W

For Khmer Republic *read* Kampuchea. *For* Malagasy Republic *read* Madagascar. *For* Rhodesia *read* Zimbabwe.

Strontian Scotland **34** 56.42N 5.33W
Strood England **27** 51.24N 0.28E
Stroud England **28** 51.44N 2.12W
Struma *r.* Greece **43** 40.45N 23.51E
Strumble Head Wales **30** 52.03N 5.05W
Strumica Yugo. **43** 41.26N 22.39E
Stryn Norway **46** 61.55N 6.47E
Stryy U.S.S.R. **47** 49.16N 23.51E
Stura *r.* Italy **40** 44.53N 8.38E
Sturgeon Falls *town* Canada **94** 46.22N 79.57W
Sturminster Newton England **28** 50.56N 2.18W
Sturt Desert Australia **80** 28.30S 141.12E
Stuttgart W. Germany **44** 48.47N 9.12E
Styr *r.* U.S.S.R. **47** 52.07N 26.35E
Suakin Sudan **69** 19.04N 37.22E
Subotica Yugo. **43** 46.04N 19.41E
Suchow China **63** 34.17N 117.18E
Suck *r.* Rep. of Ire. **38** 53.16N 8.04W
Sucre Bolivia **103** 19.05S 65.15W
Sudan Africa **69** 14.00N 30.00E
Sudbury Canada **94** 46.30N 81.01W
Sudbury England **29** 52.03N 0.45E
Sudd *f.* Sudan **69** 7.50N 30.00E
Sudeten Mts. Czech./Poland **44** 50.30N 16.30E
Sudirman Mts. Asia **61** 3.50S 136.30E
Suez Egypt **56** 29.59N 32.33E
Suez, G. of Egypt **56** 28.48N 33.00E
Suez Canal Egypt **56** 30.40N 32.20E
Suffolk *d.* England **29** 52.16N 1.00E
Sugar Hill Rep. of Ire. **39** 52.26N 9.11W
Sugarloaf Mtn. U.S.A. **95** 45.02N 70.18W
Sugluk Canada **93** 62.10N 75.40W
Suhl E. Germany **44** 50.37N 10.43E
Suir *r.* Rep. of Ire. **39** 52.17N 7.00W
Sukabumi Indonesia **60** 6.55S 106.50E
Sukadana Indonesia **60** 1.15S 110.00E
Sukaradja Indonesia **60** 2.23S 110.35E
Sukhinichi U.S.S.R. **47** 54.07N 35.21E
Sukhona *r.* U.S.S.R. **18** 61.30N 46.28E
Sukhumi U.S.S.R. **47** 43.01N 41.01E
Sukkertoppen Greenland **93** 65.40N 53.00W
Sukkur Pakistan **58** 27.42N 68.54E
Sulaimaniya Iraq **57** 35.32N 45.27E
Sulaiman Range *mts.* Pakistan **58** 30.50N 70.20E
Sulaimiya Saudi Arabia **57** 24.10N 47.20E
Sula Is. Indonesia **61** 1.50S 125.10E
Sulawesi *d.* Indonesia **61** 2.00S 120.30E
Sulina Romania **43** 45.08N 29.40E
Sullane *r.* Rep. of Ire. **39** 51.53N 8.56W
Sullom Voe *b.* Scotland **36** 60.29N 1.16W
Sulmona Italy **42** 42.04N 13.57E
Sultanabad Iran **57** 36.25N 58.02E
Sulu Archipelago Phil. **61** 5.30N 121.00E
Sulu Sea Pacific Oc. **61** 8.00N 120.00E
Sumatra *i.* Indonesia **60** 2.00S 102.00E
Sumba *i.* Indonesia **60** 9.30S 119.55E
Sumbar *r.* U.S.S.R. **57** 38.00N 55.20E
Sumbawa *i.* Indonesia **60** 8.45S 117.50E
Sumbawanga Tanzania **73** 7.58S 31.36E
Sumburgh Head Scotland **36** 59.51N 1.16W
Sumgait U.S.S.R. **57** 40.35N 49.38E
Summan *f.* Saudi Arabia **57** 27.00N 47.00E
Summer Is. Scotland **36** 58.01N 5.26W
Sumy U.S.S.R. **47** 50.55N 34.49E
Sunart *f.* Scotland **36** 56.44N 5.35W
Sunart, Loch Scotland **36** 56.43N 5.45W
Sunbury England **27** 51.24N 0.25W
Sunbury U.S.A. **95** 40.52N 76.47W
Sundarbans *f.* India/Bangla. **58** 22.00N 89.00E
Sundargarh India **58** 22.04N 84.08E
Sunda Str. Indonesia **60** 6.00S 105.50E
Sundays *r.* R.S.A. **74** 33.49S 25.46E
Sunderland England **35** 54.55N 1.22W
Sundsvall Sweden **46** 62.22N 17.20E
Sungari *r.* China **63** 47.46N 132.30E
Sungurlu Turkey **56** 40.10N 34.23E
Sunninghill *town* England **27** 51.24N 0.39W
Sunyani Ghana **70** 7.22N 2.18W
Suomussalmi Finland **46** 64.52N 29.10E
Suonenjoki Finland **46** 62.40N 27.06E
Supaul India **58** 26.57N 86.15E
Superior U.S.A. **94** 46.42N 92.05W
Superior, L. N. America **94** 48.00N 88.00W
Süphan Dağlari *mtn.* Turkey **56** 38.55N 42.55E
Sur Oman **57** 22.23N 59.32E
Sura U.S.S.R. **47** 53.52N 45.45E
Sura *r.* U.S.S.R. **47** 56.13N 46.00E
Surabaya Indonesia **60** 7.14S 112.45E
Surakarta Indonesia **60** 7.32S 110.50E
Surat Australia **80** 27.10S 149.05E
Surat India **58** 21.10N 72.54E
Surat Thani Thailand **59** 9.03N 99.28E
Surbiton England **27** 51.24N 0.19W
Sûre *r.* Lux. **45** 49.43N 6.31E
Surigao Phil. **61** 9.47N 125.29E
Surin Thailand **59** 14.50N 103.34E

Surinam S. America **102** 4.00N 56.00W
Surrey *d.* England **29** 51.16N 0.30W
Surrey Hill England **27** 51.23N 0.43W
Surtsey *i.* Iceland **46** 63.18N 20.37W
Susquehanna *r.* U.S.A. **95** 39.33N 76.05W
Sutherland R.S.A. **74** 32.24S 20.40E
Sutlej *r.* Pakistan **58** 29.26N 71.09E
Sutton G.L. England **27** 51.22N 0.12W
Sutton Surrey England **27** 51.12N 0.26W
Sutton Bridge England **33** 52.46N 0.12E
Sutton Coldfield England **28** 52.33N 1.50W
Sutton in Ashfield England **33** 53.08N 1.16W
Sutton on Sea England **33** 53.18N 0.18E
Suwanee *r.* U.S.A. **96** 29.15N 82.50W
Svartisen *mtn.* Norway **46** 66.30N 14.00E
Sveg Sweden **46** 62.02N 14.20E
Svendborg Denmark **46** 55.04N 10.38E
Sverdlovsk U.S.S.R. **48** 56.52N 60.35E
Svetogorsk U.S.S.R. **47** 61.07N 28.50E
Svishtov Bulgaria **43** 43.36N 25.23E
Svobodnyy U.S.S.R. **63** 51.24N 128.05E
Svolvaer Norway **46** 68.15N 14.40E
Swabian Jura *mts.* W. Germany **44** 48.20N 9.20E
Swadlincote England **33** 52.47N 1.34W
Swaffham England **29** 52.38N 0.42E
Swakop *r.* S.W. Africa **74** 22.38S 14.30E
Swakopmund S.W. Africa **74** 22.40S 14.34E
Swale *r.* England **33** 54.05N 1.20W
Swanage England **28** 50.36N 1.59W
Swan Hill *town* Australia **80** 35.23S 143.37E
Swanley England **27** 51.24N 0.12E
Swanlinbar Rep. of Ire. **38** 54.12N 7.44W
Swan River *town* Canada **90** 52.06N 101.17W
Swanscombe England **27** 51.26N 0.19E
Swansea Wales **31** 51.37N 3.57W
Swansea B. Wales **31** 51.33N 3.50W
Swarbacks Minn *str.* Scotland **36** 60.22N 1.21W
Swartberg Range *mts.* R.S.A. **74** 33.20S 22.00E
Swatow China **60** 23.23N 116.39E
Swaziland Africa **74** 26.30S 32.00E
Sweden Europe **46** 63.00N 16.00E
Sweetwater U.S.A. **90** 32.37N 100.25W
Swidnica Poland **44** 50.51N 16.29E
Swift Current *town* Canada **90** 50.17N 107.49W
Swilly *r.* Rep. of Ire. **38** 54.57N 7.42W
Swilly, Lough Rep. of Ire. **38** 55.10N 7.32W
Swindon England **28** 51.33N 1.47W
Swinford Rep. of Ire. **38** 53.56N 8.57W
Swinoujscie Poland **44** 53.55N 14.18E
Switzerland Europe **44** 47.00N 8.15E
Swords Rep. of Ire. **38** 53.27N 6.15W
Syderö *i.* Faroe Is. **46** 61.30N 6.52W
Sydney Australia **80** 33.55S 151.10E
Sydney Canada **93** 46.10N 60.10W
Syktyvkar U.S.S.R. **48** 61.42N 50.45E
Sylhet Bangla. **59** 24.53N 91.51E
Sylt *i.* W. Germany **44** 54.50N 8.20E
Syracuse U.S.A. **95** 43.03N 76.10W
Syr Darya *r.* U.S.S.R. **48** 46.00N 61.12E
Syria Asia **56** 35.00N 38.00E
Syrian Desert Asia **56** 32.00N 39.00E
Syzran U.S.S.R. **47** 53.10N 48.29E
Szczecin Poland **44** 53.25N 14.32E
Szczecinek Poland **44** 53.42N 16.41E
Szechwan *d.* China **62** 30.30N 103.00E
Szeged Hungary **43** 46.16N 20.08E
Szekszárd Hungary **43** 46.22N 18.44E
Szemao China **59** 22.50N 101.00E
Szenan China **63** 27.56N 108.22E
Szombathely Hungary **47** 47.12N 16.38E

T

Tabarka Tunisia **42** 36.56N 8.43E
Tabas Khorāsān Iran **57** 32.48N 60.14E
Tabas Khorāsān Iran **57** 33.36N 56.55E
Tabasco *d.* Mexico **96** 18.30N 93.00W
Table B. R.S.A. **74** 33.30S 18.05E
Tábor Czech. **44** 49.25N 14.41E
Tabora Tanzania **73** 5.02S 32.50E
Tabora *d.* Tanzania **73** 5.30S 32.50E
Tabou Ivory Coast **70** 4.28N 7.20W
Tabriz Iran **57** 38.05N 46.18E
Tacloban Phil. **61** 11.15N 124.59E
Tacoma U.S.A. **90** 47.16N 122.30W
Taconic Mts. U.S.A. **95** 42.00N 73.45W
Tacuarembó Uruguay **103** 31.42S 56.00W
Tadcaster England **33** 53.53N 1.16W
Tademait Plateau Algeria **68** 28.45N 2.10E
Tadoussac Canada **95** 48.09N 69.43W
Tadzhikistan Soviet Socialist Republic *d.* U.S.S.R. **62** 39.00N 70.30E
Taegu S. Korea **63** 35.52N 128.36E
Taejon S. Korea **63** 36.20N 127.26E

Tafersit Morocco **41** 35.01N 3.33W
Taganrog U.S.S.R. **47** 47.14N 38.55E
Taganrog, G. of U.S.S.R. **47** 47.00N 38.30E
Taghmon Rep. of Ire. **39** 52.20N 6.40W
Tagus *r.* Portugal **41** 39.00N 8.57W
Tahat, Mt. Algeria **71** 23.30N 5.40E
Taichow China **63** 32.30N 119.50E
Taichung Taiwan **63** 24.09N 120.40E
Taihape New Zealand **82** 39.40S 175.48E
Taima Saudi Arabia **56** 27.37N 38.30E
Tain Scotland **37** 57.48N 4.04W
Tainan Taiwan **61** 23.01N 120.14E
Taipei Taiwan **63** 25.05N 121.32E
Taiping Malaysia **60** 4.54N 100.42E
Taitung Taiwan **63** 22.49N 121.10E
Taivalkoski Finland **46** 65.35N 28.20E
Taiwan Asia **63** 23.30N 121.00E
Taiyuan China **63** 37.50N 112.30E
Taizz Yemen **69** 13.35N 44.02E
Tajan Indonesia **60** 0.02S 110.05E
Tajrish Iran **57** 35.48N 51.20E
Tak Thailand **59** 16.47N 99.10E
Takamatsu Japan **63** 34.20N 134.01E
Takeley England **27** 51.52N 0.15E
Takestan Iran **57** 36.02N 49.40E
Takht-i-Suleiman *mtn.* Iran **57** 36.23N 50.59E
Takla Makan *des.* China **62** 38.10N 82.00E
Talasskiy Ala Tau *mts.* U.S.S.R. **62** 42.20N 73.20E
Talaud Is. Indonesia **61** 4.20N 126.50E
Talavera de la Reina Spain **41** 39.58N 4.50W
Talca Chile **102** 36.00S 71.40W
Taldom U.S.S.R. **47** 56.49N 37.30E
Talgarth Wales **30** 51.59N 3.15W
Taliabu *i.* Indonesia **61** 1.50S 124.55E
Talkeetna U.S.A. **92** 62.20N 150.09W
Tallahassee U.S.A. **91** 30.28N 84.19W
Tallinn U.S.S.R. **46** 59.22N 24.48E
Tallow Rep. of Ire. **39** 52.06N 8.01W
Talsi U.S.S.R. **47** 57.18N 22.39E
Tamale Ghana **70** 9.26N 0.49W
Tamanrasset Algeria **71** 22.50N 5.31E
Tamar *r.* England **31** 50.28N 4.13W
Tamatave Malagasy Rep. **67** 18.10S 49.23E
Tamaulipas *d.* Mexico **96** 24.00N 98.20W
Tambacounda Senegal **70** 13.45N 13.40W
Tambohorano Malagasy Rep. **73** 17.40S 43.59E
Tambov U.S.S.R. **47** 52.44N 41.28E
Tambre *r.* Spain **41** 42.50N 8.55W
Tamega *r.* Portugal **41** 41.04N 8.17W
Tamil Nadu *d.* India **59** 11.15N 79.00E
Tampa U.S.A. **91** 27.58N 82.38W
Tampa B. U.S.A. **96** 27.48N 82.15W
Tampere Finland **46** 61.32N 23.45E
Tampico Mexico **96** 22.18N 97.52W
Tamsag Bulag Mongolia **63** 47.10N 117.21E
Tamworth Australia **80** 31.07S 150.57E
Tamworth England **28** 52.38N 1.42W
Tana *r.* Kenya **73** 2.32S 40.32E
Tana Norway **46** 70.26N 28.14E
Tana *r.* Norway **46** 69.45N 28.15E
Tana, L. Ethiopia **69** 12.00N 37.20E
Tanacross U.S.A. **92** 63.12N 143.30W
Tanana U.S.A. **92** 65.11N 152.10W
Tananarive Malagasy Rep. **67** 18.52S 47.30E
Tanaro *r.* Italy **42** 45.01N 8.46E
Tanat *r.* Wales **30** 52.46N 3.07W
Tanderagee N. Ireland **38** 54.22N 6.27W
Tandil Argentina **103** 37.18S 59.10W
Tandjungpandan Indonesia **60** 2.44S 107.36E
Tanga Tanzania **73** 5.07S 39.05E
Tanga *d.* Tanzania **73** 5.20S 38.30E
Tanganyika, L. Africa **73** 6.00S 29.30E
Tanger *see* Tangier Morocco **41**
Tangier Morocco **41** 35.48N 5.45W
Tangha Range *mts.* China **62** 32.40N 92.30E
Tangra Yum *l.* China **59** 31.00N 86.30E
Tangshan China **63** 39.37N 118.05E
Tanimbar Is. Indonesia **61** 7.50S 131.30E
Tanjung Datu *c.* Malaysia **60** 2.00N 109.30E
Tanjungkarang Indonesia **60** 5.28S 105.16E
Tanjung Puting *c.* Indonesia **60** 3.35S 111.52E
Tanjungredeb Indonesia **60** 2.09N 117.29E
Tanjung Selatan *c.* Indonesia **60** 4.20S 114.45E
Tannu Ola Range *mts.* U.S.S.R. **49** 51.00N 93.30E
Tano *r.* Ghana **70** 5.07N 2.54W
Tanout Niger **71** 14.55N 8.49E
Tanta Egypt **56** 30.48N 31.00E
Tanzania Africa **73** 5.00S 35.00E
Taonan China **63** 45.25N 122.46E
Taoudenni Mali **70** 22.45N 4.00W
Tapachula Mexico **96** 14.54N 92.15W
Tapai Shan *mtn.* China **59** 34.00N 107.40E
Tapajós *r.* Brazil **102** 2.40S 55.00W
Tapti *r.* India **58** 21.05N 72.45E
Taquari *r.* Brazil **103** 19.00S 57.22W

Tara r. U.S.S.R. **48** 56.30N 74.40E
Tara r. Yugo. **43** 43.23N 18.47E
Tarakan Indonesia **60** 3.20N 117.38E
Tarancón Spain **41** 40.01N 3.01W
Taransay i. Scotland **36** 57.53N 7.03W
Taranto Italy **43** 40.28N 17.14E
Taranto, G. of Italy **43** 40.00N 17.20E
Tararua Range mts. New Zealand **82** 40.45S 175.30E
Tarbagatay Range mts. U.S.S.R. **62** 47.00N 83.00E
Tarbat Ness c. Scotland **37** 57.52N 3.46W
Tarbert Rep. of Ire. **39** 52.34N 9.24W
Tarbert Strath. Scotland **34** 55.51N 5.25W
Tarbert W. Isles Scotland **36** 57.54N 6.49W
Tarbert, Loch Scotland **34** 55.48N 5.31W
Tarbes France **40** 43.14N 0.05E
Tarbolton Scotland **34** 55.31N 4.29W
Tardoire r. France **40** 45.57N 1.00W
Taree Australia **80** 31.54S 152.26E
Tarfa, Wadi r. Egypt **56** 28.36N 30.50E
Tarifa Spain **41** 36.01N 5.36W
Tarija Bolivia **103** 21.33S 64.45W
Tarija d. Bolivia **103** 21.30S 64.00W
Tarim r. China **62** 41.00N 83.30E
Tarim Basin f. Asia **107** 40.00N 83.00E
Tarkwa Ghana **70** 5.16N 1.59W
Tarlac Phil. **61** 15.29N 120.35E
Tarland Scotland **37** 57.08N 2.52W
Tarleton England **32** 53.41N 2.50W
Tarn r. France **40** 44.15N 1.15E
Tarnow Poland **47** 50.01N 20.59E
Tarporley England **32** 53.10N 2.42W
Tarragona Spain **41** 41.07N 1.15E
Tarrasa Spain **41** 41.34N 2.00E
Tarsus Turkey **56** 36.52N 34.52E
Tartary, G. of U.S.S.R. **49** 47.40N 141.00E
Tartu U.S.S.R. **46** 58.20N 26.44E
Tashkent U.S.S.R. **62** 41.16N 69.13E
Tasman B. New Zealand **82** 41.00S 173.15E
Tasmania d. Australia **80** 42.00S 147.00E
Tasman Mts. New Zealand **82** 41.00S 172.40E
Tasman Pen. Australia **80** 43.08S 147.51E
Tasman Sea Pacific Oc. **107** 38.00S 163.00E
Tatarsk U.S.S.R. **48** 55.14N 76.00E
Tatnam, C. Canada **93** 57.00N 91.00W
Tatsaitan China **62** 37.44N 95.08E
Tatsfield England **27** 51.18N 0.02E
Tatu r. China **59** 28.47N 104.40E
Tatvan Turkey **56** 38.31N 42.15E
Taubaté Brazil **103** 23.00S 45.36W
Taumarunui New Zealand **82** 38.53S 175.16E
Taung R.S.A. **74** 27.32S 24.48E
Taung-gyi Burma **59** 20.49N 97.01E
Taunton England **31** 51.01N 3.07W
Taunton U.S.A. **95** 41.54N 71.06W
Taunus mts. W. Germany **44** 50.07N 7.48E
Taupo New Zealand **82** 38.42S 176.06E
Taupo, L. New Zealand **82** 38.45S 175.30E
Tauranga New Zealand **82** 37.42S 176.11E
Taurus Mts. Turkey **56** 37.15N 34.15E
Taveta Kenya **73** 3.23S 37.42E
Tavira Portugal **41** 37.07N 7.39W
Tavistock England **31** 50.33N 4.09W
Tavoy Burma **59** 14.07N 98.18E
Tavy r. England **31** 50.27N 4.10W
Taw r. England **31** 51.05N 4.05W
Tawau Malaysia **60** 4.16N 117.54E
Tawe r. Wales **31** 51.38N 3.56W
Tay r. Scotland **35** 56.21N 3.18W
Tay, Loch Scotland **34** 56.32N 4.08W
Taylor, Mt. U.S.A. **90** 35.14N 107.36W
Taymyr, L. U.S.S.R. **49** 74.20N 101.00E
Taymyr Pen. U.S.S.R. **49** 75.30N 99.00E
Taynuilt Scotland **34** 56.26N 5.14W
Tayport Scotland **35** 56.27N 2.53W
Tayshet U.S.S.R. **49** 55.56N 98.01E
Tayside d. Scotland **35** 56.35N 3.28W
Taytay Phil. **60** 10.47N 119.32E
Taz r. U.S.S.R. **48** 67.30N 78.50E
Tbilisi U.S.S.R. **57** 41.43N 44.48E
Tchibanga Gabon **72** 2.52S 11.07E
Te Anau, L. New Zealand **82** 45.10S 167.15E
Te Araroa New Zealand **82** 37.38S 178.25E
Te Awamutu New Zealand **82** 38.00S 175.20E
Tebessa Algeria **42** 35.22N 8.08E
Tebuk Saudi Arabia **56** 28.25N 36.35E
Tecuci Romania **43** 45.49N 27.27E
Teddington England **27** 51.25N 0.20W
Tees r. England **33** 54.35N 1.11W
Tees B. England **33** 54.40N 1.07W
Teesdale f. England **32** 54.38N 2.08W
Tegucigalpa Honduras **96** 14.05N 87.14W
Tehran Iran **57** 35.40N 51.26E
Tehtsin China **59** 28.45N 98.58E
Tehuacán Mexico **96** 18.30N 97.26W
Tehuantepec Mexico **96** 16.21N 95.13W
Tehuantepec, G. of Mexico **96** 16.00N 95.00W

Tehuantepec, Isthmus of Mexico **96** 17.00N 94.00W
Teifi r. Wales **30** 52.05N 4.41W
Teign r. England **31** 50.32N 3.46W
Teignmouth England **31** 50.33N 3.30W
Teisenberg mtn. W. Germany **44** 47.48N 12.46E
Teith r. Scotland **35** 56.09N 4.00W
Teixeira de Sousa Angola **72** 10.41S 22.09E
Tekapo, L. New Zealand **82** 43.35S 170.30E
Tekirdağ Turkey **43** 40.59N 27.30E
Te Kuiti New Zealand **82** 38.20S 175.10E
Tela Honduras **96** 15.56N 87.25W
Telanaipura Indonesia **60** 1.36S 103.39E
Telavi U.S.S.R. **57** 41.56N 45.30E
Tel Aviv-Jaffa Israel **56** 32.05N 34.46E
Tele r. Zaïre **72** 2.48N 24.00E
Telford England **28** 52.42N 2.30W
Telgte W. Germany **45** 51.59N 7.46E
Telimélé Guinea **70** 10.54N 13.02W
Tel Kotchek Syria **56** 36.48N 42.04E
Tell Atlas mts. Algeria **68** 36.10N 4.00E
Telok Anson Malaysia **60** 4.00N 101.00E
Teluk Berau b. Asia **61** 2.20S 133.00E
Teluk Irian b. Asia **61** 2.30S 135.20E
Tema Ghana **70** 5.41N 0.01W
Tembo Aluma Angola **72** 7.42S 17.15E
Teme r. England **28** 52.10N 2.13W
Temora Australia **80** 34.27S 147.35E
Témpio Italy **42** 40.54N 9.06E
Temple U.S.A. **91** 31.06N 97.22W
Temple Ewell England **29** 51.09N 1.16E
Templemore Rep. of Ire. **39** 52.48N 7.51W
Tenasserim Burma **60** 12.05N 99.00E
Tenasserim d. Burma **59** 13.00N 99.00E
Tenbury Wells England **28** 52.18N 2.35W
Tenby Wales **31** 51.40N 4.42W
Ten Degree Channel Indian Oc. **60** 10.00N 92.30E
Tenerife i. Africa **68** 28.10N 16.30W
Tengchung China **59** 25.02N 98.28E
Tenghsien China **63** 35.10N 117.14E
Tengiz, L. U.S.S.R. **48** 50.30N 69.00E
Tenke Zaïre **72** 10.34S 26.07E
Tennant Creek town Australia **79** 19.31S 134.15E
Tennessee d. U.S.A. **91** 36.00N 86.00W
Tennessee r. U.S.A. **91** 37.10N 88.25W
Tenterden England **29** 51.04N 0.42E
Tenterfield Australia **80** 29.01S 152.04E
Teplice Czech. **44** 50.40N 13.50E
Ter r. England **27** 51.45N 0.36E
Ter r. Spain **41** 42.02N 3.10E
Tera r. Portugal **41** 38.55N 8.01W
Téramo Italy **42** 42.40N 13.43E
Teresina Brazil **102** 5.09S 42.46W
Termez U.S.S.R. **48** 37.15N 67.15E
Termini Italy **42** 37.59N 13.42E
Terminos Lagoon Mexico **96** 18.30N 91.30W
Termoli Italy **42** 41.58N 14.59E
Ternate Indonesia **61** 0.48N 127.23E
Terneuzen Neth. **45** 51.20N 3.50E
Terni Italy **42** 42.34N 12.44E
Ternopol U.S.S.R. **47** 49.35N 25.39E
Terre Haute U.S.A. **94** 39.27N 87.24W
Terschelling i. Neth. **45** 53.25N 5.25E
Teruel Spain **41** 40.21N 1.06W
Teslin r. Canada **92** 62.00N 135.00W
Tessaoua Niger **71** 13.46N 7.55E
Test r. England **28** 50.55N 1.29W
Tet r. France **40** 42.43N 3.00E
Tetbury England **28** 51.37N 2.09W
Tete Moçambique **73** 16.10S 33.30E
Tete d. Moçambique **73** 15.30S 33.00E
Teterev r. U.S.S.R. **47** 51.03N 30.30E
Tetney England **33** 53.30N 0.01W
Tetuan Morocco **41** 35.34N 5.22W
Teuco r. Argentina **103** 25.37S 60.10W
Teviot r. Scotland **35** 55.36N 2.27W
Teviotdale f. Scotland **35** 55.26N 2.46W
Teviothead Scotland **35** 55.20N 2.56W
Tewkesbury England **28** 51.59N 2.09W
Texarkana U.S.A. **91** 33.28N 94.02W
Texas d. U.S.A. **90** 32.00N 100.00W
Texel i. Neth. **45** 53.05N 4.47E
Texoma, L. U.S.A. **91** 34.00N 96.40W
Tezpur India **59** 26.38N 92.49E
Thabana Ntlenyana mtn. Lesotho **74** 29.30S 29.10E
Thabazimbi R.S.A. **74** 24.41S 27.21E
Thailand Asia **59** 16.00N 102.00E
Thakhek Laos **59** 17.25N 104.45E
Thala Tunisia **42** 35.35N 8.38E
Thale Luang l. Thailand **60** 7.30N 100.20E
Thallon Australia **80** 28.39S 148.49E
Thame England **28** 51.44N 0.58W
Thame r. England **28** 51.38N 1.10W
Thames r. Canada **94** 42.20N 82.25W
Thames r. England **27** 51.30N 0.05E
Thames New Zealand **82** 37.08S 175.35E
Thames Haven England **27** 51.31N 0.31E

Thana India **58** 19.14N 73.02E
Thanh Hoa Vietnam **60** 19.50N 105.48E
Thar Desert India **58** 28.00N 72.00E
Thargomindah Australia **80** 27.59S 143.45E
Tharrawaddy Burma **62** 17.37N 95.48E
Tharthar, Wadi r. Iraq **56** 34.18N 43.07E
Tharthar Basin f. Iraq **56** 33.56N 43.16E
Thásos i. Greece **43** 40.40N 24.39E
Thaton Burma **59** 17.00N 97.39E
Thaungdut Burma **59** 24.26N 94.45E
Thaxted England **29** 51.57N 0.21E
Thayetmyo Burma **59** 19.20N 95.18E
The Aird f. Scotland **37** 57.26N 4.23W
Thebes ruins Egypt **56** 25.41N 32.40E
The Buck mtn. Scotland **37** 57.18N 2.59W
The Cherokees, L. O' U.S.A. **91** 36.45N 94.50W
The Cheviot mtn. England **35** 55.29N 2.10W
The Cheviot Hills England/Scotland **35** 55.22N 2.24W
The Coorong Australia **80** 36.00S 139.30E
The Everglades f. U.S.A. **91** 26.00N 80.30W
The Fens f. England **29** 52.32N 0.13E
The Glenkens f. Scotland **34** 55.10N 4.13W
The Grenadines is. St. Vincent **97** 13.00N 61.20W
The Hague Neth. **45** 52.05N 4.16E
The Hebrides, Sea of Scotland **36** 57.05N 7.05W
The Little Minch str. Scotland **36** 57.40N 6.45W
Thelon r. Canada **93** 64.23N 96.15W
The Long Mynd hill England **28** 52.33N 2.50W
The Machers f. Scotland **34** 54.45N 4.28W
The Marsh f. England **33** 52.50N 0.10E
The Minch str. Scotland **36** 58.10N 5.50W
The Mumbles Wales **31** 51.34N 4.00W
The Naze c. England **29** 51.53N 1.17E
The Needles c. England **28** 50.39N 1.35W
The North Sd. Scotland **37** 59.18N 2.45W
Theodore Roosevelt L. U.S.A. **90** 33.30N 111.10W
The Ox Mts. Rep. of Ire. **38** 54.06N 8.52W
The Paps mts. Rep. of Ire. **39** 52.01N 9.14W
The Pas Canada **93** 53.50N 101.15W
The Pennines hills England **32** 55.40N 2.20W
The Potteries f. England **32** 53.00N 2.10W
The Rhinns f. Scotland **34** 54.50N 5.02W
The Six Towns town N. Ireland **34** 54.45N 6.53W
The Skerries is. Wales **30** 53.27N 4.35W
The Solent str. England **28** 50.45N 1.20W
Thessaloniki Greece **43** 40.38N 22.56E
Thessaloniki, G. of Med. Sea **43** 40.10N 23.00E
The Storr mtn. Scotland **36** 57.30N 6.11W
The Swale str. England **29** 51.22N 0.58E
Thetford England **29** 52.25N 0.44E
Thetford Mines town Canada **95** 46.06N 71.18W
The Trossachs f. Scotland **34** 56.15N 4.25W
The Twelve Pins mts. Rep. of Ire. **38** 53.30N 9.49W
The Wash b. England **33** 52.55N 0.15E
The Weald f. England **29** 51.05N 0.20E
The Woods, L. of N. America **91** 49.46N 94.30W
The Wrekin hill England **28** 52.40N 2.33W
Theydon Bois England **27** 51.40N 0.05E
Thiers France **40** 45.51N 3.33E
Thiès Senegal **70** 14.50N 16.55W
Thimphu Bhutan **58** 27.29N 89.40E
Thionville France **44** 49.22N 6.11E
Thíra i. Greece **43** 36.24N 25.27E
Thirsk England **33** 54.15N 1.20W
Thisted Denmark **46** 56.58N 8.42E
Thitu Is. Asia **60** 10.50N 114.20E
Thjórsá r. Iceland **46** 63.53N 20.38W
Thok-Jalung China **59** 32.26N 81.37E
Tholen i. Neth. **45** 51.34N 4.07E
Thomastown Rep. of Ire. **39** 52.32N 7.08W
Thomasville U.S.A. **91** 30.50N 83.59W
Thornaby-on-Tees England **33** 54.34N 1.18W
Thornbury England **28** 51.36N 2.31W
Thorne England **33** 53.36N 0.56W
Thorney England **29** 52.37N 0.08W
Thornhill Scotland **35** 55.15N 3.46W
Thornton England **32** 53.53N 3.00W
Thornwood Common town England **27** 51.43N 0.08E
Thorpe England **27** 51.25N 0.31W
Thorpe-le-Soken England **29** 51.50N 1.11E
Thorshavn Faroe Is. **46** 62.02N 6.47W
Thouars France **40** 46.59N 0.13W
Thrapston England **29** 52.24N 0.32W
Threshel r. England **31** 50.38N 4.19W
Thuin Belgium **45** 50.21N 4.20E
Thule Greenland **93** 77.40N 69.00W
Thun Switz. **44** 46.46N 7.38E
Thunder Bay town Canada **94** 48.25N 89.14W
Thuringian Forest f. E. Germany **44** 50.40N 10.50E
Thurles Rep. of Ire. **39** 52.41N 7.50W
Thurnscoe England **33** 53.31N 1.19W
Thursby England **35** 54.40N 3.03W
Thursday I. Australia **61** 10.45S 142.00E
Thurso Scotland **37** 58.35N 3.32W
Thurso r. Scotland **37** 58.35N 3.32W
Tiaret Algeria **41** 35.20N 1.20E

Tibati to **Trotternish** 167

Tibati Cameroon **71** 6.25N 12.33E
Tiber *r.* Italy **42** 41.45N 12.16E
Tiberias, L. Israel **56** 32.49N 35.36E
Tibesti Mts. Chad **71** 21.00N 17.30E
Tibet *d.* China **59** 32.20N 86.00E
Tibetan Plateau *f.* China **59** 34.00N 84.30E
Tibooburra Australia **80** 29.28S 142.04E
Tiburon I. Mexico **90** 29.00N 112.25W
Ticehurst England **29** 51.02N 0.23E
Ticino *r.* Italy **40** 45.09N 9.12E
Tickhill England **33** 53.25N 1.08W
Tidjikja Mauritania **70** 18.29N 11.31W
Tiel Neth. **45** 51.53N 5.26E
Tielt Belgium **45** 51.00N 3.20E
Tien Shan *mts.* Asia **62** 42.00N 80.30E
Tienshui China **62** 34.25N 105.58E
Tientsin China **63** 39.08N 117.12E
Tierra Blanca Mexico **96** 18.28N 96.12W
Tierra del Fuego *i.* S. America **102** 54.00S 68.30W
Tiétar *r.* Spain **41** 39.50N 6.00W
Tietê *r.* Brazil **103** 20.43S 51.30W
Tighnabruaich Scotland **34** 55.56N 5.14W
Tigris *r.* Asia **57** 31.00N 47.27E
Tihama *f.* Saudi Arabia **69** 20.30N 40.30E
Tijuana Mexico **90** 32.29N 117.10W
Tikhoretsk U.S.S.R. **47** 45.52N 40.07E
Tikhvin U.S.S.R. **47** 59.35N 33.29E
Tiko Cameroon **72** 4.09N 9.19E
Tiksi U.S.S.R. **49** 71.40N 128.45E
Tilburg Neth. **45** 51.34N 5.05E
Tilbury England **27** 51.28N 0.23E
Till *r.* England **35** 55.41N 2.12W
Tillabéri Niger **71** 14.28N 1.27E
Tillicoultry Scotland **35** 56.09N 3.45W
Tilt *r.* Scotland **37** 56.46N 3.50W
Timagami L. Canada **94** 46.55N 80.03W
Timaru New Zealand **82** 44.23S 171.41E
Timbuktu Mali **70** 16.49N 2.59W
Timişoara Romania **43** 45.47N 21.15E
Timişul *r.* Yugo. **43** 44.49N 20.28E
Timmins Canada **94** 48.30N 81.20W
Timok *r.* Yugo. **43** 44.13N 22.40E
Timoleague Rep. of Ire. **39** 51.38N 8.46W
Timor *i.* Austa. **61** 9.30S 125.00E
Timor Sea Austa. **79** 13.00S 122.00E
Tinahely Rep. of Ire. **39** 52.48N 6.19W
Tinglev Denmark **44** 54.57N 9.15E
Tingsryd Sweden **46** 56.31N 15.00E
Tinian *i.* Asia **61** 14.58N 145.38E
Tinkisso *r.* Guinea **70** 11.25N 9.05W
Tinne *r.* Norway **46** 59.05N 9.43E
Tínos *i.* Greece **43** 37.36N 25.08E
Tintagel Head England **31** 50.40N 4.45W
Tinto Hills Scotland **35** 55.36N 3.40W
Tioman *i.* Malaysia **60** 2.45N 104.10E
Tipperary Rep. of Ire. **39** 52.29N 8.10W
Tipperary *d.* Rep. of Ire. **39** 52.37N 7.55W
Tip Top Mtn. Canada **94** 48.16N 86.02W
Tiptree England **29** 51.48N 0.46E
Tiranë Albania **43** 41.20N 19.48E
Tirano Italy **42** 46.12N 10.10E
Tiraspol U.S.S.R. **47** 46.50N 29.38E
Tirebolu Turkey **56** 41.02N 38.49E
Tiree *i.* Scotland **34** 56.30N 6.50W
Tirga Mor *mtn.* Scotland **36** 58.00N 6.59W
Tirgu-Jiu Romania **43** 45.03N 23.17E
Tirgu Mures Romania **47** 46.33N 24.34E
Tirlemont Belgium **45** 50.49N 4.56E
Tirso *r.* Italy **42** 39.52N 8.33E
Tiruchirapalli India **59** 10.50N 78.43E
Tiruppur India **58** 11.05N 77.20E
Tisza *r.* Yugo. **43** 45.09N 20.16E
Titicaca, L. S. America **102** 16.00S 69.00W
Titograd Yugo. **43** 42.30N 19.16E
Titovo Užice Yugo. **43** 43.52N 19.51E
Titov Veles Yugo. **43** 41.43N 21.49E
Tiumpan Head Scotland **36** 58.15N 6.10W
Tiverton England **31** 50.54N 3.30W
Tizimín Mexico **96** 21.10N 88.09W
Tizi Ouzou Algeria **41** 36.44N 4.05E
Tlaxcala *d.* Mexico **96** 19.45N 98.20W
Tlemcen Algeria **41** 34.53N 1.21W
Tletat ed Douair Algeria **41** 36.15N 3.40E
Toba, L. Indonesia **60** 2.45N 98.50E
Tobago S. America **97** 11.15N 60.40W
Tobelo Indonesia **61** 1.45N 127.59E
Tobermory Scotland **34** 56.37N 6.04W
Tobi *i.* Asia **61** 3.01N 131.10E
Toboali Indonesia **60** 3.00S 106.30E
Tobol *r.* U.S.S.R. **48** 58.15N 68.12E
Tobolsk U.S.S.R. **48** 58.15N 68.12E
Tobruk Libya **69** 32.06N 23.58E
Tocantins *r.* Brazil **102** 2.40S 49.20W
Tocumwal Australia **80** 35.51S 145.34E
Todmorden England **32** 53.43N 2.07W
Toe Head Rep. of Ire. **39** 51.29N 9.15W
Toe Head Scotland **36** 57.50N 7.07W
Togian Is. Indonesia **61** 0.20S 122.00E
Togo Africa **70** 8.00N 1.00E
Tokat Turkey **56** 40.20N 36.35E
Tokoroa New Zealand **82** 38.13S 175.53E
Tokuno *i.* Japan **63** 27.40N 129.00E
Tokyo Japan **63** 35.40N 139.45E
Tolbukhin Bulgaria **43** 43.34N 27.52E
Toledo Spain **41** 39.52N 4.02W
Toledo U.S.A. **94** 41.40N 83.35W
Toledo, Montes de *mts.* Spain **41** 39.35N 4.30W
Tollense *r.* E. Germany **44** 53.54N 13.02E
Tolo, G. of Indonesia **61** 2.00S 122.30E
Tolob Scotland **36** 59.53N 1.16W
Tolosa Spain **41** 43.09N 2.04W
Tolsta Head Scotland **36** 58.20N 6.10W
Toluca Mexico **96** 19.20N 99.40W
Toluca *mtn.* Mexico **96** 19.10N 99.40W
Tomatin Scotland **37** 57.20N 3.59W
Tombigbee *r.* U.S.A. **91** 31.05N 87.55W
Tomelloso Spain **41** 39.09N 3.01W
Tomini Indonesia **61** 0.31N 120.30E
Tomini G. Indonesia **61** 0.30S 120.45E
Tomintoul Scotland **37** 57.15N 3.24W
Tomsk U.S.S.R. **48** 56.30N 85.05E
Tona, G. of U.S.S.R. **49** 72.00N 136.10E
Tonalá Mexico **96** 16.08N 93.41W
Tonbridge England **27** 51.12N 0.16E
Tönder Denmark **44** 54.57N 8.53E
Tone *r.* England **31** 50.59N 3.15W
Tonga Is. Pacific Oc. **107** 21.00S 175.00W
Tonga Trench Pacific Oc. **107** 20.00S 172.00W
Tongking, G. of Asia **60** 20.00N 107.50E
Tongland Scotland **35** 54.52N 4.02W
Tongres Belgium **45** 50.47N 5.28E
Tongue Scotland **37** 58.28N 4.25W
Tonk India **58** 26.10N 75.50E
Tonle Sap *l.* Khmer Rep. **60** 12.50N 104.00E
Tonnerre France **40** 47.51N 3.59E
Tönsberg Norway **46** 59.16N 10.25E
Toowoomba Australia **80** 27.35S 151.54E
Top, L. U.S.S.R. **46** 65.45N 32.00E
Topeka U.S.A. **91** 39.03N 95.41W
Topko, Mt. U.S.S.R. **49** 57.20N 138.10E
Topsham England **31** 50.40N 3.27W
Tor Egypt **56** 28.14N 33.37E
Tor B. England **31** 50.25N 3.30W
Torbat-i-Shaikh Jam Iran **57** 35.15N 60.37E
Torbay *town* England **31** 50.27N 3.31W
Tordesillas Spain **41** 41.30N 5.00W
Töre Sweden **46** 65.55N 22.40E
Torhout Belgium **45** 51.04N 3.06E
Torit Sudan **73** 4.27N 32.31E
Torksey England **33** 53.18N 0.45W
Tormes *r.* Spain **41** 41.18N 6.29W
Torne *r.* Sweden **46** 67.13N 23.30E
Torne Träsk *l.* Sweden **46** 68.15N 19.20E
Tornio Finland **46** 65.52N 24.10E
Tornio *r.* Finland **46** 65.53N 24.07E
Toro Spain **41** 41.31N 5.24W
Toronaíos, G. of Med. Sea **43** 40.05N 23.38E
Toronto Australia **80** 33.01S 151.33E
Toronto Canada **95** 43.42N 79.25W
Tororo Uganda **73** 0.42N 34.13E
Torpoint England **31** 50.23N 4.12W
Torquato Severo Brazil **103** 31.04S 54.10W
Torran Rocks *is.* Scotland **34** 56.15N 6.20W
Tôrre de Moncorvo Portugal **41** 41.10N 7.03W
Torrelavega Spain **41** 43.21N 4.00W
Torrens, L. Australia **79** 31.00S 137.50E
Torreón Mexico **96** 25.34N 103.25W
Torres Str. Pacific Oc. **61** 10.30S 142.20E
Tôrres Vedras Portugal **41** 39.05N 9.15W
Torrevieja Spain **41** 37.59N 0.40W
Torridge *r.* England **31** 51.01N 4.12W
Torridon Scotland **36** 57.23N 5.31W
Torridon, Loch Scotland **36** 57.35N 5.45W
Torrington U.S.A. **95** 41.49N 73.05W
Tortola *i.* Virgin Is. **97** 18.28N 64.40W
Tortosa Spain **41** 40.49N 0.31E
Tortue *i.* Haiti **97** 20.05N 72.57W
Tortuga *i.* Venezuela **97** 11.00N 65.20W
Toruń Poland **47** 53.01N 18.35E
Tory I. Rep. of Ire. **38** 55.16N 8.13W
Tory Sd. Rep. of Ire. **38** 55.14N 8.15W
Torzhok U.S.S.R. **47** 57.02N 34.51E
Tosno U.S.S.R. **47** 59.38N 30.46E
Tosson Hill England **35** 55.16N 2.00W
Tostado Argentina **103** 29.15S 61.45W
Totana Spain **41** 37.46N 1.30W
Totland England **28** 50.40N 1.32W
Totley England **33** 53.19N 1.32W
Totma U.S.S.R. **47** 59.59N 42.44E
Totnes England **31** 50.26N 3.41W
Totora Bolivia **103** 17.40S 65.10W
Tottenham Australia **80** 32.14S 147.24E
Tottenham England **27** 51.35N 0.05W
Totton England **28** 50.55N 1.29W
Touba Ivory Coast **70** 8.22N 7.42W
Toubkal *mtn.* Morocco **68** 31.03N 7.57W
Touggourt Algeria **68** 33.08N 6.04E
Toul France **44** 48.41N 5.54E
Toulon France **40** 43.07N 5.53E
Toulouse France **40** 43.33N 1.24E
Toungoo Burma **59** 19.00N 96.30E
Tourcoing France **45** 50.44N 3.09E
Tournai Belgium **45** 50.36N 3.23E
Tournus France **40** 46.33N 4.55E
Tours France **40** 47.23N 0.42E
Tovada *r.* U.S.S.R. **48** 57.40N 67.00E
Tovil England **27** 51.18N 0.31E
Towcester England **28** 52.07N 0.56W
Tower Hamlets *d.* England **27** 51.32N 0.03W
Tow Law *town* England **35** 54.45N 1.49W
Townsend, Mt. Australia **80** 36.24S 148.15E
Townsville Australia **79** 19.13S 146.48E
Towyn Wales **30** 52.37N 4.08W
Toyama Japan **63** 36.42N 137.14E
Trabzon Turkey **56** 41.00N 39.43E
Trafalgar, C. Spain **41** 36.10N 6.02W
Trail Canada **90** 49.04N 117.29W
Trajan's Gate *f.* Bulgaria **43** 42.13N 23.58E
Tralee Rep. of Ire. **39** 52.16N 9.42W
Tralee B. Rep. of Ire. **39** 52.18N 9.55W
Tramore Rep. of Ire. **39** 52.10N 7.10W
Tramore B. Rep. of Ire. **39** 52.09N 7.07W
Tranås Sweden **46** 58.03N 15.00E
Tranent Scotland **35** 55.57N 2.57W
Trang Thailand **60** 7.35N 99.35E
Trangan *i.* Asia **61** 6.30S 134.15E
Trangie Australia **80** 32.03S 148.01E
Transkei *f.* R.S.A. **74** 32.00S 28.00E
Transvaal *d.* R.S.A. **74** 24.30S 29.00E
Transylvanian Alps *mts.* Romania **43** 45.35N 24.40E
Trápani Italy **42** 38.02N 12.30E
Traralgon Australia **80** 38.12S 146.32E
Trasimeno, Lago *l.* Italy **42** 43.09N 12.07E
Traun Austria **44** 48.14N 14.00E
Travers, Mt. New Zealand **82** 42.05S 172.45E
Traverse City U.S.A. **94** 44.46N 85.38W
Travnik Yugo. **43** 44.14N 17.40E
Trébic Czech. **44** 49.13N 15.55E
Třeboň Czech. **44** 49.01N 14.50E
Tredegar Wales **28** 51.47N 3.16W
Tregaron Wales **30** 52.14N 3.56W
Tregony England **31** 50.16N 4.55W
Treig, Loch Scotland **37** 56.48N 4.49W
Treinta-y-Tres Uruguay **103** 33.16S 54.17W
Trelew Argentina **102** 43.13S 65.15W
Trelleborg Sweden **46** 55.10N 13.15E
Tremadog B. Wales **30** 52.52N 4.14W
Tremblant, Mont Canada **95** 46.15N 74.35W
Trenque Lauquén Argentina **103** 35.56S 62.43W
Trent *r.* England **33** 53.41N 0.41W
Trentham England **32** 52.59N 2.12W
Trento Italy **44** 46.04N 11.08E
Trenton U.S.A. **95** 40.15N 74.43W
Tres Arroyos Argentina **103** 38.26S 60.17W
Tres Forcas, Cap Morocco **41** 35.26N 2.57W
Treshnish Is. Scotland **34** 56.29N 6.26W
Treshnish Pt. Scotland **34** 56.32N 6.21W
Três Lagoas Brazil **103** 20.46S 51.43W
Treuchtlingen W. Germany **44** 48.57N 10.55E
Treviso Italy **42** 45.40N 12.14E
Trevose Head *c.* England **31** 50.33N 5.05W
Trier W. Germany **45** 49.45N 6.39E
Trieste Italy **42** 45.40N 13.47E
Triglav *mtn.* Yugo. **42** 46.21N 13.50E
Tríkkala Greece **43** 39.34N 21.46E
Trim Rep. of Ire. **38** 53.33N 6.50W
Trincomalee Sri Lanka **59** 8.34N 81.13E
Tring England **27** 51.48N 0.40W
Trinidad Cuba **97** 21.48N 80.00W
Trinidad S. America **97** 10.30N 61.20W
Trinidad U.S.A. **90** 37.11N 104.31W
Trinity *r.* U.S.A. **91** 29.55N 94.45W
Tripoli Lebanon **56** 34.27N 35.50E
Tripoli Libya **68** 32.58N 13.12E
Tripolitania *f.* Libya **68** 29.45N 14.30E
Tripura *d.* India **59** 23.45N 91.45E
Tristan da Cunha *i.* Atlantic Oc. **112** 38.00S 12.00W
Trivandrum India **58** 8.41N 76.57E
Troisdorf W. Germany **45** 50.50N 7.07E
Trois-Rivières *town* Canada **95** 46.21N 72.34W
Troitsko Pechorsk U.S.S.R. **48** 62.40N 56.08E
Trollhättan Sweden **46** 58.17N 12.20E
Tromsö Norway **46** 69.42N 19.00E
Trondheim Norway **46** 63.36N 10.23E
Trondheim Fjord *est.* Norway **46** 63.40N 10.30E
Troon Scotland **34** 55.33N 4.40W
Trostan *mtn.* N. Ireland **34** 55.03N 6.10W
Trotternish *f.* Scotland **36** 57.33N 6.15W

For Khmer Republic *read* Kampuchea. *For* Malagasy Republic *read* Madagascar. *For* Rhodesia *read* Zimbabwe.

Troup Head to **Uşak** 168

Troup Head Scotland **37** 57.41N 2.18W
Trout L. Canada **91** 51.10N 93.20W
Trowbridge England **28** 51.18N 2.12W
Troy U.S.A. **95** 42.43N 73.43W
Troyes France **40** 48.18N 4.05E
Trujillo Peru **102** 8.06S 79.00W
Trujillo Spain **41** 39.28N 5.53W
Trujillo Venezuela **97** 9.20N 70.38W
Truro Canada **91** 45.54N 64.00W
Truro England **31** 50.17N 5.02W
Trutnov Czech. **44** 50.34N 15.55E
Trysil *r.* Norway **46** 61.03N 12.30E
Tsangpo *r. see* Brahmaputra China **59**
Tsavo Nat. Park Kenya **73** 2.45S 38.45E
Tselinograd U.S.S.R. **48** 51.10N 71.28E
Tsetang China **59** 29.05N 91.50E
Tshane Botswana **74** 24.05S 21.54E
Tshela Zaïre **72** 4.57S 12.57E
Tshikapa Zaïre **72** 6.28S 20.48E
Tshofa Zaïre **72** 5.13S 25.20E
Tshopo *r.* Zaïre **72** 0.30N 25.07E
Tshuapa *r.* Zaïre **72** 0.14S 20.45E
Tsinan China **63** 36.50N 117.00E
Tsinghai *d.* China **62** 36.15N 96.00E
Tsingtao China **63** 36.04N 120.22E
Tsining Shantung China **63** 35.25N 116.40E
Tsitsihar China **63** 47.23N 124.00E
Tskhinvali U.S.S.R. **47** 42.14N 43.58E
Tsna *r.* U.S.S.R. **47** 54.45N 41.54E
Tsumeb S.W. Africa **74** 19.13S 17.42E
Tsushima *i.* Japan **63** 34.30N 129.20E
Tsuyung China **59** 25.03N 101.33E
Tuam Rep. of Ire. **38** 53.32N 8.52W
Tuamgrenay Rep. of Ire. **39** 52.54N 8.32W
Tuamotu Archipelago *is.* Pacific Oc. **106** 16.00S 145.00W
Tuapse U.S.S.R. **47** 44.06N 39.05E
Tuatapere New Zealand **82** 46.09S 167.42E
Tuath, Loch Scotland **34** 56.30N 6.13W
Tubbercurry Rep. of Ire. **38** 54.03N 8.45W
Tübingen W. Germany **44** 48.32N 9.04E
Tubja, Wadi *r.* Saudi Arabia **56** 25.35N 38.22E
Tucacas Venezuela **97** 10.46N 68.20W
Tucson U.S.A. **90** 32.15N 110.57W
Tucumán Argentina **103** 26.55S 65.15W
Tucumcari U.S.A. **90** 35.11N 103.44W
Tudela Spain **41** 42.04N 1.37W
Tudweiliog Wales **30** 52.54N 4.37W
Tuguegarao Phil. **61** 17.36N 121.44E
Tukangbesi Is. Indonesia **61** 5.30S 124.00E
Tukums U.S.S.R. **46** 56.58N 23.10E
Tukuyu Tanzania **73** 9.20S 33.37E
Tula *r.* Mongolia **62** 48.53N 104.35E
Tula U.S.S.R. **47** 54.11N 37.38E
Tulcea Romania **43** 45.10N 28.50E
Tuléar Malagasy Rep. **67** 23.20S 43.41E
Tuli Indonesia **61** 1.25S 122.23E
Tuli Rhodesia **74** 21.50S 29.15E
Tuli *r.* Rhodesia **74** 21.49S 29.00E
Tulkarm Jordan **56** 32.19N 35.02E
Tulla Rep. of Ire. **39** 52.52N 8.48W
Tullamore Australia **80** 32.39S 147.39E
Tullamore Rep. of Ire. **39** 53.17N 7.31W
Tulle France **40** 45.16N 1.46E
Tullins France **40** 45.18N 5.29E
Tullow Rep. of Ire. **39** 52.49N 6.45W
Tuloma *r.* U.S.S.R. **46** 68.56N 33.00E
Tulsa U.S.A. **91** 36.07N 95.58W
Tulun U.S.S.R. **49** 54.32N 100.35E
Tumba, L. Zaïre **72** 0.45S 18.00E
Tummel *r.* Scotland **37** 56.39N 3.40W
Tummel, Loch Scotland **37** 56.43N 3.55W
Tummo Libya **68** 22.45N 14.08E
Tump Pakistan **58** 26.06N 62.24E
Tumpat Malaysia **59** 6.11N 102.10E
Tunceli Turkey **56** 39.07N 39.34E
Tunchwang China **62** 40.00N 94.40E
Tunduma Tanzania **73** 9.19S 32.47E
Tunduru Tanzania **73** 11.08S 37.21E
Tundzha *r.* Bulgaria **43** 41.40N 26.34E
Tungabhadra *r.* India **58** 16.00N 78.15E
Tungkwan China **63** 34.36N 110.21E
Tung Ting Hu *l.* China **63** 29.40N 113.00E
Tunis Tunisia **42** 36.47N 10.10E
Tunis, G. of Med. Sea **42** 37.00N 10.30E
Tunisia Africa **68** 34.00N 9.00E
Tupelo U.S.A. **91** 34.15N 88.43W
Tupiza Bolivia **103** 21.27S 65.45W
Tura Tanzania **73** 5.30S 33.50E
Tura U.S.S.R. **49** 64.05N 100.00E
Turbo Colombia **97** 8.06N 76.44W
Turfan China **62** 42.55N 89.06E
Turfan Depression *f.* China **62** 43.40N 89.00E
Turgutlu Turkey **43** 38.30N 27.43E
Turi U.S.S.R. **46** 58.48N 25.28E
Turia *r.* Spain **41** 39.27N 0.19W
Turin Italy **40** 45.04N 7.40E
Turkana, L. Kenya **73** 4.00N 36.00E
Turkestan *f.* Asia **57** 40.00N 79.30E
Turkestan U.S.S.R. **48** 43.17N 68.16E
Turkey Asia **56** 39.00N 35.00E
Turkey *r.* U.S.A. **94** 42.58N 91.03W
Turkmenistan Soviet Socialist Republic *d.* U.S.S.R. **48** 40.00N 60.00E
Turks I. C. America **97** 21.30N 71.10W
Turku Finland **46** 60.27N 22.15E
Turneffe I. Belize **96** 17.30N 87.45W
Turnhout Belgium **45** 51.19N 4.57E
Tŭrnovo Bulgaria **43** 43.04N 25.39E
Turnu Măgurele Romania **43** 43.43N 24.53E
Turnu Severin Romania **43** 44.37N 22.39E
Turquino *mtn.* Cuba **97** 20.05N 76.50W
Turriff Scotland **37** 57.32N 2.28W
Turtkul U.S.S.R. **57** 41.30N 61.00E
Tuscaloosa U.S.A. **91** 33.12N 87.33W
Tuscola U.S.A. **94** 39.49N 88.18W
Tuskar Rock *i.* Rep. of Ire. **39** 52.12N 6.13W
Tuticorin India **59** 8.48N 78.10E
Tuttlingen W. Germany **44** 47.59N 8.49E
Tutubu Tanzania **73** 5.28S 32.43E
Tuxpan Mexico **96** 21.00N 97.23W
Tuxtla Gutiérrez Mexico **96** 16.45N 93.09W
Tuz, L. Turkey **56** 38.45N 33.24E
Tuzla Yugo. **43** 44.33N 18.41E
Tweed *r.* Scotland **35** 55.46N 2.00W
Twickenham England **27** 51.27N 0.20W
Twin Falls *town* U.S.A. **90** 42.34N 114.30W
Two Harbors *town* U.S.A. **94** 47.02N 91.40W
Twyford Berks. England **28** 51.29N 0.51W
Twyford Hants. England **28** 51.01N 1.19W
Tyler U.S.A. **91** 32.22N 95.18W
Tyndrum Scotland **34** 56.27N 4.43W
Tyne *r.* England **35** 55.00N 1.25W
Tyne *r.* Scotland **35** 56.00N 2.36W
Tyne and Wear *d.* England **35** 54.57N 1.35W
Tynemouth England **35** 55.01N 1.24W
Tyre Lebanon **56** 33.16N 35.12E
Tyrone *d.* N. Ireland **38** 54.35N 7.15W
Tyrrell, L. Australia **80** 35.22S 142.50E
Tyrrellspass *town* Rep. of Ire. **38** 53.23N 7.24W
Tyrrhenian Sea Med. Sea **42** 40.00N 12.00E
Tyumen U.S.S.R. **48** 57.11N 65.29E
Tywi *r.* Wales **31** 51.46N 4.22W
Tywyn Wales **30** 53.14N 3.49W
Tzaneen R.S.A. **74** 23.50S 30.09E
Tzekung China **62** 29.20N 104.42E
Tzepo China **63** 36.32N 117.47E

U

Ubaiyidh, Wadi *r.* Iraq **56** 32.04N 42.17E
Ubangi *r.* Congo/Zaïre **72** 0.25S 17.40E
Ubeda Spain **41** 38.01N 3.22W
Uberaba Brazil **103** 19.47S 47.57W
Uberlândia Brazil **103** 18.57S 48.17W
Ubombo R.S.A. **74** 27.35S 32.05E
Ubon Ratchathani Thailand **59** 15.15N 104.50E
Ubsa Nur *l.* Mongolia **62** 50.30N 92.30E
Ubundu Zaïre **72** 0.24S 25.28E
Uckfield England **29** 50.58N 0.06E
Udaipur India **58** 24.36N 73.47E
Uddevalla Sweden **46** 58.20N 11.56E
Uddjaur *l.* Sweden **46** 65.55N 17.50E
Udine Italy **42** 46.03N 13.15E
Udon Thani Thailand **59** 17.29N 102.46E
Uele *r.* Zaïre **72** 4.08N 22.25E
Uelen U.S.S.R. **92** 66.13N 169.48W
Uelzen W. Germany **44** 52.58N 10.34E
Uere *r.* Zaïre **72** 3.30N 25.15E
Ufa U.S.S.R. **48** 54.45N 55.58E
Uffculme England **28** 50.45N 3.19W
Ugab *r.* S.W. Africa **74** 21.10S 13.40E
Ugalla *r.* Tanzania **73** 5.15S 29.45E
Uganda Africa **73** 2.00N 33.00E
Ughelli Nigeria **71** 5.33N 6.00E
Ugie *r.* Scotland **37** 57.31N 1.48W
Uglegorsk U.S.S.R. **49** 49.01N 142.04E
Ugra *r.* U.S.S.R. **47** 54.30N 36.10E
Uig Scotland **36** 57.35N 6.22W
Uige Angola **72** 7.40S 15.09E
Uige *d.* Angola **72** 7.00S 15.30E
Uinta Mts. U.S.A. **90** 40.45N 110.30W
Uitenhage R.S.A. **74** 33.46S 25.25E
Uithuizen Neth. **45** 53.24N 6.41E
Ujiji Tanzania **73** 4.55S 29.39E
Ujjain India **58** 23.11N 75.50E
Ujpest Hungary **47** 47.33N 19.05E
Ujung Pandang Indonesia **60** 5.09S 119.28E
Uka U.S.S.R. **49** 57.50N 162.02E
Ukerewe I. Tanzania **73** 2.00S 33.00E
Ukiah U.S.A. **90** 39.09N 123.12W
Ukraine Soviet Socialist Republic *d.* U.S.S.R. **47** 49.30N 32.04E
Ulan Bator Mongolia **62** 47.54N 106.52E
Ulan Göm Mongolia **62** 49.59N 92.00E
Ulan-Ude U.S.S.R. **62** 51.55N 107.40E
Uliastaj Mongolia **62** 47.42N 96.52E
Ulindi *r.* Zaïre **72** 1.38S 25.55E
Ulla *r.* Spain **41** 42.38N 8.45W
Ulladulla Australia **80** 35.21S 150.25E
Ullapool Scotland **36** 57.54N 5.10W
Ullswater *l.* England **32** 54.34N 2.52W
Ulm W. Germany **44** 48.24N 10.00E
Ulsberg Norway **46** 62.45N 10.00E
Ulsta Scotland **36** 60.30N 1.08W
Ulster *d.* N. Ireland/Rep. of Ire. **38** 54.40N 6.45W
Ulua *r.* Honduras **96** 15.50N 87.38W
Uluguru Mts. Tanzania **73** 7.05S 37.40E
Ulva *i.* Scotland **34** 56.29N 6.12W
Ulverston England **32** 54.13N 3.07W
Ul'yanovsk U.S.S.R. **47** 54.19N 48.22E
Uman U.S.S.R. **47** 48.45N 30.10E
Ume *r.* Rhodesia **74** 16.59S 28.28E
Ume *r.* Sweden **46** 63.43N 20.20E
Umfuli *r.* Rhodesia **74** 17.32S 29.14E
Umiat U.S.A. **92** 69.25N 152.20W
Umm-al-Gawein U.A.E. **57** 25.32N 55.34E
Umm-al-Hamir Saudi Arabia **57** 29.07N 46.35E
Umm Lajj Saudi Arabia **56** 25.03N 37.17E
Umm Sa'id Qatar **57** 24.47N 51.36E
Umniati *r.* Rhodesia **74** 17.28S 29.20E
Umtali Rhodesia **74** 18.58S 32.38E
Umtata R.S.A. **74** 31.35S 28.47E
Umuahia Nigeria **71** 5.31N 7.26E
Umvukwe Range *mts.* Rhodesia **74** 16.30S 30.50E
Umvuma Rhodesia **74** 19.16S 30.30E
Umzimkulu R.S.A. **74** 30.15S 29.56E
Una *r.* Yugo. **42** 45.03N 16.22E
Unapool Scotland **36** 58.14N 5.01W
Uncompahgre Peak U.S.A. **90** 38.04N 107.28W
Underberg R.S.A. **74** 29.47S 29.30E
Undur Khan Mongolia **49** 47.20N 110.40E
Ungarie Australia **80** 33.38S 147.00E
Ungava B. Canada **93** 59.00N 67.30W
Uniondale R.S.A. **74** 33.40S 23.07E
Union of Arab Emirates Asia **57** 24.00N 54.00E
Union of Soviet Socialist Republics Europe/Asia **48** 60.00N 80.00E
United Kingdom Europe **18** 54.00N 2.00W
United States of America N. America **90** 39.00N 100.00W
Unna W. Germany **45** 51.32N 7.41E
Unnao India **58** 26.32N 80.30E
Unshin *r.* Rep. of Ire. **38** 54.13N 8.31W
Unst *i.* Scotland **36** 60.45N 0.55W
Unye Turkey **56** 41.09N 37.15E
Upavon England **28** 51.17N 1.49W
Upemba, L. Zaïre **73** 8.35S 26.28E
Upemba Nat. Park Zaïre **73** 9.00S 26.30E
Upernavik Greenland **93** 72.50N 56.00W
Upington R.S.A. **74** 28.28S 21.14E
Upminster England **27** 51.34N 0.15E
Upper *d.* Ghana **70** 10.30N 1.40W
Upper Egypt *f.* Egypt **56** 26.00N 32.00E
Upper Lough Erne N. Ireland **38** 54.13N 7.32W
Upper Taymyr *r.* U.S.S.R. **49** 74.10N 99.50E
Upper Tean England **32** 52.57N 1.59W
Upper Tooting England **27** 51.26N 0.10W
Upper Volta Africa **70** 12.30N 2.00W
Uppingham England **28** 52.36N 0.43W
Uppsala Sweden **46** 59.55N 17.38E
Upton upon Severn England **28** 52.04N 2.12W
Ur *ruins* Iraq **57** 30.55N 46.07E
Uraba, G. of Colombia **97** 8.30N 77.00W
Ural *r.* U.S.S.R. **48** 47.00N 52.00E
Uralla Australia **80** 30.40S 151.31E
Ural Mts. U.S.S.R. **48** 55.00N 59.00E
Ural'sk U.S.S.R. **48** 51.09N 51.20E
Urana Australia **80** 35.21S 146.19E
Uranium City Canada **92** 59.32N 108.43W
Urbana U.S.A. **94** 40.07N 88.12W
Urbino Italy **42** 43.43N 12.38E
Ure *r.* England **33** 54.05N 1.20W
Uren U.S.S.R. **47** 57.30N 45.50E
Urfa Turkey **56** 37.08N 38.45E
Ürgüp Turkey **56** 38.39N 34.55E
Urlingford Rep. of Ire. **39** 52.44N 7.35W
Urmia, L. Iran **57** 37.40N 45.28E
Urmston England **32** 53.28N 2.22W
Urr Water *r.* Scotland **35** 54.54N 3.50W
Uruapan Mexico **96** 19.26N 102.04W
Uruguaiana Brazil **103** 29.45S 57.05W
Uruguay S. America **103** 33.15S 56.00W
Uruguay *r.* Argentina/Uruguay **103** 34.00S 58.30W
Urumchi China **62** 43.43N 87.38E
Urunga Australia **80** 30.30S 152.28E
Uşak Turkey **56** 38.42N 29.25E

For Khmer Republic *read* Kampuchea. *For* Malagasy Republic *read* Madagascar. *For* Rhodesia *read* Zimbabwe.

Usambara Mts. to **Vis** 169

Usambara Mts. Tanzania **73** 4.45S 38.25E
Ushant *i. see* Ouessant, Île d' France **40**
Ushnuiyeh Iran **57** 37.03N 45.05E
Usk Wales **31** 51.42N 2.53W
Usk *r.* Wales **31** 51.34N 2.59W
Usküdar Turkey **43** 41.00N 29.03E
Ussuriysk U.S.S.R. **63** 43.48N 131.59E
Ustica *i.* Italy **42** 38.42N 13.11E
Usti nad Labem Czech. **44** 50.41N 14.00E
Ust'kamchatsk U.S.S.R. **49** 56.14N 162.28E
Ust Kut U.S.S.R. **49** 56.40N 105.50E
Ust'Maya U.S.S.R. **49** 60.25N 134.28E
Ust Olenek U.S.S.R. **49** 72.59N 120.00E
Ust'Tsilma U.S.S.R. **48** 65.28N 53.09E
Ust Urt Plateau *f.* U.S.S.R. **48** 43.30N 55.20E
Usumacinta *r.* Mexico **96** 18.48N 92.40W
Utah *d.* U.S.A. **90** 39.00N 112.00W
Utembo *r.* Angola **72** 17.03S 22.00E
Utete Tanzania **73** 8.00S 38.49E
Utica U.S.A. **95** 43.06N 75.15W
Utiel Spain **41** 39.33N 1.13W
Utrecht Neth. **45** 52.04N 5.07E
Utrecht *d.* Neth. **45** 52.04N 5.10E
Utrecht R.S.A. **74** 27.40S 30.20E
Utrera Spain **41** 37.10N 5.47W
Utsunomiya Japan **63** 36.33N 139.52E
Uttaradit Thailand **59** 17.38N 100.05E
Uttar Pradesh *d.* India **58** 27.50N 80.00E
Uttoxeter England **32** 52.53N 1.50W
Uusikaupunki Finland **46** 60.48N 21.30E
Uvinza Tanzania **73** 5.08S 30.23E
Uvira Zaïre **73** 3.22S 29.06E
'Uwaina Saudi Arabia **57** 26.46N 48.13E
Uxbridge England **27** 51.33N 0.30W
Uyo Nigeria **71** 5.01N 7.56E
'Uyun Saudi Arabia **57** 26.32N 43.41E
Uzbekistan Soviet Socialist Republic *d.* U.S.S.R. **48** 42.00N 63.00E
Uzhgorod U.S.S.R. **47** 48.38N 22.15E

V

Vaago *i.* Faroe Is. **46** 62.03N 7.14W
Vaal *r.* R.S.A. **74** 29.03S 23.42E
Vaal Dam R.S.A. **74** 27.00S 28.15E
Vaasa Finland **46** 63.06N 21.36E
Vaduz Liech. **44** 47.08N 9.32E
Vaggeryd Sweden **46** 57.30N 14.10E
Váh *r.* Czech. **47** 47.40N 17.50E
Vaila *i.* Scotland **36** 60.12N 1.34W
Valdai Hills U.S.S.R. **47** 57.10N 33.00E
Valday U.S.S.R. **47** 57.59N 33.10E
Valdemarsvik Sweden **46** 58.13N 16.35E
Valdepeñas Spain **41** 38.46N 3.24W
Valdez U.S.A. **92** 61.07N 146.17W
Val-d'Or *town* Canada **95** 48.07N 77.47W
Valença Portugal **41** 42.02N 8.38W
Valence France **40** 44.56N 4.54E
Valencia Spain **41** 39.29N 0.24W
Valencia Venezuela **97** 10.14N 67.59W
Valencia, G. of Spain **41** 39.38N 0.20W
Valencia, L. Venezuela **97** 10.09N 67.30W
Valencia de Alcántara Spain **41** 39.25N 7.14
Valenciennes France **45** 50.22N 3.32E
Valentia I. Rep. of Ire. **39** 51.54N 10.21W
Vale of Berkeley *f.* England **28** 51.42N 2.25W
Vale of Evesham *f.* England **28** 52.05N 1.55W
Vale of Gloucester *f.* England **28** 51.54N 2.15W
Vale of Kent *f.* England **29** 51.08N 0.38E
Vale of Pewsey *f.* England **28** 51.21N 1.45W
Vale of Pickering *f.* England **33** 54.11N 0.45W
Vale of White Horse *f.* England **28** 51.38N 1.32W
Vale of York *f.* England **33** 54.12N 1.25W
Valga U.S.S.R. **46** 57.44N 26.00E
Valinco, G. of Med. Sea **40** 41.40N 8.50E
Valjevo Yugo. **43** 44.16N 19.56E
Valkeakoski Finland **46** 61.17N 24.05E
Valkenswaard Neth. **45** 51.21N 5.27E
Valladolid Spain **41** 41.39N 4.45W
Valle Venezuela **97** 9.15N 66.00W
Valletta Malta **42** 35.53N 14.31E
Valley City U.S.A. **90** 46.57N 97.58W
Valleyfield Canada **95** 45.15N 74.08W
Valmiera U.S.S.R. **46** 57.32N 25.29E
Valnera *mtn.* Spain **41** 43.10N 3.40W
Valognes France **40** 49.31N 1.28W
Valparaíso Chile **102** 33.35S 71.20W
Vals, C. Indonesia **61** 8.30S 137.30E
Valverde Dom. Rep. **97** 19.37N 71.04W
Valverde del Camino Spain **41** 37.35N 6.45W
Van Turkey **56** 38.28N 43.20E
Van, L. Turkey **56** 38.35N 42.52E
Vancouver Canada **90** 49.13N 123.06W
Vancouver I. Canada **92** 50.00N 126.00W
Vänern *l.* Sweden **46** 59.00N 13.15E
Vänersborg Sweden **46** 58.23N 12.19E
Vanga Kenya **73** 4.37S 39.13E
Vanka Järvi *l.* Finland **46** 61.30N 23.50E
Vännäs Sweden **46** 63.56N 19.50E
Vannes France **40** 47.40N 2.44W
Vanrhynsdorp R.S.A. **74** 31.36S 18.45E
Vanuatu Pacific Ocean **107** 16.00S 167.00E
Varanasi India **58** 25.20N 83.00E
Varangerenfjord *est.* Norway **46** 70.00N 29.30E
Varazdin Yugo. **44** 46.18N 16.20E
Varberg Sweden **46** 57.06N 12.15E
Vardar *r.* Greece **43** 40.31N 22.43E
Varel W. Germany **45** 53.24N 8.08E
Varennes France **40** 46.19N 3.24E
Varginha Brazil **103** 21.33S 45.25W
Varkaus Finland **46** 62.15N 27.45E
Varna Bulgaria **43** 43.13N 27.57E
Värnamo Sweden **46** 57.11N 14.03E
Vasilkov U.S.S.R. **47** 50.12N 30.15E
Västerås Sweden **46** 59.36N 16.32E
Västerdal *r.* Sweden **46** 60.32N 15.02E
Västervik Sweden **46** 57.45N 16.40E
Vaternish Pt. Scotland **36** 57.37N 6.39W
Vatersay *i.* Scotland **36** 56.56N 7.32W
Vatnajökull *mts.* Iceland **46** 64.20N 17.00W
Vättern *l.* Sweden **46** 58.30N 14.30E
Vaughn U.S.A. **90** 34.35N 105.14W
Vavuniya Sri Lanka **59** 8.45N 80.30E
Växjö Sweden **46** 56.52N 14.50E
Vaygach *i.* U.S.S.R. **48** 70.00N 59.00E
Vecht *r.* Neth. **45** 52.39N 6.01E
Vega *i.* Norway **46** 65.40N 11.55E
Vejle Denmark **46** 55.43N 9.33E
Vélez Málaga Spain **41** 36.48N 4.05W
Velikaya *r.* U.S.S.R. **46** 57.54N 28.06E
Velikiye-Luki U.S.S.R. **47** 56.19N 30.31E
Velletri Italy **42** 41.41N 12.47E
Vellore India **59** 12.56N 79.09E
Velsen Neth. **45** 52.28N 4.39E
Veluwe *f.* Neth. **45** 52.17N 5.45E
Venachar, Loch Scotland **34** 56.13N 4.19W
Venado Tuerto Argentina **103** 33.45S 61.56W
Vendas Novas Portugal **41** 38.41N 8.27W
Vendôme France **40** 47.48N 1.04E
Venezuela S. America **102** 7.00N 65.00W
Venezuela, G. of Venezuela **97** 11.30N 71.00W
Veniaminof Mtn. U.S.A. **92** 56.05N 159.20W
Venice Italy **42** 45.26N 12.20E
Venice, G. of Med. Sea **42** 45.20N 13.00E
Venlo Neth. **45** 51.22N 6.10E
Venraij Neth. **45** 51.32N 5.58E
Venta *r.* U.S.S.R. **46** 57.22N 21.31E
Ventnor England **28** 50.35N 1.12W
Ventspils U.S.S.R. **46** 57.22N 21.31E
Ver *r.* England **27** 51.42N 0.20W
Vera Spain **41** 37.15N 1.51W
Veracruz Mexico **96** 19.11N 96.10W
Veracruz *d.* Mexico **96** 18.00N 95.00W
Veraval India **58** 20.53N 70.28E
Vercelli Italy **40** 45.19N 8.26E
Verde *r.* Paraguay **103** 23.10S 57.45W
Verde, C. Senegal **70** 14.45N 17.25W
Verdon *r.* France **40** 43.42N 5.39E
Verdun Canada **95** 45.28N 73.35W
Verdun France **40** 49.10N 5.24E
Vereeniging R.S.A. **74** 26.41S 27.56E
Verin Spain **41** 41.55N 7.26W
Verkhoyansk U.S.S.R. **49** 67.25N 133.25E
Verkhoyansk Range *mts.* U.S.S.R. **49** 66.00N 130.00E
Vermont *d.* U.S.A. **95** 43.50N 72.50W
Verona Italy **42** 45.27N 10.59E
Versailles France **40** 48.48N 2.08E
Verviers Belgium **45** 50.36N 5.52E
Vervins France **45** 49.50N 3.55E
Verwood England **28** 50.53N 1.53W
Vesoul France **44** 47.38N 6.09E
Vesterålen *is.* Norway **46** 68.55N 15.00E
Vest Fjorden *est.* Norway **46** 68.10N 15.00E
Vestmanna Is. Iceland **46** 63.30N 20.20W
Vesuvius *mtn.* Italy **42** 40.48N 14.25E
Vetlanda Sweden **46** 57.26N 15.05E
Vetluga *r.* U.S.S.R. **47** 56.18N 46.19E
Vettore, Monte *mtn.* Italy **42** 42.50N 13.18E
Vézere *r.* France **40** 44.53N 0.55E
Viana do Castelo Portugal **41** 41.41N 8.50W
Viborg Denmark **46** 56.28N 9.25E
Vicenza Italy **42** 45.33N 11.32E
Vich Spain **41** 41.56N 2.16E
Vichuga U.S.S.R. **47** 57.12N 41.50E
Vichy France **40** 46.07N 3.25E
Victor Harbor Australia **80** 35.36S 138.35E
Victoria *d.* Australia **80** 37.20S 144.10E
Victoria Cameroon **71** 4.01N 9.12E
Victoria Canada **90** 48.26N 123.20W
Victoria Hong Kong **60** 22.16N 114.15E
Victoria U.S.A. **96** 28.49N 97.01W
Victoria, L. Africa **73** 1.00S 33.00E
Victoria, Mt. P.N.G. **79** 8.10S 147.20E
Victoria de las Tunas Cuba **97** 20.58N 76.59W
Victoria Falls *f.* Rhodesia/Zambia **74** 17.58S 25.45E
Victoria I. Canada **92** 71.00N 110.00W
Victoria Nile *r.* Uganda **73** 2.14N 31.20E
Victoria West R.S.A. **74** 31.25S 23.08E
Vidin Bulgaria **43** 43.58N 22.51E
Viedma Argentina **103** 40.45S 63.00W
Vienna Austria **44** 48.13N 16.22E
Vienne France **40** 45.32N 4.54E
Vienne *r.* France **40** 47.13N 0.05W
Vientiane Laos **60** 18.01N 102.48E
Vieques *i.* Puerto Rico **97** 18.08N 65.30W
Vierwaldstätter See *l.* Switz. **40** 47.00N 8.35E
Vierzon France **40** 47.14N 2.03E
Vietnam Asia **60** 15.00N 108.00E
Vignemale, Pic de *mtn.* France **40** 42.46N 0.08W
Vigo Spain **41** 42.15N 8.44W
Vijayawada India **59** 16.34N 80.40E
Vijose *r.* Albania **43** 40.39N 19.20E
Vikna *i.* Norway **46** 64.59N 11.00E
Vila Coutinho Moçambique **73** 14.34S 34.21E
Vila da Maganja Moçambique **73** 17.25S 37.32E
Vila da Ponte Angola **72** 14.28S 16.25E
Vila de João Belo Moçambique **74** 25.05S 33.38E
Vila de Manica Moçambique **74** 19.00S 33.00E
Vila de Sena Moçambique **73** 17.36S 35.00E
Vila Franca Portugal **41** 38.57N 8.59W
Vila General Machado Angola **72** 12.01S 17.22E
Vilaine *r.* France **40** 47.30N 2.25W
Vila Luso Angola **72** 11.46S 19.55E
Vila Mariano Machado Angola **72** 12.58S 14.39E
Vilanculos Moçambique **74** 22.01S 35.19E
Vila Nova do Seles Angola **72** 11.24S 14.15E
Vila Pereira de Eça Angola **72** 17.05S 15.44E
Vila Pery Moçambique **74** 19.04S 33.29E
Vila Real Portugal **41** 41.17N 7.45W
Vila Real de Santo Antonio Portugal **41** 37.12N 7.25W
Vila Salazar Angola **72** 9.12S 14.54E
Vila Silva Porto Angola **72** 12.25S 16.58E
Vila Teixeira da Silva Angola **72** 12.13S 15.46E
Vila Vasco da Gama Moçambique **73** 14.55S 32.12E
Vila Verissimo Sarmento Angola **72** 8.08S 20.38E
Vilhelmina Sweden **46** 64.38N 16.40E
Viljandi U.S.S.R. **46** 58.22N 25.30E
Villa Angela Argentina **103** 27.34S 60.45W
Villablino Spain **41** 42.57N 6.19W
Villacañas Spain **41** 39.38N 3.20W
Villach Austria **44** 46.37N 13.51E
Villa Cisneros W. Sahara **68** 23.43N 15.57W
Villa Constitución Argentina **103** 33.15S 60.20W
Villagarcia Spain **41** 42.35N 8.45W
Villaguay Argentina **103** 31.55S 59.01W
Villahermosa Mexico **96** 18.00N 92.53W
Villa Huidobro Argentina **103** 34.50S 64.34W
Villajoyosa Spain **41** 38.31N 0.14W
Villa María Argentina **103** 32.25S 63.15W
Villa Montes Bolivia **103** 21.15S 63.30W
Villanueva de la Serena Spain **41** 38.58N 5.48W
Villanueva-y-Geltru Spain **41** 41.13N 1.43E
Villaputzu Italy **42** 39.28N 9.35E
Villarrica Paraguay **103** 25.45S 56.28W
Villarrobledo Spain **41** 39.16N 2.36W
Villa Sanjurjo Morocco **41** 35.14N 3.56W
Villefranche France **40** 46.00N 4.43E
Villena Spain **41** 38.39N 0.52W
Villeneuve France **40** 44.25N 0.43E
Villeneuve d'Ascq France **40** 50.37N 3.10E
Villeurbanne France **40** 45.46N 4.54E
Villingen W. Germany **44** 48.03N 8.28E
Vilnius U.S.S.R. **46** 54.40N 25.19E
Vilvoorde Belgium **45** 50.56N 4.25E
Vilyuy *r.* U.S.S.R. **49** 64.20N 126.55E
Vilyuysk U.S.S.R. **49** 63.46N 121.35E
Vimmerby Sweden **46** 57.40N 15.50E
Vina *r.* Cameroon **71** 7.43N 15.30E
Vincennes U.S.A. **94** 38.42N 87.30W
Vindel *r.* Sweden **46** 63.56N 19.54E
Vindhya Range *mts.* India **58** 22.55N 76.00E
Vineland U.S.A. **95** 39.29N 75.02W
Vinh Vietnam **59** 18.42N 105.41E
Vinnitsa U.S.S.R. **47** 49.11N 28.30E
Vire France **40** 48.50N 0.53W
Vire *r.* France **40** 49.20N 0.53W
Virgin Gorda *i.* Virgin Is. **97** 18.30N 64.26W
Virginia Rep. of Ire. **38** 53.50N 7.06W
Virginia U.S.A. **94** 47.30N 92.28W
Virginia *d.* U.S.A. **91** 37.30N 79.00W
Virginia Water *town* England **27** 51.24N 0.36W
Virgin Is. C. America **97** 18.30N 65.00W
Virovitica Yugo. **43** 45.51N 17.23E
Virton Belgium **45** 49.35N 5.32E
Virunga Nat. Park Zaïre **73** 0.30S 29.15E
Vis *i.* Yugo. **42** 43.03N 16.10E

For Khmer Republic *read* Kampuchea. *For* Malagasy Republic *read* Madagascar. *For* Rhodesia *read* Zimbabwe.

Visby Sweden **46** 57.37N 18.20E
Viscount Melville Sd. Canada **92** 74.30N 104.00W
Visé Belgium **45** 50.44N 5.42E
Višegrad Yugo. **43** 43.47N 19.20E
Viseu Portugal **41** 40.40N 7.55W
Vishakhapatnam India **59** 17.42N 83.24E
Viso, Monte *mtn.* Italy **40** 44.38N 7.05E
Vistula *r.* Poland **47** 54.23N 18.52E
Vitebsk U.S.S.R. **47** 55.10N 30.14E
Viterbo Italy **42** 42.26N 12.07E
Vitim *r.* U.S.S.R. **49** 59.30N 112.36E
Vitória Espírito Santo Brazil **102** 20.19S 40.21W
Vitoria Spain **41** 42.51N 2.40W
Vittória Italy **42** 36.57N 14.21E
Vizianagaram India **59** 18.07N 83.30E
Vlaardingen Neth. **45** 51.55N 4.20E
Vladimir U.S.S.R. **47** 56.08N 40.25E
Vladivostok U.S.S.R. **63** 43.09N 131.53E
Vlieland *i.* Neth. **45** 53.15N 5.00E
Vlorë Albania **43** 40.28N 19.27E
Vltava *r.* Czech. **44** 50.22N 14.28E
Voe Scotland **36** 60.21N 1.15W
Vogelkop *f.* Asia **61** 1.10S 132.30E
Vogelsberg *mtn.* W. Germany **44** 50.30N 9.15E
Voghera Italy **42** 44.59N 9.01E
Voi Kenya **73** 3.23S 38.35E
Voil, Loch Scotland **34** 56.21N 4.26W
Voiron France **40** 45.22N 5.35E
Volga *r.* U.S.S.R. **48** 45.45N 47.50E
Volga Uplands *hills* U.S.S.R. **48** 53.15N 45.45E
Volgograd U.S.S.R. **47** 48.45N 44.30E
Volkhov *r.* U.S.S.R. **47** 60.15N 32.15E
Vologda U.S.S.R. **47** 59.10N 39.55E
Vólos Greece **43** 39.22N 22.57E
Volsk U.S.S.R. **47** 52.04N 47.22E
Volta *d.* Ghana **70** 7.30N 0.25E
Volta *r.* Ghana **70** 5.50N 0.41E
Volta, L. Ghana **70** 7.00N 0.00
Volterra Italy **42** 43.24N 10.51E
Volturno *r.* Italy **42** 41.02N 13.56E
Volzhskiy U.S.S.R. **47** 48.48N 44.45E
Voorburg Neth. **45** 52.05N 4.22E
Vopna Fjördhur *est.* Iceland **46** 65.50N 14.30W
Vordingborg Denmark **44** 55.01N 11.55E
Vorkuta U.S.S.R. **48** 67.27N 64.00E
Voronezh U.S.S.R. **47** 51.40N 39.13E
Voroshilovgrad U.S.S.R. **47** 48.35N 39.20E
Vosges *mts.* France **44** 48.10N 7.00E
Voss Norway **46** 60.38N 6.25E
Votuporanga Brazil **103** 20.26S 49.53W
Vouga *r.* Portugal **41** 40.41N 8.38W
Voves France **40** 48.16N 1.37E
Voznesensk U.S.S.R. **47** 47.34N 31.21E
Vranje Yugo. **43** 42.34N 21.52E
Vratsa Bulgaria **43** 43.12N 23.33E
Vrede R.S.A. **74** 27.24S 29.11E
Vršac Yugo. **43** 45.08N 21.18E
Vryburg R.S.A. **74** 26.57S 24.44E
Vyatka *r.* U.S.S.R. **47** 55.45N 51.30E
Vyatskiye Polyany U.S.S.R. **47** 56.14N 51.08E
Vyazma U.S.S.R. **47** 55.12N 34.17E
Vyazniki U.S.S.R. **47** 56.14N 42.08E
Vyborg U.S.S.R. **46** 60.45N 28.41E
Vyrnwy *r.* Wales **30** 52.45N 3.01W
Vyrnwy, L. Wales **30** 52.46N 3.30W
Vyshka U.S.S.R. **57** 39.19N 49.12E
Vyshniy-Volochek U.S.S.R. **47** 57.34N 34.23E

W

Wa Ghana **70** 10.07N 2.28W
Waal *r.* Neth. **45** 51.45N 4.40E
Waalwijk Neth. **45** 51.42N 5.04E
Wabash *r.* U.S.A. **94** 38.25N 87.45W
Wabush City Canada **93** 53.00N 66.50W
Waco U.S.A. **91** 31.33N 97.10W
Wad Pakistan **58** 27.21N 66.30E
Wadden Sea Neth. **45** 53.15N 5.05E
Waddesdon England **28** 51.50N 0.54W
Waddington, Mt. Canada **92** 51.30N 125.00W
Wadebridge England **31** 50.31N 4.51W
Wadesmill England **27** 51.51N 0.03W
Wadhurst England **29** 51.03N 0.21E
Wadi Halfa Sudan **69** 21.55N 31.20E
Wad Medani Sudan **69** 14.24N 33.30E
Wafra Kuwait **57** 28.39N 47.56E
Wageningen Neth. **45** 51.58N 5.39E
Wager Bay *town* Canada **93** 65.55N 90.40W
Wagga Wagga Australia **80** 35.07S 147.24E
Wahpeton U.S.A. **91** 46.16N 96.36W
Waiau New Zealand **82** 42.39S 173.02E
Waiau *r.* New Zealand **82** 42.47S 173.23E
Waigeo *i.* Indonesia **61** 0.05S 130.30E

Waihou *r.* New Zealand **82** 37.12S 175.33E
Waikato *r.* New Zealand **82** 37.19S 174.50E
Waikerie Australia **80** 34.11S 139.59E
Waimakariri *r.* New Zealand **82** 43.23S 172.40E
Waimarie New Zealand **82** 41.33S 171.58E
Wainfleet All Saints England **33** 53.07N 0.16E
Waingapu Indonesia **61** 9.30S 120.10E
Wainwright U.S.A. **92** 70.39N 160.00W
Waipara New Zealand **82** 43.03S 172.47E
Waipukurau New Zealand **82** 40.00S 176.33E
Wairau *r.* New Zealand **82** 41.32S 174.08E
Wairoa New Zealand **82** 39.03S 177.25E
Wairoa *r.* New Zealand **82** 36.07S 173.59E
Waitaki *r.* New Zealand **82** 44.56S 171.10E
Waitara New Zealand **82** 38.59S 174.13E
Wajir Kenya **73** 1.46N 40.05E
Wakatipu, L. New Zealand **82** 45.10S 168.30E
Wakayama Japan **63** 34.12N 135.10E
Wakefield England **33** 53.41N 1.31W
Wakeham Canada **93** 61.30N 72.00W
Wakkanai Japan **63** 45.26N 141.43E
Walachian Plain *f.* Romania **47** 44.30N 26.30E
Walbrzych Poland **44** 50.48N 16.19E
Walbury Hill England **28** 51.21N 1.30W
Walcha Australia **80** 31.00S 151.36E
Walcheren *f.* Neth. **45** 51.32N 3.35E
Walderslade England **27** 51.21N 0.33E
Wales U.K. **30** 52.30N 3.45W
Walgett Australia **80** 30.03S 148.10E
Wallasey England **32** 53.26N 3.02W
Wallingford England **28** 51.36N 1.07W
Wallington England **27** 51.22N 0.09W
Walls Scotland **36** 60.14N 1.34W
Wallsend England **35** 55.00N 1.31W
Walmer England **29** 51.12N 1.23E
Walney, Isle of England **32** 54.05N 3.12W
Walsall England **28** 52.36N 1.59W
Waltham Abbey England **27** 51.42N 0.01E
Waltham Forest *d.* England **27** 51.36N 0.02W
Waltham on the Wolds England **33** 52.49N 0.49W
Walthamstow England **27** 51.34N 0.01W
Walton-on-Thames England **27** 51.23N 0.23W
Walton on the Hill England **27** 51.17N 0.02W
Walton on the Naze England **29** 51.52N 1.17E
Walvis B. R.S.A. **74** 22.48S 14.29E
Walvis Bay *d.* R.S.A. **74** 22.55S 14.35E
Walvis Bay *town* R.S.A. **74** 22.50S 14.31E
Wamba Kenya **73** 0.58N 37.19E
Wamba Nigeria **71** 8.57N 8.42E
Wamba Zaïre **73** 2.10N 27.59E
Wamba *r.* Zaïre **72** 4.35S 17.15E
Wami *r.* Tanzania **73** 6.10S 38.50E
Wanaaring Australia **80** 29.42S 144.14E
Wanaka, L. New Zealand **82** 44.30S 169.10E
Wandsworth *d.* England **27** 51.27N 0.11W
Wanganella Australia **80** 35.13S 144.53E
Wanganui New Zealand **82** 39.56S 175.00E
Wangaratta Australia **80** 36.22S 146.20E
Wangeroog *i.* W. Germany **45** 53.50N 7.50E
Wangford Fen *f.* England **29** 52.25N 0.31E
Wanhsien China **63** 30.54N 108.20E
Wankie Rhodesia **74** 18.18S 26.30E
Wankie Nat. Park Rhodesia **74** 19.00S 26.30E
Wansbeck *r.* England **35** 55.10N 1.33W
Wanstead England **27** 51.34N 0.02E
Wantage England **28** 51.35N 1.25W
Warangal India **59** 18.00N 79.35E
Waratah B. Australia **80** 38.55S 146.07E
Ward Rep. of Ire. **38** 53.26N 6.20W
Warden R.S.A. **74** 27.50S 28.58E
Wardha India **59** 20.41N 78.40E
Ward Hill Orkney Is. Scotland **37** 58.54N 3.20W
Ward Hill Orkney Is. Scotland **37** 58.58N 3.09W
Ward's Stone *mtn.* England **32** 54.03N 2.36W
Ware England **27** 51.49N 0.02W
Wareham England **28** 50.41N 2.08W
Warendorf W. Germany **45** 51.57N 8.00E
Warialda Australia **80** 29.33S 150.36E
Wark Forest *hills* England **35** 55.06N 2.24W
Warley England **28** 52.29N 2.02W
Warlingham England **27** 51.19N 0.04W
Warmbad S.W. Africa **74** 28.29S 18.41E
Warminster England **28** 51.12N 2.11W
Warracknabeal Australia **80** 36.15S 142.28E
Warragul Australia **80** 38.11S 145.55E
Warrego *r.* Australia **80** 30.25S 145.18E
Warren Mich. U.S.A. **94** 42.30N 83.02W
Warren Ohio U.S.A. **94** 41.15N 80.49W
Warri Nigeria **71** 5.36N 5.46E
Warrington England **32** 53.25N 2.38W
Warrnambool Australia **80** 38.23S 142.03E
Warsaw Poland **47** 52.15N 21.00E
Warsop England **33** 53.13N 1.08W
Warta *r.* Poland **47** 52.45N 15.09E
Warwick Australia **80** 28.12S 152.00E
Warwick England **28** 52.17N 1.36W

Warwick U.S.A. **95** 41.42N 71.23W
Warwickshire *d.* England **28** 52.13N 1.30W
Washington England **35** 54.55N 1.30W
Washington U.S.A. **95** 38.55N 77.00W
Washington *d.* U.S.A. **90** 47.00N 120.00W
Washington, Mt. U.S.A. **95** 44.17N 71.19W
Wasior Asia **61** 2.38S 134.27E
Wassy France **40** 48.30N 4.59E
Wast Water *l.* England **32** 54.25N 3.18W
Waswanipi L. Canada **95** 49.30N 76.20W
Watampone Indonesia **61** 4.33S 120.20E
Watchet England **31** 51.10N 3.20W
Waterbury U.S.A. **95** 41.33N 73.03W
Waterford Rep. of Ire. **39** 52.16N 7.08W
Waterford *d.* Rep. of Ire. **39** 52.10N 7.40W
Waterford Harbour *est.* Rep. of Ire. **39** 52.12N 6.56W
Watergate B. England **31** 50.28N 5.06W
Waterloo Belgium **45** 50.44N 4.24E
Waterloo Canada **94** 43.28N 80.32W
Waterloo U.S.A. **94** 42.30N 92.20W
Waterlooville England **28** 50.53N 1.02W
Watertown N.Y. U.S.A. **95** 43.57N 75.56W
Watertown S.Dak. U.S.A. **91** 44.54N 97.08W
Watertown Wisc. U.S.A. **94** 43.12N 88.46W
Waterville Rep. of Ire. **39** 51.50N 10.11W
Waterville U.S.A. **95** 44.34N 69.41W
Watervliet U.S.A. **95** 42.43N 73.42W
Watford England **27** 51.40N 0.25W
Watlington England **28** 51.38N 1.00W
Watson Lake *town* Canada **92** 60.07N 128.49W
Watten, Loch Scotland **37** 58.29N 3.20W
Watton England **29** 52.35N 0.50E
Wau P.N.G. **61** 7.22S 146.40E
Wau Sudan **69** 7.40N 28.04E
Wauchope Australia **80** 31.27S 152.43E
Waukegan U.S.A. **94** 42.21N 87.52W
Waukesha U.S.A. **94** 43.01N 88.14W
Wausau U.S.A. **94** 44.58N 89.40W
Wauwatosa U.S.A. **94** 43.04N 88.02W
Waveney *r.* England **29** 52.29N 1.46E
Wavre Belgium **45** 50.43N 4.37E
Waxham England **29** 52.47N 1.38E
Waycross U.S.A. **91** 31.08N 82.22W
Wealdstone England **27** 51.36N 0.20W
Wear *r.* England **35** 54.55N 1.21W
Weardale *f.* England **35** 54.45N 2.05W
Weaver *r.* England **32** 53.19N 2.44W
Weda Indonesia **61** 0.30N 127.52E
Weddell Sea Antarctica **106** 73.00S 42.00W
Wedmore England **28** 51.14N 2.50W
Weert Neth. **45** 51.14N 5.40E
Wee Waa Australia **80** 30.34S 149.27E
Weiden in der Oberpfalz W. Germany **44** 49.40N 12.10E
Weifang China **63** 36.44N 119.10E
Weihai China **63** 37.30N 122.04E
Weimar E. Germany **44** 50.59N 11.20E
Weirton U.S.A. **94** 40.24N 80.37W
Weissenfels E. Germany **44** 51.12N 11.58E
Welhamgreen England **27** 51.44N 0.11W
Welkom R.S.A. **74** 27.59S 26.44E
Welland Canada **95** 45.59N 79.14W
Welland *r.* England **33** 52.53N 0.00
Welling England **27** 51.28N 0.08E
Wellingborough England **28** 52.18N 0.41W
Wellington Salop England **30** 52.42N 2.31W
Wellington Somerset England **31** 50.58N 3.13W
Wellington New Zealand **82** 41.17S 174.47E
Wellingtonbridge Rep. of Ire. **39** 52.16N 6.45W
Wells England **28** 51.12N 2.39W
Wellsford New Zealand **82** 36.16S 174.32E
Wells-next-the-Sea England **33** 52.57N 0.51E
Welshpool Wales **30** 52.40N 3.09W
Welwyn England **27** 51.50N 0.13W
Welwyn Garden City England **27** 51.48N 0.13W
Wem England **32** 52.52N 2.45W
Wembere *r.* Tanzania **73** 4.07S 34.15E
Wembley England **27** 51.34N 0.18W
Wemyss Bay *town* Scotland **34** 55.52N 4.52W
Wenatchee U.S.A. **90** 47.26N 120.20W
Wenchow China **63** 28.02N 120.40E
Wendover England **27** 51.46N 0.46W
Wenlock Edge *hill* England **28** 52.33N 2.40W
Wenshan China **59** 23.25N 104.15E
Wensleydale *f.* England **32** 54.19N 2.04W
Wensum *r.* England **29** 52.37N 1.20E
Wentworth Australia **80** 34.06S 141.56E
Wepener R.S.A. **74** 29.44S 27.03E
Werne W. Germany **45** 51.39N 7.36E
Werris Creek *town* Australia **80** 31.20S 150.41E
Wesel W. Germany **45** 51.39N 6.37E
Weser *r.* W. Germany **44** 53.15N 8.30E
Wessel, C. Australia **79** 11.00S 136.58E
West Allis U.S.A. **94** 43.01N 88.00W
West Bridgford England **33** 52.56N 1.08W
West Bromwich England **28** 52.32N 2.01W

For Khmer Republic read Kampuchea. For Malagasy Republic read Madagascar. For Rhodesia read Zimbabwe.

West Burra to **Worksop** 171

West Burra *i.* Scotland **36** 60.05N 1.21W
Westbury England **28** 51.16N 2.11W
West Calder Scotland **35** 55.51N 3.34W
West Clandon England **27** 51.16N 0.30W
Westcott England **27** 51.13N 0.20W
Westerham England **27** 51.16N 0.05E
Western *d.* Ghana **70** 6.00N 2.40W
Western *d.* Kenya **73** 0.30N 34.30E
Western Australia *d.* Australia **79** 25.00S 123.00E
Western Cleddau *r.* Wales **31** 51.47N 4.56W
Western Cordillera *mts.* N. America **106** 46.00N 120.00W
Western Ghats *mts.* India **58** 15.30N 74.30E
Western Hajar *mts.* Oman **57** 24.00N 56.30E
Western Isles *d.* Scotland **36** 57.40N 7.10W
Western Sahara Africa **68** 25.00N 13.30W
Western Sayan *mts.* U.S.S.R. **49** 53.00N 92.00E
Wester Ross *f.* Scotland **36** 57.37N 5.20W
Westerstede W. Germany **45** 53.15N 7.56E
Westerwald *f.* W. Germany **45** 50.40N 8.00E
West Felton England **30** 52.49N 2.58W
Westfield U.S.A. **95** 42.07N 72.45W
West Frisian Is. Neth. **45** 53.20N 5.00E
West Germany Europe **44** 51.00N 8.00E
West Glamorgan *d.* Wales **31** 51.42N 3.47W
West Haddon England **28** 52.21N 1.05W
West Ham England **27** 51.32N 0.01E
West Hanningfield England **27** 51.41N 0.31E
West Hartford U.S.A. **95** 41.46N 72.45W
West Horsley England **27** 51.17N 0.27W
West Indies C. America **97** 21.00N 74.00W
West Kilbride Scotland **34** 55.42N 4.51W
West Kingsdown England **27** 51.21N 0.14E
West Kirby England **32** 53.22N 3.11W
West Lake *d.* Tanzania **73** 2.00S 31.20E
Westland Bight *b.* New Zealand **82** 43.30S 169.30E
West Linton Scotland **35** 55.45N 3.21W
West Loch Roag Scotland **36** 58.14N 6.53W
West Loch Tarbert Scotland **36** 57.55N 6.53W
West Malaysia *d.* Malaysia **60** 4.00N 102.00E
Westmeath *d.* Rep. of Ire. **38** 53.30N 7.30W
West Mersea England **29** 51.46N 0.55E
West Midlands *d.* England **28** 52.28N 1.50W
West Nicholson Rhodesia **74** 21.06S 29.25E
Weston Malaysia **60** 5.14N 115.35E
Weston-super-Mare England **28** 51.20N 2.59W
West Palm Beach *town* U.S.A. **91** 26.42N 80.05W
Westport New Zealand **82** 41.46S 171.38E
Westport Rep. of Ire. **38** 53.48N 9.32W
Westray *i.* Scotland **37** 59.18N 2.58W
Westray Firth *est.* Scotland **37** 59.13N 3.00W
West Schelde *est.* Neth. **45** 51.25N 3.40E
West Siberian Plain *f.* U.S.S.R. **48** 60.00N 75.00E
West Sussex *d.* England **29** 50.58N 0.30W
West Terschelling Neth. **45** 53.22N 5.13E
West Thurrock England **27** 51.29N 0.17E
West Virginia *d.* U.S.A. **91** 39.00N 80.30W
West Water *r.* Scotland **37** 56.47N 2.35W
West Wickham England **27** 51.22N 0.02W
West Wittering England **28** 50.42N 0.54W
West Wyalong Australia **80** 33.54S 147.12E
West Yorkshire *d.* England **32** 53.45N 1.40W
Wetar *i.* Indonesia **61** 7.45S 126.00E
Wetheral England **35** 54.53N 2.50W
Wetherby England **33** 53.56N 1.23W
Wetzlar W. Germany **44** 50.33N 8.30E
Wewak P.N.G. **61** 3.35S 143.35E
Wexford Rep. of Ire. **39** 52.20N 6.28W
Wexford *d.* Rep. of Ire. **39** 52.20N 6.25W
Wexford B. Rep. of Ire. **39** 52.27N 6.18W
Wey *r.* England **27** 51.23N 0.28W
Weybridge England **27** 51.23N 0.28W
Weyburn Canada **90** 49.39N 103.51W
Weymouth England **28** 50.36N 2.28W
Weymouth U.S.A. **95** 42.14N 70.58W
Whakatane New Zealand **82** 37.56S 177.00E
Whale *r.* Canada **93** 58.00N 57.50W
Whaley Bridge *town* England **32** 53.20N 2.00W
Whalley England **32** 53.49N 2.25W
Whalsay *i.* Scotland **36** 60.22N 0.59W
Whangarei New Zealand **82** 35.43S 174.20E
Wharfe *r.* England **32** 53.50N 1.07W
Wharfedale *f.* England **32** 54.00N 1.55W
Wheathampstead England **27** 51.49N 0.17W
Wheeler Peak *mtn.* Nev. U.S.A. **90** 38.59N 114.29W
Wheeler Peak *mtn.* N. Mex. U.S.A. **90** 36.34N 105.25W
Wheeling U.S.A. **94** 40.05N 80.43W
Whernside *mtn.* England **32** 54.14N 2.25W
Whickham England **35** 54.57N 1.40W
Whipsnade England **27** 51.52N 0.33W
Whitburn Scotland **35** 55.52N 3.41W
Whitby England **33** 54.29N 0.37W
Whitchurch Bucks. England **28** 51.53N 0.51W
Whitchurch Hants. England **28** 51.14N 1.20W
Whitchurch Salop England **32** 52.58N 2.42W
White *r.* Ark. U.S.A. **91** 35.30N 91.20W
White *r.* Ind. U.S.A. **94** 38.25N 87.45W
White *r.* S. Dak. U.S.A. **90** 43.40N 99.30W
Whiteabbey N. Ireland **34** 54.42N 5.53W
Whiteadder Water *r.* Scotland **35** 55.46N 2.00W
White Cap Mtn. U.S.A. **95** 45.35N 69.13W
White Coomb *mtn.* Scotland **35** 55.26N 3.20W
Whitefish Pt. U.S.A. **94** 46.46N 84.58W
Whitehaven England **32** 54.33N 3.35W
Whitehead N. Ireland **34** 54.45N 5.43W
Whitehorse Canada **92** 60.41N 135.08W
Whitehorse Hill England **28** 51.35N 1.35W
White Mountain Peak U.S.A. **90** 37.40N 118.15W
White Mts. U.S.A. **95** 44.15N 71.10W
Whiten Head Scotland **37** 58.34N 4.32W
White Nile *r.* Sudan **69** 15.45N 32.25E
White Parish England **28** 51.01N 1.39W
White Russia Soviet Socialist Republic *d.* U.S.S.R. **47** 53.30N 28.00E
Whitesand B. England **31** 50.20N 4.20W
White Sea U.S.S.R. **48** 65.30N 38.00E
White Volta *r.* Ghana **70** 9.13N 1.15W
Whithorn Scotland **34** 54.44N 4.25W
Whitland Wales **30** 51.49N 4.38W
Whitley Bay *town* England **35** 55.03N 1.25W
Whitney Canada **95** 45.29N 78.15W
Whitney, Mt. U.S.A. **90** 36.35N 118.17W
Whitstable England **29** 51.21N 1.02E
Whittington England **30** 52.53N 3.00W
Whittlesey England **29** 52.34N 0.08W
Whitton England **33** 53.42N 0.39W
Whitwell England **27** 51.53N 0.18W
Whyalla Australia **79** 33.04S 137.34E
Wiay *i.* Scotland **36** 57.24N 7.13W
Wichita U.S.A. **91** 37.43N 97.20W
Wichita Falls *town* U.S.A. **90** 33.55N 98.30W
Wick Scotland **37** 58.26N 3.06W
Wick *r.* Scotland **37** 58.26N 3.06W
Wickford England **27** 51.38N 0.31E
Wickham England **28** 50.54N 1.11W
Wickham Market England **29** 52.09N 1.21E
Wicklow Rep. of Ire. **39** 52.59N 6.03W
Wicklow *d.* Rep. of Ire. **39** 52.59N 6.25W
Wicklow Head Rep. of Ire. **39** 52.58N 6.00W
Wicklow Mts. Rep. of Ire. **39** 53.06N 6.20W
Wick of Gruting *b.* Scotland **36** 60.37N 0.49W
Widford England **27** 51.50N 0.04E
Widnes England **32** 53.22N 2.44W
Wien *see* Vienna Austria **44**
Wiener Neustadt Austria **44** 47.49N 16.15E
Wiesbaden W. Germany **44** 50.05N 8.15E
Wigan England **32** 53.33N 2.38W
Wight, Isle of England **28** 50.40N 1.17W
Wigmore England **27** 51.21N 0.36E
Wigston Magna England **28** 52.35N 1.06W
Wigton England **35** 54.50N 3.09W
Wigtown Scotland **34** 54.47N 4.26W
Wigtown B. Scotland **34** 54.47N 4.15W
Wilberfoss England **33** 53.57N 0.53W
Wilcannia Australia **80** 31.33S 143.24E
Wildhorn *mtn.* Switz. **44** 46.22N 7.22E
Wildspitze *mtn.* Austria **44** 46.55N 10.55E
Wildwood U.S.A. **95** 38.59N 74.49W
Wilhelm, Mt. P.N.G. **61** 6.00S 144.55E
Wilhelmshaven W. Germany **45** 53.32N 8.07E
Wilkes-Barre U.S.A. **95** 41.15N 75.50W
Willemstad Neth. Antilles **97** 12.12N 68.56W
Willersley England **30** 52.07N 3.00W
Willesden England **27** 51.33N 0.14W
Williamsport U.S.A. **95** 41.16N 77.03W
Willington England **35** 54.43N 1.41W
Williston R.S.A. **74** 31.20S 20.52E
Williston U.S.A. **90** 48.09N 103.39W
Williton England **31** 51.09N 3.20W
Willmar U.S.A. **91** 45.06N 95.00W
Willowmore R.S.A. **74** 33.18S 23.30E
Willunga Australia **80** 35.18S 138.33E
Wilmington Del. U.S.A. **95** 39.46N 75.31W
Wilmington N.C. U.S.A. **91** 34.14N 77.55W
Wilmslow England **32** 53.19N 2.14W
Wilrijk Belgium **45** 51.11N 4.25E
Wilson *r.* Australia **80** 27.36S 141.27E
Wilson, Mt. U.S.A. **90** 37.51N 107.51W
Wilson's Promontary *c.* Australia **80** 39.06S 146.23E
Wilstone Resr. England **27** 51.48N 0.40W
Wilton England **28** 51.05N 1.52W
Wiltshire *d.* England **28** 51.20N 2.00W
Wimbledon England **27** 51.26N 0.12W
Wimbledon Park England **27** 51.26N 0.17W
Wimborne Minster England **28** 50.48N 2.00W
Winam *b.* Kenya **73** 0.15S 34.30E
Winburg R.S.A. **74** 28.31S 27.01E
Wincanton England **28** 51.03N 2.24W
Winchester England **28** 51.04N 1.19W
Windermere England **32** 54.24N 2.56W
Windermere *l.* England **32** 54.20N 2.56W
Windhoek S.W. Africa **74** 22.34S 17.06E
Windlesham England **27** 51.22N 0.39W
Windrush *r.* England **28** 51.42N 1.25W
Windsor Canada **94** 42.18N 83.00W
Windsor England **27** 51.29N 0.38W
Windsor Great Park *f.* England **27** 51.27N 0.37W
Windward Is. C. America **97** 13.00N 60.00W
Windward Passage *str.* Carib. Sea **97** 20.00N 74.00W
Wingate England **35** 54.44N 1.23W
Wingrave England **27** 51.52N 0.44W
Winisk *r.* Canada **93** 55.20N 85.20W
Winkleigh England **31** 50.49N 3.57W
Winneba Ghana **70** 5.22N 0.38W
Winnebago, L. U.S.A. **94** 44.00N 88.25W
Winnipeg Canada **91** 49.59N 97.10W
Winnipeg, L. Canada **93** 52.45N 98.00W
Winnipegosis, L. Canada **90** 52.00N 100.00W
Winnipesaukee, L. U.S.A. **95** 43.40N 71.20W
Winona U.S.A. **94** 44.02N 91.37W
Winschoten Neth. **45** 53.07N 7.02E
Winscombe England **28** 51.19N 2.50W
Winsford England **32** 53.12N 2.31W
Winslow England **28** 51.57N 0.54W
Winston-Salem U.S.A. **91** 36.05N 80.05W
Winsum Neth. **45** 53.20N 6.31E
Winterswijk Neth. **45** 51.58N 6.44E
Winterthur Switz. **44** 47.30N 8.45E
Winterton England **33** 53.39N 0.37W
Winterton-on-Sea England **29** 52.43N 1.43E
Winton Australia **79** 22.22S 143.00E
Winton New Zealand **82** 46.10S 168.20E
Wirksworth England **33** 53.05N 1.34W
Wirral *f.* England **32** 53.18N 3.02W
Wisbech England **29** 52.39N 0.10E
Wisconsin *d.* U.S.A. **94** 44.45N 90.00W
Wisconsin *r.* U.S.A. **94** 42.57N 91.07W
Wisconsin Rapids *town* U.S.A. **94** 44.24N 89.50W
Wishaw Scotland **35** 55.47N 3.55W
Wismar E. Germany **44** 53.54N 11.28E
Wissembourg France **44** 49.02N 7.57E
Wissey *r.* England **29** 52.33N 0.21E
Witham England **27** 51.48N 0.38E
Witham *r.* England **33** 52.56N 0.04E
Witheridge England **31** 50.55N 3.42W
Withernsea England **33** 53.43N 0.02E
Witney England **28** 51.47N 1.29W
Witten W. Germany **45** 51.26N 7.19E
Wittenberg E. Germany **44** 51.53N 12.39E
Wittenberge E. Germany **44** 52.59N 11.45E
Wittlich W. Germany **45** 49.59N 6.54E
Witu Kenya **73** 2.22S 40.20E
Wiveliscombe England **31** 51.02N 3.20W
Wivenhoe England **29** 51.51N 0.59E
Włocławek Poland **47** 52.39N 19.01E
Wodonga Australia **80** 36.08S 146.09E
Wokam *i.* Asia **61** 5.45S 134.30E
Woking England **27** 51.20N 0.34W
Wokingham England **28** 51.25N 0.50W
Woldingham England **27** 51.17N 0.02E
Wolf *r.* U.S.A. **94** 44.00N 88.30W
Wolfenbüttel W. Germany **44** 52.10N 10.33E
Wolf Rock *i.* England **31** 49.56N 5.48W
Wolfsburg W. Germany **44** 52.27N 10.49E
Wolin Poland **44** 53.51N 14.38E
Wollaston England **28** 52.16N 0.41W
Wollaston L. Canada **92** 58.15N 103.30W
Wollongong Australia **80** 34.25S 150.52E
Wolmaransstad R.S.A. **74** 27.11S 26.00E
Wolseley Australia **80** 36.21S 140.55E
Wolsingham England **35** 54.44N 1.52W
Wolvega Neth. **45** 52.53N 6.00E
Wolverhampton England **28** 52.35N 2.06W
Wolverton England **28** 52.03N 0.48W
Wombwell England **33** 53.31N 1.23W
Wonersh England **27** 51.12N 0.33W
Wonsan N. Korea **63** 39.07N 127.26E
Wonthaggi Australia **80** 33.33S 145.37E
Woodbridge England **29** 52.06N 1.19E
Woodford Rep. of Ire. **39** 53.03N 8.24W
Woodford Halse England **28** 52.10N 1.12W
Wood Green England **27** 51.38N 0.06W
Woodhall Spa England **33** 53.10N 0.12W
Woodmansterne England **27** 51.19N 0.10W
Woodside Australia **80** 38.31S 146.21E
Woodstock England **28** 51.51N 1.20W
Woodville New Zealand **82** 40.20S 175.54E
Wooler England **35** 55.33N 2.01W
Woolwich England **27** 51.29N 0.05E
Woomera Australia **79** 31.11S 136.54E
Woonsocket U.S.A. **95** 42.00N 71.30W
Wooroorooka Australia **80** 28.59S 145.40E
Wooster U.S.A. **94** 40.46N 81.57W
Wootton Bassett England **28** 51.32N 1.55W
Worcester England **28** 52.12N 2.12W
Worcester R.S.A. **74** 33.39S 19.26E
Worcester U.S.A. **95** 42.17N 71.48W
Workington England **32** 54.39N 3.34W
Worksop England **33** 53.19N 1.09W

For Khmer Republic *read* Kampuchea. *For* Malagasy Republic *read* Madagascar. *For* Rhodesia *read* Zimbabwe.

For Khmer Republic read Kampuchea. For Malagasy Republic read Madagascar. For Rhodesia read Zimbabwe.